'This is a superb survey of the field of comparative political economy – including its early origins, development over time, and latest cutting-edge research. In this beautifully written book, Ben Clift manages to create genuine intellectual excitement for both aspiring and established political economists.'

Matthias Matthijs, *Johns Hopkins University, USA*

'*Comparative Political Economy* is an exceedingly erudite book. Clift navigates deftly between classical political economy theory, rival analytical frameworks, and contemporary economic issues. The discussion of current topics, like the financial crisis and political populism, is especially welcome.'

Jonah Levy, *University of California, Berkeley, USA*

'*Comparative Political Economy* provides us with some essential tools for analysing the dynamism and dysfunctionality of capitalist development in all its various forms. Ben Clift's book offers the best introduction to this approach. It places comparative political economy within the 'classical' tradition of Smith, Marx and List before providing an invaluable critical overview of the cutting-edge of the field today. The book is attentive to history and theory while marshalling an impressive breadth of empirical evidence. It will undoubtedly prove to be a key reference point for the next generation of scholars working within the field.'

Scott Lavery, *University of Sheffield, UK*

COMPARATIVE POLITICAL ECONOMY

States, Markets and Global Capitalism

2nd edition

Ben Clift

 macmillan international HIGHER EDUCATION  RED GLOBE PRESS

This edition published 2021 by
RED GLOBE PRESS

Previous editions published under the imprint PALGRAVE

Red Globe Press in the UK is an imprint of Macmillan Education Limited, registered in England, company number 01755588, of 4 Crinan Street, London, N1 9XW.

Red Globe Press® is a registered trademark in the United States, the United Kingdom, Europe and other countries.

ISBN 978-1-352-01130-2 hardback

ISBN 978-1-352-01125-8 paperback

This book is printed on paper suitable for recycling and made from fully managed and sustained forest sources. Logging, pulping and manufacturing processes are expected to conform to the environmental regulations of the country of origin.

A catalogue record for this book is available from the British Library.

A catalog record for this book is available from the Library of Congress.

Commissioning Editors: Andrew Malvern, Peter Atkinson

Assistant Editor: Becky Mutton

Cover Designer: Laura De Grasse

Senior Production Editor: Amy Brownbridge

Marketing Manager: Amy Suratia

For Charlie and Sam, whose inquiring minds and lust for life continue to inspire me daily.

Two great friends and brilliant mentors whose support, encouragement and sage counsel were major influences on my early career, very sadly died during the preparation of this second edition. This edition is dedicated to the memories of Robert Elgie (1965–2019) and Steve Ludlam (1951–2017).

Contents

List of Figures and Tables

FIGURES

TABLES

List of Boxes

List of Abbreviations

AfD	Alternative for Germany
APSA	American Political Science Association
BRICS	Brazil, Russia, India, China, South Africa (fast-growing big economies)
CCP	Chinese Communist Party
CDO	collateralized debt obligation
CME	co-ordinated market economy
CMH	capital mobility hypothesis
CPE	comparative political economy
DS	developmental state
EC	European Commission
ECB	European Central Bank
EMU	European Monetary Union
EU	European Union
FDI	foreign direct investment
GATS	General Agreement on Trade in Services
GDP	gross domestic product
GFC	global financial crisis
IAS	International Accounting Standards
IMF	International Monetary Fund
IPE	international political economy
IR	international relations
KWS	Keynesian welfare state
LIBOR	London Interbank Offered Rate
LIPC	Local Investment Platform Company (in China)
LME	liberal market economy
MDSD	most different systems (research) design
METI	Ministry of Economy, Trade and Industry (in Japan)
MITI	Ministry of International Trade and Industry (in Japan)
MSSD	most similar systems (research) design
NAFTA	North American Free Trade Agreement
NICE	non-inflationary continuous expansion
NPL	non-performing loan
NYM	New Public Management
OECD	Organisation for Economic Co-operation and Development
OEP	open economy politics
SEC	Securities and Exchange Commission

SEZ	Special Economic Zone (in China)
SSA	social structures of accumulation theory
TNC	transnational corporation
TVE	Township and Village Enterprises (in China)
UKIP	United Kingdom Independence Party
VoC	*Varieties of Capitalism*
WTO	World Trade Organization

Acknowledgements for the First Edition

This book is a product of my long-standing interest in political economy and as such owes a great debt to those who first introduced me to the field in the Department of Politics at the University of Sheffield in the 1990s. David Marquand's undergraduate teaching sparked the passion for political economy within me, and then Mike Kenny encouraged me to take the MA in Political Economy which fanned those flames. The choice proved career-defining for me. I was then introduced to the historical lineage of political economy and to contemporary international political economy (IPE) by the wonderful teaching of, in no particular order, Steve Ludlum, Mike Kenny, Andrew Gamble, Tony Payne, Jonathon Perraton, Martin Smith and Randall Germain. Thereafter, working in the Political Economy Research Centre at Sheffield strengthened my resolve that political economy was the subfield for me. It was with great pride, years later, that I accepted a role as Honorary Fellow in its successor, the Sheffield Political Economy Research Institute.

I have spent the past decade developing my interest in political economy, both comparative and international, in the Department of Politics and International Studies at the University of Warwick. In Pete Burnham, Ben Rosamond and Chris Hughes I have worked with a string of first-rate heads of department who have been unstinting in their support, generous with their time and spot on with their advice. The concentration of fine political economy minds here at Warwick is, it seems to me, second to none. It has been a tremendously stimulating environment in which to develop as a scholar. I have benefited immeasurably from corridor conversations and in-depth discussions with, among others, Matthew Watson, Ben Richardson, Shaun Breslin, Wyn Grant, Tim Sinclair, Lena Rethel, James Brassett, Jan Aart Scholte, Chris Holmes, Len Seabrooke, André Broome, Matthew Clayton, Peter Burnell, Chris Clarke, Richard Higgott, Michel Goyer, Colin Crouch and Glenn Morgan.

Thanks go to the many excellent students who have taken my 'States and Markets' and 'Theories and Issues in International Political Economy' modules over the past decade or so, and to all my doctoral students, past and present. They have made me think afresh about political economy and its study, and I am constantly impressed by their ability to help me see old debates in a new light. A number of colleagues have contributed to teaching 'States and Markets' and I am grateful to James Brassett, Dominic Kelly, Chris Rogers, Simon Glaze, Ben Richardson, Shaun Breslin, Wyn Grant and Chris Clarke for their input in refreshing the course and enriching it with their expertise.

A number of research collaborations have been particularly important in shaping my development as a political economist. These have honed and refined my understanding of comparative political economy as well as kept my intellectual curiosity levels high. First and foremost, working with Jim Tomlinson has been very rewarding and ceaselessly enjoyable over more than a decade of projects on the political economy of economic policy-making, policy autonomy and credibility in a changing world economy. Second, working with Cornelia Woll on the political economy of economic patriotism and the reinvention of political control over the economy has sparked off new avenues of inquiry. Running the research project on 'Economic Patriotism' with Cornelia was great fun, and co-authoring and co-editing together was a genuine pleasure. The research agenda we put together over five or more years remains pregnant with possibilities we have still only just begun to explore and I hope we shall find time in our busy schedules to pursue them. Working with Ben Rosamond on the lineages of British IPE was also important in shaping my thinking about the field, disciplinary politics and what it is to be a political economist. All of this underpins the approach taken in this book and indeed all the work I do. Here too there is 'power to add' to what we have written so far, and I hope the collaboration will continue to bear fruit.

In the wider field of academe, I owe much to a number of trail-blazing political economists whose work has made it such a great field to work in, and whose intellectual insights, friendship, support and sage counsel have proved invaluable to me. Andrew Gamble at Cambridge, whose throwaway comment many years ago more or less forced me to write this book, Jim Tomlinson at Glasgow and Tony Payne at Sheffield have been wonderful mentors. So too have Colin Hay and Patrick Le Galès at Sciences Po, Paris, Vivien Schmidt at Boston University, Mark Blyth at Brown University and Alan Cafruny at Hamilton College. Raymond Kuhn at Queen Mary has also been a source of support and encouragement, and organizing various conferences, workshops and special issues about French politics with him has been enjoyable and rewarding. Magnus Ryner at King's is another long-standing source of intellectual inspiration and friendship – and I hope our slow-burning research collaboration will flourish in the near future.

Those friends and colleagues who were kind enough to read parts of the book and provide invaluable comments were Michel Goyer, Renske Doorenspleet, Matthew Watson, Tony Payne, Chris Rogers, Chris Clarke, Andrew Gamble, Ben Rosamond, Tim Sinclair and Shaun Breslin. I hope I have been able to do justice to their suggestions in my revisions.

I am very much indebted to Steven Kennedy at Palgrave Macmillan for talking me into writing this book in the first place, and then for his unstinting enthusiasm for the project during its long (very long) gestation and culmination. Steven was as ever a very helpful sounding board and source of publishing wisdom, especially as the manuscript entered its final phase. Stephen Wenham at Palgrave Macmillan also carefully read the typescript and provided many useful suggestions for final tweaks. I am grateful to Keith Povey, Nick Fox and Elaine Towns for assiduous copyediting and proof-reading that improved the polish and presentation of the manuscript. I also very much appreciate the insightful and supportive comments of two anonymous reviewers of the first draft of the manuscript.

Finally, and most importantly, I am hugely grateful to all my family, and especially to Rachel, for all the love, encouragement and support.

BEN CLIFT

Acknowledgements for the Second Edition

I have been extremely gratified by how well received the first edition of this book has been, and delighted to have been given an opportunity to work on a second edition by the good people at Red Globe Press, especially first Andrew Malvern, then Peter Atkinson, who have offered fulsome and enthusiastic support. This second edition was completed under lockdown due to COVID-19's remorseless spread. I am grateful to my lovely and loving family, Rachel, Charlie and Sam, for helping keep me sane through these extraordinary and challenging times. Final tweaks to the manuscript percolated through my brain during long bike rides and walks through the Oxfordshire countryside searching for Corn Buntings, Yellow Wagtails and Grey Partridges.

I am grateful to three reviewers for their constructive recommendations on how to improve on the first draft of the manuscript. I hope to have done justice to their very good suggestions. While two remain anonymous, one revealed himself to be Matthias Matthijs, who has been a very helpful source of ideas about adjustments to make. I also benefited greatly during academic year 2018–19 from excellent research assistance from Sophie Worrall, who read the first edition and made a series of telling suggestions for updates.

A few friends and colleagues were kind enough to read parts of the revised book and provide invaluable comments on draft chapters. They were Vivien Schmidt, Gabriel Siles-Brugge, Sandy Hager and Joseph Baines. I hope I have been able to do justice to their first-rate suggestions in my revisions. The Warwick New Directions in IPE conference in May 2015 gave me the opportunity to present on key themes and arguments in the first edition of this book. The engaging discussion provided food for thought for how to revise the book. Thanks go to my fabulous colleagues who organized the conference: Juanita Elias, Lena Rethel, James Brassett, Ben Richardson and Andre Broome. Simon Glaze, Sahil Dutta and John Morris have all, at different points, done a brilliant job teaching on and overseeing the 'States and Markets' module which I developed in the early 2000s and for which this book was in part designed. I have benefited hugely from many enjoyable and engaging conversations about political economy with them. In Nick Vaughan-Williams and Juanita Elias, I have been fortunate to have more fabulously supportive, brilliant and sagacious heads of department. The friendship and camaraderie of working on the senior leadership team within PAIS with Nick, Juanita and others in recent years is a major reason why PAIS remains a great place to be a political economy scholar.

I am hugely grateful to all the fabulous PhD students I have worked with on a range of political economy topics in recent years as this second edition was planned and crafted. They are Nick Taylor, Simona Pino, Matt Kranke, Daniela Serban, Lorenzo Genito, Sean McDaniel, David Yarrow, Jack Copley and Te-Anne Robles. Many of them are already forging impressive academic careers as the next generation of political economy scholars, which is a source of great pride to me. My current PhD students all keep me inspired to think afresh about political economy and I owe them all a great debt for that: Nick Kotusha, Iacopo Mugnai, Giamacro Fifi and Jorge Quintero. Even before COVID, PhD scholarship funding was in retreat and under serious threat in UK academe. The precarity and financial strain felt by many PhD students are increasing. PAIS at Warwick's buoyant recruitment of fabulous

PhD students in the early 2010s turned out, in hindsight, to be the end of a golden era. It is far from clear that there will be anything like enough PhD scholarship funding to support the development for next generations of brilliant scholars, which is a source of grave concern.

Finally, and most importantly, once again I am hugely grateful to all my family, and especially to Rachel and my sons Charlie and Sam, for all their love, encouragement and support.

BEN CLIFT
GARSINGTON
SUMMER 2020

How to Use This Book

This book can be used to deepen your understanding of comparative political economy (CPE) and to animate different kinds of courses or modules dealing with political economy issues in a range of ways. The obvious way to proceed is to read it sequentially. Chapters 1 and 2 set up the study of the field and introduce a range of its major focal points, and I think it will always make sense to begin with those two chapters. The book is structured in such a way as to introduce those who are new to the field to the engaging and endlessly fascinating world of CPE logically, wherein each chapter builds upon what has gone before. Each chapter outlines aspects of CPE's core substantive content and central debates, and the earlier chapters in particular locate these in the broader historical and intellectual context of the field of political economy. However the curriculum of a module or course is organized, students would certainly benefit from building up their understanding of the historical evolution of comparative political economy, and in particular the core intellectual concerns of classical political economy, as provided in more depth and detail in Chapters 3 and 4.

The first four chapters, taken together, provide students with an overarching genealogy of the field, its development, evolution and core concerns. Contemporary work in all fields is building upon the shoulders of giants; so too in CPE. These early chapters map the contours of those earlier analyses and debates that provide the foundations upon which later CPE scholarship builds. Thus Chapters 1–4 provide students and researchers with crucial analytical and theoretical tools which underpin, and can be harnessed to, the analysis of contemporary developments and debates in CPE.

Alternatively, if the focus on classical political economy and the historical evolution of political economy as crucial to understanding contemporary capitalism are not the preferred approach, one could (although I would advise against it) forgo some of the historical engagement. Thus students could proceed from Chapters 1 and 2 to Chapter 5, where the detailed exploration of contemporary CPE theorizing, approaches and debates begins. Such an approach will still provide a rich understanding of the subject matter of political economy and the contours of its animating debates. Students will gain a deep appreciation of the intellectual and analytical tools needed to research CPE in depth, whether their intellectual goal is exploring contemporary issues or investigating more enduring political economy themes.

Learning how to compare is obviously a crucial dimension of CPE. After all, the comparative element within CPE provides both the definitional boundaries of the sub-field and the core analytical resource which generates many of its most important insights. Developing the wherewithal to think comparatively, and analyse political phenomena in a systematic comparative fashion, is crucial for students of CPE. This is why Chapter 13 – on the comparative method and the logic and rationale of comparative political economic analysis – is such an important part of the book. Yet it may be that the kind of methodological awareness required for effective and systematic comparative analysis is provided on other modules and courses. Depending upon how much introduction to the logic of comparative social inquiry and what level of political research methods training students have been provided with elsewhere in the curriculum, there may be scope to bring forward the reading of comparative method (Chapter 13). Thus students might choose to read the book a bit 'backwards', reading up on the comparative method straight after Chapter 1, and before the fuller familiarization with CPE provided in Chapters 2–4. A grounding in comparative method is incredibly useful because being able to work within a comparative framework for analysis helps us develop new theories about political economy, or refine the concepts which are the building blocks of these theories. The process of comparative analysis also helps us hone the theories we use when analysing politics by seeing how far they are applicable in other contexts. This improves our clarity and explanation of politics and political economy. Comparative analysis also enables us to verify or falsify theories, checking to what extent political economic generalizations hold across cases (and across what kinds of cases). For all these reasons, picking a path through the debates on the comparative method as provided in Chapter 13 may prove especially fruitful for students to read before a research essay, a research project or a dissertation on a CPE theme.

In introducing the key theories of CPE, one strategy is to introduce students to a different thinker, and attendant school of thought, each week. Thus a week on Smith could be followed by a week on Marx, then List, the Marginalists, Keynes, Hayek and Polanyi. Again, however the course is organized, students may wish get to grips with a particular political economist in more depth. Perhaps their ideas are especially key for an essay being researched, or maybe this thinker's ideas and worldview are found to be especially palatable, or objectionable. The index at the end of the book will help to make this straightforward, setting out the various parts of the book where a particular thinker's ideas and insights are discussed in depth. A careful reading of these passages should be supplemented of course by the excellent secondary literature on each. With some of the longer substantive empirical chapters (such as on the state in Chapter 8 or on *Varieties of Capitalism* in Chapter 9) reading could be split up and dealt with in sequential teaching sessions. Often a helpful way to get to grips with a new area of CPE is to familiarize oneself with the essential building blocks of the key theories and concepts first, and thereafter to seek to apply the theory to particular cases, episodes or examples. Thus, one could focus initially on the broader theory and analytical debates, followed by reading up on and thinking these through in the context of a 'worked example' of one or more concrete empirical cases. For instance, broader conceptual themes and debates could be explored in the context of Japan or China for the 'developmental' state, or of France or Germany for financial market change. One can, of course, add coverage of additional cases not covered at length in these pages by using the secondary literature in CPE and international political economy (IPE).

Students reading the book to help them study courses in IPE can use Chapters 1–4 at the outset of the course to provide a perspective on the question 'What is IPE?' The conception of IPE embodied in this texts roots it firmly in the classical political economy tradition, and sees IPE and CPE as mutually reinforcing and complementary intellectual undertakings. The ideational chapter (Chapter 7) lends itself to a week on constructivist IPE, while the interests chapter (Chapter 5) provides insights into some of the building blocks and intellectual concerns of mainstream rationalist IPE. The substantive empirical chapters, notably on the state, comparative capitalisms, financial system change and welfare state transformation, can provide the empirical colour and granularity to locate and flesh out broader IPE debates about state/market dynamics in the global political economy.

1 Introduction: The Focus and Rationale of the Book

In late 2019 and early 2020, COVID-19, a virulent respiratory pathogen, spread swiftly around the world from China and brought the global economy to its knees through the lockdowns it necessitated. The public health response was unlike anything seen before. Only by ceasing most economic activity and curtailing people's movement and contact could the spread be limited, and the number of deaths kept down. In the advanced economies and at the European Union (EU) level, enormous spending packages and state guarantees were promised to individuals, firms and whole sectors of the economy to try to cushion the economic blow of the lockdowns. The amounts of money involved were unprecedented and the levels of government spending were eye-watering in scale. Early International Monetary Fund (IMF) and other assessments indicated that the global pandemic threatened the worst global recession since at least 1920–21.

The hope was that muscular state intervention and massive public spending could bridge across what was bound to be a deep recession but, it was hoped, a short one. Governments were placing their countries on a war footing to tackle the crisis. Analogies to World War II abounded, justifying an equivalent public finance response of boosting debt-financed spending in pursuit of the war effort. 'Whatever it takes' was the mantra. The celebrated economist Olivier Blanchard noted this was 'not the time to be squeamish' about ramping up public spending and debt.

The contrast with the preceding decade of stringent public spending cuts could not be starker. A highly charged 'crisis of debt' discourse had coloured the public debate about the economy in advanced economies following the global financial crisis (GFC) of 2008–9. This ushered in 'austerity' policies centred on balanced budgets and drastic public expenditure cuts. Debt levels had risen sharply due to the GFC, and thereafter getting debt levels down had become deeply politicized as a sign of good economic management. The social contract had, it seemed, been re-drawn. The size of the public sector was being reduced.

Then the global health pandemic hit, and its economic implications meant all bets were off as to what 'sound' fiscal policy looked like. This was a 'new normal'. It was as if the previous decade of public expenditure cutting had never happened. Suddenly, debt levels shot up again as finance ministries and central banks could not spend the money fast enough. There was a wholesale transformation of debt and deficit discourse.

This graphically illustrated something that political economy as a field keenly appreciates: what passes for economic common sense and 'sound' economic policy is historically contingent. It can change, sometimes very dramatically, and also very rapidly. This malleability of economic rectitude shows us that what 'sound' economic policy looks like is not set in stone. Rather, it is always and everywhere politically and economically contingent. It is always, in short, the stuff of politics.

Suddenly, the lessons from economics about 'what is to be done' are transformed. There is a powerful underlying political debate surrounding how governments should run the

1

economy. What level of state spending is justified? What kinds of public intervention into economic activity are warranted? All seems settled, a particular balance between state and market gets struck, a particular level of public intervention in the economy, a level of taxation as a proportion of national income is seen as 'normal'. Then, in almost the blink of an eye, something happens and everything changes. One set of guiding stars, in this case those hawkish voices advocating countries 'living within their means', gets abruptly and unceremoniously dropped. Whatever happened to metaphors (such as Angela Merkel running the German state as a prudent and austere 'Bavarian housewife') misleadingly equating household finances with the public finances?

Another set of ideas – in this case those advocating a role for public intervention and a state-orchestrated public response to the crisis – is embraced as orthodoxy. The global pandemic of 2020 changed the way we thought about appropriate fiscal policy, casting doubt on whether selling off more healthcare provision to the private sector was such a good idea. The economic policy debate surrounding 2020's pandemic was like a photographic negative of 2010's strident calls for 'austerity'. Then, as economies tried to recover from a major financial crisis, advocates of 'expansionary fiscal contraction' suggested that public spending and intervention in the economy should be dramatically scaled back to enable the private sector (assumed to be inherently more efficient) to 'pick up the slack'. Come 2020, much of the private sector of the economy was effectively mothballed due to the lockdowns across most of the world's economies. In those countries with a sufficiently large public sector – like the advanced economies which are the focus of this book – the call was for massively scaled-up government intervention in the economy and public spending to 'pick up the slack'. This would enable to economy to 'bounce back' faster when restrictions were lifted and some elements of normal economic activity were scheduled to return.

However, although austerity was suddenly forgotten in the public debate, a decade of public spending cuts *had* happened. Many welfare states and health systems found themselves depleted and ill prepared to face the extraordinary challenge. The impacts of a decade of cuts could be seen in the limitations of testing capacity for the virus, the quantity and quality of protective equipment for front-line healthcare workers, and the numbers of ventilators and intensive care beds. The scale of intensive care provision was simply much lower in the UK and France compared to countries like Germany or Denmark. In some countries where austerity had been pursued harshly, health sector resources were stretched to, and sometimes beyond, their limit – with tragic consequences. The costs of how austerity had been pursued could be gleaned in the atypically high death rates in the UK, France, Italy and some other hard-hit European countries.

There is a joke about someone asking in the street for directions to an awkward location. 'Well, I wouldn't start from here ...' comes the reply. So it is with this global health pandemic visited upon the advanced welfare states in Europe. At the end of over a decade of stringent public-sector spending cuts, the scale and quality of public service provision had been eroded – with the crucial healthcare and social care sectors often the hardest hit.

The extraordinary economic measures taken by governments around the world in response to the pandemic have in some ways blown out of the water prior neo-liberal orthodoxies about the economy and economic policy. The state is no longer viewed as necessarily part of the problem, and the market is not seen to have the answers to all society's problems or the cure for all ills. This could lead to a major rethinking of how the economy works, both in terms of national and global economic governance, especially if the rethink can be harnessed to efforts to address the climate crisis. After all, the economic fallout from COVID is likely to last a very long time. Governments might find themselves owning significant stakes in a range of industries and sectors, almost by accident. Then again, we could see an all too hasty return to belt-tightening, with all the negative consequences that is likely to bring in these conditions.

HISTORY NEVER ENDS ...

This episode hints at a broader truth. There has been an ebb and flow in the prevailing orthodoxy between bigger and smaller government, from *laissez-faire* and interventionism, more regulated and less regulated markets, across the 20th and 21st centuries. Perhaps there always will be such fluctuations. We have short memories, and the upheavals tend to come as a surprise. The crisis and transformation periods always seem like bolts from the blue, as if Zeus were raining down his divine retribution capriciously upon the world. Actually, as a range of political economists we will encounter in this book point out, crises are all part of the protean operations of capitalist economies, both nationally and globally.

Sometimes, when these crises arise, the dominant economic ideas about what sound economic management looks like can change dramatically. Sometimes, they change only incrementally, or even do not change much at all. In the background, whatever the popular consensus of the day, the debate rages on regarding the appropriate size, scale and focus of state intervention in the economy. What is at stake in these debates are the fundamental principles of political economy. Sometimes these arguments seem confined to ivory towers, hidden from the public gaze in subterranean catacombs of academe. At other times, they can become front-page news. Irrespective of the level of political visibility, the battle of views still goes on, even during periods when all these matters appear largely settled in the popular consciousness. In this light, it is unwise to pronounce that any one position has won the arguments about state–market relations that – as we shall see in this book – have been animating political economy for centuries.

One such hubristic pronouncement came after the fall of the Berlin Wall in 1989, which heralded the end of the Cold War and the collapse of Soviet communism. Francis Fukuyama argued that 1989 marked 'the total exhaustion of viable systemic alternatives to Western liberalism'. His triumphalist liberal proclamation of the 'end of history' suggested that the historic dichotomy – between ordering society according to capitalist principles (private ownership and the primacy of market mechanisms) and ordering society according to communist principles (from each according to means, to each according to needs) – had been resolved. Fukuyama's Western-centric reading of world history neglected, among other things, the rising power and influence of the Chinese Communist Party on the global political economic stage. He saw no more 'fundamental contradictions in human life that cannot be resolved in the context of modern liberalism', hence the 'end of history as such: that is, the end point of mankind's ideological evolution and the universalization of Western liberal democracy as the final form of human government' (1989: 3–8). Or, paraphrasing Dr Pangloss in Voltaire's *Candide*, 'all is for the best in the best of all possible worlds'.

Freer markets and liberal democracy are the answer, whatever the question might be. Yet the free market within this brand of liberalism is understood in a highly caricatured (and deeply unrealistic) way that is derived from mainstream economics. This conceives of individuals as rational actors assumed to have perfect information and operating in perfectly competitive markets which always 'clear' – or function efficiently. Modern economics makes a further *ceteris paribus* ('all other things being equal') assumption to strip away social, historical and political context from the analysis of 'the economic', enabling increasing technical sophistication.

This account of the presumed triumph of Western liberalism, however, rested upon two fallacies. Firstly, it neglected how rising liberalization and globalization were political constructs. Secondly, it was not set in stone; its 'triumph' was *not* an inevitable outcome. It could be otherwise. As if to prove these points, in the mid-2010s in the heartlands of the Global North, the political and social foundations of the liberal international order, a seemingly unshakeable bedrock of global politics for decades, began to crumble. In the US, UK and elsewhere in Western Europe – for so long the core of the liberal globalized regime – a backlash against the established political economic order erupted. It was fuelled by stagnant wages, declining living standards and growing income inequality, spreading disaffection among many social groups who felt 'left behind' by globalization. A rise of populist movements from both the Left and the Right challenged mainstream political parties and traditional politics. Indeed, they challenged the underlying political economic principles of the established liberal order, both domestically and internationally. Meanwhile, China had steadily grown into a global political economic superpower. The guiding force behind its interventionist economic model, the Chinese Communist Party, was far less convinced of the merits of liberalism, either political or economic.

These upheavals challenged mainstream economic assumptions (about the merits of freer trade, for example) on which the international order was based. In the process, the election of Donald Trump, the Brexit vote on the UK's membership of the EU, in which a narrow majority voted to leave, and the rise of multiple forms of populist economic nationalism dramatically re-ignited political economy arguments which had been the stuff of impassioned debate for centuries. Trump as US President was hell-bent on challenging the 'globalism' and liberalism that the US had underwritten for decades, reviving economic nationalist instincts of 'America First'. As Gamble notes, these seismic shocks represent and are fuelled by a rejection of globalization. They 'have the potential to start unravelling the western economic and political order which has been the framework of world politics for the last seventy years' (Gamble 2019: 36). The idea that a rising tide would (eventually) float all boats under liberal markets was no longer believed or accepted. It was not sufficient to quell the clamour and disaffection of those citizens in advanced economies who saw themselves as 'losers' from a free market capitalism ever more riven with widening inequalities.

Political economy, arguably more so than mainstream economics, offers a useful lens to interpret such developments since it exists to ask political questions of economic processes, institutions and outcomes, exploring power relations and the (in)equality of capitalism's distributive consequences. Political economy, in contrast to economics, understands market relations as political constructions. Comparative political economy (CPE), as understood here, is not 'economics without the maths' – it is a much broader and richer intellectual undertaking which 're-embeds' analysis of the economic within the social and political realm. This desire to retain the interrelatedness of the economic, political and social is at the heart of how to think like a political economist. As I will elaborate on below and in Chapters 2–4, this underpins how *political* economy is a qualitatively different intellectual endeavour, and why CPE constitutes a very different research programme from modern economics. It is also why many comparative political economists feel that *the economy is far too important a subject to leave exclusively to economists*. This is not to deny the contribution to our understanding of many economists doing much outstanding work on the economy. After all, they do not give out those Nobel Prizes to just anyone. The point is that economists – with their particular assumptions, questions, disciplinary focus and approach – should not be the only scholars working on the economy and discussing, interpreting and analysing the economic within the social sciences.

Take, for example, the global climate crisis. The enormous and aggravating adverse global environmental consequences of free market capitalism constitute a planetary form of market failure that economists call a 'negative externality'. That means that the devastating environmental consequences of capitalism are a 'price' we must all pay, but they lie outside the price mechanism, and therefore market forces are blind to them. The *laissez-faire* economics approach has a blind spot where ecological sustainability is concerned, and cannot resolve the issue (Newell and Paterson 1998, 2010; Phelan et al. 2013). Hardin's 'tragedy of the commons' (discussed in Chapter 6) explains how self-interested actors pursuing their own interests in the market will over-exploit and ultimately put unbearable pressure on natural resources and destroy the environment, or as he puts it, 'the inherent logic of the commons remorselessly generates tragedy' (1968). Global capitalism has been relentlessly denigrating the environment at an alarming rate for the last 100 years or so. Untrammelled capitalist market activity has devastating implications for climate change and the Earth's ecosystems. The ultimate market failure of growth-addicted global capitalism is that unfettered market operations will destroy the ecological and social order in which they are embedded. Political economy has always been an ethical endeavour, envisaging how political economic orders should operate and be organized. There is scope for CPE to deliver key insights to address the global climate crisis.

The notion of a settled global future of liberal free market capitalism underpinning the 'end of history' thesis took as historically resolved fundamental questions about the principles of political economy – debates which, it turns out, were anything but over. What role should the state play within the economy? To what extent, and according to what principles, should the state intervene in the rules-based market order? How can global environmental collapse be averted?

At a deeper level, Fukuyama misses the key point about capitalism which is central to the whole undertaking of CPE: 'it may not be possible to live in a world without capitalism, but capitalism need not be a single fate' (Gamble 1999: 144). Liberalism, or for that matter economic nationalism, is not a singular, monolithic political economic tradition. There are many variants of capitalism, combining different degrees of free markets and regulation. Competing visions of political economy endure and are instantiated through differentiated practices of market-making. Differing views about the desirable distribution of the fruits of growth within firms and across society, for example, or how best to address the climate crisis, generate ongoing political struggles over how to regulate and manage capitalism.

This book provides the tools to analyse capitalism as economic activity located within sets of power relations. It underlines how the institutional context of capitalism reflects political struggles over how markets should be ordered. For example, feminist political economy puts the spotlight on gender hierarchies and gendered power relations, and how patriarchal norms shape capitalism and the way scholars analyse it. Bedford and Rai (2010) argue that feminist analysis recalibrates political economy to ask questions about the ways in which systems of production, distribution and exchange are gendered. This in turn yields a focus on social reproduction, and a wider understanding of processes of governance as forms of gendered domination. The definitions, explanations, normative judgements and prescriptions associated with welfare state theorizing, for example, while spuriously 'gender blind', in fact entail masculinist assumptions. These reinforce a gendered division of labour that gets reproduced institutionally (through the labour market and the welfare state) in different ways in different economies.

Thus, from a political economy perspective, the terrain of 21st-century political contestation centres on 'what *kind* of capitalism? With what welfare or environmental properties?' What kinds of political interventionism are to be supported, tolerated and encouraged, and which forms are to be proscribed within capitalism in any given setting? How liberal, or indeed illiberal, should it be? What gendered assumptions are made about the private or public realm, and 'productive' or 'unproductive' labour?

Even before the tumultuous rise of Trump and the Brexit vote, the reinvigoration of these debates about what kind of capitalism was amply demonstrated following the GFC which began in 2007–8. Forms of political intervention in markets which were either entirely novel or long neglected sprang up across the advanced economies and beyond. Even more striking than the vertiginous height of public expenditures and mounting public debts was the variegated nature of intervention. Governments were intervening to stimulate consumption, prop up credit markets, bail out some industrial sectors and prevent the failure of the international financial system. This illustrated how the decline since the 1970s of old-style industrial policy and heavy-handed state intervention in markets had led to the transformation of political influence over the economy, not its demise (Clift and Woll 2012a, 2012b).

These dramatically interventionist responses to the GFC seemed to break a number of neo-liberal taboos about the appropriate conduct of economic policy and management of the economy, which favour a hands-off, *laissez-faire* approach. The nature of state/market relations and interactions, which had seemingly stabilized around minimally interventionist principles in the advanced economies of the early 21st century, was suddenly thrown into flux. Traditional forms of industrial policy and interventionism revived in some advanced economies following the crash, something that resurgent economic nationalism may push further. The GFC, and responses to it, revealed a recurrent theme of this book – and a central insight of political economy: capitalist market orders, even neo-liberal ones, are always constructed and reproduced through extensive political interventionism, and require political and legal institutions to regulate them.

THE AIMS OF THE BOOK

My aim in this book about the CPE of capitalism is to provide the analytical tools to understand and interpret these dramatic evolutions in state/market relations, and the power relations that shape them. I do this by placing contemporary capitalist restructuring in the context of the key concepts and theoretical debates in the long-established field of political economy, and within that by mapping the terrain of the substantive focus and evolution of the *comparative* approach of CPE. Political economy is concerned with analysing the connections between politics and economics within capitalism, and in this book I explore the social and political implications and consequences of modern-day capitalist economic relations and institutions. The chapters that follow will provide the intellectual apparatus to evaluate competing theoretical perspectives on CPE and to explore the relationships between states and markets in the 20th and 21st centuries through a study of key theories and issues in political economy. I will also familiarize readers with debates about comparative method and how comparative analysis can enhance our ability to apply CPE insights to explore particular aspects of capitalism through systematic scrutiny of themes, issues and cases.

In order to deliver upon these aims, I introduce CPE across three different timescales. First, I situate CPE within the long-term evolution of political economy as a field of study, beginning with seminal interventions in the 18th and 19th centuries which we may group under the term 'classical political economy'. While classical political economy is a tradition which Adam Smith bestrides, here I will extend the parameters of the term, understanding it in a more encompassing way that includes the liberal (Smith), the radical (Karl Marx) and the economic nationalist (as exemplified by the German theorist Friedrich List) traditions, to name but three, and the debates between them. In locating contemporary CPE within a lineage of intellectual inquiry traceable to key thinkers such as Smith and Marx, the aim is to incorporate some of this rich and deep political economy tradition and its important critical insights to arrive at a number of useful analytical starting points for the study and understanding of modern capitalism (set out in Chapter 2). Furthermore, the expansive conception of classical political economy enables us to extend the term to brilliant and insightful 20th-century thinkers who retained the same spirit of inquiry, such as two unconventional liberal political economists – the English statesman and academic John Maynard Keynes and the Nobel Prize-winning Austrian economist Friedrich von Hayek – and the influential Hungarian anthropologist, political economist and critic of the market order, Karl Polanyi.

Second, in this book I consider the major substantive themes, empirical developments and theoretical debates within the field of CPE as they have developed over the last 70 years, asking how CPE scholars have interpreted, analysed and explained the evolving relations between states and markets in advanced capitalism. Together, the culmination of insights and concepts derived from the evolution of political economy and CPE across two timeframes provides the analytical toolkit – honed and crafted by the great political economy scholars of the past – for an in-depth analysis of *contemporary* dynamics in state/market relations. Thus third, I bring the insights of classical political economy and modern CPE to bear on more recent developments within advanced capitalism, and especially from 2000 onwards. I focus on how and why state/market relations are changing in the face of the freeing up of markets, globalization, economic crises and economic nationalist countertendencies of reviving trade barriers, frictions and conflicts. What explains the right-wing nationalism of Trump and others, the increased prevalence of discriminatory economic policies, and moreover the vocal claims for states to 'take back control' and intervene to restore the fortunes of industries and economies?

I explore these transformations, their political economic implications and how they alter the market-making activities of states. Along the way, I introduce the key debates which have preoccupied CPE scholars and shaped evolution within the field in recent times, such as the *Varieties of Capitalism* (Hall and Soskice 2001) approach to comparing capitalisms (discussed at length in Chapters 5 and 9).

I begin this chapter by defining political economy as a field of study, locating its evolution in relation to the emergence of modern capitalism and market societies, and to debates about how it should be interpreted and understood. Setting out the scope of political economy in this way establishes the groundwork for thinking like a political economist. This provides the basis for setting out the central focus of CPE, charting its genealogy via the consideration of some of the towering scholarship in the field. I then spell out the geograph-ical focus of the book on the advanced economies and how the focus on nationally differenti-ated capitalisms is reconciled to incorporation of the global dimension. Here I make the case for a dialogue between CPE and the closely related field of international political economy (IPE). The chapter then offers a detailed summary of the organization of the book and the contents of each chapter. It maps out the rationale behind the selection of focus in the chap-ters to follow, building upon the overall aims and objectives identified above, and shows why and how the focus of each chapter is crucial to achieving these.

WHAT IS POLITICAL ECONOMY?

It is important to understand something of political economy as a broad field of study first, before we can make sense of what CPE specifically has to offer. Political economy's long ancestries help account for its dynamism, developed as it was in an age before modern aca-demic boundaries had been formed to carve up the study of the social world within discrete, self-contained disciplinary specialisms. There are no clear and delineated boundaries to political economy as a field of inquiry. This 'pre-disciplinary' spirit of 'classical' political econ-omy (Clift and Rosamond 2009; Gamble 1995; Watson 2005a, 2008; Clift et al. 2021) to some extent pervades much contemporary political economy analysis, which escapes stric-tures of a disciplined parcelling up of the study of capitalism into component social science fields. Political economy's loose disciplinarity character makes possible work that scavenges readily across the social scientific spectrum (both historical and contemporary) for inspira-tion. This all offers agreeable latitude to political economy scholars to map out the terrain of the discipline somewhat on their own terms (for interesting alternative delineations, see Heilbroner 1992; Caporaso and Levine 1992; Tabb 1999; Stilwell 2012). In this book we will follow in the spirit of Andrew Gamble, Gavin Kelly and John Parkinson's definition:

> political economy has many different meanings, and does not constitute a single approach but a field of study ... [it is] interested in how political and economic systems work. Its starting point is that social orders and the institutions which make them up need to be studied as complex wholes rather than as analytically distinct parts ... in order to under-stand the interrelationships between the [economic and political] aspects, and secondly to understand the broader political and economic context in which a particular institu-tion is embedded. (Gamble et al. 2000: 2)

It follows that political economy should aspire to integrate the analysis of the economic, the social and the political. Indeed, in some ways political economy is a square peg in the round holes of modern academic disciplinarity and the way universities are organized. Social scien-tific inquiry is compartmentalized into, for example, political science, sociology and eco-nomics. Such disciplinary divides delimit how the social sciences are taught and interpreted, yet the substantive concerns and subject matter of political economy transcend them. This is one reason why, to understand what political economy entails, it is instructive to return to the forefathers and pioneers of the study of capitalism and its political, social and eco-nomic consequences. The key questions about power relations within the market order, about the nature and role of the state, its role within the economy, or about the different distributive consequences of different kinds of capitalism were all asked by the likes of Adam Smith and Karl Marx. Theirs was a holistic approach – and given the subject matter and substantive focus of political economy, this has much to recommend it. Market relations have obviously changed a great deal since they were writing. After all, in Smith's time capitalism had not fully emerged, but nevertheless many of the research questions which animated their writing continue to be those central to the modern field of political economy.

Political economy is a relatively modern area of study (compared, say, with political philosophy, which goes back to the ancient Greeks). It was only in the couple of centuries before Smith's discipline-shaping text *Wealth of Nations* was published in 1776 that political economy began to develop. This is because market relations becoming the dominant mode of distributing resources and organizing society is a 'modern' phenomenon. Only from the 1700s and 1800s onwards did the market system come to operate as a mechanism for sustaining and maintaining an entire society. Thus markets have only in recent human history become the prevailing social institutions which we recognize today. This is very different from the existence of 'markets', which have long been a part of human society, certainly as early as 3500 BC (Swedberg 2005).

A crucial corollary of the formation of 'the market system' over the centuries before Smith wrote was the emergence of an economic sphere that was to some degree separable from social life (Heilbroner 1992: 21–8). Important preconditions included changing religious attitudes to market activity, profit-making and money-lending, and advances in science and book-keeping. Most significant of all were the processes of rationalization, concentration and expansion of production in the 1700s and 1800s which drove urbanization and would come to be known as the Industrial Revolution. Notions of pecuniary gain (the search for profit) began to eclipse ideas of reciprocity and kinship as prevailing motivations behind social life. Essentially, capitalism in its recognizably modern form was taking shape, and economic processes were becoming crucial to social reproduction, in contrast to feudalism and subsistence agricultural life. The market system's rise to prevalence unleashed societal and political changes which were to provide the key substantive focus for political economic inquiry and normative debates within the field. It raised questions, for example, about the extent and nature of societal obligations of firms and other market actors, which retain their pertinence within discussions of the labour standards (and child labour) or tax-avoiding (or evading) practices of transnational corporations today.

Political economy flourished as it sought to explore and understand the social and political implications of the profound economic transformations constituted by, first, the spread of markets and then the Industrial Revolution. The growth of factories and the emergent division of labour (as in Smith's example of pin-making which begins *Wealth of Nations*) brought vast increases in productivity. The increasing scale and speed of production, and the increasing profits accruing from it, changed society and the distribution of wealth and power within it. There was a pressing need to explore and explain the production, reproduction and distribution of power and wealth, and the interactions between the political and the economic dynamics of change within society.

These concerns continued to animate the field throughout the 20th century and into the 21st. Four important episodes provided the necessary contextualization for understanding the political economy of state/market relations within contemporary capitalism. Each is outlined below and dealt with at length in later chapters. The first crucial episode was the reordering of the world economy and its institutional architecture in the 1940s following the Great Depression and World War II. The global economic collapse of the 1929 Great

Crash (Galbraith 1954), with no market-induced recovery, undermined the then prevailing economic ideas and led to a profound loss of confidence in *laissez-faire*. The protectionism and beggar-thy-neighbour policies such as high and discriminatory trade tariffs pursued by the advanced economies after the crash reflected a different set of political economic ideas, and deepened antagonisms between nations. The trauma of global conflict that followed, which many saw as at least in part caused by the 'economic warfare' in the 1930s, indicated the need for managed multilateral economic relations between states to secure the peace. The upshot was the global reordering at the Bretton Woods conference of 1944, which grouped together the allied nations, who were by then in the process of winning the war, to design a blueprint for a peacetime world economy. This took the form of a politically regulated but broadly liberal international system of trade and payments, favouring free market mechanisms and limiting restrictions, and multilateral institutions to manage trade and financial and monetary relations between countries (see Chapter 7). This 'more conscious effort at international management of the world economy' meant that 'for the first time in history the governments of the leading economies had agreed on a set of rules, on a system of collective management' (Strange 1994b: 53, 55).

In the post-World War II international economic order, there would be *adjustable* but *pegged* exchange rates with the dollar as the anchor currency, a system of capital controls and international monetary relations managed by new international economic institutions, notably the IMF. Governments were formally encouraged to make use of capital controls to maintain economic stability in the face of potentially disruptive short-term 'hot money' flows. These short-term, speculative financial flows, many felt, had fuelled the pre-war instabilities and tensions, deepening the Great Depression and fanning the flames of 'economic warfare' (see Ruggie 1982; Eichengreen and Kenen 1994; Helleiner 1994; Strange 1994b; Cohen 2002).

The Bretton Woods order was tellingly characterized by Ruggie, channelling Polanyi, as the 'embedded liberal compromise'. It was institutionalized and regulated to 'safeguard' and enable 'domestic stability' without triggering 'mutually destructive' international economic interactions. This was a new international order: 'Unlike the economic nationalism of the thirties, it would be multilateral in character; unlike the liberalism of the gold standard and free trade, its multilateralism would be predicated upon domestic interventionism' (Ruggie 1982: 393). Reordering international political economic arrangements had an important domestic purpose. The new limits on capital movements were integral to a new political settlement which enabled the pursuit of 'demand management' economic policies. Often termed Keynesianism (see Chapter 4), this approach pulled economic policy levers like sluice gates to ensure sufficient (but not excessive) demand in the economy in order to stabilize domestic economies, smooth the economic cycle and aim to secure full employment. This international context also facilitated the construction of welfare states in the advanced economies (see Chapter 11), which ensured that the fruits of economic growth would be relatively equitably distributed.

The next key episode, which began in 1971, saw the breakdown of the Bretton Woods order. On 15 August 1971, the Nixon administration closed the gold window (ending the ready convertibility of dollars into gold), which engineered a general devaluation of the dollar. The American Government was, in effect, no longer willing to bear the domestic economic costs of underwriting the 'embedded liberal' international order. Devaluation increased the competitiveness of US commodities on world markets, but brought the pegged exchange rates system of managed international economic relations in place since the 1940s to an end. As US Treasury Secretary John Connally put it: 'the dollar may be our currency, but it's your problem' (see Ruggie 1982; Eichengreen and Kenen 1994).

The instabilities and uncertainties this caused were exacerbated by the Yom Kippur war in the Middle East where, in retaliation for the Israeli response to the Syrian/Egyptian invasion, Arab states drastically raised oil prices. It suddenly became clear how much of the strong post-war economic growth had relied upon monetary stability and cheap oil. A major worldwide recession ensued – and 'stagflation' (simultaneous high inflation and high unemployment) bedevilled the advanced economies. As economic growth evaporated and public finances deteriorated, a second oil price shock in 1979 only made matters worse. Meanwhile, the oil-producing nations recycled their surpluses through 'offshore' euro–dollar markets, and these were lent injudiciously by Western banks to developing economies. With domestic US monetary policy no longer tailored to the interests of the international community, sharp rises in interest rates fuelled the debt crisis which began in 1982.

Advanced economy responses to the downturn and the 1970s world economic crisis crystallized around international financial market liberalization, the removal of capital controls and deregulation of domestic economies. The move from pegged to floating exchange rates was accompanied by a move from regulated to increasingly deregulated financial markets. The scale, instability and speed of capital flows increased markedly following the collapse of Bretton Woods in the 1970s, and the role of private actors in the process of capital mobility also greatly expanded (Germain 1997). Meanwhile, global production was being transformed by the ongoing rise of transnational corporations, and vast foreign direct investment (FDI) flows. A new international division of labour was emerging within global production networks, 'slicing up the value chain' so that parts of the production process were 'outsourced' to cheaper 'offshore' production locations around the globe. There was an intensification of economic flows, interactions, networks and processes within global production and commodity chains through which the manufacture of consumer goods now passed (Held et al. 1999). In finance, new highly complex instruments, such as derivatives (effectively bets on future market prices), and technological advances served to increase the intensity of transactions. International bank lending, international bonds and equities, new financial instruments and foreign exchange transactions all increased dramatically in the 1980s and 1990s. The era of financial globalization had arrived, with implications for state autonomy and domestic economies (see Chapters 8–11).

The GFC which began in 2007–8 was another significant upheaval. Just like the establishment of Bretton Woods, and then its breakdown, the GFC's impact on and implications for the advanced political economies led to questioning of prevailing understandings about how economies work, appropriate state/market relations and the management and regulation of economic affairs. The dynamics of the 'credit crunch' and its aftershocks undermined some of the ebullient self-confident advocacy of free market solutions to all economic problems. Many commentators thought that neo-liberalism was holed below the watermark, and anticipated wholesale political economic change. In the event, free market ideas, policies and institutions proved more resilient (Schmidt and Thatcher 2013), leading Crouch to bemoan 'the strange non-death of neoliberalism' (2010). Meanwhile, the consequences for public finances of financial sector bailouts, as well as reduced state revenues and increased expenditure accompanying prolonged downturns, generated new (and revived old) economic policy problems for advanced economy governments. What levers can and should governments pull to try to restart economic activity? How much emphasis should they place on securing growth, and how much on tackling burgeoning debt and deficit problems? These straitened circumstances augured a new focus on austerity policies (Blyth 2013; Schafer and Streeck 2013).

The last episode, which began around 2016, was doubtless fuelled by the GFC, the austerity policies that followed and rising income inequality, including in advanced economies. Another spur to this episode was a migration and border crisis in 2015, wherein ongoing war and upheaval were a key catalyst for mass migration from parts of North Africa and the Middle East towards Europe. Over a million refugees and migrants arrived, roughly half fleeing war in Syria. This was part of a longer-standing practice of migrants and refugees attempting to cross the Mediterranean in flimsy and overloaded vessels, often with tragic consequences (see e.g. Vaughan-Williams 2015: 1–4). In the face of the 2015 influx, efforts at a co-ordinated EU response underpinned by the principle of burden sharing failed, and national political responses were fractured. In the absence of a collective response or a developed sense of European solidarity, commitments to free movement, open borders and humanitarianism faltered (Stierl 2018).

Some countries welcomed the migrants, as Germany did. Others – such as Hungary and Poland – responded with hostility and xenophobia. Countries on the front line such as Greece where the flows arrived by land and sea were placed under extreme pressure. Some countries unilaterally reinstituted internal borders, and the whole issue became deeply politicized. Then UK Prime Minister David Cameron dehumanizingly referred to 'swarms' of migrants from other cultures coming to Europe. Such chauvinistic and bigoted responses by mainstream politicians 'played onside' a more strident anti-immigration discourse and fanned the flames of right-wing populism. Far right groups such as the United Kingdom Independence Party (UKIP) in Britain and Alternative for Germany (AfD) in Germany offered a racialized 'clash of civilizations' account of the crisis. In many instances this nativist xenophobia was also laced with anti-Muslim sentiment.

The kinds of border, refugee and migration practices at EU and national levels subsequently evolved to limit migration into Europe from the South and East. These shifts were politically contested, not least due to 'European border controls making safe and legal routes impossible for those fleeing conflict and poverty and a concomitant industry made up of smuggling networks and border controls that have developed alongside each other to circumvent and enforce such restrictions' (Pallister-Wilkins 2016; Andersson 2014). The role of European border policies in increasing the scale of suffering and death of migrants and refugees proved controversial (Squire 2017; Squire et al. 2017; Stierl 2020).

After seemingly decades of the political construction of more open borders and an ever freer trading order, societies had become accustomed to increasingly integrated global markets for goods, capital, labour and services. Lowering trade barriers and facilitation of large-scale migration, for so long taken for granted, were suddenly called into question. Political economic debates about *how* free markets should be and *which* markets should be more restricted suddenly re-surfaced in mainstream politics within advanced economies. Less liberal and anti-liberal political economic forces began to gain electoral success and a greater toehold in the public debate, with both Trump in the US and Marine Le Pen in France styling themselves as the 'patriots' versus the 'globalists'. Always an undercurrent within political discourse, economic nationalism and protectionism rose to prominence once more. First the Brexit vote in Britain then Trump's 2016 presidential victory were shocks that jolted the liberal order.

The assorted protectionists, economic nationalists and nativists promised re-assertion of economic sovereignty, a reordering of state/market relations and more muscular market regulation to 'take back control' over liberal global markets and to 'make America great again'. Migration flows would be restricted, key industries would be protected, trade barriers might be raised, trade wars would if necessary be fought. Following electoral setbacks for varied political forces committed to liberal values, nationalism, sovereignty and protectionism gained ground within the political debate in a range of advanced economics.

These were anachronistic political movements. 'Alt Right' parties in various countries were run by millionaires and billionaires with enormous vested interests in financial services and other sectors. Yet these politicians presented themselves as the 'voice of the people' and mobilized populist tropes to supposedly champion ordinary people – those 'left behind' by globalization – against the liberal 'elites'. The euro-sceptic right in Britain, for example, combines sovereignty-focused economic nationalists as well as 'hyper-globalist' libertarians with visions of 'global Britain' (Baker et al. 1993; Rosamond 2019; Seely and Rogers 2019). Alongside commitments to 'take back control' were dreams of a revival of the UK's 19th-century imperial trade and economic ties. The expression of this desire to open up 'global Britain' to a wider world was to withdraw it from the largest and most developed free trade order on the planet. Brexiteers such as Jacob Rees-Mogg talked up the merits of Britain (or more specifically England) 'breaking free' from the 'shackles' of the EU, while relocating the headquarters of his own large and highly profitable financial services firm to Dublin to ensure his hedge fund would continue to enjoy the economic benefits of membership of the EU's single market.

For all the anachronisms and contradictions, the period after 2016 indicated a shifting of the sands on which the political economic settlements of advanced economies were founded. The direction of travel during the globalization era had, for decades, been towards a more open, liberal trading and financial order – with extensive and ever easier movement of goods, capital, services and people. Globalization was in all likelihood too powerful a geological force to be halted by the rhetorical flourishes and electoral successes of populist politicians – but economic interdependence was bound to change in the face of these political upheavals. How deep the challenge was to the liberal international economic order which had prevailed since the mid-20th century was unclear, not least because these movements were amorphous and self-contradictory. Nevertheless, with China and the US engaged in an acrimonious trade war and Britain threatening to 'crash out' of the EU without a trade agreement, the tide was seemingly turning towards restricting and constraining the free play of market forces. One thing was for sure – these would be interesting times for political economy scholars.

WHAT IS COMPARATIVE POLITICAL ECONOMY?

We can now map out the terrain of CPE as it has evolved and matured over the last 50 or so years. One statement of CPE's contours can be found in the founding editorial mission statement of the journal *New Political Economy*:

> Its key research agenda focuses on regulation and the policy regimes and institutional patterns which characterize alternative models of capitalism. New work in this field is moving beyond the old assumptions of competition between unitary national capitalisms and government–industry relations. The public–private interface has become more

complex, with the emergence of new networks within the global economy ... [Comparative political economy's] research programme includes the organisation of financial and labour markets, changing production and company structures, corporate governance, investment and innovation, tax and welfare systems, representation and accountability, and ideology and public policy. (Gamble et al. 1996)

CPE, like political economy, does not have a clearly or tightly defined or delimited focus. Much CPE scholarship is driven by the conviction that it helps more than it hinders to organize analysis in terms of national economic spaces, within which markets are regulated by national states and regulatory structures.

In this section I illustrate some of the central concerns, theoretical and conceptual innovations and substantive focus of CPE by briefly considering some seminal interventions from the back catalogue, as it were. The selection here is illustrative, rather than comprehensive, highlighting key works and how they have cumulatively built up a research programme exploring the institutions of capitalism and the politics of their evolution comparatively. Each of these key scholars has analysed state/market relations and the politics of economic policy and economic institutions. They have shaped the debates, focus and research agendas of contemporary CPE, and their range of understandings and insights provide the base on which today's scholarship builds.

The British economist and journalist Andrew Shonfield was an important post-war era contributor. His work mapped the contours of the state/market relations, institutions and economic policies of some advanced political economies, and compared them systematically. His *Modern Capitalism* analysed 'the changing balance of public and private power' and the 'distinctive features of the new era of capitalism' (1965: 63). These themes have remained a mainstay of subsequent CPE research.

In the 1960s when Shonfield wrote, state/market relations were taking on novel forms, such as indicative economic planning and 'vastly increased influence of the public authorities on the management of the economic system' (1965: 66), regulation of industry, full employment-oriented counter-cyclical economic policy (Keynesian demand management) and welfare state expansion. Each of these, Shonfield argued, was rooted in particular institutional underpinnings, giving these broadly similar sets of political economic projects distinctive characteristics in particular countries. These national configurations of capitalist institutions and economic policies played a role in prodigiously successful post-war economic growth across Europe. Shonfield explored these developments in depth in Britain, France, Germany and the US, and developed a (slightly under-elaborated) typology, understanding the variety in capitalist evolution in the advanced economies in terms of liberalism (free market capitalism), corporatism (capitalism orchestrated by employers and unions as 'social partners') and statism (state-directed capitalism). CPE scholars, it seems, not only like categorizing and typologies – they also quite like counting to three. The depictions offered in each case became the accepted view of how we should understand the political economy of these advanced capitalisms in this post-war era. Furthermore, Shonfield's portrayal then became the explicit or implicit benchmark or yardstick by which change within capitalisms since the 1970s could be judged (see Chapters 9 and 10). In this way, Shonfield shaped much of the later CPE work on comparative capitalisms.

Susan Strange, a professor at LSE then Warwick, was another pioneering political economist. Illustrating the close proximity between the two fields of CPE and IPE, she was identified by Jerry Cohen as one of the 'Magnificent Seven' eminent scholars who shaped modern

IPE (Cohen 2008: 8; see Strange 1970, 1971: 2–3). She explored the problems and difficulties of post-war UK economic management in a wider international context, focusing on currency politics and state use of foreign currencies in particular (1971, 1976). In *Sterling and British Policy* (1971), Strange analysed 'the politics of international currencies', focusing on 'the interaction between internal economic development or the external economic relations' and 'choices of strategy and foreign policy' (Strange 1971: 2). Her aim was to use the British case to develop a theory of potentially wider applicability, notably for the US dollar (Strange 1971: 3).

The subtitle of Strange's book is 'a political study of an international currency in decline'. It charts sterling's role as a top currency in sustaining and extending the British empire in the 19th century (Strange 1971: 41–8), and efforts to preserve sterling's international currency role in the post-war era through things like the sterling area (Strange 1971: 65–71). Strange explores the adverse effects of British post-war overseas capital investment (driven by delusions of imperial grandeur) in exacerbating balance of payments constraints on domestic economic management (1971: 129–31, 144–50). She offered important insights into the British model of capitalism in comparative context, and the problems of successive UK governments' 'stop go' economic policies, instability and periodic sterling crises. These were not, she argued, due to constraints imposed by how the Bretton Woods system operated. Rather, they were the result of other economic policy choices, tied to historic views of Britain's world role, and an imperial overhang of its continued attachment to sterling as a world currency.

Britain clung to the 'sterling balances' (accumulated by Britain paying countries such as India and Egypt in sterling for imports) out of a desire to retain its imperial legacy and status as an international financial centre (Strange 1976: 60–1, 232–3). Fuelled by unrealistic aspirations to world power status, UK military spending remained higher than any other member of the Western alliance except the US. Sterling's international role was another major millstone around the neck of the British post-war economy. Yet the causes of sterling's and the UK's economic problems were construed by UK policy elites as 'inappropriate' domestic policy, not overstretch abroad. This was a reminder of the need to look beyond a narrow economic logic to understand the political dynamics and drivers of domestic and international economic policies. Contrary to the intentions of embedded liberalism, imperial overstretch was causing serious conflict between the international priorities of British policy and the needs of the domestic economy.

Peter Katzenstein, a professor at Cornell University, is another influential CPE scholar who advanced the field by placing these national political economies systematically in their international context. Another of Cohen's 'Magnificent Seven' of influential IPE scholars (Cohen 2008: 8), Katzenstein analysed varied responses to the economic crises of the 1970s. Just as nationally differentiated responses to the GFC presented tantalizing opportunities for 21st-century CPE scholars, so in the 1970s CPE could deepen understandings of stagflation, world economic downturn and the demise of the golden age of capitalism. In *Between Power and Plenty* (1978), Katzenstein and his collaborators analysed the foreign economic policies of the advanced industrial states and explored how the oil crises of the 1970s elicited nationally differentiated responses. So too, as we will explore in this book, do subsequent processes of globalization, liberalization and increasing capital mobility, as well as efforts to resist, restrain and push back against these tendencies. These advanced industrial states, the range of comparativists involved in Katzenstein's project noted, had different domestic, social and political structures which conditioned their foreign economic policies.

National responses were contingent upon the different points of insertion into the world economy, such as their export/import dependencies and the relative openness and competitiveness of their economies. In short, this work highlighted the 'different kind of limitations which the world economy imposes' on states (Katzenstein 1978: 13).

Instead of pursuing an analytical separation of the domestic and international levels of analysis, Katzenstein – like Strange – explored the interplay of international and domestic forces. The possibilities for clear-cut distinction between international and domestic realms were limited. This, Katzenstein noted, was because 'international and domestic factors have been closely intertwined in the historical evolution of the [world economy] since the middle of the 19th century' (ibid.: 11). For example, British domestic politics of the early 19th century, when combined with the country's international ascendancy, promoted free trade values internationally (see Chapter 3). Britain's domestic politics became vital to a particular world order. Hence Katzenstein's breadth of CPE focus, which includes 'political and economic forces operating at home and abroad' (ibid.: 13) and has subsequently become a hallmark of much of the best work in CPE.

Another hugely influential political economy scholar has been Theda Skocpol. Her epic historical sociology of the French, Russian and Chinese revolutions, *States and Social Revolutions* (1979), explored state/society relations and the social origins of revolutions. She focused on social structures and material conditions, and remained unconvinced of the merits of analysing institutions in terms of 'systems of meaning or normative frameworks' (1995: 105). Skocpol deployed process tracing methods to reject the view that ideologically motivated vanguard movements were the key cause of social revolutions (1979: 170–1). Skocpol has also been a key scholar of social policy who has engaged in pioneering comparative analysis of the political economy of the welfare state, exploring the drivers of its evolution – notably social class, party politics and state capacities. Her research situates analysis of state, political parties, interest groups and public policy systematically in institutional terms, and in historical and comparative context, alive to the role of deep social structures and class politics in social change.

Skocpol has a historical institutionalist's appreciation of path dependency. State structures and policy legacies, such as the emergence and mobilization of political groupings created by a policy, often play central roles in her explanations in political economy. For example, the introduction of US civil war pensions provoked veterans to mobilize politically and press for even more generous welfare provision (Skocpol 1992). She works with a Marx-inspired view of class struggle as a key driver of revolution and social change. This class struggle mobilized through working-class organization and harnessed the administrative powers of the state, leading to the emergence and consolidation of welfare states (Skocpol and Amenta 1986; Orloff and Skocpol 1984).

Skocpol's comparative historical analysis, and indeed her more contemporary work, betrays a keen interest in the autonomous role of the state within political economy. The comparative analysis of that state's role was harnessed in subsequent work to a broader project, *Bringing the State Back In* (Evans et al. 1985). The critique of prior scholarship was that the state, its capacities and potentialities, and crucially its relative autonomy from other societal pressures and actors, had been systematically overlooked in much social science research. Skocpol's role in 'bringing the state back in' to comparative political analysis underlined the catalytic role of the state as an author of political economic transformation. Taking some inspiration from Weber, she focused on 'states as organisations controlling territories' and how 'state structures and actions are conditioned by historically changing transnational contexts'. She highlighted how 'states necessarily stand at the intersections between domestic socio-political orders and the transnational relations within which they must maneuver' (1985: 8). This interest in the role of the state, and Skocpol's insight into the nation state's unique position at the intersection between national, local and international scales of political economic action, has been of enduring significance (1985). Thus state institutions, and the policies and regimes they introduce, can be key explanatory factors in a changing international economic order – for example through their effects on national economic competitiveness.

In a similar vein, a Harvard-trained professor at the University of California, San Diego, Peter Gourevitch, explored the *complex interactions* between these international and domestic levels of analysis, and how 'domestic structure ... and the international system are parts of an interactive system' (1978: 900). Gourevitch revisits in his 'second image reversed' formulation (1978) international relations scholar Kenneth Waltz's characterization of states' relationship to the international system. Waltz explained the causes of international political developments such as wars in terms of domestic political structures. For Gourevitch, the interesting focal point was, instead, the 'exigencies of the international system' (1978: 882), the international 'distribution of economic activity and wealth' (1978: 883) and 'international market forces' (1978: 884) shaping and interacting with domestic politics. Within the complex interplay of international and domestic forces, domestic politics and institutional structures are key because 'the management and the analysis of interdependence must always begin at home' (Katzenstein 1978: 22). As Gourevitch's *Politics in Hard Times: Comparative Responses to International Economic Crises* (1986) pointed out, what happens inside states influences how political economies evolve in response to crises and instabilities originating within the world economy. Exploring how international influences are mediated, contested and channelled domestically is a central focus for CPE.

Thus CPE had staked out a focus on domestic political and economic institutions, seen as crucial within capitalism. A further advance was provided, appropriately enough, from economics – which offered a novel way to theorize the importance of those institutions. The Nobel Prize winner Douglass North pursued a particular variant of 'institutional economics' and married the insights of Shonfield, Strange, Katzenstein and Gourevitch with rational choice political science (see Chapters 5 and 6). North's basic argument is that widely understood procedures reduce uncertainty and lower social interaction 'costs'. He connects this to an underlying assumption that market activities necessarily rest upon non-market arrangements – specifically interlocking institutions, both formal and informal, which he calls 'the interdependent web of an institutional matrix'. The uncertainty-reducing properties of these institutions, and the beneficial economic effects they deliver, have a dramatic effect on the logic of North's argument, overturning economic orthodoxy. The upshot is a reformulation of standard economic assumptions, replacing decreasing returns with notions of positive feedback effects and *increasing* returns accruing from particular institutional arrangements (North 1981, 1990; see also Pierson 2004: 22–30).

North emphasizes the reduced uncertainties that this 'web' or 'matrix' produces, generating 'massive increasing returns' (1990: 95). These dynamics serve to reinforce particular institutional configurations of capitalism, because efficiency gains accrue and increase from particular interconnected sets of capitalist institutions. In this way, North theorized path dependency, which denotes how initial policy choices can constrain subsequent decisions and future evolutions (see Chapter 6). Shonfield and others had already explored this from a different perspective, but North's crystallization of path dependency was of foundational importance to late 20th- and early 21st-century work on comparative capitalisms. Perhaps the most influential and pervasive contemporary research programme in CPE is that sparked off by Peter Hall and David Soskice's book *Varieties of Capitalism* (VoC; 2001). VoC garnered a 21st-century revival of comparative capitalisms analysis within CPE, as we shall see in Chapters 6 and 9, which consider VoC debates and critiques in depth. VoC takes direct inspiration from each of the key concepts theorized by North – feedback effects, increasing returns and path dependency.

The next extension of CPE was more geographical than conceptual. Californian professor Chalmers Johnson enhanced the comparative dimension of CPE through his analysis of what he termed Japan's developmental state (DS). This extended the geographical reach of mainstream CPE analysis of the institutions of capitalism decisively beyond Western Europe and North America to incorporate East Asia. Within the Japanese political economy, Johnson argued, the forces of 'social mobilization' and 'nationalism' were harnessed to a national economic development project predicated upon the state as 'guiding force' providing capitalism with the necessary direction through interventionist industrial policy (1982, 1995). This combination achieved spectacular economic growth results in the post-World War II era. Subsequent comparativists then applied the DS as a broader comparative concept, identifying different DS histories and trajectories in East Asian economies (Onis 1991; Woo-Cumings 1999; Weiss 2004), in Latin America (Evans 1995; Ban 2013) and indeed in post-war Europe (notably France; Loriaux 1991, 1999, 2003; see Chapter 8). More recently, some have explored the relevance and applicability of the DS concept to explain China's political economic transformation (Breslin 1996, 2007, 2011, 2012a, 2012b; Strange 2011).

Harvard professor Peter Hall's influential book *Governing the Economy* (1986) was another landmark CPE text, further refining the understanding of institutions within capitalist restructuring. He accentuated the focus on the politics of economic ideas within the CPE mainstream (see also Hall 1989, 1993) by exploring the rise of neo-liberalism and the demise (as he saw it) of Keynesian political economy. Informed by the insights of historical institutionalist political science (see Chapter 6), *Governing the Economy* explored how the national institutional and historical context shaped economic processes. It drew attention to the constraints imposed by the organization of the state and the political system, and its resultant constitutional and electoral practices. The socio-economic structure of society, the structure of the working class and the nature of the trade union movement and industrial relations system also shaped how advanced political economies evolved. Hall's systematic comparative analysis of the changing political economies of France and Britain in the 1980s crystallized the CPE insight that only once polity and society have been understood in their institutional complexity, and the ideational context is taken into account, can economic restructuring and economic policy change be fully understood.

Berkeley professor John Zysman's *Governments, Markets and Growth* (1983) built upon the institutionalist approach to capitalism and homed in on finance, which Zysman highlighted was not a technical topic but a deeply political one. Finance mattered because the structure of financial markets shapes the kinds of business/state relations that are possible (ibid.: 7–8). Its import had been recognized by Shonfield, Johnson and others, but Zysman offered more tools for the comparative analysis of finance than those who came before him. He made the case by focusing on 'national financial structures' in order to understand both government economic strategies and the political conflicts that surround industrial change. National financial systems rest upon 'national political settlements about economic arrangements' (ibid.: 27) and each develops over decades and centuries, shaped by national histories, political cultures and state traditions. Zysman analysed the coherence of the national financial systems of post-war Britain, France, Japan, West Germany and the US. His organizing conceptual category, the national financial system, distils the essence of the historical processes of legislative and regulatory actions and legal inscription through which financial markets are made.

National financial systems, Zysman argued, structure the various sets of relationships between firms and capital markets, and in turn the kinds of corporate capitalism that arise. He offers a categorization of national financial systems, distinguishing between those based on the capital market (which approximates to the capitalism of the UK and the US), those based on credit with government-administered prices (as in Japan or France) and those based on credit and dominated by large financial institutions (as in Germany; ibid.: 69–75). The credit-based versus capital market–based approaches to turning savings into investment form the crucial line of differentiation within capitalism – informing long-termist, trust-based 'stakeholder' relationships and short-termist, profit-prioritizing 'shareholder' logics of firm financing, respectively. As Albert Hirschman pointed out in his celebrated analysis, credit-based systems, with close, long-term links between banks and firms, prioritize 'voice', the articulation of interests and reform agendas *within* the firm. Short-termist capital market–based systems, on the other hand, facilitate 'exit' – selling up and moving on within 'liquid' capital markets, rather than transforming a corporation from within (Hirschman 1970; Zysman 1983: 57). The study was important partly because it was published just as massive changes were being unleashed following the break-up of Bretton Woods by the international liberalization of capital markets, presenting new challenges and opportunities to the national financial systems Zysman had so ably delineated and categorized (see Chapter 10).

Swedish political scientist Gosta Esping-Andersen highlighted the intimate link between welfare provision and capitalism in the advanced economies. So entwined were these, Esping-Andersen argued, that one could not really understand the political economy of advanced capitalisms without also understanding the political economy of welfare regimes. His influential book *The Three Worlds of Welfare Capitalism* claimed that the welfare regime was 'the principal institution in the construction of different models of post-war capitalism' (1990: 5). He developed this insight through a focus on the welfare institutions and properties of different capitalisms. His work was a conscious emulation of the classical political economy approach: 'the classical political economists – whether of liberal, conservative or Marxist persuasion – were preoccupied with the relationship between capitalism and welfare' (ibid.: 9). Classical political economy has thus left its imprint on contemporary CPE, which Esping-Andersen argues 'has as its focal point the state–economy relationship defined by nineteenth century political economists' (ibid.: 12).

Analysing welfare capitalism cross-nationally, Esping-Andersen noted how 'welfare-state variations' are 'not linearly distributed, but clustered by regime-types' (ibid.: 26). His mapping of three worlds of welfare capitalism is built upon an understanding of how 'in the relation between state and economy a complex of legal and organizational features are systematically interwoven' (ibid.: 2). Important sources of the differentiation between regime types include conceptions and packages of social rights, patterns of social stratification and the relations between state, market and family (ibid.: 29). This was a seminal intervention into a rich vein of research of the CPE of welfare, which I discuss at length in Chapter 11.

A final set of key interventions, by Boston-based political scientist Professor Vivien Schmidt, explore in depth the French political economy, but also Germany, the UK and others in comparative and European context. Her animating concerns are twofold – the role of the state, and the role and power of political economic ideas, within contemporary capitalism. Schmidt's meticulous qualitative empirical research into French capitalist restructuring unearthed intriguing tendencies, for example into how France's privatization process of the 1980s and 1990s reconfigured state/market relations. This seemingly re-drew the boundaries between state and market in a more neo-liberal direction, yet it *increased* the interpenetration of public and private within French capitalism. The French Government hand-picked the recipients of the corporate sell-offs, constructing 'hard cores' of stable corporate conglomerates, ensuring France's industrial patrimony ended up in safe and friendly hands. This reinforced a 'protected capitalism' logic, providing the French economy with ongoing insulation from global market forces (Schmidt 1996).

Recalling Skocpol, bringing the state 'back in' to political economy analysis is a recurring theme of Schmidt's work (2010). Yet unlike Skocpol, Schmidt foregrounds ideational factors. The central insight of her 'discursive institutionalist' approach is that discourse and ideas play an important and independent role in shaping political economy (see Chapter 7). Economic ideas matter, not only for their content, but also in the form they take – which explains why some prove more influential than others. Political economy is thus not all about the inexorable grinding out of material forces – important though these undoubtedly are. Political economic actors are not slaves to their circumstances. Rather, they use their mental resources to evaluate critically the system they are part of, and the role they play within it, in their efforts to gain and wield political influence (Schmidt 2008).

Hence how actors 'make sense' of their situation, their interests and preferences is an important focal point for analysis, crucial to a deeper understanding of political economic change. Underlining this independent and causal role for ideas, her ideationally attuned analysis avoids what Schmidt terms the 'inevitability' of rational choice institutionalist analysis and the 'inexorability' of historical institutionalist analysis (2009: 540). Schmidt puts this ideational focus into practice in her comparative analysis of Europe's political economies, exploring French '*dirigiste*' ideas about appropriate policy, as contrasted with German 'ordo-liberal' ideas and British 'neo-liberal' ideas – and the different kinds of capitalism these varied ideational conditions can foster (2002).

This whistle-stop tour through some towering CPE scholarship of the last 50 years has established some common themes and telling insights which characterize CPE as a field of study and an intellectual endeavour. CPE is particularly well placed to reveal the political economy of modern capitalism, alive to its variety and the power relations at play within its evolution. It does this by comparing and contrasting the institutional and ideational contexts of domestic policy-making and national political economies through which international economic trends, processes and dynamics are mediated. Thus the key political economic evolutions of recent decades – the long post-war boom up to the 1970s, the break-up of Bretton Woods, the financial globalization thereafter, or the GFC and the 'Great Recession' which ensued, or Trump, the revival of economic nationalism and Brexit – are refracted in different ways through these national capitalisms. Each of these various scholars deploys the comparative method and tools of comparative political analysis (see Chapter 13) to shed new light upon, and generate fresh insights within, political economy debates. Appreciative of the variegation in the trajectories of national capitalisms, CPE is also adept at revealing the *politics* of capitalist change (or indeed stability).

One facet of this politics, highlighted in the work of Shonfield, Zysman, Johnson and Schmidt, is state intervention in economic activity and the active state as 'guiding force', steering national capitalist evolution (Shonfield 1965; Johnson 1982, 1995; Zysman 1983; Schmidt 2010). In the early 21st century, many CPE scholars detected a shift in balance between state and market (in favour of the latter) within capitalism. However, CPE highlights the contingency and historical specificity of individual national state adaptation processes, and so CPE scholars are wary of hasty generalization. The nature of market liberalization and deregulation has varied in different national institutional contexts, in part reflecting diverse objectives of policy elites and other key economic actors within nation states.

The sources of differentiation are partly institutional, but they are also ideational. A market-oriented dominant political economic orthodoxy has been sedimented into very different ideational settings (see Chapter 7), affecting policy-makers from varied backgrounds, in diverse geographical locations and with distinct ideological pre-dispositions. We can identify distinct economic ideas underpinning state traditions in the UK, France and Germany. These different ideational and historical legacies of state/economy relations can provide more or less conducive environments for particular forms of market-making to develop, a theme we will return to in Chapters 8–10. Equally, there are counter-tendencies restricting freer markets, informed by economic nationalism and protectionism. Many political forces favour not level playing fields but partiality, and discriminatory regulations and policies.

COMPARATIVE POLITICAL ECONOMY AND THE GLOBAL DIMENSION

In addition to situating the modern-day canon of CPE in relation to the classical political economists, it is also instructive to connect CPE to IPE, a prominent contemporary arena of inquiry with a similar substantive focus. A dialogue between IPE and CPE, such as that conducted in this book, can help advance understanding in each area (Clift et al. 2021). While there are numerous IPE overview books (see e.g. Blyth 2009a; Ravenhill 2017; O'Brien and Williams 2016; Broome 2014), the writing of CPE texts is a path much less trodden (rare examples include Lane and Ersson 1997; Menz 2017). Compared to IPE, CPE has seen far fewer attempts at staking out its territory and mapping its contours and intellectual borders in terms of substantive focus, central debates and so on (Clift and Rosamond 2009).

In establishing a conversation with, and a cross-fertilization between, IPE and CPE (discussed further in Chapter 2), scholars can draw on IPE's insights into the international context of national political economies. For example, the establishment of the post-war Bretton Woods order, and then its collapse in the 1970s, both transformed the global conditions within which national political economies evolve. Combining comparative and international perspectives gives us a deeper understanding of the dynamics of these changes.

The focus of this book, and of much CPE scholarship, is driven by the conviction that it helps more than it hinders to organize analysis in terms of national economic spaces, within which markets are regulated by national states and regulatory structures. This may appear to some an excessively 'territorial', 'statist' and 'nationalist' approach, at odds with the advancing 'supra-territoriality' analysed by a range of globalization scholars (Scholte 2005). Given the condition of globality and multiple non-state centres of power, why focus on national states or economies as units of analysis at all? Firstly, we do not conceive of national economic spaces and political economies as hermetically sealed. They have porous borders – perhaps increasingly so. More fundamentally, however, these national economies are part of the fabric of the international system – not abstracted from it. Any dichotomous opposition between national and global is problematic. National economies are constitutive of, and woven into, the global order, and national states are both 'architects' and 'subjects' of the world economy.

Operating exclusively at the global level risks not being able to gain explanatory purchase over broad, variegated and highly complex patterns and dynamics of change. Recourse to specific cases or episodes affords greater depth of analysis and empirical understanding. Furthermore, these national economic spaces remain the prevailing units of analysis for economic data collection. Starting from national political economies gives us empirical traction upon ongoing liberalizing, deregulating processes within the global political economy. Indeed, much political economy and CPE scholarship builds its conceptual frameworks and empirical understandings with an implicit or explicit recognition of a world still in a meaningful sense organized in terms of national states, societies and political economies.

Thus an organizing theme of this book, and of much CPE work, is analysing 'national' political economies, where appropriate grouped together into regional types displaying certain commonalities, such as (Western) European and (South East) Asian capitalism. Chapters will explore the similarities and differences between different capitalisms, and will consider common trends witnessed across a variety of political economies. The book will be focused upon analysing how best to understand change within national political economies, but also on setting the analysis systematically in a global context.

Although explicitly comparative in approach, this book focuses in particular on the advanced political economies, partly reflecting the central concerns of CPE's forebears. It could be argued that one shortcoming or blind spot of CPE is that it is too Western-centric (see Hobson 2012; Helleiner and Wang 2018; Chey and Helleiner 2018). Many strands of CPE analysis have at best limited engagement with the political economy of development, and issues and substantive debates pertaining primarily to developing and emerging political economies. CPE tends to extrapolate from the particular, mostly Western European or North American, experiences of capitalist development or welfare state evolution. The concepts, theories and typologies developed to explain political economic developments in these advanced economies may not readily 'travel' to other contexts. Here I do not deny the importance of studying developing and lower–income countries, or indeed the process of economic development within CPE. These are not, however, the debates and issues this book is focused upon.

This book does focus upon the CPE of the advanced 'post-industrial' economies, the members of the Organisation for Economic Co-operation and Development (OECD), a formal grouping of the 37 most advanced economies. Broadly speaking, there is a 'most similar systems' research design rationale explaining this selection of focus, which groups together cases sharing particular key characteristics (see Chapter 13; Przeworski and Teune 1970). Certain political economic structural conditions obtain within, to put it crudely, the richer nations on the planet, where more of the economic wealth is concentrated. This differentiates political economic processes and dynamics within those national economic spaces from the rest of the world. Our focus is primarily upon those states that experienced what Polanyi called *The Great Transformation* (2001 [1944]) many decades ago, resulting from the formation and maturation of market institutions, accompanied by the expansion of regulative state activity over markets. These developments entrenched the market system as a mechanism for sustaining and maintaining the whole of society. The focus is also driven by the prominent research questions in the CPE field, such as the transformation of the state, the character and degree of welfare regime restructuring, the changing nature and role of finance at the national and international levels, the evolution of models of capitalism, and the role of institutions, interests and ideas within capitalist restructuring. Most of these questions have been most illuminatingly asked of advanced economies.

THE RATIONALE, ORGANIZATION AND FOCUS OF THE BOOK

Chapters 2–4 introduce and explore the giants of the study of political economy on whose shoulders contemporary scholarship is standing. Chapter 2 sets out this book's approach to CPE and identifies four core insights into political economy and CPE, drawn from classical political economy. These can helpfully underpin the analysis of contemporary 21st-century capitalism and its evolution. I also set out the terms on which a dialogue between CPE and IPE can be most fruitfully conducted.

Chapter 3 then engages key classical political economy thinkers and debates, focusing on Adam Smith, Karl Marx and Friedrich List in particular. The differing views on the individual's role in wealth creation of Smith, List and Marx inform distinctive understandings of capitalism's dynamics, which in turn shape their views on state/market relations and the international order. Discussion also explores the differing views on the conception of the market, individuals and their place within society, and the nature of capitalist society underpinning each variant of classical political economy. Scrutiny of these fundamental but under-discussed issues helps explain how and why these theoretical approaches to political economy differ. Comparing and contrasting these competing theoretical positions helps us to understand how to think like a political economist and to get below the surface to achieve more depth of analytical insight. In the process, the aim of Chapters 2 and 3 is to set out what modern CPE scholars can usefully learn from the classical political economists in approaching the study of 21st-century capitalism.

In Chapter 4 I then explore the later evolution of classical political economy, considering the role and legacy of 'disciplinary politics' (debates about approach and method within an academic field) in the separation of politics and economics. I discuss the *Methodenstreit* of the late 19th century, which saw the divergence of interpretive and historical analysis and methods in political economy from the marginalist political economy which was the forerunner of modern economics. Marginalism, like the neo-classical economics it spawned, adopted a range of simplifying assumptions and prioritized theoretical parsimony, deductive reasoning and generalization. This crucial phase in the evolution of modern social sciences in general and political economy in particular provides the back-story to why, today, economics and political economy differ so markedly. This historical context brings into clearer focus the nature of CPE as a field of study, how it has evolved in this particular direction and why. In exploring the legacy of this divide for political economy, I note how economics sets itself a qualitatively different set of analytical and explanatory tasks from CPE. Appreciating this indicates how earlier work in political economy can be incorporated into the modern canon of CPE scholarship.

Charting this evolution of political economy sets up engagement with a carefully selected range of central debates within the contemporary CPE literature. It also provides a theoretically informed account of how capitalism can and should be analysed and understood. Successive chapters consider CPE in terms of interests, institutions and ideas, introducing a variety of approaches. This will enable readers to compare, appropriately enough, the contributions of varied CPE theoretical approaches and perspectives to understanding contemporary capitalism.

Chapter 5 begins this charting of contemporary CPE's core substantive focus, looking at the most important theoretical and conceptual debates, and the most prevalent empirical areas of investigation. I explore interests and CPE, considering analysis that looks at political economy in an instrumental manner and, like economics, makes a set of assumptions about individual actors and their rationality. This interest-based approach reprises Harold Lasswell's classic formulation of what the study of politics amounts to: his *Politics: Who Gets What, When, How?* (1936). Similarly, celebrated political economist Susan Strange always began with the question *cui bono*? (Latin for 'who benefits?') from political economic processes and institutions (Strange 1994a: 136, 234). I consider first group-based or societal-level analysis such as corporatist analysis or Marxian class-based political economy. Thereafter, discussion considers rational choice and its methodological individualistic application of economics' methods to the study of politics. I consider public choice critiques of state/market relations and their influence on state reform, marketization and privatization since the 1970s, before finishing with an exploration of modern re-formulations of rational choice in terms of 'bounded rationality'.

Chapter 6 will consider institutions and their role within, and relationship to, economic activity and the wider society, noting how capitalism and markets require an institutional infrastructure to operate. The market economy, as Karl Polanyi once noted, is 'an instituted process' (1957: 243–70), with rules 'embedded in the market itself' (Caporaso and Levine 1992: 150). Perhaps the most celebrated debate in modern CPE is that about comparative capitalisms. This was re-invigorated by the publication of *Varieties of Capitalism* (Hall and Soskice 2001), organized around the notion of 'comparative institutional advantage'. Thus front and centre within VoC research are the nature and role of institutions, and their impact on and connection to market relations. These are identified as important sources of the distinctive qualities and properties of different kinds of capitalism. This enables us to explore key issues in institutionalist CPE, such as how one should understand the relationship between institutions, the agents who animate them and their wider social context, through VoC debates and critiques. I will note how CPE needs to pay attention to the logic and dynamics of institutional creation and thereafter reproduction. Equally central to CPE is how institutional change is explained.

One consistent theme of this book is the importance of the ideational realm to understanding CPE. Accordingly, Chapter 7 explores the role of ideas in CPE analysis, building upon foundations laid by one of the founders of modern sociology, Max Weber. Weber analysed political economy in terms of *Verstehen*, or how economic actors understand their environment and how individual action is shaped and constituted by institutional arrangements. These Weberian notions represent important insights in affording the ideational level – and the causal and constitutive role of ideas – due weight in CPE analysis. The chapter illustrates how exclusively material accounts of political economy (focusing only upon things you can see, touch or drop upon your foot) miss the role of ideational factors in shaping outcomes. It considers changing dominant political economic orthodoxies and the establishment and breakdown of Bretton Woods.

A focus on 'states and markets' captures the substantive essence of political economy as a field, and in Chapter 8 we explore the contemporary transformation of the state in a comparative context. Important conceptual categories, notably the 'developmental state'

(Johnson 1982, 1995), are outlined, illustrating how these can be deployed in a comparative analysis of state/market relations and their evolution. Following on from Chapter 7, I argue that the contingent state transformation processes are best understood within the ideational context of state traditions. An embedded conception of state/economy relations requires an appreciation of these variegated ideational particularities. This is illustrated through a comparative process tracing analysis of the evolution of the Japanese and Chinese developmental states.

Having considered VoC in relation to the theoretical and conceptual building blocks of institutionalist analysis in Chapter 6, we return to it in Chapter 9 to evaluate its explanatory purchase upon empirical developments in advanced capitalisms. To do this, we will consider VoC along with some other approaches to comparative capitalisms such as the French Regulation School and the social structures of accumulation approach. The chapter shows how, although very different, each of these rich comparative capitalisms literatures unearths the dynamics of capitalism as a negotiated socio-economic order. The nature of that negotiation takes multiple forms, plays out differently and is institutionalized in diverse ways, constituting distinct varieties of capitalism. Deploying comparative capitalisms concepts and insights to explain and understand capitalist evolution in the 21st century (through detailed exploration of transformations within Japanese and US capitalism), I make the case for 'hybridization' as the most convincing way to capture the substantive empirical realities and complexities of contemporary capitalist restructuring.

It is in the realms of finance and its liberalization that processes of international political economic change have progressed furthest since the 1970s. The end of the Bretton Woods era, and the subsequent rise and rise of international capital mobility, transformed state/market relations. This has challenged some of the stable institutional inter-relationships which underpinned post-war national varieties of capitalism. In Chapter 10 we explore the implications of this for two core building blocks of capitalism – firms and financial markets. We will explore and chart how changing global finance is reshaping national financial systems, and the firms and corporate governance practices within particular national variants of corporate capitalism. The processes of change within finance, firms and markets are all profoundly shaped by politics, and this chapter offers empirical demonstration (through in-depth consideration of the French and German cases) of how markets – including freer markets – are social and political constructs.

In advanced economies, the redistributive institutional infrastructure of social protection, what we might term the 'welfare regime', intervenes to mitigate some of the destabilizing and iniquitous effects of market competition, and to shape the labour market's norms. Indeed, the interrelationship between welfare provision and capitalist social relations of production is so fundamental that some talk of 'welfare capitalism'. Different 'welfare properties' and (in)egalitarian outcomes within capitalisms are explained by the configuration of socially embedded capitalist institutions in each country. The properties and qualities that different sets of welfare institutions impart to the particular types of market relations are considered in Chapter 11, where we also explore the relationship between welfare states and globalization.

The variety and differentiation within capitalisms explored in Chapters 8–11 are testament to the nationally differentiated distributive consequences of capitalism, and how the societal distribution of economic and social resources in different economies is crucially shaped by the institutional context of market activity. Chapter 12 explores the political, economic and social forces shaping the evolution of inequality within contemporary capitalism. Lower and median wages have stagnated in many advanced economies. Meanwhile, the very richest groups in society have become astonishingly affluent, and the wealthiest individuals and firms have managed to avoid and evade paying adequate tax on their vertiginous incomes. Furthermore, the very wealthy have exploited their political capital to make regulations laxer and loopholes larger (see Hacker and Pierson 2010). All this has increased political tensions surrounding economic inequality (Hopkin and Lynch 2016; Hopkin and Shaw 2016; Stiglitz 2012, 2015). The social and political underpinnings of liberal market capitalism have come under tremendous strain. Fractured by these widening inequalities, the social and political foundations of the political economy order began to pull apart in the early 21st century, heralding resurgent economic nationalism and populist backlashes against globalization.

The classic liberal political economy argument is that economic growth is good for all. A rising tide will float all boats. New Right US President Ronald Reagan back in the 1980s defended tax cuts for the rich on the grounds of 'trickle-down economics'. Supposedly, the increased economic dynamism unleashed by lower taxes for the rich would (in the end) benefit all economic actors, whatever their location within capitalism's social stratification. Such claims looked increasingly threadbare in the early 21st century. The decade of so-called 'great moderation' of sustained and stable economic growth in advanced economies before the GFC was, in fact, not great for many groups in society. Behind the apparent economic stability of the 1990s and early 2000s were heightening inequalities, increasing disaffection and simmering political tensions. As celebrated French economist Piketty pointed out (2014), reviving insights offered by Marx 150 years ago, capitalism has a serious inequality problem (see Chapter 12).

This book advances the case for taking a comparative approach to political economy, which is elaborated at length in Chapter 13. The comparative element within CPE provides both the definitional boundaries of the sub-field, as well as the core analytical resource which generates many of its most important insights. Returning to the theme of disciplinary politics, and how it shapes choices of method within CPE, Chapter 13 introduces the two cultures, 'qualitative' and 'quantitative', of social research, and what is 'at stake' in making these choices about methodological and explanatory frameworks for the analysis of CPE. It also sets out the logic of systematic comparative analysis and research design, issues crucial to successful CPE work.

2 Comparative Political Economy: Lineages from Classical Political Economy, Linkages to International Political Economy

INTRODUCTION

This chapter sets out the approach of this book, and distils the essence of the political economy tradition into a series of core insights which underpin and animate the CPE analysis offered here. I highlight how the pre-disciplinary character of classical political economy is a key reason why it engaged in holistic, integrated analysis of political economy and is an important source of its insights. From a contemporary standpoint, when the dominant social scientific disciplines have been shaping our views and structuring our interpretations of the political economic world for a century and more, it is not easy to rediscover such a pre-disciplinary mindset. Nevertheless, as I will argue in this chapter, the attempt to do so repays the intellectual investment required. This book's approach to political economy is also informed by the combined insights of recent developments in CPE and the IPE literature, and assumes that dialogue between the two areas of the political economy canon can help to advance understanding in each area. For this reason, the final section sets out how the conversation between CPE and IPE can best be approached to improve the prospects of fruitful cross-fertilization.

DISCIPLINARY POLITICS AND CLASSICAL POLITICAL ECONOMY

Embrace of the 'pre-disciplinary' character of classical political economy within modern CPE is an important stance within what we will encounter in Chapter 4 as 'disciplinary politics', or the decisions made about what a field of study or academic discipline amounts to and should focus on, what is at its core, and what lies outside it. For now, suffice to note that between different academic disciplines (and even between different schools of thought within disciplines) there can be important, indeed trenchant, disagreements on these issues (Rosamond 2007; Clift and Rosamond 2009; Clift et al. 2021), and that disciplinary political divides have been crucial elements within political economy's evolution.

Today, as a result of the sedimented effects of disciplinary politics, intellectual endeavour tends to be much narrower in scope than in the 18th and 19th centuries. Social scientific research often operates within fairly strict, self-defined academic disciplinary borders which render large swathes of social scientific inquiry outside their remit. Thus much exploration of what one might think 'should' be political economy analysis takes place in the fields of sociology or geography. The silo mentalities of academic disciplines mean that such work can be obscured from view to those working in politics, for example. Here part of the problem is the disciplining effects of academic fields as they have grown up over many decades, with economics studied according to one set of prior assumptions and attendant theories, methods and techniques, and political science developing along a very different path. Politics scholars developed tools for studying political institutions and processes, but often paid little, or limited, attention to the economic context of such political dynamics. Political science and economics can thus seem rather hermetically sealed and unable to engage with each other. At least, they often appear uninterested in such engagement because of the chasm that has emerged over time between how each respectively goes about studying politics and the economy.

One very influential strand of economic thought, marginalism (which we shall encounter in Chapter 4), made a set of assumptions about 'naturally' emerging, perfectly competitive and efficiently operating markets. These 'marginalist' assumptions underpinned the development of neo-classical economics in the late 19th and 20th centuries, which continues to form the bedrock of modern mainstream economics today. The assumptions and foundations upon which economics is built matter because they reflect different ideological pre-suppositions about how efficient markets are, and how and in what way agents are rational. Such assumptions have political consequences, since different pre-suppositions can entail very different policy ramifications and corollaries.

Moves in this marginalist direction were taken further in the 1970s with the rise of 'New Classical' macroeconomics (Lucas 1976; Lucas and Sargent 1981). The discipline of economics has since become increasingly focused on processes of individual 'optimization' wherein economic agents, assumed to be possessed of perfect information and seemingly infinite forward-looking calculative abilities, constantly adjust their selection of the optimal course of action or basket of goods to maximize their utility. This view of utility maximization, assuming perfect information and forward-looking constant optimization, was at the core of New Classical economics' challenge to earlier Keynesian economics. Keynesianism had shone the analytical light on significant market imperfections and failures. New Classical economics, by contrast, assumed *a priori* the superior efficiency of markets.

New Classical economics' animating desire was to provide rigorous 'micro-foundations' (incorporating forward-looking, constantly optimizing agents) for macroeconomic theorizing and analysis. Yet building economic models on the foundations of these constantly optimizing and efficient understandings of how actors and markets behave had important political implications. Assuming constantly optimizing forward-looking agents, possessed of complete and perfect information, fuels a conviction that market mechanisms and the private sector will allocate resources optimally. These *a priori*-presumed efficient functioning markets, in this vision of the economy, can and should be left to their own devices to steer the economy back to (full employment) equilibrium (see e.g. Quiggin 2012: 80–4, 109–10; Backhouse 2002: 298–301; Stiglitz 2018: 75).

The discipline of economics from the marginalists onwards also made *ceteris paribus* (all other things being equal) assumptions, holding factors relating to political, social and historical context constant in order to separate out analytically the study of the economic. Most economists decided, for perfectly respectable intellectual reasons, to follow this lead in homing in on the economic factors and processes in which they were most interested, and such a starting point can be put to very good use. As I show when discussing rational choice approaches to CPE in Chapter 5 on 'interests', appropriating economic assumptions about individuals and their preferences in the comparative study of political processes can be a source of revealing insights. At the same time, the assumptions of most mainstream economics tend to exclude the state, politics and society from their models. Indeed economics, as in the example above, often incorporates forms of normative bias *against* state intervention in the economy. This has profoundly affected how the realm of the economic is understood, not only within the discipline of economics, but across the social sciences more broadly.

Classical political economy spanned what today we would separate out as political science, economics, philosophy, sociology and history, to name but five. Most obviously, this was because modern academic disciplines had not yet come into being when the classical political economists were thinking and writing. But more importantly, the intellectual project and animating concerns of classical political economy held that the political *could not* and *should not* be separated from the economic and the social. The classical political economists further thought that processes such as the division of labour within the production process had profound social and political implications. The Industrial Revolution was in its infancy when Adam Smith was writing in the 18th century, but by the mid-19th century it was transforming economy and society out of all recognition. These economic changes needed to be analysed and understood in their political, social and historical context.

Seeking to avoid the silo mentality which academic disciplining can elicit involves two main intellectual moves. First, in terms of substantive focus, analysis needs to recognize that the political, the economic and the social are always intertwined, and should be understood as such. Second, CPE, as part of the political economy tradition, is a broad and pluralistic field of study, and thus we draw on ideas and analysis from a range of academic disciplines, including, for example, sociology, economics and history as well as political science and IPE, a field we will discuss in more detail below. Inevitably, one's own intellectual development as a political economist trained in and working in politics departments has been shaped by those same disciplining effects within academia. Hence within the 'genetic' material out of which this book has grown, political science and IPE are very much the dominant genes.

Classical political economy's intellectual pluralism can be one of CPE's strengths. The predisciplinary spirit of classical political economy opens up possibilities here which can seem closed off by how academic disciplines have developed and delineated their borders and 'external relations' with each other since the late 19th century. For example, economic sociology is a somewhat neglected source of intellectual inspiration for political economy analysis and CPE. This is both curious and regrettable, since it has valuable lessons (about appropriate conceptions of the state and state/market relations, and how to understand capitalisms comparatively) for CPE analysis (see e.g. Granovetter and Swedberg 2001; Smelser and Swedberg 2005). Central to economic sociology is the recognition of the role and significance of the 'embeddedness' of the economic within a societal context (Granovetter 1985; Polanyi 2001 [1944]). This concept, as we shall see below, can offer much within CPE analysis. It helps us to understand major upheavals in state/market relations, and underlines how politics matters within such a transformation. For example, the intertwining of the political, the economic and the social is illustrated in the birth of modern welfare states (which we discuss in Chapter 11), which was linked to the economic crisis in 1870s Bismarckian Germany (Esping-Andersen 1999; Hay and Wincott 2012: 9).

WHY IS THE HISTORY OF POLITICAL ECONOMY SO IMPORTANT FOR CONTEMPORARY COMPARATIVE POLITICAL ECONOMY?

The insights of the classical political economists about the nature, functioning and dynamics of capitalism, this book argues, are very useful points of departure and analytical tools for the comparative study of the advanced capitalist economies in the 21st century. To understand political economy's distinctive intellectual, analytical and explanatory agenda, it is necessary to trace back the evolution of thinking about and analysis of the economy to the latter parts of the 19th century, and indeed further. While the immediate pertinence of these issues might not be at first glance self-evident, how economic thought evolved a long time ago is actually of burgeoning contemporary relevance, as will become clear. It affects the way we think about the economy and the kinds of questions we can and do ask about economic issues in different academic disciplines. Furthermore, arguably some of the greatest minds in human history were political economists. Given the prodigious intellectual gifts of Smith and Marx, in particular, it seems churlish not to draw on their insights. Their penetrating analyses of early industrial capitalism and state/market relations, even if written 200 or so years ago, are in fact remarkably prescient for our own times, as I will demonstrate.

Marxian ideas about the logic of capital accumulation driving capitalist social reproduction and the structural power of capital can offer telling insights into the nature and narration of responses to the GFC. When the financial crisis morphed into a debt crisis, governments apparently felt compelled to prop up financial institutions and sectors on a massive scale through a socialization of risk which saw bad bank debts end up on the public's books. Securing the balance sheets of the big banks is, it seems, treated as a 'public good'. Accusations of moral hazard (excessive risk-taking by economic actors who can avoid or pass on the costs and liabilities of their actions) were directed towards supposedly fiscally profligate national governments (many of whose finances had been in good shape before they had to bail out the banks), but not towards the excesses of risk-taking in investment banking. Marxian ideas about the structural power of capital, specifically what Hilferding later termed 'finance capital' (1910), offer one highly plausible account of why governments intervened on a gargantuan scale to save major finance houses and investment banks – at colossal expense to the taxpayer and to the extreme detriment of the state of the public finances in advanced economies.

Meanwhile, Adam Smith and the liberal political economic principles he espoused continue to be appealed to regularly to justify or decry 21st-century economic institutions and policy choices. Smith made a distinction between 'natural' prices and 'market' prices. Natural prices pertained to the abstract model of a perfectly competitive price-adjusting economy. Yet this, Smith recognized, was an abstraction and not an account of how markets or economies really work. In the real world, he was all too aware, markets are *not* perfectly competitive, and all kinds of distortions can enter the price adjustment process. What emerge in these real-world situations are not 'natural' but 'market' prices. Smith's distinction between natural prices and market prices portrays how real prices are set in a social context pervaded by sets of economic and political power relations, and by institutions (Smith 1993 [1776]: 36–62; Watson 2005a: 104–6). For this reason, market prices will in all probability not align with the natural prices.

This one distinction is pregnant with a number of hugely significant insights, and suggests analytical moves which are central to thinking like a political economist. In this one conceptual distinction, we get a feel for how the political and social context of economic activity shapes outcomes and distorts a 'pure' or 'free' operation of market mechanisms or forces. We get some useful pointers on how comparative political economists can begin to bring together the social and political along with the economic into a holistic understanding of political economy. This insight that real prices ('market prices') are arrived at in a social context stratified with power relationships which affect all economic outcomes remains as pertinent to understanding 21st-century sub-prime mortgage holders (Schwartz and Seabrooke 2008; Schwartz 2009) and those 'left behind' by globalization (Crouch 2019) as it was to understanding poor labourers in 1776 (Rothschild 2001: 69). Then, as now, comparative analysis of these processes in different contexts throws into relief how the prevailing balance of political forces in society, and unequal power relationships, influence economic outcomes.

The 'economic nationalist' ideas of Friedrich List about strategies for achieving economic development in a liberalizing world economy, characterized by uneven development and unequal power relations between states, have much to offer in seeking to understand the seemingly inexorable political and economic rise of China within the contemporary world order. The advanced economies struggle to achieve economic growth, while the increasingly influential 'BRICS' economies (Brazil, Russia, India, China and South Africa) have enjoyed prodigious growth. The changing configuration of economic and political power, shaped by differing economic trajectories, is transforming the nature of the world order and economic interdependence. In advanced and emerging economies alike, governments have become creative at politically managing their exposure to international competition and their point of insertion into the world economy by new means and old. The multiple policy instruments in support of national or regional economic actors are today more fragmented and less coherent than under post-World War II capitalism, but no less prevalent (Clift and Woll 2012a, 2012b). The pertinence of Listian ideas was graphically demonstrated with the revival of economic nationalist discourse and policies under the Trump administration in the US. Protectionism and 'America first'-oriented discriminatory practices to favour domestic industries, which recall Alexander Hamilton's political economic vision of the 1790s, more so than free trade and liberalized markets, became the hallmarks of American foreign economic relations. Thus in order to understand better the contemporary transformation of political influence over the economy, much can be learned from the writings of List and Smith on freer trade, its political management and regulation, and sources of resistance to it.

Most contemporary CPE scholarship, explicitly or implicitly, wittingly or otherwise, is in fact 'standing on the shoulders of giants', and that is why Chapters 3 and 4 take the reader through the key ideas, concepts and insights of the most influential classical political economists. While they disagreed about a great deal, they shared some important assumptions about how to study and conceptualize political economy – notably a *pre-disciplinary* view of political economy as a holistic field of study. In order to grasp fully what CPE is all about, it is necessary to understand something of what was at stake in decisions taken at crucial phases by influential scholars about what was, and what was not, the appropriate central focus for economic analysis. The interrelationship between the political, the economic and the social which some strands of economics have been at pains to assume away is precisely what is most crucial to the study of political economy and CPE.

The charting of the historical evolution of political economy enables us to understand some of the differences between diverse approaches within contemporary CPE – for example, why a rational choice approach to understanding capitalism (see Chapter 5) is significantly different from an 'ideational political economy' approach (Chapter 7). Understanding the disciplinary and pre-disciplinary back-story sheds light on the distinctive kinds of insights that each approach can offer. This backdrop also deepens our understanding of the ideas of towering 20th-century figures in political economy such as Keynes, Hayek and Polanyi, whose insights and arguments continue to animate debates about state/market relations today. This intellectual lineage informs a richer understanding of contemporary state/market relations in the 21st century.

COMPARATIVE POLITICAL ECONOMY: THE CORE INSIGHTS

This section sets out how best to use insights originating in classical political economy, and refined by modern CPE, to explore contemporary developments in CPE by identifying four core analytical insights which underpin the analysis of CPE as set out in this volume. As will be clear from previous sections, these insights, although not necessarily always to the fore in much contemporary analysis, are not new. They are as old as the field of political economy. All were keenly appreciated by the progenitors of the modern field of political economy such as Smith, Marx, List and Weber. Unpacking these four classical political economy insights provides the rationale and justification for the approach to CPE taken in this book. Each in its way conveys a sense of why making the kinds of assumptions that modern economics does can only paint a partial picture. Each one reinforces how a pre-disciplinary approach or mindset can enrich our comparative understanding of capitalism.

Core insight 1: state/market relations

The first point is about how to approach the understanding of state/market interaction and the dynamics of capitalism. One of the most important normative debates over the principles of political economy surrounds the appropriate role of state and market (see Chapters 4, 6 and 7; Gamble 1986). More recently, many of the more interesting analytical debates and controversies in the empirical investigation of political economic developments within the discipline have focused on the trajectory, fate and potentialities of the nation state within a changing global political economy (see Chapters 8 and 11). However, while all agree that a focus on states and markets is central to political economy, there are widely differing normative positions on and understandings of the nature of each, and of their complex relationship.

Susan Strange's classical IPE text entitled *States and Markets* (1994a) remains open as to the nature of the relationship. Other important political economy volumes have been *States Versus Markets* (Schwartz 2010) and *States Against Markets* (Boyer and Drache 1996). These titles (if not necessarily the analysis within the volumes) display a tendency to view the two elements as separable and engaged in a 'zero-sum' struggle for prevalence, pertinence and relevance within political economy. As if both were perched on the ends of a seesaw, one prevails or predominates at the other's expense. I argue that such a conception constitutes an analytical wrong turn. It is unhelpful to think of states and markets as 'analytically separate realms each with its autonomous logic', a tendency which economic sociologists Fred Block and Peter Evans call 'state–economy dualism' (2005: 512). The temptation towards such a dichotomizing opposition of state and market should be resisted. This is because the idea of a tug of war between 'state' on the one hand and 'market' on the other is a very unhelpful way to conceptualize state/market relations in CPE.

The classical political economy mindset offers a number of correctives to avoid this unhelpful mischaracterization of the relations between state and market. Adam Smith understood that capitalist market relations existed in a social order involving state intervention in the defence from external threat, securing law and order and the sanctity of private property and contracts, as well as protection from 'injustice' and 'oppression'. However, his vision for state intervention in the good society extended much further to include a range of 'publick goods' and 'publick works', including – very radically for his time – a commitment to public education. Thus, for Smith, state intervention was an inevitable, a necessary and indeed a desirable element within commercial capitalism (see pp. 49–50, 169–70).

From a Polanyian perspective, there is a similar emphasis on the state's role in setting the rules and framework for market activity and on state intervention that is necessary for the governance of, indeed the existence of, markets. Karl Polanyi's *The Great Transformation* demonstrated how 'regulation and markets, in effect, grew up together' and that 'no market economy separated from the political sphere is possible' (Polanyi 2001 [1944]: 71, 205). The 19th-century 'liberal state' which he described was in many ways the architect of the misnamed 'self-regulating' market and central to the processes of regulation without which *laissez-faire* capitalism could not have existed (ibid.: 146–7; see also Block 2003; Krippner and Alvarez 2007).

Alternatively, and directly inspired by Karl Marx, contemporary historical materialist political economy argues for the need to move away from 'those frameworks which insist on regarding "states" and "markets" as fundamentally opposed forms of social organisation' (Burnham 2001: 108). Marxian political economy scholars refuse 'to fetishize' either the 'market' or the 'state'. Burnham's 'Open Marxism' 'locates the development of the capitalist state in the establishment and maintenance of generalised commodity production' (ibid.: 106–7). Thus 'states are not to be thought of as "thing-like" institutions losing power to the market' (ibid.: 108). Thinking about the state as a 'moment' or 'nodal point' in a circuit of capital reaffirms how state and market are inseparable both empirically and analytically (ibid.: 107; see also Clarke 1983: 118; Phillips 2005: 85–6).

One illustration of this point is the interaction of states and markets as the 'Great Complacence' (Engelen et al. 2011) of the NICE (non-inflationary continuous expansion) decade from the late 1990s to the mid-2000s, which then gave way to first the GFC and thereafter the 'Great Recession'. This was characterized *not* by a reassertion of state power at the expense of a retreat of market forces, but by the coexistence of pervasive liberalized markets and emboldened, more activist and interventionist states in many advanced economies. Substantial parts of modern social scientific academic disciplines have evolved over many decades on foundations of 'state–economy dualism'. Within much mainstream neoclassical economics, for example, the state is often exogenous to the model. By contrast, the approach to CPE adopted in this volume argues, along with like-minded IPE scholars, for a move away from a dichotomous opposition between states and markets (see Gamble 1995; Higgott 1999; Underhill 2000; Watson 2005a), towards studying political economy as an integrated whole. Inspired by classical political economy, and thinkers like Smith, Marx and notably Polanyi, it is helpful to think in terms of the mutual constitution of state and market. The fundamental premise here is that 'the notion that markets could exist outside of state action is simply inconceivable' (Krippner and Alvarez 2007: 233).

Core insight 2: markets as politically constructed, not natural

The second core insight, which follows on from the first, is that there is inevitably and always political intervention in and shaping of the operation of markets. Markets are *not* natural phenomena, but have to be politically constructed and politically maintained. Markets, in short, have to be made; and this is a deeply political process. We need to understand political economy not just in terms of the operation of markets, or the reproduction of market relations, but also in terms of processes of market-making which always accompany such operations. Thus the high levels of inequality within contemporary advanced capitalisms (see Chapter 12) are not the natural outcome of market mechanisms. Rather, they result from political forces mobilizing to engage in market-making and to shape laws, regulations and tax regimes in particular ways.

We can see how political interventionism shaped and made markets historically. The chain of historical developments that culminated in the 'national revolutions' which saw the formation of modern European nation states (Lipset and Rokkan 1967) were precursors to the spread of markets and the rise of modern capitalism. These political developments facilitated the political acts of market-making that were the midwife of modern industrial capitalism. The standardization of currencies, measures and so on, the advent of modern company law and the regulation of financial markets and transactions, were all crucial to the smoother operation of markets on increasingly large scales. A series of political, legislative and regulatory reforms had to accompany and nurture, at each stage, the emergence and development of markets (see Chapters 9 and 10). The intertwining of the political and the economic within market-making processes takes different forms in different societies. This is both a key finding from, and an important focus for, CPE analysis. Friedrich List highlighted this in his *National System of Political Economy*, and the theme has been taken up by subsequent CPE scholars.

List saw international economic relations against the backdrop of a struggle for wealth and power of different nations, and market relations and institutions as always subject to political intervention. His critique of 19th-century British free trade liberalism is not that free trade is undesirable in theory, but that the hypocritical British economic strategy was highly protectionist in practice, and only very selectively liberal. List's analysis underscored how political intervention in economic activity will always be pervasive (List 1856 [1841]: 250). In the real world where the world order is configured around national political economies striving for what List termed 'civilisation and power', 'free trade' is not really free and it is 'folly to speak of unrestricted competition between individuals of different nations' (ibid.: 261).

In some ways, this is a reiteration of Smith's point about natural and market prices – but offers a little more by way of explanation of the contours of the political struggles which shape market outcomes and what is at stake within them. It is an irony that the capitalist national markets which Smith and other liberals so revered could only come into existence as a direct result of the earlier actions and market-making interventions of the mercantilist statesmen Smith decried in the *Wealth of Nations* (Swedberg 2005: 236–7). Mercantilism 'strove to create a unified domestic market for commodity production. Aiming to increase the power of the State relative to that of all other States, it encouraged export of goods, while banning exports of bullion or coins, in the belief that there was a fixed quantity of commerce and wealth in the world' (Anderson 1974: 35). Smith thought their policy approach wrong-headed, but without mercantilists establishing national markets, and the institutional infrastructure that sustained them, liberal classical political economy would never have been able to advocate the anti-mercantilist free market agenda.

The centrality of political acts of market-making also comes through vividly in Polanyi's work. The supposed 'liberal' political economic character of 19th-century Britain is, as Polanyi points out, misleading. In fact the spread of markets was the result of political forces and interventions making and shaping markets: 'there was nothing natural about laissez-faire; free markets could never have come into being merely by allowing things to take their course ... Laissez-faire was planned' (2001 [1944]: 146, 147). State actors, acting in concert with prevailing social forces, had to manage the process of freeing up markets, constructing the international, legal and regulatory frameworks which enabled these markets to operate, and maintaining the impetus of market-making in the face of opposition. Along the way, the establishment of markets needed to compensate or exclude 'losers' from socio-economic change, and keep the social peace. Thus 'the road to the free market was opened and kept open by an enormous increase in continuous, centrally organized and controlled interventionism' (ibid.: 146).

Understanding capitalism in terms of market-making helps incorporate a range of insights from classical political economy. It also draws attention to important empirical realities of the intertwining of the political and the economic in the real-world operation of markets. If we consider executive wage determination in the banking and finance sector, we can see evidence of the politicized processes of arriving at market prices and the wielding of economic power which Adam Smith identified. These processes have become further politicized in public debates about, and outrage at, levels of bankers' remuneration since the GFC. Some governments sought to step in to impose or encourage limits on pay and bonuses, often with limited success. Similar political struggles surround efforts by states and campaigners to get large multinational corporations to pay adequate tax on their enormous profits in the various jurisdictions where they operate. Yet while such efforts and struggles render the political intervention in market outcomes highly visible, this is nothing exceptional. Virtually all capitalist markets are sustained by extra-economic regulation (relating, for example, to environmental or labour standards, health and safety provisions or the outlawing of child labour) – 'pure' exchange relations are rare (see e.g. Chang 1996, 1999). In this book we shall operate with the notion of markets as social and political constructions, and foreground these political acts of market-making.

Core insight 3: economy embedded in social and political context

The third foundational assumption, which is a logical corollary of the second, is that the operation of markets does not take place separately from its societal, historical and political context, and therefore market relations should not be analysed in isolation from this context. Unlike the 'all other things being equal' assumptions of economics which strip away social, historical and political context, CPE as understood here is driven by the desire to retain the interrelatedness of the economic, political and social within its understanding and analysis.

The classical political economy tradition, once again, provided torch bearers who were pursuing similar intellectual ambitions. As Matthew Watson points out, classical political economy 'focused on economic *relations* as a sub-set of the broader social relations into which individuals were integrated as members of a society that was based on asymmetric distributions of power' (Watson 2005a: 48). Although not expressed in these terms, for Smith the key economic category of capital was understood as what Marx would later call a set of *social* relations of production. Much of Smith's writing on capitalism embedded his economic analysis in a wider cultural, social, historical and political context (see ibid.: 108). Within the liberal classical political economy approach of Smith and Ricardo, and the radical approach of Marx, society was analysed in class-based terms, identifying socio-economic categories of land, labour and capital as sources of a stratified social order. This was but one reflection of their appreciation that economic activity is rooted in, shapes and is also shaped by society. Thus an individual's relationship to capital, to land and to wage labour created what Marx called 'estates' and 'classes'.

Marx saw the nature of the dynamic evolution of capitalism as contingent upon particular forms of capital, state and labour relations. This offers one route to understanding differentiated capitalism and the particular social contexts in which market relations are embedded. Market relations and commodity forms exist in a social context shaped by power relations, and society and economy must therefore be analysed together, not separated out. Robert Cox, whose Marx-inspired 'critical political economy' we will encounter in Chapter 7, talks in terms of specific 'state/society complexes' (1981). These are understood to be generative of specific sets of understandings of market relations, and of the economic, particular to a given setting.

Economic sociologists use the term 'embeddedness' to capture this interrelatedness of the economic, political and social (Granovetter 1985). Embeddedness is multidimensional, including the social, legal, political and cognitive dimensions of political economic activity (Krippner 2001; Block and Evans 2005). Following Polanyian trains of thought, Block thinks in terms of economic activity and markets that are 'always politically embedded' in their social context, requiring legal rules and a set of institutions (Block 2003). The embeddedness of the economy is one route into an appreciation of dynamics of differentiation between capitalism in different national political economies (see also Streeck 2001, 2009; Block and Evans 2005: 506–7). The influence of different national, social, political, institutional and ideational contexts on how capitalism evolves is an issue we return to in Chapters 6 and 9.

Whether inspired by Smith, Marx or Polanyi, the implications for studying political economy from this insight are similar. Instead of positing sets of relationships between 'the state' and 'the market' or 'society', which might be deemed capable of application across space and time, I argue for a historically contingent comparative analysis of particular state/ market relationships.

Core insight 4: capitalism as a dynamic, not static, social order

The fourth foundational assumption may seem obvious – capitalism can and does change. Yet the *ceteris paribus* assumptions which underpin the static or 'equilibrium'-based models of much economic analysis assume away much of what political economy is interested in, namely how and why political economic orders change. The interactions of economic, social and political forces to which capitalism gives rise are dynamic and constantly evolving. Capitalism is the social condition of the advanced economies, and has been for decades, indeed centuries in many cases. Yet the enduring prevalence and pre-eminence of capitalist social relations have not been accompanied by stability, still less stasis. Like the other insights, this does not make our task as scholars of political economy any easier.

List's national political economy is attuned to how economic development is 'a diachronic phenomenon', which is 'learned and perfected over time, through a long process of institutional adaptation' (Woo-Cumings 1999: 15). To gain 'intellectual and social power', List argues, nations 'must sacrifice present advantages to secure future benefits' (1856 [1841]: 223). This is what Ha-Joon Chang means when he talks of 'dynamic efficiency' as opposed to 'static efficiency'. The 'static efficiency' approach, following current price signals, is the only one of which neo-classical economics and static equilibrium thinking can conceive. 'Dynamic efficiency', on the other hand, is informed by 'a "vision" for the future of the economy' to address long-term development. This 'cannot be adequately dealt with by blindly following current price signals' (Chang 1999: 194), as dynamic, diachronic approaches to CPE readily appreciate.

Understanding the dynamic nature of capitalism is also important because 'the boundary between the economic and the political is not something "naturally" given but something that can vary across time and place' (ibid.: 197). Thus all 'free' markets are deeply politically conditioned, and free markets differ across time and space: for example, changing norms relating to slavery have changed the nature of 'free' labour markets, just as changing norms regarding food safety have affected agricultural product markets for commodities such as hormone-treated beef. Sometimes the shifts can be abrupt, as with changing financial market regulators' attitudes towards mortgage-backed securities and collateralized debt obligations during 2007 and 2008.

Marx's historical materialist approach recognizes capitalism to be a dynamic, changing system. This requires political economists to understand the particular sets of historical conditions and social relationships involved. Such a dynamic account of capitalism illustrates how re-establishing the connection to classical political economy helps to restore to analysis a grasp of the *politics* of capitalist change. Appreciation of how economic and political power stratifies society informs our understanding of the crucial role of power relations, for example those between organized labour and big business, where the political power that control of economic resources conveys (Lindblom 1977) influences how capitalism changes.

For a long time, institutionalist analysis in CPE was content to think in terms of 'punctuated equilibrium' explanations of institutional change within capitalism. Thus there are 'critical junctures' such as economic crises, wars and so on, when institutions are in flux. A path is decided upon in a contingent manner (Lehmbruch 2001: 43); thereafter, until at the next critical juncture, institutions deliver significant degrees of stability. However, this way of thinking about change fails to acknowledge 'shifts that are gradual and incremental, though cumulatively transformative' (Streeck and Thelen 2005; Mahoney and Thelen 2010; Thelen 2010: 45).

Path dependencies, like embeddedness, need to be approached as dynamic concepts. As John Campbell puts it, 'institutional reproduction and change are flip sides of the same coin' (Campbell 2010: 108). This is because 'many of the forces that change institutions ... conflict and struggle – also stabilise them' (ibid.: 98). Paul Pierson similarly notes that static equilibrium analyses ignore how ideas and institutions evolve, and how 'social life unfolds over time. Real social processes have distinct temporal dimensions' (2004: 1, 5). How best to conceptualize, understand, explain and characterize change was a source of lively debate between the classical political economists, and it remains so today (Streeck and Thelen 2005), as we shall explore further in Chapters 6 and 7. The best contemporary comparative political economists, like classical political economy scholars before them, understand both the reproduction of existing capitalist institutions and evolutions towards new ones as political struggles (ibid.; Campbell 2010; Thelen 2010).

These insights reflect only a fraction of the contribution that classical political economy can make to our understanding of the political economy of 21st-century capitalism. They distil the essence of how best to use insights originating in classical political economy to explore contemporary developments in CPE. They offer pointers as to what to bring with us from classical political economy to a reading of and engagement with the modern CPE litera-ture and its framing debates. They can also provide a solid basis from which to undertake an exploration of present-day developments and dynamics within capitalism in the advanced economies.

COMPARATIVE POLITICAL ECONOMY: LINKAGES TO INTERNATIONAL POLITICAL ECONOMY

One last issue to address is the relationship between CPE and the closely related field of IPE. This is important, because integral to my purpose and approach is the view that both these contemporary political economy fields can benefit from increased cross-fertilization (see Clift et al. 2021). Susan Strange famously argued that there had been a case of 'mutual neglect' between economics and international relations, noting that analysis in each field was the poorer for it (1970). Something similar could be argued about a case of mutual neglect between CPE and IPE. That these similar intellectual undertakings can sometimes proceed in relative isolation from each other may reflect that CPE and IPE struggle to agree on how best to analyse and interpret political economic change. Take, for example, the impact of changes in international financial markets on domestic political economies. On the one hand, as Strange pointed out, some comparativists are liable to overstate national institutional continuity, at times failing to pick up significant qualitative change at the international level (1997). On the other hand, IPE scholars focused at the global level of analysis are at risk of neglecting how domestic institutional and ideational structures and processes mediate and shape global pressures. There is a tendency, within some debates about capitalist restructuring, especially among those positing convergence, to over-emphasize evolutions (notably deregulation and liberalization) at the international level, and to underplay continuities (such as economic and corporate law and governance struc-tures, or labour relations) at the national level, and how pre-existing norms and structures endure and *interact* with new influences (see e.g. Hollingsworth 1997; Hollingsworth and Boyer 1997).

IPE is often mistakenly thought to have 'begun' as a sub-discipline around the 1970s (Cohen 2008). It is more helpfully thought of as a longer-standing political economy tradi-tion (see Clift et al. 2021; Clift and Rosamond 2009; Watson 2005a, 2016; Cohen 2019: 3–4; Ravenhill 2008), which traces its lineages back to classical political economy. Moreover, many aspects of IPE's research agenda and the central intellectual questions that animate the field intersect and overlap with CPE. Hence increased dialogue and engagement with IPE scholarship have the potential to enhance CPE analysis, because IPE has grown to become a large and vibrant field of study. IPE scholars can enable comparativists to locate their spe-cific understandings of political economic developments within broader patterns of change. The German, French, Japanese, American, British and other capitalisms of the post-war era discussed in this book rested upon the Bretton Woods order (see pp. 10, 142–9, 255–6; Ruggie 1982; Streeck 2001: 37). This particular world order which obtained for the decades following World War II was a crucial condition of what some have called the 'golden age of capitalism' (Marglin and Schor 1992). This combined, in the advanced economies, strong economic growth, rising living standards, full employment and relative economic stability in the post-war decades.

In the wake of see pp. 10–11, 206–8, 250–1, 256–7, many IPE scholars have charted significant increases in the prevalence and pervasiveness of markets and market mechanisms at the national and international levels. Some of these trends seem to be particularly important for the analysis of comparative capitalisms, such as the internationalization of financial markets. Increased levels of stock market capitalization and activity represented significant shifts in formerly co-ordinated market economies and relatively closed national financial systems where capital markets hitherto played limited roles (see Chapters 8–10). A good part of the explanation of *why* contemporary capitalism is changing links back to the unravelling of the regulated international monetary system in the 1970s and 1980s. IPE has much to offer on this changing international context of the advanced political economies (see e.g. Helleiner 1994; Germain 1997; Pauly 1997; Cohen 1996, 2002). At the same time, CPE can expand understanding of how general international political economic trends and processes manifest themselves in different forms within, and are mediated and shaped by, specific historical and institutional contexts. Furthermore, actors within these national institutional contexts are not passive recipients of global political economic change, but play an active role in shaping its dynamics. Appreciation of this suggests a focus on the complex interplay of international and domestic forces, as explored in the pioneering analyses of Strange (1971, 1976), Katzenstein (1978, 1985) and Gourevitch (1978, 1986) discussed in Chapter 1. This book sets out how CPE provides the tools and insights to analyse and understand better the processes of political economic change, both nationally and internationally.

There is increasing recognition in both IPE and CPE that, given the complexity and diversity of increasing economic interdependence, driven in part by differentiated liberalizing re-regulation, 'the convergence thesis is no longer a reliable or useful heuristic tool to frame our investigations of this world' (Engelen and Konings 2010: 609; see also McGrew 2011). The diversity of responses to globalization, and the coexistence of dramatic changes (many along similar lines in different cases) and enduring and highly significant particularities, are the real story of what is happening within the global political economy. Common patterns within responses to globalization as well as mediation by diverse 'domestic' institutions and politics are all part of the 'variable geometry' (Castells 2000) of globalization. Linear understandings of economic globalization, rooted in a textbook neo-classical economic model and the theoretically threadbare 'logic of no alternative' argument, simply do not cut the mustard in explaining differentiated processes of change within contemporary capitalism.

As the threats to the liberal international order posed by resurgent political forces of economic nationalism, nativist anti-'globalism' and illiberal populism gained ground in various societies across the advanced capitalist world, the trajectories of national capitalisms appeared likely to alter in response. These political forces represented a challenge to the institutional and regulatory edifice upon which liberal economic internationalism had been built over many decades. This suggested fresh evolutions in the kinds of interactions between domestic and international forces, different from those that obtained during the complex economic interdependence that prevailed from the collapse of Bretton Woods in the 1970s up to the early 21st century and the GFC.

These are insights and fresh avenues of inquiry that many working within CPE and IPE have helped to develop, and such thinking prepares the ground for further cross-fertilization between IPE and CPE. However, the success of this exercise crucially depends upon how IPE is conceived. The vision defended here is of IPE as a broad-based, inclusive and multidisciplinary field of study which draws on and grows from classical political economy (see Watson

2005a; Clift and Rosamond 2009; Clift et al. 2021). Yet this is not necessarily the majority or consensus view of IPE. At the risk of caricature, a prevailing narrative of IPE as a field presumes there to be two versions of how to understand what IPE is, an American and a British 'School' (see Cohen 2008; Lake 2006; Maliniak and Tierney 2009; for a critique see Hveem 2009; Blyth 2009a & b). This, once again, is the stuff of the 'disciplinary politics' discussed above and in Chapter 4. Of course, the European, Antipodean, Asian, Latin American, African, Canadian and other academic environments all have their own particularities, but there is not space to address all of those here. The character of work in IPE is likely to differ across intellectual communities (which are to some extent national, though the boundaries are porous) because of different societal negotiations regarding what constitutes an appropriate focus for and method of analysis, and where the limits of the discipline lie (see Rosamond 2007). One version – perhaps the dominant one globally – reflects the US academic context, where there is a very clear and disciplined ordering of political science into component sub-fields, hence pedagogy and scholarship are subdivided into political theory, American politics, comparative politics and international relations (IR). In this version, IPE is understood as an offshoot from or sub-field of IR, which takes all its cues from IR theories. Looked at in the wider international scholarly community, such a disciplinary location is at least debatable. Not all IPE scholars see IR as a necessary, or necessarily helpful, point of departure for analysing the global political economy (though, of course, many do; Clift et al. 2021).

An alternative view of IPE is as a broader multidisciplinary field, sometimes termed the 'British School IPE' (Cohen 2008). Unlike the development of IPE in the US, there has never been a pervasive sense of a 'parent discipline' (or disciplines) of which British IPE is a sub-field. There is no requirement to choose between a comparative politics or IR pathway in UK universities, and doctoral research is not defined in strictly delineated disciplinary terms. This relatively relaxed disciplinarity within the British academic environment makes possible work that scavenges more readily across the social scientific spectrum (both historical and contemporary) for inspiration. This kind of IPE work has been able to develop by exploiting the potentialities of loose disciplinarity, grazing on the sunlit uplands of (to name but a few) Marxist sociology, economic history, economic geography and heterodox institutional economics. In essence, at its best, this British IPE reflects the 'pre-disciplinary' intellectual spirit of classical political economy discussed above. Thus the pervasive US notion of IPE as a sub-field of IR brings with it intellectual baggage which British IPE scholars have largely been spared (see Clift and Rosamond 2009).

The dialogue between the IPE and CPE literature advocated in this book can fruitfully best proceed if IPE is conceived of *not* as a sub-discipline of or offshoot from IR, but rather as the application of the insights of political economy, classical and contemporary, situated within an international context. Such an approach builds a bridge between CPE and those operating within the related sub-field of IPE who argue that the revitalization of that field can helpfully proceed via a return to classical political economy (Gamble 1995, 2009; Watson 2005a, 2005b, 2009, 2012; Holmes 2009, 2012; Breslin 2011; Strange 2011; Hobson 2013a, 2013b; Knafo 2013). This bridge between CPE and IPE is also manifest in the work of leading scholars such as Mark Blyth (2002a & b 2009, 2013) and Peter Katzenstein (1978, 1985), and in the prestigious *Cornell Studies in Political Economy* book series, which Katzenstein edits. These and other IPE scholars have noted, or simply demonstrated, the appeal to CPE for inspiration. Similarly, Nicola Phillips argues that 'states must be understood not in the sterile terms of a strengthening/weakening dichotomy … but rather as undergoing variegated processes of adaptation and transformation' (2005: 95). She goes on to evoke concepts drawn into IPE from outside its mainstream, notably from CPE, as a means to arrive at a more fruitful analysis of state transformation (see Chapter 8).

Thus certain types of IPE scholarship and CPE can be and increasingly are brought together in a mutually advantageous dialogue and engagement. Within this enterprise, the reason to avoid the IPE as an 'offshoot of IR' conception is because the IR theoretical foundations of some variants of IPE can rather get in the way and obscure the insights which CPE can offer. One strand of IPE – realism – is focused on states as key actors in the global political economy, but can tend (for reasons of IR theoretical lineage – see Kirschner 2009) to assume common structural properties or preferences of, say, all advanced economy states (Gilpin 1971, 1975, 1981; Krasner 1976, 1978, 1984; Waltz 1979). CPE scholarship, on the other hand, tends towards a more nuanced appreciation of the changing relationship between a given state, its scope and its capacities, and the wider global political economy.

Another US IPE example is 'open economy politics' (OEP), which its advocates see as an 'emergent paradigm' which 'structures and guides research among many scholars' and as an important intellectual advance for the field (Lake 2009; see also Rogowski 1989; Frieden 1991). On one level, with its focus on the domestic sources of foreign economic policy, and given that it affords a 'central explanatory role to institutions at both the domestic and international levels' (Lake 2009: 225), it seems well suited to a dialogue with the kind of CPE set out in this book. However, its privileging of 'certain assumptions, methods and epistemologies over others' (ibid.: 220) presents some problems (for a critique, see Oatley 2011). OEP focuses exclusively on the domestic sphere, ignoring the complex interplay between the domestic and the international highlighted earlier by Strange, Katzenstein, Gourevitch and others. Rather, OEP uses statistical analysis to examine domestic causes of foreign economic policy.

OEP, as Lake notes, 'adopts the assumptions of neoclassical economics and international trade theory. But by incorporating political variables more explicitly into its analysis, OEP provides a bridge between economics and political science' (2009: 224–5). Its conscious appropriation of the techniques and assumptions of open economy macroeconomics, in particular its simplifying assumptions and the omission of important factors in the interests of parsimony, is problematic for the reasons laid out earlier in this chapter and throughout the rest of this book. As Lake puts it, 'for tractability, scholars ... bracket many obviously varying features of a political-economic environment by treating them as exogenous for purposes of isolating and studying a single causal effect' (ibid.: 225). CPE's approach differs from the reductionism of both OEP and realist IPE. CPE wants to ink in all the institutional and ideational texture and granularity of national political economies, in their historical and social contexts and their complex interactions with the world economy, in order to arrive at a richer understanding of the politics of capitalist change in a given setting.

CONCLUSION: CONCEPTIONS OF THE MARKET, DISCIPLINARITY AND POLITICAL ECONOMY

Within the analysis of the economic across various social scientific fields, we can draw a distinction between 'the market' as a conceptual abstraction (assumed to exhibit certain properties) on the one hand, and 'the market' understood as the site (perhaps even a physical space) of social interaction on the other. The notion of 'the market' as a conceptual abstraction can be found in parts of Adam Smith's *Wealth of Nations* (in Book 1), and under-pins the marginalist political economy of the late 19th century which delivered neo-classical economics (see Chapter 4), and thereafter modern 'New Classical' economics. Obviously, the market as a conceptual abstraction can take different forms depending on the underpinning assumptions. One particularly prevalent and influential set of assumptions about markets within many branches of economics is that they are in some sense natural and that they tend to work efficiently in allocating resources.

Each of the four core insights of the approach to CPE taken in this book, as set out above, stands at odds with a conception of the economy and the market as natural. Neo-classical economic theory is adept at explaining pure free markets as theoretical abstractions. However, CPE analyses regulated markets that are subject to political intervention. The core analytical insights derived from escaping the dichotomous opposition of state and market, understanding that markets are made, how economic activity is always embedded in socie-ties, and that capitalism is a dynamic, not a static, social order, help us understand these real-world market relations. From these starting points we can appreciate better how vari-ous forms of state interventionism and political, legislative, legal and regulatory activity are all preconditions of the very existence of market relations. These are all the subject of politi-cal and societal contestation – of *politics*.

This book combines the classical insights about political economy with the key substan-tive focus of and central debates within contemporary CPE scholarship. In the chapters that follow, the aim is to incorporate important political economic insights, old and new, and to arrive at a number of useful analytical starting points for the analysis and understanding of modern capitalism. CPE, in rediscovering the spirit of classical political economy analysis, is able to offer an in-depth analysis of the political economy of modern capitalism, which is appreciative of the variegation within it. It is to the influential scholarship of Smith, Marx and List that we turn in the next chapter.

3 Capitalism and Classical Political Economy

INTRODUCTION

In Chapters 1 and 2 I argued that returning to the insights, concepts, theories and arguments of classical political economy is an extremely instructive launch-pad for exploration of contemporary CPE. We will engage with the classical political economy tradition to discover more about how to think like a political economist and how to study political economy comparatively. We will encounter three schools of classical political economic thought in this chapter – liberal (focusing on Smith, but also on David Ricardo), radical (Marx) and economic nationalist (List) – each understanding the nature and source of wealth differently. I will offer a brief summary of their most important insights and standpoints from which to analyse capitalism, taking care to avoid the crude caricatures of their positions sometimes found in the literature.

We will explore the distinctive conceptions of the capitalist market underpinning Smith's, List's and Marx's views on state/market relations, and highlight differing views on how to understand the individual and his or her relationship to society. In addition, we consider their understandings of the international order within which national political economies operate. This chapter thus explores the implications of these differing views on markets, individuals, capitalist society and international order that underpin each variant of classical political economy. Thinking about capitalism, markets, institutions and society – and their interactions – from each of these perspectives constitutes good brain training, arranging the mental furniture in a way conducive to fruitful CPE analysis. Thus the aim of this chapter and the next is to set out what modern CPE scholars can usefully draw on and learn from within classical political economy for the comparative study of 21st-century capitalism. Exploring the ideas of key classical political economists in this chapter and the next provides more context, background and depth for understanding how the four core political economy insights identified in Chapter 2 are so central for the field. These chapters flesh out how these four insights animated debates in political economy, and how they were approached and theorized by towering scholars who shaped the early evolution of the field.

CLASSICAL POLITICAL ECONOMY AND CAPITALISM

Adam Smith is arguably the godfather of modern political economy. There were many precursors. Marx calls the 17th-century scholar William Petty 'the father of Political Economy' (1974: 259), and Smith certainly drew on Petty. Smith's defence of *laissez-faire* and free markets built upon Bernard Mandeville's earlier, less systematic arguments about private vice for public benefit in *Fable of the Bees* (albeit Smith rejected Mandeville's selfishness hypothesis as too simplistic, neglecting the human capacity for sympathy). Smith also benefited from discussions with François Quesnay, originator of the idiosyncratic physiocrat system of political economy. This focused on agricultural production and asserted that wealth sprang from nature, flowing through the nation like blood through the body (Heilbroner 1992: 49–51). Nevertheless, we begin with Smith because he synthesized earlier contributions into the first holistic, comprehensive and – in an important sense – modern account of pre-industrial and early industrial capitalism.

Smith's focus was the historical development of economic relations, not 'the economy'. His was 'a grand vision of the interrelatedness of society' (Landreth and Colander 1994: 67), which analysed social institutions in which economic relations were embedded. This holistic, interrelated approach became a hallmark of classical political economy, as did the appreciation that a proper understanding of the *politics* of this complex and interrelated whole requires giving special explanatory importance to *economic* structures and processes.

Custom, religion, reciprocity, feudal hierarchies and familial ties had all at one time been important in economic activity. From the 1500s onwards, but advancing apace from the 1700s, the market, and market institutions, profit-seeking and pecuniary gain increasingly crowded out these earlier organizational drivers behind economic activity. Adam Smith's piercing insights into two economic categories – changes to labour and capital – demonstrate this well. The onset of modernity saw the formation of land, labour and capital as abstract, impersonal and dehumanized entities – as factors of production. Classical political economy understood market forms as political constructs, and analysed the 'invention' of land, labour and capital as commodities essential to the emergence and evolution of modern capitalism. Classical political economy focused on these crucial sources of the changes to society, economy and politics that the Industrial Revolution was auguring.

The commodification of labour engendered social transformation as wage labour became the norm, and ever more members of society were subject to the dictates and vagaries of labour markets (Polanyi 2001 [1944]). Political economy explored the social consequences and dislocations of these emerging and evolving *capitalist* economic forms and processes. In his conclusion to Chapter 11 of Book 1 of *Wealth of Nations*, Smith analyses a stratified social order divided into 'three great, original and constituent orders of every civilised society', reflecting three different sources of wealth – rent of the land, wages of labour and profits of stock. This class-based understanding of the capitalist social relations created by the then still emergent Industrial Revolution spelt out power relations rooted in the economy and pervading society. Such a class-based analysis proved very influential with political science and sociology, becoming the dominant orthodoxy for much of the 20th century. It still has many advocates today.

ADAM SMITH AND CLASSICAL LIBERAL POLITICAL ECONOMY

Smith elaborated a theoretical framework unveiling the nature of capitalist social relations of production and of distribution. The liberal assertion that human society should best be organized around free market principles is perhaps its most important and enduring contribution to political economy. Smith's endorsement of free markets is linked to his understanding of the sources of wealth. Individuals pursuing their own economic activity are, for

Smith, the well-spring of wealth. Particularly important is the (increasingly efficient) production of commodities and their trade in a competitive environment. This was a fundamentally modern conception of wealth and its social implications.

The conception of capitalist market relations

Liberal classical political economy elaborated a robust argument and theoretical apparatus to defend the free market as a theoretical construct and as a 'real-world' institution. Faith in the market was as integral to Adam Smith's political economy as it was, in the mid-20th century, to Hayek's neo-liberal political economy (see Chapter 4). In the 21st century, these same arguments in favour of free trade and free markets, and the conceptual toolkits underpinning them, continue to resonate through policy and academic debate. Smith's system was built upon a conviction that the market would ultimately deliver optimal outcomes. This view was underpinned by assumptions about the market's properties, and about individuals as social and ethical beings. As the Industrial Revolution took off and markets became more pervasive, this liberal defence was an important intellectual bulwark to the societal transformation it yielded. That said, Smith's emphasis on ethical individuals received much less attention than assertions about free markets.

The beneficial societal outcome arising from free market exchange was not down to intentionality. Rather, in Smith's model, benefits arise as *unintended* consequences of each individual pursuing only (or so they think) their own 'self-love' (Smith rarely if ever talked in terms of 'self-interest'), within a context of freely competitive markets. For each individual, Smith argues that 'the study of his own advantage *naturally*, or rather *necessarily* leads him to prefer that employment which is most advantageous to the society' (Smith 1993 [1776]: 289; emphasis added). The good society is an unintentional side effect of pursuing 'self-love'. This does not rest on individual intentional action, making it bulletproof, since each individual 'neither intends to promote the public interest, nor knows how much he is promoting it', but is 'led by an invisible hand to promote an end which was no part of his intention' (ibid.: 291–2). This bold and counter-intuitive argument's power and durability derive from both its seductive appeal and the difficulty of conclusively disproving its initial assumption. It can be deployed ubiquitously as an argument against interference in markets.

The term 'invisible hand' was used only three times, each time in cursory fashion, in all Smith's writings. Only once, in the passage quoted above, does it convey the notion subsequently considered Smith's most telling insight. Indeed, Rothschild argues that for Smith it was perhaps 'a mildly ironic joke' (2001: 5, 116). Whether or not the invisible hand metaphor really captured the essence of Smith's understanding of the societal consequences of the marketplace, its assumed operation has evolved into the fulcrum of liberal accounts.

Smith's free market defence is built on assumptions of pursuing self-love, which combined with competition will allocate economic resources efficiently. Smith imparts to his theoretical discussion of the free market economic system the terms 'natural' and 'necessary' repeatedly, for example in Book 1, Chapter 7. Here he sets out how, left to itself, the free market will 'naturally' produce the balance of supply and demand (Heilbroner 1992: 56–8). Later economists would call this 'perfect equilibrium', though Rothschild argues that Turgot, rather than Smith, was the 'true visionary of general equilibrium' (2001: 176). This cornerstone of all liberal political economy was subsequently elaborated by the French political economist Jean-Baptiste Say. Say's law stated simply that supply called forth demand. The cost of every good was income for someone – be it in rent, wages or profits. Therefore the market system would, in a self-regulating manner, generate buoyant demand. In a manner similar to much subsequent liberal political economy analysis, Smith subtly asserts that the free market is both inevitable and the normal state of affairs. It was these assumptive foundations that enabled Smith, in the conclusion to Book 4, to refer to commercial capitalism as 'the system of natural liberty' and 'the system of perfect liberty' (Smith 1993 [1776]: 392).

This tone of argument partly reflects Smith as moral philosopher, seeing individuals as ethical and moral beings, and the free market as the best environment in which they could realize their potential. While the moral and ethical dimensions were subsequently downplayed, the claimed inevitable character of the market's delivery of socially optimal outcomes still dominates. This liberal defence of markets almost forecloses any further debate (in liberal eyes). These asserted 'natural' and 'necessary' beneficial social outcomes of untrammelled market activity are what most divides liberals from the radical Marxist and economic nationalist critics, as we shall see later.

Smith's legacy for thinking about the market, however, is complex and multifaceted. On one level, he *a priori* assumes the market's potential to resolve societal problems, reinforced by his tendency to naturalize the market and render its optimized outcomes inevitable. Yet in the same book, but with a different voice, he rails against the shortcomings of particular real markets, distorted by powerful cartels and price fixing by producer groups. Smith makes the crucial distinction between 'natural' and 'market' prices which goes to the heart of this potential disjuncture (see pp. 30–1). The real world of 'market' prices is, Smith keenly recognized, one where state and market are intertwined, where the market order is shaped by political intervention. Real-world market relations are not self-regulating, but predicated upon state authority and action (e.g. to enforce contracts and property rights).

Smith was well aware of commercial capitalism's shortcomings and was at times careful to calibrate his claims in favour of free markets. Such judicious calibration is often lost when Smith's ideas are appropriated by subsequent liberal scholars. Smith underscored, in Chapter 11 of Book 1, his deep suspicion of the 'mean rapacity' of merchants and manufacturers, and in Chapter 10 of Book 1 criticized their 'conspiracy against the publick' in a 'contrivance to raise prices' (ibid.: 129), ideas taken up by later public choice theorizing about 'rent-seeking' (see pp. 101–4). Thus Smith was no apologist for ruthless, self-seeking profiteers. His discussion of market society's potentially dehumanizing properties, and the division of labour (Book 5, Chapter 1), as Watson notes, highlights how 'the economics of the division of labour are infused with relations of power and powerlessness, privilege and exploitation' (2005a: 103). Smith's critical insights into the actual operation of real-world markets presaged critiques of capitalism from Marx to Polanyi. Yet these were reduced to a footnote by subsequent liberal political economists. Smith observed existing historical and institutional circumstances, and made a contextualized assumption that freer markets will probably usually produce the least worst outcome. His was no abstract assertion of market perfection.

Yet Smith did at times adopt a naturalistic view of markets working effectively. This view was subsequently sustained by the foundational assumptions of marginalist political economy (see pp. 74–8), and thereafter of neo-classical economics about the inevitability of the efficient operation of markets. This transmuting of Smith's theoretical defence of the idealized market into the liberal assumption about how markets actually work does considerable violence to Smith's own nuanced position. Modern free marketeers' liberal advocacy which claims Smithian foundations often neglects how his *Wealth of Nations* not only set out important principles of economics, but also sought to embed those economic writings in a wider cultural, social, historical and political context.

What CPE can most usefully draw from Smith's writing is first the enormous potential benefits of the market as an allocator of resources and the possibilities of beneficial social outcomes bound up with its operation. However, for Smith price setting was socially constructed, reflecting the prevailing political power distribution within this class-based society (Watson 2005a: 105–6). Equally important is Smith's often neglected appreciation that market activity occurs in a social context characterized by unequal power relations. These can and do shape and distort economic processes like price setting and market outcomes.

The individual and society

Liberal political economy shares much common ground with liberal political theory. The overlap is exemplified by J. S. Mill, who was influential as both political theorist and political economist. Liberalism prioritizes individual freedom and accordingly seeks to order affairs affording maximum autonomy to individuals making decisions about their own affairs. Thus a liberal perspective entails a methodological individualism – the individual is the fundamental unit of analysis. Society is understood as a collection of individuals, and it is from the perspective of the impact on the individual (and his or her autonomy) that policy and institutions are evaluated.

Smith's account of wealth creation is about individual economic activity. Individuals and their endeavours are the source of wealth, not precious metals. Smith assumed a world of individual producers (and individual private ownership). Yet important misunderstandings pervade liberal political economy regarding the nature of Smith's attachment to individual self-love, self-reliance and free markets. The prevailing conception of the individual within much modern liberal political economy (see pp. 87–8; Rogowski 1989; Frieden 1991) is a somewhat impoverished understanding by comparison with Smith's rich account. The individuals that are the building blocks of Smith's 'system of natural liberty' (1993 [1776]: 392) bear little or no relation to the 'rational fools' (Sen 1977) of modern economic theory or rational choice political science (see pp. 97–100). Smith's individual was not restrained simply by law, but by a complex code of moral assumptions about what would increase the regard of others (Wilson 1976; Viner 1984).

Smith was first and foremost a moral philosopher, and his political economic writings are imbued with a powerful moral argument. This remained deeply suspicious of the (a)morality of markets. He favoured a capitalist *economy*, held together by a *society* bound by non-capitalist moral values. He thought that 'self-love' must have a stabilizing social context (Tabb 1999: 38), but his situating of the economic in a moral and social context is often forgotten, or underplayed. A crucial concept for understanding Smith's view of the individual and their place within society is 'sympathy'. First developed in his *Theory of Moral Sentiments* (2009 [1759]), this refers to the relationship between the passions and actions of an individual and how they are perceived by others; it equates roughly in modern terminology with empathy. For Smith, there exists an idealized 'other' who views one's actions and sits in moral judgement upon them – the 'impartial spectator' (ibid.: 13–33). The economy is a *social process*, wherein individuals are guided by moral notions of propriety.

The nature of capitalist society was much debated within liberal classical political economy. Smith saw a potentially harmonious, though class-based, social order. David Ricardo's view was more antagonistic, homing in on perhaps *the* core question for political economy: *Cui bono?* (Who benefits?). Ricardo wrote to Thomas Malthus that 'political economy ... should rather be called an inquiry into the laws which determine the division of produce of industry among the classes which concur in its formation' (quoted in Hartwell 1971: 15–16). Ricardo's account of industrial capitalism highlights the *differential* impacts of capitalism on different classes, and shares none of Smith's assumed social harmony.

Ricardo analysed economic activity taking place within a societal context stratified along class lines – the causes of which were to be found in the economic system. His, then, was a socially embedded vision of economic activity, highlighting the mutual influence of the economic on the political and social. His approach revealed a range of antagonisms – presaging Marx in identifying a negative wage–profit relationship: 'in proportion then, as wages rose, would profit fall' (1971 [1817]: 131, 134–5, 146) – and historical tendencies of falling profit rates. One source of antagonism, for Ricardo, was that those who toiled and created value did not reap the rewards. He had in mind diligent and entrepreneurial wealth-creating manufacturers as those sold short by the system, though later Marx would take a similar analytical tack to theorize worker exploitation.

We can draw from Smith the benefits of situating the analysis of individuals within a social context and developing an appreciation of the prevailing societal ideas and norms. This adjusts our eyes to appreciate the social context within which economic activity is embedded, and to understand individuals as socially embedded. From Ricardo we grasp the unequal and differential consequences of liberal market capitalism for different classes in society. This jars with modern liberal political economy, which normally assumes that society as a whole benefits from free markets and *laissez-faire*. From both we also get arguments and insights setting out the potential benefits of free markets and fairly consistent intimations that, though free market capitalism has its shortcomings, leaving as many decisions as possible to individuals operating in markets that are as unrestricted as possible is going to deliver superior alternatives to any other mode of social and economic organization. It is the benefits, more than the shortcomings, which modern liberal political economy has taken to its heart.

The standard jibe, from List first and foremost, against Smith's liberal defence of the market is that it is based on an idealized understanding of the economy which assumes the politics and power relations out of the equation. This is certainly unfair to Smith, who was very keenly aware of the discrepancy between his theoretical system and the operations of real-world economies. Liberal political economy's failure to *politicize* economic relations and processes sufficiently, given its 'blind spot' regarding the crucial concept of power, can be overstated. It is an inaccurate and decidedly uncharitable reading of Smith that finds him 'guilty' of such offences.

The international order

Mercantilist ideas favoured protectionism and saw international economic interactions as 'zero-sum' (i.e. one gains at others' expense). Smith's was a very different understanding of the nature of liberal market capitalism's international context. Mercantilist political economy understood national economic wealth in terms of gold and silver reserves held in the

Treasury, and its policy prescriptions involved restrictions geared to delivering a favourable balance of trade. For centuries before Smith, this was the prevailing wisdom. So deep-seated were these precepts in the collective consciousness that Smith dedicated over 200 pages to debunking mercantilism. Indeed, Smith ascribed more coherence to mercantilist theory than was warranted (Ahmad 1990).

Smith argued that mercantilism's emphasis on precious metals as sources of wealth was thoroughly misguided. The prohibition on exporting gold or silver – a classic mercantilist policy (hoarding it against the cost of future wars) – was economically and commercially damaging. So too were other restrictions on trade and the competitive operation of markets. This was wrong-headed because economic activity (especially commodity manufacturing and exchange), not precious metal, was the *real* source of wealth. Smith emphasized how the division of labour led to huge productive gains, and thereby a massive expansion of wealth. A focus on gold and silver was a distraction from this. They have no special status as commodities, and indeed, as a proportion of all commodities bought and sold, they are of marginal importance. The empires and protectionist barriers mercantilism gave rise to were inimical to free trade and international competition, and thus – for Smith – to wealth creation.

Unlike mercantilism's beggar-thy-neighbour predispositions, Smith envisaged the possibility of a mutually beneficial, indeed harmonious, international order. His position internationalized his assumptions about the social benefits and productivity gains arising from free markets. The transformation of manufacturing detailed in the *Wealth of Nations* showed how the division of labour, and the improvements in productive process of the Industrial Revolution, was raising productivity by staggering amounts. He projected this dynamic onto the world economy, arguing that the international division of labour would have a similar impact. Just as, domestically, free markets were beneficial to society, so too internationally would free trade benefit international society. The resultant rising tide of productivity gains, international trade and economic activity would float all boats, so that the wealth of *all* nations would be secured and enhanced.

Ricardo's refinement of Smithian thinking developed a more rigorous theory of comparative costs, which clarified the gains to be made from international specialization and trade (1971 [1817]: 147–67). It contained probably his most important theoretical contribution to political economy – comparative advantage. His was an abstract account based on a set of simplifying assumptions. His fundamental theoretical insight was that international trade should be undertaken on a free market basis because it constituted a *positive sum game*, or a win/win scenario. It is easy to see the potential gains when two states trade goods in which they are each a low cost producer. Rather harder to understand is why trade is worthwhile for two states when one is better at producing everything than the other. Comparative advantage, and the benefits of industrial specialization, provides the answer.

Although one country may be more efficient at producing all goods than another, it is usually the case that the more efficient country is particularly efficient (has less cost disadvantage) at producing some commodities compared to others. This is that nation's *comparative advantage*. Ricardo used trade between England and Portugal as his example. England is a less efficient producer of wine or cloth than Portugal. Even though Portugal is better at producing both than England, it pays Portugal to *specialize* in wine and to import cloth from England. This is because Portugal is much *more* efficient at producing wine than making cloth. The bottom line is that comparative advantage means trade can be advantageous for both parties regardless of the level of economic efficiency, productivity and overall economic development of the trading partners (Ricardo (1971 [1817])).

Few read the argument in its original form. After all, as Robert Heilbroner puts it, 'there is no more difficult economist to understand than Ricardo' (1992: 85). This is a highly abstract, very simplified model of international economic relations, and some of its assumptions are not terribly 'safe' within contemporary capitalism. For example, Ricardo assumed national capital controls, immobile capital and a 'natural disinclination' to invest abroad (1971 [1817]: 155). In a globalizing world economy dominated by transnational corporations, this is scarcely credible, but nevertheless Ricardo's theoretical 'proof' that international trade is a win/win scenario retains great power. It still underpins trade theory in economics. The theoretical demonstration of this in Ricardo's *Principles* dovetailed with Smith's ideas about the invisible hand and internationalized the liberal classical political economy defence of freer markets and more liberalized economic relations.

At the international as well as the domestic level, the self-interest of one becomes the general interest of all. Comparative advantage has been crucial to the theoretical and practical evolution of political economy ever since, providing scholars and trade policy-makers with a means of showing the mutual advantages of free trade. Arguably, in the decades following its elaboration, the theory of comparative advantage changed the world. As Heilbroner puts it, 'gone is the notion of gold, treasures, kingly hoards; gone the prerogatives of merchants or farmers or working guilds. We are in the modern world, where the flow of goods and services consumed by everyone constitutes the ultimate aim and end of economic life' (1992: 53).

Ricardo's theory of comparative advantage offers an example of how to deploy theory within policy debates, harnessed to a political commitment to tariff reform and freer trade. The abstract academic insight was a weapon in the battle for the repeal of the protectionist Corn Laws. This was to transform the British and international political economy in the mid-19th century. Ricardo exemplified not abstract theorizing but 'socially embedded' political economy. In the social context of late 18th- and early 19th-century Britain, Ricardo was focused on class conflict between emerging industrialists – who were demanding political representation and wanting freer markets to bring food prices (and therefore wages) down – and the vested interests of landowning classes. Tariff reformers argued that parasitical landlords were siphoning off profits which should rightfully belong to the industrialists generating the economic wealth. This 'pernicious distribution of the general funds of society' (Ricardo 1971 [1817]: 313) was politically sustained by the landed gentry's dominance of Parliament, where industrialists were very much under-represented until, and even after, the Reform Act of 1832.

The Corn Laws were trade barriers erected during the Napoleonic wars, restricting the British import of wheat from the Continent. Through sliding high tariffs on imported grain, they kept cheap foreign grain permanently out of the domestic market. This protected the landowners – 'country gentlemen' as Ricardo called them (ibid.: 311) – at the expense of both workers (as consumers) and of merchants and industrialists (Barber 1967: 89–92; Watson 2011). Ricardo wrote two pamphlets, in 1815 and 1822, putting the theoretical and empirical case for tariff reform: 'the natural price of labour' depends on 'the natural price of those necessaries on which the wages of labour are expended' (Ricardo 1971 [1817]: 118). If wheat could be imported, the price would drop dramatically, reflecting continental comparative advantage in wheat production. Thereafter, British subsistence wages would drop accordingly (ibid.: 150–1, 163–4). This, combined with Ricardo's assumption that only lower wages could boost industrial profits, meant that Corn Law repeal would improve profitability for industrialists, given British comparative advantage in industrial production.

Ricardo's advocacy of free trade could and would bring cheap grain into Britain. The resulting higher industrial profits would increase industrial investment, and Britain could concentrate more economic resources (specialize further) on those areas of production in which it had *comparative advantage*. This meant the beneficiaries of Britain's economic pre-eminence would be the 'deserving' manufacturers, not 'undeserving' landowners. This would benefit the political economy of Britain and indeed everyone else. After Ricardo's death, following much political wrangling, his free trade arguments won the day. The growing political power of the industrialists eventually broke the landlords' grip on Parliament. The Corn Laws were abolished in 1846 and the liberal political economic view became the prevailing wisdom of the age. Thereafter, a free trade agenda characterized foreign economic policy under the British empire, changing the face of the world economy (Katzenstein 1978: 9).

CPE can learn much about how to understand markets and locate national economic activity within an international context from classical liberal political economy. Alongside the important defence of free markets and free trade, there is the appreciation of political struggles arising from the unequal distribution of resources in capitalism's class-based social order. The liberal view of individuals and of economic activity as socially embedded is also instructive for CPE. Liberal ideas about harmonious and beneficial consequences of free markets have been most powerfully influential in shaping the political economy of the modern world. Smith's and Ricardo's qualifications and clarifications about the shortcomings of the market order have tended (unjustly) to receive less attention. These interventions provoked critique and response from competing standpoints, sparking the debates that animated classical political economy. We will consider in turn the economic nationalist and the Marxian views.

ECONOMIC NATIONALIST POLITICAL ECONOMY

The debate about tariff reform, raging in the early 1800s, is still a hot political potato in the World Trade Organization (WTO) today. Debates about the merits of protectionism 'versus' free trade revived under the Trump presidency amid tariff disputes verging on an all-out trade war between the two 21st-century economic superpowers – the US and China. Such political struggles over fractious and increasingly contentious trade relations lay bare some of the key points of disagreement between classical liberal political economy and the economic nationalist school. It was and is an argument about how restricted international trade should be. More fundamentally, the economic nationalist account of political economy was rooted in a very different conception of markets and of the international order. We focus in this section on the conception of the market, of wealth, of the individual and their places within capitalist society underpinning economic nationalist political economy. We will then consider the economic nationalist view of politics and of international economic relations. Before exploring these, however, I need to offer some definitional clarification.

Economic nationalism is sometimes casually equated to 'neo-mercantilism'. This refers back to the older doctrine of the mercantilism of the 1500s–1700s which Smith railed against (see pp. 48–50). Significantly, mercantilism's intellectual ascendancy as 'a theory of the coherent intervention of the political State into the workings of the economy' (Anderson

1974: 36) coincided with the rise of modern nation states. However, the term 'economic nationalism' is preferable to neo-mercantilism for two important reasons. Firstly, as modern economic nationalist scholars note, mercantilism's exclusive focus on the state is in fact a very different beast from economic nationalism's emphasis on the *nation* (Harlen 1999; Levi-Faur 1997a, 1997b; Crane 1998; Helleiner and Pickel 2005). From an economic nationalist perspective, it does not make sense to assume that all nations or all states in the world economy face the same incentives, as in mercantilism or some neo-realist IR theory and IPE that we discussed in Chapter 2. Instead, economic nationalism appreciates differentiated national trajectories and histories. The second reason, dealt with below, is that economic nationalists accepted much of Smith's critique of mercantilism.

Alexander Hamilton offers a useful example. His famous 1791 Report on Manufacturers (see Crane and Amawi 1997: 37–47), written in his capacity as President Washington's first Treasury Secretary, was a key statement of early US economic nationalism. Furthermore, it was an effort to tackle the specific economic policy problems faced by the fledgling American republic. His report challenged prevailing understandings of 'productive' and 'unproductive' labour (a distinction at the heart of classical political economy). Agriculture had been prioritized for reasons of food security. Hamilton argued that manufacturing had been 'improperly represented as unproductive', and he championed manufacturing on a par with agriculture (hitherto seen as a more worthwhile pursuit; Hamilton 1997 [1791]: 38–9). If regulated appropriately, he argued, manufacturing could confer wide-ranging benefits on economy and society. Manufacturing, for Hamilton, was especially crucial for national security. Controlling within the nation 'the essentials of national supply' was deemed key to 'the means of Subsistence, habitation, clothing, and defence' (Hamilton 1997 [1791]: 43–4). The incapacity of Americans to supply themselves during their war of independence was a painful lesson. Moreover, Hamilton appreciated the substantial economic gains that accrue for promoting domestic manufacturing. His boosting of manufacturing aimed to secure national prosperity, partly through the knock-on positive effects on the wider economy.

The interpenetration of state and market and the predication of market relations on political intervention are central insights much emphasized within economic nationalism. The influential 19th-century German political economist Gustav von Schmoller saw state intervention in the economy as a culturally and historically informed practice of nation-building and national advancement. He talked of 'state making and national-economy at the same time' (1902 [1884]: 50–1). His focus was 'the social and economic forces underlying the development of the German state'. He offered an 'ethical evaluation of the state' and a 'historical and ethical view of the state and society' (Tribe 2007: 223–4). Based on this appreciation of national differentiation, and its impact on historically contingent trajectories of economic development, economic nationalists think in terms of culturally conditioned national paths of capitalist evolution. These remain an important empirical reality and crucial theoretical building blocks within analysis. In a contemporary context, this obviously jars with bolder assertions of globalization often advanced from a liberal standpoint (Pickel 2005: 5–7).

From a similar perspective to Schmoller, Friedrich List, whom we encountered in Chapters 1 and 2, emphasized how national 'productive power', which crucially determines a nation's power, prosperity and influence in the world economy, 'depends chiefly upon social and political conditions' (1856 [1841]: 253) prevailing within the nation. This hinges on the 'social economy of a nation' and the division between 'intellectual labour' and 'material labour' (ibid.: 240). Economic nationalism embeds the national economy, state policy, institutions and actions within the context of a broader national project and sets of historical, social and cultural conditions. The resultant differentiated, contingent paths of development contrast with the one-size-fits-all prescriptions of mercantilism – namely, protectionism and hoarding precious metals. Indeed, economic nationalism can encompass and accommodate a range of policy prescriptions and economic strategies (Helleiner 2002). It is not confined to mercantilism's protectionism.

Another economic nationalist focused on capitalism's societal context was the American Henry Carey (1793–1879). Though less widely known than List or Hamilton, he influenced US shifts towards protectionism in the mid-19th century (Helleiner 2020: 3). Carey's books *The Past, the Present and the Future* (1848) and his three-volume *Principles of Social Sciences* (1858–9) demonstrated him to be an original theorist of economic nationalism (Helleiner 2020). Carey saw the benefits for national prosperity of cultivating localized manufacturing: more stable local markets, reduced transportation costs, an increasingly diversified economy, and a boost to productivity flowing from the division of labour. Carey's subtle theorizing added a focus on domestic distributional and social consequences of free trade, themes absent from much other economic nationalist work. Downward wage pressure arising from trade liberalization was a significant concern, and Carey highlighted how workers, farmers and women in general were often substantial losers from freer trade. Their unjust suffering threatened the 'social harmony' that was crucial to Carey's political economy, and his appreciation of the broader societal context and consequences of economic policies and national economic development.

The second reason to avoid the neo-mercantilist label is that the economic nationalism of Hamilton, List and others largely accepted Smith's critique of mercantilism in the *Wealth of Nations*. The source of wealth, for economic nationalists, is indeed economic activity, not bullion. However, unlike Smith and liberal political economy, the crucial difference for economic nationalists is that wealth is a national, not an individual, phenomenon. Wealth creation arises out of collective endeavour, harnessed within a national project; it is the augmentation of 'civilization and power', not individual self-reliance. For List, Schmoller and Hamilton, wealth reflects the ability to harness the potential of national intellectual, physical and other resources to raise productivity and increase economic activity. Furthermore, List, Hamilton and others appreciated the power relations that pervaded international economic interactions. Thus their sustained critique of British classical liberal political economy was that under the conditions of the British empire, 'free trade' worked solely to sustain UK dominance and keep down emerging nations like the US and Germany. Only once other nations had been able (through protectionism and other means) to acquire similar levels of economic development to Britain could free trade prove more beneficial to all.

List and Schmoller were part of an intellectual movement, the German Historical School of political economy, which challenged classical liberal political economy and its prevailing wisdoms (see e.g. Tribe 1988, 2007: 218–25; Hodgson 2001). Max Weber was their most famous associate. They had major reservations about the liberal notion that free markets and free trade gave rise to a harmonious economic order sustained by mutual advantage. List, despite being the least academic and scholarly, was 'a popularizer' of scepticism about free trade. He was a journalist and 'never an economist by qualification or academic position', 'in conventional terms, a third-rate economist and, consequently, a non-runner in the history of economic theory', yet this 'should not be permitted to obscure the significance of the work which List did' (Tribe 1988: 17–9). Reading List's key work, *The National System of*

Political Economy, the anecdotal nature of the evidence base and the unevenness of the quality of argument are striking. His critique of Smith is at times unfair, based on a caricatured version of Smith's views (Watson 2012). Nevertheless, List offers some piercing insights and reflects an important body of academic and political opinion which was (and remains) suspicious of, or outright hostile to, the postulates of liberal political economy. List's ability to capture the essence of these sentiments and popularize them arguably justifies his long-standing influence.

The conception of the capitalist market

The understanding of the market underpinning economic nationalist political economy differs in important respects from the liberal view of 'self-regulating' markets and the asserted 'natural' or 'necessary' character of free markets. Economic nationalists point out that markets are *not* natural phenomena – they have to be politically constructed and politically maintained. It is a difference of degree, not of kind. As noted above, Smith and Ricardo appreciated the political context of market activity and how this affected the operation of free markets. At root, however, there was a conviction within liberal classical political economy that freer markets had the potential to overcome these impediments to improve, even optimize, the distribution of economic resources.

List's foundational assumption was that nations, seeking self-preservation, were always looking for their own particular advancement in power and strength within the world economy. This is the point of departure, for List, in understanding market relations. Political intervention and the shaping of market outcomes in pursuit of these aims are inextricably part of capitalism, even liberal capitalism. This inevitability of political interference means that all economic activity is profoundly shaped by, and perhaps subordinated to, power relationships and political institutions such as the state. Hence there is no such thing as 'free' trade, and no such thing as 'unrestricted' competition (List 1856 [1841]: 261). Political authorities, in pursuit of national interests, will always attempt to shape market operations and outcomes. They will also often succeed.

Hamilton, similarly, saw the inevitability and necessity of politics shaping the economy. He highlighted the benefits for national prosperity of developing the domestic market and increasing the stability of demand, for example for domestic agrarian production. More goods produced and sold locally in a more diversified economy would increase employment opportunities and the 'diversity of talents' (Hamilton, quoted in Crane and Amawi 1997: 40). Yet left to its own devices, the market could not be relied upon to deliver the goods. Government intervention is necessary to build up the emergent manufacturing sector: 'the public purse must supply the deficiency of private resource' (Hamilton 1997 [1791]: 47).

To demonstrate the point, List holds up a mirror to 19th-century Britain – which proclaimed free trade and projected a self-image as a paragon of liberal virtue. List points out the linchpins of the British empire: 'a prosperous manufacturing industry, a considerable marine, and a vast external commerce', which 'can only be acquired by the intervention and aid of government' (ibid.: 265). This interpenetration of state and market, and the recognition of political intervention shaping market relations, was at the core of List's political economy and central to how he understood capitalism. Despite centuries of interventionism, the British were hypocritically professing *laissez-faire* and free trade to the world.

Beneath the façade of intellectual commitment to a political economic doctrine, List discerned the naked pursuit of national self-interest at the expense of Britain's emerging economic and military competitors.

Carey's conception of the capitalist market had some similarities with those of Hamilton and List. All embraced the necessity of interventionist policies of infant infantry protection state subsidies and tariff measures to support and nurture fledgling firms and shelter them from international competition though for Carey this was more through ongoing tariffs than subsidies, and all were keen to attract foreign capital and inward immigration. Where Carey was distinctive was in identifying the adverse social and distributional effects of freer trade on ordinary workers and ordinary citizens. He saw disproportionate benefits accruing to 'traders' and financiers through rent-seeking. Traders were viewed sceptically as monopolists and manipulators of prices, lacking sufficient commitment to the community or the workers (Helleiner 2020: 12–13). This increased the exposure of social groups, heightening the dependence of domestic workers on the vicissitudes of international markets.

Carey saw farmers and the agricultural sector as equally vulnerable to exploitation by 'traders', not least through monocrop production diminishing soil quality. Indeed, Carey's was an early environmental critique of 19th-century free trade capitalism: 'It is singular that modern political economy should so entirely have overlooked the fact that man is a mere borrower from the earth, and that when he does not pay his debts, she does as do all other creditors – expelling him from his holding' (Carey *Principles* v.1, 336, quoted in Helleiner 2019: 12–3; 2020: 12–13).

Another atypical element in Carey's economic nationalism, picking up elements of feminist political economy (see pp. 5–6, 88–91, 132–3, 225–7, 231–4, 299), is his highlighting of the disproportionate suffering of women from lower wages and job loss through the unequal gendered impacts of free trade. 'Social harmony' is key to economic well-being for Carey, and this is undermined by what modern feminism would term patriarchal power relations in society: 'Unfit to dig the earth, [women] find themselves driven from the light labor of conversion, in every country subject to the system [of free trade] … What, then, remains to them? In millions of cases, little else than prostitution; yet are we constantly assured of the civilizing effects of that trading system' (Carey *Principles* v.3, 377–8, quoted in Helleiner 2019: 13). This is an unusual focus for the perennial economic nationalist appreciation of how the economy is riven with power relations.

Carey embraced localism and decentralizing the economy, and tackled the adverse environmental and gendered consequences of free trade, in addition to the more familiar themes of safeguarding the domestic economy from international competition. His was a harmonious view of a decentralized economy, driven by rising (agricultural) productivity and decisively at odds with Ricardo's view of antagonistic class relations. There is none of Ricardo's zero-sum struggle between wages, rents and profits (Helleiner 2019: 12–4). Carey's case for significant levels of protectionism centred on countering the adverse social and distributional implications of freer trade to restore social harmony. This would increase productivity, raise wages and generate the benefits of a diversified economy.

These 19th-century arguments in political economy bear the imprint of the world order of the time and its politics. Hamilton wanted to bolster the independence and self-reliance of America's emergent national economy. List's whole oeuvre is in effect an instruction manual to help Germany (which was not yet unified as a nation) escape the yoke of British imperial, economic, military and political dominance. There is, however, a conceptual point underpinning his railing against the perfidious British. As List notes, in critiquing classical liberal political economy, 'to the end that free trade may operate naturally, it is necessary that the nations less advanced than England, should be raised by artificial means to the same degree of development at which England arrived artificially' (ibid.: 207). This artificiality denotes the inevitability of political intervention in the economy underpinning the economic nationalist conception of the capitalist market.

The individual and society

Economic nationalism entailed a rejection of the methodological individualism central to classical liberal political economy. As List pointed out, Smith's is 'not a system of national economy, but of individual economy', and therefore classical liberal political economy 'does not comprehend nationality' or 'national interests' (ibid.: 253, 261). By contrast, the nation, *not* 'the state' and *not* the individual, is the core analytical category in List's methodological nationalism. Smith's error is that 'individuals are regarded merely as producers and consumers, and not as citizens of a nation' (ibid.: 261). Hamilton's goal was to confront both the mercantilism of foreign governments and the monopolistic tendencies of domestic producers in order to strengthen 'national independence and safety' (Hamilton 1997 [1791]: 37). For economic nationalists, citizen nationals are engaged in a collective endeavour of economic development and progress. This is what makes the national economy greater than the sum of its parts. Biological metaphors abound in German Historical School and economic nationalist descriptions of society. Schmoller, for example, sought 'the creation of real *political* economies as unified organisms' (1902 [1884]: 50–1).

Instead of the liberal methodological individualism, economic nationalism is focused on what List termed 'the social economy of a nation' (List 1856 [1841]: 240). Furthermore, by bending individual wills to serve the national interest, in potentially *illiberal* ways, greater feats of economic development can be achieved: 'only where private interest has been subordinate to public interest ... have nations attained an harmonious development of their productive power' (ibid.: 243). Economic nationalist political economy interprets this not necessarily as coercion, but as mobilization behind a national ideology (see e.g. Johnson 1982; Woo-Cumings 1999). This jars with liberalism's sanctity of individual freedom as espoused by Smith, Mill and Hayek. It also sees the pursuit of private self-interest as (at least potentially) inimical to social goods, and is in that sense at odds with the liberal notion of the 'invisible hand'.

The conception of the individual underpinning List's analysis is distinctive and important. This is crucial because, for List, so much of a nation's 'productive power' (the ultimate source of a nation's wealth) hinges on the development and refinement of intellect, skill and 'mental capital'. From List's perspective, learning reconstitutes the individual (Hodgson 2001: 61–2) in a manner attuned with national culture and nurtured within specific sets of national institutions. This contrasts with modern liberal political economy's assumed fully formed and fixed preferences of rational individuals, discussed in Chapters 4 and 5.

List is ungenerous to Smith in asserting that he failed to appreciate the importance of productive power and its immaterial, intellectual underpinnings. Nevertheless, List emphasizes repeatedly how mental capital is rooted in, and nurtured by, particular kinds of social relationships and strongly affected by the quality of education. In this, Listian political economy speaks to modern concerns about enhancing 'human capital'. List's focus on education and mental capital as sources of wealth explains his famous critique of bagpipe producers:

'those who manufacture bag-pipes or pills, are indeed productive; but the instructors of youth and manhood, musicians, virtuosos, physicians, judges, and statesmen, are productive in a much higher degree. The former produce exchangeable values; the latter productive power' (1856 [1841]: 221). Social and political context, and crucially the division of labour between 'intellectual labour' and 'material labour', conditions a nation's 'productive powers' and 'public prosperity' (ibid.: 240).

Economic nationalism rests upon national identity, taking account of specific national traditions, ideas and institutions. It is rooted in what some ideational scholars in political economy call 'social purpose' (Ruggie 1982, 1998; Helleiner 2005; see pp. 134–8). Individuals in Listian and economic national political economy are socially embedded (Jackson and Deeg 2008: 683). Historically and culturally specific paths of political economic evolution channel the learning and mental capital enhancement processes along distinct developmental trajectories, guided by national traditions of economic thought. Accordingly, 'economic nationalism should be understood simultaneously as political action in a specific historical context, rather than as economic doctrine in a universal context of ideas' (Pickel 2005: 8). Liberalism's methodological individualism tends to admit no conception of national differentiation among individuals' world views and fails to grasp fully 'the nature of social labour', which is crucial to understanding and augmenting productive power.

The international order

Arguably the most significant quality of economic nationalism is its situating of domestic political economic activity and policy in the wider global context (Tribe 1988: 30). Obviously, List had a very different view from Smith as to how that world order should be conceptualized. This was one of List's main disputes with classical liberal political economy, yet the nature of that disagreement, and the distance between Smith and List, is often misrepresented.

The liberal view of harmonious and mutually beneficial interaction, economic nationalist political economy argues, ignored the importance of nations as intermediaries between individuals and humanity. It thus underplayed how the politics of international economic relations involves national competitive struggles. The Smith/Ricardo view of the world economy can only operate if trading nations compete at comparable levels of economic development (which will only be possible, if at all, in the very long run). Until then, the hierarchies and inequalities of power relationships, especially between nations, always skew the capitalist system. This will prevent the win/win international trading scenarios theorized and predicted by Smith and modelled in Ricardo from arising. Rather than the liberal school's 'cosmopolitical economy', List's 'political economy' instead 'merely teaches how a nation, in certain circumstances, may attain, by means of agriculture, manufacturing industry, and commerce, to prosperity, civilisation and power' (List 1856 [1841]: 189–90).

It is important to avoid overstating the distance – in policy and indeed theory – between economic nationalism and liberalism. List did acknowledge the scale of Smith's contribution as the originator of the science of political economy. He did not reject Smith's insights, arguing that Smith's work should be further developed. List built on Smith by situating liberal postulates within an understanding of the long-term uneven development of capitalism in different nations, generating unequal power relationships. His critique argued that Smith's 'cosmopolitical' vision did not *yet* apply because of differences in power, 'civilisation' and wealth among nations. In time, List felt, by following his policy prescriptions, more nations could attain economic development comparable to the UK. At that point, the pertinence of Smithian insights would increase. That is why List claims that 'the protective system ... will be the most effective promoter of universal association among nations, and consequently free trade' (ibid.: 201).

Hamilton also built on Smith's contribution, evoking the division of labour and the spirit of enterprise as key motors of national economic wealth and growth (Hamilton 1997 [1791]: 39). Yet Hamilton was sceptical of wider Smithian arguments about the 'system of perfect liberty', finding them not relevant to the US context of the 1790s. Hamilton's rationale for protectionism was partly that government intervention in the national economy was essential to confront the mercantilist interventions of competitor nations. His report voiced scepticism that the free play of market forces, or the market's invisible hand, would deliver optimal outcomes. Interventionism was necessary and beneficial in developing the fledgling US manufacturing economy – not least given the advantage earlier industrializing nations already enjoyed (Hamilton 1997 [1791]: 41–3).

Mutually beneficial free exchange did not reflect the real-world 'general policy of Nations'. Instead, Hamilton noted, the international trading system was 'regulated by the opposite spirit', such that the US finds itself 'precluded from foreign Commerce'. He identified numerous 'injurious impediments' and 'serious obstructions' imposed by America's trading partners. Discriminatory economic nationalist interventionism of other governments skewed the international marketplace such that 'the United States cannot exchange with Europe on equal terms' (Hamilton 1997 [1791]: 41). Bolstering domestic US manufacturing would reduce dependence on European powers and their mercantilist economic policies. Hamilton remained sceptical that free trade would increase the chances of international peace. He saw international economic relations as conflictual, since power relations between unequal nations would shape and skew international interactions (Hamilton 1997 [1791]: 41). For Hamilton, foreign commerce was inherently bound up with power relations between nations.

Similarly, List dedicates much attention to what he terms 'the protective system', the tariffs and commercial regulations imposed by nations to shape market outcomes and reshape international competitive pressures. Hamilton and List both appreciated the inescapable fact of market-shaping political interventionism (List 1856 [1841]: 249–50, 261) and the inevitability of unequal power relationships between rival nations at different stages of economic development. The subtitle of List's *The National System of Political Economy* was 'International Trade, Commercial Policy, and German Customs Union' (Henderson 1983: 166), indicating how crucial tariffs and protectionism were to his diagnosis of Germany's economic development in a world economy dominated by the British empire. The protective system, List argues, 'is the only means by which nations less advanced can be raised to the level of that nation which enjoys supremacy in manufacturing industry' (List 1856 [1841]: 201). It is the 'ladder' which he accuses Adam Smith, William Petty and countless British governments of 'kicking away' (ibid.: 440; see also Chang 2002). List's is a diachronic approach to political economy, appreciating that political economies change over time and need to be understood and analysed as dynamic, developing systems.

The most celebrated element of the protective system is List's advocacy of infant industry protection, given that 'in the actual state of the world, an infant industry, deprived of protection, is not able to sustain the competition of an industry long established, of an industry protected on its own territory' (List 1856 [1841]: 223–4). Infant industry protection ideas can also be found in classical liberal political economy – notably in J. S. Mill's writings (1970 [1848]: 487). Adam Smith, too, argued for a gradual opening up of domestic industry to international competition (Harlen 1999: 737–8). Yet protecting infant industries is more central for List and other economic nationalists such as Hamilton. Liberals tended to view these protective measures as an unpalatable and temporary necessity. List's was a much more fulsome defence of them as an appropriate, legitimate, medium-term (though *not* permanent) policy tool for nations seeking economic development. Schmoller's analysis was equally attuned to the 'role of the state in moderating the negative effects of economic progress' (Tribe 2007: 223). Both List and Schmoller advocated protective legislative measures to assist firms and highlighted the state's interventionist role (see also Weber 1994 [1895]: 1–28). These illustrate well the economic nationalist conception of state/market relations.

Yet List foresees the possibility of a different politics of international economic relations emerging. The distorting effects of political intervention on market outcomes would only present problems to the effective operation of markets while the inequalities between nations were very pronounced. List defined 'the mission of political economy' as being 'to furnish the economical education of the nation, and to prepare it to take its proper place in the universal association of the future' (List 1856 [1841]: 263). This refers to an approximation of an international society where mutual gains from trade would indeed accrue in roughly equitable measure to all. Thus, for all the important differences with liberal political economy, List entertained a conception of potential future freer capitalist markets and liberalized international trade which drew on Ricardo's ideas of comparative advantage.

The key insight which CPE scholarship can helpfully draw from this economic nationalist approach to markets and capitalist society is the merits of a historically and culturally contextualized approach to a particular set of state/market relations, and its institutional and ideational embeddedness. Economic nationalist political economy has much to offer CPE scholars as a way to approach an understanding of the political economy of the international order. The principal merit of economic nationalism's diachronic account of uneven capitalist development is to bring to the fore political interference in and shaping of markets and market outcomes. It encourages scepticism as to the possibility of 'free trade' and indeed 'free markets'.

MARXIAN POLITICAL ECONOMY

Listian political economy pays close attention to the historical context of political economic development and to the national social context of economic activity. The last school we consider here, Marxian political economy, does likewise, but arrives ultimately at a radically different account of capitalist society and its dynamics of change. Karl Marx's contribution to political economy has been described as 'a heroic attempt to project a systematic general account of the "laws of motion" of capitalism' (Blaug 1996: 215). He ranks alongside Smith as a hugely ambitious political economist, engaged in a Herculean intellectual endeavour, which in important respects continues to shape our thinking about capitalism today (Wolff 2002; Fasenfest 2018). A central theme of Marx's entire oeuvre is a 'critique of political economy', by which he meant the liberal school originating with Smith. Marx was part of the classical political economy tradition and drew quite extensively on the liberal school that was the subject of his damning critique.

He assimilated, for example, Ricardo's insights into the 'labour theory of value' (see Meek 1956; Dobb 1973) and into social stratification between classes arising from the negative wage/profit relationship that generates antagonisms and conflict within capitalist society. As Harvey notes, 'when he takes on Adam Smith ... Marx accepts much of what Smith had to say but then searches for the gaps or contradictions which, when rectified, radically transform the argument' (Harvey 2010: 5).

Marx's legacy is a complex and multifaceted one, and can easily be misunderstood. One should perhaps follow David Harvey's sage counsel: 'try, as best you can, to set aside everything you *think* you know Marx said so that you can engage with what he actually has to say' (ibid.: 1). Marx is obviously famed as a godfather of communist or socialist political economic visions of a differently ordered society and economy. He is unfairly associated with numerous 'communist' societal projects in the 20th century – in Soviet Russia and Mao's China, among others. They erected statues of Marx, proclaimed him as a demi-god (without always reading his work very closely) and prosecuted appalling human rights abuses. All these communist projects were – in human, economic and social terms – failures. Yet all of this is largely irrelevant to Marx's importance for understanding CPE. After all, *Capital*, arguably his most important work, 'has a great deal to say about the scientific understanding of capitalism, but not much to say about how to build a communist revolution' (ibid.: 6). This is equally true of the rest of his oeuvre. What little Marx said about communism simply does not concern us here. As *comparative* political economists, we are interested in the huge amount Marx wrote about capitalism and how his method (which we discuss further in Chapter 4) encouraged people to think about and analyse capitalism comparatively.

Marx's understanding of wealth differs from those of both liberals and economic nationalists. Ricardo developed elements of a labour theory of value (Meek 1956; Dobb 1973; O'Brien 1978: 84–90) which Marx took on board. The distinctiveness of Marx's understanding of value was that it revolved around exploitation by the capitalist class of the surplus value generated by labour power through the labour process and commodity production. Capital is arguably *the* central concept for Marx. Smith advanced political economy by identifying capital as a crucial category. Marx refined and enhanced our understanding of capital by placing it front and centre within his explanatory model, and noting how the circulation of commodities is the starting point of capital. Capital, for Marx, is a social, not a technical, category. From a Marxian standpoint, capital is best understood 'as a set of social relationships which are always capable of being contested politically and ideologically, rather than as a quantity of resources which are simply utilised in production' (Gamble 1999: 142).

Capital can be thought of as 'value in motion', and this shapes the entire capitalist economy and society. Labour, as the sole source of value, underscores the dependency of 'capital as value in motion' on exploitation. The Marxian account of political economy can be reduced to the circuit of capital, or M – C – M′; that is, the transformation of money into commodities, the sale of which realizes the surplus value contained within commodities and generates more money – this is 'the movement that converts [value] into capital' (Marx 1977: 448). All of this arises out of the inexorable systemic drive to generate profits, augment pecuniary gain and increase wealth (through exploitation; ibid.: 445–55; Harvey 2010: 87–92). To understand how exploitation is at the heart of wealth creation, we need to understand how Marx used the labour theory of value not to determine prices, but to capture a social system in which labour power is transformed into a commodity. This underpins Marx's theory of exploitation and how social relations of production determine relations of exchange (Meek 1956; Dobb 1967: 7–8; O'Brien 1978: 78–109).

Exploitation, as Marx set out in Chapter 10, Volume 1 of *Capital*, is an inherent dynamic of capitalism. The capitalist (owner of the means of production) employs the worker (buys the 'commodity' of their labour power). Labour power is a unique commodity within capitalism. It alone creates value. The 'exchange value' (market price) of labour power is only its subsistence (paying the worker just enough to live on). But the 'use value' (literally how useful something is – this for Marx constitutes the substance of wealth) is greater. In six hours, the capitalist has got their 'money's worth' out of the worker in terms of goods manufactured. But the worker still has more hours, perhaps even six hours, of their shift to go. All the commodities produced in this time create extra 'value' (sale of these commodities make more money for the capitalist than they spent in the overall production process) – that is, surplus value. The surplus value created by the labourer but appropriated by the capitalist in the form of profit-generating commodity sales is the source of wealth within capitalism. This exploitative process underpins the Marxian account of the market, capitalist society and the international order.

Conception of the capitalist market

Marx attempted to discern the historical dynamics of industrial capitalist development (and crisis). In the preface to *Capital* he stated his goal: 'to lay bare the economic law of motion' of capitalist relations of production (1977: 417). His economic analysis is infused with an understanding of the power relations at work within society, economy and polity. Indeed, the economic processes and institutions of capitalism, crucially the market exchange of commodities and private property, are, in Marx's view, what instantiate and sustain the power relationships stratifying society. These are the social relations of production, and their constant reproduction is the central focus of his analysis. Even though he was writing between the 1840s and the 1880s, his analysis of the political economy of capitalism still resonates today.

That said, it is not always easy going. Marx himself described some chapters of *Capital* as 'rather arduous', and that was no understatement. Nevertheless, Marx was one of the great social scientists of the 19th century, and delving into his writings, perhaps guided by the excellent secondary literature (see e.g. McLellan 1980; Harvey 2010), certainly repays, with interest, the intellectual investment it requires. Whether or not one endorses any or all of Marx's normative critique of capitalist society and economy, as comparative political economists we can learn a huge amount about capitalism as a social order, and how it changes, by analysing it in his terms, using his key concepts and ideas.

To grasp Marx's political economy, in addition to seeing it as a critique of classical liberal political economy, we also need to grasp his theory of historical materialism and the notion of dialectics. Marx's 'historical logical' approach to political economy is holistic, as was Smith's, yet it differs in being more 'dynamic'. Like economic nationalism, Marx offered a diachronic account of capitalist development – but one with much more precisely defined drivers of change. Most fundamentally, Marx's disagreement with Smith rejected the allegedly natural laws of bourgeois society. In contrast, Marx pointed to the transitory nature of the capitalist social order. His aim was to analyse 'the birth, life, and death of a given social organism and its replacement by another, superior, order' (1977: 420).

His historical materialist method, discussed further in Chapter 4, led Marx to discern the existence of different modes of production through history, such as the transition from feudalism and agriculture to capitalism and industry with the onset of the Industrial Revolution. Each mode of production has its own historically specific internal laws of motion which give rise to characteristic relations and forces of production. These are essential, for Marx, to understanding why change and development occur. He wrote mostly about the internal laws of capitalism, both how it started in England and why it would in time transform the rest of the world.

His was a theory of 'dialectical materialism'. Dialectics (see pp. 72–3) involve the contradictory interaction of ideas, and human action, with material (economic) conditions. Capitalism is highly unstable, and it is these dialectical internal conflicts and contradictions, according to Marx's theory, which propel change. His is not a static picture but one of constant movement – *circuits* of capital, capital as value *in motion*, labour *processes* and *ever-evolving* social relations of production (see Harvey 2010: 11–13). Marx's writings offered analytical elaboration of these dialectical contradictions within the capitalist economic and social order, rooted in destabilizing unequal relations of power and wealth. His method breathes life into capitalism and our appreciation of how and why it changes. He situates analysis of modes of production within the context of continual reproduction of particular social relations, which have particular outcomes in terms of the distribution of power and resources (Gamble 1999: 143).

The individual and society within the capitalist social order

The most important driver of the dynamic evolution of capitalist society and economy is class, in particular the bourgeoisie (capitalists) or owners of the means of production, and the proletariat (wage labourers) who have to sell the commodity of their labour power. A Marxian account eschews the methodological individualism of much liberal political economy, situating individuals in a social context of class relations, and seeing their actions as explicable only with reference to that social order. As Engels put it, 'production, and with production the exchange of its products, is the basis of every social order ... the division of society into classes or estates, is determined by what is produced and how it is produced, and how the product is exchanged' (quoted in Heilbroner 1992: 144). Thus society is stratified based on people's relationship to production, and this, as Marx states in his preface to *A Critique of Political Economy*, is why 'the anatomy of civil society is to be sought in political economy' (1977: 389).

Marx noted the systemic drive to exploit the proletariat within capitalism, and he sets out in Chapters 6 and 7 of Volume 1 of *Capital* how the forces inherent in the capitalist mode of production *impel* capitalists *inexorably* to extract ever more surplus through the profit motive (ibid.: 445–70; Bonefeld 1992; Clarke 1992). Marx also highlighted the dialectical manner in which the antagonisms and contradictions generated by capitalism would lead to more and bigger economic and social crises within the system. As *The Communist Manifesto* puts it: 'what the bourgeoisie produces, therefore, above all, are its own gravediggers. Its fall and the victory of the proletariat are equally inevitable' (1977: 231). Such a historical transformation was, Engels noted, driven by the underlying deep structures within the system: 'the ultimate causes of all social changes and political revolutions are to be sought … in changes in the mode of production and exchange' (quoted in Heilbroner 1992: 144).

The 'inevitable' aspect of this historical process of transformation is a source of much debate about Marxian political economy. Marx is often accused of economic determinism, or that his economic 'laws of motion' – capital accumulation, exploitation and class antagonism – mean that people, or even whole societies, have no autonomy, being driven by systemic forces. We will consider Marx's view of the relationship between the individual and the structures of the capitalist economic order at length in Chapter 4. The deterministic reading is unfair to Marx, who offers a subtle, open-ended and deeply politicized account of the dynamic evolution of capitalism. As he notes in a famous passage: 'men make their own history, but they do not make it just as they please; they do not make it under circumstances chosen by themselves, but under circumstances directly encountered, given, and transmitted from the past' (Marx 1977: 300; see also Harvey 2010: 196–9). As Bob Jessop points out, very few Marxian accounts argue that the economic sphere in and of itself plays a determining role in change (1990; see also Burnham 2001; Harvey 2010).

From such a non-deterministic position, the Marxian method can gain a deeper comparative understanding of the operations of free market capitalism. It can reveal how apparently neutral, technical and economic categories can conceal antagonisms and dialectical struggles. As a theorist of the capitalism of the Industrial Revolution, Marx, like Smith, appreciated the crucial social and economic shift that the commodification of labour entailed. Yet Marx was perhaps more penetrating in developing a sophisticated understanding of commodities – and how they instantiate and sustain capital accumulation for the bourgeoisie and unequal power relationships within capitalism. This is a good illustration of how the Marxian method of abstraction can change the way we think about commonplace economic phenomena within capitalism, in this case the commodity. So central are commodities to his account of the dynamics of capitalism that it is with a rather impenetrable and 'particularly arduous' discussion of commodities that *Capital* begins (see Holloway 2002: chs 4, 5; Harvey 2010: 8).

It is necessary to grasp the 'double character of commodities'. A key feature of the commodity phase of capitalism is that 'the social character of men's labour appears to them as an objective character stamped upon the product of that labour' (Marx 1977: 436). Marx refers to this as the 'fetishism of commodities'. The commodification of labour conceals the fundamental aspect of the capital/labour relationship – the exploitation of the proletariat and the expropriation of surplus value (profit) by the bourgeoisie inherent within capitalist social relations of production. On the surface it appears that the labour market is just like any other commodity market. Commodification conceals both how wage labour entails exploitative social relations and how the production of other commodities entails the expropriation of surplus value by the capitalist, generating capitalist profits from worker exploitation (ibid.: 421–70; Holloway 2002: chs 4, 5; Harvey 2010: 109–34).

From a Marxian perspective, these antagonistic class relations shape the political economy. They are always manifest in political, economic and legal forms (Bonefeld et al. 1992; Burnham 2001: 105) within capitalist society, because the political and the economic are inseparable. This recognition of different 'forms' that capitalist social relations can take presents opportunities for CPE scholars. One modern variant of Marxian political economy – the 'Regulation School' – operationalizes these Marxian insights in the comparative analysis of late 20th- and early 21st-century capitalism. This approach deconstructs particular capitalist economies into 'regimes of accumulation', the underlying economic structure; and 'modes of regulation', the political, economic and legal forms that class relations take in the political and institutional infrastructure developed to sustain capital accumulation and manage arising tensions (Boyer 1990). We explore this Regulation School approach further in Chapter 9.

Marxian political economy thus offers concepts and tools for analysis that are potentially particularly useful for the comparative study of political economy. Marx makes us think differently about commodities, locating them in relation to the notion of class struggle. It is with the concept of capital, and the book *Capital*, that Marx is most readily associated. His view of capital as 'value in motion' transforms our understanding of this economic category and entails a profound shift away from much liberal political economy and neo-classical economics towards understanding economic activity in particular historical, political and institutional contexts.

The international order

The emergence of capital as a social form is what gives capitalism its revolutionary character, and this has implications for the wider international context of capitalist social relations of production. Marx saw capitalism as a 'world-historical' transformation of social order. In Chapter 6 of Volume 1 of *Capital* he notes that 'capital ... announces from its first appearance a new epoch in the process of social production' (1974: 167). He fleshes out the 'immanent laws of capitalistic production' in Chapter 32 of Volume 1, noting how capital drives the 'annihilation' of 'the old social organisation' and the 'ever-extending scale' of capitalism. He predicted the universalization of social relations of capitalist society. Marx and Engels noted in *The Communist Manifesto* that the bourgeoisie had 'through its exploitation of the world market given a cosmopolitan character to production and consumption' and brought 'distant lands and climes' within capitalist relations of production and exchange (1977: 224–5).

Marx argued that the antagonistic, exploitative social relations of production cause the 'expropriation of the great mass of the people'. The inexorable drive to increase profits induces ever fiercer competition between capitalists, and the concentration of capital, as 'one capitalist always kills many'. As he puts it: 'the bourgeoisie cannot exist without constantly revolutionising the instruments of production, and thereby the relations of production, and with them the whole relations of society' (ibid.: 224). Harvey calls this the 'transformative dynamism of capital' (2010: 13). This draws disparate cultures and formerly national groupings into the same worldwide social and economic system.

Capitalism, Marx discerned, is 'growth-addicted', only surviving if the accumulation of wealth increases and accelerates. Just like Alice in Wonderland, capital has to run to stand still. Capital, as 'value in motion', shapes the entire capitalist economy and society through M – C – M', as discussed above. Capital, Marx sets out in Chapters 4 and 6 of Volume I of *Capital*, constantly attempts, unsuccessfully, to avoid the systemic crises to which the whole social order is prone (Marx 1974: 145–55, 164–72; Bonefeld 1992). The repeated capitalist crises, caused by the system's inherent contradictions, spur on further economic and social change (Marx 1974: 713–15). This is why Marx and Engels argue in *The Communist Manifesto* that 'the bourgeoisie, during its rule of scarce 100 years, has created more massive and more colossal productive forces than have all preceding generations together' (Marx 1977: 225).

So powerful are these transformative forces and drivers that they cannot be contained within national borders. As Marx and Engels put it in *The German Ideology*, capitalism 'made all civilised nations and every individual member of them dependent for the satisfaction of their wants on the whole world, thus destroying the former natural exclusiveness of separate nations' (1970: 78). Marx identified, though did not develop at great length, this internationalizing dimension wherein 'the need of a constantly expanding market for its products chases the bourgeoisie over the whole surface of the globe ... cheap prices of its commodities are the heavy artillery with which it batters down all Chinese walls' (Marx 1977: 225). This leads to 'the entanglement of all peoples in the net of the world-market, and with this, the international character of the capitalistic regime' (Marx 1974: 713–15; see also Marx 1970: 72–9). Thus the capitalist mode of production is dynamic, entailing the *almost constant* transformation of national economies, and the world economy, and the linkages between them: 'the bourgeois mode of production ... creates a world after its own image' (Marx 1977: 225).

Marx's method fosters a fine-grained appreciation of particular sets of social relations of production in specific contexts, and as such is helpful for the comparative analysis of the political economy of capitalism. It enables us to see afresh important economic categories – such as the commodity and capital – and to scratch beneath the veneer of capitalist social relations to reveal what Marx deemed to be underlying exploitation and antagonism. Whether or not one signs up to any or all of his account of the nature of capitalist social relations, his method facilitates deeper analytical engagement with the economic drivers behind dialectical and open-ended processes of societal change. It also brings to the fore the economic underpinnings of extant power relations and the extant institutional configuration of society, located in their international context. These aspects offer scope for contemporary CPE analysis of capitalism.

CONCLUSION

Smith, Marx and List, as well as Hamilton, Carey, Schmoller and others, were part of a broad, encompassing, pre-disciplinary field of social, political and economic inquiry unlike anything in modern academia. Classical political economy's development of a holistic analysis and understanding of the intricate workings, and social and political implications, of global capitalism is a forbiddingly difficult task. The Herculean attempt to analyse the entire social system of capitalism in all its complexity – as Smith and Marx did – is rare for a reason. The more modest task which contemporary CPE scholars might set themselves is to identify and avail themselves of classical political economy scholarship that offers illuminating avenues into a deeper understanding of how 21st-century capitalism works.

Smith, List and Marx all in their different ways make the case for a historically contextualized understanding of political economic processes. Each has something distinctive and interesting to say about how to understand the market, state/market relations, the social order, and the individual's place within and in relation to it. Each of them also has a distinctive account of how to conceive of the international context within which political economic activity takes place, and its ramifications. Such a locating of capitalism in institutional and international context remains the stuff of CPE today. Appreciation of their insights, and what was at stake in their debates, increases our acuity as political economists, facilitating a deeper understanding of the connections between the political and the economic and how they should be analysed. This provides a fruitful foundation on which to build a comparative understanding of political economy. In their different ways, each offers a promising line of inquiry so as to understand, unpack and unpick contemporary capitalism. In the next chapter, I explain why the classical political economy approach became marginalized within the academic study of things economic, and suggest ways to rehabilitate it.

4 Disciplinary Politics and the Genealogy of Comparative Political Economy

INTRODUCTION

We have seen in Chapters 1–3 how getting to grips with the historical evolution of political economic thought is important for learning how to think like a political economist. Appreciation of this lineage, we noted in Chapter 1, explains the significant differences between political economy and economics. In this chapter we will develop this theme further as we introduce more analytical tools required to understand and interpret contemporary state/market relations by exploring the important issue of *how* to engage in CPE analysis. We will unearth disagreements about method and the merits of simplifying assumptions, abstract modelling and generalization in political economy. This divided Ricardo and Malthus over two centuries ago, divisions which continue within contemporary CPE (see Chapter 13). These debates have been going on long enough for us to be confident that there is merit on both sides and that there is no imminent prospect of resolution.

In this chapter, we are interested primarily in addressing the question: 'Where did the tradition of classical political economy go?' Answering this question draws our attention to particular norms, assumptions and practices associated with different schools of thought regarding the most appropriate method for studying CPE and political economy. In the process, we will learn more about the legacy for contemporary scholarship of the genealogy and history of CPE as a field. Central to the explanation is the disagreement on method beginning in the 1880s known as the *Methodenstreit*. This had a profound transformational effect not only on CPE, but on all social scientific inquiry. It entrenched differences over substantive focus and method which, during the 20th century, became institutionalized as academia separated out into the disciplines we know today (Gamble 1995; Hodgson 2001; Watson 2016). We analyse this as the stuff of disciplinary politics (Rosamond 2007; Clift and Rosamond 2009; Clift et al. 2021), and how powerful disciplinary norms can be in shaping what is deemed appropriate conduct in the pursuit of social scientific (and other) knowledge.

The classical political economy tradition, with its foundational assumptions about the need to analyse the political, the economic and the social as a complex interrelated whole, struggled to survive the advent of this academic specialization. The 20th century saw a much more modest place for political economy – marginalized as a sub-discipline within economic sociology, political science and economic history. CPE's development and evolution were hindered by the need to straddle these academic divides. The assumptive foundations of mainstream economics, which came to dominate academic social scientific inquiry into all things economic, largely shifted the focus away from the differentiated institutions of market capitalism so central to CPE. Indeed, following the *Methodenstreit*, economics as a discipline confined itself to a substantive focus which would have been virtually unrecognizable by Smith, Marx and List.

Before we consider the implications of the *Methodenstreit*, we first need to know how and why it happened and what the disagreement was about. After spelling out what disciplinary politics entails, we will explore the origins of the rift between Gustav von Schmoller in the historicist corner, and Carl Menger – a key member of the Austrian School of Economics and a teacher of Hayek – in the marginalist corner. The Austrian School had a radically different understanding of knowledge and the market process from mainstream economics, stressing the uncertainty and subjectivity in human affairs. They distrusted the idea of economics as a science, and this gave Austrian marginalism a distinctive quality.

We will consider how the insights, methods and techniques of the German Historical School and Marxism were and are important for exploring and comparing political economic differentiation across time and/or geographical locations, which is at the core of CPE. Yet this kind of historically and institutionally attuned analysis was, as we shall see, very much at odds with the marginalist approach. Marginalism was very influential, homing economics in on a restricted set of questions which became the bedrock of neo-classical economics.

Having considered what was at stake in this academic rift, and its outcome, we will turn to the *Methodenstreit*'s consequences and implications for CPE as a modern field. We will look at isolated examples of heterodox scholarship which carried on the classical political economy spirit in the earlier 20th century. This includes the Marxist economist Rosa Luxemburg, British anti-imperialist scholar J. A. Hobson, the influential economist and political scientist Joseph Schumpeter, and the unconventional founder of American institutional economics Thorstein Veblen. We will then chart how the discipline-defining debates between Keynes, Hayek and Polanyi over the role of the state in the economy shaped later 20th- and 21st-century debates in political economy.

Thereafter, we consider how disciplinary politics shapes underlying assumptions about the appropriate subject matter of political economy. We can readily appreciate this if we consider the marginalization of feminist political economy – and issues of gender and social reproduction – within CPE analysis. Feminist political economy underlines that many taken-for-granted assumptions about what the field should focus upon – how the public and private sectors should be understood, for example – are in fact contested.

The chapter ends by noting the emergence of IPE as a self-defined field, which to a degree made the intellectual climate more hospitable for CPE scholarship. Meanwhile, work ongoing in other fields, such as economic sociology, history and law, offered insights and source material which CPE scholars willing to escape disciplinary boundaries could draw upon. By the 1990s, new journals were founded and CPE's core focus and insights were again central to major debates in fields such as political science, IPE and economic sociology. Thus a new respectability has been achieved, such that CPE is returning from the periphery towards the core of political science and IPE.

The upshot of this somewhat complicated genealogy is that modern CPE has a range of available methods and approaches. In this chapter, I argue for a methodologically pluralist approach (see also Chapter 13), recognizing that each method and approach can have much to offer CPE. More is lost than is gained by asserting one single way of doing political economy as superior, let alone as the only legitimate approach. None is intrinsically better, but each offers a different kind of undertaking, setting itself distinctive intellectual and analytical goals. The rich variety of different approaches to CPE analysis is a considerable source of strength within the field, as we shall see in later chapters.

DISCIPLINARY POLITICS

Sociologists of knowledge highlight the disciplinary power of academic disciplines, sometimes described as 'knowledge production regimes' (Rosamond 2007: 231). Within these regimes 'the production of knowledge ... is not a neutral or innocent exercise', because 'the conditions of intellectual knowledge production reflect assumptions, biases, trends, and debates within the academy' (ibid.: 232). This is what Ben Rosamond calls 'disciplinary politics' (see Box 4.1), and it involves 'the idea that the course of academic work is governed by power games and that there are likely to be significant disagreements about best practice and progress in a field' (ibid.; see also Clift et al. 2021). We will encounter such 'biases' and 'prior assumptions' in this chapter, and again in Chapter 13. Below we show how disciplinary disagreements about the best way to conduct political economy research can lead to rifts which can reshape whole fields of study. We will also see the emergence of 'monistic claims about propriety in the field' (ibid.: 233), wherein some deem their set of prior assumptions to be the only legitimate starting points for research in the field.

Box 4.1 Disciplinary politics

National, and sometimes international, disciplinary communities tend to institutionalize in distinct ways at least four aspects of academic inquiry within a field:

- *Admissibility*: what is considered to be acceptable or admissible work and knowledge in a given field?
- *Conduct*: what are the legitimate means and methods by which knowledge may be garnered? How should work be conducted and how and where should its results be presented?
- *Borders*: where do the limits of the discipline lie? What substantive issues, topics and theoretical frameworks are deemed to lie outside the discipline?
- *External relations within a field*: what is the nature of the engagement with and/or the interaction between (and potentially the 'othering' of) cognate social scientific disciplines?

Sources: Based on Rosamond (2007: 235); see also Clift and Rosamond (2009: 95–8); Clift et al. (2021); Klein (1996); Mancias (1987).

Significantly, these disciplinary political issues never faced the classical political economists, partly because not all were academics, but mostly because they wrote in a predisciplinary era when no disciplinary divisions had become institutionalized. On the whole, disciplinary political contestation surrounding conduct and admissibility can be quite healthy. It is important, however, that these biases and assumptions are worn 'on the sleeve' and not smuggled underneath appeals to 'science' or 'rigour'.

TO GENERALIZE OR NOT TO GENERALIZE? THE ORIGINS OF THE RIFT IN POLITICAL ECONOMY

These differences of method straddle many issues relating to the nature and purpose of social scientific inquiry. Here we flag an important methodological difference which to some extent divided the classical political economists we discussed in Chapters 2 and 3. At issue here are different logics of analysis that hinge upon the distinction between inductive and deductive reasoning (see Hay 2002: 30–1). The intellectual justification for each approach is impeccable, and importantly the two logics of inquiry are not mutually exclusive. Adam Smith's political economy, for example, attempted to 'judiciously blend induction and deduction' (Hodgson 2001: 5), and legions of social scientists have followed in these footsteps. Nevertheless, these approaches encompass different understandings of the logic guiding social scientific inquiry. Taken to extremes, they can lead to stark scholarly differences. Within CPE, debates as to their relative merits endure (see pp. 97–6, 116–17).

A deductivist perspective starts with a theory, which is derived from established facts and which posits a set of relationships. Deductive approaches 'seek to derive (or deduce) testable propositions or hypotheses from pre-established facts' (see Hay 2002: 30), and these hypotheses are then tested against the evidence. The models established within deductive analysis make a set of simplifying assumptions – as in the case of marginalist political economy explored below. Deductive approaches tend to favour theoretical parsimony – or having the fewest possible explanatory variables in the model. These initial theoretical assumptions, and the model built from them, generate a series of predictive hypotheses about, in our case, how political economic activity will unfold. The logic of research seeks observations that confirm or confound the predictive hypotheses. The early mover in this direction was Ricardo, who 'pursued more and more an axiomatic and deductivist method' (Hodgson 2001: 5). Ricardo's abstraction from reality to reveal (what he supposed to be) the system's essential workings is likened by Heilbroner to removing the back of an (analogue) pocket watch to reveal the cogs and springs which make it tick (1992: 102).

The inductive approach is sometimes described as the 'mirror image' of deductivism (Hay 2002: 30). Inductive social scientific inquiry prioritizes empirical observation of the world, searching for patterns and regularities. Inductive inquiry infers from these observations causal connections, relationships and ultimately theories. The logic of inductive inquiry begins with empirical observation and infers from the observed empirical phenomena or relationships broader, more generalizable, perhaps even universal 'laws', propositions or theories. An inductive generalization based on all observed cases of X aims to arrive, eventually, at a theory about X.

Ricardo had an important methodological spat with Thomas Malthus which in some ways captures the essence of the struggle over how to do CPE and political economy. They argued about what constitutes the appropriate mode of political economy analysis. Malthus criticized the 'precipitate attempt to simplify and generalize' (quoted in Hodgson 2001: 5) of Ricardo's axiomatic approach. The problem, for Malthus, was that Ricardo's analytical techniques, though adopted with impeccable scholarly intentions, had important side effects. This presaged an analytical separation of the political and the economic. Ricardo's penchant for abstraction contrasted with Smith and Malthus and their holistic accounts and explanations. These differences continue within CPE and political science today. Basically, not all see generalizability as the most important goal of social scientific research, theories or findings.

It is important to recall, however, that for Ricardo abstraction was an analytical device, not a political move. His analysis was, as we saw in Chapter 3, deeply politically engaged in the Corn Laws reform debates. Nevertheless, in less careful hands, the Ricardian method of abstraction and rigorous deduction could lead to a tendency to separate 'economic man' from any social or political context. Tabb sees it as auguring the 'depoliticization' of political economy (1999). Indeed, Ricardo's analytical turn began the shift towards abstraction from political context, later exaggerated by the marginalist revolution. Hodgson characterizes the ascent of marginalism and thereafter neo-classical economics as 'the triumph of barren universality' (2001: 232).

THE DEBATE ON METHOD IN POLITICAL ECONOMY: THE GERMAN HISTORICAL SCHOOL

Before drawing any lessons from the *Methodenstreit*, we need to understand it. The German Historical School that we encountered in Chapter 3 came to represent, in the mid to late 19th century, one side of a struggle for the soul of political economy. The German Historical School was united by its 'reaction against the individualist assumptions and deductivist methods of British classical political economy' (ibid.: 58; Backhouse 2002: ch. 8). Pitted against Ricardo's followers who favoured abstraction in search of universal law–like generalizations, the German Historical School instead championed detailed empirical research into concrete political economic phenomena.

This approach was not the unique preserve of German scholars, but empiricist and historicist ideas had most lasting impact within German academic political economy and policy debates. The political context was a German nation seeking unification and identity, and autonomy from British imperial dominance of international trade. This concentrated the minds of the School on a similar set of substantive analytical themes, focused on differentiated national paths of economic development (Hodgson 2001: 56–8). They sought to develop a historically sensitive study of political economy, fully acknowledging nationally specific conditions of evolution. This focus on concrete empirics was a world away from the abstraction of Ricardo's parsimonious model. Subsequently, the Younger German Historical School, notably Schmoller, directed their attacks at the marginalist political economy of Leon Walras, William Stanley Jevons and especially the Austrian economist Carl Menger.

Classical liberal political economy in the 18th and 19th centuries saw economic phenomena as natural forces. This irked – to different degrees – List (1856 [1841]), Wilhelm Roscher (1843) and Bruno Hildebrand (1848). As Tribe notes, List et al. considered that the universal political economic laws discerned by Smith and his followers amounted to 'expounding an economics of spurious generality and limited utility' (1988: 17). The German Historical Schools rejected the posited regularities of natural laws of economics, arguing for contingent, historically specific, approaches to economic law and economic policy. They wrestled with what Geoffrey Hodgson calls 'the problem of historical specificity' (2001: xiii, 21–40).

Another important point of contention between the marginalists and the German Historical School was the balance between theorizing and evidence gathering. At the extreme, some German Historical scholars felt there was simply no need for theory. This standpoint has not stood the test of time. For one thing, evidence gathering is a very time-consuming endeavour. (Where does one start looking for empirical evidence? At what point should one stop, if ever?) As leading Austrian marginalist Carl Menger cogently criticized, this approach is based on a misrepresentation of the relationship between research (evidence gathering) and theorizing. In truth, all empirical research – however purportedly atheoretical – has to rely on some prior assumptions, concepts and theorizing in order to know how to make sense of the social world, where to look for evidence, and how to interpret and afford priority to that evidence once found (ibid.: 75–81). Schmoller, Weber and Werner Sombart were perhaps the most convincing on these issues (ibid.: 113–32), seeing the need for economic propositions and theorizing, but basing this on detailed empirical observation and evidence.

The German Historical School's context-specific, contingent analysis resting upon particular national historical and cultural circumstances finds echoes in much CPE work today, including historical institutionalism (Chapter 6), economic nationalist scholars working with concepts such as the developmental state (Chapter 8) and critics of 'self-regulating' market understandings of 21st-century capitalism (see e.g. Chang 1999, 2002).

THE DEBATE ON METHOD IN POLITICAL ECONOMY: MARX AND HISTORICAL MATERIALISM

It may seem odd to consider Marx's approach in the context of the *Methodenstreit*, since he was not a protagonist in the argument. However, we are seeking to understand better how to think like a political economist and what analytical tools and techniques are particularly useful for undertaking *comparative* political economy analysis. In this light, the Marxian perspective offers important insights and stakes out a revealing approach. Marx's materialist conception of history provides a powerful methodological critique of the whole enterprise of marginalist political economy and its underlying method (Clarke 1983; Burnham 1994, 2001). There are some affinities between Marx and the German Historical School, since Hegelian philosophy is an important influence on both. However, Marx was much more enamoured of abstraction as a mode of reasoning and analysis, and his case for historicized, contextualized analysis is built on different foundations.

Marx was inspired by Hegel, whose method saw history as 'the development and conflict of abstract "principles" – cultures, religions, and philosophies', propelled by 'a tension between any present state of affairs and what was becoming', so that 'every state of affairs contained within itself the seeds of its own destruction and transformation to a higher stage' (McLellan 1980: 134). This process, sometimes called 'the power of the negative' or 'the interpenetration of opposites' (ibid.: 152), Hegel called the 'dialectic'. For Marx – the historical materialist, as opposed to Hegel the idealist – it was the economic basis of society (the mode of production, forces of production, social relations of production and class antagonism) which was the driver of historical development, not abstract principles in people's minds (ibid.: 134–8; Buckler 2002: 181–5; Harvey 2010: 11–13). Marx stood Hegel's concept of the dialectic on its feet, as he once put it.

From this starting point, Marx sought 'to recreate and reconfigure what social scientific method is all about' (Harvey 2010: 6). The preface to *Capital*, Volume I states: 'it is the ultimate aim of this work to lay bare the economic law of motion of modern society' (Marx 1977: 417). Marx saw historical development in terms of successive economic phases, each distinct, and each containing within it the seeds of its own demise and of the transition to its successor. Subsequent Marxists call his methodology 'dialectical historical materialism'. Marx himself called it the 'materialist conception of history', recognizing that theorizing was historically specific to each distinct stage of capitalist development.

Marx thought that any social scientific concepts, 'laws' or analysis can only be pertinent to one specific historical phase – since each one had its own internal logic. Thus Marx's analysis in *Capital* could only ever apply to the capitalist mode of production – and its contingent structures, processes and social relations of production. That is why Engels noted that 'political economy is therefore essentially only ever a *historical* science' (quoted in Hodgson 2001: 48). According to Marx, one methodological problem with liberal political economy was its attempt to ground theory in timeless, universal postulates about human nature. This might be a bit unfair to Smith, who viewed habits such as 'trucking' and 'bartering' as being inculcated within commercial society, rather than derived from the essence of human nature. Other liberals, however, were not so careful, and Marx was understandably suspicious of their universal, timeless assumptions about human nature, or indeed anything else.

Marxist theory argues that human nature cannot be separated from society. These assumptions about the character of social reality are one important way in which Marxist approaches differ from the liberal political economy. Marx thought that social relations define what humans can become within *specific historical and geographical contexts*, therefore political economy needed to understand historically specific social relations and structures, such as the capitalist mode of production, to grasp how and why human beings act as they do. This, of course, is an important insight for *comparative* political economy in particular, since the comparative element inevitably involves analysing political economic phenomena from more than one temporal or geographical context. Indeed, the comparative method (see Chapter 13) is one particularly useful way to explore these historically specific social relations and structures.

In a key passage to his Preface to *A Critique of Political Economy*, Marx set out how social relations of production determine consciousness:

> In the social production of their lives, men enter into definite relations that are indispensable and independent of their will, relations of production that correspond to a definite stage of development of their material production forces. The sum total of these relations of production constitutes the economic structure of society, the real foundation, on which rises a legal and political superstructure and to which correspond definite forms of social consciousness. The mode of production of material life conditions the social, political and intellectual life process in general. It is not the consciousness of men that determines their being, but, on the contrary, their social being that determines their consciousness. (Marx 1977: 389)

This crucial passage conveys Marx's view of social reality, of the individual and their place within and relationship to political economy. It differs markedly from liberal conceptions of these issues, both in its classical political economy and modern forms. Arguably, this famous passage, and the understanding of the character of social reality which flows from it, underpins the critique of liberal political economy which was Marx's life's work.

Marx uses this understanding of how social relations of production determine consciousness as a stick to beat the likes of Smith and Ricardo. He is excoriating about these 'bourgeois economists who regard … economic categories as eternal laws and not as historical laws which are laws only for a given period of historical development, a specific development of productive forces' (quoted in Hodgson 2001: 45). Here he has in mind, among other things, the assertions from Smith and others about the free market as a 'natural' or 'necessary' order. This is not dispassionate, value-free political economy, according to Marx, but an ideological project – an intervention in the class struggle. After all, as he notes in *The Communist Manifesto*, 'intellectual production changes its character in proportion as material production is changed ... The ruling ideas of each age have ever been the ideas of its ruling class' (Marx 1977: 236). This, according to Marx, is how to account for the dominance of classical liberal political economy and its *laissez-faire* agenda in the 19th century.

The key point for CPE scholars is that the nature of human consciousness will alter across different phases of historical development. This explains why concepts cannot be transposed out of a stage in economic development (from feudalism to capitalism, say), or indeed out of a particular phase in the evolution of the capitalist mode of production. Therefore, social scientific concepts and theories cannot hope to stretch across historical phases because they will be addressing profoundly different social realities (even if talking about the same country or similar-looking institutions). This is because, as Marx put it, 'politico-economic categories' should be seen 'as abstractions of actual social relations that are transitory and historical' (quoted in Hodgson 2001: 45). Comparativists in political science warn of the dangers of 'conceptual stretching' (Sartori 1970), trying to apply notions outside their appropriate frame of reference. This is something CPE scholars need to be mindful of, and a dose of dialectical historical materialism *à la* Marx can help. As Hodgson remarks, Marx's 'formulation of the problem of historical specificity has been a major achievement' (2001: 49–50). Using concepts and theories to compare political economic developments in different contexts is central to CPE, and Marx's careful approach situating analysis and concepts in their appropriate historical context is a salutary lesson for all CPE scholars.

THE DEBATE ON METHOD IN POLITICAL ECONOMY: MARGINALIST POLITICAL ECONOMY

Marginalist political economy was at loggerheads with the German Historical School on the *other* side of this titanic academic schism. The key protagonists in what became known as the 'marginalist revolution' were pioneering economists working contemporaneously but independently of each other – Carl Menger in Austria, William Stanley Jevons in England, and Leon Walras in Switzerland. They sought to change not just the method, but also the object of political economy analysis. Their intellectual project sought to refine analysis of the economic in a more rigorous direction. Marginalism wanted to escape the all-encompassing holistic visions of Smith or Marx and avoid the unmanageable complexities of a classical political economy overrun with factors, variables, historical contextualization and thick description. They erected new disciplinary boundaries and a narrowly defined set of research questions to reflect this. The new marginalist paradigm revolutionized economic analysis, shifting focus decisively away from the comparative analysis of capitalist institutions and market relations. The new marginalist conception of value 'directed attention away from analysing the social basis of capitalism towards analysing how choices are made between alternative ends under conditions of scarcity' (Gamble 1995: 518). The analytical turns taken by the marginalists were to render economics a 'science' of the study of relationships between *given* ends and *given* scarce means (Blaug 1996: 278).

For Jevons, and legions of economists who followed in his wake, the 'problem of economics', its central question, is 'given a certain population, with various needs and powers of production, in possession of certain lands and other sources of material', what is 'the mode of employing their labour which will maximise the utility of the produce' (quoted in Blaug 1996: 279). This was not just *a* problem, it was *the* economic problem *to the exclusion of all others*, certainly to the exclusion of comparative institutional analysis of social relations of production or capitalist restructuring. This was marginalism's most revolutionary element. It is this specialization and narrowing of focus in academic inquiry about the economy which herald the shift from political economy as an ethical endeavour, to economics as a supposedly, but spuriously, 'value-free' science.

In addressing this much narrower question, the notion of, and assumed sources of, value was the key source of division with classical political economy. On this, Jevons' theory of political economy took issue with Ricardian value analysis (Backhouse 2002: 168). For Ricardo, value was assumed to be 'objectively' determined by production cost and 'natural' rates of reward for the three key factors of production – land, labour and capital (O'Brien 1978). The classical political economists provided a theory of the distribution of each factor. For Ricardo, as for Smith, value was discerned through a historical institutionalist account of the social relationships which define capitalism. This placing of the understanding of value in its social and political context is why classical political economy comfortably aligns with and informs the concerns of CPE. Marginalism, by contrast, denied any objective determinant of value and hence took no interest in objective institutional conditions within the economy (Dobb 1973: 31–3).

The three key protagonists – Menger, Walras and Jevons – were united in conceiving of value as wholly *subjectively* determined. It is the nature of this subjective determination which gives marginalism its name, the 'marginal utility theory of value'. This draws on Jeremy Bentham's theory of utility, which assumed that human behaviour sought to increase pleasure and avoid pain. Both Jevons and Walras called economics 'a calculus of pleasure and pain' (Jevons 1871: vi). Individual consumers, making buying decisions, would evaluate the degree of 'utility' (the amount of pleasure) derived from any purchase. For Jevons, 'value depends entirely upon utility' (ibid.: 77). This ignores prevailing objective social conditions and takes all political and ethical considerations out of discussions of value by resting them on a (as we shall see below, very unrealistic) conception of human subjectivity. This is why Walras and others referred to marginalism as 'pure theory' (1954 [1873]: 71).

Marginalists developed a notion of diminishing marginal utility, or as Jevons put it, 'the degree of utility varies with the quantity of commodity, and ultimately decreases as that quantity increases' (1871: ch. 3). It is termed 'marginalism' because it emphasizes small subjective adjustments (at the margin) within consumption decisions about which combination of commodities will yield maximum utility (the greatest satisfaction). As one acquired more of a good (two dozen apples, say), the additional pleasure gleaned from purchasing the twenty-fifth apple would be considerably lower compared to the first. The consumer's subjective determination of the twenty-fifth apple's value drops accordingly, and they might well choose to buy something else. Economic analysis becomes all about small subjective adjustments of consumers deciding which combination of commodities will yield maximum utility. A dominant role in this process is played by the concept of 'substitution at the margin', or as Stilwell puts it, 'a little more of this and a little less of that' (Stilwell 2012: 152). This incrementalism in individual decision-making is, for marginalists, the essence of understanding the economy.

This focus enabled the marginalists to make some momentous (for the future of social scientific inquiry) methodological decisions and choices. Jevons wrote in the Introduction to *The Theory of Political Economy* that 'economics, if it is to be a science at all, must be a mathematical science' (1871). Jevons and Walras saw mathematics as the panacea for economic inquiry. Menger, by contrast, with his Austrian School emphasis on uncertainty in human affairs, had no time for an economics based on mathematical modelling. Jevons and Walras wanted to achieve increased analytical precision by using more sophisticated maths and calculus because they saw economics (as they were beginning to call it) as inherently mathematical. This was central to their desire to move economics in a more scientific and rigorous direction.

Jevons and Walras' mathematical modelling approach required a very highly simplified model of the economy. In order to achieve refinement and increased precision in analysis true to their scholarly intentions, the marginalists needed to make a series of heroic prior assumptions (see Box 4.2). Their foundational pre-suppositions enabled them to assume away the messy realities of political economic life which are the core substantive focus of modern CPE. Marginalism disregards *a priori* Smith's distinction between natural and market prices, or Marx's class struggle. This was the essence of the 'marginalist revolution'.

Building from these particular assumptive foundations, the marginalists sought to assert that economic laws operated in all times and all places. They deployed deductive reasoning and mathematics to address political economic questions in a more technical, scientific manner. These assumptions became the bedrock of neo-classical economics. Having identified what they deemed the core of economic activity as value determination through marginal utility, the marginalists wanted to strip away everything else. Hence *ceteris paribus*, by assuming that everything else – all historical, institutional, political, social and whatever other factors – will hold constant, the marginalists could focus their attention on what they thought really matters. They assumed all kinds of relationships (which were in political economic reality dynamic and changing) to be constant.

Box 4.2 The foundational assumptions of marginalist political economy

- The focus of political economy should be the study of relationships between *given* ends and *given* scarce means, and how choices are made under conditions of scarcity.
- The maximization of utility is *the* economic problem to be addressed – *to the exclusion of all others*.
- Value is wholly *subjectively* determined.
- *Ceteris paribus*, or all other things being equal, all historical, institutional, political and social factors will, for the purposes of parsimonious analysis, be held constant.
- Individuals are rational, calculating utility maximizers in possession of perfect information.
- Markets are perfectly competitive and they 'clear', allocating resources efficiently and balancing supply and demand.

Sources: Gamble (1995), Blaug (1996) and Hodgson (2001).

This approach abstracts economic analysis from a social and political context, and makes it, in one sense, deeply unrealistic. It attenuates the connection between economic analysis and the real world of political economy. That is what the *Methodenstreit* was all about. All social, political, historical factors – which, back in the real world, are bound to intervene in economic decision-making – are kept out of economic analysis by means of the *ceteris paribus* assumption. In reality, these factors are not constant, of course. On the positive side, if we (or if neo-classical economists) make these assumptions, then greater refinement, specialization and technical precision can be achieved. The *ceteris paribus* assumption enables a more scientific economic analysis, because it avoids attempting to develop a holistic overarching theory as Smith and Marx did. As Mark Blaug argues, neo-classical economics 'indeed achieved greater generality but only by asking easier questions' (1996: 282). Yet economics could develop increasingly sophisticated answers to these simpler questions.

The next assumption is about the nature of individuals within the economy. Classical political economy was interested in analysing entire social orders as complex, interrelated wholes, and tended to understand individuals in socially embedded terms. For Smith they were ethical, social beings. Ricardian techniques began a different analytical tack towards the abstract modelling of individuals' preferences. The marginalists took this up enthusiastically and proposed a radical shift from analysing the social and institutional basis of capitalism to a particular variant of 'methodological individualism'. For Jevons, Walras and Menger the individual is – effectively – the only unit of analysis.

Yet how to understand these individuals? Here the marginalists made further bold assumptions. The individual is assumed to be an atomistic, *asocial* being ('there is no such thing as society', as former British prime minister Margaret Thatcher once said). Although Menger's view was distinct, emphasizing uncertainty and partial knowledge, Jevons and Walras assumed the individual to be a rational, calculating 'utility maximizer' in possession of perfect information. This is the famous *homo economicus* – or economic man (Bowles and Gintis 1993; Persky 1995; Anderson 2000; Tsakalotos 2005). Like *ceteris paribus*, this is an unrealistic assumption, since real-world individuals do not consistently behave in this way, nor do they possess perfect information (Veblen 1919: 73–4; Sen 1977). Nevertheless, this conception of individuals – *all* individuals – enables the generalization of marginalism's models and theorizing, and is justified on these grounds. This understanding of the individual, it need hardly be added, contrasts starkly with Smith's conception of individuals as social and ethical beings, and with Marx's view of the social and historical specificity of consciousness.

We come now to an assumption very dear to, and familiar within, liberal political economy. We encountered Smith's version of it in Chapter 3. It is that markets are perfectly competitive, and allocate resources efficiently, balancing supply and demand. It is a huge assumption to make, and the empirical evidence to the contrary is often substantial. Nevertheless, it is an assumption underpinning marginalist political economy and thereafter neo-classical economics. Marginalists assumed that, within the economy as a whole, markets would 'clear' as a result of multitudinous incremental individual subjective valuing processes. The sum of all the micro-level individual subjective decisions about marginal utility would, at the macro level, determine the value of commodities in a way that balances supply and demand.

Some, like Schumpeter, argue that this amounts to a formalized version of Smith's idea of the invisible hand, though that is debatable. The notion that, by this mechanism, markets *will* tend towards stable equilibrium is a prior assumption fundamental to marginalism and economics, but it is also an ideological assertion, not rooted in an empirical evidence base. Walras in particular analysed this assumed tendency within markets, and posited a process of '*tâtonnement*', or 'groping' towards the point at which all markets clear simultaneously. This state of affairs economists came to call 'general equilibrium'. Walras undertook to develop a mathematical proof that general equilibrium is possible. Yet the status of this proof should be clarified: it only worked on the back of a series of 'heroic abstractions' (Blaug 1996: 279), such as perfect competition and perfectly distributed perfect information.

The assumed active equilibrating mechanism in Walras' model was another 'heroic abstraction'. He posited a hypothetical, perhaps mythical, 'auctioneer' who would simultaneously set *all* prices across *all* markets to bring about equilibrium. As Matthew Watson has pointed out, Walras himself always stressed that his model was *purely* hypothetical. He *never* claimed his models accurately reflect how markets work in practice. In updating his work, Walras eventually assumed away the possibility of disequilibrium exchange (i.e. markets ever not 'clearing' perfectly). He also took the temporal (groping towards perfect equilibrium) element out, so that general equilibrium is assumed at the outset, but never actually demonstrated. Indeed, individuals are not part of what was, for Walras, an impersonal, pure competition mechanism (Watson 2005b: 150–3).

These underlying assumptive foundations of marginalism (adopted to enable economic analysis to become more scientific) entailed the separation of the economic from the social and the political. Important implications of this included a profound *depoliticization* of political economy (Tabb 1999). However, we should be a little careful about casting aspersions about the political character of the marginalist revolution (Winch 2009). Both Jevons and Walras were active social reformers. Indeed, Walras called himself a socialist (Backhouse 2002: 172). Both should be situated on the 'progressive' left side of politics. Yet what history, or more importantly the discipline of economics, learnt from Jevons and Walras was a profoundly conservative lesson – that the market should be left to its own devices, and that political interference within it should be kept to a minimum.

Crucially, marginalism assumed away all the historical, institutional, ideational and contextual variety of capitalist market relations which are the substantive focus, perhaps even the *raison d'être*, of *comparative* political economy. Indeed, Walras' approach seemed to remove the need to make the case for freer markets; one can simply assume that markets clear *a priori*. That Walras never claimed that his models accurately reflect how markets work in practice was subsequently overlooked as economists and advocates used this theoretical proof as a bulwark for their *laissez-faire* arguments. Meanwhile, economists built models assuming an inherent propensity towards general equilibrium within free markets.

THE *METHODENSTREIT* AND COMPARATIVE POLITICAL ECONOMY

The *Methodenstreit* augured a hugely influential shift in the conduct of academic political economy research – heralding the birth of modern economics with its foundations in abstraction and the simplifying assumptions of the marginalists about markets, information, rationality and individual preferences (see Gamble 1995; Hodgson 2001). The marginalist revolution was disciplinary politics at its rawest. Each of the marginalists' central assumptions is contentious and contestable. Essentially, the *Methodenstreit* was an argument about how sensible and defensible these assumptions were. Each one is very important for the evolution and character of political economy analysis. Thus, while on one level the *Methodenstreit* was a dispute about method, it was in fact about much more than that.

The two conceptions of the study of the economic – classical political economy and marginalist economics – were profoundly different, rooted in such widely divergent methodological assumptions and scholarly intentions. As Gamble notes, 'the two camps of the *Methodenstreit* became entrenched in separate academic disciplines, and economics and politics were increasingly treated as separate spheres, which needed to be studied in quite separate ways' (Gamble 1995: 520).

Underpinning the difference between marginalism and classical political economy was a profound disagreement over the nature and purpose of social scientific inquiry. Marginalism directed attention away from the broad-ranging concerns of classical political economy to a narrowed focus, based on a static, ahistorical conception of markets and economic activity where institutions played little or no part. As neo-classical economics specialized as a technical discipline, it became increasingly divorced from any consideration of the historical, social or political context of economic activity. This shifted economic analysis away from classical political economy's holistic modus operandi (Gamble 1995; Tabb 1999; Hodgson 2001; Watson 2011: 58–62).

Of course, marginalism or the economics that followed are interesting, helpful or enlightening ways to explore economic phenomena. Simply, the assumptive foundations and analytical intent upon which they are built point in a very specific, restrictive direction. Marginalist political economy, and thereafter neo-classical economics, shines its light on aspects of economic processes it deems to be particularly revealing. Almost by definition, shining its torch in this direction leaves a wide array of substantive issues in darkness. They are exogenous to economic models because economics is not trying to explain or address them. It is important that we understand the nature of modern economics, what it is trying to achieve, and perhaps more importantly what it is *not* trying to do. After the *Methodenstreit*, academic economics sets itself very dissimilar intellectual tasks and conceives of itself in very different terms compared to its classical political economy forebears.

The variant of methodological individualism underpinning marginalism, and the ensuing singular conception of individuals within mainstream economics, had profound implications. It meant the social and political questions that had ignited the passions of political economy for centuries were, to all intents and purposes, assumed away. There were especially significant implications for *comparative* political economy of choosing a path of abstraction and generality in a way which assumed away, for example, national, institutional, ideational and historical specificities and contexts.

COMPARATIVE POLITICAL ECONOMY AFTER THE *METHODENSTREIT*

Neo-classical economics, built on marginalist foundations, proved to be a cuckoo's egg in the 'nest' of academic exploration of the economy. Political economy, especially the classical political economy approach, was somewhat crowded out thereafter. Yet the marginalist revolution was not a complete victory. This section highlights scholarship carrying the torch, retaining the spirit of classical political economy, in the decades following the *Methodenstreit*. This provided important insights on which modern CPE could draw and build. It is indicative, not comprehensive, considering some exponents of political economy who were interested in comparative study of the economic institutions of capitalism. Classical political economy had established a central focus on growth, accumulation of capital and the dynamic evolution of social relations of production. As this book underlines, these themes remain centre stage within modern CPE scholarship and its research agendas.

Some very eminent early 20th-century scholars attempted to bridge the gap between economics and other disciplines such as sociology and political science. These included towering figures like Max Weber (Djelic 2010) and Joseph Schumpeter. They, like Smith and Marx before them, saw the impossibility of developing adequate economic theories without considering the social and political conditions of economic activity. Weber's magnum opus *Economy and Society* (1978 [1922]) and Schumpeter's intellectual project of '*Sozialokonomik*' (Gamble 1995: 519) kept the spirit of classical political economy alive. Another was Rosa Luxemburg, an important scholar in the Marxist tradition. Her *Accumulation of Capital*, published in 1913, revisited the drivers of capitalist development, offering significant insights into economic imperialism. She identified non-capitalist origins of capitalist development, challenging and taking forward aspects of Marx's political economy. Many of her central insights into the 'transformation problem' surrounding the international dynamics of capitalist development were taken up by subsequent neo-Marxist scholars – not least Immanuel Wallerstein and Fernand Braudel (Kowalik 2003: xii). Her ideas about demand proved salient, in amended form, for Keynesian economics (Robinson [1951] 2003: xxix; Kowalik 2003: xi–xii).

The institutionalist political economy of Thorstein Veblen, focused on institutions, individuals and emergent social phenomena and on habituation over rational thought, is another example of scholarship keeping the spirit of classical political economy alive (Hodgson 2001: 140; Watson 2005a: 120–40). As Hodgson notes, Schmoller's 'extremely rich' institutional analysis 'foreshadowed the transaction cost theory hinted at by Thorstein Veblen (1904: 46–8) and developed more explicitly and extensively by Ronald Coase (1937) and Oliver Williamson (1975)' (2001: 115). Thus Veblen and the German Historical School were influential in founding American institutional economics (ibid.: 137–77).

The early 20th-century economist J. A. Hobson also retained a classical political economy mindset, and applied it comparatively. Hodgson notes how Hobson 'openly embraced the metaphor of society-as-an-organism' central to the German Historical School (ibid.: 111). Hobson was a self-confessed 'economic heretic' (Hobson 1988a [1938]: 29), at odds with Alfred Marshall, who was founding the British discipline of economics on marginalist foundations (Hodgson 2001: 95–112). Hobson advocated a 'human interpretation of cost and utility, and economic value' which 'brings economic values into close organic relations with other human values' (Hobson 1988a [1938]: 31). Appreciating these 'intricate interactions' had important implications, precluding 'the specialism and separatism which economic, political, and other social theorists have been prone to' (ibid.: 32).

Hobson railed against the reorganization of the social sciences into separate disciplines during his professional life. He lamented 'the whole trend of orthodox economics ... to keep economics within the limits of quantitative measures of markets, and to prevent the intrusion of ethical considerations into its field' (ibid.). His critique of an earlier 'new political economy', that of Mill, Jevons and Marshall, was that it remains a 'commercial science', its scope and method had not been 'humanized' and it fails to provide a framework through which to address 'the Social Question' (Hobson 1988c [1901]: 34–9). The lifeblood of classical political economy is coursing through these veins.

His analytical standpoint refuted the separation of politics and economics, and this was in evidence when arguing against protectionist tariffs in Germany in *The New Protectionism* (1988d [1916]: 168–72). His comparative framework for the analysis of imperialism saw the political and foreign policy consequences of the new 'machine economy' as 'the taproot of Imperialism' (Hobson 1988b [1938]: 80–1). The 'economic nature of the new Imperialism' (ibid.: 71) was rooted, Hobson argued, in a crisis of over-production combined with capital-ist firms evolving into ever larger 'trusts' and 'combines'. Imperialism amounted to 'the endeavour of the great controllers of industry to broaden the channel for flow of their sur-plus wealth by seeking foreign markets and foreign investments to take off the goods and capital they cannot sell or use at home' (ibid.: 85). This also drove imperial policy in the US, Great Britain, Germany, Holland and France, generating enormous profits for 'industrial and finance magnates' (ibid.: 74, 78–81).

Thus fine-grained analysis of the empirical reality of firms and their institutional embed-ding within market relations generated an array of revealing insights into the political econ-omy of early 20th-century capitalism. Yet the firm does not exist in marginalist political economy – which assumes the firm to be a rational utility-maximizing individual. This blind spot was further exposed by other comparative analyses of firms and their complex institu-tional make-up. Berle and Means' *The Modern Corporation and Private Property* (1932) was a landmark corporate governance text, exploring the capitalist joint-stock enterprise and highlighting the disempowering of shareholders at the expense of management arising from a divorce of ownership from control. This is part of a rich tradition of corporate govern-ance scholarship on which CPE can draw (see Chapter 10).

COMPARATIVE POLITICAL ECONOMY AND DEBATES OVER THE ROLE OF THE STATE IN THE ECONOMY: KEYNES, HAYEK AND POLANYI

A central substantive theme of modern CPE has been comparative analysis of the evolution and dynamics of state/market relations in the advanced economies. Three political econo-mists in particular deserve special mention for shaping how these relations were discussed in the 20th century. None of them was particularly enamoured of mainstream neo-classical economics, albeit for very different reasons. Keynes, Hayek and Polanyi were all hugely influential on conceptions of appropriate state/market relations within political economy. Keynes and Hayek also shaped the economic ideas informing policy-making. In many ways, these three seminal political economists' different views on the appropriate role of the state within capitalism set the terms of political economic debate in advanced countries. This debate continues, returning to centre stage following the GFC, and again with the revival of economic nationalism and protectionism in the mid-2010s.

Keynes

John Maynard Keynes, whom we discuss further in Chapter 7, kept the spirit of classical political economy alive. His was a fundamental theoretical critique of some tenets of neo-classical economics, notably the assumed efficient operation of capitalist markets. The assumptions about markets underpinning marginalism and Say's Law (that supply auto-matically calls forth demand, which we encountered in Chapter 2) were overturned by

Keynes. Writing before and during the Great Depression, he identified a potential systemic failure of the market to deliver adequate demand, purchasing power and hence full employment.

Capitalism, Keynes observed, 'seems capable of remaining in a chronic condition of sub-normal activity for a considerable period without any marked tendency either towards recovery or towards complete collapse. Moreover, the evidence indicates that full, or even approximately full, employment is of rare and short-lived occurrence' (1964 [1936]: 249–50). In his recognition of inherent market instability, Keynes denied the intrinsic ability of markets to reproduce themselves smoothly and maintain employment. Capitalism may not necessarily always be violently unstable, but left to its own devices outcomes may well be sub-optimal. A further implication of Keynes' approach reinforced one of the core insights of political economy identified in Chapter 2 – namely, the interpenetration of state and market. The management of the capitalist economy entailed letting free markets play their role, but also state policies and intervention to maintain confidence and mitigate shortcomings. Key policy goals were countering tendencies towards instability, crises of confidence and slumps.

Acceptance of such a fundamental market failure has very powerful political implications. It challenges classical and neo-classical assumptions about the appropriate relationship between public and private sectors, between state and market (Worswick and Trevithick 1983; Eatwell and Milgate 2011). Keynes emphasized the necessity of government intervention to sustain capitalist social relations and correct inherent failings within markets. Thus Keynesian political economy entails an intrinsic appreciation of the inevitable interpenetration, perhaps the mutual constitution, of state and market. The Keynesian 'revolution' heralded key changes in economic policy-making and, more fundamentally, altered assumptions about the appropriate role of the state in the economy (Leijonhufvud 1968; Clarke 1988).

In response to the Great Depression, Keynes highlighted the positive role in demand, confidence and economic activity of expanding public employment. He once famously quipped:

> If the Treasury were to fill old bottles with banknotes, bury them at suitable depths in disused coalmines which are then filled up to the surface with town rubbish, and leave it to private enterprise on well-tried principles of *laissez-faire* to dig the notes up again ... there need be no more unemployment and, with the help of the repercussions, the real income of the community, and its capital wealth also, would probably become a good deal greater than it actually is. It would, indeed, be more sensible to build houses and the like; but if there are political and practical difficulties in the way of this, the above would be better than nothing. (1964 [1936]: 129)

As Keynes noted, normally public works find a more beneficial focus for their labours than this, not least through investment in public infrastructure (transport and communications networks and the like) which can help improve the overall productivity of the economy. The state can create public-sector employment to offset job losses in the private sector, and more generally public-sector jobs can be used to smooth the economic cycle.

This re-evaluation of the relation between state and market opened the scope for political economy in terms of both policy prescription and the analysis of capitalism. Where the market was liable to fail, government policy should step in to stabilize capitalism, ensuring sufficient aggregate demand through fiscal and monetary policy or 'demand management', as it became known. Central to economic policies of 'stabilization' (Gamble 1984) was the advocacy of boosting public spending during downturns. One theoretical bulwark of this is the notion of 'multipliers' associated with public spending, which is derived from Richard Kahn (1931) and closely associated with the classical Keynesian position as set out in *The General Theory* (Keynes 1964 [1936]: 113–31). As Backhouse puts it, following the Keynesian assumption that 'the expenditure multiplier [is] greater than one … a rise in investment or government spending would produce a rise in income that was larger than the initial increase in spending' (2006: 32). This recognition of the potentially beneficial effects of increased public spending and positive spillover effects of the aggregate demand boost on consumption, economic activity and confidence is important for the politics of economic policy. It strengthens the case for a focus on demand and the need to sustain it, and for increased public spending and activist, expansionary fiscal policy, in a recession.

As Clarke puts it (1996: 67, 2009), before World War II no government claimed to have a macro-economic policy because the concept did not exist. Following Keynesian economic thinking and techniques, it was deemed to be within governments' powers to deliver economic growth and full employment. The government could and should pull the levers of economic policy-making to sustain effective demand, and therefore confidence in the economy. A Keynesian policy orientation could deliver 'stabilization' of the economy, smoothing the economic cycle like a hydraulics engineer of the plumbing system of the economy (Tabb 1999: 156–8). Policy-makers could attempt to regulate flows (of money) through the economy, most obviously by raising or reducing taxes and government spending, thus raising/lowering the 'sluice gates' ensuring the correct amount of effective demand flows through the system (see Phillips 1950). The Keynesian-inspired policy paradigm changed the face of political economy in the mid-20th century, altering approaches to economic policy-making. More fundamentally, Keynesianism shifted assumptions about the appropriate balance between state and market.

This increased role and ambition for government in the economy also focused greater attention on the political and institutional context of economic policy. As Kalecki pointed out, there was a danger, in a full employment economy, of inflationary wage spirals (1943). In order to prevent this, labour market and wage bargaining institutions and industrial relations structures needed to induce norms of wage moderation. These were precisely the kinds of roles for capitalist institutions in sustaining economic growth and stability which, in the post-war world, became the focus of pioneering CPE scholars such as Shonfield (1958, 1965) and the other exemplars of the CPE tradition discussed in Chapters 1–3. Other important political economists in the post-war period who took up these themes of explaining comparative economic performance and analysing different nexuses of capitalist institutions (not necessarily from a Keynesian standpoint) included J. K. Galbraith (1956), Albert Hirschman (1970, 1995), Mancur Olson (1965, 1982) and Susan Strange (1971, 1976, 1994b).

Hayek

Friedrich von Hayek was a towering intellect who won the Nobel Prize for economics, but who was also a world-leading scholar of the philosophy of knowledge and political philosophy. Although both were liberal political economists, Hayek's thinking was almost diametrically opposed to Keynes'. Indeed, while Hayek was at the London School of Economics in the early 1930s and Keynes was at Cambridge, they got into a heated academic argument about monetary policy and appropriate interest rates during a recession. Keynes advocated inducing particularly low interest rates, whereas Hayek thought that if interest rates fell below what he termed their 'natural rate', this would cause inflation. Thereafter, Hayek became less concerned with narrow technical debates and more interested in the basic principles of social and economic organization. His focus moved from the narrow issues of economics to the wider political economy questions.

Hayek was trained in the Austrian School of political economy by Carl Menger, and this shaped his broad vision of political economy. Hayek shared Menger's Austrian view of uncertainty, tacit knowledge and markets. This deep anti-rationalism set Hayek apart from neo-classical economists and many other neo-liberal thinkers, such as Milton Friedman. Markets, for Hayek, are a means of disseminating information in a highly uncertain world where knowledge is tacit and uncodifiable. This is why it is nonsensical, from a Hayekian or Austrian political economy viewpoint, to assume that all individuals are alike and share identical preferences, as a mathematical approach must (see e.g. Gamble 1996).

Hayek was an unconventional and highly original thinker, the richness and subtlety of whose ideas are often lost when appropriated by subsequent neo-liberal political economists. He resembles Adam Smith in this regard. Keynes also sold Hayek short, saying of him (one hopes tongue in cheek) 'of course he is crazy, but his ideas are also rather interesting' (quoted in Gamble 1996: 2). Hayek was the founding father of the 'New Right' and his radical political economy shaped the ideology of neo-liberalism. His subsequently famous 1945 book *The Road to Serfdom* was a profound criticism of statism, collectivism and socialism. It argued that even moderate state interventionism and redistribution were economically damaging and could lead to totalitarianism. This contradicted the immediate post-war zeitgeist wherein welfare states were being founded across Europe by collectivist governments, including socialists (see Chapter 11).

Seen as an archetypical neo-liberal, Hayek's views on the appropriate role of the state are indeed fairly tightly delimited. Yet the state's role was not as minimal as one might expect (see Gamble 1996: 206–7). In Hayek's vision of a political economic order, the state secured what was for him the most important value in society – personal liberty. Although in *The Road to Serfdom* Hayek did not specify where to draw the line between state and market, between the public and private realms, he viewed a strong state as crucial for individual freedom and market order. A strong state was needed to 'police the market order, maintain the value of money, protect life and property, and enforce contracts' (see Gamble 1996: 134). Within these areas – seen by Hayek as essential to the preservation of individual liberty, and therefore legitimate realms of state activity – the state should enjoy unlimited power. Thus, for all Hayek's commitment to free markets and individual liberty, the state played a vital and relatively expansive role.

Hayek's vision of a constitutionally instituted market order was predicated upon a strong state as 'the guarantor of the set of rules which made a market order and therefore civilisation itself possible' (Gamble 1996: 134). This is Hayek's way of reflecting that core political economy insight outlined in Chapter 2 of the interpenetration and mutual constitution of state and market. For all his hostility to statism, he nevertheless saw a necessary state role in enforcing rules of just conduct. Furthermore, the state should restrain the destructive features of markets, provide certain public goods and even undertake counter-cyclical intervention (Gamble 1996: 134, 206–7). Unlike many neo-liberals, Hayek saw state income provision as appropriate under certain conditions, though he rejected both redistribution and progressive taxation as interfering too much with market signals.

Following years of neglect, both Hayek and *The Road to Serfdom* became highly influential in the 1970s. Aspects of Hayek's distinctive understanding of the state's role, which flowed from his views on knowledge and markets, shaped neo-liberalism. Politicians such as Margaret Thatcher and Ronald Reagan pursued this agenda vigorously in the 1980s, seeking to challenge and 'roll back' the size and scope of the state within the affluent political economies (see pp. 154–63). Hayek saw trade unions as coercive organizations whose wage claims interfered in natural market mechanisms, fuelled inflation and damaged prosperity. Trade union powers, Hayek argued in *The Constitution of Liberty*, 'gravely threatened' the 'whole basis of our free society' (1960: 269). This view was keenly embraced by the New Right, and enacted in Thatcher's union reforms (Gamble 1996: 170–3).

Keynes' insight was that markets can fail; Hayek's conviction was that governments will fail. Hayek's faith in markets as the best possible processor and adjudicator of information in a highly uncertain world was profound and unshakeable. This partly reflected his philosophy of knowledge work and the import he attached to local knowledge. Hayek's liberalism was deeply anti-rationalist, and this informed his view that society is not amenable to rational planning, because no state planner can be aware of the infinite complexities of the subjective interests of all actors in their local situations (Gamble 1996: 18–25). Hayekian political economy is preoccupied by an insistence that any attempt to control the marketplace, however honourable in intent, necessarily makes things worse. What makes markets work, in the Austrian view, is enabling individuals to act on their unique appreciation of their own situation and interests.

The conviction that markets are superior to states reflects the Hayekian idea of 'cosmos' or spontaneous social order. Hayek used the term 'catallaxy' in preference to 'economy' to describe a particular market form of spontaneous social order (Gamble 1996: 36–9). Crucial to Hayekian political economy is the view that 'spontaneous and uncontrolled efforts of individuals' are 'capable of producing a complex order of economic activities' (Hayek 1945: 11–12). A successful 'great society' (a term Hayek drew from Adam Smith) requires a social realm with no single directing centre and an absence of organization of society as a whole. This 'catallaxy' or spontaneous market order arises, like the 'invisible hand', as the unintended consequence of all agents using their local knowledge to pursue their interests. Catallaxy is not a perfect social order, nor is it wholly stable or in equilibrium. Indeed, Hayek rejected the general equilibrium assumptions which underpin neo-classical economics (Gamble 1996: 22). Nevertheless, catallaxy provides the best context for individuals to use information which is inherently imperfect, fragmented and local. For Hayek, this spontaneous social order, though pervaded by uncertainties, uses knowledge in a way no government can ever hope to match. As Hayek put it, 'the market order ... [is] the only way in which so many activities depending on dispersed knowledge can be effectively integrated into a single order' (1973: 42).

Competition would, Hayek argued, always deliver outcomes superior to the centralized direction and organization of economic activities. Market competition would also secure the maximum individual liberty and avoid what he termed 'coercive interference with economic life' (Hayek 1945: 26–7). Hayek deemed entrepreneurship and innovation the engines of economic development. State intervention tended to impede both (Backhouse 2002: 279). For Hayek, the post-war state planners and welfare state constructors had extended far beyond the necessary and appropriate realms of state action. In so doing, they had placed obstacles in the path towards the spontaneous market order and trampled upon three vital elements of political economy, prosperity and the good society – competition, entrepreneurship and individual freedom of choice.

Polanyi

Karl Polanyi was another unconventional, wide-ranging and influential thinker who enriched our understanding of political economy and of the (dis)functioning of capitalist market orders. He was a renaissance man, an educator, journalist and political organizer, as well as an academic anthropologist, economic historian and political economist. Compared to both Keynes and Hayek, Polanyi was much more sceptical and critical of markets. His distinctive conception of the symbiotic relationship between state and market, and his insights into the social consequences of capitalist markets, constitute important counterpoints to Hayek, Keynes and others.

Polanyi's was a trenchant critique of the capitalist system's negative effects; his work was excoriating about the liberal tradition and the liberal conception of markets. He contributed to different fields and academic debates, but it is for *The Great Transformation* (published in 1944) that political economists know him best. In it, Polanyi charted the 19th-century origins of the market economy in Britain, and the dynamics of its international spread. Polanyi's core concerns include economic ideas, the role of the state within capitalist economy and society, and the nature and structure of the international economic system. He is particularly interested in the domestic political, social and economic implications of the gold standard.

Polanyi's eclectic political economy approach combined some Marxist and socialist thought with residual influences of his marginalist training. He had a penchant for bringing together concepts from different traditions of thought (see Dale 2010: 6, 12–14, 101–2, 2016: 7, 10). Polanyi's political economy had two dominant characteristics which link to CPE's core insights outlined in Chapter 2. Firstly, he highlighted the embedding of economic activity in a broader social and political context. Secondly, Polanyi located British political economy in a broader global context – the international liberal system of the gold standard and free trade. Polanyi's articulation of national and international levels of analysis has inspired many IPE scholars (Germain 2019).

The *embeddedness* of the economic system in social order (Polanyi 2001 [1944]: 134–5), such that there 'is no strict demarcation between "economic" activities and "political" or "social" activities' (Holmes and Yarrow 2019: 16; see also Dale 2010: 188–205), is key to Polanyi's political economy. He charted the advent of 'market society' (Polanyi 2001 [1944]: 257–8) – a contradictory and unstable social order where economic institutions exist increasingly separate from political ones (see Dale 2010: 50). The market system was becoming a mechanism for ordering and maintaining the whole of society, and the substance of society was becoming subject to its logic and laws. This, for Polanyi, entailed a perilous transgression of the principle of embeddedness. It was only thanks to this embeddedness that people did not 'perish from the effects of social exposure' (Polanyi 2001 [1944]: 76) to markets. Economic activity 'dis-embedded' from social context is, for Polanyi, a 'stark utopia' which 'could not exist for any length of time without annihilating the human and natural substance of society' (2001 [1944]: 3).

What Polanyi objected to so vehemently about market society was 'a worldview which sought to understand human affairs in general from within the parameters of the market self-regulation idea only' (Holmes and Yarrow 2019: 10). *The Great Transformation*'s historical analysis of the 19th century exemplified the social dislocation caused by marketization. The abolition of the Poor Law in 1834, in Polanyi's interpretation, led to the modern integrated labour market (Polanyi 2001 [1944]: 81–9, 225; Dale 2010: 52–3). Within Polanyi's schema, this constituted a move towards the 'self-regulating market', the lodestar of the 19th-century political economy. Polanyi rejected such 'market utopianism' as deeply flawed, destabilizing and socially dangerous, leading to starvation and deprivation.

Polanyi took a keen interest in economic ideas. His was a critique of the neo-classical view of the economy and of economic actors. He rejected so-called *homo economicus* assumptions that rational, self-interested market exchange reflected some inner timeless acquisitive characteristics or propensities of human nature. Polanyi problematized how neo-classical economics saw 'the economy' as the same thing as 'the market', and rejected the view of the market as the natural way to order social affairs (Holmes and Yarrow 2019: 7–11). For Polanyi, 'the supposedly universal principles of neo-classical economics' were a 'social fiction' (Watson 2005a: 145). He focused on economic ideas in public life, perhaps at the expense of the political processes and institutions through which their domination was carried through society (Holmes 2019). This is ironic, since he underlines how market orders are always *political* constructs.

The apparently paradoxical yet crucial observation that 'Laissez faire was planned' opens up Polanyi's interesting critiques of liberalism. His account of 19th-century Britain, often misleadingly associated with minimal state activity, pointed out how expansive state intervention was integral to the spread of markets: 'There was nothing natural about laissez-faire; free markets could never have come into being merely by allowing things to take their course' (2001 [1944]: 146, 147). Indicating the symbiotic state/market relationship, 'regulation and markets', Polanyi notes, 'in effect, grew up together' (Polanyi 2001 [1944]: 71). The development of the market system was an act of political construction: 'the road to the free market was opened and kept open by an enormous increase in continuous, centrally organized and controlled interventionism' (2001 [1944]: 146).

Polanyi's nuanced and complex oeuvre challenged the view of markets as a natural order. Rather; 'the market has been the outcome of a conscious and often violent intervention on the part of government which imposed the market organisation on society for noneconomic ends' (2001 [1944]: 258). A pure free market is, from a Polanyian perspective, a practical impossibility. Positing a 'self-regulating' market fails to recognize the integral role of the state in constructing, maintaining and shaping these markets.

The gold standard approximated the self-regulating market on an international scale, although some have questioned Polanyi's grasp of its actual operation (Knafo 2019). While free market orders, both nationally and internationally, may resemble the 'self-regulating' market, this end state could never be fully attained. This was because 'leaving the fate of soil and people to the market would be tantamount to annihilating them' (Polanyi 2001 [1944]: 137). As this intimates, Polanyi saw capitalism's ecological threat in the pernicious tendencies of commercialization of land and the exploitation and marketization of the planet's natural resources (Dale 2010: 50–1); 19th-century market expansion wrought havoc on the natural and social order. These tendencies spread on a global scale through the internationalization of markets and colonial exploitation (Polanyi 2001 [1944]: 166–9). Societies' 'human and natural substance', he argued, needed to be 'protected against the ravages of this dark satanic mill' (2001 [1944]: 76–7).

Polanyi's celebrated concept of the 'double movement', which entailed the extension of the market domain into ever more aspects of human society (Polanyi 2001 [1944]: 136), is identified as a key motor of historical change. As the socially damaging consequences of market liberalization advance, socially protective resistance arises. Continuous market expansion was 'met by a countermovement checking the expansion in definite directions'. This countermovement, although 'vital' for the 'protection of society', was 'incompatible with the self-regulation of the market, and thus with the market system itself' (Polanyi 2001 [1944]: 136). This contradiction is a key source, for Polanyi, of the inherent instability of regulated capitalism (Dale 2010: 15–17).

Britain's 19th-century social order was not impassive to the advent and spread of desta-bilizing market forces (see Dale 2016: 96–9). Varied counter-mobilizations of social protec-tion challenged marketization: 'historically contingent class-based forces: one-nation conservatives, feudal landlords, trade unionists and socialists' (Dale 2010: 61). Polanyi scholars disagree on how the 'dis-embedding' of market activity sparks protective 're-embedding' counter-measures. Some identify a 'pendular swing' between the two forces locked in a Manichean tussle over capitalist society (Shrank and Whitford 2009), while oth-ers decisively reject this view (see e.g. Dale 2016: 5–7). Nevertheless, for Polanyians, the nature of any capitalist political economy arises from the ongoing *dialectical* struggle between these dual forces within society.

DISCIPLINARY POLITICS, (COMPARATIVE) POLITICAL ECONOMY AND GENDER

The discussion of disciplinary politics which began this chapter shed light on how underly-ing assumptions about the appropriate subject matter for political economy inform a series of choices about both *what* is studied and *how* it is studied. These understandings of the nature of CPE as a field shape what constitutes 'mainstream' scholarship, and what work occupies more liminal spaces at the margins. We can readily appreciate this by considering the position, perhaps the marginalization, of feminist political economy within CPE analysis.

The story of central debates in CPE told in Chapters 2–3 is one which largely sidesteps gender. It is important to revisit this and include feminist political economy, which has become more prominent since the 1990s. The inclusion of gender as a central concept in (comparative) political economy radically transforms understandings of what the field's basic subject matter should be. Thus incorporating gender into CPE involves a rather more dramatic transformation than merely 'adding women and stirring' (Bedford and Rai 2010; Elias and Roberts 2016; Elias and Roberts 2018a, 2018b; Griffin 2007a, 2007b, 2010; Peterson 2005; Steans 1999; Hozic and True 2016). Using gender as an optic to explore political economy immediately reconstitutes what political economy actually is. Bedford and Rai (2010) argue that feminist analysis recalibrates political economy to ask ques-tions about the ways in which systems of production, distribution and exchange are gen-dered. This in turn yields a focus on social reproduction and a wider understanding of processes of governance as forms of gendered domination. It leads to an empirical concern within capitalism on the instantiation of economic process in the realm of the intimate and the everyday (see Bakker 2007).

These are concerns that the standard CPE debates between Keynes, Hayek and Polanyi about state/market relations discussed above cannot begin to equip us to explore intellectually. Keynes, Hayek and Polanyi disagreed in their normative evaluations of state intervention in markets and their prescriptive policy discourse differed widely. Yet they shared (perhaps unthinkingly) taken-for-granted gendered assumptions about what political economy is. From a feminist perspective, we find that many of these premises, for example about what constitutes the public and private spheres, are in fact problematic and contested. Feminists focus on an implicit distinction made – harking back at least to Adam Smith – between 'productive' and 'unproductive' labour that foregrounds the production of commodities for sale in formal markets. This shapes how economic activity is measured – and what gets counted in assessing economic performance of nations and firms. Feminist political economists argue that the scope of political economic research, and the nature of political action, have been defined in ways that exclude women *as women* from political economy. The conventional account of the economy occludes, among other things, the production of daily necessities, and care work sustaining family life and looking after the sick and elderly. Thus gendered assumptions about productive/unproductive labour and the public/private realm mean that vital social reproduction work is systematically under-valued and under-reported (Hozic and True 2016: 6). Yet without these activities economies would crumble. In this way, feminism challenges the standard definitions, explanations, normative judgements and prescriptions of political economy.

Feminists critique mainstream theorists purporting to define the political terrain in genderless terms. Ironically, this supposedly 'gender-blind' analysis has deeply iniquitous gendered effects, masking enduring masculinist assumptions and structural gender bias in both political economic activity and its analysis (Beneria 2003). The apparently 'universalist' traditions of political science and CPE are in fact built on *masculine* norms, and this results in problematic silences on unequal gender power relations (Steans 1999). The modern economy is so deeply encoded with masculinized conceptions that we usually fail to recognize the fact.

Thus superficial 'gender blindness' and apparent 'equality' of treatment mask deep-seated underlying patriarchal assumptions, norms and practices. Patriarchy is a key concept in feminist scholarship, but is conspicuously absent from nearly all other political economy analysis. It refers to systemic, structural and enduring male/masculine dominance and gender bias that pervade culture, society, institutions (including academia) and economic practices and power relations within contemporary capitalism. Feminist political economy explores gender hierarchies, patriarchy and gendered power relations, and how they shape (and are shaped by) capitalism. Focusing on the arbitrary inequalities that are manifest in social constructions of femininity and masculinity offers a different perspective for understanding the politics of market-making within contemporary capitalism.

The footprints of these patriarchal assumptions are revealed when we reconsider the focal points of mainstream political economy analysis, and how some core concepts are understood. How 'public' and 'private' are constructed as systems of meaning is not gender neutral (Steans 1999: 115). This gendered imposition of conceptions of public and private on political analysis is, Anne Phillips argues, 'the major sleight of hand that had excluded women from centuries of debate on citizenship, equality, freedom, rights, for having been subordinated to men in the private sphere they were then subsumed under men in the public' (Phillips 1992: 17). Indeed, written into the classical definitions of politics itself were premises that precluded women's political participation: 'women's exclusion from public life was predicated on their "natural" inability to transcend their biological and economic subordination in the household' (Jones 1988: 13). Patriarchal assumptions that men were more rational, therefore better suited to public life, lead to women's 'ghettoization' within the private sphere. The consequences of these delineations are what Benhabib calls a privatization of the intimate sphere (1994).

Yet political and economic relations transcend this artificial public/private divide (Youngs 1999), for example through gender-differential inheritance rights. Feminists critique societal decisions about what is deemed the private or public realm. For example, financial scandals are construed in ways that 'reconstitute the divide between the public and the private spheres' and 'turn systemic problems into individual failing' (Hozic and True 2016: 10). In response, 'Feminists have challenged the conceptual boundary between the public and private realms' (Steans 1999: 115) and focused on structures of power that 'operate across the so called public/private divide' (ibid.: 113).

Political economy and economics have historically defined the economic in overly narrow terms of the production of goods and services for sale in the formal market. This affords primacy to the formal economy, but utterly neglects social reproduction and the informal economy. These are certainly no part of the conventional story of national wealth. All kinds of work caring for, sustaining, maintaining and reproducing the households and families of which society and economy are comprised get excluded from a consideration of 'the economy' or 'economic activity' (True 2016: 44–5, 53–5). This is but one way traditional 'gender-blind' political economy analysis leaves women's unpaid labour in the family outside of economic analysis.

Another way feminist political economy broadens the analytical framework of mainstream CPE is to acknowledge gender as 'a signifying code'. Interrogating the social meaning of words used to discuss the economy and their associated concepts, we find they are deeply encoded with masculinist understandings of the world. Masculinities constitute a common sense, not only of modern economic theory but also of modern economic practice. Mainstream views of the economy include assumptions about the innate competitiveness of human agents, the centrality of pursuing self-interest, and individuals as isolated, autonomous, calculating beings. These masculinized character traits of *homo economicus* are so deeply ingrained that we usually fail to recognize this (Hozic and True 2016: 6, 10). Focusing on processes of *social construction* deepens understanding of 'how identities are formed and mapped into symbolic and political identifications' (Steans 1999: 113). Thus gender is about knowledge, and knowledge construction; it informs and is reproduced by the practices of actors, institutions and organizations.

V. Spike Peterson's constructivist 'analytical gender' approach focuses on masculinity and femininity as systems of meaning. Gender is 'a *governing* code that pervades language and hence systematically shapes how we think, what we presume to "know" and how such knowledge claims are legitimised' (Spike Peterson 2005: 502). It explores hierarchies that devalue feminized bodies, identities and activities: 'the feminisation of identities and practices effectively devalues them in cultural as well as economic terms' (ibid.: 507). Unequal gender power relations are instantiated and sustained through discourse, subjectivities and culture, including academic culture. Examples include notions of 'women's work', the 'productive economy' and 'unproductive labour' (ibid.).

These social construction processes mould social reality and even shape the process of political research. 'Analytical gender' thus represents a profound challenge to traditional political economy conceptions such as public/private, productive/unproductive labour. 'Gendering' CPE analysis '*entails* a questioning of orthodox methods and foundational inquiries', and re-assessing 'gendered assumptions and biases' inherent in taken-for-granted terms like 'work' or 'development' (ibid.: 506). An analytical gender perspective exposes how these taken-for-granted conceptions entail the denigration of feminized labour and prioritization of the masculine. This challenge to traditional concepts and assumptions helps explain why just 'adding women' to traditional political economy fails to address underlying problems.

This indicates what is 'at stake' within disciplinary politics. It also shows how earlier intellectual moves in the field's development have effects in the present. Feminist scholars argue that our focus on political and economic activity needs to be broadened and re-conceptualized. Feminist political economy looks beyond the realms of formal politics, and formal economic activity, to incorporate vital economic activity (the reproduction of social relations – and of people) and power relations traditionally thought of as in the 'private sphere'. Pre-existing patriarchal norms surrounding the gendered division of labour, and their institutionalization within economic and social policies (see Chapter 11), mean that women have been denied social and economic and political equality. Feminism's re-evaluation of the place of women within society, economy and the workplace has brought new understandings of what constitutes political, social and economic equality.

CONCLUSION

In this chapter I have set out how disciplinarity shapes CPE, its evolution, its central concerns, and how one effect of disciplinary politics is a blind spot around gender. The genealogy of modern CPE offered here explores some aspects of that disciplinary politics by situating it within the context of the *Methodenstreit*. It is only against that backdrop that we can fully appreciate how to think like a political economist, and how CPE in its modern form emerged with its substantive focus and central research questions. Economics developed as an academic discipline built upon assumptive foundations which would have been virtually unrecognizable to Smith, Marx and List. After marginalism, the new discipline of economics was no longer *political* economy. An interest in power and societal power relationships was not part of the discipline of economics as it came to define itself. The institutional context of capitalism – so central to classical political economy and to modern CPE – is hidden from view within marginalism. These silences were sources of the depoliticization of the study of the economy. For Tabb, 'neoclassical economics, starting with its founders, removed the political element from political economy' (1999: 98). Economics became the 'hardest' of the 'soft' social sciences, and acquired a superiority complex rooted in that fact. The after-effects of this late 19th-century intellectual rift are still visible in the widely divergent research agendas of economics and political science. Much economics research is today wholly impenetrable to political scientists.

The prior assumption of markets operating efficiently and being beneficial to society seemed to foreclose all discussion. Yet the burgeoning reality of global capitalism during the 19th, 20th and 21st centuries is a deeply unequal and unstable societal order. This could not easily be accounted for with marginalist assumptions about markets or individuals. Institutions, like the state, profoundly affected the operation of markets and economic outcomes. Thus, the need for a political economy based on non-marginalist foundations endured, and in the post-war era CPE found its distinctive place and voice within the social sciences. Despite a much more modest place for political economy as a sub-discipline within economic sociology, political science and economic history, CPE scholars could draw on a rich and diverse genealogy which included Weber, Schumpeter, Hobson, Keynes and Hayek, in addition to the authors discussed in Chapters 1 and 2. The burning questions about capitalism as a dynamic economic and social order, raised by Smith, Marx, List and others, continued to be explored as CPE scholars analysed power, institutions, the state and the unequal distributional consequences of capitalism.

When IPE began to develop as a self-defined field of study from the 1970s, comparativists such as Peter Katzenstein and Peter Gourevitch were able to connect CPE to this emergent cognate inter-discipline. Then, in the 1990s, new journals such as the *Review of International Political Economy* and *New Political Economy* emerged as natural homes for revitalized CPE research programmes, bringing together an eclectic range of political economy scholarship focused on issues of gender and environment, as well as the more familiar staple topics of CPE analysis (Gamble 1995; Gamble et al. 1996). In this fertile scholarly environment CPE flourished, some of it emulating the classical political economy spirit. All the while, major CPE volumes such as Gosta Esping-Andersen's *The Three Worlds of Welfare Capitalism* (1990), Peter Hall and David Soskice's *Varieties of Capitalism* (2001) and Gourevitch and Shinn's *Political Power and Corporate Control* (2005) continued to stake out a central place for CPE analysis within a range of social scientific fields, including comparative politics, political science and IPE. In the remaining chapters of this book I set out in more detail how the field of CPE in its diversity can shape and deepen our understanding of contemporary capitalism and its evolution.

5 Interest-Based Analysis and Comparative Political Economy

INTRODUCTION

One way to explain outcomes in CPE is through the interests of political economic actors, which sees self-interest and egoism, as opposed to altruism, as the driving motivations behind political economic activity and behaviour. The marginalist political economy we encountered in Chapter 4 analysed political economy in terms of individuals maximizing 'utility', following Bentham's 'utilitarian' logic which centres on the maximization of pleasure and the avoidance of pain. Political economic actors are seen as engaged in a continuing tussle to secure the highest possible level of satisfaction through their choices in the marketplace. Mainstream economics has retained this basis in the realization of individual self-interest as crucial for analysing and understanding economic processes. The 'constant optimization' of contemporary economics sees actors continually re-calculating (on the basis of perfect information and forward-looking calculative abilities) what is in their best interests and acting accordingly (see p. 28).

An interest-based approach to political economy need not be rooted in these exacting micro-foundations, but assumes in any given situation, presented with any given choice, actors will ask: 'What is in it for me?' The celebrated political economist Susan Strange was an exemplar of a particular type of interest-based approach to political economy, beginning with the question: *cui bono*? (Latin for 'who benefits?'). Her conviction was that the key to answering this question lies in understanding power relations (Strange 1994a: 136, 234; Tooze and May 2002: 7; see also Lasswell 1936).

At the risk of some over-simplification, an interest-based approach to CPE reduces the focus of analysis to Strange's two-word question: who benefits? It focuses attention on why bureaucrats might tend to seek to increase their power and the size of their budgets, and why politicians might be inclined to make promises to increase public provision and reduce taxes to electorates to secure re-election (whether or not they realistically think these promises can be kept after the election). It can also account for why unions have a propensity to bargain for more pay, and why executives might be pre-disposed to seek higher remuneration. It can explain how and why financial market actors secured such light-touch regulation for decades through close lobbying links with political elites in the advanced economies. Equally, once the GFC hit and the costs of risky financial innovation were revealed to be huge and system-threatening, these same powerful economic groups were able to ensure that governments bailed out financial institutions and socialized the debts so that taxpayers, not the bankers themselves, bore the brunt of the costs (see Blyth 2013).

As I show in this chapter, an interest-based approach to CPE can take many forms, operating at the 'macro' level of broad societal groups such as classes or at the 'micro' level of individual economic or political actors. Societal-level interest-based approaches to political economy have affinities with the materialist political economy of Marxian class-based analysis which we encountered in Chapters 3 and 4. The bulk of this chapter, however, concentrates on the 'micro-level' individualized approach of rational choice, with its strong attachment to methodological individualism. This 'asserts that all social phenomena can and should be explained in terms of the actions of individuals operating under prevailing constraints' (Tsebelis 1990: 21).

Standing on the other side of the *Methodenstreit* (see Chapter 4; Gamble 1995) from the integrated, holistic analyses of classical political economy, rational choice CPE embraces theoretical parsimony. It shares the same intellectual ambition as marginalism and uses its *homo economicus* ('economic man') assumptions. Deploying economics-based modes of reasoning to analyse and explain individuals and their behaviour, its sparse explanations derive an actor's preferences from a small amount of information. From these austere foundations, rational choice can generate striking explanations, notably of how difficult it is proving to mitigate the adverse environmental consequences of capitalism, despite the now longstanding and well-established scientific consensus that the problems of global warming are a very real and very pressing issue.

Some see the three 'I's – interests, ideas and institutions – as three separable ways to approach explaining political economic outcomes. Such a view can lead to a naive and unhelpful interrogation as to which of the three matters more, or explains more, in a given instance. That question cannot be ultimately resolved with satisfaction, since it is formidably difficult to come to firm conclusions on the interactions and relative importance of the three 'I's. Rather, the three 'I's represent different but not mutually exclusive ways to focus attention in explaining political economy (see Clift 2016). In what follows, I set out a number of ways to incorporate interest-based explanations, considering some group-level or societal-level variants before concentrating on rational choice and its close cousin, 'public choice' theory. Later in this chapter we explore recent evolutions in interest-based accounts which have problematized the notion of an actor's interests or preferences being fixed or 'given' by his or her material situation. This, as we shall see, immediately opens up the discussion to the role of ideas and institutions in shaping preferences – but in an explanation which can remain at root interest-based.

USING INTERESTS TO EXPLAIN OUTCOMES: MARXISM, CORPORATISM, CORPORATE GOVERNANCE AND TRADE POLICY COALITIONS

The Marxian approach to political economy discussed in Chapters 3 and 4 offers one illustration of the potential fruitfulness of interest-based approaches to political economy (Caporaso and Levine 1992: 55–78). Marx's materialist conception of history sets out how an individual's position in relation to the means of production determines his or her interests. From the interests of the proletariat and the bourgeoisie we can explain the structure of society, economy and polity. Marx thought that individuals did not always accurately discern their class interests because of the ideological superstructure in society, hence his discussion of 'false consciousness'. Nevertheless, a historical materialist approach views interest (be it of worker, capitalist or state manager) as capable of being objectively derived from an analysis of the structure of the social relations of production in any given social order. For example, the factory owner's interest is extracting more surplus value from the workers by depressing wages further, or increasing productivity. The workers' interest is in raising the price at which they sell the commodity of their labour power through increasing wages. This is the essence of the wage bargaining process which operates within firms, or sometimes at a broader sectoral or societal level within corporatist industrial relations institutions.

Other Marxian interest-based approaches include influential scholars such as Rosa Luxemburg, who developed a novel account of the drivers of imperialist rivalries between major powers seeking colonial expansion. Imperialism was, for Luxemburg, 'the political expression of the accumulation of capital in its competitive struggle for what remains still open of the non-capitalist environment' (2003: 426). Other early 20th-century Marxists were thinking along similar lines: Austrian-born former German finance minister and Social Democratic Party theorist Rudolf Hilferding (1981 [1910]), and two protagonists in the Bolshevik Revolution which established the Soviet Union, Nicolai Bukharin (1971 [1917]) and V. I. Lenin (1950 [1917]). Analysing early 20th-century capitalist social relations of production, these scholars noted how more and more parts of the globe were becoming integrated to different degrees because of the *unevenness* of capitalist development into the world economy. At the heart of this, for Hilferding, was the merging of bank capital with industrial capital into *finance capital* – a small group of very powerful, very wealthy owners of enormous corporations which dominated the economy. Finance capital had a direct interest in maximizing the extent of protected national economic territory (increasing access to markets and raw materials), and this explained state policies of imperialist expansion. The foreign economic policies of imperialism pursued by advanced states in this period were interpreted as economic interests of 'finance capital' filtered through the political and foreign policy process.

The interests of monopoly capitalists led to the transformation of *laissez-faire* capitalism into monopoly capitalism and the ever greater scale of production (Hilferding 1981 [1910]). Competition, which might normally be seen as crucial to securing low prices for consumers, was not a priority for finance capitalists. Close links between finance capital and political elites enabled finance capital to shape the market of its day, inducing governments to legislate a permissive regime allowing trusts, combines, cartels and quasi-monopolies to flourish (see p. 205). Marxian scholars saw this concatenation of forces as resulting from the interests and power of finance capital. Though they were writing about the 19th and early 20th centuries, many have seen the parallels between these accounts and the rise of transnational corporations in the later 20th and 21st centuries to positions of enormous economic and political significance (see e.g. Crouch 2011, 2016; Dicken 2011; Atal 2019; Zuboff 2019).

In the 1970s and 1980s in particular, a large body of political economy work focused on corporatist institutions and organized interest intermediation and wage bargaining between unions and employers' associations. Focused primarily on Western Europe, these scholars explored the influence these economic interest groups exerted over economic policy through 'tripartite' policy-making institutions which afforded organized labour and organized business considerable power (Crouch 1982; Dunleavy 1991: 27–30; Schmitter 2010: 249, 1974). This research programme is perhaps less fashionable than it once was. Its relevance has been reduced by the erosion of 'encompassing' industrial relations systems and the diminution of collective bargaining in many advanced economies in the wake of labour market deregulation and flexibilization since the 1980s. Nevertheless, it has some useful insights into how and why post-war advanced capitalisms evolved in the way they did and how we can mobilize economic interests in explaining these outcomes.

The power and resources model (Stephens 1979; Korpi 1983; Esping-Andersen 1990) of welfare state analysis (see pp. 223–4) explains country differences in terms of how redistributive economic policies are with reference to how powerful the organized labour movement is in a given society. In short, unions pursue their economic interest of distributing the fruits of capitalist growth towards wage earners and lower-income groups through policies such as unemployment insurance. Where they have power within the political system through their size or through corporatist structures of policy-making, these redistributive interests are translated into labour market and welfare state policies and institutions. An alternative account looks at the interests of powerful business associations (Iversen 1999; Swenson 2002; Mares 2003; Martin and Swank 2008; Iversen and Soskice 2010: 210), noting that business benefits from the social stability and increased demand and consumption that can ensue from a broadly redistributive economic policy regime and limited economic inequality in society. In each case the explanation of distinctive paths of capitalist development is in terms of the economic interest of particular groups within the political economy.

Another way to explain capitalist variety from an interest-based perspective has been advanced by Peter Gourevitch and James Shinn (2005), who, looking at the political economy of corporate governance, ask Lasswell's perennial political question: Who gets what, when and why? Gourevitch and Shinn's masterly comparative study (see pp. 201–3) foregrounds interests in charting the changing approaches to who has power and authority within the firm, and how this is reflected in national company law and economic and financial regulation. They highlight the key role of 'economic preferences and political institutions – in short ... politics' (Gourevitch and Shinn 2005: 8). Coalitions can form between these groups where their interests coincide: 'owners and manager ally to contain workers' demands on wages and job security; workers and managers combine to secure employment and stable wages in the firm; and workers and owners combine to contain management agency costs and preserve the security of their investments and pensions, and even jobs' (ibid.: 8, 22–5, table 2.3). The ensuing 'political explanation' of evolving corporate governance generates a 'complex causal pattern' and an interest-based account of differing systems (ibid.: 10–12).

A further set of influential, systematically applied and interest-based approaches to political economy, operating at the level of large economic groups within society, has been advanced in the realms of trade policy and its explanation. This builds on Ricardo-inspired standard trade theorizing in economics. Stolper and Samuelson advanced the thesis that the abundance or scarcity of key factors of production – notably land, labour and capital – affects how far a country will benefit from trade liberalization as opposed to protectionism. Inspired by this, in his influential book *Commerce and Coalitions*, Rogowski argued that 'increases or decreases in the costs and difficulty of international trade should powerfully affect domestic political cleavages and should do so differently, but predictably, in countries with different factor endowments' (1989: xiii). He developed and applied this insight to explain the comparative political economy of trade policy, deriving trade policy positions towards less regulated trade or protectionism. Rogowski interprets the manifestation of either class conflicts or urban rural conflicts within political systems and societies as arising from the interests of economic actors (ibid.: 7–10).

At the firm level, the Ricardo–Viner model of trade theory sees different configurations (and degrees of advantage) accruing differentially to economic sectors. Thus certain sectors and firms within them, which are export oriented and competitive on world markets, seek to expand market access through trade liberalization. Meanwhile other sectors and firms that are not export oriented and/or less competitive favour more regulation of trade. Jeffry Frieden has applied this insight to explain sets of interests of different actors in the economy *vis-à-vis* trade openness (1991). This kind of work has been updated by the open economy politics (OEP) scholars in IPE discussed in Chapter 2 (see e.g. Lake 2009; for a critique, see Oatley 2011). Each of these diverse approaches to political economy builds explanations from the interests of groups within society and exemplifies some of the rewards offered and insights gleaned from such an approach. Yet the most prominent interest-based approach looks not at the broad societal level of social groups, but at individuals' interests. It is to this approach, known as rational choice, that we now turn.

WHAT IS 'RATIONAL CHOICE'?

Rational choice is a long-standing approach to political science. In essence, rational choice applies some of the methods and assumptions of neo-classical economics, discussed earlier in this book, to the study of politics, positing rational political economic actors animating the political economy (see e.g. Mueller 1979, 2003: 1; McLean 1987; Hindmoor 2006: 1). Methodological individualism is integral to rational choice. The assumption that, as Hindmoor puts it, 'political process and outcomes are *completely* determined by the actions of and interactions between these individuals' (Hindmoor 2006: 1; see also Caporaso and Levine 1992: 145) is a strong one, and leads to a particular focus for and style of analysis wherein 'macro-political phenomena must have micro-foundations in the behaviour of individuals' (Dunleavy and O'Leary 1987: 91).

Rational choice more or less equates political processes to market exchange, and therefore, as Hindmoor puts it, 'it is inappropriate to assume of individuals who are entirely self-interested in the economic arena that they somehow become entirely public-spirited and self-sacrificing in the political arena' (2006: 165; see also Brennan and Buchanan 1985). This kind of analysis seeks to 'identify the preferences and the parameters of the individual actors ... and show how, after the event, the outcomes can be understood as the result of rational calculated behaviour' (Marsh and Furlong 2002: 37; see also Elster 1989: 22; Ward 2002: 65). This instrumental approach to rationality evaluates policy and institutions in terms of delivering what people want, not 'how society ought to be' (Hindmoor 2006: 1). This is perhaps its most significant debt to economics, not just in the unit of and focus for analysis, but also in how that individual is conceived. Some have gone so far as to claim that rational choice offers the potential for bringing together the disciplines of political science and economics, which have remained divided over the many decades following the *Methodenstreit* (Lake 2009).

In terms of the logic of inquiry, rational choice involves a deductive approach to social science (see pp. 70–1). In spirit, it echoes Ricardo's logic and reasoning, arguing 'from the general to the particular' (Marsh and Furlong 2002: 37). Rational choice CPE analysis embraces a 'positivist' view of social science. For positivists, social science can stand outside the social world and observe it dispassionately and objectively (Ringer 2000: 19–26; Hay 2002: 80–8; Creswell 2008: 6–8). The analogy is with natural scientists performing experiments under laboratory conditions. Positivism assumes that all salient phenomena in the social realm are deemed to be observable (and measurable). The model of knowledge and methods centres on gathering evidence to test hypotheses, akin to the research process in the natural sciences (see Chapter 13). Rational choice CPE's positivist methodology favours *parsimonious* explanation, using theory to generate hypotheses and testing them empirically (Dunleavy and O'Leary 1987: 87–8). Rational choice has come to be very influential in political science for a reason. These methodological predispositions are in alignment with mainstream US political science and its view of what counts as scientific rigour (see pp. 277–87; Hindmoor 2006). The kinds of formal, sometimes mathematical, modelling which these approaches favour fill the pages of numerous leading US journals.

A rational choice method comes with no inherent or necessary baggage attached, as a distinguished line of rational choice Marxist scholarship (see Elster 1985) co-existing with more mainstream work illustrates. The rational choice approach can be harnessed to widely divergent approaches in terms of ideological predispositions and political agendas. As Ward puts it, 'what you get out of a rational choice model depends on what you feed in by way of assumptions, and the questions you pose' (Ward 2002: 67). Nevertheless, there can be something of an alignment between much rational choice political economy and right-wing politics (King 1987), as with the highly influential 'Virginia School' of public choice political economy of Niskanen (1971), Buchanan (1975) and Tullock (1965, 1989). This uses rational choice methods to focus on economic interest groups extracting special privileges, or what Ricardo called 'rents', from government and the policy and regulatory process. Its focus on rent seeking and on budget maximizing by bureaucracies has a fairly clear Conservative agenda. It advocates the constitutionalizing of fiscal conservatism and balanced budget rules. As Hindmoor points out, 'there is something slightly incongruous about the way many rational choice theorists claim the mantle of scientific neutrality whilst issuing partisan policy proposals' (2006: 178).

In ways that reveal and underscore the core political economy insight about the interpenetration of state and market (see Chapter 2), public choice favours privatization and marketization of public service provision and of the state more generally. Public choice has advocated and informed state reform projects that see the market increasingly penetrate the state. Through marketization and privatization, market mechanisms have become increasingly imbricated into the state in various policy realms in ways that have durably altered the nature of the state (see Thatcher 2017).

Some reservations about rational choice relate not to the politics of its influential protagonists, but to the implications of its theoretical parsimony. A rational choice approach presupposes less need for historical understanding of context because the explanation proceeds via *a priori* assumed preferences of actors. Hay notes the danger, with the incorporation of rational choice micro-foundations and reasoning into CPE analysis, of adopting 'a rather agentless and apolitical conception' of political economy (2005: 107). Preferences are derived from a reading of an actor's material position and his or her interests which are seen to ensue. This 'calculus' approach, Hay notes, runs the risk of 'substituting the contingency of agency with a utility function' (ibid.: 109, 112). Nevertheless, stripping away to an individual's posited 'what's in it for me?' calculation has a certain attraction as an analytical strategy. It helps to distil the essence of what is at stake in a given political economic context.

In short, there are very good intellectual reasons for making some of the choices rational choice makes in terms of how to approach analysing CPE. This kind of thinking has thrown up some very interesting insights about democratic politics – such as that the interests of society as a whole cannot be aggregated satisfactorily (Arrow 1951), or that it is never rational to vote (Olson 1965). Rational choice also indicates that the ideological struggle in pursuit of the good society is not the heart of electoral politics. Rather, it is the politician's instrumental, self-interested desire to secure office. Politicians produce policies for voters to consume. Voters always want to consume more goods, and politicians have an interest in promising to deliver them. It is this, more than ideology, which shapes electoral manifestos. As such, in a two-party system, it is always in politicians' interests to offer policies that secure the broadest majority appeal and hence to tend towards the middle ground to secure electoral victory (Downs 1957). One of rational choice's merits is as a yardstick for measuring deviation from rationality: 'it provides a standard against which action can be judged and indicates variables that might lead to departures from rationality' (Ward 2002: 70).

Rational choice and environmental degradation: Hardin's tragedy of the commons

What thinking in this way about self-interested political economic actors can do is to show how difficult it can be to co-ordinate social and economic activity. This has burgeoning relevance for political economy analysis of the climate crisis, and the difficulties democratic politics and global capitalism face in seeking to limit global warming and environmental degradation. Perhaps the best example is Garret Hardin's 'Tragedy of the Commons', which offers a rational choice account of the pathologies of ecological devastation under capitalism and the difficulties of addressing and halting it (Hardin 1968). Hardin's highly influential argument took on underlying assumptions within liberal political economy. Adam Smith's thinking, Hardin noted, contributed to 'a dominant tendency of thought ... to assume that decisions reached individually will, in fact, be the best decisions for an entire society' (ibid.: 1244). However, this premise, and the *laissez-faire* approach to economy and society it gives rise to, are fundamentally flawed – as Hardin illustrates with reference to the use and abuse of common land. Hardin underlines a contradiction between untrammelled freedom to pursue one's own interests and environmental sustainability; his argument demonstrates how self-interested actors will destroy the environment, or, as he puts it, how 'the inherent logic of the commons remorselessly generates tragedy' (ibid.).

It is in each rational herdsman's interest to graze his cattle on common land as often as possible. As the number of herdsmen and cattle increases, this will put ultimately unbearable pressure on natural resources, and eventually the commons will become a barren wasteland: 'each man is locked into a system that compels him to increase his herd without limit – in a world that is limited. Ruin is the destination toward which all men rush, each pursuing his own best interest, in a society that believes in the freedom of the commons' (ibid.).

Nobel Prize–winner Elinor Ostrom calls this kind of situation a 'social dilemma' because 'at least one outcome yields higher returns for *all* participants, but the rational participants making independent choices are not predicted to achieve this outcome' (2007: 186). We will return to this 'tragedy' below to discuss different interest-based political economy approaches to how it might be addressed. This has come to be known as the common resource pool problem – a particularly trenchant form of a wider genus of problem called the 'collective action problem'. We owe this term to the pioneering political economist Mancur Olson (1965, 1982), who was at the forefront, in the 1960s, of the development of an approach which has become known as 'public choice'.

PUBLIC CHOICE THEORY

Public choice theory applies the economic approach to the design and dynamics of political institutions, rules and procedures, and to government, the public sector and the public economy (Buchanan 1975; Mueller 1979; McLean 1987). It has become a highly influential way of thinking about interest group organization and influence, and bureaucratic behaviour. Public choice 'assumes that citizens do in fact act on the basis of self-interest (in the economist's sense) so that actual political outcomes are explained on that basis' (Caporaso and Levine 1992: 138). We can trace processes of privatization, 'contracting out', new public management (NPM) and the marketization of public services and public sectors in advanced economies and beyond to the ideas of public choice (Self 1993). As such, it has had a profound effect on state reform and the transformation of state/market relations, pushing the interpenetration of state and market further in many advanced economies.

Mancur Olson: the political economy of interest groups

Olson's seminal contribution to political economy was to theorize collective action problems, introducing terms such as free riding (1965). Olson's study takes apart the assumption that groups and organizations exist to pursue common interests. This had been a mainstay of the dominant pluralist approach to political science of Dahl (1961) and others, which argued that all interests in society can organize themselves politically and find their interests reflected in government actions. Olson discusses lobbying organizations and trade unions who pursue the economic interests of their members. He put a spanner in the works of pluralism's assumed interest articulation process by pointing out that some interests never organize, but remain 'latent'.

Olson notes, first, that '*rational self-interested individuals will not act to achieve their common or group interests*' (Olson 1965: 2). It is not rational to join groups or act to secure provision of collective or public goods (ibid.: 15–17). It makes sense to let others do the work, though you can still reap the rewards since the 'good' is 'non-excludable'. In other words, the higher wages for workers, or increased contracts for the firm, will in all likelihood be extended to all workers/members of the firm, whether or not they made the effort to secure the 'good'. Thus 'free riding' is the optimal strategy for a rational actor, but if everyone pursues it – nothing gets done! Olson's central claim is not that collective action is impossible or irrational, but rather that it is difficult to achieve (Hindmoor 2006: 127). Group organization and activities 'take on the characteristic properties of public goods: they are undersupplied and subject to free riding' (Caporaso and Levine 1992: 142). In explaining why groups ever do organize despite it not being rational, Olson appeals to notions of 'selective incentives' and to the notion of privileged groups and group members accruing benefits in excess of the 'costs' of group participation.

Olson's account was an early outing in political science for 'game theory', though he did not use the term. Game theory offers illustrations of the deductive method and how to build up explanations of political economic outcomes from the posited or derived interests of a restricted number of actors. It lays bare some of the difficulties of co-ordinating political economic activity by exploring how choices are arrived at when outcomes depend not just on your own choice, but on the choices and actions of others. Key examples include the 'prisoner's dilemma' and 'chicken' games, where an actor's best course of action depends on what others will do, and on whether the other protagonists can be trusted to act in a way consistent with the realization of one's best interests (Hindmoor 2006: 105–12). So, in the prisoner's dilemma, if both guilty parties, A and B, keep quiet during their separate inter-rogations, they will get light sentences, but if one implicates the other, the snitch may get off scot-free, at the expense of a higher sentence for the other. However, if each prisoner implicates the other, both will get stiff sentences. In the chicken game, both A and B would benefit from some laborious activity being undertaken, so each may hold out hoping the other will do the work – and it becomes a question of 'who blinks first'. Of course, if both stubbornly dig their heels in and do not do the work, no one benefits.

In game theory, the nature of the game (the institutional and structural context) con-strains strategic choices. Game theory has been used to model and explain outcomes and policy dynamics in a wide range of areas of political economy. George Tsebelis took this interest in games forward in comparative politics, adding more layers of complexity by developing the idea of 'nested games'. These take the form of either a 'network of games' in 'multiple arenas' that actors are playing simultaneously or alternatively when actors are 'in a game about the *rules* of the game', which Tsebelis calls 'nested game institutional design' (1990: 7–8). Apparently sub-optimal choices in one 'game' can normally be explained by tak-ing into account the other games and arenas in which one game is 'nested'.

One way to think about the relatively stable configurations of institutions which, as I show in Chapter 6, are integral to sustaining capitalism is as a series of 'repeated games' (Aoki 2000). A variety of capitalism could be seen as a large-scale example of what game theorists call a 'strategy equilibrium'. This 'is a set of strategies, one for each player, such that no player can increase their pay-off by changing strategy given that no other player changes strategy ... equilibria are self-reinforcing' (Ward 2002: 68–9; see also Green and Shapiro 1994). This follows from game theory logic: repeated game playing may lead to sta-ble solutions. Institutions are stable as long as shocks are small and they change only irregularly.

Public choice, rent seeking and state/market relations

Writing after several decades of growth of the extended state in the post-war era, public choice theorists helped to shape an influential ideological movement – the 'New Right' (see King 1987; Gamble 1988) – which sought to challenge and overthrow the perceived legiti-macy and acceptance of expansive state intervention in economic activity. Within public choice, the state and the public sphere are conceived in the same way as the private sphere. Voters, politicians, bureaucrats, consumers and producers 'all follow the dictates of rational self-interest' (Ekelund and Tomlinson 1986: 440).

The New Right of Thatcher and Reagan appropriated Olson's insight into groups and the instrumental pursuit of self-interest to argue for political economic reform to tackle organ-ized 'vested interests' in the private and especially the public sector. They questioned the state's size, its cost to the public purse and the scale of its intervention in and influence on the economy. Olson provided a lens which sees state and market not as separable spheres with different logics, but rather as complex terrain upon which self-interested political eco-nomic actors have to navigate to achieve their goals. This was taken further by later public choice theorizing. In its distinctive fashion, public choice shone a light on how state and market were intertwined, not hermetically sealed off from one another.

Interest groups, be they oligopolistic business interests or powerful trade unions, seek to shape government policy and market outcomes, extracting 'rents' from government and the policy and regulatory process, leading to less than efficient organization of economic activity (Becker 1983, 1985; Tullock 1990). Industrial lobbies will seek to secure from the state the regulation which most suits and sustains the dominant position of a few powerful producers in the industry (Stigler 1971). As Tullock puts it when discussing rent seekers, monopolists do not 'get their monopolies through divine favour. In the real world, they have to work for them' (1990: 197–8). Sub-optimal outcomes arise because producer interests concentrated within a few groups with powerful members are likely to prevail over consumer interests in lower prices or in freer competition because their interests are dispersed.

Olson saw the overall effect of corporatist institutions (through which these economic groups could shape policy and outcomes) as fostering 'institutional sclerosis' (1982). This has been applied within CPE to explain the impeding of market efficiency through the hold on public policy of powerful economic insider groups, and following on from that differential economic performance of varieties of capitalism. Varying levels of success of rent-seeking and market-shaping behaviour by economic interest groups in different societies can, in some accounts, explain differential rates of economic growth (ibid.; North 1990).

The public choice account of rent seeking proved highly influential. As Hindmoor puts it, 'rent seeking also flourished because it offered to rational choice theory a distinctive and distinctively hostile theory of the state' (2006: 162; see also Dunleavy and O'Leary 1987: 43, 108). The key methodological move for a public choice account of the state involves analysing the state not in terms of its overarching structures or institutional make-up, but from the perspective of the preferences and interests of individual citizens, bureaucrats and state actors: 'political institutions and structures must be understood from the ground up, as resultants of self-interested actions' (Caporaso and Levine 1992: 145).

The point of departure for Niskanen's influential work was that bureaucrats always 'rent seek' or look to 'maximize' their budgets and increase the size of their bureaucracies, and that public bureaucracies are accordingly always distended and inefficient (Hindmoor 2006: ch. 6). Across the public sector, these selfish and profligate public office holders seek to expand and increase their authority and offices, not in the national interest but in their own particular interests. Since private economic activity is assumed *a priori* within public choice to be more efficient than the public sector, economic growth is undermined. The results are increasing public expenditure and adverse effects on private-sector entrepreneurs. This illustrates how an account of state/market evolution can be built up from a focus on the self-interested instrumental actions and behaviour of individuals – in this case, senior bureaucrats. However, rather than seeing this as a possible tendency of some states and bureaucrats, Niskanen and many public choice theorists argued that this was an inherent tendency in any public-sector bureaucracy.

A similar ideological predisposition in favour of free market mechanisms and against state, political or bureaucratic interference, built on similar assumptions about the self-interested behaviour of state actors, found expression in other areas of New Right economic thought, notably in relation to macro-economic policy-making (King 1987; Gamble 1988). The neo-liberal bottom line was a concern to secure 'sound money' (low inflation), a distrust of governmental interference in free markets, and a desire to limit governmental latitude to intervene. The historic origins of hostility to discretion in monetary policy can be found in the belief that the authorities (stretching back to medieval kings) have an incentive to generate unexpected inflation and thus gain benefits from a depreciating currency (Haldane 1995: 5).

This thesis was not formalized until the 1970s, when it became known as the 'time-consistency' argument by public choice theorists, as it suggested that the authorities faced incentives to expand the economy in a run-up to an election to try to get re-elected, with the likely effect of increasing inflation in the short run even though this would be destabilizing in the long run (Kydland and Prescott 1977). The policy corollary of this was to develop rules-based policy regimes to tie irresponsible state actors to the mast of economic rectitude (Gill 1998; Burnham 1999; Clift and Tomlinson 2012).

Some of the problems with Niskanen's positing of budget maximizing as an inherent tendency within the state and public sector argument relate to his lack of rigour in applying the comparative method which is so integral to CPE (see Chapter 13). Niskanen's account was based partly on his own experiences in the US bureaucracy of the 1960s, extrapolating from the particular circumstances of American civil service budget-making. These ceased to obtain in the US in the 1980s, and never obtained in the other advanced democratic states in the same way. There is a problem of 'parochialism' at the heart of Niskanen's account, because of his extrapolating from a particular case (see Hindmoor 2006: 149–51).

Ideological predispositions aside, as Hindmoor rightly points out, when welfare economics theorizes certain market failures, such as monopoly, imperfect competition or the provision of public goods, the theoretical case for state intervention to correct them assumes that the state will not fail to deliver in the way the market has in these specific instances (ibid.: 132–3). What public choice theorists have done is to cast a more critical eye over state intervention in the economy and question the motives of policy-makers and bureaucrats, and ask the question as to whose interest they are really serving. Public choice recognizes the possibility – or perhaps the probability – of state failure. The analysis chimes with the Hayekian critique of state intervention which we encountered in Chapter 4.

Niskanen's original thesis was based on some fairly tendentious premises, under-elaborated causal mechanisms and was strongly ideologically driven. Niskanen eventually toned down his assumptions about the budget-maximizing behaviour of bureaucrats, restricting it to their discretionary budgets, not the overall budgets of their bureaux (1991; see Hindmoor 2006: 143–4). In a similar vein, Dunleavy, from a somewhat sceptical position, reformulated the thesis in terms of 'bureau shaping', where state actors were engaged in 'sufficing' – or making their conditions of work more agreeable, not maximizing their budgets (1991: ch. 7).

Despite at best limited empirical support for public choice presumptions about how bloated and inefficient states and public sectors were (see Tomlinson 1990: 248–9), the 'time was right' for such ideas to come to prominence. Public choice spawned the highly influential 'new public management' analytical and policy agenda for state and public-sector reform. This seeks changes to the structure and operation of public service provision by emphasizing a focus on outputs, performance measurement, contracting out and the introduction of markets and market-like mechanisms (see Pollitt 2002; Hindmoor 2006: 153–4). NPM-inspired privatization and marketization reforms have profoundly transformed the state across the advanced economies and beyond since the 1970s (Thatcher 2017; Vaughan-Whitehead 2013). All of this shone a spotlight on one of the core political economy insights (Chapter 2) – about the interpenetration of state and market. The policy instruments of NPM engendered the intertwining of state and market – always a facet of capitalism, even if often under-appreciated – more evident. While the state-regulating aspects of how markets work were familiar, NPM entailed new market forms and mechanisms being constructed within the public sector, altering the nature of the state and how public policy was delivered.

The rhetoric surrounding these state reform programmes was hostile to state provision, equating it with inefficiency and vested interests. Without public choice theory, and its enthusiastic take-up by the likes of Reagan and Thatcher, these dramatic transformations in state/market relations, which are now part of a new settlement in the 21st century, would not have occurred in the way they did.

REFORMULATED RATIONALISM: RETHINKING INTEREST-BASED COMPARATIVE POLITICAL ECONOMY

Rational choice, as we have seen, offers considerable advantages in affording a certain parsimonious explanatory power. The parsimony of its approach is appealing in some respects, but like all intellectual choices about method, it has advantages and disadvantages (see pp. 277–87). Most rational choice work in CPE remains substantially wedded to the utility-maximizing assumptions about the individual and his or her relationship with institutions and the social order found in marginalist political economy. Thus it is open to the kinds of critiques of the implausibility of assuming perfect information, perfectly competitive markets and 'all other things being equal', as discussed in Chapter 4.

There remains, for example, a difficulty in explaining things like institutional development in 'pure' game theory terms, because we come back to the question: How did the institutions arise? Thus game theory may take account of particular 'rules of the game', but the problem of infinite regress pushes us back to the question of where the game's rules arise from in the first place (Field 1984; Mirowski 1986; Hodgson 2002; Ward 2002). As Blyth puts it, 'institutions themselves are collective action problems' (2002b: 303). The kinds of collective action problems identified by Olson (1965) indicate that self-interested rational egoists would not, in short, go to the trouble of creating social institutions, even ones they knew would be socially and personally beneficial.

However, there is scope within interest-oriented explanation in CPE to at least circumvent some of these difficulties. Rationalist assumptions about individuals, and their relationship to institutions and social order, lie on a continuum. In this last section of this chapter, we explore ways of rethinking an interest-based account of political economy rooted in rational choice, admitting more complexity to its 'micro-foundations' by relaxing certain *homo economicus* assumptions to admit conditions of uncertainty and imperfect information. Once again, this comes with costs and benefits. Some of the parsimony, and the spare and sparse character of 'pure' rational choice analysis, is lost as more complex 'micro-foundations' are imported. However, on the plus side, arguably more realistic accounts of the social world can be developed as a result.

Douglass North exemplifies an approach which remains faithful to many aspects of rational choice, but which navigates around some of the pitfalls through a judicious relaxation of certain assumptions (North 1990). He began with quite orthodox underlying assumptions and conceptions of individual action and rationality (1981). Over time, North has been picking away at a number of *homo economicus* assumptions, and in the process he opened up more space for 'play' between institutional and material contexts and the individuals who animate them. There is much scope within North's later work to understand interests in ways that admit ideas and motivations other than utility maximization. North (1990: 96) and others have subsequently emphasized the role of 'mental constructs' such as ideologies and theories, and how 'mental models' and different conceptions of rationality directly shape individual choice (Knight and North 1997: 216; Table 5.1).

This thinking connects to the concept of 'bounded rationality', which recognizes that actors operate 'in the face of limited information, limited time and limited cognitive capacity to process information' (Ward 2002: 72; Simon 1982, 1985). Herbert Simon identifies the use that individuals make of what Ward calls 'heuristics built into standard operating procedures as a shorthand guide to getting a satisfactory result' (2002: 72). Individuals deal with the limits of their knowledge and understanding, and when the 'games' they are playing are rendered more complex by not being sure whether to trust and reciprocate with other actors, 'individuals develop a range of heuristics to deal with the problem of when and when not to reciprocate. They rely on communication and others' reputations for trustworthiness, and they internalize norms of appropriate behaviour which there are intangible costs to violating' (ibid.: 73; see also Ostrom 2007: 190–4).

Another refinement of rational choice political economy, inspired by New Keynesian economic thinking (see Hargreaves Heap 1992, 1994), entails a departure from standard economic assumptions about equilibrium. In the orthodox model, perfect information, costlessly and uniformly distributed, determines the beliefs individuals entertain about the

Table 5.1 Varieties of interest-based accounts of political economy

	Micro-foundations	Object of analysis	Conception of society	Some core concerns
Rational choice	Homo economicus	Voters, economic actors	Individualized, atomized	Varieties of capitalism; collective action problems
Public choice	Homo economicus	Interest groups, state bureaucracy	Individualized, atomized, rent-seeking behaviour	State failure; public-sector reform
Marxism	Materialist conception of history – social classes	Social relations of production; regimes of accumulation	Antagonistic, collectivized, class-based	Capitalist instability and exploitation
Actor-centred institutionalism	Bounded rationality; imperfect information	Decision environment; social constructs	Social norms and social facts situated, strategic actors; logics of appropriateness	Varieties of capitalism; political parties
Corporatism	Sectoral or class-based interests (business and unions)	Welfare states – labour market structure	Power resources model; collectivized, class-based	Industrial relations; incomes policies

behaviour of other agents, and this results in a single equilibrium. That reflects what economists call a 'Walrasian' view of market propensities (after the Swiss economist Leon Walras)
that assumes markets are efficient and possess inherent tendencies towards optimal outcomes. The spanner which the refinement throws into mainstream economics' tidy Walrasian
mechanism is the possibility of multiple equilibria. Drawing on the insights of Herbert
Simon, Elinor Ostrom and New Keynesian theorists about lack of information and uncertainty, 'there are a number of expectations any *one* of which will prove to be a rational expectation if expected and acted upon by *all* agents, and any *one* of which will *not* prove to be
rational if held in isolation' (Hargreaves Heap 1994: 39).

The existence of multiple possible equilibria has significant implications. As Ward points
out, 'the existence of multiple equilibria reduces the predictive power of the method' (2002:
72). Some of rational choice's parsimony has been compromised. Thus 'the clear and unambiguous predictions of earlier theories have been replaced with a broad range of predictions
... the theoretical enterprise has, however, become far more opaque and confused' (Ostrom
2007: 195). The 'game' in game theory becomes a more complex one of selection of an equilibrium among a number of options – and this requires co-ordination. As Hargreaves Heap
puts it, 'multiple equilibria occur under the assumption that individuals are instrumentally
rational ... Hence it requires the introduction of some other guide to action to explain equilibrium selection' (1994: 40). This co-ordinating role is played, within the New Keynesian
macro-economic framework, by the institutions and mechanisms which provide the context
within which the economy operates. For Ostrom and others, norms, heuristics and actors'
bounded rationality are crucial.

We will consider three applications of these insights to illustrate how reformulated
rational choice built on bounded rationality and acknowledging multiple possible equilibria
can enhance CPE analysis through a nuanced appreciation of differentiated 'micro-
foundations'. The first brief example takes us back to the comparative capitalisms debates
much discussed in this book. The various possible equilibria may have widely divergent welfare properties – hence this co-ordinated equilibrium selection constitutes a political choice
of the appropriate social institutions of capitalism. The corporatist institutions discussed
earlier in this chapter, and the welfare provision regime considered in Chapter 11, can under
certain conditions help to maintain co-operation, social cohesion and trust within capitalism. This can in turn uphold a political economic bargain, or in rational choice and game
theory parlance an equilibrium, which sustains high employment and moderate wage
increases (Therborn 1986). There are numerous examples of 'social pacts' in countries such
as Ireland, the Netherlands and parts of Scandinavia which have coincided with relatively
equitable economic growth and relatively low unemployment (see Becker and Schwartz
2005). These can be explained if 'inflation and the medium term level of unemployment
[are] viewed as the outcome of the "distributional struggle" – the tug of war where the rope
is income and the teams are firms and workers' (Driver and Wren-Lewis 1995: 28; see also
Glyn 1995). The state may be one institution playing a key role in shaping market mechanisms to facilitate selection of a possible equilibrium, or one kind of capitalism, over another
(see pp. 151–4, 203–6).

The second example focuses on norms and bounded rationality. Ostrom has taken forward this work on bounded rationality to address collective action problems, and in particular the common pool of resources problem, namely Hardin's tragedy of the commons
discussed earlier in this chapter (1990, 2007). In tackling 'social dilemmas' such as over-
harvesting and crowding, Ostrom argues for 'a theory of boundedly rational, norm-based

human behaviour' as a foundation for explaining collective action wherein 'individuals can use reciprocity and reputations to build trust in dilemma situations' (2007: 187, 189, 1990). The work of Simon, like that of Ostrom, encourages what Ostrom terms 'a broader theory of human behaviour', in which 'humans learn norms, heuristics, and full analytical strategies from one another, from feedback from the world, and from their own capacity to engage in self-reflection' (ibid. 195, 196–201). This is similar to North's incorporation of 'mental constructs – ideas, theories and ideologies' into his later model of rationality.

Ostrom uses an interest-based approach rooted in bounded rationality to explain relatively successful management of limited environmental resources in cases related to fisheries and irrigation systems. One enlightening contribution of rational choice, here, is to explain *departures* from pure rationality. As Blyth puts it, 'if all fishermen were the self-interested agents portrayed in rational choice theory, then the last tuna would have been hauled out of the Mediterranean Sea a few hundred years back. Why then are there, even now, some tuna left?' (2002b: 301). The answer is that, without heavy-handed state intervention, but guided by enlightened self-interest, rational actors have developed norms about resource allocation, increased transparency and reinforcing reciprocating strategies to sanction and monitor behaviour through 'tit-for-tat' (Ostrom 2007: 197–8). Actors have been able to manage seemingly intractable common-pool resource problems (Ward 2002: 87; Blyth 2002b: 302–3; Hindmoor 2006: 120–1) and found ways to at least mitigate, if not fully resolve, Hardin's tragedy of the commons.

The final CPE example offers a different illustration of bounded rationality – through what Fritz Scharpf calls 'actor centred institutionalism' (1991, 1997). This, as Crouch summarizes it, depicts 'boundedly rational and imperfectly knowledgeable' actors with a variety of goals 'acting within contexts which constrain them in various ways, but with the actors having some capacity to change the constraints' (2005b: 62). It retains, but at the same time relaxes, some rational choice assumptions. It does not assume a singular rational response *a priori*, but seeks to contextualize its account of rationality. In this way, Scharpf's approach 'gives equal weight to strategic actions and interactions of purposeful and resourceful individual and corporate actors and to the enabling, constraining, and shaping effects of given (but variable) institutional structures and institutionalized forms' (1997: 34).

Thus, 'economic policy makers', Scharpf notes, are likely 'to be guided by their own interpretation of the situation'. This is because, 'like all human action, economic policy is possible only within a cognitive framework that pairs goals with available means and the critical conditions of the decision environment' (Scharpf 1991: 11–13). This approach presupposes much more need for historical understanding of the context or 'decision environment' than standard rational choice, because its explanation does not proceed straightforwardly via the assumed preferences of actors. Leaving behind unrealistic assumptions of perfect information, actor-centred institutionalism views the knowledge on which strategic calculations are based as impressionistic and partial at best (Hay and Wincott 1998: 954; Hay 2001, 2002: ch. 6).

This approach has affinities with Tsebelis' 'nested games' (1990). Scharpf has applied it to explain changing West European mainstream left political parties from the 1980s onwards. Social democratic parties are viewed as responding to changing economic, ideological and electoral conditions not as completely dependent actors, but as independent, reflective and relatively autonomous actors. This autonomy means they are able to respond to and indeed reshape these changing conditions in innovative ways (Scharpf 1991; see also Przeworski 1985; Koelble 1991: 4; Kitschelt 1994). The organizational structure of a party conditions and influences its internal debates about how to respond to external changes and challenges. This crucially affects the dominant 'frame of reference' through which the situation is interpreted. Different parties, with different intellectual traditions and lineages, may approach strategic dilemmas and electoral or ideological difficulties in significantly different ways, as Scharpf illustrates through his in-depth comparative analysis (1991; Koelble 1991; see also Anderson and Camiller 1994; Sassoon 1996).

CONCLUSION

Interest-based approaches to and explanations in CPE have much to recommend them, distilling the essence of the question to an age-old political economy question: 'Who benefits?' Building political economy explanations from this question can take many forms. Rational choice, with its foundations in a stark form of methodological individualism which sees all political phenomena – including large-scale structures like the state – as explicable in terms of motivations for individual action, has been used to throw new light on a range of important issues in CPE. These include the size and scope of the state and attempts to mitigate environmental degradation.

Public choice lays bare the difficulties of mobilizing and orchestrating collective action. It also exposes some of the incentives, notably 'rent seeking', which can lead powerful economic and political actors to shape market outcomes to their advantage in ways that adversely affect broader economic efficiency. The 'budget-maximizing' bureaucrat theories make similar points about the proclivities towards inefficiency within the state sector. Powerful economic interest groups 'extracting rents' from the wider economy and society by using their political power to shape the market (in sub-optimal, economically inefficient ways) became a mainstay of public choice theorists. These insights can contribute to CPE explanations of comparative capitalist performance across advanced economies.

Yet some feel that an interest-oriented account of political economy built upon marginalist foundations and *homo economicus* assumptions is incomplete. It can seem to offer a somewhat unrealistic account of how the social world really operates, and it struggles to account for how crucial social goods and institutions come into being. However, North, Ostrom, Scharpf and others exemplify ways to relax certain assumptions and use an interest-based rational choice approach to political economy that thinks of individuals outside the *homo economicus* framework in ways that are rich with potential. They also open up increased possibilities for cross-fertilization with institutional and ideational approaches to political economy that we will discuss in the next two chapters.

6 Institutional Analysis and Comparative Political Economy

INTRODUCTION

The study of political institutions is as old as the study of politics. Within political science the focus on institutions was revived by 'new institutionalism' (Peters 1999) in the 1980s and 1990s. Within CPE, comparative institutional analysis of capitalism has long been a mainstay of the discipline (see e.g. Shonfield 1965). Spelling out how capitalist evolution becomes channelled along particular paths of development is the central contribution of institutionalist CPE. The comparative dimension enables appreciation of the nationally differentiated paths of institutional development, and the dynamics and implications of their attendant configurations of institutions.

When seeking the best ways to plot the institutional terrain of capitalism, modern scholars can also 'consult the charts' mapped out by pioneering political economy analyses by the likes of Weber, Veblen, Hayek, Polanyi, Schmoller and List, among others. This distinguished lineage of political economy scholarship on institutions has long explored how institutions play an important role in economic activity. Many economists tend to either ignore the role of institutions or see them as impediments to the free operation of markets. Yet, as Chang points out, non-market institutions are in fact 'integral parts of socio-economic life' and 'not necessarily unfortunate rigidities that are best eliminated' (Chang 1996: 4). Institutions, as Hay puts it, 'configure social and political space and are constitutive of the opportunities and constraints which characterise that space' (Hay 2016: 523). The classical political economy scholars all grasped the constitutive role of institutions for market activity. They appreciated that without such institutions, capitalism could not survive.

Unsurprisingly, the place of institutions, and institutional reproduction, in explaining trajectories of capitalist evolution is front and centre within this modern revival of CPE. Indeed, Hall and Soskice go so far as to characterize their influential *Varieties of Capitalism* (VoC) approach as the analysis of 'comparative institutional advantage' (2001). Institutions are integral to capitalist market relations, and as the protean capitalist social forces evolve and shape-shift, political struggles arise over the institutional embedding of market activity. This in turn leads to changes in the empirical realities and character of markets as political constructions. I will demonstrate below how *comparative* analysis can enhance political economy's ability to understand and explain the varied nature and extensive scope of the institutional circumscribing and framing of market activity within capitalism.

Schools of institutionalist analysis within political science differ as to how to approach the individual and his or her relationship with the institutional and social context. I illustrate some of this variety by highlighting the evolution of historical institutionalist analysis of the CPE of comparative capitalisms. In considering different theoretical approaches to the problem of how to incorporate the institutional realm, the central contention is that a full account of institutionalist CPE should take care to conceive of the interrelationship between actors, institutions and their social context in a way that does justice to the dynamics of change within capitalism.

The institutions of capitalism, which as noted above play a constitutive role in configuring the political economic space of a particular capitalist order (Hay 2016: 523), are subject to change over time as economies evolve and develop. Yet one shortcoming of institutionalist political economy has been the difficulty of capturing such change adequately. We will explore below recent institutionalist attempts to recognize and address prior weaknesses in explaining change. Such work connects to the core insights of CPE discussed in Chapter 2: an appreciation that markets, and the institutions necessary to sustain market orders, are not naturally occurring phenomena, but rather inherently political constructs. A full account of the institutional context of capitalism requires that we appreciate that it is dynamic rather than static.

Institutions are the result of shared understandings, and they exist 'by virtue of human agreement', as Hay puts it. It follows from this that they 'are socially and politically contingent' (Hay 2016: 524), an aspect not always to the fore in some CPE treatments. Institutional creation, evolution and reproduction are not automatic, still less 'natural'. Institutionalist analysis that pays especially close attention to the political processes through which institutions are created, changed and re-created can reaffirm this contingency and indeterminacy. This view of social processes and outcomes problematizes the idea of institutions or orders as inevitable, or unchanging. We should study institutional orders comparatively, and in ways that are mindful to 'bring the politics back in'. This needs to go beyond merely noting that there is a politics surrounding the design of institutions – to appreciate that institutions (their design, creation and reproduction) are inherently political. Understanding 'politics as intrinsic to institutions' (Hay 2016: 525), we can explore in historical context the changing institutions which surround and sustain market activity as potential sites of such political struggle.

THE ARGUMENT: CAPITALISM, POLITICAL ECONOMY AND INSTITUTIONS

In this chapter, I argue that approaches to political economy which neglect or ignore institutions and the rich insights offered by their analysis are problematic. Institutionally blind analysis of political economy, as in marginalist political economy and some strands of economics, is flawed because it simply does not make sense to talk about 'the economy' in isolation or abstracted from this institutional context.

The starting point for a CPE of institutions returns us to political economy's foundational assumptions discussed in Chapter 1:

> social orders and the institutions which make them up need to be studied as complex wholes rather than as analytically distinct parts ... institutions need to be studied as a whole first in order to understand the interrelationships between the different aspects, and secondly to understand the broader political and economic context in which a particular institution is embedded. (Gamble et al. 2000: 2)

The patterns of institutional interlinkages take different forms in different national historical contexts. Hence *comparative* analysis is uniquely well placed to reveal the multiple forms
that 'the market's' predication upon the institutional context takes. For example, in their
analysis of the 'spatial fragmentation of production', as parts of the production process
move 'offshore' within complex transnational global commodity chains, Bair and Mahutga
discern the 'dispersion of disaggregated manufacturing processes' at the heart of 21st-
century capitalism (2012: 270). Transnational production chains and networks mean that
semi-finished manufactures and components cross national borders multiple times before
finished products are ready for sale. The import content of exports for many advanced economies is between 20 and 30 per cent (Crouch 2019: 44). Given what Feenstra has termed the
'integration of trade and the disintegration of production' (1998), it is these institutional
particularities that account for *which* parts of global production and commodity chains are
reorganized *where* within globalizing commodity and production chains. Bair and Mahutga
note how this evolving international division of labour hinges on the role of 'institutional
context in producing persistent cross-country or cross-regional variation in economic
organization' (2012: 270–1).

In order to advance my argument, I first need to define the term 'institution'. Much ink
has been spilled dwelling on this, but we will satisfy ourselves with a straightforward definition. March and Olsen (1984: 738) identified institutions as 'collections of standard operating procedures and structures that define and defend interests'. They can be formal or
informal. In Douglass North's classic statement:

> Institutions are the rules of the game in a society or, more formally, are the humanly
> devised constraints that shape human interaction ... Institutions reduce uncertainty by
> providing a structure to everyday life. They are a guide to human interaction, so that
> when we wish to greet friends on the street, drive an automobile, buy oranges, borrow
> money, form a business, bury our dead or whatever, we know (or can learn easily) how to
> perform these tasks. We would readily observe that institutions differ if were trying to
> make the same transactions in a different country. (North 1990: 3–4)

The focus here will be primarily on formal, concrete institutions (though the interaction
of ideational and material matters – as we discuss in Chapter 7) and on those institutions most important to economic processes, political economy and the reproduction of
capitalism. The institutionally informed and attuned account of capitalism developed
below understands that 'individual action is influenced by the hold that institutions
have on individual decision-making' (Hollingsworth and Boyer 1997: 3; see also
Campbell et al. 1991). Institutionalist scholars in political economy are keen to highlight what some term 'the constitutive nature of institutional contexts' (Farrell and
Newman 2010: 611; Hay 2016).

As Adam Smith pointed out, and Hayek reiterated, capitalism needs a settled legal framework and mechanisms for the enforcement of contracts. But the scale and density of institutions needed for the stable continuation of capitalist social relations of production are much
broader than that (see e.g. Hodgson 1988; Chang 1996: 49–50, 1999; Polanyi 2001 [1944];
Clift and Woll 2012a, 2012b). When we dig deeper, we find that there is a very wide array of
aspects of the ordering of social life which are required for market relations to operate
smoothly. To give some obvious examples of the institutional framing of capitalism, things

like stable currencies, common weights and measures, a reliable banking system, bank-ruptcy laws, product and process standards, and educational, professional or artisanal quali-fications and their recognition are all required for market exchange in advanced economies. These all require institutions to sustain them, and those institutions require a state or some form of public authority to establish and underpin them. This illustrates the core CPE insight (see Chapter 2) – the co-constitution of state and market. Thus the state, through its regula-tory actions and its establishment and maintenance of the institutional and legal frame-work, permeates the market economy.

Karl Polanyi took a keen interest in institution building, and this co-constitutive relation-ship between state and market, in his analysis of the establishment of *laissez-faire* capital-ism at the hands of the 'liberal state' in 19th-century Britain. He argued that markets and regulation 'grew up together' (2001 [1944]; see also Block 2003; Dale 2010; Holmes and Yarrow 2019). The expansion of market activity was contemporaneous with the vast expan-sion of infrastructure and institution building to sustain market activity; the expansion of markets and the growth of state activity were intimately intertwined.

Liberal market capitalism is inherently unstable, given the dynamic dislocating tenden-cies of markets and capital analysed by Marx, Polanyi, Hayek, Keynes and others. The sys-tem requires a degree of social stability to operate which it cannot itself provide. Adam Smith, for example, noted how capitalism rested on an ethical base, which was necessary to secure such constituent parts as the respect for a contract (Smith 1993 [1776]; Watson 2005a). This ethical base is institutionally embedded in the social institutions of capitalism, though it is exogenous to the capitalist model, since capitalism cannot create these institu-tions or embed them. Firms, after all, do not manufacture ethics as a commodity for sale in the marketplace. Colin Crouch notes that this need for an ethical foundation on which capi-talism and markets are sustained is a 'kind of meta-instance of the more general problem of market failure, the inability of market processes to produce public goods' (Crouch 1993: 83; see also Streeck 2010: 23).

In the wake of the GFC, a number of politicians, appalled by the scale of greed and reck-lessness in the financial sector and the havoc this wreaked on the real economy and citizens, called for the 'remoralization of capitalism'. Such a clarion call (which arguably went largely unanswered) indicates the pertinence of Smith's point about the ethical base on which capi-talism needs to rest. To return to another of Chapter 2's core political economy insights, economies and market activity are always embedded in a social context. Comparative analy-sis can reveal the variation of the ethical norms of capitalism in different national contexts. For example, Japanese labour market norms (about security and duration of employment) and norms regarding the nature of the firm and the rights of workers within it differ pro-foundly from those in the UK. These institutional differences can be traced back to the ethi-cal base on which each capitalism rests. To capture these aspects, we need to extend our gaze beyond marginalism's focus on utility maximization and look at shared normative values (such as trust, obligation or reciprocity), and how institutions sustain them, to get at how capitalism really works (Streeck 2010: 16).

In the rest of this chapter we focus on VoC and comparative capitalisms debates within CPE as a means to illustrate and explore the institutional dimensions of capitalism and their differentiation. Comparative capitalisms is also one of the most vibrant sub-fields within CPE, and it is in relation to this substantive area that many broader issues in institutionalist political economy analysis have been brought into sharper focus in recent times.

INSTITUTIONALISMS, PATH DEPENDENCY AND COMPARATIVE CAPITALISMS

Institutionalist analysis in political science and political economy takes a variety of forms. In this section we will see how contemporary comparative capitalisms analysis draws inspiration from two dominant strands of institutional analysis – 'historical institutionalism' in political science and institutional economics. Historical institutionalism constitutes the often implicit default methodological position or starting point for analysis in interpretive political science. At its most elemental, historical institutionalism highlights how historically developed institutions matter politically and have enduring effects (see Peters 1999: 19, 63–77; Fioretos 2011; Fioretos et al. 2016).

Perhaps the most important concept and theme for historical institutionalist analysis is path dependency (Pierson 2000; Fioretos et al. 2016). This underscores how initial choices early in the history of any policy field or system have an enduring impact as they shape both the strategies and goals pursued by political actors (Thelen and Steinmo 1992: 8; Goodin 1996). Policy choices are dependent upon an initial path that has been adopted. A metaphor often used is the 'branching tree' view of history (Levi 1997: 28; Pierson 2000: 252–3). So, when analysing policy choices at any given moment, historical institutionalists highlight the import of analysing established political traditions and prior policy practices and decisions. These become institutionalized in ways which will, they argue, limit the conditions of possibility for current policy evolution (see e.g. Hall 1986).

While economics on the whole has not been very focused on institutions, there are (and have always been) honourable exceptions to that rule. The 'new institutional economics' of Douglass North, Oliver Williamson and others (Williamson 1985; Hodgson 1988; North 1990) are shining examples from which CPE institutional analysis takes inspiration in thinking about individuals' preferences and behaviour. This uses economics-based modes of analysis and reasoning to explore and explain individuals and their behaviour within institutional settings. Williamson deploys neo-classical economic conceptions of the individual rationalities at play within the institutions, focusing on transaction costs (e.g. within firms), and sees institutions as efficient solutions to economic co-ordination problems (1985). This generates insights into institutional creation, reproduction and development.

The pioneering analysis of Douglass North (1990) discussed in Chapter 1 is important here in building a bridge between institutional economics and political science. North's basic argument is built on an underlying assumption, similar to that outlined earlier in this chapter, that market activities necessarily rest upon non-market arrangements. The institutional relations which surround economic activity have evolved to form mutually reinforcing ensembles, reducing uncertainty and delivering positive feedback effects. North argues that the reduced uncertainties this 'web' or 'matrix' of institutions delivers generate 'massive increasing returns' (ibid.: 95; see also Pierson 2004: 22–30). These dynamics serve to reinforce particular institutional configurations of capitalism, because efficiency gains from particular interconnected sets of capitalist institutions accumulate and augment. In this way North turned some orthodox economics assumptions on their head, positing not the diminishing returns familiar since marginalism, but rather *increasing* returns accruing from path dependency. This can explain both why some combinations of capitalist institutions can facilitate stronger economic growth than others, and why those institutional matrices endure. The 'dynamics of self-reinforcing or positive feedback processes' identified by North constitute the causal mechanisms at play within capitalist path dependency, and 'once a particular path gets established ... self-reinforcing processes make reversals very difficult' (Pierson 2004: 10; Fioretos et al. 2016).

Institutional path dependency and positive feedback effects are important because they 'generate branching patterns of historical development' (Pierson 2004: 21). There remain multiple possible outcomes from a given starting point, but the evolution of capitalism is far from open-ended because early decisions limit subsequent options (Arthur 1989; Perraton and Clift 2004: 197; Pierson 2004). Policy evolutions and political economic changes can and do occur, but developments are constrained by the initial conditions, the formative period of the institution and histories of adjustment (Peters 1999: 65; Fioretos et al. 2016). These path-dependent tendencies are powerful because they are found in a wide array of different embedded institutional arrangements, as noted above.

It is important to understand path dependency in ways that are non-deterministic (Fligstein 1996; Lehmbruch 2001; Campbell 2004: 71, 2011: 226). Social processes do not proceed inexorably along 'tram tracks'. Often, 'path dependency is sustained by a dominant political coalition successfully fending off all attempts by minorities to alter the political course' (Peters et al. 2005: 1278; Eisner 2011: chs 1, 2). This is perhaps what Johnson had in mind when coining the term 'path contingency' (Johnson 2001; see also Djelic 2010; Thelen 2010: 54). Comparative 'process-tracing' analysis of evolving capitalist institutions in different countries can help to reveal the key 'branching' moments, the configurations of institutions they have given rise to, and the contested politics surrounding their reproduction (see Chapters 8–12).

Perhaps the most salient example of path dependency in CPE is the evolution of particular capitalisms along institutionally framed paths. Most contemporary CPE work on comparative capitalisms implicitly or explicitly builds on the logic of institutional path dependency. Hall and Soskice's VoC (2001) takes direct inspiration from the concepts of feedback effects, increasing returns and path dependency theorized by North and others. VoC has come to dominate the field and has contributed to a wider revival of interest in CPE as an undertaking since the early 2000s.

Hall and Soskice's reinvigoration of comparative capitalisms analysis has combined many insights of historical institutionalism with some from institutional economics to explain capitalist diversity and trajectories of continuity and change within national capitalisms. A variety of institutional co-ordinating mechanisms are identified, including legal frameworks, education and training systems and industrial relations systems, as well as rules or codes of conduct regarding labour relations or corporate governance. The institutionalization of co-ordinating mechanisms also occurs through networks and associations such as trade unions and employers' organizations. Nationally differentiated but enduring configurations of capitalist organization and the attendant institutional infrastructure are conceived, in broad terms, as meta-examples of path dependency, since the institutional infrastructure will tend to guide evolution along a particular path.

These institutions evolved in the particular historical, social and political conditions of capitalist market development that prevailed in Western Europe and North America in the 19th and 20th centuries. It was these cases that VoC was developed to explain. It may be that the institutional context of the emerging dominant economic powers of the 21st century – the BRICS – is so different (Gough and Therborn 2010) that VoC has only 'limited portability' (Pierson 2004) to explain developments in these economies. It is certainly the case that the VoC framework has not been so widely applied outside the long-established advanced economies (although see e.g. Becker 2013; Bohle 2018; Feldmann 2019; Kiran 2018; Nolke 2010; Ebenau 2012; Schneider 2009; Vasileva-Dienes and Schmidt 2019).

Hall and Soskice's OECD-centric framework generated a typology of modern capitalism and an influential argument about capitalist evolution and its trajectory (2001). They identified two central ideal-typical institutional forms that capitalism could take. First, there are co-ordinated market economies (CMEs; such as Germany or Japan) that are reliant on a variety of non-market-based co-ordinating mechanisms and networks such as social partnerships between unions and employers' associations, and that are characterized by long-term trust-based relationships within firms and between economic actors. Second, there are liberal market economies (LMEs; such as the US or the UK), which are reliant primarily on markets and market mechanisms for co-ordination, and which emphasize shorter-term contractual relations. These sets of institutional interactions and relationships underpin Hall and Soskice's fundamental 'market' versus 'non-market' co-ordination pathologies of posited institutional ensembles – the liberal and co-ordinated market economy types. Each type of capitalism is institutionalized in different ways in different national settings (see Chapters 7 and 8).

Path dependency and feedback effects, then, are crucial mechanisms within the VoC schema which deliver Hall and Soskice's central concept – 'comparative institutional advantage' (2001). The posited 'comparative institutional advantages' that Hall and Soskice identify are assumed to flow for economies organized along either CME or LME lines. The VoC approach involves assessing the degree of coherence of any given institutional configuration of capitalism (Hall and Gingerich 2009), identifying its comparative institutional advantages, and assessing its proximity to either ideal-typical position (see pp. 178–83). More generally, comparative capitalisms scholars, in the VoC tradition and outside it, have used concepts of positive feedback and increasing returns to explain institutional reproduction (North 1990; Pierson 2004; Deeg 2005).

The remainder of our engagement with institutionalist political economy analysis is organized around the theme of comparative capitalisms and VoC, because much recent critique of institutionalist analysis in political economy has cropped up within and in relation to VoC debates. Many of the questions raised about VoC are often not specific to it. They are mostly broader concerns faced by most or all institutional analysis in political economy. We use VoC to illustrate issues and conundrums that all institutionalist comparative political economy faces, and consider ways these problems or shortcomings can be addressed (Table 6.1).

Table 6.1   Varieties of institutionalist analysis in political economy

	Rational choice institutionalism	*Historical institutionalism*	*Constructivist institutionalism*
Object of analysis	Rational behaviour	Historical structures	Ideas, social norms, social facts
Micro-foundations	*Homo economicus*	Bounded rationality	Situated, reflective actors
Logic	Instrumental rationality	Path dependency	Intersubjective meanings; logic of appropriateness; discursive construction
Scope of institutions	Limited – reducing transaction costs	Expansive – formal and informal	Expansive – ideational as well as physical
Conception of society	Atomistic	Institutionally mediated	Ideationally, culturally conditioned

INDIVIDUALS AND THE INSTITUTIONAL AND SOCIAL CONTEXT: DETERMINIST TEMPTATIONS

In thinking through how and why particular paths are selected, and how development of that path is reproduced, we need to pay close attention to one of the central themes of this chapter, namely the relationship between the individual, his or her institutional context, and the wider social order. The assumptions made about these connections and relationships can generate some markedly different accounts and explanations. Put differently, the micro-foundations of institutional analyses vary. We can illustrate this if we consider briefly the rational choice approach (see Chapter 5) which, along with institutional economics and historical institutionalism, has supplied some of the building blocks for VoC's explanation of the institutions of capitalism.

There are sometimes close affinities, in terms of how it sees behaviours as being shaped and reproduced, between some work in the VoC paradigm and rational choice political science (for critiques, see Crouch 2005a, 2005b; Hay 2005; Jackson and Deeg 2008). VoC explains the reproduction and evolution of a given capitalism in terms of rationalist assumptions about how economic actors will behave and respond to their institutional and economic environment. Hall and Soskice talk about how national patterns of political economic specialization should reflect 'rational responses' (2001: 41) to the institutional frameworks they set out. This helps to impart coherence to the typological schema generated by VoC which can be used to categorize different kinds of economies. Levy identifies 'borrowings from game theory' within VoC's 'formalistic' approach to the CPE of capitalism (2006a: 23). The 'reading off' of actors' or even entire systems' responses to sets of institutional conditions according to posited rational pathologies is an element of the scaffolding of VoC.

However, not all are so comfortable with these rationalist micro-foundations as the best way of thinking about individuals, institutions and their relationships with the wider social and economic order. A particular concern in the comparative analysis of the political economy of capitalist institutions is the positing of a singular, uniform notion of economic rationality. This rather flies in the face of one of the core insights of political economy as outlined in Chapter 2 – that capitalist market relations are always embedded in specific social contexts. It follows from this that economic understandings and norms – indeed conceptions of economic rationality itself – may be shaped over time by distinct social contexts, cultures, histories, state traditions and so forth.

Assuming uniformity of rational response risks overlooking how, within national capitalisms, with distinctive histories, trajectories and institutional contexts, different kinds of approaches to economic behaviour might develop over time. From a CPE perspective, this variety in approaches to economic action and market relations is one of the central things to be explored and explained. In assuming it away so readily, rationalist comparative capitalisms analysis may be missing a trick. Indeed, one of the great merits of the comparative analysis of capitalism is the ability of such work to reveal nationally differentiated understandings, approaches and practices and their institutionalization. So, rather than positing a single rationality, it makes sense to admit the possibility of multiple traditions of economic thought and of anticipated patterns of 'economic rationality' flowing from them.

While the default VoC position is a fairly narrow understanding of economic rationality (Hay 2005; Jackson and Deeg 2008), a more differentiated conception of economic rationality is not incompatible with VoC. German and Japanese models of capitalism have been analysed in terms of distinctive 'discourses of embedded capitalism' (Lehmbruch 2001), French understandings of the market have been used to explain its model of capitalism (Schmidt 1996; Clift 2012), and Japanese social norms have explained the political economy of its limited labour market restructuring (Vogel 2005, 2006). The market, then, is 'not a neutral norm but a political and social construct' (Jabko 2006: 33, 34). Jabko discerns 'many different meanings of the market' (2006: 32) and highlights differentiated social construc- tions of 'the market' and their implications. The idea of 'building a market' can be reconciled to different political economic visions, including 'a free market economy' and 'a socially ori- ented market economy' (2006: 26–7). If we accept this 'broader conception of market rationality' (Jabko 2006: 40), we can understand how varied understandings of economic rationality can be constructed. Each conception of the market should be interpreted in its 'given meaning context' (Schmidt 2008: 314). The market can, after all, be shaped in differ- ent national contexts by understandings of state capacities and traditions of political eco- nomic interventionism (Schmidt 2009).

Adopting a more differentiated approach to economic rationalities constitutes a step in the right direction, presenting a more nuanced analysis. Nevertheless, even once armed with this more nuanced and differentiated view of capitalism and the individuals who ani- mate it, analysis can still fall prey to a deterministic view of individuals within institutional and social contexts.

Institutionalist analysis, interested in the constitutive nature of institutions (Farrell and Newman 2010), inevitably highlights and underscores the constraining effects of institu- tions. Yet the strictures of these constraining effects can be such that the room to manoeu- vre of agents within the institutions is lost from sight. Where institutions and actor behaviour are very closely related, it can seem as though there is little or no space for 'play' between them (Streeck and Thelen 2005: 11). Jackson and Deeg note that VoC tends to 'emphasize rational, strategic behavior within a set of fixed institutions' (2008: 688). This is a deterministic view of the relationship between institutional context and individual action, wherein actors are drones, unable to (re)interpret their institutional environment. As I dem- onstrate in a later section, there are more satisfactory alternative approaches (see also Campbell 1998; Seabrooke 2007; Schmidt 2008).

THE FUNCTIONALIST TEMPTATION AND INSTITUTIONAL COMPLEMENTARITY

Another issue raised by VoC's account relates less to the individuals, and more to the institu- tions and their social and economic context. In the VoC account, which hinges on 'compara- tive institutional advantage', institutions seem to be 'called forth' by the systemic demands of the capitalist economy to perform functions needed to sustain the system. This is a ten- dency in explanation critiqued as 'functionalism' within the social sciences (see Crouch 2005b: 61–8). Watson detects a 'latent functionalism' in VoC wherein 'political choice to construct social institutions in one way, thus foregoing all possible alternatives, appears to be an epiphenomenon of a more essential economic logic' (2003: 232; see also Blyth 2003; Radice 2004; Deeg 2005).

To illustrate this functionalist tendency, one strand of comparative capitalisms analysis of the relation between institutions and economic performance focuses on 'institutional complementarities' and the nature of the interconnections between institutions (see Deeg 2005; Crouch 2005b). Such a focus recognizes the importance of not treating each institution in isolation, but as part of a complex whole (Gamble et al. 2000: 2; Streeck 2009, 2010). The notion of institutional complementarities rests on North's ideas about increasing returns and posits particular beneficial qualities of certain interrelationships between institutions.

Within the influential VoC approach, 'two institutions can be said to be complementary if the presence (or efficiency) of one increases the returns from (or efficiency of) the other' (Hall and Soskice 2001: 17). These posited interrelationships are complemented, within VoC analysis, by an asserted trend: 'nations with a particular type of coordination in one sphere of the economy should tend to develop complementary practices in other spheres as well' (ibid.: 18). In this way, interconnections between the labour market, the financial market and the firm form parts of a jigsaw. This is then connected to a (disputed) claimed empirical relationship – the more coherent the institutional mix, the more efficient and successful the economy – so that purer breeds of capitalism outperform institutional mongrels (Hall and Gingerich 2009; Thelen 2010; for a critique, see Crouch 2005a, 2005b; Kenworthy 2006).

Germany and Japan are widely recognized as exhibiting institutional complementarities which have at various times been identified as sources of their economic successes. Typical co-ordinated market economy institutional complementarities, for example, include extensive in-firm training, developing the 'human capital' and skills of the workforce, and its dovetailing within regulated labour markets where hiring and firing are relatively difficult. In a labour market which makes 'poaching' of skilled workers by competitors difficult, in-firm training and 'upskilling' the workforce operate particularly successfully. This enhancing of human capital is good for the firm, the employees, the economy and society as a whole. Firms and employers have more incentives to invest in it and can anticipate that their firm will reap the rewards in terms of increased productivity or the potential to move into higher value-added commodity production. Each aspect is sustained by an institutional infrastructure within the labour market and the education system.

At a more micro level, there is also a particular nexus of institutions *within the firm*, where corporate governance practices fit together with the other aspects of the political economic system (see pp. 200–3). In contexts where capitalism is co-ordinated via long-term trust-based relationships, internal corporate governance structures tend to induce loyalty and empower the workers through representation on the board – prioritizing 'voice' over 'exit' (Hirschman 1970). The financing of firms tends to operate through long-term relations with regional or local banks, thus remaining at arm's length from financial markets, which enables firms to prioritize long-term firm strategy over considerations of short-term profit and shareholder value (boosting dividends). VoC's 'institutional complementarities' thus describe how parts of the matrix of economic institutions within a political economy dovetail together and how efficiency gains accrue from these felicitous interconnections and symbiotic, synergistic interrelationships (see North 1990; Pierson 2004). However, as we will discuss further in Chapters 9 and 10, the real story of the development and evolution of capitalist institutions is a much more *political* process than this focus on economic efficiency suggests.

When thinking about how and why capitalist structuring takes particular paths, there is a danger of post hoc rationalization in reading the VoC argument, and its functionalist undertones, back into the historical development of particular configurations of capitalist institutions. Functionalist arguments that root an institutional selection process in efficiency criteria, which in VoC's case involves the identification of 'comparative institutional advantage', are problematic. We must be careful not to ascribe to institutional innovators the kinds of perfect information which neo-classical economics unrealistically ascribes to *homo economicus*, and compound the problem by adding the foresight of decades into the future to the list of assumed mental powers supposedly possessed by the individuals who create and animate institutions. This exposes a problem for VoC analysis, what Watson calls its 'chronological contradiction' (2003: 232).

There is a danger of problematically assuming perfect prescience and foresight on the part of actors about what courses of action, and which combinations of institutions, will prove most economically advantageous and functionally efficient within a given system. Such an account also assumes their ability to co-ordinate and orchestrate the development of national institutions according to their economically efficient blueprint (for a critique, see Clift 2020). The questions which functionalist thinking evades, but which really need to be central to comparative research on the institutions of capitalism, are why and how these particular institutional configurations prevail. How did these arrangements withstand the myriad influences, constraints, contingencies and obstacles of the highly complex social and political context within which these institutions were established and developed over decades, indeed centuries? We should not assume that it was ever thus, nor necessarily thus. Nor indeed is it safe to assume that it became thus *because of* economic efficiency concerns or criteria. As we will see in Chapters 9 and 10, it is important to bring the politics back in when thinking about the selection, development and reinforcement of economic institutions. Politics and power relations play fundamentally important roles, as do accident and unintended consequence.

Again, the comparative element – the central quality and distinctive offering of CPE – can swiftly dispel some of the above functionalist misconceptions. Gregory Jackson's historical discussion of the origins of the Japanese and German models indicates that the original motivations of foundational actors were *not* primarily rooted in any economic logic or a desire to impose efficient economic institutions. In the German case, political expediency (managing and delaying demands for democratization among the working class under the Weimar Republic) was key. Jackson identifies a similar story within the roots of Japanese capitalism (Jackson 2001). Yet each has been heralded at various points in the later 20th century as a highly desirable, efficient and perhaps even optimal mode of capitalist organization (Kamata 1983; Hutton 1994; Gamble et al. 1997).

Jackson's account of the evolution of the economic institutions, institutional complementarities and corporate governance in Japan and Germany details how their coherence was 'not inevitable and resulted from an unintended fit' (2001: 126). That such unintended fits and happy accidents can and do occur does not, of course, hole VoC below the waterline. What this highlights, however, is how such accounts leave some very important questions unanswered, or at best under-answered. How, for example, do institutional innovators know that these institutional configurations, with these particular interrelationships, are going to be efficient? At the very least, it is surely difficult to confirm they were established because of mooted expected future efficiency.

What really needs explaining, but what tends to be simply assumed within functionalist accounts, is how economically efficient institutions 'win out'. To address this issue, we need to bring the politics back in, for institutional survival will probably be a result of political skirmishing. If and when congruence between institutional elements emerges, we should not assume as a historical inevitability that some kind of political economic glue will spring forth to cement it in perpetuity. As Wolfgang Streeck argues of modern Germany and Japan, concerning their histories, 'the two national models of embedded capitalism had to be continuously established, restored, redefined, and defended against all sorts of disorganising forces' (2001: 30–1, 2009, 2010).

The post hoc rationalizations and functionalist pitfalls are not an issue only for VoC, but for all institutionalist analysis in political economy. Nor are they pitfalls that all VoC analysis necessarily falls prey to. Contextualized understanding and analysis of how the politics of capitalist institutional development has played out help to counter these tendencies. So too does a nuanced understanding of the relationship between individual actors and institutional contexts. In the next section, we will see how relaxing some orthodox economic assumptions can facilitate such an understanding.

INSTITUTIONAL ANALYSIS AND POLITICAL ECONOMIC CHANGE

We have identified in this book from a number of theoretical perspectives how a dynamic notion of capitalist evolution underpins much of the best writing about capitalisms from the classical political economy scholars onwards (Smith, Marx, Polanyi, Hayek and List). It follows that this dynamism should also be incorporated into CPE analysis of institutions. Institutional change, Streeck contends, 'should be regarded not as a subject of its own, but as a constitutive feature of any social formation' (2009: 1, 2011: 5; see also Campbell 2010; Thelen 2010). Change is endogenous and integral to social orders.

Yet the explanation of change is a perennial tricky issue for institutionalist analysis. As Pierson notes, historical institutionalism has always been more focused on the institutional rather than the historical dimension, 'examining the impact of relatively fixed institutional features of the political landscape' (Pierson 2004: 8). The standard approach to change within historical institutionalism is known as 'punctuated equilibrium', a terminology which derives from evolution biology. This conveys how 'periods of comparatively modest institutional change are interrupted by more rapid and intense moments of transformation' (Hay 2002: 156, 161–3). This discontinuous view of time describes a pattern of change where long periods of relative stability are interrupted by brief flurries of fairly dramatic change. Change, then, is concentrated within turning points that are episodic and dramatic (Krasner 1984: 234). As a way of understanding political time, punctuated equilibrium is much deployed in historical institutionalism (Skocpol and Ikenberry 1983; Thelen and Steinmo 1992; Pierson 1996).

Yet punctuated equilibrium obviously does not exhaust the possibilities of how change might play out. In the realms of comparative capitalisms the default assumption of relative stasis may be problematic because the institutions of capitalism should be analysed 'as elements of the larger social system to which they belong', which is not a 'static structure' but a 'dynamic process' (Streeck 2009: 1). VoC's understanding of 'institutional reinforcement' involves 'path dependent change in line with certain logics' (Hancké et al. 2007: 11), though Blyth argues that 'the concepts of institutional complementarity, feedback, increasing returns and the like all suggest a rather static and indeed functionalist picture' (2003: 219; see also Crouch 2005a: 444; Hay 2005; Jackson and Deeg 2008). Certainly, some institutionalist CPE analysis has difficulty accounting for change, and could engage more systematically with it.

In this section and the next I set out evolutions in institutionalist CPE which counter these tendencies by emphasizing the comparative appreciation of particular historically contingent trajectories of capitalist development and by highlighting the contested politics of institutional reproduction which is rooted in multiple possible rationalities. This dynamic approach is inspired by leading CPE scholars including Wolfgang Streeck, Gregory Jackson, Kathleen Thelen, Vivien Schmidt and John Campbell. While drawing on historical institutionalism, this approach recaptures some of the spirit of classical political economy. The key analytical move is a reconsideration of the relationship between individual institutional orders and the wider social context. The method adopted in pursuit of this reconsideration is *comparative* analysis of capitalist institutional development and change.

HISTORICAL INSTITUTIONALISM REVISITED: IDEATIONAL INSTITUTIONALISM

Calls to refine our understanding of change, and to use the tools of CPE analysis to do so, have been taken up in a book edited by Wolfgang Streeck and Kathleen Thelen entitled *Beyond Continuity* (2005). With the above critiques ringing in their ears, the ideationally attuned reworking of historical institutionalism focused on explaining processes of change. I will illustrate the benefits of this kind of institutionalist political economy analysis by exploring arguments about convergence which abound within discussions of contemporary capitalist change and globalization.

Streeck and Thelen seek to establish 'an empirically grounded typology of institutional change that does justice to the complexity and versatility of the subject' (ibid.: 1). The frustration with some work in comparative capitalisms, such as much VoC analysis, is that 'many arguments in support of the idea of distinctive and stable national models lack the analytical tools necessary to capture the changes that are indisputably going on in these countries' (ibid.). They identify a 'conservative bias' in much CPE literature on comparative capitalisms, whereby the highly sophisticated frameworks for the analysis of continuity and stability are not matched by sophisticated accounts of frameworks for the analysis of *change* and discontinuity (ibid.: 1, 16–18).

Lurking beneath standard comparative capitalisms analysis they detect an exaggerated 'punctuated equilibrium' model. Yet this conception risks overstating both the degree of stasis (assumed to be the prevailing norm) and the scale of change (very rare but dramatic). Furthermore, it assumes this to be *the* way in which institutional change occurs – to the exclusion of all other patterns of change. Critics have noted how the punctuated equilibrium framework can overstate change, overlook continuities and overrate the efficiency of punctuated change (Clift 2020). Escaping dichotomous opposition between 'incremental change supporting institutional continuity through reproductive adaptation' and 'disruptive change causing institutional break-down', Streeck and Thelen alert us to the possibility of change that is both 'incremental and transformative' (2005: 8, 2).

Critical junctures (radical or dramatic shifts in the logic, nature and functioning of political economic institutions), while exciting and revealing, do not exhaust the possibilities of types of institutional change. Furthermore, 'external shocks' or exogenous factors may not be the 'smoking gun' causing the change. Change may originate *from within* (see Carstensen 2011a, 2011b), as Richard Deeg argues of the transformation of the German financial system (see pp. 218–21). Using the comparative method both diachronically (analysing the same case at two points in time) and synchronically (analysing the processes of change within two or more different cases), this broader menu of types in institutional change can be revealed, as can the politics underpinning the dynamics of such change. Focusing on 'frequently overlooked mechanisms and modes of change', *Beyond Continuity* sets out 'an empirical inventory and analytical typology of modes of *gradual transformative change* of modern political-economic institutions' (Streeck and Thelen 2005: 2). For Streeck and Thelen, the story of contemporary capitalism and its liberalization is one of 'incremental processes of change' which are causing 'gradual institutional transformations that add up to major historical discontinuities' (ibid.: 8).

In this contingent, open-ended account, institutional reproduction is best understood as 'a dynamic political process' (ibid. 2005: 6; Thelen 2010; Campbell 2010). Political institutions are 'not only periodically contested; they are the object of ongoing skirmishing' (Streeck and Thelen 2005: 19; Pierson 2004: ch. 4). Historical institutionalist analysis has long been attuned to the significance of temporality and sequence, and their systematic incorporation into the analysis of the establishment and evolution of institutional orders (Pierson 2004; Streeck 2009). This attention to 'theorizing the conditions under which temporal processes matter' and exploring 'how historical processes shape political outcomes' (Fioretos 2011: 369) is crucial to grasping the location of this political skirmishing and what is at stake within it. This helps us establish *where* change is most likely within a political economic order at any given time, and why there.

Institutions are on the whole not chosen, and rarely built from scratch. Rather, they evolve as 'different actors with different interests build layers taking as their starting point not a blank canvas, but existing arrangements'. This is because 'attempts at institutional redesign have been carried out against a backdrop of a set of past practices, which brings with it its own peculiar set of constraints and possibilities' (Goodin 1996: 30). Hence at any one time, only a few areas can be altered. That said, Thelen argues that the static nature of institutionalist analysis can be overstated. While path dependence constrains the range of options, there is a good deal 'up for grabs', amenable to contingent processes of change. Furthermore, the importance of positive returns and feedback effects (which might tend to 'lock in' existing institutional configurations) can be overstated (Thelen 2004: 27–30).

One means to escape the overstating of lock-in and stasis is to rethink the individuals who give life to the institutions under scrutiny: 'the practical enactment of an institution is as much part of its reality as its formal structure' (Streeck and Thelen 2005: 18). Thus institutions are understood in non-deterministic terms, recognizing the enactment of rules by creative agents whose interpretation of the 'rule' or institution they are giving life to imparts their agential input into the structure. As Streeck and Thelen put it, 'the enactment of a social rule is never perfect', partly because 'the meaning of a rule is never self-evident and always subject to and in need of interpretation' (ibid.: 14). If the agents within institutions are conceived as reflexive actors, then it becomes possible to appreciate that 'what an institution "really means" must *and therefore can* be continuously re-invented by actors' (Streeck 2010: 12).

This more nuanced and complex conception of institutions admits a good deal more 'play' between institutions and behaviour, between institutions and individual actors (see Streeck and Thelen 2005: 11; Crouch 2005b: 19), as well as a good deal more indeterminacy in trajectories of change. Actors are not slaves to their institutional context or bearers of institutional logics following pre-programmed scripts, but are autonomous reflective actors able to reinterpret and recreate their environment (Weber 1978 [1922]; Seabrooke 2007). The 'ideational turn' in political economy in recent times, increasingly appreciative of the multiple rationalities associated with different institutions and contexts, leads to a similar focus on meaning contexts and cognitive frameworks and processes (see e.g. Campbell 1998; Woll 2008; Schmidt 2008; Clift 2012). Variously termed 'discursive' (Schmidt 2008), 'constructivist' (Hay 2009, 2016; Clift 2018) or 'ideational' institutionalism, this sees actors as reflective, thinking actors 'whose ideas, discourse, and actions ordinarily make sense (and can be made sense of) within a given meaning context' (Schmidt 2009: 532–3).

In terms of tools of analysis which can help to bring these insights to life and enable researchers to operationalize them in their analysis, Campbell has developed two useful concepts. He deploys the notions of 'translation' and 'bricolage' in analysing institutional change within contemporary capitalism, and these illustrate how this more reflexive approach to individuals and agency within institutional analysis can enhance its ability to explain change. Translation involves 'the combination of locally available principles and practices with new ones originating elsewhere', whereas bricolage is a process 'whereby actors recombine locally available institutional principles and practices in ways that yield ... path dependent evolutionary change' (Campbell 2004: 65). Campbell argues that actors 'craft new institutional solutions' through recombinative bricolage 'whereby new institutions differ from but resemble old ones' (ibid.: 69). This focus on creative processes serves to 'infuse our understanding of path dependence with a greater sense of agency' (ibid.: 71). These are, after all, political choices, and certain recombinations win out over alternative possibilities. We will see applications of these concepts in relation to comparative capitalisms, financial systems and welfare states in Chapters 9, 10 and 11.

The conception of actors and their relationship with the institutional and social context underpinning these discursively and ideationally attuned accounts seeks to avoid what Schmidt terms the 'inevitability' of standard rational choice institutionalist analysis and the inexorability of historical institutionalist analysis (2009: 540). Once the actors who animate institutions are conceived in these active, creative, reflective terms, it becomes easier to escape a static conception of the social realm. At the same time, though, the parameters of change are very likely to be delimited by the established institutions which frame, contain and reproduce capitalist social relations (Campbell 2004: 28–9). The cross-national comparative analysis of such processes demonstrates their contingent quality and how they play out differently in diverse national institutional and ideational contexts. Comparative analysis has the distinct contribution of unearthing nationally differentiated ideational conditions and how these shape processes of capitalist development.

INSTITUTIONALISM AND CAPITALIST CONVERGENCE

We will round off this consideration of institutionalist CPE by looking at an influential argument within the comparative capitalisms debate – the notion of capitalist convergence among the advanced economies (Strange 1997; Cerny 1997a, 1997b; Rajan and Zingales 2003; Eichengreen 2008). Many convergence theories tend to have their roots in a particular strand of IPE which remains largely blind to the differentiated appreciation of particular contingent national trajectories of change. This style of analysis tends to present the free mobility of capital globally as an immanent reality. The convergence argument goes that, as liberalization proceeds, and more and more aspects of economic life, sectors and markets become more opened up to international competitive pressures, the space for national particularities shrinks. This is a parsimonious, simplistic and bold account. The convergence thesis has its roots in a textbook neo-classical economic model and the 'logic of no alternative' argument. These linear interpretations equate economic globalization's effects with global economic convergence (McGrew 2011). This idea of a *telos* at work inducing capitalism to converge towards an LME end point within a liberal international order characterized by ever freer markets looks less compelling in the wake of the backlash against international liberalism and globalism, and the revival of economic nationalism. Trump, for example, has questioned the foundations of the liberal international order, and placed more impediments in the way of freer markets and global flows, for example by pursuing beggarthy-neighbour trade policies. Meanwhile, Britain's departure from the EU augurs the erection of significant new barriers and frictions to trade and economic flows (see e.g. Clift and McDaniel 2019).

The convergence view assumes *a priori* the innate superiority – in economic terms – of the purest possible form of market relations. It then superimposes an abstract model of a perfectly competitive market economy on real existing economies as *if it were* an account of their actual properties. Assumptions about the efficient operation of markets provide the posited economic logic behind the convergence dynamic, delivering the theoretical (and indeed ideological) bulwark for the convergence thesis. These assumptions deliver the micro-foundational mechanisms which will induce change in this more efficient direction and which are relied upon in lieu of a careful specification of the causal mechanisms involved in inducing change along more LME lines. The core insights of political economy (see Chapter 2) indicate significant limits to the convergence thesis. Capitalism is embedded in distinct social contexts, and sustained by the institutional infrastructures discussed in this chapter. The logical corollary of this is not a monoculture, but a variegated world of different capitalisms. Furthermore, the real world of market economies is a far cry from the textbook neo-classical economics model that underpins convergence theorizing.

Though an arresting theory, it has understandably attracted much criticism, both empirically and theoretically (Drezner 2007). Empirically, a wealth of studies carried out over recent decades continues to point to significant enduring 'home bias' in investment flows, as well as limits of flows measured, and the lack of profit equalization between markets (Feldstein and Horioka 1980; Epstein and Gintis 1995; Epstein 1996; Watson 1999; Sinclair 2001: 96). Thus, the real world of international finance remains a more parochial place than the textbook globalized financial market.

From our reformulated historical institutionalist perspective, a number of theoretical critiques of convergence stand out. At the institutional level, social embeddedness explains how 'common pressures may be refracted through different sets of institutions, leading to different sorts of problems and calling forth distinct solutions' (Jackson and Deeg 2008: 683; see also Hay 2004a). Even where transnational tendencies towards 'institutional isomorphism' (the reproduction of similar institutions, policies or paradigms in different locations) are identified (DiMaggio and Powell 1983), we would anticipate the institutional and ideational terrain to generate national differentiation. CPE flags up how flawed convergence assumptions are by demonstrating how market relations play out differently in different national historical contexts.

Mindful of the Polanyian insights about how markets require institutional and regulatory framing, Steven Vogel has analysed international processes of liberalization since the

1980s in terms of 'freer markets, more rules' (1996). This neo-liberal shift towards market liberalization has often been interpreted as convergence. Yet, as Campbell pointed out, the 'translation of the neoliberal model into local institutional practice resulted in much diversity across countries in the character of regulatory reform' (Campbell 2004: 164). Regulatory reform 'combined with long standing institutional traditions' generated 'new styles of regulation, often with more, not fewer, rules, and new regulatory capacities that varied substantially across countries' (ibid.: 165). For example, China's financial system has undergone substantial reform since the late 1970s, introducing market mechanisms to supplant earlier state direction. Coupled with this have been internationalization and privatization. However, it remains a political economy *very* unlike the LME archetypes in terms of the dynamics of its financial system (Breslin 2014; Gruin 2013, 2019).

The economic processes such as liberalization which are the driving force behind mooted convergence do not paint themselves onto a blank institutional canvas, but onto a dense web of interrelated institutions. In-depth comparative cross-national process-tracing analysis of regulatory reform processes reveals the variations in outcomes that these varied institutional contexts give rise to (see Levy 2006a; Cioffi 2006; Howell 2006). Even common international processes and trends – such as trade liberalization or financial market deregulation – are refracted through and mediated by these matrices of institutions, meaning that the outcomes follow distinctive paths. Thinking along similar lines, Colin Hay (2004a, 2005, 2016) has highlighted the manifold institutional and ideational mediations between international economic forces and domestic political economy within contemporary capitalism. He urges an unpacking of these mediations of exogenous economic change by disaggregating the notion of convergence into inputs, paradigms, policies, legitimatory rhetorics, outcomes and processes. Given the diversity of institutional arrangements framing markets across national economies, which earlier CPE masterpieces demonstrated (Shonfield 1965; Zysman 1983; Hall 1986; Gourevitch 1986; Schmidt 2002), we would therefore expect to see – and do indeed see – that specific configurations of institutions and markets mediate and channel change and adjustment in distinctive directions, leading to more variation than convergence (see Macartney 2011; Clift and McDaniel 2019).

The sophisticated account of institutions set out in this chapter involves thinking about the agents who animate institutions as reflexive, thinking actors. The comparative analysis of political economy is especially well disposed to explain the diversity of responses to similar circumstances. There are two elements to this. Firstly, we unearth important social phenomena that intervene 'between' actors and material and institutional drivers, and open up space for 'play', which tells against reading off responses *a priori*. Secondly, we note the implications of thinking about institutions as politically contested in their creation and reproduction. In these ways, we can restore contingency and also agency to explanations in political economy.

Convergence theories both deem a single mode of capitalist organization to be the most efficient and then assume that the 'fact' of its mooted superior efficiency will be sufficient to 'make it so'. Both elements are deeply problematic and empirically at odds with the findings from the comparative analysis of the actual development of capitalist economies. They also fly in the face of recent and not so recent insights about institutions and capitalism that tell against expectations of convergence in response to common exogenous developments (Hodgson 1999: ch. 6; Thatcher 2007; Jackson and Deeg 2008). 'Bricolage' and 'translation' are much more likely outcomes than convergence (Campbell 2004). For Campbell, Hay and others, the space for 'play' between institutions and actors is recognized at every turn, at

which point 'the likelihood of common pressures, associated, for example, with globalization, driving processes of convergence even in institutionally isomorphic political and economic systems recedes' (Hay 2004a: 246).

CONCLUSION: INSTITUTIONS AND CAPITALISM

Institutions are constitutive of markets and, within each economy, markets are sustained,
contained and reproduced through institutions. Institutions are thus fundamental to capitalism's workings, and each political economy, even the most liberal one, has a dense institutional infrastructure. In each country case, path dependency tells us, these institutions
have distinct histories and trajectories of evolution. Yet to draw the appropriate conclusions
from this, CPE scholars need to think through the relationship between institutions, the
agents who animate them, and the wider social context within which they exist. It is helpful
to recognize that much hinges, within institutionalist accounts of comparative political
economy, on the way the individuals who animate the institutions are understood. What
nature of rationality is posited? Put differently, what are the micro-foundations of institutionalist analysis?

VoC has successfully revived interest in institutionalist CPE. However, it has done so in a
way which arguably can obscure some of CPE's most telling insights about differential
dynamics of capitalist development and institutionalization. The functionalist temptations
within VoC can lead to a neglect of the *politics* of institutional development as it plays out.
The timing and sequencing of institutional change are crucial, affecting the likelihood and
degree of transformation. Institutional 'solutions' are not chosen by some impersonal
mechanism which ensures efficiency, but arise out of political struggles.

It is important not to assume away all the rich granularity of evolution and change of
capitalist institutions. The recalibrated historical institutionalist approach understands the
relation between institutions and the actors which animate them in dynamic terms. Using
the comparative method, CPE analysis can throw into relief nationally differentiated institutional conditions, admit more differentiated conceptions of rationality, and in the process
make it easier to bring out the politics and history in the explanation of capitalist institutional development and reproduction.

Common international economic pressures or trends, such as the liberalization and
deregulation (or, more accurately, re-regulation) witnessed within the advanced political
economies since the 1970s, are not situated in a barren institutional landscape. Rather, they
are overlain on an undulating institutional terrain, densely packed with pre-existing institutional structures and relationships. Globalizing pressures have to adjust to fit these contours, and processes such as economic liberalization are *refracted through* these institutional
complexes. This helps to explain why liberalization and deregulation do not 'mean' political
economic monocultures. In the next two chapters, I will complement this consideration of
institutionalist CPE with explorations of interest-based and ideas-based approaches.

7 Ideational Analysis and Comparative Political Economy

INTRODUCTION

In this chapter I explore the ideational element within CPE analysis and consider different theoretical approaches to the problem of how to factor ideas and shifts in prevailing understandings of political economic wisdom into the study of political economy. Max Weber was an important forebear of this kind of political economy analysis, introducing the concept of *Verstehen*, or how economic actors understand their environment. His work explained political economy in terms of individual action and perception, noting that understandings of economic rationality can vary (Weber 1978 [1922]; Swedberg 1998: 36). Building on these foundations, I will underline how shared understandings of, among others, markets, the state and capitalism all shape how political economic change is enacted. These have been important foundations for the 'ideational turn' in political economy.

Firstly I will highlight the contingency and ebb and flow of economic ideas, and then underline how incorporating the ideational into political economy analysis requires engagement with the structure/agency problematic. I then highlight how Keynes' understanding of economic conventions is important for grasping both the power of economic ideas and how these come to structure political economic activity. I then go on to explore two theoretical approaches to 'ideational' CPE – constructivism and Coxian critical political economy. Finally I illustrate how these approaches can be deployed to explain developments in CPE by analysing the changing economic policy paradigms and prevailing economic orthodoxies which were involved in the shift from *laissez-faire* to embedded liberalism in the mid-20th century.

THE POWER AND CONTINGENCY OF ECONOMIC IDEAS

One task of CPE as a field of study is to chart and explain the ebb and flow of political economic ideas from orthodoxy to heresy, and sometimes back again. For example, orthodoxies about economic policy were overturned in the wake of the GFC. Remarkably, the co-ordinates of economic orthodoxy, apparently set in stone over many years, were thrown into flux. The extraordinary turbulence within the world economy led to unprecedented macro-economic policy responses. What constituted appropriate economic policy was being redefined (Clift 2018, 2019). Debt and deficit levels rose in ways almost unimaginable before the crisis, yet some countries pursued a more expansive, activist role for fiscal policy by *increasing* their budget deficits still further. 'Quantitative easing' involved pumping money into the economy on a mind-boggling scale, throwing away the rulebook for prudent monetary policy.

The radically changed economic policy context was a spur for significant shifts in the ideas that underpin economic policy.

What was considered appropriate fiscal policy and monetary policy was evolving dramatically by comparison with pre-crisis 'great moderation' norms of the non-inflationary continuous expansion 'NICE' decade. So too were understandings about management of the public finances and acceptable levels of debt and deficit. More fundamentally, the underlying theory of how the economy worked, and how it should work, was challenged by the severity of the crisis and the prolonged nature of the ensuing downturn. An activist role for fiscal policy within economic stabilization, a cornerstone of Keynesian economic thinking but long neglected, once again returned to prominence in the early years of the GFC. In a later phase, opinions were divided between governments and international economic organizations as to the appropriate balance between fiscal activism to boost anaemic or absent economic growth and recovery on the one hand, and fiscal consolidation to restore the parlous state of public finances on the other. This austerity debate took centre stage across the advanced economies (Blyth 2013; Hay 2013; Schafer and Streeck 2013). At its heart were perennial disputes about the appropriate role of the state in the economy, which recalled the intellectual debates between Keynes, Hayek and Polanyi discussed in Chapter 4 that had in part been instigated by the Great Depression of the 1930s and responses to it.

This lays bare the historically contingent and *contested* nature of economic ideas, and the economic policies and practices which sometimes follow on from them. Economics and the economic are often presented as technical matters, abstracted from political debate and ideological argument, but in fact this supposedly apolitical representation is spurious. There is always a set of underlying assumptions on which any economic analysis, prognosis or policy recommendation is based. These foundations – the particular set of assumptions – have been selected over other possible choices for a variety of reasons, which include normative preference and ideological predisposition. For example, the advent of the market society within the advanced economies in the 19th and 20th centuries, the 'great transformation' that Polanyi analysed, was built on the ideological bulwark of what he termed 'the liberal creed' (2001 [1944]: 141–70), or classical liberal political economy. This political project, and its prevailing set of political economic understandings and assumptions, facilitated and drove forward the spread of *laissez-faire* capitalism.

Economic prescriptions are always couched in a discourse that is ideological and normative. Thus any economic analysis is built upon a politics. So, for example, the British media debate in the late 1990s and early 2000s as to whether a putative future entry into the single European currency would be a 'political' as opposed to an 'economic' decision was based on false premises. Any such decision would be inextricably both. How the economic aspects of that decision were interpreted, assessed and presented would be a crucial determinant of the outcome, but that process of interpretation and presentation would be deeply political.

The same was true, more recently, of debates surrounding Brexit and its effects on the British economy and model of capitalism (Rosamond 2019, 2020; Siles-Brugge 2019). Assessments of the likely economic effects of Brexit, both before and after the referendum, were all refracted through the political debate. More or less the entirety of mainstream economic thinking envisaged significant negative economic effects from leaving the largest and most developed free trade area and single market in the world. The real question, perhaps, was about how sizeable the negative effects would be (for an overview, see Tetlow and Stojanovic 2018). Yet when any forecasting body set out the case, it was vilified as 'project fear' by ardent 'Leave' supporters (Rosamond 2019). How the likely economic effects of

Brexit were interpreted, assessed and presented was deeply political, each assessment constituting an intervention in a highly charged and febrile public and popular debate about Brexit. This was even true of the British Government's own 'Operation Yellowhammer' no deal planning work – which was dismissed as scaremongering by some Brexiteer members of that self-same Government.

CPE seeks to expose and explore the political underpinnings of economic ideas, analysis and policy prescription. This approach is sometimes called 'the politics of economic ideas' (see e.g. Hall 1989; Hay 2001; Blyth 2002a; Clift 2018, 2019, 2020), and it reveals how the underlying assumptions of any economic analysis are always contestable. As one famous quip about Keynes puts it, 'where five economists are gathered together there will be six conflicting opinions, and two of them will be held by Keynes' (quoted in Steele 2001: 10). As historians of economic thought tell us, and as I have demonstrated in Chapters 3 and 4, the evolution of economics has been as fraught with political and ideological argument as the development of political philosophy (Barber 1967; Heilbroner 1992, 1996; Hollander 1992; Backhouse 1994, 2002; Hodgson 2001). Today, those ideological struggles and arguments may be obscured by the technical, 'scientific' evolutions of economics as a pseudo-science, but those ideological positions are still present within sets of (often implicit) assumptions made in economics (see pp. 76–8).

A modern parallel for the *Methodenstreit* is the contemporary differentiation between reflectivist and rationalist approaches to CPE. In Chapter 5 we encountered the archetypal rationalist approach to political economy: rational choice. This at first sight seems to be 'about ideas', since they root their explanations in the minds of actors. However, on reflection, many rational choice approaches are not really about ideas, or the ideational. The rationalist assumptions (modelled on neo-classical economics) about what goes on in those minds posit *a priori* what actors (conceived as pre-social beings) want, how they think and how they act. Rational choice then seeks to explain outcomes in the light of this set of *prior* assumptions. While this may be a fruitful way to develop rigorous explanatory frameworks for CPE analysis, it can be a rather crude way to factor the role of ideas into political economy. This is because the range of possible ideational elements within the decision matrices of actors in political economy extends beyond the limited menu which the rationalist approach admits.

What I do in this chapter is to explore a different approach, highlighting not the timeless certainty of *homo economicus*, operating according to something like a pre-programmed script (Ruggie 1998), but the contestability, contingency and changeability of prevailing economic ideas in the minds of economic actors (and the behaviours of actors that may flow from them). This is achieved by exploring two approaches within CPE which have sought to grapple with the complexities of how to think in these more nuanced terms about the role of ideas: constructivist and critical political economy.

Constructivist approaches, for example, assert at least a relative autonomy of the ideational from the material conditions which – for many rationalist approaches – provide the limits of the explicable world. Thus, for constructivism, rationalities (*plural*) cannot be 'read off' from a given set of material conditions, but are seen in Weberian terms as varied and variable. Mental frames of reference and interpretive leeway enter the picture and give actors a degree of autonomy in terms of how they respond to (and indeed how they perceive and interpret) a given set of material conditions (see e.g. Hay 2009, 2016). The Coxian 'critical' political economy approach highlights the need to historicize accounts of how particular sets of ideas come to prevail in particular institutional contexts (with particular sets of social forces and forms of state given the configuration of the broader world order; Cox 1981). The analytical tool of policy paradigms provides a means to put these approaches into practice, capturing how these interpretive frameworks can shape political behaviour, but also how they can evolve and change in response to changing conditions.

'NEW' POLITICAL ECONOMY: IDEAS, STRUCTURE AND AGENCY

These approaches can be seen as emulations of classical political economy. Each in its different way retains a commitment to historically contingent and socially and politically embedded approaches to the study of political economy. That commitment has informed a strand of political economy scholarship throughout the 20th century (see Gamble 1995; Clift and Rosamond 2009; Clift et al. 2021). The late 20th-century revitalization of CPE and IPE discussed in Chapters 1, 2 and 4 looked afresh at the role of ideas, and the ideational, within political economy (see Tooze and Murphy 1991; Higgott 1994, 1999; Gamble et al. 1996; Campbell 1998; Blyth 2002a; Watson 2005a). This attention to the role of ideas requires a (mercifully brief) venture into one of the age-old debates in social scientific inquiry – the structure/agency problematic (for an excellent overview, see Hay 2002: 89–134). One of the classic statements which sums up the essence of the problematic is Karl Marx's:

> Men make their own history, but they do not make it just as they please; they do not make it under circumstances chosen by themselves, but under circumstances directly encountered, given, and transmitted from the past. (quoted in Marx 1977: 300)

The relationship between agency and structure is, for Marx, dialectical. Such an interactive, dynamic, potentially conflictual conception has informed thinking about the role of the ideational in CPE. As Hay puts it, 'a dialectical understanding of the relationship between the ideational and the material is logically entailed by a dialectical understanding of the relationship between structure and agency' (2002: 209–11). Structures are not just physical institutions but also ideational phenomena, thus the conception of structure used here extends to include norms and shared understandings which are 'the parameters of our existence' (Cox 1995: 33). For ideationally oriented comparative political economists, emphasizing the importance of the 'ideational' is one way to counter the tendency to structuralism, or structural determinism (the overemphasis on structures at the expense of agents). It is important 'to give equal weight to both structure and agency rather than concentrating on one to the exclusion of the other' (Gamble 1995: 522).

Agents are the 'bearers' of structures, but in 'bearing' these structures they (re-)interpret them (and their position in relation to them). Structures are thus dynamic, not static, and one of the reasons they change is because of the strategic decisions of the agents who give life to and reproduce them. For Robert Cox, 'historical change is to be thought of as the reciprocal relationship of structures and actors' (1995: 33). The dialectical relationship between agency and structure entails a conception of agential action as empirically open-ended, but – as Marx pointed out – materially conditioned and historically circumscribed. Institutions constrain and shape the desires, motives and habits of agents. However, agents' 'intersubjective' construction of structures (the cognitive and ideational filters through which structures are understood and expressed) enables them in turn to reshape institutions (Hay 2016). Every action that disrupts the social order, breaking conventions and challenging established hierarchies, is mediated by structural features that are reconstituted by that action, albeit in a modified form.

Structural contexts impose pressures and constraints on actors, but they *do not* determine outcomes. This is in part because historical structures are *expressed through* political agency (see Weber 1978 [1922]). Structure and agency are interconnected aspects of social relations and Cox, like other political economy scholars attuned to the significance of the *ideational* in their analysis and understanding, stresses the *intersubjective* nature of structures and the role of agents in the constitution of their structural contexts. A similar approach (on this issue at least) is taken in Ruggie's work, which sets out a 'constructivist' political economy (discussed further below). For Ruggie, understanding the *dynamic* structure/agency relationship can be achieved by recognizing the ability of actors (agents) to shape and reshape the ideational parameters which circumscribe what agents consider politically possible, feasible and desirable.

For this range of political economy scholarship – from Hay to Cox to Ruggie – this intersubjective element, whereby agents give life to their structural contexts, is crucial in shaping political economic behaviour (see also pp. 117, 121–3). This way of thinking about political economy attributes to ideational factors, such as norms, ideas (e.g. prevailing orthodoxies), conventions and culture, an important causal role. This operates by moulding how actors understand and interpret the world and their place and interests within it. In CPE analysis, it is helpful (though very difficult) to try (as far as it is possible) to (re-)construct the cognitive framework within which actors are operating in order to understand what is driving change. We will explore two well-developed ways to attempt this challenging task within political economy scholarship below, but first it makes sense to say a bit more about the role and power of ideas.

THE POWER OF ECONOMIC IDEAS AND THE IDEATIONAL TURN IN POLITICAL ECONOMY

In recognizing and insisting upon the significance of the ideational, as political economists we want to insist specifically on the crucial role played by the political power of *economic* ideas. These ideas, and the differing understandings of how the economy works (or should work) that they generate, seem to be particularly powerful. This is particularly fertile ground for CPE and we align with a well-established and distinguished body of scholarship (see e.g. Hall 1989, 1993; Blyth 2002a; Hay 2001; Clift 2020). Indeed, the power of economic ideas was one of the central preoccupations of one of the greatest political economists of the 20th century – John Maynard Keynes. One of his more famous passages reads:

> the ideas of economists and political philosophers, both when they are right and when they are wrong, are more powerful than is commonly understood. Indeed the world is ruled by little else. Practical men, who believe themselves to be quite exempt from any intellectual influences, are usually the slaves of some defunct economist. Madmen in authority, who hear voices in the air, are distilling their frenzy from some academic scribbler from a few years back. (Keynes 1964 [1936]: 383)

Yet elsewhere Keynes offered a more measured and honed account of how and why economic ideas matter and shape political economic outcomes. A point of departure for this,
and a pervasive theme of Keynes' *General Theory*, is the prevalence, almost omnipresence, of
economic uncertainty. This recognition is, for an economist, somewhat heretical, given that
neo-classical economics tends to assume perfect information, perfectly distributed. Keynes,
though, is best understood as part of the classical political economy tradition (see pp. 27–9;
Watson 2005a: 47–8) and a liberal critic of neo-classical economics. For Keynes, this economic uncertainty was fundamental to his understanding of the economy (Klaes 2006:
261). As he wrote a year after he published the *General Theory*, 'the fact that our knowledge
of the future is fluctuating, vague, and uncertain, renders wealth a peculiarly unsuitable
topic for the methods of classical economic theory [here, confusingly, Keynes is referring to
neo-classical economics] ... About these matters there is no scientific basis on which to form
any calculable probability whatever. We simply do not know' (Keynes 1937: 213–4; see also
Blyth 2002a: 42; Klaes 2006: 262).

Economic activity, and in particular business confidence, is for Keynes bedevilled by this
uncertainty. As Mark Blyth points out (2002a: 41–4), this prevalent uncertainty underpins
Keynes' sophisticated account of how economic ideas structure political economy behaviour
through ideas as 'conventions' (Keynes 1964 [1936]: 152, 1937: 214). Conventions are ideational mechanisms which influence behaviour through their use by economic actors to counter prevalent uncertainty. An earlier approach to the role of conventions in shaping political
economic behaviour was advanced by Thorsten Veblen in his analysis of the significance of
'habits of thought' (see e.g. Veblen 1919; Watson 2005a: 133–9).

Keynes sets out three of the most important techniques which generate these conventions. Firstly, 'we assume that the present is a much more serviceable guide to the future
than a candid examination of past experience would show it to have been hitherto'; secondly, 'we assume that the *existing* state of opinion ... is based on a *correct* summing up of
future prospects'; and thirdly, 'knowing that our own individual judgement is worthless, we
endeavour to fall back on the judgement of the rest of the world which is perhaps better
informed ... the psychology of a society of individuals each of whom is endeavouring to copy
the others leads to what we may strictly term a *conventional* judgement' (Keynes 1937: 214).

There are, Keynes points out, good grounds to doubt the usefulness and accuracy of each
of these methods, but they are the best available tools for economic actors at sea in an ocean
of uncertainty (and unpredictability). That actors cling to these for security explains how
they can help to stabilize an uncertain economic world. Keynes' 'beauty contest' analogy
(based on tabloid newspaper competitions of the time wherein the aim was to identify cor-
rectly the contestant most people would choose as the winner) helps us to understand the
stabilizing role of these conventions. In order to assess how financial markets might move
in the immediate future, the key is to predict accurately the prevailing average sentiment
about particular assets. This highlights the significance of 'conventional' judgements as to
how people conceive of and react to economic signals: 'we have reached a third degree where
we devote our intelligences to anticipating what average opinion expects the average opinion to be' (Keynes 1964 [1936]: 156). This, for Keynes, helps to explain the functioning and
the psychology of financial market activity. The herd behaviour and irrational exuberance of
financial bubbles are in part explained by these conventions.

Another way to reveal the importance of ideational factors is feminist political economy
that analyses and explores the gendered construction of economic subjectivities and identities. Notions of 'irrational exuberance' in finance are instances of the gendered ideational

construction of the economic, which is part of a wider process of the social construction of gendered identities and meanings (Steans 1999; De Goede 2001; Whitworth 2006). Feminist political economy explores how the practices that led to the GFC were rooted in 'masculinized ways of governing the global economy' (Hozic and True 2016: 19) and 'hyper masculine excess' (Elias 2016). These masculinized understandings of the economy come at the expense of feminized understandings (economies of care, nurture, mutual co-operation, empathy, sympathy, etc.). Ideationally attuned feminist political economy understands gender not as a synonym for women, but as 'a signifying code'. For Spike Peterson, gender is 'a *governing code* that pervades language and hence systematically shapes how we think, what we presume to 'know' and how such knowledge claims are legitimised' (Spike Peterson 2005: 502; Whitworth 2006). Thus masculinized notions constitute the common sense, not only of modern economic theory but also of modern economic practice.

Socially constructed gender stereotypes also 'help to normalize high levels of financial risk-taking as appropriate and normal behaviour' (Hozic and True 2016: 10). De Goede has identified 'gendered representations of financial crisis as instance of madness, delusion, hysteria and irrationality' which 'simultaneously constructs the sphere of financial normality or rationality' (De Goede 2001: ch. 2). Gendered identities, feminist scholars point out, are social constructions shaped by prevailing patriarchal power relations. This generates 'specific gendered narratives' of financial crisis, for example 'habitually masculine selfishness (generator of economic growth)' and 'feminine altruism (protector of family)' (Hozic and True 2016: 10; see also Brassett and Rethel 2015). These gendered discursive constructions had impacts on the consequences of the crisis, and who bore the burden of adjustment. Patriarchal norms and power relations meant that, both before and after the crash, women were also over-represented in precarious and low-paid positions in the labour market. Meanwhile, the social provisioning no longer delivered by the state in the wake of austerity was disproportionately provided by women. Thus 'the gendered poor and marginalized ended up as the disproportionate targets of austerity measures' (Hozic and True 2016: 3). Post-GFC some feminist political economists identified a '"new normal" of gendered and racialized inequality and heightened sexualized and domestic violence' (ibid. 2016: 4).

What these different kinds of ideational work explore is the relative autonomy of the discursive construction of political economy from material underpinnings. This phenomenon is particularly well illustrated in the political economy of finance and the construction of financial credibility. Financial markets are often less interested in the economic fundamentals than in other actors' (not necessarily exhaustively well-informed) perceptions. Thus, for example, even if, as a financial market actor, you know that the vertiginous growth in opaque mortgage-backed securities, which was at the root of the GFC which rocked the global financial markets from the summer of 2007 onwards, is bound to come crashing down sooner rather than later (and many financial market actors did), it still makes sense to keep trading (and lending) as long as everyone else still believes the market is sustainable. Nobel Laureate Paul Krugman likens these dynamics to Wile E. Coyote defying the laws of gravity and running in thin air high above the canyon floor until he realizes he is no longer on firm ground, 'for only then, according to the laws of cartoon physics, does he plunge' (2012: 48).

As financial markets have become deregulated, and the scale and speed of financial flows have increased in the decades since the collapse of Bretton Woods (discussed below), these confidence and credibility dynamics have become increasingly significant. This is because, as the eurozone sovereign debt crisis which followed on the coat-tails of the GFC demonstrated, the volume and velocity of economic (capital) flows, mobilized and channelled by the presence or absence of credibility, have grown almost exponentially. A similar growth has been seen in the political and social consequences of all this financial activity, as the financialization scholars discussed in Chapter 10 have underlined. By looking at the ideational and material forces that shape understandings of credibility, we can gain a greater insight into the nature and limits of economic policy autonomy in the context of international capital mobility.

Keynes' insight is an important one for grasping how the ideational realm matters for political economy analysis. Blyth notes that 'in essence, the economy for Keynes is as much a subjective construct as an objective reality' (Blyth 2002a: 42). Supposedly material facts of the world economy in fact rest upon an intricate interweaving of ideational and material elements. Keynes explained how 'economic actors mediate uncertainty by stabilizing co-ordinating economic conventions through discursive practices' (Klaes 2006: 262). Yet what is striking about these ideas or conventions is that these highly significant 'inter-subjective constructions' have 'at best a tenuous relationship to market fundamentals and no precise calculable metric' (Blyth 2002a: 43).

The role of such conventions in mediating actors' perceptions and judgements about the economy helps to explain how prevailing political economic orthodoxies take hold and wield their influence. Such orthodoxies, with the ability to shape and sway perceptions, may in turn not be closely rooted in an analysis of the economic fundamentals. As Blyth puts it, 'there is no truth about markets "out there" apart from the prevailing wisdom that markets have about themselves, and this can be a very fickle thing' (ibid.). This somewhat under-reported contribution of Keynes to our understanding of the importance of the subjective and the ideational to a thorough understanding of political economy has recently been recognized and taken forward by a range of 'ideational' political economy scholars.

In the remainder of this chapter we look at two different attempts to incorporate system-atically ideational variables into the analysis of CPE: firstly, constructivist political economy; and secondly, the ideas of Robert Cox. A sizeable body of mainstream political economy lit-erature affords primacy, sometimes to the exclusion of all else, to measurable material fac-tors and to things that you can drop on your foot. These approaches set themselves apart from such a view, highlighting the political economic importance of intangible ideas.

CONSTRUCTIVIST POLITICAL ECONOMY

There is an increasingly well-established social constructivist approach developed by a range of like-minded scholars working in CPE and IPE. Inspired (wittingly or otherwise) by Keynes' thinking, as outlined above, this approach shares the recognition of the independent, *causal* and *constitutive* role of ideas, of the *ideational*, in shaping political economic outcomes and practices (Blyth 2002a; Rosamond 2002; Hay 2004a, 2004b, 2016; Sinclair 2005; Abdelal et al. 2010; Schmidt 2008, 2010; Widmaier 2003a, 2003b, 2004; Baker 2013a; Woll 2008). As one leading constructivist summarizes the approach, 'social constructivism ... attributes to ideational factors, including culture, norms and ideas ... a role in shaping the way in which actors define their identity and interests' (Ruggie 1998: 4).

It makes sense to talk of more than one 'constructivist turn' in political economy which leads along a number of different avenues of social scientific inquiry. One variant of con-structivist political economy launches off less from Keynes' economic conventionalism described above, and more from Veblen's account of rites and rituals – and how they become behaviourally embedded through habits of thought (see Veblen 1919; Watson 2005a:

133–9). This has been explored by a body of scholarship on 'the political economy of the everyday' which highlights the significance of the activity of ordinary people as agents within political economy (Hobson and Seabrooke 2007; Widmaier 2009). This work is in an important sense about the role of ideas in shaping political economy, and its focus is on the societal development of perceptions of self-interest, and how these inform and guide behaviour in everyday economic life (see e.g. Langley 2004, 2008; Seabrooke 2006). This is an interesting research agenda for CPE (see e.g. Schwartz and Seabrooke 2008), and we will explore some of these ideas when we examine financialization in Chapter 10 and welfare state restructuring in Chapter 11. However, in this chapter we focus not upon these 'bottom-up' societal processes and transformations in intersubjective constructions of what it means to be an economic subject, but rather upon the role of ideas and intersubjective constructions in relation to more 'top-down' policy-makers and policy-making.

Both strands of constructivism recognize (following Marx's interpretation of structure/agency outlined above) that material conditions do establish parameters which delimit the range of possibly prevailing ideational constructions of political economic reality. Nevertheless, there is significant room to manoeuvre within these parameters. Furthermore, there is a degree of what Marxists call 'relative autonomy' of the ideational realm from material conditions. As Blyth puts it, ideas 'do not "really" need to correspond to the "real" world in order to be important in that world' (Blyth 2002a: viii). This fairly diverse body of scholarship is perhaps best characterized in opposition to the approach that all proponents, in their different ways, reject. All constructivism takes issue with the rationalist analysis built on neo-classical economic micro-foundations, which (according to constructivists) conceives of agency as 'the enactment of pre-programmed scripts' (Ruggie 1998: 4).

In contrast, 'social constructivism' understands actors and agency very differently, as 'reflective acts of social creation, within structured constraints' (ibid.). This difference is explained by the very different 'micro-foundations' of constructivism. Constructivism challenges the methodological assumptions of rationalist political economy analysis (Box 7.1). It involves an interpretive mode of understanding, recognizing many social phenomena to be unquantifiable. Constructivism understands actors' preferences as shaped in a social environment, where preference formation entails socially constituted shared understandings and meanings (Hay 2016). Actors are inherently social, and inevitably, therefore, their identities and interests are socially constructed, the products of intersubjective social structures (Campbell 1998, 2004; Woll 2008; Schmidt 2008). Actors are socially embedded and communicatively constituted. If we accept this social character of economic activity, and market relations, then assumptions of rationality (singular) appear less helpful in understanding how and why markets, and political economies, work in the way they do.

Tim Sinclair's work on global finance, which recalls Keynes' points about the (inter)subjective nature of finance, credibility and confidence, illustrates the point. Sinclair's constructivist approach rejects a mainstream view that 'markets reflect fundamental economic forces, which are not subject to human manipulation' (Sinclair 2005: 5). Recalling the core political economy insight outlined in Chapter 2, such an approach recognizes how (financial) markets are social and political constructs – not naturally occurring phenomena. For Sinclair, as for Keynes, reality is socially constructed, and this makes its study so complex and interesting. In recognizing 'the social nature of global finance', Sinclair's work highlights how, given prevalent and increasing risk and uncertainty, a crucial mediating role is played by 'the institutions that work to facilitate transactions between buyers and sellers', which 'have a central role in organizing markets and, consequently, in governing the world' (ibid.).

Box 7.1 Constructivist political economy

Understanding of the social world

- Material conditions establish parameters delimiting possibly prevailing ideational constructions of political economic reality.
- Crucially there is significant interpretive room to manoeuvre within these parameters.
- Economic orthodoxy and economic rationality, for example, are changeable and contingent – shaped by national traditions of economic thought.

Role of ideas

- Independent *causal* and *constitutive* role of ideas.
- A focus on culture, norms and ideas.
- These intersubjective structures shape outcomes through collective intentionality and social facts (shared beliefs and understandings).

Conception of agency

- Actors are seen as reflective, creative – not following pre-programmed scripts.
- Key is how these actors make sense of the world, within their 'meaning context'.

Sources: Ruggie 1998; Hay 2006, 2016; Schmidt 2008; Blyth 2002a; Abdelal et al. 2010; Widmaier 2004; Clift 2018; Sinclair 2005.

Sinclair analyses bond rating agencies as 'reputational intermediaries' which have enormous influence as the gatekeepers of financial credibility in the context of the deregulated global financial markets. These 'specific institutions and associated "micropractices" at the core of contemporary capitalism' are selected because prevailing understandings within the ratings process are both somewhat arbitrarily arrived at and enormously important for the allocation of global credit (ibid.: 10–11). What ratings agencies say about the state of a firm's credit worthiness matters. Thus this ratings process becomes the site for the exercise of highly significant political power. The GFC, wherein huge volumes of mortgage-backed securities rated 'A' by these reputational intermediaries turned out to be worthless, illustrates how powerful these agencies are and how dramatic the consequences can be when they get their judgements wrong (see Sinclair 2010; Langley 2010).

This episode throws into dramatic relief 'the "reconfiguring" effect these institutions and practices have on global economic and political life' (Sinclair 2005: 10–1; see also Ruggie 1998: 27). The fundamental point is that 'financial markets are more social – and less spontaneous, individual or "natural" – than we tend to believe' (Sinclair 2005: 5). Thus without the unorthodox conceptions of markets, and of actor behaviour (which abandon rationalist assumptions by focusing on the ideational), these crucial power relations and dynamics (and indeed the political economy of the GFC) cannot be analysed adequately and understood.

For constructivists, the focus is always on ideational as well as material structures. Thus it is not just the gold standard that matters in understanding the political economy of the 19th century, but equally the 'liberal creed'. This brings us to the other key conceptual elements of constructivism, namely the 'reflective acts of social creation', which is how Ruggie et al. understand that agency can 'express not only individual but also collective intentionality' and 'the meaning and significance of ideational factors are not independent of time and place' (Ruggie 1998: 33). Collective intentionality is important in the constructivist account (and something which the methodological individualism and the assumptive basis of much rational choice political economy find it difficult to deal with).

When particular intersubjective beliefs become sufficiently embedded, they develop the quality of social facts, resting on 'collective intentionality' (Searle 1995: 24–5; Ruggie 1998: 13, 20–1; Sinclair 2005: 53–4; Hay 2016). Social facts differ from 'brute' facts in that what makes the 'true' or 'false' is not 'independent of anybody's attitudes or feelings about them' (Searle 1995: 8). Constructivist political economy highlights just how many political economically significant understandings are not 'brute' facts (independent of any institutions), but are social facts (ibid.: 27). For example, financial credibility can ebb away from a government and its borrowing costs can rise – sometimes dramatically – not because of any adverse change in the economic fundamentals of the country's economic position or prospects, but because market sentiment turns against it. That happened to Italy in the international context of the eurozone sovereign debt crisis. This illustrates how social facts play a constitutive role in shaping political economic outcomes in that they guide collective intentionality, shaping the meaning and significance attached to economic phenomena. These social constructions can, as in the case of the ratings agencies, acquire sufficient influence so as to shape material conditions in the political economy.

Collective intentionality involves shared understandings, and a good example in political economy is the prevailing political economic orthodoxy on a given issue. The social facts which are the building blocks of such an orthodoxy are not timeless, impermeable, ideational structures. Thus the social constructivist enterprise entails a 'space–time contingent' conception of macro-structures in the global political economy, since structures are 'the aggregation of specific social practices that are situated in time and space' (Ruggie 1998: 26). Given the relative autonomy of the ideational from the material within their 'mutually conditioning relationships' (ibid.: 32), it follows that these intersubjective beliefs can change over time.

Constructivist political economy analysis is motivated in part by an ambition to explore the historical development of 'intersubjective structures' or 'interpretive frames [that] actors use to understand the world' (Sinclair 2005: 10–2). This body of scholarship is interested in how 'economic ideas provide agents with an interpretive framework, which describes and accounts for the workings of the economy by defining its constitutive elements and "proper" (and therefore "improper") interrelations' (Blyth 2002a: 11). The prevailing political economic wisdom, as Watson has demonstrated in relation to prevailing orthodoxy on inflation (Watson 2002: 189–92), is a set of social facts which rest upon particular (contingent social constructions of) political economic assumptions (see also Clift 2018, 2020). It can be subject to quite dramatic changes over relatively short time periods, as with the 'great reversals' in the history of financial regulation to be discussed in Chapter 10 (see Rajan and Zingales 2003), or the shift from state socialism towards a distinctive brand of authoritarian state-directed capitalism within the Chinese political economy since 1978 (see pp. 166–70). These changes shift perceptions of the underlying 'economic fundamentals' and judgements of economic rectitude (or its lack) which are ascribed to particular economic situations. Similarly, the bond ratings agencies discussed above can change their assessment as the prevailing wisdom evolves.

How ideas of economic rectitude are constructed is a deeply political process. There is a crucial role of policy elites within this process in shaping which economic policy practices are understood as sound, and which are not. These shared understandings are sites for the exploration of power relations, and they have significant policy impacts. Furthermore, work focusing on the role of ideational factors in shaping economic policy rectitude rests upon the recognition of the mutability of economic orthodoxy (Clift and Tomlinson 2004, 2012). These intersubjective structures matter (Rosamond 2002) and they can and do change (Clift 2018, 2020). Work on balance of payments assessment (Clift and Tomlinson 2008) and financial credibility in global bond markets (Mosley 2000, 2003) indicates that the way these judgements are arrived at, although often highly consequential, is also somewhat arbitrary. Below we will explore an example of the transformation of the 'embedded liberal compromise' as a highly significant set of political economic social facts, and how this ideational shift transformed the nature of global capitalism.

CRITICAL POLITICAL ECONOMY: ROBERT COX ET AL.

Since the mid-1980s, a new stream of Marx-inspired (though not necessarily Marxist) theory has developed in IPE, and it makes sense to incorporate this approach into CPE analysis. This remains faithful to the historical materialist method used by Marx, and is built partly on the thinking of the influential Italian Marxist theorist Antonio Gramsci. The instigator of this new thinking is Robert W. Cox (1981, 1983, 1995; see also Gamble and Payne 1996; Payne 2005). Its common name – critical theory – hints unsubtly at its other inspirations, namely the 'Frankfurt School' of Marxist sociologists such as Adorno and Horkheimer (see Devetak 2001). This approach is also termed neo-Gramscian IPE, as it argues – as did Gramsci – that culture and ideas ('the ideational') are of particular importance in political economy, and that the ideational element should balance the materialist emphasis of much earlier Marxian analysis. Coxian critical political economy (Box 7.2) could be seen as modern historical materialism (see pp. 59–65, 72–4), because it seeks to *operationalize* Marx's insight of conceiving of capital as a set of social relations of production (Cox 1987: pt 1).

The understanding of social forces within critical theory involves what Cox calls 'a fresh approach to the dynamics of class formation' (ibid.: 3–4), and he specifies a particular role for ideas within this fresh approach. As Cox argued in his famous 1981 article, understanding the conditions under which particular sets of social forces attain and exercise power requires analysis of the *indeterminate* interactions of three types or 'spheres of activity': social forces, forms of state and world orders. This approximates different levels of analysis within Cox's schema. The evolution of the CPE of capitalism is, in this view, understood as arising from the interaction of social forces, forms of state (derived from state/society complexes) and world orders (1981: 138). Thus elsewhere Cox identifies 'complexes of production relations, classes and historic blocs ... linked to a world order that bears directly on them, as well as influencing them through their nation state' (1987: 6–7). 'Historic bloc' is a term Cox draws from Gramsci. It refers to a relatively coherent and stable political economic order, spanning the levels of social forces, forms of state and world orders.

Box 7.2 Critical political economy

Understanding of the social world

- Marxian-inspired analysis of capitalism focused on social relations of production.
- Cox identifies three 'spheres of activity': social forces, forms of state and world orders. Capitalism arises from the interaction of social forces, forms of state (derived from state/society complexes) and world orders.
- State/society complex – a Gramsci-inspired conception of the interpenetration of state and society.

Role of ideas

- Cox identifies 'historical structures', the interaction of which shape the path of its evolution. These are *ideas*, *material capabilities* and *institutions*.
- A Gramscian emphasis on culture and ideology, alongside material conditions.
- Ideas matter – the ideational realm as a 'determining sphere of action'.
- Intersubjective meanings are politically important, as are 'shared notions of the nature of social relations'.

Conception of world order

- A 'historic bloc' – 'a coherent conjunction or fit between a configuration of material power, the prevalent collective image of world order (including certain norms) and a set of institutions which administer the order with a certain semblance of universality' (Cox 1981: 139).
- A key concept is 'hegemony' – dominant power relations in the global political economy being reproduced through both coercion and (arguably more importantly) consent.
- Hegemony hinges on material capabilities, but also on the power of ideas (to legitimate the status quo).

Sources: Cox (1981, 1983, 1987).

Within that configuration, Cox's framework for analysis posits the interaction of sets of historical structures. His 'method of historical structures' is to be applied to the three spheres of activity. Cox is seeking to identify regularities and repeated (repeating) patterns of interactions within political economy (nationally and globally). These reveal the fingerprints of the 'historical structures' which Cox identifies as the interaction of *ideas*, *material capabilities* and *institutions* (1981: 136). Cox thinks of these three sets of historical structures as a 'heuristic device', rather than as 'categories with a predetermined hierarchy of relationships' (ibid.: 137). They demonstrate their worth in the insights they generate from being *applied* empirically to the three spheres of activity. Obviously, it is the presence of ideas which is of particular importance for our purposes. The three elements – though analytically separable (i.e. it is analytically helpful to separate them out in theory) – are always intimately interlinked. These historical structures are, in essence, 'persistent social practices, made by collective human activity, and transformed through collective human activity' (Cox 1987: 4). Thus the historic bloc rests on and is supported by a particular set of understandings about the tasks and limits of the state, rooted in the class structure on which the state rests; that is, the social forces arising out of a particular state/society complex.

The goal of what Cox calls 'a political economy perspective' is not merely identifying and categorizing these historical structures, but also, echoing Marx, 'explaining their origins, growth and demise in terms of the interrelationships of the three levels of structures' (1981: 141). These historical structures are conceived as frameworks for action. To recall our earlier discussion of structure and agency, agents (people) are not merely 'bearers of structures'. For Cox, 'actions are shaped either directly by pressures projected through the system or indirectly by the subjective awareness on the part of actors' (ibid.: 144). 'Intersubjective meanings' are politically important, as are 'shared notions of the nature of social relations' which, 'though durable over long periods of time, are historically conditioned' (ibid.: 136). This historical conditioning indicates the role of the historical materialist method 'to find the connections between the mental schema through which people conceive action and the material world which constrains both what people can do and how they can think about doing it' (Cox 1985: 243). The ideological realm is, for Cox, 'a determining sphere of action which has to be understood in its connections with material power relations' (Cox 1981: 141).

Gramscian notions of hegemony underpin this connection between the ideological and material realms. For Gramsci, hegemony entails both coercion and (arguably more importantly) consent, and hinges on material capabilities, but also on the power of ideas. The ideational aspect of hegemony involves the ability to shape perceptions of the general interest in such a way that particular groups or outcomes are favoured. Norms and shared understandings, which are 'the parameters of our existence' (Cox 1995: 33), in fact embody power relations. In this way ideas can legitimate the status quo. Cox argues that culture and ideas are important in the creation and maintenance of a hegemonic system (or world order), by generating consent within state/society complexes.

Although not at the core of CPE, this approach is possibly a rich and fertile analytical device for comparative political economists. One of the limitations of critical political economy is in applying the elegant theoretical edifice to concrete conditions. It has, for example, been applied to the political economy of European integration (Gill 1998; Cafruny and Ryner 2003, 2007a, 2007b, Ryner 2015; Ryner and Cafruny 2016). This work has offered glimpses of how the comparative method – and focused, case-specific work – is one viable arena in which to use and develop the Coxian approach to CPE.

TOOLS FOR COMPARATIVE POLITICAL ECONOMY ANALYSIS: POLICY PARADIGMS

These two approaches to incorporating the ideational within CPE are useful, but in both cases they entail abstract theoretical concepts which can be difficult to 'operationalize' and apply. With that in mind, we will deploy a more obvious concept – that of the policy paradigm – to demonstrate how these approaches can be used. What matters, and what does not, in affecting political economic outcomes is filtered through what Thomas Kuhn called 'paradigms' of ideas (Kuhn 1970; see also Carstensen 2011a). In our case these are sets of economic ideas (Hall 1989, 1993; Blyth 2002a: 11; Hay 2001, 2004b; Clift 2020). Paradigms are ideational structures of internally consistent and coherent understandings of the world and how it works. Policy paradigms help us to understand the limits of the possible (and the feasible) in the minds of political actors in terms of policy responses to changing conditions.

Policy paradigms can be thought of as part of the political economists' analytical toolkit, helping them to understand the role of economic ideas in policy-making. The policy paradigm is a tool for analysis which helps to organize the analysis of the 'intersubjective frameworks' discussed above. It can be taken up and deployed in the context of a range of differing theoretical approaches. Though not developed exclusively by or for constructivist or critical political economy analysis, it can be made compatible with either.

Within a paradigm, cohesion is provided by a set of underlying assumptions leading to an approach to explanation, and to policy, which all policy actors share. Analysis in terms of policy paradigms focuses attention primarily on how 'normative structures restrict the set of policy ideas that political elites find acceptable' (Campbell 1998: 378). By 'providing cognitive templates through which policy-makers come to understand the environment in which they find themselves', policy paradigms explain how 'state-managers and policy experts alike may become institutionally embedded in norms, conventions and standard operating procedures' (Hay 2004b: 504–5; see also Hall 1993; Campbell 1998: 378, 389–92).

Political economic ideas (which are always contestable) are the building blocks of these paradigmatic ideational structures. It is important to underline that what is 'at play' in the rise and decline of economic policy paradigms is a contingent and to some extent open-ended struggle between different *socially and politically constructed* interpretations of economic phenomena. These processes of change are not (or at the very least not necessarily) subject to deterministic, inexorable logics. Equally, the policies and policy prescriptions which flow from these are built on *socially and politically constructed* interpretations of economic rectitude.

While a useful tool, there are certain caveats attached to the use of policy paradigms as tools for analysis. Firstly, policy paradigm analysis is a cosy environment for 'punctuated equilibrium'-style accounts of change which, as discussed in Chapters 1 and 4, are somewhat problematic. During periods of what in Kuhnian terms we might call 'normal science', paradigmatic 'border police' within policy communities are instrumental in sustaining (relative) stasis, if not complete inertia. These stable discursive patterns and practices tend to be associated with 'normal' periods of policy-making, which scholars often differentiate sharply from the discursive patterns accompanying rare 'crisis' moments or periods of 'exceptional' policy-making (for a critique, see Streeck and Thelen 2005). The 'normal' is very infrequently overthrown by radical transformative change as inconsistencies within the prevailing paradigm undermine it and lead to a revolution: 'the very parameters that previously circumscribed policy options are cast asunder and replaced, and in which the realm of the politically possible, feasible and desirable is correspondingly reconfigured' (Hay 2004b: 505). Taking such a paradigmatic view of economic ideas and their relationship policy orders can overstate change, overlook continuities and overrate the efficiency of punctuated change (see Clift 2020).

Secondly, as scholars in science studies have pointed out, although the Kuhnian frame-work admits the possibility of dramatic change, it is in truth a rather conservative mode of understanding social and ideational change (Fuller 2003). This tendency towards conserva-tism also informs the 'punctuated equilibrium' approach to explaining political economic change. This struggles to account for small, incremental but cumulative changes in prevail-ing ideas which, over time, amount to a profound transformation of the ideational context of political economy (see Carstensen 2011a, 2011b).

Thirdly, a somewhat problematic tendency towards what social scientists call functional-ism can bedevil policy paradigm analysis. Consider the following passage:

> A set of ideas is selected because it 'offered clearer and simpler programmatic policy guidelines for resolving important economic problems, better fit the existing cognitive and normative constraints that policy makers faced, and was more effectively framed for discursive purposes'. (Campbell 1998: 378)

There is a sense here that ideas are 'called forth' and fit the context (in a manner which seems to assume perfect information, perfectly distributed). But, as Mark Blyth has pointed out, crises do not come with instruction sheets (2002a: 10). Political economic reality is always more ideological and political than that. It is incumbent upon ideational political economy scholarship to explore and explain *how* and *why* one set of ideas is selected over another. This involves setting ideational choices in the context of power relations. This helps to counter the problems of functionalism and the somewhat antiseptic, depoliticized view of ideas and change which can accompany it.

Blyth's account offers a more politicized view, but perhaps contains its own shortcom-ings. Blyth argues that paradigm shifts involve actors who 'propose particular solutions to a moment of crisis, and empower agents to resolve that crisis by constructing new institu-tions in line with these new ideas' (2002: 11). Yet it is questionable how far novel institu-tions are created 'in line with these new ideas' (Blyth 2002: 11). This arguably overlooks the 'thwarted operationalisation' of economic ideas. This can result from the practical exigencies of economic management, the complexity of the policy process, or enactment by policy practitioners less convinced by the underpinning economic ideas. All this can lead to the development of policy regimes, orders and mechanisms and models at odds with the origi-nal paradigmatic principles (see Clift 2020).

Those provisos notwithstanding, deploying the policy paradigm toolkit is one useful way to analyse political economic change and the role of the ideational within it. In the remain-der of this chapter we will use the policy paradigm toolkit and the two broader theoretical approaches outlined above to show the insights they can offer in explaining the crucial changes in political economy in the mid-20th century – the onset of 'embedded liberalism'.

CHANGING DOMINANT ECONOMIC ORTHODOXIES: FROM THE 'LIBERAL CREED' TO 'EMBEDDED LIBERALISM'

The power and significance of political economic ideas are amply demonstrated by one par-ticularly important shift in the prevailing political economic paradigm, and thus the domi-nant economic orthodoxy, in the middle of the 20th century. In a manner which builds on Polanyi's insights, John Gerard Ruggie characterized the establishment of a regulated international economic order, instigated at the Bretton Woods conference in 1944 which sought to design the shape of a post-war world economy, as the era of 'embedded liberalism' (Ruggie 1982). The 'embedded liberal compromise' was rooted in the political economic ideas of Keynes, and it transformed economic policy-making, state/market relations and the processes of market-making within states, as well as the inscription of those processes (and the understandings on which they rested) within legislative and regulatory activities.

We have already encountered the set of prevailing political economic understandings – the policy paradigm – which held sway in the minds of policy-makers in the advanced economies of the 19th and early 20th centuries. The ideological accompaniment to the international self-regulating market was a particular variant of liberal political economy, sometimes referred to as the 'Manchester School' because of the debt it owed to the free trade writing of British political economists such as Richard Cobden, John Bright and Louis Mallet, and the anti-Corn Law league based in Manchester (a centre of 19th-century British industrial capitalism; see Winch 2009: 179–202). The ideas extend from free trade to include *laissez-faire* more broadly, and advocacy of a minimal role for the state in the economy.

The prevailing variant within the British state was the 'Treasury View' that Keynes railed against in the early 20th century. This policy paradigm was inspired by the policy prescriptions of neo-classical economics and held that the free play of market forces was always the optimal policy response. Thus, for example, public expenditure always 'crowded out' (inherently more efficient) private spending and investment. As R. G. Hawtrey put it to the Macmillan Committee of 1930: 'whether the spending came out of taxes or loans from savings, the increased government expenditure would merely replace private expenditure' (quoted in Klein 1968: 45–6). Corollaries of this view include Say's Law, that supply will call forth demand and that the free market has an inherent tendency towards full employment of resources which does not require government stimulus. This view of state/market relations assumes that increases in public spending will not enhance economic growth or economic activity, no gains are to be made from public works, and government deficits are always problematic because the lack of a balanced budget always damages business confidence (see e.g. Tomlinson 1990: 60–1, 85–6; Clift 2019).

Recalling the core political economy insight outlined in Chapter 2, this 'liberal creed' perpetuates a myth of the possible separation of state and market. It argues for 'less state' and 'more market' in ways assuming a zero-sum struggle between the two that fly problematically in the face of the inherent interpenetration and co-constitution of state and market. Nevertheless, 'the liberal creed' came to be accepted within domestic political economy as orthodoxy because of its compatibility and congruence with global political economic conditions. From a Coxian perspective, one explanation of the dominance of these liberal ideas was the alignment of social forces, of a particular form of state and of world order. This all coalesced, in the 19th century, into a liberal 'hegemonic world order' dominated by the British empire which Cox called Pax Britannica. Particular sets of social forces were created by the prevailing social relations of production (the growth in economic and political power of the industrial bourgeoisie and the growth in size, though not at this stage political power, of the proletariat). Pax Britannica was 'an order based ideologically on a broad measure of consent, functioning according to general principles' which secured British dominance 'but at the same time offer[ed] some measure or prospect of satisfaction to the less powerful' (Cox 1987: 7).

The prevalence of the liberal policy paradigm discussed above was aligned to the minimally interventionist 'liberal state' as a distinctive and particular form of state (ibid.: 129–43; see also Polanyi 2001 [1944]: 3, 29–31). World order was sustained through the interaction of Cox's three sets of historical structures – institutions (such as the gold standard or the Cobden–Chevalier free trade treaty between Britain and France), ideas (the liberal creed) and material capabilities (British military and economic dominance). This configuration between particular sets of social forces (the bourgeoisie at the heart of British industrial capitalism), the liberal state and Pax Britannica coalesced into a 'historic bloc'.

Yet the pervasive influence of that 'liberal creed' was such that it continued to dominate, even after political economic conditions which underpinned its emergence had changed and the congruence of that historic bloc no longer obtained. Thus despite the suspension of the gold standard, and all the upheavals of World War I which changed the configuration of the world order, politicians retained their faith in liberal ideas. As Skidelsky put it, 'politicians in the 1920s deployed a stock of economic wisdom which was a kind of codification of what they assumed to be the successful practice of the 19th century' (1970: 6).

The acceptance of these liberal political economic principles began to be undermined as the economic slump of the 1920s and 1930s wore on. The 19th-century liberal policy paradigm was under threat. The politically and socially destabilizing consequences of the spread of the 'self-regulating market' became ever more apparent as economic turmoil and rising unemployment left populations poorer, hungrier and more vulnerable. A range of political movements challenged the liberal capitalist order, with politicized and enfranchised labour movements drawn to a variety of ideologies from communism and socialism to fascism. The tectonic plates of economic ideology were shifting from the 1920s onwards. Eventually, the inconsistencies and anomalies within the existing policy paradigm were such that it was holed below the water line.

The Great Depression politicized economic issues and ideas, and demonstrated the potentially dire adverse consequences of the kinds of untrammelled free markets that the liberal creed advocated. It also illustrated more eloquently than any academic treatise could that the underlying assumptions of neo-classical economics (that free markets tend towards equilibrium at full employment) do not necessarily obtain in the real world, certainly not in the short run. The global economic collapse, with no market-induced recovery, undermined the policy paradigm and led to a profound loss of confidence in *laissez-faire*. On a lesser scale, there were similar dynamics underlying policy and regulatory changes following the 2008 GFC. The rejection of *laissez-faire* principles by those who considered themselves the 'losers' from globalization was also at the heart of the rise of xenophobic economic nationalism in the mid-2010s in the forms of Trump and the Brexit vote.

From a constructivist perspective, the effect of these episodes was to gnaw away at intersubjective societal understandings of (and faith in) the free market economy. In the face of these tumultuous events, shared understandings of the right way to order the political economy were in flux as the old recipes and solutions (balanced budgets and 'sound' public finances) were deployed without beneficial effect. During the 1930s and 1940s, this in concert with the war (and the everyday experience of state intervention in economic activity and collectivism within the war economy) coalesced into new 'social facts'. A different policy paradigm was finding favour within academia and among policy elites, notably within the British and American states (Weir 1989; Hirschman 1989; Salant 1989). By the 1940s, this flourishing of new economic ideas among the policy elites of Western allies who were in the process of winning World War II was crystallizing into a conscious desire to 're-embed' (international) economic relations in their social and political context, from which they had become 'dis-embedded' through adherence to the self-regulating market in the 19th century and the first half of the 20th.

A very different ideational context would encompass international economic relations after World War II. The questioning of *laissez-faire*, which had been proceeding within academic economics by Keynes and a number of other fellow travellers, was spilling over into the public policy debate. This provided economic justification and rationale for debunking *laissez-faire*, giving credence and respectability to the new policy paradigm. As Keynes put it, 'what used to be a heresy is now endorsed as orthodox' (quoted in Helleiner 1994: 25). The emergent new political economic orthodoxy – the embedded liberal paradigm – was central to the reconfiguration of the world order. The US Treasury Department Secretary Henry Morgenthau told the Bretton Woods conference he wished to 'drive the usurious money-lenders from the temple of international finance' (ibid.: 4). This colourfully captured the reservations about the liberal creed and its attendant free-flowing global finance. Bretton Woods constructed a politically regulated but broadly liberal international system of trade and payments wherein governments were formally encouraged to make use of capital controls to maintain external balance in the face of potentially destabilizing short-term 'hot money' flows (see Helleiner 1994; Ruggie 1982; Strange 1994b; Cohen 2002). The alteration of the regulatory institutional context of capitalism to enable the imposition of capital controls illustrated once again the core political economy insight that the economic and political are not separate or separable spheres. There is no such thing as a pure 'free' market, because markets are always politically maintained and subject to regulation.

Such a blueprint for the world economy would have been unthinkable 15 years earlier. So what had changed? At the Bretton Woods conference in 1944, attitudes to international capital movements were shaped by a new understanding which distilled the essence of the embedded liberal policy paradigm. A significant part of the problems of the inter-war international economy, policy-makers agreed, had been caused by flows of short-term 'hot' money (Eichengreen 1996). This had, for many, demonstrated what Polanyi called 'the pernicious effects of a market-controlled economy' (2001 [1944]) (Table 7.1).

This *new* prevailing wisdom (which questioned the benefits of short-term capital mobility) fed through into a new framing of economic policy debates. The new system should limit such (destabilizing and problematic) movements (de Vries 1987: 8–11; James 1996: 32, 37–9).

Table 7.1   Economic ideas and world order

Epoch	International order/world order	Dominant orthodoxy/economic policy paradigm	State/society complex
19th century up to World War I	Gold standard	Polanyi's 'liberal creed', *laissez-faire*	Nightwatchman state
Post-war era – 1940s–1970s	Bretton Woods institutions – pegged exchange rates regulated (liberalizing) capital flows, ever freer trade	Embedded liberalism; Keynesian stabilization through demand management	Keynesian welfare state
1980s–21st century	Advancing globalization – freer trade; financial deregulation and increased capital mobility	Dis-embedded neo-liberalism; monetarism and the New Right	'Schumpeterian workfare state' (Jessop)/competition state (Cerny)

The distinction between short-term and long-term capital flows was a crucial part of the mental furniture used to describe and understand the international context of economic policy. The policies that resulted from these ideas involved extensive capital controls to prevent destabilizing flows, while not ruling out long-term 'productive' international investment (Eichengreen 1996: 93–6). The approach to capital mobility was thus transformed. The free market for money which the gold standard had represented was curtailed – instead there would be *adjustable* but *pegged* exchange rates, a system of capital controls, and international monetary relations managed by new international economic institutions, notably the IMF.

This reordering of international political economic arrangements had an important domestic purpose, delivering a new political settlement which enabled the pursuit of a new economic policy paradigm – Keynesianism (see Chapter 4). The new limits on capital movements were to allow national governments to pursue full employment policies without disruption by speculative flows (de Vries 1987: 8–11; James 1996: 32, 37–9). Full employment, social welfare provision (see Chapter 11) and Keynesian demand management policies to stabilize domestic economies – these were all policy priorities which the architects of the new economic order sought to deliver (Eichengreen and Kenen 1994: 12). This amounted to a new set of intersubjective understandings about how a political economy should be ordered, distilled into a policy paradigm.

In concrete terms these were the new policy instruments developed to secure this new political economic settlement:

> controls on trade and financial flows allowed governments to pursue domestic policy goals, most notably full employment, without seriously violating international rules. They could tailor their fiscal and monetary policies to domestic needs, take welfare-state initiatives, and still meet the objective and obligations embodied in the postwar institutions, including the commitment to liberalize their trade and payments. (Ibid.: 5)

The late lamented Oxford economist Andrew Glyn cited an important passage from Keynes which indicated the centrality of the policy instrument of capital controls for the Keynesian policy paradigm: 'the whole management of the domestic economy depends upon being free to have the appropriate rate of interest without reference to the prevailing rates elsewhere in the world. Capital control is a corollary of this' (Glyn 1995: 40). The introduction of capital controls significantly altered the scope for governments (of advanced industrial economies at least), granting them some 'policy space' to pursue their domestic economic policy goals of full employment and welfare provision without bumping up against international constraints. Thus these controls formed foundational elements of the emergent Keynesian policy paradigm. The policy space was fundamentally altered, probably in ways not anticipated, by capital controls. The root cause was a 'paradigm shift' which transformed notions of the desirability (or otherwise) of heightened short-term capital mobility, which in turn reshaped international and domestic economic policy and politics.

In Ruggie's celebrated constructivist account of this episode, he underlines how 'collective intentionality creates meaning' and how the 'embedded liberal' compromise of the Bretton Woods era 'established intersubjective frameworks of meaning that included a shared narrative about the conditions that had made these regimes necessary' (Ruggie 1998: 21). The Bretton Woods negotiations to establish a monetary and trade regime 'produced more than standards of behaviour and rules of conduct. They also established intersubjective frameworks of meaning that included a shared narrative about the conditions which made these regimes necessary and what they were intended to accomplish, which in turn created a grammar, as it were, on the basis of which states agreed to interpret the appropriateness of future acts that they could not possibly foresee' (ibid.).

Embedded liberalism thus refers not just to a set of real concrete historical institutions established after World War II, but – arguably more importantly – also to a set of social facts (about appropriate – and inappropriate – ways to organize political economies and conduct economic policy) which generated a 'grammar' among policy-makers and political economic actors as the basis for their interpretation, in the decades following 1944, of the appropriateness of acts (see also pp. 253–6). Embedded liberalism, like any other prevailing political economic orthodoxy, is, for constructivists, a set of social facts, resting upon (contingent social constructions of) economic assumptions. It is historically contingent, and time and space specific.

From a Coxian 'critical' political economy perspective, the transformations of the mid-20th century need to be understood in terms of Pax Britannica, the previous prevailing world order. The old 'historic bloc' had been displaced, having lost its hegemonic status, and was now challenged by an emergent new hegemon. The two world wars saw the erosion of Britain's pre-eminence as an economic and military power. This undermined its material capabilities, and ushered in the rise of American economic and military power. Pax Britannica was replaced with Pax Americana (Cox 1987: 211–67).

The growth of American 'Fordist' capitalism, combining mass production and mass consumption (discussed further in Chapter 9), generated different 'social forces' – sets of social relations of production. The social forces arising from the social relations of production of American Fordism saw the empowerment of the labour movement, the rise of the managerial class. Transformations within world order and social forces were also interlinked with institutional transformations which saw the emergence of a new form of state. As Cox notes, 'a particular configuration of social forces defines in practice the limits or parameters of state purposes, and the modus operandi of state action' (ibid.: 105). Whereas after World War I the tide of expansion of state intervention into the war-time command economy had retreated with the onset of peace, after World War II there was no such receding. The emergent world order of Pax Americana and its attendant social forces entailed a new form of state – not the (minimalist) liberal state of the 19th century, but the (interventionist) Keynesian welfare state. This new Keynesian welfare state was born in part to redistribute wealth to sustain the patterns of mass consumption which underpinned Fordist capitalism (Block 2011). The embedded liberal policy paradigm discussed above was the ideational element aligned to this new form of state.

Over time, the world order was reconfigured and stabilized around the embedded liberal compromise. A new hegemon and a new historic bloc meant a new world order configuration. Pax Americana (the post-World War II configuration of world order) was sustained through the interaction of Cox's three sets of historical structures – institutions (Bretton Woods institutions such as the IMF), ideas (embedded liberalism) and material capabilities (American military and economic dominance). The new political economic order of the post-war period proved to be a conducive environment for sustained growth of Western liberal capitalism in general, but American capitalism in particular. It rested on an emergent coherence between world order and domestic forces: 'a coherent conjunction or fit between a configuration of material power, the prevalent collective image of world order (including certain norms) and a set of institutions which administer the order with a certain semblance of universality' (Cox 1981: 139). Thus, in the 1940s and 1950s, new 'ideas' as well as new 'material capabilities' and 'institutions' explain how and why the realms of the possible for domestic economic policy changed so significantly. Understanding political economic changes in any given national context also requires grasping these broader international patterns of change (and configuration of world order).

This major political economic shift in the mid-20th century demonstrates the malleability and historical contingency of dominant economic ideas and the institutions to regulate capitalism that arise from them. In a more contemporary context, the impact on and implications for the advanced political economies of the GFC have led to similar questioning of prevailing understandings about how economies work and the management and regulation of economic affairs. Though nothing comparable to the shift to embedded liberalism has emerged, a constant refrain of commentary and analysis of the GFC is the historical parallel with the 1920s and 1930s. The dynamics of the 'credit crunch' and its after-shocks certainly undermined the ebullient self-confident advocacy of free market solutions to all economic problems espoused by the likes of former US Federal Reserve Chairman Alan Greenspan. Re-examinations of accepted political economic wisdom, albeit on a more modest scale than in the 1930s and 1940s, shaped the post-GFC evolution of the international economic architecture.

The mode of economic regulation (in particular of financial markets) began to shift away somewhat from the 'self-regulating market' norms which had prevailed over the past few decades, towards a more 'hands-on' supervisory and monitoring role for various forms of public authority. Neo-liberal economic ideas have become deeply entrenched, and this reduces the probability of a Polanyian 'double movement', with an attendant 'great transformation' in state/market relations. Nevertheless, the GFC reignited a debate about capital controls within the IMF and beyond (Moschella 2015; Chwieroth 2014). Apparently settled in the decades following the breakdown of Bretton Woods in the 1970s in favour of capital account liberalization (and decisively *against* the acceptability of capital controls, equating them always with 'financial repression'), suddenly the GFC threw some elements of economic orthodoxy into flux. Capital controls have enjoyed a thorough rehabilitation as a crucial part of the 'macro-prudential' policy toolkit protecting against economic systemic risk (see Baker 2013a, 2013b). Through revisions to its prescriptive economic discourse which nudged back in a 'Keynesian' direction, the IMF rehabilitated counter-cyclical fiscal policy as an economic stabilization tool (Clift 2018, 2019).

Yet, even though the GFC unleashed a deep crisis within global capitalism, there was nothing like the scale of revisiting the principles on which liberal market capitalism was founded that we saw in the 1940s. Indeed, scholars soon inquired into the *Strange Non-Death of Neoliberalism* (Crouch 2011) and sought to explain 'the resilience of neo-liberal ideas in Europe' (Schmidt and Thatcher 2013). Political economists were interrogating why relatively little had changed in terms of the political economic order in the wake of the GFC (Helleiner 2014). What the crash of 2008 did, perhaps, was sow the seeds of discontent within advanced capitalist societies. This discontent was aggravated when the bankers that caused the crisis were bailed out by the state (Woll 2014). To make things worse still, ordinary citizens were forced to bear the burden of adjustment through a decade of austerity policies which ate away at social provisioning (Blyth 2013). A decade or so after the GFC, fuelled by post-crash austerity policies and widening inequalities in advanced economies, this discontent erupted into a backlash against globalization (Crouch 2019). It was manifest in resurgent populist, protectionist ideational challenges that shook the foundations of the liberal creed and the liberal international order, as I explore in Chapter 12.

CONCLUSION

In this chapter I have shown how ideas matter in CPE. Economic orthodoxies have real and powerful impacts, including gendered impacts, on how political economies are ordered and operate. Yet these are contingent historical phenomena, rooted in prevailing ideational conditions. Their political salience is shaped by the international economic and institutional context. What is deemed an 'appropriate' way to organize a particular nation's articulation with the wider global political economy is – as Ruggie and Cox in their different ways both highlight – space and time contingent. This historical contingency is unearthed through comparative analysis, both across time and across different geographical locations.

In drawing attention to context specificity and the contested nature of dominant economic ideas and understandings of how the economy works, ideationally attuned analysis can help to restore sufficient *contingency* to explanations of capitalist change (see also Campbell 2004: 71; Schmidt 2009: 540). The underlying political economic assumptions (rooted in prevailing political economic orthodoxy) upon which policy paradigms rest are social constructs. For constructivism, the social realm and the intersubjective construction of social facts shape this process. For Coxian critical political economy scholars, it is the configuration of social forces, forms of state and world orders that do this. Nevertheless, the key point here is that a full understanding of the changing CPE of capitalism requires appreciation of the shifting ideational sands and the ebb and flow of political economic ideas and orthodoxies. In the next chapter, we will see how differing visions of political economy have shaped and reshaped notions of appropriate levels and focus for state intervention in the economy.

8 The Comparative Political Economy of the State

INTRODUCTION

Conceptualizing and analysing the relationship between state and market arguably capture the substantive essence of political economy, and constitute CPE's most important contribution to social science. Many interesting analytical debates and controversies within CPE have focused on the trajectory, fate and potentialities of nation states within a changing global political economy. However, while most agree that focusing on states and markets is central to CPE, there are widely differing normative positions on, and understandings of, their complex relationship.

As we noted in Chapters 1 and 2, the temptation towards a dichotomizing opposition of state and market, or 'state–economy dualism' (Block and Evans 2005: 512), is resisted in this book. The idea of a tug of war wherein more market equals less state is erroneous. This chapter charts a route out of the 'state versus market' cul-de-sac, through recognition of the mutual constitution of state and market (Block and Evans 2005; see also Crouch 2004, 2011). This draws on classical political economy traditions and intellectual antecedents encountered earlier in this book – Marxian, Polanyian and Listian. In this chapter I develop a framework for analysing the CPE of the state using the comparative method to capture the contingency and historical specificity of individual national state adaptation processes. This is situated within influential accounts within CPE (and IPE) which introduce different 'forms of state' as comparative conceptual categories to chart state transformation.

Given that state and market are inextricably interlinked, and there is inherent interpenetration between state and market, it makes sense to think of the liberalization of markets since the 1970s not as deregulation, but as active re-regulation (see e.g. D. Vogel 1995; S. Vogel 1996; Levy 2006a, 2006b; Clift and Woll 2012a, 2012b; King and Le Gales 2017: 1–13, 21–5). This has implications for the questions we ask about the state, and the evidence we gather to adjudicate on its evolution. I argue that the most revealing and interesting questions surround not the *size* of the state (important though this issue is), but rather the recent evolutions of the *scope* of the state. CPE debates got rather bogged down in the 'more state' or 'less state' issue, which yields valuable insights, but at times hinders more than it helps in understanding the trajectory of contemporary state/market relations.

The empirical sections below illustrate how the political economy of the state is changing, first through a brief quantitative assessment, and then through qualitative analysis of changing state capacities and new modalities of state intervention. Later we will explore the variegated evolution of advanced economy states, illustrating how 'state forms' as analytical categories can be reconciled to historically contingent analysis of developmental state transformation in the cases of Japan and China. The aim here will thus be to demonstrate how the combined elements of our approach – the emphasis on state forms, and on deploying these conceptual categories in a manner sensitive to particular national legacies and contexts – can be operationalized. The final section explores the transformation of state capacity and 'new' state activism in the 21st century.

CONCEPTUALIZING THE STATE AND STATE/MARKET RELATIONS

Many CPE scholars have argued for the need to 'bring the state back in' to analyses which, they felt, neglected this key actor, arena or variable (Evans et al. 1985; Levy 2006a, 2006b; Schmidt 2009). For this re-incorporation to succeed, we need to consider carefully how that state is conceptualized – and here, classical political economy can help. Polanyi's *The Great Transformation* sees political economies as negotiated socio-economic orders, within which state and economy are mutually constitutive. The state sets the rules and framework for market activity, indicating the necessity of state intervention for the governance of, indeed the existence of, markets: 'no market economy separated from the political sphere is possible' (Polanyi 2001 [1944]: 146–7, 205; Krippner and Alvarez 2007: 233). Given the 'ubiquity of state intervention' (Perraton and Clift 2004: 209), Block's notion of the 'always embedded market economy' is a helpful one (Block 2003).

Informed by Marxist state theory, historical materialist scholarship, notably 'open' Marxism (Burnham 1994, 1999, 2001; Rogers 2009), offers surprisingly similar insights. Marxian political economy identifies an intimate connection between capitalism and state institutions, wherein state and market are inseparable both empirically and analytically. State and market are not opposing modes of social organization. The state is an active process of forming social relations, and a 'moment' of the process of reproduction of capitalist relations. It should not be thought of as losing power to the market. The Coxian critical political economy approach (Chapter 7) thinks in related terms, identifying 'forms of state' understood in the context of 'state/civil society complexes'.

Listian economic nationalist political economy locates a particular state within a national culture and a societal project of economic development, generating context-specific (contingent) analysis (Crane 1998). A Listian understanding of the state is shaped by the view that economic activity is always and inevitably suffused with political power relations. Political intervention shaping market outcomes is inextricably part of capitalism (List 1856: 249–50). Genuine free trade and *laissez-faire* are thus both distant prospects (see also Hamilton [1791] 1997). The nature of capitalism, and the role of the state within it, means that such intervention is *always* the case, in the 19th, 20th and 21st centuries, including in archetypal 'neo-liberal' political economies such as the UK or the US.

These conceptual reformulations of state/market relations offer helpful pathways into the CPE of the state. They have been articulated with varying degrees of precision and clarity, with some being systematically applied to empirical work (Evans 1995; Burnham 2003), while others remain more like thought experiments (Cox 1981). All share a basic understanding of the mutual constitution of state and market. Their focus is not 'the state' or 'the market', but market relations embedded in particular state/society complexes. From this vantage point, we can explore further CPE debates about the state and its evolution.

THE COMPARATIVE POLITICAL ECONOMY OF THE STATE

CPE scholars tend to be (rightly) wary of generalizations about the fate or trajectory of 'the state' within contemporary capitalism. As noted in Chapter 2, the CPE approach can differ starkly from some (realist) IR theorizing about 'the state', which posits in the abstract certain qualities, characteristics and properties of states in the international system. Most obviously, states at different levels of economic development are faced with very different problems, constraints and opportunities within the global political economy. State/market relations in the BRICS economies, for example, differ in some respects from the advanced industrial states, as the comparison between China and Japan below illustrates. But there are many other potentially important points of difference.

The reluctance to generalize about the fate, properties or potentialities of '*the* state' reflects a recognition of the embeddedness of societal negotiations of state/market relations, and the contingency and historical specificity of individual (national) state adaptation processes (Crouch 1993: 295–311). Accordingly, state and market will be intertwined in varied and distinct ways across different political economies. These historically specific interpenetrations of state and market herald significant national differentiation in the range and nature of state interventions in economy and society. To give an example, 'in Germany and the Netherlands the provision of postal services is privatised and fully marketised, while the provision of health services is seen as the concern of government; in the USA it is the other way around' (Crouch 2011: 20).

State transformation should not be discussed in apolitical terms. Bringing the state back in will not necessarily bring the *politics* back in. It is important not to depoliticize, 'naturalize' or 'necessitate' any state transformation in accordance with assumed or mooted economic imperatives (Hay 2004c: 41–2). If markets are socially embedded, then their governance will reflect power struggles between competing groups. In this vein Hay calls for 're-politicising the state' (ibid.: 38), avoiding a conception of natural adjustment to changing economic imperatives of a pliant state.

One fruitful analytical move is for states to enter the research design as *independent* variables (see Chapter 13; Levy 2006a, 2006b; Jackson and Deeg 2008; Schmidt 2009). States are (to a degree) independent entities that mediate external factors and shape trajectories of capitalist change, remaining, as Marxist scholars describe it, 'relatively autonomous' from their social and economic context. Therefore explanations for state retreat or transformation should entail not only external factors, but also the state's internal organization and workings, and the actions and strategies of state managers.

Contemporary CPE delineates qualitatively different forms of state emerging within advanced economies. 'Forms' of state can be incorporated into analysing what Phillips calls 'variegated processes of adaptation and transformation' (2005: 95; see also Cox 1987). Often these forms of the state concepts are drawn into CPE from comparative politics or Weberian historical sociology. With each form of state comes an attendant new mode of state/market interaction. Prominent examples within CPE include Polanyi's 19th-century 'liberal state' (2001 [1944]), the Keynesian welfare state (KWS; see e.g. Przeworski 1985), the 'developmental' or 'plan rational state' (see Johnson 1982 and pp. 183–7), the 'competition state' (Cerny 1997a), the 'managerial state' (Burnham 1999, 2001) and the 'Schumpeterian workfare state' (Jessop 1993). More recently, the 'debt state' and then the 'consolidation state' (Streeck 2014, 2017), the 'market supporting state' (Levy 2006b) and the 'market making state' (Crouch 2004; King and Le Gales 2017: 21–5) have been added to the canon. All can be deployed in a manner which recognizes the mutual constitution of state and market, and remains sensitive to the historical contingencies of market relations embedded in specific state/society complexes.

These ideal-typical characterizations serve to underline the qualitative changes in state–market interaction. For example, Mick Moran charts how the nature of interpenetration of state and market evolves as forms of state action and intervention in the market change with the rise of the 'regulatory state' (Moran 2001, 2003). With privatization, 'marketization' of public service provision and re-regulation of economic markets, the state oversees more, but directly delivers less (see also Thatcher 2017; King and Le Gales 2017). As the protean advanced capitalist state changed form in response to privatization and liberalization, advanced states came to *control* a smaller public sector, and *regulate* a larger private sector, requiring a very extensive and expensive infrastructure (Figure 8.1).

State forms are not necessarily mutually exclusive, and any single empirical case can manifest tendencies of more than one. The developmental state (DS), for example, has been evolving, with the growth of contemporary, more market-conforming and 'lean' state forms. Some identify 'regulatory state' elements as emergent in advanced democracies previously associated with the DS, without abandoning all its vestiges, dynamics and elements (see Walter 2006). States, and state actors, are considered agents of the transformation process heralding a shift in state form. These changes will be shaped by political forces and social embeddedness. Crucially, these forms of state are not settled realities, but ideal-typical characterizations of emergent processes of transformation (see e.g. Jessop 1993, 2002).

State forms can be deployed in different ways. Some seek to 'map' the changing prevalence of state forms across time onto shifts with global capitalism, such as from Fordism to post-Fordism (Lash and Urry 1987). Before that, the 19th-century nightwatchman or 'liberal state' was superseded by the embedded liberal KWS (Cox 1987). Some accounts detect the emergence of new state forms bound up with an inexorable logic, or necessary adjustment path. Cerny's 'competition state' argument claims that global competition induces national states to compete to attract inward foreign investment, providing infrastructure and attractive (low) taxation regimes (1997a; for a critique, see Hay 2004c: 41–2). Cerny's account aligns somewhat with the convergence analysis and logic we discussed in Chapter 6. There is limited recognition of possible alternatives to the competition state, the latter prevailing in 'an almost natural process of competitive selection' (Hay 2004c: 42). Globalization and economic imperatives may instil somewhat similar adaptations, yet the sheer volume of different 'forms' in the comparative literature suggests a

Scale and scope of Public provision	Logic of state action	
	Market directing	*Market conforming*
High / expanding	Developmental state	Keynesian welfare state
Low / reducing	Regulatory state	19th-century liberal state 21st-century competition state/consolidation state

Figure 8.1 State forms and characteristics

more open-ended, contingent process, and significant political and institutional media-tion of such exogenous forces.

Another approach differentiates geographically, rather than temporally, identifying the prevalence, for example, of the DS in East Asia, liberal or neo-liberal state forms in the US and the UK, and more embedded versions of KWS in continental Europe (see e.g. Perraton and Clift 2004). To some extent these strategies can be combined. State/society complexes in advanced political economies (and elsewhere) are historically contingent (Hay and Lister 2006) and different societal negotiations of state/market relations may make particular 'forms of state' more or less likely to emerge in particular contexts. National state traditions will also shape how new state forms manifest themselves empirically.

STATE TRANSFORMATION AND THE POLITICS OF ECONOMIC IDEAS

State transformation involves political contestation underscored by ideological struggles over the principles of political economy. As David Coates notes, analytical debates about the state within capitalism since the 1970s are as much ideological as empirical arguments (Coates 2000: 191–2). We can repoliticize discussions of state evolution by locating them against the backdrop of competing normative views of how the state *should* operate in the economy.

The economic ideas which inform and underpin public policy and economic policy-making operate at two different levels. Campbell distinguishes these as 'programmatic' and 'paradig-matic' (1998: 386–92; see also Schmidt 2008: 306–7). 'Programmatic' or operational eco-nomic policy ideas are used in day-to-day policy-making. 'Paradigmatic' ideas, which recall the policy paradigms discussed in Chapter 7, are rooted in underlying normative assump-tions about how political economies should be ordered. There has been a highly significant shift in overarching paradigmatic ideas about the appropriate balance between state and market since the 1970s. When Charles Lindblom wrote *Politics and Markets* in 1977, he exposed the 'myth' that the market was 'dying' in the face of ascendant planning (1977: 4–5). From a 21st-century perspective, this seems a strange thing to need to convince any-one about.

After the 1970s, in advanced economies and beyond, ascendant neo-liberal political econ-omy challenged the embedded liberal compromise and Keynesian ideas of extensive state interventionism within capitalism (Helleiner 1994: 144–5; Blyth 2002a: 126, 139–51). Crouch identified the core of neo-liberalism as the 'fundamental preference for the market over the state as a means of resolving problems and achieving human ends' (Crouch 2011: 7). As seen in Chapters 4 and 7, Keynes and Polanyi underlined how markets can fail; the neo-liberal New Right asserted that governments will fail.

Milton Friedman's monetarist ideas and Hayekian political economy (see pp. 83–6) influ-enced neo-liberalism. In Chapter 4 we noted Hayek's insistence that the state *should* not act: 'since the state can never know more than markets because of the way knowledge is dis-persed in a modern economy ... all forms of intervention are likely to be harmful and desta-bilizing' (Gamble 1986: 42). Yet Hayek appreciated that a strong state was necessary to police the market, ensuring that the value of money, the rule of law and contracts and prop-erty rights were sacrosanct. These all reflected the interpenetration and co-constitution of state and market. Indeed, the state was ultimately the guarantor of rules that made market order possible (see Gamble 1996: 134, 206–7).

Hayek's antipathy to state intervention resonated with the public choice theorists Niskanen, Tullock and Buchanan, whom we encountered in Chapter 5, and their assault on rent-seeking and 'budget-maximizing' state actors. The New Right rejected the benign, Keynesian or embedded liberal view of the state's positive stabilizing role within capitalism, and the Listian view of the state as catalyst enhancing efficiency and economic dynamism (Johnson 1982; Chang 1996, 1999). Neo-liberals argued that the state had performed far too many functions over the post-war period. The state was necessarily inefficient and a far less effective goods and services provider than the market, which it often 'crowded out' (Spencer and Yohe 1970).

Public choice inspired New Public Management (NPM), which offered policy solutions to a supposedly bloated and inefficient public sector – these included contracting out public services and marketization of public provision, integrating the market and market-like structures into the state and public policy. New Right ideas like NPM (see p. 103–4) were catalysts for neo-liberalism that shifted the embedding of market relations in state/society complexes along more market-conforming (rather than market-directing) lines. Both privatization and marketization became significant international trends, opening up more fields of state activity to markets, quasi-markets, competition and the private sector. Figures 8.2 and 8.3 indicate the ensuing multi-dimensional state transformation processes.

From the 1990s to the mid-2010s, social democrats and neo-liberals alike accepted the primacy of markets within a new market-conforming political economic settlement (see pp. 103–4, 243–7). This was a seismic shift for political economy and its study. Some discerned the replacement of the KWS with an emergent 'Schumpeterian post-national Workfare Regime' (Jessop 1993; Hay 2004c). That said, the extent to which neo-liberalism,

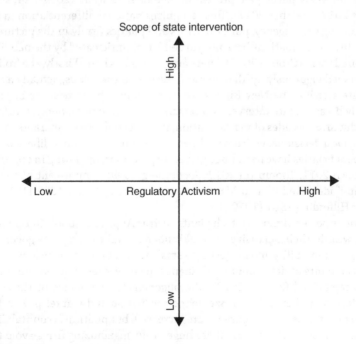

Figure 8.2 Logics of state restructuring

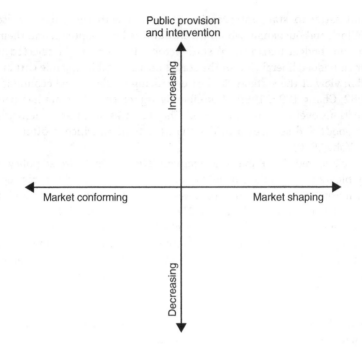

Figure 8.3 Dimensions of state transformation

privatization and marketization took hold varied across time and place. Hay identifies a 'gradual' and 'unevenly developed' process of 'neo-liberalisation' (2004c: 44; see also King and Le Gales 2017; Thatcher 2017). This recognizes national differentiation in state transformation, putting contingency, political actors and politics firmly in the picture.

Yet the state transformations have not turned out as anticipated by the neo-liberal thinkers who inspired them (Crouch 2017). There are two ironies here. Firstly, the 'rolling back' of the state, pursued vigorously by Thatcher and Reagan in the 1980s, actually expanded and extended state activity. The New Right's ability to reduce the state's size or scope proved limited, partly because state intervention remains integral to neo-liberal state/market relations. Secondly, after decades of marketization, it is not competitive markets, or small-scale firms making local decisions, which have been the beneficiaries of neo-liberalizing reforms. Rather, the beneficiaries have been huge global corporations, operating in oligopolistic markets (see Crouch 2011; Thompson 2012; Soederberg 2009), reminiscent of the imperialist 'finance capital' identified by neo-Marxists (see Chapter 5; Lenin 1950 [1917]; Bukharin 1971 [1917]; Hilferding 1981 [1910]).

The enormous power of modern tech giants such as Apple, Facebook and Google is linked to their vast wealth, their pervasive societal influence, and to corporate governance structures limiting accountability and protecting a small group of founding insiders. Their control of enormous amounts of data about us all shapes the power relations within contemporary 'surveillance capitalism' (Zuboff 2019). The oligopolistic dominance of these global tech firms is reinforced by their colossal size, market valuation and market power. We live in a world where some forms of transparency are increased, but political accountability of transnational corporations (TNCs) is not. These huge profit-maximizing firms avoid tax, distort, ignore and control knowledge, and use and shape public knowledge to their own ends

(Crouch 2016). Some compare them to the East India Company of earlier centuries in their ability to pervade and shape society, and their scope to operate as fiefdoms outside public authority or popular control (Atal 2019). The power of neo-liberal economic ideas, and the political projects which championed them, has transformed states and state/market relations in the advanced economies. However, the result has not been increased individual freedom or a more competitive and accountable corporate environment. Increased competition and local knowledge informing decisions, two key priorities for Hayek, are substantially absent from many aspects of the current political economic order in advanced economies.

The 21st century witnessed still further ebb and flow of economic ideas about state intervention. Responses to the GFC saw states, through bank bail-outs, fiscal stimulus programmes and the like, take on a more visible role in regulating capitalism (Thatcher 2017; King and Le Gales 2017; Woll 2017). Following a decade of post-crash austerity policies, reduced welfare provision, stagnating living standards and widening inequalities fuelled anti-*laissez-faire* movements advocating protectionism and economic nationalism (Crouch 2019; Hopkin 2017). These challenged the prevalence and acceptance of liberalized markets, favouring a more restricted, regulated market order. They renewed the emphasis, rhetorically at least, on state capacity and intervention – styled as 'taking back control' by populists (see Chapter 12).

THE EMPIRICAL ASSESSMENT: ADVANCED STATE CAPACITIES IN A GLOBAL ECONOMY

Before engaging in historically contextualized qualitative analysis, we need to gauge the broader empirical patterns of state transformation. To do this, we review CPE research engaging in large-scale quantitative cross-national studies of state activity in advanced economies, asking what this data tells us about how the political economy of the state is changing. The neo-liberal sea change in political economy and the cross-national trends in state transformation discussed above were catalysts generating a rich literature exploring the role of the state within CPE. This became somewhat fixated around the 'more state' or 'less state' issue.

Susan Strange advanced the notion of a 'retreat of the state' since the 1970s, explained by the growth, liberalization and internationalization of global production and markets (Strange 1996). The post-war era of 'organized' capitalism (Lash and Urry 1987), where the state played a key directive and orchestrating role within society and economy, has, in this view, given way to eroding state capacities and increasingly powerful market actors and institutions. State retreat theorists argue that CPE scholars' focus on differences between national political economies blinds them to global processes of state erosion and attrition. CPE fails to see the wood for the trees, unable to appreciate the 'general decline in the ability of governments to manage their national economies' (Strange 1996, 1997: 188).

Strange harnessed her retreat of the state thesis to predictions of capitalist convergence (see pp. 123–6). Crouch and Streeck also identified a 'rapidly advancing attrition of national state capacity in relation to the economy' (1997: 10). Increasing financial capital mobility constrains state autonomy generally, and macro-economic policy activism specifically. Allegedly, this reduces state interventionism as governments eschew expansionary fiscal and monetary policies in favour of sound money and balanced budgets (Andrews 1994). Some go further, hyperbolically asserting the 'end' of the state (Ohmae 1995).

The antithesis of these arguments is the 'compensation thesis', which claims that states are becoming *more*, not less, significant players (Cameron 1978; Rodrik 1998; Garrett 1995, 1998). This work builds on Katzenstein's classic study *Between Power and Plenty* (1978). As societies within increasingly open economies seek responses to (and insulation from) the vulnerabilities caused by globalizing economic pressures, the state has to step in to bolster economic and social stability (Swank 2002; Hobson 2003; Weiss 1998, 2003; Garrett and Lange 1991, 1995).

Large-scale quantitative analysis of data collected by various agencies – including the states themselves – about state capacities can unearth patterns, regularities and commonalities in changing state/market relations. This section concentrates on these empirical assessments of the state within contemporary capitalism. Many of these issues are taken up in the three following chapters, which explore state activity in relation to varieties of capitalism (Chapter 9), financial systems (Chapter 10) and welfare provision (Chapter 11). States, and international organizations such as the OECD and the IMF, gather a large amount of economic data, demarcating national economies and measuring aspects of state capacity. As Broome and Seabrooke put it, international organizations such as the IMF 'attempt to construct cognitive authority', partly by creating 'analytic institutions' to 'make their member states "legible"' (2012: 1; see also Scott 1998; Rosamond 2002). This is all useful raw material for political economists of all hues to evaluate and adjudicate upon the competing theories and assessments of the fate and trajectory of the state and its potentialities.

This data offers valuable insights into the evolving political economy of the state. For example, patterns of change in public expenditure as a proportion of gross domestic product (GDP) in OECD states provide a barometer of the state's displacement within advanced economies (see e.g. Perraton and Clift 2004; Hay 2011). This data can be harnessed to varied explorations of state transformation. In addition to quantitative evaluation of state activity and involvement in the economy, we can analyse data on different aspects of state capacity. Do patterns of change or continuity align with state transformation accounts aligned with particular forms of the state?

Public expenditure

The ability to raise revenue, borrow money and spend money is a key state capacity. Public expenditure as a proportion of total economic activity measures this spending capacity, giving indications about the public sector's size and scope. Counter-intuitively, through the neo-liberal heyday of 'rolling back' the state, total public expenditure *rose* a great deal. Thereafter it stabilized, but it continues to rise in real terms as economies grow (Coates 2000: 193–201; Swank 2002: 86–94; Perraton and Clift 2004: 209; Glyn 2006: fig. 1.8, table 7.2). Even in the neo-liberal heartlands of the UK and the US, the state has not reduced in size. The extended state remains alive and well, an enduring feature of advanced capitalism (Rodrik 1998; Hay 2011: 324–7, table 10.1), not least because state intervention and welfare remain integral to neo-liberal state/market relations. This scale of government spending cannot but influence patterns of economic activity, for better or worse. Neo-classical economics, built on marginalist foundations that exclude the state as exogenous to its models (see pp. 74–8), clearly overlooks crucial aspects of political economic activity.

There are thus good empirical grounds to question the 'retreat of the state' thesis. That said, snapshots of expenditure volumes tell us nothing about what money is spent on, and to what end. Stability in state expenditure levels may not equate to stasis in state/market relations. The nature of state interventions in, and the shaping of, economic activity could conceivably change dramatically without altering aggregate spending. Indeed, over many decades, stability would be remarkable and unlikely given the scale of political economic change. Thus expenditure levels, while instructive, are but a spur to further investigation, since the jury is still out on state transformation at this stage.

Taxation

A second key state capacity, closely linked to spending, is revenue-raising ability, especially through taxation. This is clearly crucial to the state's size, scope and potentiality for economic intervention. It captures the notion of state capacity better than aggregate expenditure levels. One prevalent debate argues that states' tax-raising abilities are undermined by downward tax competition resulting from globalization and increasingly mobile international capital (Strange 1996, 1997; Cerny 1997a). For the retreat of the state thesis, and indeed Cerny's competition state thesis, this mooted 'race to the bottom', especially in corporate taxation, is a crucial mechanism eroding capacity.

Furthermore, increasingly hard to tax but incredibly wealthy global corporate giants, embedded in what Seabrooke and Wigan call 'global wealth chains' (2017), shift their profits to low tax environments and tax havens (Sharman 2006) through 'transfer pricing' and other questionable accounting techniques. Campaigning groups like the tax justice network highlight the sheer range and complexity of tax avoidance and evasion strategies. Advanced states struggle to gain fiscal traction over these massive TNCs and their enormous profits.

Counter-intuitively, given globalization's mooted diminishing of state capacities, evidence indicates *increased* tax revenue as a proportion of GDP across a range of affluent economies between 1980 and 1999, from 33.2 to 38.2 per cent. There is no race to the bottom in taxation, but 'evidence of continuing divergence', albeit with 'some evidence of lower dispersion'. Through neo-liberalism's heyday, the average OECD tax take was increasing slightly, from 38 per cent of GDP in 1980 to 41 per cent in 1994 (Perraton and Clift 2004: 205–7, table 12.1). States in 21st-century affluent economies raise *more* revenue from taxing individuals, corporations and economic activity than in the 1960s, before international capital mobility really took off (Hobson 2003; Hay 2011: 316–29).

Swank's analysis of changing corporate taxation patterns finds an 'absence of systematic, downward pressure' on overall business tax burdens from 'internationalization' (2002: 249–50, 86–94, 2003). Reductions in 'headline rates' of corporate taxation have been largely revenue neutral, offset by broadening corporate tax bases and eliminating business exemptions, credits and allowances. Corporate taxation has thus become more market-conforming, but it has not reduced significantly. Increased international capital mobility was met with 'concomitant changes in tax policy (e.g. cuts in rates, base broadening, and related tax policy reforms) which produced moderate increases in tax revenues from capital' (Swank 2002: 255). Confirming the earlier analytical point that states need to be conceived as independent variables, state actors as agents of transformation have not submitted blithely to the inexorable forces of tax competition. Rather, they have adjusted their taxation practices, continuing to shape their own paths of economic development. Indeed, Swank concludes that 'the general fiscal capacity of democratic governments to fund a variety of levels and mixes of social protection and services may be relatively resilient in the face of internationalisation of markets' (ibid.: 249–50, 255).

Evidence indicates different societal negotiations of state/market relations and contingent national trajectories of state income and expenditure evolution in advanced economies (see pp. 238–41). Alongside these nation-specific patterns, there is also evidence of the geographical clustering of states, or forms of state, in expenditure and revenue-raising. We can identify Anglo-Saxon, Continental European and East Asian groupings in taxation levels, with some high tax 'outliers', notably Scandinavian countries (Perraton and Clift 2004: 209–15). All this tells us much about the state's size and some of its capacities. To explore the *scope* of the state further, we need more disaggregated analysis of state capacity, finding out what public expenditure is used for. One crucial state capacity is mitigating inegalitarian market outcomes (see Chapter 12) through redistributive policies. Despite its centrality to the state transformation debate, I will save the story of welfare and social provision for Chapter 11. Here we concentrate on other state capacities to intervene in and shape economic activity and market relations. This survey is not exhaustive, focusing on public employment and industrial policy, selected according to their importance and the quality of available data.

Public employment

The state plays an important role in the economy as an employer. This can fit with the compensation thesis, the state cushioning society from the vulnerabilities of enmeshment in a globalizing economy. It also links to Keynesian ideas about counter-cyclical economic policy, smoothing the economic cycle by expanding public employment to offset private-sector job losses (see pp. 81–3). Overall, public employment as a proportion of total employment has not declined since the 1970s. In most advanced affluent economies, there was a steady expansion during the 1960s and 1970s of civilian government employment as a percentage of the working age population, which was then followed by stabilization (Huber and Stephens 2001a, 2001b: 358–9; Huber et al. 2004). The results again group certain political economies together. Scandinavian states have most public-sector employment, around 20 per cent of the working population, France is in an intermediate position, and most other states are at between 5 and 10 per cent (Hay 2011: fig. 10.3).

This is another counter-intuitive finding given the neo-liberal emphasis on rolling back the state. We should, however, be mindful of data limitations in charting complex public-sector change. As a result of marketization, privatization and the NPM discussed above, advanced economy public sectors have been reconstituted, and the co-constitution of state and market has been reconfigured. The empirical complexities of the changing contours and logic of state activity raise important methodological issues. With private agencies delivering many public services, the boundaries of modern advanced states are more porous, less clear. Public–private partnerships blur these boundaries still further (Burnham 2001; Crouch 2011: ch. 1; Thatcher 2017).

Furthermore, following the GFC, states intervened to prop up the private sector. In some instances, the scale of state support amounted to or approximated re-nationalization. These more interpenetrated connections between public and private sectors raise interesting questions for CPE, such as: Where does the state end? And how do you measure it? We need to exercise some caution in interpreting the quantitative data on the size and scope of the state. Nevertheless, the data suggests that state employment is by no means diminishing in significance in contemporary advanced economies.

Industrial policy

In the post-war era, industrial policy was an important aspect of state involvement in the economy (Shonfield 1965; Zysman 1983). Quantitative assessments of industrial policy indicate an overall decline (Perraton and Clift 2004: 209). This aligns with the rise of neo-liberalism, the retreat of the state and a decline in state capacities. CPE analysis has high-lighted how the policy levers and mechanisms of industrial interventionism used by European and North American economies earlier in their history (List 1856), and in post-war Japan (Johnson 1982) and South Korea (Pirie 2005, 2008; Hundt 2009), are decreasingly viable in the contemporary global political economy (see e.g. Perraton & Clift 2004: 219–25; Clift and Woll 2012a, 2012b).

Traditional tools of industrial policy, such as governments subsidizing strategically important firms, are not readily available to developing countries because of global and regional trade rules on unfair competition (Chang 2002; Clift and Woll 2012a, 2012b). Direct industrial support through trade protection, local content requirements, subsidies and tax breaks are now severely restricted by the WTO, for example (Damro 2004; Hocking and McGuire 2004). Most countries find it harder to 'pick winners' or systematically use trade policy or selective industrial interventionism to promote sectors or firms (Perraton and Clift 2004: 215–19). Nationalized industries have largely been sold off, and industrial policy has shifted away from favouring 'national champions' towards 'horizontal' economy-wide human capital and infrastructure investment support for smaller, flexible firms.

Direct state intervention has reduced partly due to the changing political economy of finance (see Chapter 10). As private capital markets eclipse states and banks as sources of company financing, state capacity to induce firms' strategic choices is undermined. Yet states have not abandoned their ambitions to shape the industrial profile and steer the tiller of economic development. The GFC demonstrated that these ambitions endure, but the means to pursue them are being reinvented to avoid flouting international trade rules (Clift and Woll 2012a, 2012b).

That said, we should not overstate the erosion of industrial policy (Chang 2011; Wade 2012). Even before the GFC, though overall subsidy levels were diminishing, public subsidization of industries still cost between 1.0 and 0.5 per cent of GDP on average for the EU states between 1992 and 2007 (Zahariadis 2008; European Commission 2009). When the GFC hit, the co-ordinates of industrial policy rectitude were thrown into flux. The German, US, UK, French and other governments introduced enormous state aid packages to support large financial institutions and major automobile producers. This indicates the ongoing reality of interventionism and industrial policy. After a gentle decline in state aid from around 1.0 to 0.5 per cent between 1992 and 2007, there was a sharp spike up to 2.5 per cent of GDP in 2008 (European Commission 2009: fig. 1). The European Commission – which polices unfair competition rules – revised its directives to permit more state aid, not once but twice. This is further evidence of the enduring strength of the industrial policy reflex, especially in times of recession (Wilks 2009; Clift 2013; Mosconi 2015).

Following the GFC, even the OCED and IMF discovered an enthusiasm for industrial policy. The tectonic plates of orthodoxy surrounding economic interventionism were shifting (Wade 2012). Industrial policy has undergone a revival, with more countries, scholars and policy-makers recognizing its merits. Policy frameworks have strengthened commitments to strategic economic interventionism (Berger 2013; O'Sullivan et al. 2013; Chang and Andreoni 2016; Chang et al. 2013; Pisano and Shih 2013).

Trump's economic nationalist discourse noisily vaunted reviving US industrial policy, state interventionism and tariffs to protect, perhaps even revive, struggling US industries (Helleiner 2020). Indeed, support for a more muscular US industrial policy has crossed partisan divides (see e.g. Tucker 2019). Even economists like Rodrik (2004) and Stiglitz (Stiglitz et al. 2013) re-emphasized industrial policy commitments – albeit channelling neo-classical economics more than Friedrich List, Alexander Hamilton or Henry Carey (see Chapter 3). Economy-wide 'horizontal' approaches developing human capital and infrastructure superseded efforts to 'pick winners'. Heterodox economist Ha-Joon Chang found his reinvigorating industrial policy ideas becoming increasingly mainstream (Lin and Chang 2009; Chang 2011). Meanwhile, in Europe, industrial policy's revival accompanied the downturn following the sovereign debt crisis (Mosconi 2015; Chang et al. 2013). Competition policy and anti-trust rules did not constrain preferential interventionism as much as neo-liberals and ordo-liberals might have hoped.

Overview

The 'more state' (Cameron 1978; Rodrik 1998; Swank 2002) versus 'less state' (Ohmae 1995; Strange 1996, 1997) debates shed fresh light on the CPE of contemporary advanced capitalism. Yet state 'retreat' arguments often assume a passive state, subject to burgeoning exogenous forces. The state often enters debates as a dependent variable, its fate determined by external independent variables – variously globalization of finance and production (Giddens 1998), demographic change (Schwartz 2001) or European integration (Martin 2004; Offe 2005). This state is a price taker in world markets (see Streeck 2009, 2010). Yet states can be independent variables, market-making agents of transformation (see Levy 2006a; Clift and Woll 2012a, 2012b). Furthermore, the more state/less state framing jars with the mutually constitutive conception of state/market relations. Thus the 'retreat of the state' thesis can be challenged both theoretically and empirically.

Judged empirically by indicators of what states do in the economy, evidence indicates a *lack* of state retreat. How can this be explained? Partly, it reflects the co-constitution of state and the market. Another explanation, recalling the 'compensation thesis', is that societal pressures prevent any retreat. In Polanyian terms of the 'double movement', the damaging consequences of freer markets provoke social and political resistance. An ongoing dialectical struggle plays out between dual forces of 'economic liberalism' (dis-embedding economic activity from society) and 'social protection' (re-embedding economic activity within society; 2001 [1944]: 136–9).

More puzzlingly, why did state retreat arguments gain such ground? Partly, it is because evidence of new or enhanced capacities in the economic is hard to acquire. Some of the enduring, even expanding, state intervention – market-making, market-shaping re-regulatory activity – is hard to capture empirically (Clift and Woll 2012a, 2012b). Certainly, it is difficult to capture in large cross-national quantitative studies.

This broad-brush overview is only part of the story. It is easy, when looking at OECD tables and graphs, to presume that each state is essentially similar. They are all advanced industrial democracies, but this category stretches very widely. We should recognize states as independent variables and appreciate different state/society complexes. Each distinct national path of development reflects particular ideational and cultural conditions. All this is difficult to capture in large-scale quantitative assessments – hence the need to complement this overview with a more qualitative, fine-grained, empirical assessment of particular cases.

QUALITATIVE ASSESSMENT: STATE FORMS AND STATE TRANSFORMATION

In-depth case studies of the changing political economy of the state add the necessary granularity. We can locate the ideal-typical state forms discussed earlier in concrete historically and nationally specific empirical contexts. Even among the advanced economies, state characteristics differ significantly. In combining the analysis of broad trends of state change with specific case studies, we face the perennial trade-off between large-scale studies, knowing 'less about more', and detailed analysis of a few cases, knowing 'more about less' (see Chapter 13). Below we demonstrate the relevance of the conceptual and methodological points made above through exploration of the capitalist DS in Japan and China. These illustrative examples indicate how to incorporate state forms into the analysis of the political economy of the state and its transformation.

The Japanese developmental state

The DS has played a particularly important role within CPE analysis of the state and its evolution (Johnson 1982, 1995; Amsden 2001: 125; Gotoh 2019). DS analysis aligns with many of the themes developed above: state and society need to be understood as a complex whole engaged in a joint enterprise of societal (and industrial) transformation across the 20th century (see also Kohli 2004: 390). For Chalmers Johnson, who introduced the DS concept, the social forces of 'social mobilization' and 'nationalism' were crucial. Johnson (1982) charts how the Japanese 'plan rational state' used its key agencies (in tandem with business elites) to steer the nation's economic development in the 20th century. Japanese capitalism is not simply state-directed, but entails complex interactions within the state/society complex. Reflecting the mutual constitution of state and market, the DS 'is not an imperious entity lording it over society but a partner with the business sector in a historical compact of industrial transformation' (Woo-Cumings 1999: 16; see also Evans 1995: 59).

Johnson (1995) offered a 'thick description' of Japanese development, and saw the DS as a *sui generis* ('one of a kind') Japanese phenomenon. He prioritized historical specificity, and did not see the concept as readily transportable beyond Japanese borders. Some scholars prioritize detailed contextualized understanding of particular cases, and others favour more theoretical and conceptual abstraction in pursuit of generalizations. There is clearly tension between the historical, specific uniqueness which Johnson favours, and the analytical rewards of comparing similar trends across cases. Yet Johnson is right to underline that the DS is rooted in national specificities of historical and ideational context. Therefore caution is needed in attempting to apply the Japanese 'model' across national borders.

In Chapter 13, I will make the case for Pierson's 'limited portability' of concepts across space and time as a useful middle ground. In this spirit, subsequent comparativists have applied the DS outside Japan – identifying different DS trajectories and histories in East Asian economies (Weiss 2004), in Latin America (Evans 1995; Ban 2013) and indeed in post-war Europe (notably France; Loriaux 1991, 1999, 2003). Levy et al. note, for example, similarities in the DS interventionism in post-war Japan and France: both used meritocratic state education to recruit the brightest talent to the prestigious state bureaucracy; both engaged in indicative economic planning to guide economic development; both used a plethora of policy instruments (such as managed exchange rates, price and credit controls and state aid) to allocate economic resources strategically (2006: 97). Japan and France were, in this account, the East Asian and European DS exemplars. Below we explore the applicability of the DS concept in the contemporary Chinese case.

State capacities are central to DS analysis, which understands the CPE of development primarily through the lens of state-led industrialization (Weiss 1998). Finance is the 'tie that binds the industrialists to the developmental state' (Woo-Cumings 1999: 10). The DS as 'gatekeeper' controls access to investment, attaches strings to subsidies, rations credit and maintains artificially low interest rates. Illustrating the state as an independent variable, which shapes paths of economic development, DS managers use credit-based financial structures as conduits of industrial policy, to support and restructure key industries.

Japanese DS scholars emphasize how prior institutions and state traditions shape trajectories of change (Johnson 1982; Vogel 2006: 3–4). Decisions taken and acts of institutional creation undertaken are the stuff of political struggles, and these shape subsequent developments through path dependency (discussed in Chapter 6). At critical junctures, one path is selected over alternatives, as in Japan under the Meiji dynasty from the late 1860s until the early 20th century (Lehmbruch 2001: 59–68; Gotoh 2019: 7–12) or at the end of World War II. In each case, the norms, practices and expectations established early in a phase of development had a profound impact on the subsequent parameters of possible evolution.

The distinctive national social and ideational context within which state institutions are embedded shapes state/economy relations. This perhaps explains Johnson's reticence about using his DS concept beyond Japan. In each DS case, social networks and social norms (for example, about the nature and role of the firm in society and employment security) play their role in shaping state actors' interactions with business elites (see pp. 134–8; Vogel 2006). Lehmbruch terms this the 'discourse of embedded capitalism' (2001), another dimension of which is the expectation of and accepted legitimacy of state interference within private economic activity (Johnson 1982; Vogel 2005, 2006).

Organized business interests have significant influence within the Japanese state, and economic sectors are dominated by '*keiretsu*' (oligopolistic conglomerates of financial and industrial firms). These close-knit business elite/state relations are cemented by job mobility – the so-called 'descent from heaven' in Japan, where senior state bureaucrats leave the ministries to take up positions on corporate boards. A similar process within the French DS is called *pantouflage* – literally shuffling between top state and business posts in one's carpet slippers. This fusing of state and business within individual career trajectories highlights the important temporal dimension. The DS is, in Woo-Cumings' phrase, 'a diachronic phenomenon' (1999: 15), its evolution and logic only understandable over a lengthy period. These important sources of co-ordination within Japanese capitalism were 'learned and perfected over time, through a long process of institutional adaptation' (ibid.).

As noted above, the CPE of the state needs to portray a dynamic, not a static, picture (Streeck 2009, 2010). The DS is a dynamic, evolving project. Ha-Joon Chang talks of 'dynamic efficiency' as opposed to 'static efficiency' (the latter he equates with neo-classical economics). The DS is a 'catalytic agency' with 'a "vision" for the future of the economy'. Rather than 'blindly following current price signals', the DS entails 'an important "entrepreneurial" dimension' (Chang 1999: 194). Over decades, 'entrepreneurial' DS interventionism shapes the nature of the market economy. The DS is not solely a financial 'gatekeeper' but shapes many, perhaps all, aspects of market relations.

Finance is rightly seen as 'the defining aspect of the developmental state' (Woo-Cumings 1999: 11). Yet given the dense networks linking public and private sectors, and the proximity of state institutions to economic activity, the tentacles of the DS extend much more widely and deeply into the fabric of market and society. The economic policy mechanisms the DS deploys seek to perform four functions: 'developmental banking; local-content management; "selective seclusion" (opening some markets to foreign transactions and keeping others closed); and national firm formation' (Amsden 2001: 125). In addition to state subsidies and aid to industry, state policy and actions shape economic development through a wide range of possible market-making interventions. These include public procurement (giving government contracts to favoured firms), price controls, regulating company law and corporate governance, and controlling market access, not only through trade barriers but also by regulations of product and labour standards.

These long-term structural and historical processes shape business/state bureaucracy relations (Evans 1995). Along with the legacies of other tentacles of DS intervention, they mould the very nature of markets and property rights in societies. This role of the DS as the 'ultimate guarantor of property and other rights in the society' (Chang 1999: 196) is crucial to how capitalism works. It underlines the fundamental role the state plays in sustaining the market economy. Politics shapes market outcomes in a very evident fashion in, for example, the East Asian DS political economies after World War II. Revealing how the political and the economic are intertwined in the co-constitution of state and market, Chang notes: 'in the end, all prices are potentially political, and there is no "scientific" rule that will tell us which prices should be "political" and which should not be' (ibid.: 197).

This (potential) politicization of virtually any aspect of economic activity exemplifies the notion of the 'always embedded' market economy. Listian insights into the nature of capitalism, and the state's role within it, are also particularly pertinent to the DS (List 1856: 194, 250, 261). The labour market is one of the central features of any capitalist economy. It is always and inevitably (even in supposedly deregulated, flexible and 'freer' labour markets) shaped by political regulations (including labour standards and immigration controls). Given 'numerous regulations in the product markets regarding safety, pollution, import contents, and so on, there is virtually no price that is free from politics' (Chang 1999: 197). Other examples of politically managed prices can include interest rates and exchange rates.

DS and Japanese state transformation

Given its 'diachronic' character, change over time is integral to DS analysis. In the 2000s, Japanese scholars explored how, compared to the post-war era (Coates 2000: 54–64), state agencies no longer enjoyed their earlier dominant position. The proportion of the economy under Ministry of International Trade and Industry (MITI, the key agency of the post-war Japanese DS) measures fell with the structural change in the Japanese economy. MITI was renamed METI – the Ministry of Economy, Trade and Industry – and moved from strategic industrial policy towards more incremental, less targeted programmes, responding to a changing international regulatory environment. Consistent with the quantitative evidence presented above (pp. 157–63), METI's ability to protect its industry through tariffs and an artificially low exchange rate has been reduced. Its power within the government apparatus diminished as its budget and number of personnel fell relative to the rival competition agency, the Japanese Fair Trade Commission (Matsuura et al. 2004; Vogel 2005, 2006; Levy et al. 2006).

Some interpret this undermining of capacity within the archetypal Japanese case as symbolizing the 'end' of the DS (Beeson 2003, 2009; Wade 2003). For others, what is afoot is something akin to Streeck's 'redesigning of state capacity' (2001). Japanese state interventionism is not 'in retreat' (Levy et al. 2006). Rather, METI is reinventing itself, taking on new missions: promoting investment abroad and in Japan, and 'deregulation, cultivating market infrastructure, and facilitating corporate restructuring' (Vogel 2005: 163).

The Japanese government actively intervened in the financial system attempting to resolve Japan's protracted economic slump. Vogel outlines Japan's 21st-century industrial policy as 'cultivating new mechanisms to help turn around troubled corporations', working with the market, but using some familiar tools, such as tax breaks, subsidies and low-interest loans (2006: 85–8). In 2003 the government launched the Industrial Revitalisation Corporation to buy up non-performing loans (NPLs), working with the main bank investors to reorganize struggling companies (Vogel 2005: 163–4, 2006: 85–8; Walter 2006; Jackson et al. 2008).

Consistent with the institutional and ideational path dependency discussed earlier, prior Japanese societal institutions and state traditions continue to shape the trajectory of the DS (Matsuura et al. 2004; Vogel 2006: 3–4; Jackson and Miyajima 2008; Lehmbruch 2001; Gotoh 2019). Vogel identifies how preferences within Japanese society, business associations and bureaucracy are diverse, hindering fast and further liberalization: 'given the embedded nature of ... sectoral bargains, liberalisation requires a complex process of renegotiation' (2006: 62). Tendencies associated with changing 'forms of state' are refracted through these renegotiation processes. This suggests caution before asserting that one state form has been replaced, for example grafting a neo-liberal 'regulatory state' onto the long-established DS.

Andrew Walter explores how far the neo-liberal 'regulatory state' has taken hold in Japan (2006: 410). Evaluating the transformation of Japanese banking regulation, Walter argues that despite significant evolutions in institutions and regulatory codes, change to business/state relations on the ground is less than dramatic. Crucially, levels of discretionary regulatory action remain high, and the degree of independence of regulatory agencies is low. Thus a variant of the regulatory state is present within the Japanese political economy, yet its manifestation is unlike the neo-liberal ideal type because of Japan's social context within which it is embedded. Similarly, within labour market deregulation and liberalization, Japanese social norms limit 'Anglo-Saxon' hire and fire practices (see pp. 185–7; Vogel 2006; Jackson 2008; Sako 2008; Gotoh 2019).

In the case of Japan, then, state transformation is clearly a reality, but *not* state erosion or retreat. Erosion of the DS's characteristic financial 'gatekeeper' leverage has been a major body blow, but Japan's interventionism has not been abandoned. Developmental states have always adapted policy instruments to new circumstances, and this continues. Meanwhile, some argue that DS dynamics are becoming increasingly relevant in China.

Is China a capitalist developmental state?

Contemporary CPE scholars have sought to use the DS concept to analyse the transformation of China's state/market relations and its rise as a global economic power since the 1970s. From a Maoist or communist political economy heavily influenced by Marxism, China has evolved dramatically since 1978 'from a state planned and state owned economy towards state regulation of a hybrid economic system with the existence of a private economic sphere that remains very close to the state system that spawned it' (Breslin 2007: 40).

China's societal project was redefined from Chinese-style socialism to an emphasis on economic modernization and 'quasi-capitalism with Chinese characteristics'. Within this ongoing evolution, private-sector expansion co-exists with an enduring key role for the authoritarian Chinese Communist Party (CCP) as central in orchestrating state/society relations (McNally 2019; Gruin 2019).

The DS concept (Breslin 1996, 2011) highlights the unambiguous link between Chinese economic nationalism and the country's economic rise, with the CCP defining Chinese national interest. Like earlier DS projects, China after 1978 faced a hostile international environment, with competition from the US globally and Japan locally. The CCP felt a pressing need to catch up with, perhaps even overtake, economic rivals. This recalls Johnson's 'status inconsistency' logic of the Japanese DS (1982). Wan (2011) argues that China's liberalizing trade agenda in East Asia is a strategy to counter US dominance in the region.

DS analysis also aligns well with the public- and private-sector interrelationships developing within Chinese quasi-capitalism. From the late 1970s onwards, the basis of party rule shifted from ideological attachment to Marxism to emphasis on securing economic modernization and growth. This heralded the emergence of a Chinese 'private sector', though this term has a distinctive meaning in China. During the decollectivization of agriculture, small-scale township and village enterprises (TVEs) were an interim evolution, which were non-state yet not fully private economic activities notionally outside state control. Thereafter, partial privatization of state-owned enterprises further blurred the lines between public and private (Breslin 2011; see also McNally 2019; Gruin 2019).

The non-state sector proved economically more successful, and the CCP, prioritizing capital accumulation, encouraged private ownership and expanded the non-state sector (Breslin 2007: 49). Yet economic success in China's 'private sector' still hinges on clientelistic relations between firm and Party. All Chinese markets remain subject to CCP regulation and oversight, especially by local government officials. Business success is all dependent on political decisions, networks and support. Thus, as Breslin puts it, 'commercial rationality in China is less about searching for market opportunities than searching for strong ties with local officialdom that in turn will guarantee those market opportunities' (ibid.: 73). This is very unlike a free market capitalist economy in the European or North American sense. These blurred public/private boundaries arguably increase the DS's relevance for understanding China's political economy. Breslin talks of the 'coalescence of political and new economic elites' in contemporary China, where 'state elites and new economic elites' have 'co-opted each other into an alliance' (ibid.: 78, 79). This all recalls Johnson on the DS in Japan (1982) and Evans on Latin America (1995). However, decades of authoritarian party rule in China means that there is no civil society independent of the Party. Rather, the Chinese authorities seek passive acceptance of CCP orchestration of economic development. The tentacles and legacies of party–state intervention continue to shape outcomes, and the 'non-state' sector remains 'heavily connected to officialdom through various mechanisms' (Breslin 2007: 76; McNally 2019).

Chinese finance has shifted since the 1970s from plan-based to bank-based credit. China's financial system is bank-based, though underwritten by the state through quasi-government debt (Breslin 2007: 56). Offering further evidence of blurred public/private boundaries, there remains extensive political interference in lending decisions. In essence the financial system serves local state and party elites by maintaining employment, generating taxes and allowing favoured companies to flourish. Chinese financial system reform also reinforced the internationalization of the economy, seen by the CCP as key to sustaining economic growth, development and modernization. Before China's new economic strategy began in 1978, foreign economic relations had been outlawed. The partial opening up of the Chinese economy began with the creation of four Special Economic Zones (SEZs) – with limited freedom to engage in international economic relations such as joint ventures – and permitting, then later encouraging, foreign investment and foreign ownership of firms. Residual domestic protectionism co-exists with the gradual opening up of (parts of) the Chinese economy and society to global capitalism (and neo-liberal economic ideas and reforms).

Integral to changing China's articulation with the global political economy was joining the WTO (in 2001) and signing other bilateral free trade agreements. The country's exports have grown rapidly following liberalization. Some see China's trade policy as resulting from struggles between protectionists and liberalizers, and thus driven by economic beneficiaries of liberalization (Jiang 2010), while others interpret it in more DS-style terms, emphasizing the role of China's autonomous government bureaucracy (Wan 2011). Compliance with WTO regulations remains incomplete given the 'less than full liberalisation of the Chinese economy' and the 'less than even playing field for external economic actors' (Breslin 2008: 27). Thus, by combining liberal and Listian economic nationalist elements, Chinese authorities are able to interpret WTO rules in ways that continue protecting some Chinese firms and sectors (Ravenhill and Jiang 2009: 42–3; Jiang 2010).

The politically managed low valuation of the renminbi is another facet of China's foreign economic relations. This exchange rate policy secures the competitiveness of Chinese exports on world markets, but causes tensions, notably with the US and Japan, who periodically threaten to withhold market access. US/China economic relations became highly politicized with Trump's 'America First' policy. This entailed increasingly vociferous opposition to what the Trump administration saw as unfair Chinese currency manipulation, discriminatory trading and indeed industrial espionage practices. The Trump administration's 'trade war' with China resulted both from resurgent US protectionism and economic nationalism, and from China's combination of liberal and Listian economic nationalist elements.

After 1978, economic modernization was initially DS-style and state led. Extensive state aid to industry accounted for a quarter of government expenditure by the late 1980s. Since then, Chinese state interventionism has changed nature and form, evolving mechanisms of economic control and arguably creating 'a new regulatory state' (Breslin 2007: 64), shifting from government control to supervision and regulation. However, because of enduring local political autonomy, it is largely a 'voluntary regulatory state' (ibid.: 72) and thus very different from advanced economy variants. Moreover, the Chinese state still uses multiple traditional interventionist means, channelling funds to favoured firms through local government, as influencing economic outcomes through levying fees, awarding public contracts and granting of tax relief (Breslin 2007, 2008).

Thus evolving Chinese state/market relations have not fully introduced market forces. The lack of transparency and of established institutions of corporate governance (which help limit corporate abuses in other contexts) means that Chinese privatization has been insider-oriented, dominated by 'bureaucrat capitalists'. It is more akin to insider dealing or asset stripping. Chinese stock markets proved 'efficient' at taking money from private investors and redirecting it to 'networks of insiders clustered around the local party-state machinery' (Breslin 2007: 74). Interestingly, these problems resemble the corruption and clientelism found in other DS cases, including Japan, Korea and Latin America.

Breslin terms the Chinese political economic settlement an 'Embedded Socialist Compromise', an uneasy alliance combining some competition-promoting market reforms with protecting those who suffer through a concern for employment and social stability (Breslin 2007; see also Ravenhill and Jiang 2009: 40). Yet this compromise is not easily maintained given uneven development across the enormous extent of China's political economy. Within China's 'fragmented authoritarianism' (Lieberthal and Lampton 1992), power operates at many sub-state levels, with a 'diffused and differential nature of centre–local relations' (Breslin 2007: 61).

The economic power structure is also fragmented. The southern coastal provinces (sites of the initial SEZs) have become highly internationalized and enmeshed in global networks of production and capital and trade flows. Many other inland provinces remain much less integrated and much less economically advanced. The geographically uneven impact of China's economic modernization means that the state sector dominates in the interior and the north-eastern provinces. Meanwhile foreign-owned enterprises, TVEs and the like dominate the coastal regions in the south, such as Guangdong, Shanghai and Liaoning, recipients of 90 per cent of FDI since 1978. Yet there are weak, shallow linkages between export-oriented sectors and the wider Chinese national economy. Technology transfer has been lacking from assembly for export plants by foreign-owned TNCs, and this limits FDI's effectiveness as a motor of Chinese 'indigenous' economic development.

Furthermore, China's economic development came at enormous environmental cost (Shapiro 2001, 2016). The ecological degradation that Polanyi (pp. 255, 298, 309) and Hardin (pp 5, 99) warned of has been one dark side of China's economic 'miracle'. This, compounded by uneven economic development and the relative backwardness of rural agricultural areas, is potentially socially destabilizing (Lai 2010). Two manifestations of the tensions are popular protests and massive labour migration. These social and geographical tensions are compounded by a highly variegated political infrastructure. Decentralized economic authority means that local authorities impose fees on economic actors to raise revenue, and there are extensive internal tariffs (local protectionism) encountered when moving goods around within the country (Breslin 2007: 66–7). All this hinders Chinese internal market development. These were exactly the problems List sought to resolve with his proto-DS plans for Prussia/Germany in the 1840s.

The GFC layered new vulnerabilities upon these existing ones. The crisis refocused attention on the scale of bad loans and bad debts within the Chinese banking system. Before the crisis, bad loans were transferred to asset management companies at enormous cost – perhaps US$260 billion – but the fundamental problems were not addressed (Breslin 2012a: 7–8, 2014). Local governments, establishing Local Investment Platform Companies (LIPCs), circumvented restrictions on local government borrowing. Following the crisis, much of the vast RMB4 trillion (US$586 billion) stimulus package was channelled through local government lending on infrastructure projects, adding to the potential for more NPLs (Breslin 2012a, 2012b, 2014; Gruin 2013, 2019). These problems arise because of ongoing political manipulation of lending practices.

The interlinkages between party and state, between local government and business, as well as among public, semi-private and private sectors, remain deep and complex. At a local level, 'the relationship between the state, the financial system and economic actors is often quite intimate on a daily basis' (Breslin 2012a: 24). The character of Chinese state/economy relations, including widespread corruption and political interference in economic decision-making, may present considerable difficulties for growth and economic performance. Furthermore, the Chinese economy is not immune to speculative bubbles, notably in land prices. Breslin detects 'an unsustainable link between banks, local government, and land prices' (ibid.: 4). This is particularly problematic since local governments derive much of their income from land sales.

There have been moves towards 'rebalancing' Chinese economic activity towards a more sustainable growth path. Before 2008, state actors sought to steer Chinese economic development to reduce the vulnerable reliance on FDI and exports, to boost domestic private consumption and to 'trade up' towards higher value-added production. These efforts were downgraded amid needs to restart the Chinese economy, since the political and social consequences of stagnation were deemed too unpalatable to contemplate (Breslin 2012a, 2012b).

In summary, the DS concept has some explanatory purchase over the desire to steer recent Chinese economic development, the capacity to do so and the policy mechanisms used. China's financial system has undergone substantial reform, introducing market mechanisms to supplant earlier state direction. Despite wide-ranging internationalization and privatization, China remains a political economy *very* unlike other liberal capitalist economies, retaining some DS characteristics in terms of financial system dynamics (Breslin 2014; Gruin 2013, 2019). Following these evolutions, China's leadership finds the political direction of national economic development harder to achieve. Given the deep but uneven articulation of China with the global political economy, China's DS variant is arguably more globalized than others. China's modernization and state-led developmentalism are not purely nationalistic, because they are driven partly by external sources with a key role for international economic actors. The repatriation of profits by foreign TNCs means that they were 'winners', as well as China. Chinese economic development arises out of Chinese state politics acting in concert with foreign companies (Breslin 2007, 2011, 2012a, 2012b). Nevertheless, Chinese state elites demonstrate significant capacity to orchestrate their national economic developmental path.

THE TRANSFORMATION OF STATE CAPACITY: 'NEW STATE ACTIVISM' AND THE REINVENTION OF CONTROL IN THE ECONOMY

Both the Japanese and Chinese cases demonstrate that the state's relation to the economy is changing, especially surrounding the traditional DS 'gatekeeper' role in finance. International financial liberalization and re-regulation substantially undermined domestic governments' capacity to direct credit and channel economic development. This was a linchpin of earlier DS interventionism. Since the 1970s, this has reduced state managers' leverage to cajole and influence business elites, hindering the effectiveness of DS policy instruments (Perraton 2003, 2009). Yet this erosion is not complete, as the China case illustrates. Responses to the GFC (see Grant and Wilson 2012) further underline ongoing market-shaping activities by interventionist states, including subsidies to prop up troubled firms and sectors. Under normal circumstances, however, state interventions have not so much eroded as changed form.

The global integration of markets and the concurrent weaving together of regulatory frameworks put pressure on national economic interventionism to comply with WTO rules, other international trade agreements or European competition policy. All of these increasingly proscribe traditional industrial policy and direct intervention, as analysed by Shonfield (1965) and Johnson (1982). As noted above, industrial policy revived following the GFC, and its death should not be exaggerated. Overall, governments have become creative to achieve traditional economic policy objectives with new means. The multiple policy instruments of economic interventionism are more fragmented and less coherent than in Shonfield's era; they may be no less prevalent.

The CPE of the state requires an understanding of this transformation of political influence over the economy. For example, industrial support has become bound up with regional policy and urban policy (OECD 2006; Crouch and le Gales 2012), in part to circumvent strict state aid rules (e.g. in the EU) and anti-trust rules (within the WTO). Some policies are designed to support insiders without in principle excluding outsiders, yet they strengthen the position of national or regional target groups, such as risk regulation or competition rules that prohibit standards that are common abroad. This is a reinvention of political control of the economy (Clift and Woll 2012a, 2012b).

Analysing this changing scope of state intervention is one way to explore 'new state activism' identified by Levy (2006a). Levy argues that as *'the state also rises* ... globalisation and liberalisation has spelled not the erosion of state activism but rather the redeployment of state initiatives on behalf of new missions' (ibid.: 2–3). Of the various forms of state intervention and state/economy relations, the DS is particularly vulnerable. Its penchant for authoritative market direction clashed with shifts towards a 'market supporting' role for states in affluent political economies (Levy 2006b: 385–7). Ascendant neo-liberalism was a cold ideological climate for DS interventionism. Wolfgang Streeck sees this in Polanyian terms of a 'second Great Transformation of the state' (2001: 38), a profound 'redesigning of state capacity' in the face of 'changed international conditions of state action'. The 'emerging nation state of the future', he argues, is 'much more market-making and market-conforming than market-limiting and market-distorting' (ibid.; Figure 8.4).

With these new modes of intervention, industrial policy has become somewhat Janus-faced, combining older and newer interventionist modes. New missions of 'market support' involve logics of state intervention that may be 'corrective' or 'constructive'. All this

		The varied political economy of industrial policy	
		Liberalizing	Protectionist/ Defensive
Policy logic	Market-supporting, favouring insiders	Q1 e.g. selective liberalization in strategic sectors	Q3 e.g. regulation to maintain home product and process standards; state subsidies
	Market shaping, resisting outsiders	Q2 e.g. regulation or competition rules that prohibit standards common abroad	Q4 e.g. classic barriers to trade

Figure 8.4 State transformation and new instruments of economic interventionism (see also Clift and Woll 2012a, 2012b)

illustrates 'the state's innovative capacity ... [for] forging new state policies and regulations for a new competitive environment' (Levy 2006a: 3). Thus 'market support is not synonymous with state withdrawal'; rather, 'the move towards the market has generated a raft of new state missions' (ibid.: 3; 2006b: 382–91). State intervention, as Levy puts it, 'is not just a one-shot deal' and the state 'does not simply set up' market regimes, 'it also helps them to adapt' (ibid.: 374).

Whether interpreted as a second great transformation, the rise of new state activism or the reinvention of political control over the economy, all these accounts recognize the state as co-constitutive of the market economy and always integral to the process of re-regulating the free market. State activism is inscribed within contemporary processes of market-making and market-shaping through its re-regulatory activity which frames capitalist markets. CPE analysis of the state must look beyond traditional industrial policy to a broader range of legislative and regulatory interventions to shape markets and their outcomes (Chang 1999). As Vogel (following Polanyi) puts it, the 'irony of state-led deregulation' is that of 'freer markets, more rules' (1996). These new rules for the regulatory frameworks are designed by states, often to promote particular outcomes (Perraton and Clift 2004: 218–19; Gamble 2004; Weiss 2004; Clift 2004, 2007, 2012). Within this transformation of state influence over the economy, the precise contours of these market-shaping and market-supporting re-regulatory interventions will be moulded by the historical specificities of particular state legacies, as discussed above.

Another evolution, reflecting the changing scope and nature of state activism, is nations and firms intervening in national and transnational re-regulation, shaping it to their advantage. Braithwaite and Drahos (2000) highlight the importance of transnational business regulation in contemporary capitalism. They ascribe significant similarities and convergence between national regimes to the emergence of an international epistemic community of business regulators. A less teleological interpretation identifies 'transnationalization' and the increasing scope and breadth of regulatory and governance activities. This 'proliferation of regulatory activities, actors, networks or constellations' heralds an 'explosion of rules' and ultimately 'the profound re-ordering of our world' (Djelic and Sahlin-Andersson 2006: 1). This 'complex compound of activities bridging the global and the local' that constitutes the regulatory order is 'taking place at the same time within, between and across national boundaries' (ibid.: 3). Thus the boundaries of capitalist regulation 'do not necessarily coincide with national boundaries'. States are actively embedded in and constrained by a transnational regulatory order which remains 'very much in the making' (ibid.: 2; Djelic and Quack 2010).

This emergent, 'in-the-making' quality intersects with our approach to states as independent variables. This new regulatory terrain may be not just a source of state constraint, but also a site of reinvented state activism (see e.g. Fioretos 2009, 2010). Behind new regulatory initiatives and activism is the new politics of industrial policy. Regulation enshrines traditional product or process standards, thus favouring insiders already acquainted with the system through licensing procedures or professional qualifications. The German *Meister*, for example, does not discriminate explicitly against foreigners, but defends national quality standards difficult for producers or service providers abroad to meet. The defence of national interests has thus moved from tariffs to regulatory standard-setting. Governments can simultaneously open up markets and enshrine standards offering home advantage to domestic producers in global markets. For example, within the General Agreement on Trade in Services (GATS) we will be sure to find national interests buried in the details of its sectoral agreements.

These evolutions in state intervention require a rejoinder to the empirical assessment of industrial policy decline set out above. The object of analysis – industrial policy-type, market-shaping or market-making interventions – is changing. The difficulty for empirical assessment, however, is knowing what to measure and how to measure it. These kinds of missions and interventions are hard to quantify. This suggests caution when interpreting declining quantitative indicators of traditional industrial policy. Firstly, the trend can be reversed, as happened post-GFC. Moreover, that decline may mask rises in other kinds of interventions not captured by conventional industrial policy data.

CONCLUSION

The CPE of the state involves the intertwining of the political and the economic, the combination and recombination of public and private within the economy. The rejection of the retreat of the state thesis here takes aim at its underlying theoretical assumptions. While state/market relations became more free market oriented in character from the 1970s, it would be erroneous to equate this with an erosion, a retreat, still less the 'end' of the nation state, given the mutual co-constitution of state and market. To capture state transformation in its complexity, the ideational context of particular state/society complexes needs to be appreciated. Different liberal states, drawing on varied political economic traditions and intellectual legacies, arrive at distinctive kinds of state/market relations and forms of interventionism. These different political, institutional and economic conditions can provide more or less conducive environments for particular forms of state to develop.

Furthermore, the state is dynamic, not static. The various ideal-typical state forms are tendencies – rising, declining or perhaps recombining in novel ways. They do not exist in a stable equilibrium. The 'state forms' approach must remain faithful to the contingency at play within differentiated, variegated processes of state transformation. The state can helpfully be conceived of as an independent variable, and state actors as potential agents of transformation. Accordingly, we may need to seek state intervention in the economy in novel places and attempt to gauge it in new ways. Comparative political economists, therefore, have their work cut out in taking account of the changed parameters and logics of state activism. Mapping this terrain, as Shonfield (1965), Johnson (1982) and Zysman (1983) did for an earlier phase of state/market relations, is challenging. In the next chapter, we will see how comparative capitalisms scholars have taken up this challenge.

9 Comparative Capitalisms

INTRODUCTION

We encountered the *Varieties of Capitalism* (VoC; Hall and Soskice 2001) approach to comparative capitalisms in Chapter 6 when discussing institutions and CPE. In this chapter we return to this theme, which has become so pervasive and dominant within CPE that VoC has been criticized for falling short of providing a unifying theory of everything for the study of comparative capitalisms. As more sympathetic scholars note (Hancké et al. 2007; Hancké 2009), this is all rather unfair as it never claimed to be anything so all-encompassing. Notably, VoC may not offer the same explanatory purchase over the emerging market economies and the rising 21st-century economic powers. A 'VoC of the BRICS' research programme has been relatively slow to develop, and most comparative capitalism work inspired by this framework remains empirically centred on the core OECD economies in Western Europe, North America, Japan and East Asia. That said, there is an increasing body of work looking at and applying VoC-type frameworks beyond these horizons (see e.g. Becker 2013; Becker and Vasileva 2017; Bohle 2018; Feldmann 2019; Kiran 2018; Nolke 2010; Ebenau 2012; Schneider 2009; Vasileva-Dienes and Schmidt 2019). The relatively underdeveloped nature of the VoC research programme beyond the advanced economies may be for good reasons, linked to the historical specificities of capitalist development in the countries VoC was first developed to explain. Those political economies had experienced some version of what Polanyi called *The Great Transformation* (2001 [1944]) many decades ago. This entailed the protracted formation and maturation of market institutions, accompanied by the expansion of regulative state activity over markets, and the entrenching of the market system as a mechanism for sustaining and maintaining the whole of society.

VoC can provide a useful and potentially revealing starting point for the comparative analysis, interpretation and interrogation of processes of capitalist restructuring in the advanced economies. Though VoC has become dominant of late, there are other, older and broader traditions of comparative capitalisms scholarship (see Coates 2000 for an overview) and we will encounter a number of alternative approaches below. These include 'social structures of accumulation theory' (SSA; Hollingsworth 1991; Kotz et al. 1994; Hollingsworth and Boyer 1997; Duménil and Lévy 2004; McDonough et al. 2010; Block 2011), the 'French Regulation School' of political economy (Aglietta 1979; Boyer 1990; Boyer and Saillard 1995, 2002) and the important *Capitalism Against Capitalism* intervention of Albert (1993; see also Marquand 1988; Hutton 1994). Some of this work built on still earlier seminal comparative capitalisms analysis. Indeed, the CPE of post-war capitalism as described and analysed by Shonfield (1965) is an implicit point of departure for most analysis of how capitalism is changing in the contemporary period. In the 21st century, VoC has been used to explain differential impacts of and responses to the GFC, with some initially seeing LME capitalisms as hardest hit, while CMEs have reportedly 'sailed through' (Schmidt 2012: 156–7). Which varieties of capitalism are most threatened, and how, by pressures such as globalization, financial crisis and European integration remains a disputed topic within the field (see e.g. Clift and McDaniel 2019; Johnston and Regan 2016, 2018; Hopner and Shafer 2010; Hay 2019; Hall and Gingerich 2009). We will explore the linkages between the pathologies of the US's particular neo-liberal variant of LME capitalism and the GFC in a later section.

While comparative capitalisms scholars find much to disagree about, all this work shares an appreciation of path dependency and institutional complementarity, and how institutions are necessary to the reproduction of capitalist social relations of production. As noted in Chapter 6, answering calls to admit contingency and dynamism into analysing the institutions of capitalism, path dependency and institutional complementarity need not necessarily equate to or entail stasis and fixity. A more dynamic appreciation also flows from the particular analytical moves of what we might term a second wave of post-VoC comparative capitalisms scholars, including John Campbell, Colin Hay, Gregory Jackson, Richard Deeg, Vivien Schmidt and Kathleen Thelen. Thelen, for example, highlights the need to 'move institutional analysis beyond its traditional "comfort zone" of comparative statics to generate a more genuinely dynamic account of institutional reproduction and change' (2010: 46). This is a challenge that comparative capitalisms analysis has begun to rise to in recent years (Hay 2004a, 2005, 2019; Crouch 2005a, 2005b; Jackson and Deeg 2006, 2008).

The core argument of this chapter is twofold. Firstly, that Hall and Soskice's highly influential initial framework for analysis fails to give due weight to the mutual constitution of state and economy, of state and market (see Chapters 2 and 8). Secondly, that comparative capitalisms analysis can benefit from more systematic attempts to incorporate ideational factors (see Chapter 7), such as different state traditions and varied conceptions of the market, into its analysis. Consistent with the intellectual endeavour of this book, I argue for approaching the study of comparative capitalisms in the spirit of classical political economy, inspired by the likes of List, Marx, Polanyi, Keynes and Weber, seeing market relations as socially embedded and capitalist restructuring as resulting from political choice. In the process, comparative capitalisms analysis can also answer the calls for more dynamic, contingent analysis.

Recognition of such dynamism within capitalism is important because, as discussed throughout this book, key features of the advanced political economies *have* changed as global capitalism has been transformed since the 1970s. The positing of two (or more?) types of market capitalism raises the question which this chapter addresses – namely, how should we best characterize the trajectory of contemporary capitalist restructuring? How successfully can we map evolutions onto the backdrop that VoC offers? Possible answers are that capitalist restructuring is inducing convergence on the LME model, or that enduring clear divergence persists between LMEs and CMEs, or that we are witnessing fragmentation of coherent capitalist 'types', or indeed hybridization (see Clift 2007; Clift and McDaniel 2019).

To adjudicate on this, first we need to inspect further the theoretical foundations on which comparative capitalisms analysis is built. We then move on to explore its empirical explanatory purchase through in-depth qualitative comparative analysis in the form of 'process tracing' of particular trajectories of national capitalisms. The CPE of capitalist restructuring will be analysed as a differentiated, open-ended process – mediated by a range of institutional and ideational factors at national and other levels. In the next section I consider the contribution of classical political economy to a richer understanding of state/market relations within contemporary comparative capitalisms. I then reflect on the use (and abuse) of ideal types in comparing capitalisms, before setting out, with illustrative examples, how to incorporate ideational factors and concepts of social embeddedness into the analysis of capitalist restructuring. The final two sections engage in in-depth process-tracing analysis of the changes within Japanese and American capitalism, using the empirics to illustrate the 'pay-off' of both VoC and the conceptual and theoretical critiques of it.

CLASSICAL POLITICAL ECONOMY AND COMPARATIVE CAPITALISMS

The contemporary scholarship comparing capitalisms, whether inspired by VoC, SSA, Regulation Theory or some other conceptual framework, is in different ways and to different degrees standing on the shoulders of the giants of classical political economy analysis of capitalism (Hodgson 2016). Recalling the core insights of political economy outlined in Chapter 2, the underlying themes of classical political economy which pervade the best comparative capitalisms analysis are the recognition of how politics shapes markets and economies, how states and markets are intimately intertwined, and how market relations need to be understood as embedded in social contexts. The pre-disciplinary classical political economy approach is conducive to a fine-grained appreciation of the importance of (historically specific) embedded institutional and legal arrangements for capitalism. Within this, how the state's relationship to the wider economy and its role in capitalist restructuring and development are conceived is crucially important.

One curious aspect of VoC's influential framework is its silence about the role of the state. As Hancké notes, 'the VoC approach starts – axiomatically – with the firm at the centre of the analysis' (2009: 2). Partly because of this, VoC-inspired analysis can leave the state out of its story (see Hancké et al. 2007: 4, 14–16; Schmidt 2009). The VoC framework does not really offer a useful, compelling or plausible conception of state/market or state/economy interactions and relations (see Levy 2006a: 22–4). Given the centrality of the state/economy nexus – the interrelationship between state and market – to capitalist diversity and variety, this is an important issue. The state and politics always matter in the development of capitalism (Campbell and Lindberg 1990; Dobbin 1994; Fligstein 1996; Davis 2009: ch. 6; Campbell 2010: 94–8; Krippner 2011). Here we argue that what unites the best work in the field is how, aligned with the insights of classical political economy, it avoids what Block and Evans (2005) call 'state-economy dualism' (*either* state *or* market) and recognizes the mutually constitutive nature of state and economy, rejecting notions of state and market as 'distinct and opposing modes of organising economic activity' (ibid.: 505; Block 1994; Evans 1995; Fligstein 2001).

The commonalities of purpose between classical political economy and contemporary comparative institutional analysis of capitalism have been highlighted previously (Gamble 1995). Similarly, Djelic notes that the German Historical School we encountered in Chapters 3 and 4 understood that 'economic "laws" were contingent upon the particular historical, social and institutional context' and analysed and in some cases advocated 'a combination of highly organized capitalism and strong state intervention' (2010: 18–24). The terminology may differ, but these insights still underpin contemporary comparative capitalisms analysis. Institutions matter and are consequential for economic growth, activity, (re)distribution and development. This institutional infrastructure is integral to the reproduction of market relations.

There is an obvious affinity between List's national political economy and the focus of comparative capitalisms. List saw the mission of political economy as exploring 'how a particular nation in the actual condition of the world, regard being had to its special circumstances, may preserve and improve its economic condition' (List 1856: 194). His focus on 'law and institutions' as crucial sources of 'productive power' shares much with contemporary comparative capitalisms analysis. Contemporary scholars continue to explore how these capitalist institutions differ cross-nationally, in part because politics always and everywhere shapes market activity and outcomes. They also report, as List and others did, how this intertwining of the political and the economic takes different forms in different national and societal contexts. Attempts within contemporary debates to discern how far institutional context can ultimately explain rates of economic growth (see e.g. Coates 1999, 2000) recapture directly the spirit and focus of inquiry of classical political economy.

Thus the lessons from classical political economy loom large within the contemporary analysis and interpretation of comparative capitalisms. Marx, for example, understood and analysed how capitalist institutions, notably the state, were crucial to circuits of capital. He analysed the key role of institutions sustaining particular forms of capitalism, and this influenced a range of capitalism scholarship, notably the critical engagement with VoC of David Coates (2005). Robert Boyer and the French Regulation School have also built explicitly on these Marxian foundations in exploring national institutional differentiation within global capitalism. Regulation School analysis discerns successive stages in capitalist development, such as Fordism – a combination of mass production assembly lines and emergent mass consumerism – understood as 'regimes of accumulation' (Lipietz 1992: ch. 1).

The Fordist mass production regime increased economic efficiency through the 'Taylorization' or rationalization of work practices; that is, the scientific application of Smithian insights into massive productivity gains accruing from the division of labour. Workers performed repetitive, often menial, tasks on large production lines. Each regime of accumulation has its own underlying logic and is sustained by a 'mode of regulation' – a nexus of institutions in which the economy is embedded, reproducing its accumulation path (Boyer 1990; Boyer and Saillard 1995). These institutionalization processes take different forms in each political economy, delivering a variety of national Fordisms. These 'institutional forms of Fordism', Boyer and Juillard note, 'provided codification of growth in parallel with production and consumption' (1995: 239).

The Marxist political economist Giovanni Arrighi places the development of 'Fordism-Keynesianism' within the sweep of a much longer historical perspective on the global political economy, and 'changes in the spatial configuration of processes of capital accumulation' (2010: 1) linked to the greater geographical mobility. He sees the inequality and instability of US capitalism at the end of the 20th century as rooted in the collapse of US Fordism, and inherent instabilities, contradictions and tensions within a changing international political economy context (1994, 2010).

The emphasis on institutions to provide the necessary conditions for capital accumulation to flourish, and on capitalist instability, is no less pronounced in SSA scholarship. A Marxian emphasis on the inherent crisis-prone tendencies within capitalism leads SSA scholars to place great emphasis on the crucial role of institutions in providing some stability to what would otherwise be a perpetually unstable socio-economic order. SSA also draws on Keynesian political economy, with its emphasis on the instabilities of market economies and especially the psychology of investment decisions and practices (McDonough et al. 2010: 2). Fred Block also highlights influences from economic sociology, and notably Polanyi, on both Regulation Theory and SSA analyses: 'markets are always and everywhere embedded in certain political, legal and ideational elements ... market societies are always hybrids that combine market and non-market institutions' (2011: 33).

Another link from economic sociology and from the German Historical School discussed above to contemporary comparative capitalisms analysis is provided by Max Weber (Hodgson 2001). Djelic talks of the 'embeddedness' of Weber in German Historical School debates (2010: 23), and one strand of his work inspired an economic sociology attuned to explanations rooted in individual action, and indeed perception, as well as the shaping role of institutions. Jackson and Deeg (2006) note the influence of Weber (1978 [1922]) on comparative capitalisms analysis, notably how 'economic action is viewed as a special case of social action', how each is shaped and constituted by institutional arrangements (see also Hollingsworth et al. 1994: 4; Swedberg 1998: 23). Drawing on these Weberian influences, the 'ideational turn' in CPE (see e.g. Schmidt 2002; Clift 2012) can be harnessed to the goal of comparative capitalisms analysis, a theme we return to below (Table 9.1).

VARIETIES OF CAPITALISM: INTERPRETING THE TRAJECTORY OF CAPITALIST RESTRUCTURING

Contemporary debates about comparative capitalisms have been framed by VoC to some extent. As Thelen puts it, VoC theory 'emphasizes the constitutive power of institutions in shaping the strategies of key political economic actors ... and sees powerful feedback loops

Table 9.1   Approaches to comparative capitalisms analysis

	Historical materialist, e.g. Regulation School	*1st-wave VoC*	*2nd-wave VoC*
Micro-foundations	Class-based	*Homo economicus*	Bounded rationality; embedded actors
Conception of social order	Social relations of production, class antagonism	Institutionally circumscribed rational choice	Constructivist institutionalism
Logic of institutions	Facilitate accumulation; mode of regulation determined by capitalist drivers	Efficiency; reducing transaction costs	Logic of appropriateness; social norms; navigate uncertainty
The state	Node or 'moment' in the circulation of capital	Under-stated, role obscured by focus on firms	Market-making intervention, rooted in national traditions
Temporality	Periodic crises then transformation (to new regimes of accumulation)	Comparative statics	Dynamic account of institutional reproduction
Stable social order?	No	Yes	Not necessarily
Exemplars	Boyer, Coates, Amable	Hall and Soskice, Iversen	Schmidt, Hay, Crouch, Thelen, Campbell

at work that sustain distinctive trajectories of development cross-nationally, even in the face of common challenges' (Thelen 2010: 42). VoC identifies two prevailing ideal types of capitalism, the liberal market economy (LME) and the co-ordinated market economy (CME) (Hall and Soskice 2001: 1–70).

Within the LME ideal type, Hall and Soskice emphasize 'competitive market arrangements' in relation to labour, goods and services, with the price mechanism and contracts used to co-ordinate firm activities. More specifically, 'highly competitive markets' are relied upon to 'organise relations' with firms' 'suppliers of finance' (ibid.: 8–9). These are free markets for goods and services, supplied by companies depending on market-based firm financing and reliant on capital markets rather than bank or institutionally based processes. In CMEs, by contrast, 'non-market' interactions, institutions, relationships and 'modes of co-ordination' are crucial to labour relations, corporate governance, interfirm relations and so on. Firms rely on these non-market-oriented networks to 'co-ordinate their endeavours'. Long-termist relations with banks and other private, public or para-public financing institutions are characteristic CME modes of firm financing (see pp. 200–3). These lead to 'network monitoring based on the exchange of private information inside networks' (ibid.: 8; see also Hancké 2009).

The crucial distinction at the heart of VoC, that between CME and LME, hinges on the role of markets. The differences between the two kinds of capitalism crystallize around contending conceptions of the relative import of, and degree of prevalence of, market mechanisms as organizing principles of political economy. In the LME model, markets are the default. As Hall and Soskice put it, 'nations with liberal market economies tend to rely on markets to coordinate endeavours in both the financial and industrial relations systems, while those with coordinated market economies have institutions in both spheres which reflect higher levels of non-market coordination' (2001: 19). Within the more regulated CME or 'institutional economy' (Crouch and Streeck 1997) model, there is much greater reliance on and prevalence of 'institutionally regulated economic transactions', and on regulation by 'institutions *other than* markets' (Streeck 2001: 7).

Some have criticized this framing for being devoid of politics and excessively oriented around economic efficiency considerations (Hay 2004a, 2005, 2019; Crouch 2005a, 2005b). There are functionalist overtones within some accounts of how particular sets of capitalist institutions 'win out' and get reproduced (see pp. 117–20). Particular configurations of institutions are mysteriously 'called forth' by the systemic requirements of what might either be termed economic efficiency or capital accumulation, depending on one's approach. In fact, careful historical analysis indicates that outcomes are not determined by pure economic logics or the imperatives of efficiency, but by politics, accident and unintended consequence as well (Jackson 2001).

The exclusive focus on economic drivers is something Hall and Soskice themselves resist: 'although efficiency considerations of the sort our analysis identifies are relevant to institutional change, the latter is ultimately a political process driven by many factors' (2003: 245). To counter the tendency towards unsatisfactory explanations couched exclusively in terms of economic efficiency, it is important to keep in view the intertwining of the political and the economic so vividly depicted within classical political economy.

A range of comparative capitalisms scholars are agreed on the notion that, in analysing capitalist change, 'politics matter' (Campbell 2011: 226), because 'processes of institutional reproduction and change are contested. They involve considerable struggle, conflict and negotiation. Power is central to all of this' (Campbell 2010: 88). Thelen, for example, in her take on VoC focuses on 'the power-political distributional foundations of the institutions of the political economy' and 'the political struggles that shape and reshape these institutions over time' (2010: 43, 53–7; see also Hall 2007; Streeck 2009, 2010). Politics matter, not just at the institutional formation stage, but through processes of institutional reproduction in the face of political opposition (Streeck and Thelen 2005; Block and Evans 2005: 506–7). The reason why institutions may be reproduced is not primarily because of economic efficiency – it is first and foremost because of politics. One key dimension of this is employer prefer-ences in favour of sustaining these 'institutional arrangements around which they have organised their strategies in the market' (Thelen 2010: 48; Swenson 2002).

It should be recalled that the whole point of the Hall and Soskice book was to restore a degree of contingency and open-endedness to discussion of contemporary capitalism's tra-jectories (Hall and Soskice 2001: 57–66, 2003: 245). Specifically, theirs is an argument *against* the capitalist convergence thesis we explored in Chapter 6. Hall and Soskice's work represents a departure from predictions of teleological convergence towards LME capitalism (Rajan and Zingales 2003; Eichengreen 2008) or 'institutional monocropping' (Evans 2004). With its dichotomous approach to understanding the regulation of economic affairs, VoC offers a conception of CPE 'in which alternative social bases of organizing capitalist econo-mies freely coexist' (Watson 2003: 227).

As Colin Hay's critique points out, however, what Hall and Soskice offer is not so much a rejection of the convergence thesis, but a more nuanced variant of it. They posit not simple convergence, but rather 'dual convergence' on *either* the liberal *or* co-ordinated varieties of capitalism (and no other; Hay 2004a: 232–8, 2005, 2019; Hall and Soskice 2001). Intermediate cases supposedly pay what Goodin terms 'a hermaphrodite's penalty' (2003: 206). Such a view is contested, with Kenworthy among others arguing that mongrels or hybrids (a theme we return to below) may convey economic advantages (2006). Nevertheless, VoC does assume or assert powerful dualizing tendencies within capitalism in the face of international economic competition (Hancké 2009). Colin Crouch goes further, noting how those comparative institutional advantages with which VoC credits CMEs are in traditional, declining sectors, whereas those for LMEs are 'future oriented industries and services sec-tors', such that 'in the long run, all institutions other than the pure market fail to cope with the future' (2005a: 443). Thus, for critics such as Crouch and Hay, lurking within the Hall and Soskice approach is a convergence account, albeit one parading as a critique of conver-gence arguments (Hay 2005).

There are, as we saw in Chapter 6, good reasons to question the mooted telos of capital-isms converging on a similar, singular (LME) norm (see e.g. Clift and McDaniel 2019). Equally, there are good reasons to question that capitalist restructuring will lock capitalist systems into one of two (and only two) sets of institutions and norms (CME and LME). The convergence thesis and indeed the 'dual convergence' thesis skate on fairly thin ice in that they lack recognition of the importance of (historically specific) embedded institutional and legal arrangements (see e.g. Hay 2019). These institutions underwrite the functions of busi-ness and the market economy in ways richly appreciated in the work of Polanyi, Weber, Schmoller, List, Veblen and others. Thus this thesis 'ignores the basic logic of embeddedness' (Block and Evans 2005: 511).

Re-establishing the connection to classical political economy can help foster understand-ing of both the reproduction of existing capitalist institutions and evolutions towards new ones as processes of political struggles (Streeck and Thelen 2005; Campbell 2010; Thelen 2010). Appreciation of the institutional and ideational context of domestic policy-making through which international pressures and drivers are mediated is important for understanding capitalist diversity and variety. This can be enhanced by recognition of the embeddedness of capitalisms and of production regimes in societies, systems of national economic law and state traditions, each being shaped by the balance of political forces within society and national traditions of political economic thought.

HOW TO COMPARE CAPITALISMS: USING AND ABUSING IDEAL TYPES

VoC places the LME and CME ideal types front and centre within the analysis of comparative capitalisms. The ideal type is a heuristic device, a hypothetical construction 'built' out of empirical observations. It is not intended to describe the facts, but can facilitate comparison or indeed theoretical explanation. Its purpose is to capture certain characteristics of a system. Ringer calls ideal types 'simplifications or "one-sidedly" exaggerated characterizations of complex phenomena that can be hypothetically posited and then "compared" with the realities they are meant to elucidate' (Ringer 2000: 5; see also Crouch 2005a: 445). Ideal types can be tremendously helpful and enlightening in comparative analysis, but they must be handled with care (see Hay 2019: 1–7).

Colin Crouch spells out the problem with the way that ideal types are being constructed within VoC: 'the authors are not building their theory deductively, but are reading back empirical detail from what they want to be their paradigmatic case of an LME – the US – into their formulation of the type' (Crouch 2005a: 445–6; Hay 2019: 8–9). This is one facet of a broader issue within some VoC analysis, namely the conflation of different levels of abstraction (Watson 2003: 228–9). The problems really start, as Matthew Watson points out, when slippery elisions occur between 'arguments that exist at two very different levels of abstraction' (ibid.: 230); that is, between ideal-typical models and empirical discussions of actual political economies. Thus empirical analysis of institutional specificities of real economies becomes conflated with conceptual claims about a 'model' of capitalism. Going one step further, these conceptual 'models' are treated *as if they are* empirical analyses of real phenomena. What really needs to happen is that such conceptual assertions need to be subjected to empirical investigation and adjudication (ibid.: 230; Crouch 2005a: 445–6; Hay 2019). Watson points out (2003: 231) the need to distinguish more clearly between the *explanans*, 'that doing the explaining', and the *explanandum*, 'that to be explained'.

Not all influential political economy work on comparative capitalisms operates using (and abusing?) such ideal types. In Shonfield's pioneering analysis, each economy is treated *sui generis* (as one of a kind) and not representative as cases of a broader category (1965: ch. 9; Goodin 2003: 203). This avoids the pitfalls detailed above, though it limits the ambition of the explanation which can be drawn from the analysis (Hancké 2009). Hall and Soskice clarify their ambition for the *Varieties of Capitalism* volume as 'to develop new formulations about the principal dimensions distinguishing one political economy from another in more general terms, with an emphasis on dimensions of difference consequential for national policy and performance' (Hall and Soskice 2003: 243–4). Thus the ambition is to escape context specificity in order to contribute to a set of understandings and propositions about capitalist restructuring which are, perhaps, generalizable across the advanced economies (see Hancké 2009: 12–17).

However, the way ideal types are constructed and deployed within VoC analysis runs the risk of doing violence to the facts in particular cases. At the very least, the casual use of ideal types leads to a stylized, caricatured version of the 'Anglo-Saxon' or LME capitalist model becoming the central focus of analysis. The problematic desire to place the US economy at the centre of this latter ideal type has profoundly shaped how it has been defined, described and analysed (Hall and Soskice 2001: 27–33). Hall and Gingerich (2009) have the US scoring a perfect 0 on their 'co-ordination index' (see Goodin 2003: 24–5), indicating it to be the exemplary LME. They might consider this a success, demonstrating the worth of their model. However, these results are arguably revealing of the conflation problem noted above.

Political economic reality is considerably messier. Indeed, in a surprisingly large number of respects, the US political economy often fails to conform to the ideal type supposedly so closely modelled upon it (Thompson 2004; Martin 2005). For example, at the heart of US capitalism is massive state intervention in, financial support for and subsidization of 'an extremely powerful, scientifically oriented military sector, tying a number of contracting firms into close and necessarily secretive relations with central government departments'; and these are crucial to its innovative capacities, notably in aerospace and computing (Crouch 2005a: 441–2; see also Coates 2000: 201–10; Wilson 2012; Weiss 2014). Across the 20th century, with a vertiginous 'spike' during World War II, Eisner characterizes the 'long-term growth in the size of the American State' as 'striking' (2011: 9–12). Indeed, such is the scale of governmental financial and other support for the commercialization of new technologies that Fred Block charts over recent decades 'the rise of the hidden developmental state in the United States' (2008; see also Block and Keller 2009).

Similar issues arise with the other paradigmatic political economy, Germany, and its relation to the CME model it spawned (Hall and Soskice 2001: 21–7). There have been significant evolutions in German labour market practices, including defection by employers from co-ordinating institutions, and financial market liberalization in recent years (see pp. 218–21; Hassel 1999: 485–93; Thelen 2000, 2001: 83). As Blyth puts it, 'actually existing Germany may not be the Germany that the VoC literature portrays' (2003: 220; see also Streeck 2009).

Lurking in the shadows of much empirical analysis of comparative capitalisms are the Hall and Soskice LME and CME ideal types, often deployed not as one-sided accentuations but as supposed descriptions of reality (Hay 2019). Furthermore, often assertions are made about developments within actual existing economies to force the square peg of empirical reality into the round hole of the conceptual ideal type. As Levy puts it, 'France finds itself in typological purgatory, neither CME fish nor LME fowl' (2006a: 23). That is an interesting empirical phenomenon to be explained and explored using the ideal types to understand better both French capitalism and the ideal types themselves. However, some VoC-inspired analysts are determined to bludgeon France into the LME pigeonhole (Culpepper 2005; discussed in Clift 2012).

Second-wave VoC scholarship has gone some way to addressing the excessive restrictions of the dichotomous typology. Thelen highlights the problem of the 'rather broad and dichotomous categories on which the theory rests' (2010: 48). Jackson and Deeg suggest countering the shortcoming of VoC's silence about the state through recognition of 'alternative types of capitalism distinguished by the extent and character of state intervention in the economy' (2008: 699). Indeed, Schmidt has argued the case for statist France as an exemplar of a third variety of capitalism (2002, 2003, 2009). Furthermore, Hancké et al. discuss '"mid-spectrum" mixed market political economies, or MMEs' (2007: 13–14; Molina and Rhodes 2007; Hall and Gingerich 2009). Yet the risk here is that every capitalism ends up with its own type and opinion is divided as to 'whether the gains in empirical coverage and possibly even depth outweigh the losses in terms of analytical sharpness' (Hancké 2009: 15). The bottom line is that ideal types, as heuristic devices, should be handled and deployed with great care (Hay 2019).

IDEAS, EMBEDDEDNESS AND INSTITUTIONAL CHANGE WITHIN COMPARATIVE CAPITALISMS

CPE scholars, often drawing explicitly on Polanyi, have in recent times come to understand the relation of institutions to their social, economic and political context in terms of embeddedness (Polanyi 2001 [1944]; Granovetter 1985; Hollingsworth and Boyer 1997; Granovetter and Swedberg 2001; Krippner 2001; Block and Evans 2005; Smelser and Swedberg 2005). As Streeck puts it, 'embeddedness runs through most or all the current work on capitalist diversity' (2001: 2), and this connects to the points made earlier that it is not economic efficiency considerations which primarily account for how a particular trajectory of capitalism is sustained, but rather that it is socially embedded institutions which have to provide that which the market left to its own devices cannot.

This is not to say, however, that capitalist institutional orders necessarily ossify and induce stasis. Embeddedness, like the path dependency discussed above, needs to be understood as a potentially dynamic phenomenon (Block and Evans 2005: 507). Thus a degree of continuity within socially embedded market relations along a given path is not a matter of inertia (Polanyi 2001 [1944]; Amable 2003; Crouch 2005a, 2005b; Streeck 2011), nor of social determinism (Fligstein 1996; Campbell 2004: 71, 2011: 226).

The above reference to 'understandings' within embeddedness recalls Weberian notions of individual perceptions of economic phenomena. This opens the door to weaving in the ideational realm and the crucial role played by the shared understandings whose significance we explored in Chapter 7. A socially embedded account of comparative capitalisms appreciates how social context has ideational as well as institutional dimensions, and how these shape the behaviour of economic actors, their understanding of markets and the trajectory of a national capitalism (see e.g. Campbell 2004). Diverse national traditions of economic thought leave their footprints on how economic phenomena are understood. This is because actors' 'background ideational abilities' are consistent with 'the ideational rules or "rationality" of that setting' (Schmidt 2008: 314; see also Weber 1978 [1922]; Swedberg 1998: 36; Campbell 2004: 149; Jackson and Deeg 2008). Campbell labels these underlying shared understandings – which are taken-for-granted unthinking scripts, cued rituals and habits of thought – as 'cognitive frameworks'; 'actors rarely subscribe to them self-consciously or deliberately … [they are] virtually invisible to the actors themselves' (Campbell 1998: 378–82).

Any capitalist market relations evolve in the context of a distinctive state tradition (Dyson 1980) and a prevailing set of understandings of state market relations. For example, as Lehmbruch notes, German and Japanese capitalism – that is, the archetypes of the CME variety – were sustained by a 'discourse of "embedded capitalism"' (Lehmbruch 2001: 46), which took different forms in each case. This 'core discourse' of embedded capitalism involves a 'shared cognitive framework', most visible at moments of crisis (such as the economic crisis in Germany in the 1870s, or during post-war reconstruction) which can act as 'catalysts for the building of market-embedding institutions' (ibid.: 45; Streeck 2001: 9).

In Germany, the 'ordo-liberal' tradition of economic thought is important (see e.g. Nicholls 1994; Dyson 1999; Bonefeld 2012; Young 2014), which entails a 'market-conforming interventionism', which places emphasis on rule-bound economic policy-making, with competition seen as a condition for economic efficiency (Lehmbruch 2001: 80–1). This was a crucial element of the post-war German 'discourse of embedded capitalism' that underpins the central organizing concept of the 'social market economy', which can be summarized as 'a pragmatic and eclectic combination of ordo-liberal concepts with social policy postulates of the Social Catholic tradition' (ibid.: 84). This combined corporate governance norms, which empowered workers as 'industrial citizens' within the firm (see p. 251); redistributive welfare with the market economy; and a commitment to full employment (of which ordo-liberals were sceptical). Regulation of the economy was justified if 'in conformity with the market' (ibid.: 84–5).

In this way an appreciation of embeddedness can help incorporate important ideational elements into the understanding of comparative capitalisms, notably how the institutions of capitalism bear the imprint of national political economic traditions of thought. An important part of these are sets of shared societal understandings about the nature of the market and about state capacities and traditions of political economic interventionism (see pp. 134–8, 163–5; Jabko 2006; Woll 2008; Schmidt 2009; Clift 2012). These elements are all brought into the mix of a more socially embedded view of capitalist institutions (Jackson and Deeg 2006, 2008; Deeg and Jackson 2007) and the reproduction and evolution of capitalism. In this light, the most helpful way to think about actors within comparative capitalisms is *not* neo-classical economic rational actors following micro-level signals (as VoC sometimes does; Hay 2005, 2019). Rather, CPE needs to recognize a range of rationalities, rooted in societal norms surrounding economic activity, and traditions of political economic interventionism at play in the reproduction and evolution of embedded market relations. These ideational dimensions (and the more nuanced conception of micro-foundations they generate) help to explain comparative capitalisms and their ongoing particularities.

TRACING PROCESSES OF CAPITALIST CHANGE: THE CHANGING JAPANESE POLITICAL ECONOMY

Having dealt with the most pressing conceptual and theoretical issues, we have now established the rationale behind our ideationally attuned approach to comparative capitalism, rooted in appreciation of the intricate interweaving of state and market, the political and the economic. We can now shift emphasis to the interrogation of empirical developments in two important cases, the Japanese and American political economies. Each is an exemplar of one of the two capitalist types which make up VoC's dichotomizing typology. Each process-tracing exercise is approached diachronically, first establishing the parameters of the post-war model and then exploring contemporary evolutions within it. A number of themes emerge in analysing the degree and nature of transformation within contemporary capitalisms. Firstly, path dependencies are not static, nor indeed are institutional complementarities. Politics profoundly shapes how capitalist institutions change, and the extent of that change. Also crucial are shared societal understandings about market relations and about capitalism. In terms of interpretation of the trajectories of change, hybridization suggests itself as a helpful framework (Clift 2007).

THE POST-WAR JAPANESE MODEL OF CAPITALISM

Tracing the restructuring processes within Japanese capitalism, chosen as an exemplar of the CME capitalist type, offers an illustration of the importance of socially embedded norms to understanding capitalist change comparatively. Hall and Soskice talk about how national patterns of political economic specialization should reflect 'rational responses' (2001: 41) to the LME/CME institutional frameworks they set out. But what kind of rationality do they have in mind? This takes a particular form in the Japanese case, as a range of scholars have noted. Vogel (2005, 2006), in his analysis of relationships of reciprocity within Japanese capitalism, notes 'they have both a rational and a normative element' and that 'actors facing new circumstances do not rationally calculate costs and benefits so much as they fall back on pre-existing norms and routines' (2005: 150–1). National capitalisms rest in part on different underlying principles of economic governance and the institutions, regulations and legal arrangements (and the actors who give life to them) that operationalize these principles. The Japanese market system is, Vogel notes, 'embedded in a complex web of laws, practices and norms' (ibid.: 145), such as trust and reciprocity (see also Coates 2000: 54–64).

Where Japanese capitalism does sit very comfortably with the Hall and Soskice approach is in offering considerable empirical corroboration for the existence of institutional complementarities so central to their account and the co-ordinating properties that their CME ideal type highlights. The interconnections between the labour market, the financial market and the firm within Japanese capitalism form parts of a jigsaw (see e.g. Vogel 2006: 11–13). They dovetail together, and increasing returns and efficiency gains accrue from these felicitous interconnections and symbiotic, synergistic interrelationships. A range of institutions have arisen over many decades to inscribe 'stakeholder' norms into the fabric of economic society, such as the notion of an 'implicit contract' between firms and between firms and banks (Matsuura et al. 2004: 137, 142).

Industrial relations in Japan have been organized around pervasive norms of lifetime employment guarantees and enterprise unionism fostering loyalty to the firm (Coates 2000: 58–62). This is very different from the antagonistic 'class war' politics found in some post-war European industrial relations contexts. Consensual Japanese industrial relations involve employers and employees unified in a 'community of fate' where wage differentials are low. This all built on the earlier foundations of the Meiji period (1868–1912), when the German Historical School of economics was influential in Japan, inculcating paternalistic norms in industrial relations and social policy (Lehmbruch 2001: 59–68; Gotoh 2019: 7–10). Japan, with its strong post-war growth, long-termist relations and dense co-ordinating economic and social networks, was for a long time lauded as an economic miracle – with predictions that it would overtake the US economically in the 1970s and 1980s (Kamata 1983).

Some of these complementarities are reinforced by the state as well as firms, such as government regulation imposing strong legal restraints on dismissals, bolstering system coherence and hindering worker mobility which would threaten firm cooperation (Matsuura et al. 2004: 134). The mutual commitment to long-termism between workers and managers within firms finds expression in job security and the seniority wage system linking increased remuneration to length of service with the firm. This, along with lifetime employment norms, 'provide[s] the incentives by which both workers and firms are willing to accumulate firm-specific labour skills'. Firms are able to 'take workers as "hostages"' since workers realize they 'can "invest" in their firm while young and recoup their investment when older' (ibid.: 141).

There is a very high degree of stability for actors operating within the institutional arrangements of Japanese capitalism. This is one key reason why 'pre-existing institutions leave an especially heavy imprint on the trajectory of change' (Vogel 2005: 147). The traditional Japanese model of capitalism, influenced by state-led developmentalism (see pp. 163-6; Yamamura 1997), and traditions of collective family ownership can be traced back to the Meiji period. Societal norms grew up which saw the businessman 'as benefactor of the community and servant of the state' (Jackson 2001: 139; see also Clarke 1979: 29). There was substantial restructuring of the institutions of Japanese capitalism after World War II. A transition was orchestrated towards stable, large shareholders, including large banks, that dominated the capital ownership of firms. It was complemented by cross-shareholdings and other social ties and networks that shaped interfirm relations (Jackson 2001: 143-5). This reduced the power and holdings of the dominant families, though the underlying relationship between business elites and the community did not change.

As we saw in Chapter 8, the history of capitalist development in Japan has been interpreted within CPE in terms of the 'capitalist developmental state' (Johnson 1982). The powerful industry ministry MITI helped Japanese firms and sectors develop through administrative guidance, subsidies, protections and credit allocation, acting as a gatekeeper for access to finance. Each key aspect of Japanese capitalism – corporate governance and finance, labour market and industrial relations, and welfare provision – was influenced by the state and its regulatory activities (Jackson and Miyajima 2008: 3-5; Coates 2000: 62-4).

In post-war Japan, stringent state regulation of and disincentives to corporate bond and share issuing and regulated access to capital markets meant these were rarely used to generate external finance for industry. Banks were much the preferred option for industrial finance from the 1940s until the 1990s (Vitols 2003: 255), and this complementarity between state regulation and firm financing created an environment conducive to the dominant role of bank finance. The bank/firm nexus sustained system coherence, strengthening MITI's orchestration of Japanese capitalism through state allocation of finance (Johnson 1982; Zysman 1983: 234-51; Vogel 2005: 146; Gotoh 2019: 48-52). Returning to the ideational context of capitalist institutions, Lehmbruch's 'discourse of embedded capitalism' underpinned post-war Japanese 'managerial capitalism', emphasizing a strategic role for the state in export-led growth (2001).

The organization of large firms also has particular characteristics. Interfirm networks of *keiretsu* (corporate groups sustained by cross-shareholdings, often linking firms to their suppliers) have long been a central feature of Japanese capitalism (see pp. 164-5; Hollingsworth 1997: 279-84; Jackson 2001; Vogel 2005: 145). These *keiretsu* involve 'reciprocally held cross-shareholdings among corporations and banks' wherein 'the web of small reciprocal cross-shareholdings often account for 20% of the shares, and stable shareholders over 40%'. These form 'a dense and stable network of long-term relationships' which can be horizontal (bank-centred) or vertical (buyer–supplier; Jackson and Miyajima 2008: 3-4). These networks, combined with state-orchestrated allocation of finance, insulated Japanese firms against stock market pressure in general and hostile takeover in particular (Vogel 2005: 146).

Following market signals and short-term economic returns are not the only considerations shaping capitalist development. Within post-war Japanese capitalism, its dynamism and competitiveness 'seemed not to rest on the allocative efficiency of the market, but the organizational efficiency of firms generated by the investment of stakeholders in developing and maintaining firm-specific capabilities' (Jackson and Miyajima 2008: 3). Japanese rates of return on industrial capital were, as Coates has pointed out, relatively poor, while the Japanese economy was growing strongly (Coates 2000: 148). This was sustainable in the relatively closed financial system of that era, wherein Japanese firms were insulated from capital market pressures.

Illustrating Thelen's points above, the distributional politics of Japan has been central to sustaining a stable path of capitalist development (2010). In the 'golden age' of Japanese capitalism between the 1950s and 1980s, the corporate governance system arrived at a social pact surrounding the distribution of the fruits of growth within the 'J-firm' (Tsuru 1993; Lehmbruch 2001: 87–93). This nexus of institutions, social practices and norms coalesced into an economically successful ensemble for many post-war decades, after which it hit the buffers in the 1990s with a decade and more of low growth and deflation in the 'bubble economy' crisis (Grimes 2001). Some predicted that the foundations of the Japanese model of capitalism were doomed. We will now consider the contemporary restructuring of Japanese capitalism.

JAPANESE CAPITALISM INTO THE 21ST CENTURY

As many comparative capitalisms scholars have pointed out, dramatic changes in the international political economic context have been one key facet in instigating change within capitalisms. This is certainly the case for the Japanese political economy. One arresting feature of transformation has been the internationalization of Japanese capitalism, which advanced in the 1980s and 1990s, in part under US pressure (Matsuura et al. 2004: 135). We will look at the labour relations and financial system aspects of Japanese capitalism and trace the processes of change. As we shall see below, the 'protected capitalism' logic (Schmidt 1996) underpinning the *keiretsu* stable cross-shareholdings, which insulated firms against stock market and takeover pressure (Jackson 2001; Matsuura et al. 2004: 134, 143–7; Vogel 2005: 145–6), began to be challenged and attenuated.

For what was previously a relatively insulated and sheltered financial system, Japanese capitalism's internationalization has been swift and dramatic. Foreign investor holdings of Japanese stocks rose from just 6 per cent in 1992 to 23.7 per cent by 2005, and stable cross-shareholdings were eroded (Jackson and Miyajima 2008: 10, 6–7). Through Campbell's processes of 'translation' (see pp. 122–3), international standards, codes and regulations, such as OECD corporate governance standards and International Accounting Standards (IAS) accounting norms, came to play a greater role within Japanese capitalism (Jackson and Miyajima 2008: 11). From the 1990s onwards, there were increasing attempts to incorporate liberalization into the firm/finance nexus, seeking to reconcile international standards and codes to Japanese norms, networks and relationships (Vogel 2005: 152).

One of the ties that historically have bound Japanese interfirm networks together is the role of the main bank (Matsuura et al. 2004: 137–40). Most large Japanese firms traditionally have one main source of financing, a main bank, and this bank plays a crucial role in monitoring, information sharing and corporate governance, as well as financing. With the progressive liberalization and internationalization of Japanese capital markets, there was also an expansion of corporate bonds, which displaced bank loans as sources of corporate finance. The role and significance of main banks at the core of firm financing have been challenged, as firms could now raise funds easily on capital markets (Jackson and Miyajima 2008: 31).

Stable ownership patterns still insulate firms against stock market pressure and hostile takeover, but to a lesser degree. Cross-shareholdings and long-term relations between banks and firms endure, albeit with negotiated restructurings of holdings (though see Miyajima and Kuroki 2008). Significantly for the VoC typology and its key distinguishing features, these restructurings are interactions based on the network, not the market. The move to equity financing and corporate bond market development represents a major change within Japanese capitalism. Nevertheless, familiar Japanese norms such as reciprocity remain important, and long-term bank/firm relations still provide system coherence (Vogel 2005: 155).

Japan's industrial relations system discussed above, founded on job security and long-termist relations, historically dovetailed with social provision. Firms provide certain social goods, such as non-portable pensions and firm-specific benefits. These all further sustain loyalty, generating complementarities between industrial relations and welfare provision (Estevez-Abe 2008). As Japanese capitalism began to change, these interconnections also revealed the limits of firm flexibility. The absence of a more established publicly provided social safety net places limits on firm restructuring and the social acceptability of lay-offs. The reputational damage that lay-offs would cause would adversely affect future recruitment of the graduates who, firms envisage, will spend their working life at the firm. This, combined with enduring strong legal restraints on dismissals, means that, unlike the Anglo-Saxon capitalism in LMEs, an external labour market in Japan remains underdeveloped (Vogel 2005: 158–9; Jackson 2008). Thus Japanese adoption of LME-style labour market practices and institutions is limited, and industrial restructuring still does not involve lay-offs (Vogel 2006: ch. 5).

That said, the Japanese labour market has undergone considerable change in recent times – partly because of the financial pressures felt by firms through the long economic slump and the need to cut costs. There has been an increasing tendency to introduce more non-core or non-regular workers into companies' workforces (who do not enjoy all the privileges and benefits noted above). Thus, the norm of lifelong employment is circumvented with increased use of part-time workers, and Japan today is an increasingly dualistic labour market (Matsuura et al. 2004: 141–3; Vogel 2006: 115–26; Estevez-Abe 2008; Jackson 2008: 283). The norm of lifetime employment endures, but the number and proportion of lifetime employees are gradually reducing (Jackson and Miyajima 2008: 31). In terms of pay structure, the seniority wage norms are being replaced by, or in some firms exist alongside, 'Anglo-Saxon'-style merit-based pay (Vogel 2005: 154; Jackson and Miyajima 2008: 31; Jackson 2008).

Within comparative capitalisms debates, internationalization coupled with financial liberalization seem inevitably to raise questions as to whether these are strides on a path converging towards Anglo-Saxon capitalism (Strange 1997; Cerny 1997a, 1997b; Rajan and Zingales 2003; Eichengreen 2008). Yet such a mooted transformation is forbiddingly difficult to achieve given the importance of the state and the wide range of social and economic institutions oriented towards non-market forms of co-ordination within Japan's institutional economy. It would entail what Polanyi called a 'great transformation' (2001 [1944]). As Steven Vogel points out, 'for Japan to shift toward the liberal market model, it would not simply have to dismantle existing institutions but also create new ones' (2005: 145).

Thus there is evidence from labour market and financial market practices within Japanese capitalism that Japan has moved in a more market-oriented direction. However, the shared view among numerous Japan specialists (Vitols 2003; Vogel 2005, 2006, 2019; Jackson 2008; Jackson and Miyajima 2008: 31; Gotoh 2019) is that the empirical case for convergence on the LME model is weak. The notion of the 'implicit contract' between economic actors and norms of trust, honour and reciprocity remain powerful forces within Japanese capitalism (Matsuura et al. 2004: 137, 142). Actors have been able to incorporate elements of liberal adjustment strategies and reconcile them to Japanese norms, networks and relationships (Vogel 2005: 152, 2006: 3). There has been a selective adaptation process and numerous creative modifications and examples of what Campbell (2004: 70) calls 'bricolage' and 'translation' (see pp. 122–5). Unsurprisingly, perhaps, given the dense web of institutions on which Japanese capitalism rests, 'the existing institutions of Japanese capitalism are shaping their own transformation' (Vogel 2006: 4).

Japanese financial markets and corporate governance are changing much more quickly than the labour relations and welfare elements of Japanese capitalism (Vogel 2005: 162–3). This could suggest tensions between formerly dovetailing institutional complementarities, as the 'jigsaw' may be pulling apart. Other commentators, however, argue that a new kind of coherence, of relatively stable hybrid forms, is being developed. Institutional complementarities are dynamic, not static; and new ones might emerge as older ones wane (see Crouch 2010; Campbell 2011). At the level of the firm, we have not seen root-and-branch change to its nature or to shared societal conceptions of what the firm is for. As Jackson and Miyajima put it, 'the idea that corporations should first and foremost serve the interests of their shareholders remains at odds with other elements of solidarity and equality within Japanese society' (2008: 10).

Recalling the ideas of Campbell, Crouch, Thelen and second-generation comparative capitalisms scholars, Jackson detects 'the recombination of corporate governance practices which result in new "hybrid" forms ... which are unlike either the past Japanese model or the US model' (ibid.: 32). These hybrid forms are a major new feature of Japanese capitalism, covering approximately a quarter of large firms (ibid.: 38, fig. 1.2). Methodologically, in the analysis of this hybridization process, the classic Japanese model (and – at the more abstract level – the CME) is deployed as a yardstick to evaluate change. It is not anticipated that this will or should provide an accurate description of reality, but the logic and dynamics identified within the classic model – what made it cohere, fit together and 'work' – are used as clues as to how to interpret contemporary changes and what is happening within existing Japanese capitalism today. Similar observations about hybridity and increasing diversity could be made about German (see pp. 218–21), French (see pp. 215–18), South Korean (see Pirie 2005, 2008; Thurbon 2016), Chinese (see pp. 166–70).

Institutional isomorphism (one institution in a given setting emulating or resembling another; Di Maggio and Powell 1983), or what Streeck and Thelen call 'diffusion' (2005), generated strong similarities between Japanese firms in the 'golden age' between the 1960s and the 1990s (Jackson and Miyajima 2008: 6). This, however, contrasts with 'a growing diversity of corporate governance practices across firms' in the contemporary period (ibid.: 3). This 'increasing heterogeneity' and diversity *within* Japanese capitalism (ibid.: 38) in recent years are a result of structural transformations of Japanese capitalism, notably increased internationalization of investment and ownership patterns. Increased diversity arises, Jackson and Miyajima argue, because 'not all firms are equally exposed to pressures for change and existing institutions also constrain change along particular trajectories' (ibid.: 31). Jackson and Miyajima see emerging from this process relatively stable hybrid firms and forms of capitalist organization. Indeed, some comparative capitalisms scholars even suggest that hybrids outperform 'purer' capitalisms (Kenworthy 2006).

Convergence accounts posit that increased deregulation and liberalization of capitalism, and the internationalization of investment and ownership patterns, cause a teleological convergence on LME capitalism. Counter-intuitively, the upshot of these changes in Japan has been the opposite: an increasing heterogeneity and diversity *within* Japanese capitalism. Interestingly, in these examples, sources of increased efficiency are the enduring departures from pure market relations. This relates back to Hall and Soskice's fundamental 'market' versus 'non-market' co-ordination pathologies of LME and CME types, respectively. For example, with Japanese as compared to US managers, trust is much more prevalent in the former context, given societal norms of honourable behaviour. These cultural differences explain the reduced need to incorporate sub-contracting relationships within 'vertically integrated multidivisional firms' in the Japanese context. This may help to explain why globalization has not induced more convergence, because 'cultural and social relations may mediate the degree to which changes in the technical environment necessarily precipitate institutional transformations' (Campbell 2010: 93–4; Dore 1983, 2000; Granovetter 1985; Jacoby 2005). Thus the ideational element – social norms and how market relations are understood in different contexts – has its part to play in explaining ongoing diversity as capitalisms transform.

TRACING PROCESSES OF CAPITALIST CHANGE: THE AMERICAN POLITICAL ECONOMY

As the archetype of the LME model, deemed in some quarters to be more compatible with liberalization and increasing economic interdependence in the world economy, one might anticipate the American model not to exhibit significant change as globalization advances. This analysis of its contemporary evolution indicates, firstly, that its path-dependent trajectory is not static but dynamic; secondly, it demonstrates how the evolution of American capitalism is a deeply political process, shaped by powerful forces and the contours of the US political system (King and Wood 1999; Prasad 2006; Hacker and Pierson 2010) as much as by economic efficiency considerations. It also reveals enduring 'impurities' within American capitalism, such as impediments to the market for corporate control, generating a disparity between US corporate governance and the LME ideal type (Monks and Minow 2004; Clift 2009: 72). The Trump administration revealed further counter-tendencies in US capitalism – towards more protectionist trade policies, and some more interventionist economic policies. Yet the US remains a free market economy characterized by low taxation, market-oriented regulation and limited employment rights. It remains a political economy with comparatively limited welfare provision (though see pp. 227–8; Hacker 2002) where market modes of co-ordination are the norm economy.

As noted above, one decidedly un-LME prevailing structural feature of American capitalism is the ongoing massive state intervention in and financial support for a scientifically oriented military sector which drives much of America's vaunted innovatory capacity in areas such as aerospace and computing (Coates 2000: 201–10; Crouch 2005a: 441–2; Block

2008; Block and Keller 2009; Weiss 2014). The presence of such departures from the LME ideal type, to different degrees in different phases of the country's historical development (see also Thompson 2004; Martin 2005), offers further support to the interpretation of contemporary capitalist change in terms of hybridization.

A brief look at American economic development indicates how politically contested and interrupted the emergence of its liberal market capitalism has been. There have been political upheavals, dramatic shifts and 'great reversals' (Rajan and Zingales 2003) along the way. In the early 1800s the American political economy was characterized by a state-led project to develop manufacturing through activist, interventionist industrial policy and protectionism, theorized by Alexander Hamilton ([1791] 1997: 35–47) and Henry Carey (see Helleiner 2020). This bore many hallmarks of List's economic nationalism and Johnson's developmental state (1982). Later in the 19th century the US political economy portrayed many of the traits of CME capitalism, from 'trusts, combines, main banks, interlocking directorships' to 'restricted retail competition', flourishing apprenticeships and government intervention 'to promote railroads, harbours, canals', as well as industrial policy whereby 'specific industries were subsidised and sheltered' (Gourevitch 1996: 239; see also Galbraith 1956).

A range of market-making interventions transformed US capitalism in the early 20th century. Anti-trust laws were introduced to prevent cross-shareholdings and close links between banks and large firms, shifting the logic along the liberal lines accentuated within the LME ideal type. One important driver here was ideational – the ideological attachment to liberty as realized through free markets which has a powerful hold within American societal norms (see e.g. Galbraith 1956: ch. 1). The American political economy tradition (see Lindblom 1977; Block et al. 1987; Ferguson and Rogers 1987; Hacker and Pierson 2010: 167) has analysed how policies, politics and state intervention play key roles, especially at critical junctures, in shaping the trajectory of American capitalist development (Gourevitch 1996; see also Campbell 2010, 2011; Thelen 2010). The Great Depression and World War II saw another bout of market-making intervention to arrive at another post-war US political economic regime, shaped by the political forces of the New Deal coalition (Eisner 2011; Deeg 2012). Active intervention by government created 'new institutions ... that allowed the government to play a central role in stabilizing the business cycle and assuring a pattern of income distribution that supported mass consumption' (Block 2011: 33).

The Fordist post-war American model

Just as in Japan, American capitalism has dovetailing institutional complementarities, albeit underpinned by a more liberal logic, oriented around market mechanisms and following market signals (Hall and Soskice 2001; Amable 2003: 60; Hancké 2009). Between the 1950s and the 1970s, US industries were highly competitive internationally, and US productivity was comparatively high (Coates 2000). US firms were able to offer relatively generous wages, feeding growing consumption in the large domestic market, a dovetailing of mass production and a society predicated upon expanding mass consumption.

American capitalism in this era is often termed 'Fordist', a term the comparative capitalisms debate derives from Gramsci via Michel Aglietta (1979), doyen of the French Regulation School. What Boyer and Juillard term 'the institutional forms of Fordism' provided a crucial underpinning for Fordist accumulation: 'a post-1945 labour-capital compromise that codified the principle of sharing the productivity gains created by scientific management' (Boyer and Juillard 1995: 238). Thus, once again, the distributional politics underpinning the model of capitalism (Thelen 2010) were crucial to its stability, endurance and success.

The long period of post-war prosperity is explained in Regulation School terms by a Fordist 'accumulation regime' which comprised 'major transformations in the wage–labour nexus, forms of competition, the monetary regime and insertion into a special international regime, the *Pax Americana*' (Boyer and Juillard 1995: 238; see also Block 2011). The latter point underlines how the post-war American model of capitalism was predicated upon the international context of embedded liberalism (see pp. 10, 142–9, 255–6) to whose construction US statesmen were so integral (Ruggie 1982; Ikenberry 1992; Helleiner 1994). In terms of national-level institutions, this 'regime of accumulation' was sustained and accompanied by a 'mode of regulation' – an industrial relations system, education and training system and other elements which sustained the variety of capitalism. For example, the priority was not highly skilled but semi-skilled workers, and the education system was tailored to provide these, another case of institutional complementarity (Hollingsworth 1997: 270–1).

Fordist mass production techniques were accompanied by a broadly Keynesian approach that managed demand in the macro-economy (Salant 1989; Hirschman 1989; Eisner 2011: 80–8). This reached its zenith in the 1960s with Johnson's 'aggressive brand of Keynesianism' (Eisner 2011: 100) and the consumption-fuelling generous welfare provision, education, housing and social spending which formed part of the 'Great Society' legislation. This provided the social basis of the US political economy in the 'golden age' of post-war capitalism (Marglin and Schor 1992; Block 2011: 34), and Keynesian demand management techniques were an important source of the business confidence needed to sustain high levels of productive investment.

Other institutions within the political economy aligned with this Fordist configuration. US unions lacked the institutions of corporatist representation, entrenched workers' rights or employer/employee co-ordination (Martin 2005) prevalent in some co-ordinated or corporatist economies such as Germany (Soskice 1999) and Sweden (Pontusson 1992). The limited employment rights of workers meant a 'fluid' labour market – with ease of hiring and firing being a key means for firms and managers to adapt swiftly to changing economic circumstances and market conditions. This worker/firm relationship fostered a short-termist horizon reinforced by other elements of the system – such as firm financing arrangements. This limited 'up-skilling' and training provision within firms, and limited mobility within the firm as a route to acquire skills. Such a 'rigid internal labour market' is a corollary of the flexible external labour market (Hollingsworth 1991, 1997: 292–3).

The politics underpinning its distributional settlement was an important element within US Fordism. David Coates terms US organized labour 'the absent guest at the capitalist feast', but notes an important if subordinate role for unions in supporting the post-war Fordist growth model (1994: 219, 221, 2000: 249; see also Davis 1986: 190–1; Kotz et al. 1994). The New Deal legislation of the 1930s heralded a peaking of unionization at around 35 per cent in 1945, but subsequent decades were characterized by long-term decline (Martin 2005: 190–1; Hacker and Pierson 2010: 185–9; Eisner 2011: 23–4). Deeg claims that the institutional complementarities arising from the weak corporatist institutions in Fordist post-war America were not very great (2012). Similarly, King and Wood identify in weak, peak business associations and unions unable to deliver sustained negotiated wage outcomes the 'structural roots' for the failure of corporatism in the US (1999: 378).

The post-World War II American financial system was formed under the New Deal regime, the result of political acts of market-making: 'regulatory legislation and institutions literally created the various financial industries and defined the relationships between them' (Eisner 2011: 23; see also Hacker and Pierson 2010). Orienting US firms towards capital markets, the system tended to 'institutionalise arms-length relationships between firms and finance' (Lindberg and Campbell 1991: 392). In general, large US firms have relied on stock markets, rather than banks, for financing. This feeds a focus for 'the management embedded in such a system' on rates of return on equity in corporate strategy. Managers have 'a high incentive to maximise short term considerations at the expense of long term strategy' (Hollingsworth 1997: 271; see also Coates 2000: 36).

These labour market, industrial relations, financial system institutions, along with firm organization elements and Keynesian demand management, aligned into a relatively coherent LME model (Coates 2000; Deeg 2012: 1250–4). This was, as is always the case with any capitalist regime (see e.g. Streeck and Thelen 2005; Streeck 2010), underpinned by political and social forces, what Deeg terms the US Democrats' 'New Deal coalition' (2012: 1250–1). This New Deal regime was established before World War II and consolidated over the following decades (see Eisner 2011: chs 4–6). These provided the political support for the more 'embedded' aspects of US capitalism, which proved sufficiently resilient to sustain this growth path while economic growth and productivity gains were being delivered.

This strong economic growth and rising living standards of US workers faltered somewhat from the 1970s onwards, with real wages stagnating and firm restructuring leading to higher unemployment (Coates 2000: 249). US workers were working longer hours than their parents and often needed more than one job. While still boasting comparatively high productivity, the US economy was losing competitiveness in some key sectors (ibid.: 24–31). Worsening economic results domestically fuelled fears of deteriorating international competitiveness of the US economy and its firms. David Coates identifies the 'erosion of the American dream' from the 1970s onwards as US growth faltered, median wages stagnated, people worked longer hours and living standards ceased to improve for millions of Americans. US society became ever more unequal (Coates 2000: 24–5) and this sparked increased political contestation over distributional outcomes within US capitalism (Hacker and Pierson 2010; see Chapter 12).

As Regulation School analysis put it, flagging productivity and contradictions within the wage–labour nexus eventually generated a crisis within Fordist accumulation in the US (Boyer and Juillard 1995). SSA scholarship was highlighting similar crisis-prone tendencies, weaknesses and instabilities with the Fordist model (Duménil and Lévy 2004). Regulation Theory and SSA scholarship (see Coates 2000: 41–3) inspired a range of interpretations of US capitalist change focused on the US model and its contradictions and perceived crisis. Some saw a collapse of the Fordist accumulation regime. A feature of this work was a mooted (or desired) transition to a 'post-Fordist' production regime of 'flexible specialisation' (Piore and Sabel 1984; Amin 1994).

After Fordism: US capitalism into the 21st century

The difficulties experienced by American Fordism spawned successive waves of debates as to whether liberal American capitalism was more successful than, for example, Japanese co-ordinated capitalism, which had seen comparatively very strong economic growth in the post-war world (see e.g. Albert 1993; Coates 2000: 23–4). For a time, some advocated US emulation of Japanese capitalism to escape the short time horizons of management and the lack of investment in the human capital of workers which the LME model induced (Reich 1984; Lazonick 1993; Coates 2000: 37–40).

However, transition to a different model of capitalism, if possible at all, would be an enormous upheaval – requiring massive political capital outlay to reform each of the different sets of interlocking institutions: labour markets, education system, financial system and corporate governance arrangements, to name but a few. After all, such a new 'regime of accumulation' required a new 'mode of regulation' (Lipietz 1992: ch. 1). The social and political forces that would have been needed to mobilize such a profound restructuring of capitalism and the social institutions which sustained it were lacking. The path of reform for American capitalism in the end coalesced around a neo-liberal trajectory emphasizing 'deregulation', or rather liberalizing *re*-regulation.

These changes in the governance of American capitalism were backed by a mobilization of political forces within society, notably the defection of the Southern Democrats from the old New Deal coalition to support Reagan's neo-liberal reform agenda (Deeg 2012: 1251). Neo-liberalism held sway in the Reagan era, and in the 1990s the Democrats largely aligned with the neo-liberal agenda under Clinton (King and Wood 1999; Prasad 2006). This neo-liberal variant of America's LME was more market-oriented. Its institutional complementarities included 'limited financial regulation, strong anti-trust law and decentralized labour markets', generating 'incentives for radical product innovations that enhance economic competitiveness' (Campbell 2011: 212; see also McDonough et al. 2010; Eisner 2011: 34–5, 113–38).

The recalibration of the American capitalist model along more neo-liberal lines resulted from political acts of market-making intervention by the US regulatory state (Campbell et al. 1991). Federal and state governments engaged in substantial lightening of the regulatory burden within American capitalism in the 1980s and 1990s across a range of areas, including labour, financial and product markets, and environmental, consumer and worker protections (King and Wood 1999: 391–4; Prasad 2006: 67–70, 82–96; Hacker and Pierson 2010).

The distributional settlement of neo-liberal American capitalism, and the politics which it reflected, were again distinct from the Fordist period. Hacker and Pierson, thinking about American politics and political economy in terms of 'politics as organised combat', detect the crucial 'role of organised interests in shaping large-scale public policies that mediate distributional outcomes' (2010: 154). Crucially, business interests became much more mobilized and lobbied much more effectively from the late 1980s onwards (ibid.: 175–7). This business lobby became much more focused on influencing 'the specific ways in which the government structures the economy' (ibid.: 170), enabling a skewing of the income distribution dramatically in favour of the very very rich (Krugman 2012: 71–90).

The neo-liberal shift, and the stark increases in US income inequality which resulted from it, occurred both through specific laws and policies, and through 'drift' where extant policies change their effects (in this case making society much more unequal; Hacker and Pierson 2010: 170). This led to 'major changes in the governance of the American economy', enriching America's very top earners, notably by overcoming opposition to push through changes in taxation, industrial relations, corporate governance and executive pay, and financial market regulation (ibid.: 183–96). The weakening of US organized labour, subjected to successive erosion of rights by governments and employers, has been one significant shift within US capitalism (Brenner 1998: 191–6; Hacker and Pierson

2010: 179, 185–9). Arguably the resulting 'intensification of the labour process and stagnation in real wages' have been important elements in US firm profitability and economic
growth since the 1970s (Coates 2000: 249). The consequences for US firms of the industrial relations and labour market context are 'enormous wage dispersion, limited worker
protections, and few incentives to make long-term investments in skills development'
(Martin 2005: 190–1, 196–200). The political consequences of this shift in the distributional outcomes and power relations within American capitalism are explored at length in
Chapter 12.

Though the neo-liberal 'regime of accumulation' delivered economic growth during the
1990s and 2000s, the vulnerability and instability within neo-liberalized American LME
capitalism were amply demonstrated when the GFC erupted in 2007–8. The prevailing political forces in society had shaped how financial regulation evolved in the lead-up to the crisis.
Bhagwati has talked of the Wall Street/Treasury nexus (1998), with powerful interests
within large-scale finance lobbying hard for reforms, which lightened the regulatory touch
and opened up new profit-making opportunities, and massive hikes in remuneration. Key
players within Congress and Government had very close ties to (and previous careers within)
major financial firms (Hacker and Pierson 2010: 193–7). Liberalization within US financial
capitalism involved a slew of changes to ensure an ever lighter touch by US financial services
regulation (Gourevitch 1996; Wilson 2012; Deeg 2012; Tooze 2018). Pursued by an active
state (Cioffi 2006; Davis 2009: ch. 6; Krippner 2011), these crucial shifts facilitated the
emergence of the 'shadow banking industry' (Ban and Gabor 2016), freed from the capital
reserve requirements of normal banks and financial institutions. The advent and growth of
asset-backed securities trading, which the US Government decided not to regulate, fuelled
the expansion of this elusive financial underworld (see Hardie et al. 2013a, 2013b;
Nesvetailova 2015; Campbell 2011: 220–4; Krugman 2012). The global shadow banking
industry exploited 'regulatory arbitrage' opportunities and poorly designed financial regulation to grow quickly, both before and after the crash, heightening levels of systemic risk
within global finance (Thiemann 2014, 2018; Helgdottir 2016; Fernandez and Wigger 2016;
Gabor and Ban 2016).

The New Deal regulation and legislation had arrived at a political settlement on which
the American financial system rested for some decades. In challenging this, the lighter
touch re-regulation of US finance under the neo-liberal regime involved political struggles
and contestation: 'the gradual shredding of the post-New Deal rulebook for financial markets did not simply result from the impersonal forces of "financial innovation"' (Hacker
and Pierson 2010: 194; see also Eisner 2011: ch. 7). To give one example, the Glass–
Steagall Act of 1933 sought to prevent conflicts of interest (and financial crises) by separating the investment and commercial arms of banks. By introducing what would in
today's parlance be termed 'firewalls' into the finance industry, the aim was to reduce the
ability of a banking crisis to spread what is now known as 'systemic risk'. This legislation,
however, was relaxed in the 1980s and then repealed in the 1990s, following political
mobilization and lobbying pressure from Wall Street interests keen to exploit the profitable opportunities which the enforced separation proscribed (Hacker and Pierson 2010:
194–6; Campbell 2011: 226).

These, like the decisions not to regulate that enabled the rise of the shadow banking
industry, were political acts of market-making, with the state a key player and the political
decisions backed by powerful groups (see Gourevitch 1996; Hacker and Pierson 2010: 197).
The 'light touch' content of LME market-making had significant implications for the

American financial system and the US model of capitalism. Hacker and Pierson underline the importance of permissive regulations on 'crucial issues as what constitutes insider dealing or an unacceptable conflict of interest, how much monitoring and transparency there will be in major financial transactions, and what levels of leverage and risk are acceptable given the potentially massive externalities associated with large-scale speculation' (2010: 193–4). The ever lighter touch re-regulation of the financial services industry, especially mortgage markets and derivatives trading, is part of what Campbell terms the 'deeper institutional roots of the crisis' (2011: 214) which rocked global markets in 2008.

The causes of the GFC relate to the social basis of consumption within the US political economy. Within America's deregulated labour market from the 1980s, firms sought to keep production costs low to remain internationally competitive. Disempowered workers had to accept low or no wage growth (Coates 2000). This has fuelled the increasingly unequal distribution of wealth within the US political economy – with the top 1 per cent becoming much richer (and within that the top 0.1 per cent becoming *very* much richer), as I explore in Chapter 12 (see also Krugman 2012; Hacker and Pierson 2010; Clarke et al. 2019). A 2017 Oxfam report *An Economy for the 99%* found that just eight men own the same as half the global population (2017).

Substantial tranches of the US population in the lower middle and working classes are becoming much poorer as their real incomes have stagnated. This is detrimental to a revitalization of the consumption dynamics which underpinned the earlier Fordist accumulation regime (see Block 2011: 44–5). American households used debt, notably mortgage debt, as a means to fuel the mass consumption on which the US model of capitalism remained predicated (see Langley 2004, 2008, 2010; Montgomerie 2006, 2007, 2009; Davis 2009; Deeg 2012). US consumers were 'using their homes as automated teller machines', and 'this dramatic expansion in consumer credit worked to breathe new life into the exhausted model of suburban-based mass consumption' (Block 2011: 41). The housing bubble fuelled this dynamic, which Colin Crouch has felicitously termed 'privatised Keynesianism' (2009). Campbell interprets this as a shift in American capitalism's institutional complementarities to sustain consumption practices, although he notes that such complementarities may not provide efficiency gains or economic stability over time (2011: 227).

The above lighter touch re-regulation of financial services fuelled this credit boom, for example making mortgage-backed securities more attractive investments and second mortgages more attractive options for homeowners through changes in the tax system (ibid.: 218). The ever-increasing focus on 'shareholder value' (see pp. 200–3) in the financial services industry, and short-term return on (potentially risky) investments, became more pronounced within US capitalism. The role of accident and unanticipated consequence should not be underplayed. The repeal of Glass–Steagall permitted the 'bundling and rebundling of asset-backed securities and swaps in ways that linked virtually everyone involved in the shadow banking system'. Campbell argues that the 'complimentary effect of these two institutional reforms proved to be devastating in the long run' (Campbell 2011: 228).

This brief tour of US capitalism's recent evolution indicates a number of themes of this chapter. Embeddedness of markets in social context and institutional complementarities have been features of US capitalism, but they have not paralysed it. Change has been path dependent, since evolution has taken place within the LME type. However, changes over recent decades have resulted in a decidedly different manifestation of LME-type capitalism. In industrial relations, the disempowering of labour from the 1970s onwards, compared to the post-war period, has seen this aspect of American capitalism approximate more closely to the LME ideal type. This has entailed successive regulation and legislation reducing employment and social rights, and reducing the taxation burden on the very wealthy (Coates 2000: 249–50; Martin 2005: 185; Hacker and Pierson 2010). These social pathologies of contemporary US capitalism were a significant cause of the recent crisis, from which it has struggled to emerge. On the other hand, the scale and scope of government intervention in the wake of the GFC have introduced 'impurities' into American capitalism (Wilson 2012). Instability, institutional change and institutional reproduction have co-existed, and political contestation has surrounded the political acts of market-making which have shaped the trajectory of American capitalist evolution.

CONCLUSION: INTERPRETING CAPITALIST RESTRUCTURING – NOT CONVERGENCE BUT HYBRIDIZATION?

Comparative capitalisms analysis, when informed by the insights of classical political economy, can benefit from the latter's explicit recognition of how the market, and capitalism, is predicated upon a necessarily dense network/web of social institutions. A more differentiated political economy of capitalism can be discerned – one alive to the diversity of possible responses to economic interdependence and to the GFC. The particularities of each political economy's trajectory are mediated by 'domestic' institutions and politics, thus conditioned by interaction with domestic ideational and institutional factors (Vogel 2005: 147, 2006). Thus ongoing capitalist variety has its roots in the differential embedding processes of state/economy relations, which give rise to distinct histories, legacies and politics of capitalist change (see Hay 2004a).

Many comparative capitalisms scholars have characterized evolutions in terms of 'hybridization' (Boyer 1998, 2005a, 2005b; Jackson 2001: 169, 2008; Streeck 2001: 33; Perraton and Clift, 2004: 258; Lütz 2004: 189; Streeck and Thelen 2005: 21; Vogel 2005: 147; Clift 2007; Clift and McDaniel 2019). The key merit of this is that it 'rejects both an economic determinism of a single best model, as well as societal determinism which suggests that practices can never be transferred across social contexts' (Jackson and Miyajima 2008: 39). It is compatible with the more dynamic and contingent approaches to social embeddedness of capitalist institutions, to path dependency and to institutional complementarity, which have been advanced in this chapter. Hybridization is helpful because it captures the qualitative nature of change, doing less violence to the facts than a rather too loosely and liberally applied notion of convergence, or co-convergence. In its account of change, and of institutional reproduction, in its characterization of the relation between abstract ideal-typical model and real political economy, and in its rejection of 'state-economy dualism' (Block and Evans 2005), it involves a number of important moves away from the VoC mainstream. The approach to comparing capitalisms advanced in this chapter takes greater heed of the insights of classical political economy, and of the core insights into political economy outlined in Chapter 2.

Proposing hybridization as the most persuasive descriptive characterization of capitalist evolution offends the clean lines of the VoC typology, certainly in its initial formulation. It challenges the VoC notion that either one logic or the other logic prevailing consistently across actual existing capitalism is more likely to endure and stabilize, and more likely to deliver superior success. More significantly, it does not accept the VoC logic of argument regarding institutional reproduction, and sees institutional evolution as more open-ended and less 'locked-in'. A number of accounts have highlighted how the 'jigsaw' dovetailing of institutional complementarities *does not* cement stasis and prevent change (Goyer 2003, 2006; Hancké et al. 2007: 11; Campbell 2010). Similarly, Gregory Jackson and Hideaki Miyajima talk in terms of 'co-evolution' or 'rebundling' or 'conversion' (2008: 2). Thus hybridization thinking understands the role of institutional complementarities differently, seeing them as potentially explaining the *differential* effects of *similar* kinds of changes within capitalisms, potentially generating increased diversity. In the next chapter, we will consider the explanatory purchase of 'hybridization' over changes in financial systems and corporate governance.

10 The Comparative Political Economy of Finance and Corporate Governance

INTRODUCTION

The market and the firm are two of the central institutions of capitalism. Building on the discussion of comparative capitalisms in Chapter 9, and the state in Chapter 8, in this chapter I analyse the CPE of finance through an exploration of the interconnected developments of financial markets (at both national and international levels) and firms. Analysis underlines how both markets and firms are political constructs. It is not 'the market' per se which shapes how firms and capitalism evolve in a given context. Instead, primacy in explanation goes to political processes of market-making, notably inscription of the rights and responsibilities of firms (and the actors within them) into the legislative and regulatory environment. These determine what the company is, how it operates, and crucially how it is financed and its relationship to its financiers.

These political settlements over the ordering of finance, corporate governance and capitalism are never set in stone, but subject to contestation and change. Corporate scandals such as Enron and WorldCom, or the post-GFC London Inter-Bank Offered Rate (LIBOR) scandal over major banks fixing interest rates, illustrated the inefficiencies and scope for abuse within the status quo. Such developments eroded confidence in 'light-touch regulation'. Further financial scandal erupted in 2016 when the leaked 'Panama papers' exposed a dubious offshore finance industry which facilitated tax evasion on a colossal scale. Hundreds of politicians, celebrities and members of the global elite, as well as criminals, concealed their wealth and business interests with varying degrees of legality through hard-to-trace offshore companies in numerous tax havens. All of this generated a conducive environment for a politics which challenged the nature of company law, banking and capital market regulation. However, as the dust settled on the 2008 crash, the scale of post-crisis financial re-regulation looked somewhat limited (Helleiner 2014). It was not clear that the state had been empowered vis-à-vis the financial sector (Woll 2014, 2017).

How far was the enormous financial power of big banks and major finance houses really curtailed? The debate continues as to whether enough was done to clip the wings of dominant financial market actors, still prone to explore a variety of highly complex investment opportunities with potentially systematically risky consequences. The political and market power of major financial market operators, and their capacity to shape the regulatory environment to their advantage while neglecting resultant systemic risks, seemed largely undimmed. To make sense of this, it is important to recall two of the core insights of political economy outlined in Chapter 2. Firstly, markets are political constructs sustained by market-making interventions, not naturally occurring phenomena. Secondly, financial markets, like other markets, are embedded in distinctive national social contexts. The evolution of financial markets and firms within advanced capitalism has not been a smooth, linear, teleological process, but a drawn-out wrangle shaped by financial politics and struggles over the appropriate level, form and scale of financial regulation (see e.g. Germain 2010; Baker and Wigan 2017). This evolution of national financial systems has been a profoundly political process, mediated through distinctive national institutional settings, corporate and market cultures and legal and regulatory environments. Marxian insights into the structural power of capital (see pp. 30, 62–4, 251) help us make sense of the power relations at work (see e.g. Crotty 2009).

Firms and markets remain socially embedded, and this imprints upon their nature and functioning. Distinct understandings about firms and finance shape the regulatory edifice which has been built up to sustain capitalism in each setting. Each national institutional context reflects the influence of past political settlements about the nature and role of the firm, and the distribution of power and authority within it. To illustrate the differentiated processes of building finance capitalism, we will consider in this chapter two modes or ideal types for the ordering of finance: long-termist, relationship-oriented, 'stakeholder' capitalism, and short-termist, rate-of-return-oriented, 'shareholder' capitalism.

Stakeholder and shareholder forms of corporate organization, and the modes of firm financing and national financial systems which align with them, generate particular incentive structures for political economic actors. Each can deliver economic returns, growth, productivity gains and economic efficiency, and each leads to the instantiation and reproduction of qualitatively different understandings of the firm. A different politics prevails in stakeholder and shareholder capitalism because different groups tend to be empowered. Both within firms and in society, the fruits of growth and the profit share from economic activity accrue differentially to the various social groups. At the societal level, the income distribution across the economy and society as a whole can vary widely (see p. 241; Chapters 11 and 12).

The main focus for this chapter is how international trends towards the liberalizing re-regulation of markets, which have been particularly pronounced in the realms of finance, have unleashed common pressures on diverse political economies and 'national financial systems' (Zysman 1983). International financial flows have in some cases partially undermined the coherence of national financial systems of post-war capitalism. As the comparative capitalisms scholars we encountered in Chapter 9 would anticipate, the transformations that globalizing finance has brought about within capitalism have been refracted through 'national financial systems', mediated by prior institutional settings. The various sets of relationships between firms and capital markets interact differently with changing international financial conditions. I illustrate this in the empirical sections of this chapter through process tracing of the contemporary evolutions of firms and financial markets in two advanced political economies – France and Germany – arguing that the contemporary evolution of their firms and financial systems is best understood in terms of 'hybridization': combining elements from both stakeholder and shareholder capitalism in varied ways.

THE COMPARATIVE POLITICAL ECONOMY OF STAKEHOLDER AND SHAREHOLDER CAPITALISM

How the company is organized (where power lies within it, who is accountable to whom and what interests the power holders serve) is a crucial political question, as a rich tradition of corporate governance and comparative capitalisms analysis has demonstrated. The distribution of rights and responsibilities, of authority and oversight between firms and their sources of finance, can take many forms. How the legal and regulatory environment of the company is ordered (according to which principles, serving which interests) is equally a central political question. The different stakeholder and shareholder understandings of the nature of the firm find different solutions to these political questions, and this helps us explain important differentiation between capitalisms. This is because where firm financing comes from, and the nature of relations between financiers and firms which it generates, have important implications for the nature of capitalism. At root, they may reflect different understandings of what the firm is for. Obviously, at one level, firms exist to conduct business and make profits, but there are many ways those objectives can be fulfilled, and perhaps reconciled to other social goals.

As we saw in Chapter 8 when we looked at the political economy of the developmental state, control over sources of finance can be a crucial source of power and influence, and this can shape behaviour and outcomes in capitalist economies. Different kinds of relationships between firms and their financiers influence behaviour in diverse ways, predicated upon particular kinds of expectations. Most obviously, the difference can be temporal – whether the return on an investment is calculated in weeks, months, years or decades. Firm financing arrangements can also have implications for the balance of priorities – between generating profits, offering stable employment and other societal obligations which might impinge upon the firm, depending on its legal and regulatory context.

Specifically, stakeholder capitalism prioritizes 'voice', whereas the shareholder capitalism model facilitates 'exit' (Hirschman 1970; Zysman 1983: 57). The prevalence (or not) of corporate takeovers is important within comparative capitalisms as indicators of broader logics. Generally speaking, to the extent that market mechanisms can operate unimpeded, the shareholder capitalist approach prevails (Manne 1965). A freer-functioning market for corporate control (facilitating takeovers) results in increased emphasis on 'shareholder value', the core organizing principle of shareholder capitalism (Sternberg 1998: 34–5; Lazonick and O'Sullivan 2000; Aglietta and Rebérioux 2005; Boyer 2005b). To the extent that states and firms are able to introduce or rely upon impediments to a free market for corporate control, a more stakeholder capitalist approach prevails.

These differing logics nurture dovetailing interrelationships of the kind discussed within comparative capitalisms debates (see pp. 117–20, 174–5). Stakeholder capitalism tends to co-ordinate activities through long-term network relationships, wherein trust and loyalty play their part. In shareholder capitalism, market mechanisms, the following of market signals and contracting tend to be the prevailing modes of interaction between economic actors; that is, between firms. Gourevitch and Shinn (2005) note a range of 'institutional complementarities' between firm/financial market relations and other aspects of the political economy such as product market regulation. Thus there are points of overlap and common influences, such that 'shareholder' and 'stakeholder' capitalism map fairly closely onto the LME and CME 'varieties' of capitalism, respectively (see Chapter 9).

That said, shareholder and stakeholder capitalism connote broader societal issues – extending the focus beyond just firms to the role of finance within society. Different configurations can induce particular distributions of wealth and distinctive patterns of behaviour on the part of economic actors within and between companies. Patterns of ownership and control of firms shape wider societal outcomes such as how the fruits of economic growth are distributed, both within firms but also within society. One body of work explores the 'societal foundations' of financial systems, and how society's degree of reliance on capital markets (for example, for pension provision) affects societal norms and preferences for shareholder or stakeholder capitalism (Jackson and Vitols 2001; Vitols 2003: 244–7). The outsider, capital market–based 'shareholder capitalist' systems tend to be among the least egalitarian societies of the world's richest economies (Glyn 2001, 2006: ch. 7; Bastagli et al. 2012: table 1). That said, inequality levels have been rising in all advanced economies, spanning the shareholder/stakeholder capitalism divide, as I explore in Chapter 12.

Drawing attention to the social context within which particular firm financing arrangements are embedded facilitates appreciation of the *politics* of finance. Different social and economic groups are likely to enjoy significant political power in a stakeholder capitalist society compared to a shareholder one (Roe 1994, 2003, 2006; Gourevitch and Shinn 2005; Goyer 2011). Indeed, a number of different coalitions can form around issues such as disclosure of information and where power lies within the firm (between, for example, labour, management and the owners of capital). As Perraton and Clift note, 'a coalition of interest groups around labour and entrepreneurs/managers may have a common interest in avoiding hostile takeovers which would lead them to promoting a legal framework limiting investor protection but promoting workforce rights; a coalition of interest groups around entrepreneurs and investors would lead instead to a strong framework of investor protection but limited labour rights' (2004: 224–5; see also Roe 1994, 2003; Fehn and Meier 2001; Gourevitch and Shinn 2005).

More broadly within capitalism, the power resources model underlines how different social groups are empowered depending on how capitalism is organized. Thus in 'stakeholder' capitalist societies, organized labour is likely to enjoy a more prominent role within national politics. Powerful unions are able to shape the policy and wage-bargaining process such that more wealth accrues to the workers in wages, and towards welfare state development (Korpi 1983; Stephens 1979). In shareholder capitalist societies, owners and managers are likely to enjoy more scope to divert disproportionate wealth towards themselves through executive remuneration and other channels (Hager 2018: 13–15). This is especially likely in political economies where processes of 'financialization' prioritizing shareholder value within the financial system (Epstein 2005), and within capitalism more broadly (see below), are more advanced (van der Zwan 2014: 104; Table 10.1).

Thus the political settlements over how capitalism works take different forms, empowering workers and owners of capital to different degrees in Germany and the US, for example. The more solidaristic 'stakeholder' preferences prevalent within some societies can be reflected in corporate organization through worker representation on the board. This helps us to understand how national financial systems, and the firm/financing relationships which align with them, are reproduced. Thus it is possible to trace the 'footprints' of shareholder and stakeholder capitalism influences in looking at how firms are ordered, the distribution of wealth within the firm, within society, and the market-making interventions and regulation within a particular capitalist order. These can explain the varied economic and social impacts of the GFC.

Below we will discuss 'financialization' and how the increasing encroachment of financial dynamics into all aspects of society is affecting the everyday life of citizens, for example how prospects for adequate caring and pension provision in retirement are increasingly linked to one's portfolio of financial assets. In a financialized economy, an individual's credit scores and their debt profile increasingly shape their life chances and opportunities. CPE scholarship explores varieties of financialization (Deeg 2010; Engelen and Konings 2010; Berghoff 2016; Maxfield et al. 2017; Van Gunten and Navot 2018; Van Treeck 2009) and how these

Table 10.1   Modes and properties of firm financing and of corporate governance

	Stakeholder capitalism	Shareholder capitalism
Prevailing conception of firm	A social entity – to deliver social goods, livelihoods and profits	A private entity – to generate profits
Firms' internal power relations	Worker representation on company boards	Executive dominance and managerial hierarchy
Firm financing	Bank-based, 'patient' capital	Financial market–based, 'footloose' capital
Stock market pressure	Limited – management insulated by e.g. multiple voting rights	Strong – threat of hostile takeovers, shareholder demands for dividends
Logic	'Voice'; trust, loyalty, networks, favours company insiders	'Exit'; follows market signals, favours return on equity
Sources of efficiency	Strategic vision, developing human capital, skills and training	Innovation, flexible labour markets, competition
Priorities	Secure long-term 'dynamic' efficiency	Increase short-term shareholder value
Regulation of capitalism	Extensive	Limited
Political economic ideas	Organized capitalism, industrial citizenship, social cohesion	Free markets, profit motive, *laissez-faire*

contemporary evolutions of the financial sector and corporate governance take particular national paths or forms because of the distinctive ways that processes of financial innovation operate within and interact with their societal context. The prioritizing of shareholder value which aligns with financialization was most entrenched in the Anglo-Saxon political economies, notably the US and the UK (Engelen and Konings 2010: 617–8), and in these political economies the GFC hit particularly hard. These intertwinings of financial markets and ever more aspects of society, and the increasing dominance of shareholder value norms, arguably mean that the instabilities and vulnerabilities that can beset financial markets have deeper and broader social effects and implications than once they did.

BUILDING FINANCE CAPITALISM

A focus on market-making interventions and regulation highlights another important aspect of the relationship between finance and capitalism. Capitalist development and evolution are at one level driven by technological advances and innovations which can increase productivity and lead to growing profits. The expansion of capital accumulation in the 19th century, fuelled by technological advances, combined with an international expansion of investment opportunities and a conducive context for international capital mobility, generated by the fixity and stability provided by the gold standard (see e.g. Eichengreen 1996), created new potential channels for wealth and financial capital. Major projects such as railway and canal building were crucial to the further success and expansion of accumulation, as well as being potentially highly profitable ventures in themselves (Kindleberger 1993: 190–8).

Yet in order for technological advances to transform industrial capitalism, certain political pre-conditions had to be met. For example, new legal and corporate forms and financial instruments were needed to channel the available capital for investment into such lucrative ventures (Gamble and Kelly 2000: 28–34). Yet these did not emerge naturally or inevitably, but were the result of political struggles and acts of market-making. A focus on technological development tells only part of the story. Market orders are political settlements, the result of previous political and social struggles over the distribution of economic gains or over where power lies within the company. These political struggles and settlements are reflected in the law and financial, product and labour market regulation in any given national capitalism.

For Gamble and Kelly, the modern company, the central institution of the modern economy, is 'a contrivance' which is 'constructed through political and legal agency' and 'bears the imprint of the various historical contexts and social and political systems in which it was fashioned' (ibid.: 22). This is equally true of the complex overlapping array of legal and regulatory obligations and entitlements within which firms operate, as comparative analysis of this 'building' of finance capitalism (Cioffi 2006) illustrates. From the mid-19th century onwards, small-scale individual capitalist owner-managers were eclipsed by the rise of the large-scale corporate economies.

In Britain, for example, the political forces of the day shaped the nature of the new legal environment of joint-stock companies and established what rights and responsibilities would accompany the new privileges of limited liability (Hunt 1936). Extensions of the franchise in the mid-19th century empowered some social groups such as the industrial bourgeoisie, but not, in Britain and many other countries, the workers. Key British market-making milestones were the joint-stock company and limited liability laws passed between 1844 and 1862, reflecting the empowerment of investors and owners within the firm and the constitution of the company (Gamble and Kelly 2000: 32). In relation to accountability, disclosure or internal organization of the firm or workers' rights, no requirements were stipulated as a *quid pro quo* for the enormous privilege that limited liability bestowed upon a firm's financiers, its shareholders.

Once the laws had been passed, the new political and corporate settlement over the relationship between a firm's financiers and the firm's liabilities transformed both capitalism and society. For example, in the UK in the second half of the 19th century, the dramatic expansion of the joint-stock company displaced the individual capitalist from control of the enterprise and created a new corporate economy (Hannah 1983). The growth of stock markets and trading in the shares of joint-stock companies in Britain and then beyond made these financial mechanisms for allocating resources increasingly significant within capitalism. The qualitative shift in the nature of capitalism was rooted in a transformation of how capital could be channelled to fund firms' activities. The subsequent ubiquity of large joint-stock enterprises, and the advent of shareholding on a significant scale, had profound implications for societies and for the process of industrial development. Without these key legal and political changes, the modern corporation, stock markets, shareholders and corporate capitalism as we know it today could never have come into being.

The shareholder-friendly *laissez-faire* British approach contrasts with the constitutionalism of the German company law framework, or those developed in Japan and France during the 20th century. In Germany and Japan, for example, Jackson details 'the constraints placed by industrial citizenship on property rights' (2001: 126) and how a very different politics of the company arose. The workers in these societies enjoyed more rights, power and representation within the firm. Greater recognition of their interests imposed constraints upon the pursuit of profit at all costs in pursuit of 'shareholder value'. However, the very notion of such constraints on shareholder interests within the firm, or indeed ideas of 'industrial citizenship', were and are anathema in a British context.

We can see the footprints of these different approaches to building financial capitalism, and the differing societal understandings of the role of the firm and finance they reflect, within the 'battle of the systems' logic identified by scholars of international financial regulation (Story and Walter 1997). Within notionally technocratic regulatory commit-tees overseeing, for example, the development of the European financial space since the 1970s, an economic nationalist struggle played out, pitting distinct French and German stakeholder visions against British shareholder capitalism (see Jabko 2006; Rosamond 2002). National policy elites all seek to mould European financial regulation in ways aligned with their own domestic financial system, and in the interests of their national financial services champions (Quaglia 2007, 2010; Quaglia and Howarth 2018; Clift and McDaniel 2019).

The variety is not just across space, but also over time. A glance back into history reveals some 'great reversals' (Rajan and Zingales 2003; see also Roe 1994, 2003; Gourevitch and Shinn 2005) and some archetypal 'shareholder' or 'stakeholder' societies have at times organized their firms, markets and financing in very different ways. Economic crises and corruption scandals have triggered political struggles between those favouring liberal capi-tal market development and others seeking more stringent, corporate and financial market regulation. As a result of the ebb and flow of these political forces, political economies have shifted their approach dramatically to questions of firm financing and company and compe-tition regulation.

The US case is often seen as an archetypal stock market–based liberal capitalism model (which is the 'end point' lurking behind much teleological convergence thinking). Yet, as we saw in Chapter 9, it contains many non-liberal impurities. Before the 1920s US corporate capitalism was organized around the protected blocs of insiders more familiar to contempo-rary continental European co-ordinated capitalism. Political opposition to cartels, oligopo-listic markets and unfair competition provoked a series of legislative changes in the late 19th and early 20th centuries. The 1890 Sherman Antitrust Act actually unintentionally *increased* oligopoly by triggering mergers and advancing industrial concentration (Fligstein 1990: 23, 59; Jackson 2001: 135). Thereafter, anti-trust measures and competition law ini-tiatives such as the 1914 Clayton Act managed to limit mergers and help to break up the cartels and 'trusts' which previously prevailed, dramatically transforming American corpo-rate capitalism (Peritz 1996; Rajan and Zingales 2003: 41–2; Quack and Djelic 2005: 257; Eisner 2011: 20–1).

At a similar time, between the world wars, Japan and France went in the opposite direc-tion, from liberal towards co-ordinated or state-dominated financial capitalism (Rajan and Zingales 2003: 38–41; Gourevitch and Shinn 2005: 4–12). Germany in the 1920s and 1930s offered a relatively permissive environment for cartels. Thereafter, ordo-liberal principles of strong state regulation of market competition reshaped the post-war German political econ-omy, which developed very strong anti-trust, anti-cartel and anti-monopoly laws. These sig-nificant shifts were the subject of political struggles, rooted in social forces.

To give one vivid contemporary example of how a corporate governance settlement is a power struggle, post-communist Russia saw the dominant party, organized crime and secret service elites seize the enormous corporate assets released through privatization as the communist system collapsed. They emerged as the new dominant corporate elite: the so-called oligarchs. Thereafter, 'after a decade of rampant corporate governance abuse and outright theft, the managers of leading Russian firms rushed to introduce international standards of corporate governance'. This apparently curious turnaround is again explicable in terms of political struggles – this time between corporate elites seeking 'anti-state insurance' against expropriation. In this case, 'the corporate governance "fashion" among Russia's top firms' is designed to counter 'the Kremlin's attack on the independence of big business' (Markus 2008: 70).

The historical and comparative method (see Chapter 13) unearths numerous 'great reversals'. This warns against presuming that evolutionary trends within the CPE of finance are a teleological progression towards a liberal, Anglo-Saxon 'end point' of history. They also warn against a depoliticized view of finance as being driven and shaped exclusively by inexorable forces of economic efficiency. Revived economic nationalism and interventionism further underline these points.

GLOBAL CAPITALISM, INTERNATIONALIZING FINANCE AND NATIONAL FINANCIAL SYSTEMS

In the second half of the 20th century, two seminal CPE texts on the relationship between finance and capitalism were Andrew Shonfield's *Modern Capitalism* (1965) and John Zysman's *Governments, Markets and Growth* (1983). Even though the key substantive issues have moved on since they were writing, there is much to be gleaned from their approach and many of their insights remain pertinent. Zysman's organizing conceptual category, the national financial system, distils the essence of the historical processes of building finance capitalism and the legal inscription of market-making into a national legislative and regulatory environment, as described above. In this section we explore whether national financial systems *still* play the crucial role in shaping the evolution of contemporary national capitalisms that Zysman discerned for them, despite the sharply rising scale of transactions in international capital markets.

National financial systems rest upon 'national political settlements about economic arrangements' (Zysman 1983: 27). Thus, as Goyer puts it, 'the diversity of institutional arrangements across advanced capitalist economies reflects context-specific settlements of political and social conflicts' (2011: 7). Understanding these 'political settlements' and their institutional and historical context helps explain the dynamics and institutional characteristics of these national financial systems – and their impact on economic actors' incentives and behaviour. It also helps explain distributive outcomes within a political economy (see Chapter 12). Zysman makes the case for focusing on 'national financial structures' in order to understand both government economic strategies and the political conflicts that surround industrial change, because the structure of financial markets shapes the kinds of business/state relations that are possible (1983: 7–8). By sub-dividing stakeholder capitalism into two, Zysman arrives at a categorization which identifies three ideal-typical financial systems and three 'models of finance'. These are the capital market–based model (which approximates to the shareholder capitalism of the UK and the US), the credit-based model with government-administered prices (as in stakeholder capitalist Japan or France) and the credit-based model dominated by large financial institutions (as in stakeholder capitalist Germany; Zysman 1983: 69–75; see also Story and Walter 1997: ch. 5; Perraton and Clift 2004: 221–35).

The credit-based versus capital market–based approaches to turning savings into investment form the crucial line of differentiation here. Capital market–based systems favour 'exit' and shareholder value norms, seeing firms as tools to generate return on equity. Credit-based systems, on the other hand, prioritize 'voice' and stakeholder values such as inclusion, trust, solidarity and protecting the broader interests of the firm as a social entity (Hirschman 1970; Zysman 1983: 57). The second dimension of the categorization highlighted by Zysman is how prices are set in these markets – in competitive markets, in institutionally dominated markets or by the government. The final element is the role played by the government in the financial system (Zysman 1983: 69).

How has the rise and rise of international capital markets and financial flows affected these national financial systems? The increased volume of international financial activity is indeed remarkable, and the scale and speed of flows can be dizzying. In terms of trading in currencies, the Bank of International Settlements recorded overall daily foreign exchange trading at US$6.6 trillion per day in April 2019, up from $5.1 trillion per day three years earlier (BIS 2019), dwarfing the levels recorded back in the 1980s (Glyn 2006: 66). Charting this helps us to grasp the implications and impact of a changing context of global finance and the degree of internationalization of savings and investment practices (see e.g. Deeg and O'Sullivan 2009). The impact of this international expansion of capital market activity on national political economies varies. By and large, the advanced economies which are the central focus of this book have become much more deeply enmeshed in global financial flows than have developing economies (Held et al. 1999). Stock market capitalization to GDP ratios are one useful way to attempt to measure the overall displacement of capital markets within the domestic political economy. Evidence indicates substantial and often dramatic increases in capital market activity in the advanced economies since about 1980 (see Rajan and Zingales 2003: 15; Gourevitch and Shinn 2005: table 2.3; Thatcher 2007: tables 2.1, 2.2).

The internationalization of stock market trading is demonstrated by evidence of the penetration of foreign portfolio investors within 'domestic' financial systems and firms' capital bases (Gourevitch and Shinn 2005: tables 5.1, 5.2; Thatcher 2007: table 2.3). The key changes have been the dramatic internationalization of equity issuing and ownership, and corporate bondholding. These have changed the way firms secure finance and how national financial systems engage with global financial markets. As well as foreign investors buying up shares in firms and overseas listings, there is an increasing incidence of cross-border mergers and acquisitions, and the advent of foreign hostile takeover bids (UNCTAD 2003). This all means that firms are enmeshed in a set of international or global networks of financing and ownership.

Key players in these hugely expanded internationalized equity markets, a range of scholars have pointed out, are not individual shareholders but large institutional investors (Verdier 2002: 176–7; Thatcher 2007: 41–4; Goyer 2011; Hertig 2018; Miyajima et al. 2018). The growth in institutional investor assets has been spectacular (Gourevitch and Shinn 2005: table 5.3). In terms of the overarching distinction between shareholder and stakeholder capitalism around which this chapter is organized, this change in the cast of key characters is important. Pre-eminent among the major institutional investors are large US- or UK-based pension and mutual funds. As the equity holdings of these Anglo-Saxon institutional investors grew, their preferences for shareholder value capitalism began to make themselves felt in boardrooms. Thus as inward investment from Anglo-Saxon institutional investors, steeped in the shareholder value paradigm, flows onto the balance sheets of large firms all around the advanced industrial world, these new dominant players within internationalized equity and bond markets may be the Trojan horses of shareholder value capitalism. This interpretation of US institutional investors as the vanguard of Anglo-Saxon capitalism is widespread (Morin 2000; Goyer 2001; Aglietta and Rebérioux 2005). In a later section we will consider the differential impact of institutional investors within German and French firms and finance.

A caveat should be offered, however. The internationalization of financial markets and investment is considerable – but it is not complete (Hirst and Thompson 1999). The real world of international finance remains a more parochial place than the textbook globalized financial market, with ample empirical evidence of significant enduring 'home bias' in investment flows (Feldstein and Horioka 1980; Epstein and Gintis 1995; Sinclair 2001: 96). Nevertheless, the above evidence suggests that the boundaries of national financial economies have become much more porous. The rise in transnational capital market actors in global flows and networks, and the spread of global rules, is evident. We would anticipate a diminished ability to contain, channel or control investment and savings flows within a national economic space.

The evidence presented above (see also Glyn 2006; Deeg 2010: 309–20; Engelen and Konings 2010: 601–5) suggests that, with more pervasive, more liquid, more powerful international capital markets changing the face of a range of political economies, national financial systems are increasingly penetrated by global financial flows. Much hinges, for Zysman's categorization and his argument, on administered, controlled prices and credit lines in the non-capital market–based financial systems. Given decades of liberalizing re-regulation and neo-liberal orthodoxy, the prevalence of politically or institutionally allocated finance within national financial systems is considerably reduced. This is true across a wide range of political economies, including statist France, Japan and China, as well as hitherto bank-based systems such as Germany, all of which were, when Zysman wrote, outside the capital market category.

One consequence of this increased scale and speed in financial flows for the global financial system is increased systemic risk. This became all too apparent as the turbulence unleashed by the GFC, and notably the collapse of Lehman Brothers, created a crisis of confidence and a 'credit crunch' that threatened to bring down entire financial systems (Tooze 2018). The governments desperately trying to prop up their financial systems were made painfully aware that their 21st-century capacities to 'direct flows through capital markets' and engage in the 'selective allocation of credit' (Zysman 1983: 71, 76) are much more limited compared to the early 1980s.

This changed context makes traditional industrial policy, wherein states or banks act as 'gatekeepers' controlling access to strategic long-term financial investment flows, a much trickier proposition. The transformation of finance and corporate governance increases 'exit' options for investors at the national, regional and international levels (Hirschman 1970). Inducing this 'patient' capital to remain patient and content itself with significantly below-'par' returns on its capital investment is likely to prove harder and harder to achieve. More broadly, with advancing financial internationalization, firm financing structures and practices associated with shareholder capitalism are becoming more significant and influential, including within stakeholder capitalist political economies.

THE COMPARATIVE POLITICAL ECONOMY OF FINANCIALIZATION

The above changes in finance have the potential to transform not just firms and capital markets, but also the society within which they are embedded. More solidaristic 'stakeholder' values (such as trust, reciprocity or indeed equality) may be progressively undermined by the role and import of capital markets in more aspects of people's lives. This can have implications for the stability of the socio-economic order and for the distribution of wealth within society. Financialization as a concept has been part of political economy for a long time and has been discussed by Marxist theorists such as Hilferding (1981 [1910]). Similar themes were discussed, albeit using different terms, by radical scholars such as Hobson (1988a [1938]) and Tawney (1961 [1921]; see also Clift and Tomlinson 2002) early in the 20th century. Since then, Marxist scholars (Harvey 1982; Arrighi 1996) have kept the flame alive. In the last 30 years, neo-liberalism and globalization played a transformative role for the economic landscape, allowing financial capital accumulation to take a predominant role over a productive economy (Arrighi 2010). One consistent theme of research on financialization is the increasing liquidity and the size and depth of financial markets, and their growing import for and influence on individuals and societies (Boyer 2000; Massó 2016; Aglietta and Bretton 2001; Pike and Pollard 2010; Palley 2008).

The rapid expansion of financial services, especially in the US, is much focused on, with some scholars identifying financialization as a finance-led capitalist regime in which capital accumulation is anchored around financial motives, instruments and markets as integral to the growth process (Guttman and Plihon 2008). Indeed, financialization scholarship draws so heavily on US experience (Fine 2012) that its insights might not all be readily applied in all other political economies. That said, much work has been done on the UK and on other developed economies such as Germany and France (Nölke 2017; Berghoff 2016; Alvarez 2015; Van Gunten and Navot 2018; Godechot 2012, 2016). Financialization has also begun to be applied beyond the core advanced economies (see e.g. Bonizzi 2014, 2016; Lagna 2016; Karwowski and Stockhammer 2017). Many commentators note how financialization was a key driver of the GFC, and furthermore financialization dynamics have become more pronounced since the crash (Assa 2012, 2016). After the crisis, financial institutions and financial markets increased their relevance as important actors shaping contemporary economics and social life (French et al. 2011).

The focal points of different strands of financialization scholarship vary. Some focus on the distributional effect at the firm level, transforming the managerial culture of companies and increasing the prioritization of shareholder value maximization (Froud et al. 2000; Erturk et al. 2007: 556; Shin 2014). Others take a more bottom-up approach to the political economy of financialization, exploring changes at a household level and the social transformation they provoke in the 'everyday life of global finance' (Langley 2006; French et al. 2011), for example as individuals assume financial responsibilities and risk via pension schemes, private insurance and investments to compensate for declining benefits and public social provision (Langley 2007; Martin 2002).

Recent CPE work on financialization has highlighted changes in the political economy of social provision, notably the increasing displacement of private (as opposed to state or public) pension provision within societal insurance against old age. Across the advanced economies, financialization is accompanied by the erosion of 'state-backed guarantees' and social safety nets, increasing the vulnerability of citizens. This has forced households 'to turn to the financial markets to secure access to goods that used to be provided publicly, i.e. housing, higher education, unemployment benefits, health care and pension benefits' (Engelen and Konings 2010: 602; see also Thatcher 2007: 43). This can leave more people more reliant on the stock market, or on the increasing value of their assets in the housing market, for their welfare or pension income. As a consequence, the argument goes, shareholder value capitalist norms may become increasingly pervasive (Thatcher 2007: 43), not only at the level of the boardroom of the firm and among shareholders, but in society more broadly. In this reading of financialization, the shareholder value paradigm can be seen as part of a broader societal 'project', wherein increasing returns and stock market performance matter more and more for ordinary citizens (see e.g. Engelen et al. 2011).

In recent years financialization has become widely used across a range of social sciences, in economic sociology, critical accounting studies and in business administration as well as in political economy (Engelen and Konings 2010: 605). Financialization can have different emphases when discussed in these different disciplinary contexts, but common themes include the increasing profitability of the financial sector and this sector's more pervasive role within the economy and society. For example, financialization scholars note the increasing tendency of non-financial firms to derive profits from financial transactions (Nölke and Perry 2007a, 2007b; Deeg 2010: 328; Engelen and Konings 2010; Maxfield et al. 2017). The transformation of corporate governance, and the increasing focus within firms on generating shareholder value (van Apeldoorn and Horn 2007), are also underlined as evidence of financialization. Financial innovation is another crucial element of financialization – going beyond the traditional distinction between the 'real economy' and finance to explore 'the production of financial products that are at two or three removes from real financial assets (e.g. derivatives, securitized assets, and futures)' (Engelen and Konings 2010: 610). Leyshon and Thrift discuss 'the capitalisation of almost everything' (2007). Engelen and Konings note 'the transformation of an increasing number of assets into financial commodities that can be easily traded on liquid financial markets' (2010: 608).

The above-noted levels of internationalization, increasing capital mobility and deeper, more liquid capital markets are all integral to financialization. So too is the declining role of banks in the traditional intermediation practices within capitalism (Rethel and Sinclair 2012; Hardie et al. 2013a, 2013b; Ban and Gabor 2016; Gabor and Ban 2016). The shifts within these capital markets towards disintermediated investment and trading (Sinclair 2005) are empirical manifestations of financialization. These new practices, financial intermediation techniques and exotic financial products are transforming not just finance, but cultural norms within capitalism more broadly (Langley 2004, 2008, 2010). The transformations of the financial services industry entail 'the penetration of relations of credit and debt into new areas of social life', such that financialization becomes 'embedded in the wider structure of social life' (Engelen and Konings 2010: 607; Froud et al. 2006). Profound changes in state/society relations resulting from financialization include changing public pension provision and welfare state retrenchment (see Chapter 11). Indeed, arguably the boundaries where the welfare state ends and the financial market begins have become blurred. This offers another prime example of the core political economy insight outlined in Chapter 2 on the interpenetration of state and market (Table 10.2).

Engelen and Konings argue with some justification that VoC and other comparative capitalisms scholars (see pp. 174–80) have neglected finance and financial innovation. The dizzying array of financial product innovations and vertiginous rises in the size of these markets entail seismic changes for capitalism. This gets neglected because of VoC's 'near

Table 10.2 The political economy of financialization

	Effects	*Drivers*
Firms	Salience of shareholder value in firms (e.g. executive remuneration); non-financial firms increasingly derive profits from financial transactions; corporate governance prioritizes financial returns, profits, dividends	Systemic power of global finance; shareholder power within corporate governance; financial innovation; institutional investors; asset management industry
Macro-economy	Instability, systemic risk, securitization, rising inequality, excessive consumer credit, housing bubbles, financial crises, consumption-oriented growth model	Market and political power of dominant financial sector interests; accumulation imperatives of a finance-led growth model
Households	Asset-based welfare – individuals assume financial responsibilities and risk via pension schemes, private insurance and investments, to compensate for declining benefits and public social provision	Financialized investor subjectivities; burgeoning private debt; welfare state restructuring; financial innovation
Society	Shareholder value capitalist norms are increasingly pervasive in society; 'the capitalisation of almost everything' (Leyshon and Thrift 2007)	Neo-liberal economic ideas; cultural hegemony of finance, 'we live in financial times' (pre-crash *Financial Times* ad campaign)

exclusive focus on the production of goods that one, in the memorable phrase of *The Economist*, can drop on one's foot' (2010: 604). The broad thrust of many variants of financialization analysis explores the 'erosion of institutional differences between national political economies' (ibid.: 608). Deeg, for example, notes a 'common trend towards financialisation and internationalisation of finance' undermining the coherence of national financial systems amid 'a rapid expansion of financial markets vis-à-vis the real economy' (2010: 310, 315). Yet, at the same time, there is appreciation that 'financialisation processes assume fundamentally different forms in different polities', and recognition that 'to consider national institutional frameworks as reacting to financialisation trends is to downplay their active role in shaping and constituting these dynamics' (Engelen and Konings 2010: 609).

Different patterns of 'residential capitalism' (Schwartz and Seabrooke 2009), for example, rest on diverse national practices in home ownership, renting and mortgage markets. These are sustained by political acts of market-making that instantiate such national characteristics. There are important distinctions in the 'type and extent of credit extended from the financial sector to firms, households, and governments' (Deeg 2010: 310) in each political economy. Pension conditions and systems differ, as do the profiles of banking sectors and financial services industries, as well as different welfare state regimes (see Chapter 11). These all shape how the financial services industries central to financialization operate in particular societies, meaning that financialization plays out differently in each societal context (ibid.: 327–30; Engelen and Konings 2010). Thus, for reasons of the political acts of market-making which shape financialization, and for reasons of the diverse social contexts within which financialization practices are embedding, 'the convergence thesis is no longer a reliable or useful heuristic tool to frame our investigations of this world' (Engelen and Konings 2010: 609).

Engelen and Konings offer some empirical adjudication upon financialization across five advanced economies (the UK, the US, France, Germany and the Netherlands), using IMF and OECD data. They note the difficulties of finding indicators that 'get at' the complex financialization processes. Nevertheless, they do find that bond and stock market levels as a proportion of GDP are high, and highest in the US, the UK and the Netherlands; these three countries also have much more institutional investment activity (ibid.: 609–20). An LME or Anglo-American financialization trajectory can be discerned, for example, by the 'combination of large pension funds and deep and liquid financial markets' (ibid.: 611) and high levels of bank disintermediation. The US and the UK unsurprisingly populate this category, but, interestingly from a comparative capitalisms perspective, the Netherlands appears as a consistent outlier – a supposedly stakeholder economy which outstrips the UK and the US on a range of financialization indicators, suggesting that it is more shareholder capitalist than the archetypes.

The differential impacts of the 'credit crunch' and the GFC revealed differing degrees of financialization prevalent in the societies of the advanced political economies. As noted above, the US and the UK, where financialization is most deeply embedded, were hardest hit. Initially, continental Europe appeared less dramatically affected in the initial phase up to 2010. However, Europe's banks (deeply imbricated in financialization practices) turned out to be very heavily exposed to massive financial liabilities, especially in the southern periphery of the Eurozone. This proved an Achilles heel that prompted a major *banking* crisis in Europe, which got discursively constructed by Germany and the European authorities as a deep *sovereign debt* crisis (see Chapter 12; Blyth 2013; Tooze 2018). The varied nature of financialization across the Eurozone helps explain the different national forms that the European crisis took. In Ireland and Spain, pre-crash growth had been fuelled by enormous real estate bubbles that resulted from the way these economies were financialized. When property values collapsed, the effects on the construction sectors, the banking sector and the wider economy were sudden and enormously damaging. Economic activity and tax revenues collapsed while state liabilities for the damaged financial sectors skyrocketed.

Yet there has been limited substantive challenge in the US and the UK to the financial sector and an ongoing faith in self-regulation in post-GFC reform discussions and measures (Grant and Wilson 2012; Wilson 2012). This, many financialization scholars argue, can be explained because many pre-crisis financial sector practices are woven into the fabric of the social order in these political economies (Finlayson 2009; Watson 2008, 2010; Langley 2006, 2008). Thus initiatives such as the UK Government's 'Help to Buy' scheme seek to reinstate the lending practices which created the damaging pre-crisis bubble in the UK housing market, as the IMF critically observed (IMF 2013). Financialization practices are, it seems, seen by governments as integral to the economic growth model (Hay 2013; Gamble 2019; Lavery 2019).

Yet within European societies there are important differences, partly because states assume different roles and encourage different characteristics in their financial systems, and partly because market-making practices play out in diverse ways. For example, 'in terms of household investment patterns, Germany and Italy retain a strong bank orientation, while France has moved quite substantially towards the UK market-based pattern' (Deeg 2010: 328; see also Byrne and Davis 2002; Gourevitch and Shinn 2005). Overall, work at the interface of CPE and financialization unearths 'different paths or trajectories of financializa-tion – not just international in the sense that universal processes of financialization are refracted differently in different institutional contexts, but rather as shaped by the contin-gent outcomes of actors' political struggles and compromises' (Engelen and Konings 2010: 617). Financial systems are embedded in particular societal contexts, and they entail dis-tinctive demand conditions and market opportunities.

CPE scholars situate their analysis of financialization within broader societal shifts and transformations in state–market relations. Notable here are reduced public provision, the erosion of social safety nets and the increasing vulnerability of citizens (see Chapter 11). Individuals and families have to provide, through their own financial asset bases should they be lucky enough to have them, for their own social protection, for example through private pensions. Similar dynamics are identified in health (e.g. private health insurance and funding care for the elderly) and education (increasing private education, higher university fees) across some advanced economies. Citizens who once enjoyed extensive social rights to public services have morphed into financialized investor subjects who have to make up the shortfall of reduced public-sector provision. Furthermore, these political economies rely increasingly on private household debt, rather than stimulus from macro-economic policies, to fuel consumption and sustain economic growth (Crouch 2009; Streeck 2014). These are some of the reasons why widening inequalities (Kwon et al. 2017), growing precarity and disaffection with the political economic order are common features of increasingly financial-ized societies (see Chapter 12).

WHAT IS LEFT OF NATIONAL FINANCIAL SYSTEMS? TRACING PROCESSES OF FINANCIAL CHANGE

In this section we explore processes of change and dynamics of evolution unleashed by increasingly mobile capital and a more lightly regulated financial realm, through detailed consideration of how internationalizing finance is changing the German and French finan-cial systems. We will take two historically 'stakeholder' capitalist cases in order to explore how different institutional configurations can lead to diverse changes within capitalism as capital market liberalization advances. Shareholder value practices may have increased in each of these CME economies and stakeholder societies, but in different ways through inter-actions with different institutional contexts. Before coming to the detailed case studies, we will consider briefly the broader empirical picture.

There is evidence of reduced reliance on banks for industrial and firm financing in a range of political economies. Because of the bank disintermediation which is integral to financiali-zation, banks are by-passed as investors buy up bonds or shares and firms borrow directly from bond markets (Byrne and Davis 2002; Deeg 2010: table 11.1). Deeg discerns a 'long-term trend towards increasing self-finance and market finance by European firms' (2010: 327; Byrne and Davis 2002). This is an important shift when placed in the context of Zysman's typologies. It is happening in the political economies associated for much of the 20th century with Zysman's bank-based national financial systems. So, for example, in Sweden, following financial liberalization in the 1980s and 1990s, finance came much less from bank loans and much more from retained income – which is a typical 'Anglo-Saxon' mode of firm financing (Perraton and Clift 2004: 227–8). Oxelheim also finds evidence of increasingly 'Anglo-Saxon' patterns of finance – both in terms of sources and of deployment – across Scandinavia more broadly (1996). Interestingly, Pontusson argues that an influx of shareholder value–oriented, mobile international capital, and the practice of Anglo-Saxon capitalism more broadly, can be reconciled to the Swedish model of embedded capitalism with its egalitarian and solidaristic norms (2011).

Similar shifts have occurred in the once archetypal bank-based Japanese political economy (as discussed in Chapter 9). Corporate bonds have displaced bank loans, reducing the role of the main bank (Jackson and Miyajima 2008: 10, 31). The once crucial 'Keiretsu cross-shareholdings' have partially unravelled because of liberalized, internationalized financing practices and financial markets (Matsuura et al. 2004). When set against the backdrop of our distinction between stakeholder and shareholder capitalism, these developments lead some to identify a convergence in firm nature, organization and behaviour towards the latter. As stock markets and bond markets become the primary source of financing and are increasingly central to firm operations, 'shareholder value' – which involves not just a short-termist focus on return on equity, but also a reconceptualization of the nature and role of the firm – becomes an increasingly pervasive organizing principle of corporate capitalism.

For some (see Hardie et al. 2013a), the changes in the role of financial markets and in banking practices brought about by financialization and international financial market liberalization were so profound that Zysman's typology differentiating 'bank-based' and 'capital market–based' systems was no longer useful or operable. Banking has increasingly, albeit to varying degrees, become 'market-based' as the prevalence of bond-based and equity-based financing has increased across advanced economies. Furthermore, bank lending has become increasingly market-based, as loans are sold on into the market, either directly or via securitization. Bank funds come not from depositors, as in the traditional banking model, but from the financial markets. Banks also use financial markets to shore up their positions, engaging in hedging activities to insure against risk using complex financial instruments. These have led to important changes in the nature of banks and banking. For Hardie et al., this rise of 'market-based banking' has 'rendered the bank-based/capital market-based dichotomy of the varieties of capitalism obsolete. We cannot understand change in national financial systems, or the onset and impact of the financial crisis, without understanding the actions of banks as agents of change' (Hardie et al. 2013a; see also Hardie et al. 2013b; Adrian and Shin 2008, 2010; Gabor 2018). Thus the insight into market-based banking indicates a fresh focal point for the analysis of finance – seeing banks as crucial drivers of recent transformations.

For all these increasing complexities, some scholars continue to see a convergence of all advanced political economies towards Anglo-Saxon financial systems (see Rajan and Zingales 2003). That said, many are sceptical. Gourevitch and Shinn, for example, argue that 'the economy is too complex; there are too many ways of putting the pieces together. Convergence assumes a relentless and powerful selection mechanism, clearly rewarding some behaviours as it clearly punishes others' (2005: 12). So even if finance, capital markets and shareholder value 'matter more' within a broad range of advanced industrial political economies today, precisely *how* they matter more will continue to vary considerably. Empirically, there has been considerable reduction in 'stakeholder' patterns of firm financing, such as concentrated ownership and 'insider' bloc-holding, but they remain prevalent firm/finance configurations in many political economies (ibid.: table 2.1; Barca and Becht 2001; Enriques and Volpin 2007). Also prevalent are a variety of practices contrary to the 'shareholder value' wish list. This reiterates the point made above regarding domestic mediation of international pressure for change – at the firm or societal as well as state level – which gets neglected in political economy analyses that underplay the interaction between global and domestic forces.

Internationalization and financial liberalization can lead to sometimes quite rapidly changing patterns of financing, including in stakeholder capitalist societies. What impact such changes have on how capitalism works in a given setting is a trickier question to answer. The following two sections explore how French and German capitalism have been trans-formed in the wake of these broad changes of internationalization of financial markets and financialization detailed above. We find important evolutions in firms, in terms of both who is empowered within them and the prioritization of stakeholder or shareholder values within the firm. There is also evidence of hybridization, as national financial systems and corporate capitalisms are becoming increasingly enmeshed in international financial flows and networks. Shareholder value–oriented mechanisms, norms and practices come to play a greater role within corporate governance and financial regulation, while much of the pre-existing institutional architecture of capitalism endures and interacts with these novel influences and elements.

FRANCE'S CHANGING FINANCIAL SYSTEM AND CORPORATE CAPITALISM

The dramatic pace of financial change in France is evident. In the early 1980s, French finan-cial markets were quiet backwaters, international investment was heavily regulated and for-eign ownership was in some cases proscribed. France has lacked a culture of investment in financial savings instruments such as pension funds or mutual funds. Companies did not traditionally look to financial markets for investment. The historic reliance on institution-ally allocated credit (orchestrated through the state) rationed industrial investment (Zysman 1983; Loriaux 1991). This led the French economy to be caricatured as 'capitalism without capital' (Stoffaes 1989: 122). Dominant bloc-holder groups tended to own large stakes in each other's firms and sit on each other's boards, making up *noyaux durs* ('hard cores') of insiders. France was an archetypal 'insider-dominated' stakeholder capitalist system, offer-ing insulation from capital market pressures. The tentacles of these 'hard core' networks of investors covered much of large-scale corporate France. Illustrating the core political econ-omy insights outlined in Chapter 2 about mutual constitution of state and market and how market orders are political constructions, there was deep interpenetration of state and mar-ket within French capitalism. The state was a substantial shareholder and had considerable means of influence through controlling access to institutionally allocated finance (via public and para-public banks).

The 1980s and 1990s changed the nature of state/market interpenetration within French capitalism. Privatization and state-orchestrated liberalizing re-regulation of the French financial system revitalized French stock markets amid extensive liberalization of the French model of capitalism (Schmidt 1996: 140; Cerny 1989; Clift 2004, 2012). At the same time, internationalization of capital and securities markets has enmeshed French firms in a set of global financial markets and networks which provide capital and offer opportunities for mergers and acquisitions. French overseas acquisitions expanded dramatically, along with foreign holdings of French stocks and shares.

As a result the 'hard cores' were reconfigured, and their grip on French capitalism was considerably reduced. However, this new, more liberal environment was reconciled to prior French 'protected capitalism' in a number of ways. Indeed, paradoxically, the privatization process expanded its insider-oriented stakeholder norms. Illustrating the French state's directive role in the re-constitution of French capitalism, Finance Minister Balladur's hand-picking of the benefactors of privatization between 1986 and 1988 deliberately *reinforced* the *noyaux durs* within France's 'financial network economy' (Schmidt 1996: 369–92).

The regulatory environment of French finance changed. As part of the process of (re-) building finance capitalism in France, new corporate governance and financial markets rules were introduced, influenced by 'Anglo-Saxon' shareholder capitalist notions (Abdelal 2006; Clift 2007). In general, while capital markets have flourished, shareholder capitalism has not fully taken hold. In various ways, 'insiders' are privileged and advantaged both in the historical structure of capitalist institutions in France and also through the deliberate design of policy-makers. The state's long-standing *présence tutélaire* (interventionary presence) within the banking sector (Jabko and Massoc 2012) continued the deep interpenetration of state and market within French capitalism.

Illustrating another core political economy insight from Chapter 2, the social context within which French firms and capital markets are embedded is another important mediating factor of how far liberalization transforms practices within French firms and capitalism. Elitist stakeholder-style networks operate at the summit of French corporate capitalism, with insiders sharing close personal ties, forged at France's *grandes écoles* (Offerlé 2009; Dudouet and Grémont 2010; Jabko and Massoc 2012). These networks co-exist with the new modalities of state intervention which operate more with the grain of the market, though French capitalism retains a prevailing comfort, with markets dominated by a few 'national champions' wielding significant market power.

In the mid to late 1990s, the *noyaux durs* groupings of insiders began to unravel amid dramatically increasing international mergers and acquisitions – especially in the bonanza period around 1999–2000 (UNCTAD 2003; Culpepper 2005). The erosion of the *noyaux durs* since the mid-1990s is considerable but not complete (Morin 2000: 39; Loriaux 2003: 116). Their cross-shareholding legacy remains in the capital structure of many firms. French state actors and elites within French corporate capitalism have found new mechanisms to protect their firms, for example through regulatory and legal impediments to hostile takeovers (Clift 2009). The elitist social networks still exist, with insider orientation privileged today through interlocking board directorships (Clift 2012; Jabko and Massoc 2012). This mitigates the Anglo-Saxon shareholder capitalist emphasis on market-based firm financing, 'competitive market arrangements' to co-ordinate firm activities, and more specifically 'highly competitive markets' to 'organise relations' with firms' 'suppliers of finance' (Hall and Soskice 2001: 8–9). While firm finance *is* increasingly reliant on capital markets, the network based co-ordination of stakeholder capitalism remains a prevalent feature in French capitalism.

More broadly, the micro-foundations of the shareholder value paradigm are not, it seems, taking root. This is partly because schemes have not been opened up to most employees, but also because popular capitalism is not that popular in France (O'Sullivan 2003: 42; see also Hancké 2002: 51–5). In part this relates to a suspicion of Anglo-Saxon liberalism (Hayward 2007) and an attachment to the distinctive *dirigiste* French model of capitalism (Clift 2004, 2007, 2012).

One final dimension worth reporting is the nature of the firm in France. Firms, as noted above, are 'a contrivance' (Gamble and Kelly 2000), and in France a particular view of what firms are for characterized their legal inscription. The distinctive understanding of what firms are for in the French social and legal context is captured in the idea of the 'social interest' of the company. Firms are not construed exclusively as vehicles of shareholder value (as in UK or US corporate law), but as social entities with social obligations – to their employees and others (Alcouffe 2000; Clift 2007).

The shareholder-oriented market-making reforms to financial markets and firms introduced in France in recent years combine and interact with elitist social networks, elements of insider-oriented corporate governance, societal ambivalence towards shareholder value capitalism and a legacy of state intervention. This is likely to produce different consequences than pro-shareholder mechanisms combined with principles of shareholder value, as for example in the US or the UK. Offering evidence of hybridization within French capitalism, despite the liberal character of French takeover law, there is plenty of sand in the wheels limiting the free operation of a takeover market in France's legal and regulatory context and the state's desire to protect 'strategic' sectors.

Another way of assessing the transformation of French firms and finance is to 'drill down' into processes of inward capital flows from shareholder capitalism–oriented investors and assess their impacts. This is what Michel Goyer has focused upon (2003, 2011). His research highlights the importance of the points made above about how the politics, and the degree of empowerment of different social and economic groups, differs between capitalisms. This differentiation is evident between stakeholder capitalism and shareholder capitalism, but also between different variants of stakeholder capitalism. This becomes a live issue as financial opening and market liberalization progress, when financial reforms and mechanisms seek to prioritize shareholder value. This is likely to benefit owners and shareholders, and have adverse distributional effects for workers and other stakeholders.

In stakeholder societies, worker empowerment within the firm and the social obligations of firms can be an impediment to shareholder value–oriented reforms (see Goyer 2011: 14; Roe 1994, 2003). It can also affect the contours of liberalization and internationalization – and which kinds of investors take up stakes in firms. The French firm and societal context is characterized by relatively weak (though vocal) unions within society, and weak worker rights and powers within the firm (see e.g. Goyer 2003; Howell 2006). Relatively low unionization levels have a long historical pedigree in France's slow, late and only partial industrialization. The conditions which fostered strong unionism elsewhere in Europe never obtained in France to the same degree (Labbé 1994; Milner 1995). Thus, despite the reputation of France for powerful unions, in truth union density is low and declining. Outside parts of the public sector, French unions are not powerful actors within firms or within French capitalism more broadly.

Conversely, a striking feature of French bosses and management has traditionally been a distinctive set of corporate governance arrangements, characterized by Napoleonic boardroom power relations. In a system characterized as 'capital without sanction', company bosses are highly autonomous, a position reinforced by the elitist networks they operate within. Boards tend to be rubber stamps for the largely autonomous Président Directeur Générale (Charkham 1995: 131; Maclean 1999: 104; Hancké 2002; Clift 2004, 2007; O'Sullivan 2007).

This creates a context where unions struggle for purchase and traction at the national level within corporate reform debates, or at the firm level in decisions about firm restructuring. On the other hand, company bosses can, within the limits of the social context of the firm out-lined above (the social interest of the company), push through change as they see fit. Appreciative of this very limited worker empowerment and management autonomy, particular kinds of foreign institutional investors have taken up stakes in French firms. As Goyer's research reveals, different degrees of short-termism and shareholder value maximization underpin the investment strategies of different kinds of institutional investors. Risk-averse 'defined benefit' pension funds seek longer-term, stable, predictable, modest returns. Mutual funds' investment strategies, in contrast, are riskier, shorter term and more aggressive in pursuit of maximizing returns. These marry up differently with the changing incentive structures and opportunities of the transformed financial systems and corporate capitalism in different countries. Goyer unearths how the high degree of autonomy of company bosses in France enables greater profit maximization and higher returns, and this in turn attracts more international investment from mutual funds and hedge funds (2011: 70–6).

As we will see below, this picture contrasts with investment strategies and practices within German capitalism. This highlights the need for fine-grained analysis of the changing political economy of finance, appreciative of different kinds of capital and its mobility. Not only is investment capital different from more short-term currency speculation, but even within 'Anglo-Saxon institutional investors' there is significant differentiation (Goyer 2011).

These findings reveal the merits of drilling down into particular kinds of internationalizing finance and their interactions with national financial systems. Goyer's research invites thinking not of 'international capital mobility' in abstract, general terms, but focusing on specific actors, flows and networks, and asking which particular kinds of investment flows are attracted to French firms. This can reveal different opportunities and possibilities for internationalization and liberalization. It further underlines the complex impacts of internationalization, mediated by national and firm-level structures and norms. The resulting evolutions are best understood in terms of hybridization (see pp. 25, 175–6, 189–90, 197–8).

GERMANY'S CHANGING FINANCIAL SYSTEM AND CORPORATE CAPITALISM

Germany has been considered the archetypical 'stakeholder' capitalist political economy, as well as a CME par excellence (see pp. 178–9). Many comparative capitalisms scholars have evoked ideas of path dependency (see pp. 113–16) to capture the institutional evolution of German capitalism (Deeg 1999, 2001; Jackson 2001; Goyer 2003, 2011). Concepts of institutional complementarity and increasing returns (North 1990; Pierson 2004) are deployed to explain the dovetailing between, on the one hand, the mode of firm/financing relationships and, on the other, the education system, vocational training infrastructure, labour market regulation and the industrial relations system more broadly. Germany's financial system has evolved to foster long-term firm financing relationships and patient capital. Gregory Jackson identifies 'financial commitment' and 'industrial citizenship' as crucial underpinnings of firms and how capitalism works in Germany (2001: 145). 'Voice' is favoured in Germany over exit. The reverse is true for the UK and the US. Links between small and medium-sized firms (the *Mittelstand*) and local and regional banks who tend to be represented on company boards have been much-vaunted features of Germany's diversified high-quality mass-production variety of capitalism (Streeck 1997, 2009; Deeg 1999).

Post-war Germany was the archetype of Zysman's credit-based system dominated by large financial institutions (1983: 69–75; see also Story and Walter 1997: chs 5 and 6; Perraton and Clift 2004: 221–35).

Reflecting the social context in which German capitalism is embedded, historical elements within German ideas of the firm, and indeed the market economy (Lehmbruch 2001: 80–5), dating back to at least the 1870s continue to shape the corporate form and corporate governance. The firm has since the 1870s been organized around the stakeholder capitalist idea of 'industrial citizenship' (Jackson 2001: 145), with workers enjoying extensive rights and responsibilities within the firm. The constitutionalization of rights and obligations (and the public interest) in the make-up of the firm, with its two-tier board system, dates from 1884. These 19th-century innovations, incidentally, were another 'great reversal' in the politics of finance. They resulted from a backlash against liberal *laissez-faire* and shareholder rights triggered by the economic crisis of the 1870s (see ibid.: 131).

After World War II, the German political economy retained its incorporation of labour rights and power through worker representation within the firm and co-determination through corporatist collective bargaining institutions. These were important elements of the 'social market economy'. This generates a very particular form of mutual constitution between state and market drawing inspiration from 'ordo-liberal' thought, wherein the state constructs and ensures a constitutionally ruled free market order (preventing monopolies and unfair competition, for example). The social market economy pragmatically combined a rules-based free market system with 'social policy postulates of the Social Catholic tradition' (Lehmbruch 2001: 84). Jackson details 'the constraints placed by industrial citizenship on property rights' (2001: 126) within the social market economy, which prevented 'shareholder value'–style pursuit of profit at all costs.

Corporate ownership and financing developed along 'stakeholder' lines in Germany (ibid.: 123). Family, bank and interfirm networks of insiders came to dominate the *Aufsichtsrat* or supervisory board of German firms through cross-shareholdings, among other mechanisms. There were multiple interactions between banks and large firms, going beyond just lending, and these cemented the close ties and the 'financial commitment' (ibid.: 133). 'Patient capital' was focused on long-term expansion, rather than short-term profit maximization (Deeg 1999).

'Big' banks like Deutsche Bank, Commerzbank and Dresdner Bank, and smaller regional, local or co-operative banks, have been the dominant players within German firm financing. This has been so ever since the 1884 reforms raised barriers to small-scale individual investment in the stock market, ensuring that 'banks were the central actors mediating access to outside capital' for firms (Jackson 2001: 133; see also Deeg 1999). Between the 1940s and the 1990s, access to German capital markets was controlled and equity and bond markets were discouraged as industrial financing sources through public policy and the tax system (Vitols 2003: 250–1). The interpenetration of state and market took the form of the state playing a background role as mediator, codifying agreements arrived at consensually by private actors within the banking system (Lütz 2000: 152–5, 1998).

The transformation of this post-war German financial system came to fruition in the late 1990s and the 2000s. It began with political acts of market-making in the 1980s, policies pursued by the state but driven by the 'big banks' in search of new sources of revenue as their returns within the old system dwindled (Deeg 1999, 2001: 23). Internationalization and attracting 'Anglo-Saxon' institutional investors through new financial products and market liberalization were seen as crucial to German financial reform (Lütz 1998; Deeg

2001). German state actors, acting in concert with the 'big banks', began to engage more actively in market-making, reforming the stock market and creating a new short-term commercial paper market in the 1990s (Deeg 1999: 88, 2001: 25, 31; Lütz 1998).

The state was more directive in the financial reform and re-regulation process than at earlier stages in Germany's post-war history. German state actors and key players within the sphere of finance were able to plan and time their financial market reform process, passing a series of laws promoting financial market development (Deeg 1999, 2001; Vogel 2003; Vitols 2003: 251–13; Cioffi 2006; Gourevitch and Shinn 2005: 162–7). This saw the advent of a single centralized federal securities regulator, modelled on the US Securities and Exchange Commission (SEC), which banned insider trading and introduced strong disclosure requirements. International accounting standards were introduced, increasing transparency and improving German firms' access to foreign financial markets and investors (Lütz 2000; Deeg 2001: 26; Cioffi 2006: 212–13).

Financial and company law reforms sought to reduce levels of insider protection, hitherto characteristic of German stakeholder capitalism. The 1998 KonTraG law legalized and brought in a number of other 'Anglo-Saxon', shareholder capitalism– and shareholder value–oriented mechanisms – such as stock options and buy-backs – which constituted a conscious shift away from stakeholder capitalism (Deeg 2001). This influential law reduced the power of banks within German corporate governance by abolishing multiple voting rights, which had previously afforded banks and other insiders disproportionate power and influence on company boards (Gourevitch and Shinn 2005: 162–7; Cioffi 2006: 214–5; Goyer 2011: 94–5). Insider insulation from market pressure was reduced, and this served potentially to expose German firms to hostile takeovers (a crucial dimension shaping the behaviour of economic actors within shareholder capitalism; Deeg 2001: 27–8). That said, hostile takeovers remain rare in Germany, one notable exception being Vodafone's takeover of Mannesmann in 2000.

Nevertheless, firm/bank relations changed significantly. Shares trading increased and the government encouraged the unwinding of cross-shareholdings in 2000 by eliminating capital gains tax on their sale (Deeg 2001; Gourevitch and Shinn 2005: 162; Cioffi 2006: 215). Banks became less of a presence on large firms' supervisory boards, and the cross-shareholdings which had 'locked up' capital began to unravel (Goyer 2011). As Deeg puts it, 'the financial and industrial systems in Germany are "decoupling"' (2001: 29), partly because large firms and banks want access to international bond and equity markets. The likes of Deutsche Bank were key players in orchestrating a move towards investment banking – buying up British and American investment banks. They saw the evolution of the German financial system along US lines as key to their success as international investment banks (Vitols 2003: 252). This period also saw the listing of major German firms, including Siemens and Deutsche Telekom, on the New York Stock Exchange (Borsch 2007).

The timing of the German financial system's transformation is interesting, coming after the onset of capital market deregulation and liberalization in the UK, France and elsewhere. Those powerful actors within the German financial system committed to reform found an opportunity in the Single European Act of 1986, with its 'Single Market' and attendant liberalization and internationalization. Deeg sees this as a 'tipping point', after which 'the incremental expansion of financial market internationalization suddenly had much greater determinative force over the German financial system' (Deeg 2001: 20). This changing financial context disturbed the equilibrium of German capitalism, and the German state was a key orchestrator of the transformation, with new practices mediated through existing institutions. The drawn-out process (between the mid-1980s and the early 2000s) is explained in part by the fact that new practices had to be reconciled to existing social norms (Deeg 2001).

Many of the legal and regulatory reforms were a compromise between shareholder and stakeholder capitalist norms. The German company still has its dual board, with constitutionalized worker-interest representation. Many firms retain their close links with long-term financial backers such as regional banks. A 2001 law even *expanded* the scope for insider protection through pre-bid takeover defences (Cioffi 2006: 216). Some of the core institutional structures of 'industrial citizenship' – such as co-determination and works councils – were not considered for reform, and this ensured 'the preservation of Germany's stakeholder model' (ibid.: 217–18). What reforms were undertaken revealed quite how much political capital had to be expended to transform German capitalism's legal and regulatory environment, and how difficult it was to mobilize broad-based support for shareholder capitalism–oriented shifts. In some spheres, such as securities regulation, the reform process ran out of steam (ibid.: 219–21).

Nevertheless, the enduring stakeholder elements now co-exist with augmented reliance on increasingly active capital markets, counter-balancing traditional stakeholder influences. So the stakeholder capitalist conception of the firm endures, alongside new shareholder value–oriented norms. While large firms and large banks in Germany pursue internationalized and increasingly 'Anglo-Saxon' or shareholder value–oriented corporate strategies, the medium-sized and smaller firms and banks remain more wedded to the previous stakeholder model. Thus, 'the new path of the financial system encompasses elements of the bank-based system and those of the new market-oriented system. The new path or model is a hybrid' (Deeg 2001: 34). Germany's national financial system has shifted considerably from an insider-dominated, primarily bank-based stakeholder system towards a capital market–based financial system (Zysman 1983), more outsider oriented and involving more market-based interactions. Yet the shift is not complete, nor uniform throughout German capitalism. The upshot, Deeg argues, has not been convergence on shareholder capitalism, but hybridization (2001: 7, 34).

Goyer's analysis of institutional investment into Germany reveals that – while both France and Germany have 'hybridized' financial systems – large firms within them exhibit somewhat different properties. In particular, the 'industrial citizenship' in Germany and 'constitutionalized' rights of workers (Jackson 2001) limit how far and how fast corporate strategies can evolve towards shareholder value norms. Prioritizing shareholder value would probably have adverse distributional effects for workers and other stakeholders (see Goyer 2011: 14; Roe 1994, 2003). German firms, with inclusive notions of 'industrial citizenship' generating workforce rights, power and participation in the governance of the firm, offer less scope for decisive changes in firm practice, but instead foster the stable long-term pursuit of economic success by the firm as a whole. Hence German firms attract different kinds of institutional investors than France, fewer short-term mutual funds or hedge funds, and more pension funds seeking longer-term, stable, modest returns (Goyer 2011: 70–6).

CONCLUSION

More pervasive, more liquid, more powerful stock markets and bond markets have become conspicuous features of a range of economies and societies, with financial logics, products and drivers pervading the everyday lives of citizens to greater degrees, as 'financialization' scholars underline. Thus financing structures and practices associated with shareholder capitalism are becoming more significant and influential, including within stakeholder capitalist political economies. In the process, 'shareholder value' – which involves not just a short-termist focus on return on equity, but also a reconceptualization of the nature and role of the firm – becomes an increasingly pervasive organizing principle of corporate capitalism.

Yet stakeholder conceptions of the firm, and power relations within firms and society, have not disappeared. Stakeholder capitalist mechanisms and institutions, such as concentrated ownership bloc-holding to sustain insider-oriented corporate governance and insulate firms from market pressures and takeovers, are also still prevalent (Gourevitch and Shinn 2005: 18). The transformations of finance in advanced economies entails the ongoing mutual constitution of state and market, with the changing interpenetration of state and market altering to some extent the logic of capitalism – yet not in uniform fashion and not in a single unambiguous direction. This is why hybridization, rather than convergence, is the likely outcome of the changes in financial capitalism. In both France and Germany, the national financial system has become more enmeshed in wider global capital flows. Liberalizing re-regulation has rendered their financial systems much more open, their borders much more porous. But inflows and influences that now permeate these national financial systems more readily continue to be refracted through the institutional ensembles of each national financial system. Attention must be paid to this institutional, societal and ideological context within which finance and firms operate and to distinctive state traditions, shaped by different political forces and underpinned by different visions of the market economy.

As liberalizing financial market internationalization advanced in the 1980s and 1990s, it provoked a variety of responses from governments, firms and other actors within national financial systems. The political acts of market-making involved in building finance capitalism offer states latitude to shape the contours of the political economic settlement. Thus the paths of adjustment do not simply emerge, but are the subject of political struggle and contestation, through which the path is forged by political actors and other key players. There remain distinctive kinds of markets and distinctive kinds of firms, even if many are more reliant on capital markets and more attuned to 'shareholder capitalist' norms than once they were.

Building financial capitalism by shaping and channelling the evolution of finance, while apparently somewhat arcane and technical, is, as I have underlined, a deeply political process. Thus the nature and structure of firms, and of capital markets, have profound implications for the distribution of wealth within society. The outsider, capital market–based systems are the least egalitarian societies among the world's richest economies. Furthermore, financial market dynamics pervade increasingly individualized pension practices and shape aspects of social and welfare provisioning, deeply affecting the conduct of people's everyday lives. This pervasive influence of shareholder value norms and dynamics can also have implications for conceptions of society, social rights and social policy in increasingly financialized political economies. Such distribution and re-distribution of wealth and social provisioning questions, and the changing nature of social rights within contemporary advanced capitalisms, are the focus of the next chapter – on the political economy of welfare.

11 The Comparative Political Economy of Welfare

INTRODUCTION

One of the biggest changes in the nature of capitalism within the advanced affluent democracies during the 20th century was the extension in the scope and scale of social welfare provision. In this chapter I explore the CPE of welfare regime restructuring and how to understand the relationship between capitalism, inequality and the social order. In the next chapter, I explore further how rising inequality is destabilizing the social and political settlement upon which capitalism rests. In this chapter, firstly, I consider the changing international context of advanced welfare states and interrogate the relationship between welfare and capitalism and between globalization and the welfare state, arguing that the strictures imposed on welfare states by international capital mobility can be overstated. That said, welfare provision is facing real and increasing political and economic pressures. Welfare states in advanced economies since the 1970s exist in what Pierson has termed 'a context of essentially permanent austerity' (2001: 411). This arises from reduced growth (and therefore lower tax revenues) and pressures to keep taxes lower, compounded by increased social provision demands from an ageing population and escalating healthcare costs. However, a wide array of CPE research indicates that these pressures are more endogenous, domestic and demographic than exogenous and international.

The first 'take home' point is the intimate relationship between capitalism and welfare. The appeal to the classical political economy approach, a theme throughout this book, helps the analyst appreciate this fact and recognize its implications by foregrounding an understanding of the economic as socially embedded. Hay and Wincott, in negotiating the myriad labels applied to welfare states and welfare state–like phenomena, make the case for 'welfare capitalism' because it connotes the 'profound interdependence of the economic, the social and the political' (2012: 4). The core insights of political economy outlined in Chapter 2 underline the intricate intertwining of market relations and their social context, as captured in the terms 'welfare capitalism' and 'welfare state regime' (Esping-Andersen 1990: 2). Chris Pierson evokes a similar 'logic of symbiosis between the welfare state and capitalism' (2006: 15).

Classical political economy also draws attention to the mutual constitution of state and market. Welfare and social policy reveals this interpenetration of state and market especially well, with laws and regulations shaping how a range of markets operate. The labour market is profoundly shaped by levels of unemployment benefit and other social entitlements, for example. Minimum wage regulations are very clear government acts of market shaping – but there are many more subtle instances. Understanding the CPE of welfare state change requires grasping the inherent intertwining of state-orchestrated social protection and capitalist market relations (see e.g. Pierson and Castles 2000; Schwartz 2001: 18, 31–44). The relation between welfare states and capitalism can helpfully be understood as symbiotic. Indeed, in a counter-intuitive twist to the relationship between welfare and globalization, some argue that it was the development and growth of post-war welfare states that made possible later 20th-century increasing trade openness and economic interdependence. Welfare states delivered social protection from adverse consequences of increased trade openness (see Polanyi 2001 [1944]: 136–9) that would otherwise have been delivered through protectionism (Rieger and Liebfried 2003: 13; Gough and Therborn 2010: 710).

As I demonstrate below, the supposed 'race to the bottom' of welfare provision, like the mooted 'rolling back' of the state in Chapter 8, is not empirically verified. The marginalist or neo-classical economic assumptions on which 'race to the bottom' theorizing is predicated struggle to recognize the economically beneficial effects of social provision, social stability and so on (see e.g. Swensson 2002). Social protection in this view is a public good, crucial for macro-economic stability, not simply an economic cost or an impediment to freer markets (see Clift and Robles 2020). The previous head of the IMF even called social protection 'a core component of the social contract' needed to fulfil IMF missions (Lagarde 2019). These constitute further good reasons to revisit pre-marginalist classical political economy in analysing the CPE of welfare.

Furthermore, welfare state restructuring involves the marketization and contracting out of social and public services provision, reorganizing the state and public sector according to the ideas of public choice and NPM (see pp. 100, 103–4, 155). NPM-oriented reforms are increasingly applying market efficiency structures and criteria in public healthcare, social care and education. Thus rather than 'less state' and 'more market' operating in separate spheres (as marginalist political economy would see it), there is increasing interpenetration of market and state within welfare state restructuring. The CPE of changing welfare state institutions, regimes and programmes is more complex and contingent than 'race to the bottom' thinking can admit. Domestic institutional and ideational factors mediate global economic influences, with each aspect of welfare expenditure facing different pressures and drawing on diverse constituencies of support. State actors also enjoy enduring policy autonomy within the parameters set by complex economic interdependence. Politics matters, and the politics of retrenchment are fraught, so cutbacks are very difficult to enact (Pierson 1994, 2001). This politics and constituencies of support for particular programmes also help explain ongoing differentiation within welfare state and labour market reforms across advanced economies.

The persistence and resilience of social provision within welfare capitalism result from institutional path dependency (see Chapter 6) and a range of intervening variables, including domestic electoral and political structures, veto players and points within welfare state institutions and programmes (Bonoli 2001). More fundamentally, however, welfare states provide necessary social foundations for market relations to operate in advanced political economies. Many 'public goods' are delivered by welfare provision – outputs which are not only economically beneficial, but necessary for the very reproduction of capitalism. These include social stability, social cohesion and an educated, skilled, healthy workforce (see Gough 1996; Hay and Wincott 2012). These all have positive effects on productivity and economic growth through human capital development, for example, but a purer free market order could not deliver these goods. This is an example of Crouch's 'meta-market failure' (1993), discussed in Chapter 6. The fundamental reason for welfare state persistence is the integral, symbiotic link between social welfare provision and liberal market capitalism. Without sufficient welfare provision to limit inequalities and instability, political contestation within capitalist market orders becomes extremely fraught (see Chapter 12).

I begin by defining the welfare state, before exploring the politics of retrenchment and insights from classical political economy. Thereafter, I consider the interconnections with comparative capitalisms analysis and issue health warnings about the Eurocentric foundations of welfare state analysis (Gough and Therborn 2010). This may limit its explanatory purchase on evolving welfare provision and capitalism in the rising economic powers of the 21st century. Finally, I adjudicate on the empirical evidence regarding welfare state trajectories, and note the emergent contours of a new welfare settlement in the advanced economies.

DEFINING AND ANALYSING WELFARE RESTRUCTURING

There is an important methodological and conceptual issue to address at the outset, namely: What *is* a welfare regime? What are the limits of the welfare state? What should we measure in order to adjudicate on its evolutionary dynamics (Hacker 2002: 24)? The answers to these questions can profoundly shape accounts of welfare state evolution. Thus identifying and specifying the object of analysis form a crucial pre-condition for analysing the CPE of welfare.

Which questions get asked, how they get asked and the answers provided are often influenced by past welfare state scholarship. This literature, as Schwartz puts it, 'provides a lamp post around which enquiries naturally cluster ... ignoring areas of darkness away from the lamp' (2001: 17). In analysing the CPE of welfare state change, there are a number of data-sets measuring potentially relevant factors (see Stephens 2010 for a discussion). But this raises Schwartz's 'looking under the lamp posts for lost keys' problem. Welfare state data is out there, but the contention is over what, exactly, it tells us. Technical questions around measurement and research design can have a major impact on findings and interpretation. For example, was Esping-Andersen's pioneering analysis correct in identifying three 'families' of welfare states? Debates about concepts and coding – how you measure and what you measure – underpin ongoing disagreements about whether there are in fact two or three prevailing 'families' of welfare state regimes (see e.g. Esping-Andersen 1990; Pierson 2006: 20; Scruggs and Allen 2008; Hay and Wincott 2012).

As regards what 'counts' or merits measurement, much hinges on differing conceptions of the welfare state. A choice has to be made between broad and narrow definitions (see Figure 11.1; Esping-Andersen 1990: 1–2). The conception of the welfare state is often limited to the formal institutions of welfare provision, focusing on social spending as a proportion of GDP data. Yet this might hinder as much as it helps in clarifying the CPE of welfare. Long ago, Titmuss noted the 'iceberg phenomenon of social welfare' and the need to analyse 'submerged' aspects of social provision such as tax breaks and workplace benefits (1963, 1965; see also Pierson 2006; Hacker 2002: 12–13). After all, the 'familiar policy instruments' of 'direct public spending or provision', Hacker points out, 'do not exhaust the available strategies of intervention' (2002: 11). Other means to pursue social welfare ends can, and perhaps should, be incorporated into the analysis.

Feminist political economy has problematized welfare state boundaries and more fundamental boundaries between public and private spheres, focusing on issues such as unpaid caring work within the family (see pp. 5–6, 88–91, 132–3, 231–4, 299). They explore this through a lens of gender understood as 'systems of sexual difference whereby "men" and "women" are socially constructed and positioned in relations of hierarchy' (Haraway 1991:

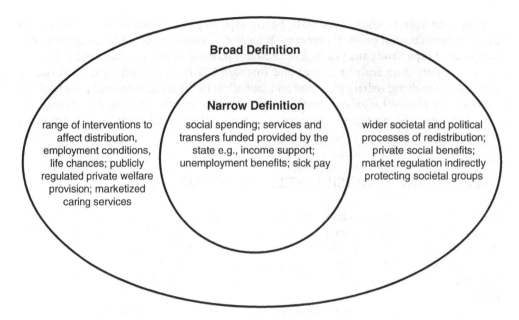

Figure 11.1 Defining the contested boundaries of the welfare state

131; see also Steans 1999: 114–17). Is the welfare state an agent of patriarchal oppression (as suggested by the male breadwinner model) or the means for its redress? One strand of feminist scholarship analyses 'the empowerment of women through the welfare state' and 'feminism from above' (O'Connor 2015: 483). Helga Hernes explores the possibility of a 'Woman-friendly state' (1987: 15) which could eliminate gender injustices through 'state feminism', 'gender equality and social policies' and the 'feminization of welfare state-relevant professions' (Hernes 1987: 153). Scholars have focused on specific policies for combining employment and paid and unpaid caring work, exploring how social and employment policies affect gendered employment patterns. More broadly, feminist welfare scholars analyse the significance for gender and women's welfare of state activities such as family and employment law (Williams 1995), housing and the regulation of those who receive benefits (Orloff 2010: 254).

Feminist political economy rejects the gendered premises of mainstream work on welfare. Orloff highlights the 'falsely universalizing (implicitly masculinist) analytic frames' of most welfare state analysis, which 'occlude the gendered underpinnings of systems of social provision and the specific situations of women' (2010: 253). Feminists critique the gendered division of labour, allocating social reproduction and care work to the private (unproductive) sphere, as opposed to recognizing it as contributing to national wealth and productive labour (True 2016: 44–5, 53–5). They underline how social reproduction and domestic work are key to women's oppression (Orloff 2010: 256). The gendered division of labour endures, despite the advent and growth of marketized caring services and of some state provision of childcare and other services.

Where does the welfare state begin and end? What care work is in the private realm of the family and what is in the public realm of the economy? As Orloff points out, 'the construction and transformation of public-private divides' are a 'critical moment in the gendering of

welfare' (2010: 258; Lewis 1992; O'Connor et al. 1999). This leads to reassessing the definition of (social) citizenship, the fundamental distinctions between market and family,
between public and private, between paid and unpaid and productive and unproductive
labour. Most CPE work on welfare fails to take up the gauntlet thrown down by feminist
political economy of re-evaluating these core concepts and distinctions. These silences on
gendered inequalities and processes of social reproduction are significant caveats to attach
to CPE discussions of welfare restructuring.

These kinds of re-evaluations of the welfare state's accepted boundaries lead some to look
beyond 'formal' welfare state institutions (understandably the focus of much welfare state
literature) to include wider societal and political processes of redistribution. Esping-
Andersen alights on the term 'regime' because it denotes 'the fact that in the relation
between state and economy a complex of legal and organizational features are systematically interwoven' (1990: 2). For Hacker, too, 'welfare regime' connotes such a broader conception, including some (publicly regulated) private provision of welfare as well as public
programmes (Hacker 2002).

Following Chris Pierson, we note the merit of tightly-focused analysis specifying a narrow definition of the 'welfare state' as 'state measures to meet key welfare needs (often
confined to health, education, housing, income maintenance and personal social service).
This provision may take the form of either *services* (provided by, or funded by the state) or
income *transfers*.' Like Pierson, however, we complement this with a broader notion of 'the
welfare state under capitalism', a 'specific type of society' in which 'the state intervenes within
the processes of economic reproduction and distribution to reallocate life chances between
individuals and/or classes' (2006: 10). The narrow definition is useful for understanding the
specificities of particular social provision arrangements. Locating this within a wider welfare 'regime' helpfully captures 'the inherent interconnectedness of the economy, on the one
hand, and public and social policies, on the other' (Hay and Wincott 2012: 38).

In this chapter I adopt a broad conception, since focusing solely on formal institutions
and 'conventional social amelioration policies' (Esping-Andersen 1990: 2) is rather restrictive. The means to the end of social protection extend beyond formal welfare institutions
and policies, and therefore it makes sense to extend the definitional boundaries of the welfare regime accordingly. Our definition encompasses not only specific government policies
and programmes, but also how state regulation of markets can indirectly protect sections of
society against particular risks (Schwartz 2001). The idea of liberal market capitalism and
the provision of social welfare existing in a symbiotic relationship (Pierson 2006; Hay and
Wincott 2012: 74) aligns with this definition, as does the notion of 'welfare capitalism'.

The merits of the broader conception are well illustrated in the US case. At first sight, it
appears at the extreme liberal end of the spectrum, not really comparable to European welfare states (P. Pierson 2001: 420). Traditional social spending as a proportion of GDP measures (rooted in a narrow welfare state conception) see the US as a residual, minimal outlier:
'US spending is not just the lowest in the group, it is barely more than half the average level
of the other nations' (Hacker 2002: 13). Yet that impression is somewhat misleading. The US
welfare regime is substantially hidden (Hacker 2002, 2005; Seabrooke 2006). Hacker's analysis of 'America's broader framework of social provision' unearths 'the rise of private benefits as a preeminent source of social protection' as 'one of the most important "unseen
revolutions" of American political history' (Hacker 2002: 9). The qualitative particularities
of US welfare arise from a distinctive ideational context averse to public provision, where
Marshall's notions of *social* rights of citizenship (discussed below) 'have been less firmly
entrenched' (King and Wood 1999: 260).

Within 'America's public–private welfare regime', private actors are 'encouraged to provide benefits by a diverse range of subsidies and regulations'. It is important to recognize the 'impressive scope and dense policy underpinnings of private social benefits' (Hacker 2002: 7). These are not 'an autonomous market development' and they 'do not spontaneously arise through decentralized market processes'. These 'private social benefits', and 'the less visible subsidies and regulations that shape them', must be incorporated into analysing the US welfare regime. In another illustration of the interpenetration of state and market, this demonstrates the interlinked nature of private and public aspects of social provision, which are 'systematically inter-twined' in US public policy-making (ibid.: 8). These are 'an active, if not always deliberate, construction', politically constituted through government regulatory intervention and driven by 'subterranean political and judicial processes' (ibid.: 9).

Thus, by adopting a broader 'welfare regime' conception and incorporating 'relative tax burdens, tax expenditures, and publicly subsidized private benefits', the picture changes dramatically: 'the United States rises to the middle of the pack' (ibid.: 13). Due to the 'dense sinews of state authority and private power that together define America's unusual social policy amalgam' (ibid.: 27), even in the US liberal archetype, welfare provision is extensive. Hacker argues that it is not levels of provision, but the extent of private provision within public orchestrated social welfare which distinguishes the US from other advanced economy welfare regimes. Thus, contrary to conventional wisdom, 'properly measured, the United States does not devote a markedly smaller proportion of national resources to social services and transfers than do other affluent democracies' (ibid.: 16). This extensive social provision, even within the liberal, minimal welfare archetype, demonstrates the co-constitutive character of social provision and capitalism.

WELFARE CAPITALISM AND THE POLITICS OF RETRENCHMENT

Welfare regimes, like varieties of capitalism (see pp. 174–80), are complex historical phenomena, shaped by multiple factors and the 'interactive and cumulative effects of a number of interdependent causal factors' (P. Pierson 2001: 428). As Allan and Scruggs point out, welfare state expansion was not mono-causal (2004: 497) and nor is its contemporary evolution. Differentiated labour market and welfare institutions, programmes and histories are sedimented into their national landscapes. Globalization and marketization are not geological forces powerful enough to erode these national particularities. We may see some common directions of travel (towards more 'activation', incentivizing labour market participation) confronting some common problems (health and pensions cost containment in the face of demographic and technological change). That said, we can expect differing paces of change and varied qualitative transformation of welfare regimes. Processes of bricolage and translation (see pp. 122–5), along with institutional path dependencies, mean that welfare state reform takes different forms in each case, fuelling ongoing diversity.

The politics of this co-evolution of complex sets of social institutions is key: 'welfare states face severe strains and they retain deep reservoirs of political support' (P. Pierson 2001: 416). This is why Paul Pierson recommends Charles Ragin's 'complex conjunctural causation' approach (1987), discussed in Chapter 13, as the best methodology to analyse welfare state restructuring. From such a perspective, arguing for 'a linear relationship between independent and dependent variables' makes no sense, because welfare state regimes 'are the products of complex conjunctural causation, with multiple factors working together over extended periods of time' (Pierson 2001: 429).

The symbiotic view taken here suggests that expanding welfare provision was a necessary condition of economic development. Some identify a 'growth to limits' in advanced economy welfare state trajectories, wherein, as growth waned, the fruits of growth ceased to accrue readily to all social strata (Castles 2004: 45; C. Pierson 2006: 206). In the contemporary context, funding generous welfare becomes harder given electoral competition and neo-liberal low tax agendas bearing down on headline tax rates, combined with hard-to-tax TNCs and other fiscally elusive forms of footloose capital. This fiscal pressure is compounded by demographic change reducing the size of the working-age population (and the tax base). Meanwhile the costs of, and demands for, social provision continue to grow. Ageing populations, crises of social care and rising healthcare costs only increase the fiscal stress. Against this backdrop, sometimes termed 'permanent austerity' (P. Pierson 2001: 411), the political economy of welfare has become increasingly fraught. It becomes ever harder to meet competing claims and satisfy all constituencies. These pressures and tensions were only augmented in the wake of the GFC and its austerity-reinforcing impact on public finances (see Hay and Wincott 2012; Blyth 2013; Vaughan-Whitehead 2013; Streeck 2014, 2017).

Growing demands and increasing welfare costs, set against still high but *not growing* aggregate levels of social spending, indicate that welfare retrenchment has been a reality since the late 20th century. If we 'drill down' into the nitty-gritty of social provision in specific programmes (which is hard to do), we find reduced entitlements and lower replacement rates (the ratio of unemployment benefits to an unemployed worker's last wage level). We also find shorter benefit duration and increasingly strict eligibility criteria. While there is no far-reaching contraction in advanced economies, intensifying fiscal pressures means that differentiated processes of welfare state 'recalibration' are transforming 21st-century welfare states (Stephens et al. 1999; P. Pierson 2001; C. Pierson 2006; Hay and Wincott 2012). Welfare state recalibration refers to remodelling welfare provision – changing its function (which risks it protects against), rebalancing its distributive characteristics (towards which social groups), reforming the institutions through which welfare is delivered, and sometimes revising the values or norms it upholds (see e.g. Hemerijck 2006; Johnston et al. 2011; Ferrera and Hemerijck 2003).

Some familiar political economy arguments help explain the limits of retrenchment. As Paul Pierson puts it, following Mancur Olson's logic (see pp. 100–1), 'huge segments of the electorates of advanced industrial societies rely on the welfare state for a large share of their income. It is one of the few basic axioms of political science that concentrated interests will generally be advantaged over diffuse ones' (P. Pierson 2001: 413). Institutional complementarity, path dependency and self-reinforcing patterns (see pp. 113–16; North 1990; Soskice 1999: 109; P. Pierson 2004) also play their role within a multi-variable approach to welfare politics. Potential losers from retrenchment are concentrated and organized into mobilized, politicized constituencies protecting cherished social entitlements. Welfare provision creates and entrenches clienteles (Esping-Andersen 1990; Skocpol 1992). The CPE of welfare state restructuring involves 'bounded change' (P. Pierson 2001: 415; North 1990: 98–9), combining resilience, recalibration and retrenchment. Below we explore the dynamics driving welfare trajectories within modern capitalism, but first I will reiterate salient insights of classical political economy.

CLASSICAL POLITICAL ECONOMY AND THE POLITICAL ECONOMY OF THE WELFARE STATE

Inequality has always been a key focus of classical political economy, exemplified in Adam Smith's concern for the well-being of the whole of society. He thought the benefits of growth would spread throughout society, and this underpinned his ethical case for capitalism. As we shall explore in Chapter 12, the relationship between capitalism, inequality and capitalism's ethical basis has evolved significantly since Smith's time. In recent decades, widening inequalities within and across globalizing capitalisms have destabilized the social and political settlement underpinning the liberal capitalist order. It is less clear that 21st-century welfare states, facing pressures of permanent austerity, retrenchment and recalibration, can restrain political and social discontent. Increasing inequality sees rising society-wide poverty and precarity levels co-existing with pockets of enormous wealth. The existing welfare settlement, and the traditional political parties that constructed and defended it, find themselves buffeted by populist disaffection mobilizing the 'losers' from globalization.

For all the political economic strain on welfare provision, it remains a prevalent structuring feature of advanced capitalism. Capitalism's socially disruptive consequences always generate political pressures for social protection: 'even in the less generous welfare states', Block and Evans note, 'virtually every new welfare state program produces new institutional connections between the state and civil society' (2005: 513, 514). Welfare regimes do not exist alongside a capitalist regime of accumulation (as the Regulation School theorists we encountered in Chapter 9 would call it). Rather, in those advanced (post-)industrial economies which have undergone some variant of Polanyi's 'great transformation', capitalism and welfare provision are co-constitutive of the political economic order.

The nexus of political intervention in the market is central to crucial concepts in welfare state debates: de- and recommodification. This encapsulates the relation between political institutions and policies of welfare provision (and their consequences for individuals' labour market position) and the labour market (Esping-Andersen 1990: 21–3). Decommodification refers to interventions reducing labour market discipline by limiting reliance on wage labour, such that 'a person can maintain a livelihood without reliance on the market' (Esping-Andersen 1990: 22). Thus one can exit the labour market without suffering a major loss of income (due to unemployment benefits and other forms of social provision). Recommodification (Offe 1984), by contrast, refers to reforms that reinstate labour market disciplines, heightening labour market competition and intensifying reliance on markets. This may include new forms of administrative control of workers and job-seekers (Greer 2016). Though Smith was writing before the Industrial Revolution could unleash its seismic effects on economy and society, his distinction between 'natural prices' and 'market prices' (see pp. 30–1, 46–7) is pertinent here. Decommodification and recommodification dynamics, and the reform struggles they give rise to, illustrate how the labour market is not a naturally occurring phenomenon (a self-regulating market). Rather, it is a politically and legally instantiated and sustained nexus of institutions (a regulated market; see also Chang 1996, 1999).

The social impact and consequences of the Industrial Revolution, notably urbanization, the decline of agriculture and 'the creation of a landless (manual) urban working class, concentrated in particular economic sectors and based in distinctive urban neighbourhoods' (C. Pierson 2006: 15), shaped the relationship between capitalism and welfare. The social transformation of growing inequality, appalling working and living conditions and widespread working-class destitution, combined with pockets of bourgeois opulence, fuelled Marx's view of the inherent incompatibility of welfare and capitalism. Social welfare represented a challenge to the logic of the market because it could mitigate the compulsion of the worker to sell their labour power, undermining the system of capitalist accumulation. For Marx, worker exploitation was so crucial to capitalist social relations of production that, as Chris Pierson puts it, 'radical inequality of welfare outcomes is [seen as] endemic to capitalism' (2006: 13).

The growth of factory employment, the capitalist labour market and the advent of the industrial proletariat were 'deep-seated economic, social and political changes in the structure of the developing capitalist societies' (ibid.: 15). Over time, the rampant and widening inequality and fears of societal breakdown generated new approaches and policy initiatives to address industrial capitalism's social instability problem. Throughout the later 19th and early 20th centuries, these changes in attitudes and approaches to public social provision were integral to Polanyi's *Great Transformation* (2001 [1944]). One key factor underpinning changing attitudes to welfare was novel ideas about citizenship and rights. Smith, though he advocated public education and assistance for the poorest in society, did not think in terms of social rights and attendant state duties to provide welfare (C. Pierson 2006: 11).

Thinking about the nature of social rights, however, has evolved since Smith's time. T. H. Marshall, a mid-20th-century towering scholar of welfare, analysed the nature of citizenship. His account of the slow emergence of encompassing notions of social citizenship set out the ideational pre-conditions for welfare state development. Marshall charted in Britain the development of social citizenship through incremental expansion of rights – first civil, then political and then finally social. These social rights gradually extended towards the broader populace in the early to mid-20th century. This historical expansion of citizenship culminates in the emergence of 'social rights' to welfare (1963: 70–4; C. Pierson 2006: 24–6). This notion of citizenship, and the attendant social rights, had the potential to mitigate the exploitative social consequences of capitalism, envisaged by Marx as inexorable. The key qualitative shift within advanced capitalism was the potential for 'Marshall's notion of citizenship replacing the market as a distributive mechanism' (Stephens 2010: 513).

The idea of welfare states resting on foundations of social rights remains central to welfare state scholarship. Marshall's 'social citizenship' saw the welfare state as an essential ingredient of modern civilization, such that every (advanced economy) citizen enjoys the right to social support (pension, unemployment relief, education, social services and healthcare) which is free at the point of use. Entitlement is based on citizenship status, not ability to pay. This, according to Marshall, was a fundamental egalitarian challenge to existing capitalist private property rights: 'the preservation of economic inequalities has been made more difficult by the enrichment of the status of citizenship' (Marshall 1950: 29).

Yet some feel the challenge represented by Marshall was not fundamental enough. Feminist political economists contend that these ostensibly gender-blind definitions of social citizenship and social rights remain problematic because they rest on the inequalities of a gendered division of labour. This is part of a wider concern to 'contest gender hierarchies' (Orloff 2009: 318) in welfare research and analysis, and to challenge the patriarchal premises of welfare states. Mainstream accounts of welfare neglect unequal social reproduction roles, and assume that women will undertake unpaid care work. Feminist political economists argue for reconceptualizing notions of citizenship and equality in ways that recognize and redress such gendered inequalities (Orloff 2010: 254).

Marshall's approach to social citizenship, while failing to deal adequately with gender inequalities, did extend social rights across broad swathes of society. The welfare state was not just the province of the poorest, nor only supported by vulnerable sections of society. After all, the beneficiaries from the social stability and redistribution that welfare provision delivers extend beyond 'the workers' and 'the poor'. They include business interests, those on a middle income and more affluent groups (Therborn 1986: 240; Rothstein 1998; Schwartz 2001: 18; Hacker 2002; Swenson 2002; Mares 2003; C. Pierson 2006: 36; van Kersbergen and Manow 2009). The range of social groups with a stake in the welfare state helps explain the difficulty of achieving retrenchment (see e.g. P. Pierson 1994, 1996, 2001). Welfare states include the middle classes and affluent social groups among their core clientele, and this makes them politically difficult to reform. Furthermore, path dependency (Chapter 6) means that 'past reforms have contributed decisively to the institutionalization of class preferences and political behaviour' (Esping-Andersen 1990: 32; see also P. Pierson 1994, 1996, 2004; Hacker 2002). This has implications for the CPE of welfare restructuring, making institutional and political mediation of any changes to welfare provision highly likely. This will vary according to national, historical trajectories of welfare state development.

Welfare states shape the structures of capitalism and also the agents: the citizenry. Esping-Andersen exhorts that 'we have to think in terms of social relations, not just social categories' (1990: 18) in relation to distinct welfare regimes. The politics of welfare provision affects processes of 'class formation' as well as 'coalition building' (ibid.: 23–4, 32). For example, the role of 'social partners' in managing Germany's welfare state was a crucial source of their legitimacy. It shaped German 'industrial citizens' as economic actors (see pp. 219–20; Streeck 2001: 12–3; Jackson 2001). Indeed, some argue, contrary to Marx, that social classes are less products of the social relations of production, and more products of public policy, notably welfare provision (Marshall 1950; Esping-Andersen 1990: 23–6; Manow 2001b: 148).

In a slightly different vein, Mikko Kuisma's discussion of the 'Nordic model' (encompassing the welfare regime and model of capitalism) extends beyond just its redistributive economic and social policies to include the role of 'nation-state building and the constitution of citizenship'. Indeed, through the socio-cultural development of a Nordic conception of citizenship and social rights, 'social democratic ideals and policies became embedded in ... national societies' (2007: 87).

Kuisma highlights the interlinking welfare, citizenship and national society, 'a shared legacy of values, norms, and morals, which are largely passed on in collective traditions and inter-generational collective memory' (ibid.: 88). These understandings became what the constructivists we discussed in Chapter 7 would call 'social facts'. Thus Nordic welfare regime development over the 19th and 20th centuries created configurations of citizen expectations about who they were and what sort of economic future they would allow themselves to be politically mobilized into (ibid.). Kuisma demonstrates these welfare regime effects on the everyday assumptions that Finnish and Norwegian citizens form about their rights. These ideational foundations continue to influence contemporary welfare state developments, and Vartiainen finds evidence that the high and stable levels of social spending and high taxation in Scandinavia reflect citizens' preferences (2004).

COMPARATIVE WELFARE STATES, COMPARATIVE WELFARE CAPITALISMS

The urge to cluster political economies into types exerts, it seems, a powerful gravitational pull on comparative political economists. Thus the broad distinction between more regulated continental (European) CME capitalism and more free market–oriented Anglo-American LME capitalism (see Chapters 6 and 9) is an undercurrent of and backdrop to contemporary CPE analysis. Similar to varieties of capitalist institutions, there are several 'worlds' of welfare institutions and of welfare capitalism. Esping-Andersen's influential book claimed that the welfare regime was 'the principal institution in the construction of different models of post-war capitalism': 'welfare-state variations' are 'not linearly distributed, but clustered by regime-types' (1990: 5, 26; see also Huber and Stephens 2001a, 2001b; P. Pierson 2001; Scruggs 2006; Scruggs and Allen 2006). Furthermore, consistent with the symbiotic relationship between welfare and capitalism, Paul Pierson identifies 'a strong co-evolutionary aspect to the intersection between varieties of capitalism and systems of social provision' (2001: 423).

Despite these close interconnections, a peculiarity of sub-disciplinarity within contemporary CPE is that the rich literatures on comparative capitalisms and comparative welfare states do not 'speak to' each other as explicitly as they should. This is problematic because welfare and production regimes are inextricably interlinked. There are honourable exceptions (e.g. Ebbinghaus and Manow 1998; Huber and Stephens 2001a, 2001b; Manow 2001a, 2001b; Estevez-Abe et al. 2001; Mares 2001; Iversen 2005), but the continuation of these debates in relative isolation is regrettable because they share similar central themes. Issues of path dependency, interlocked institutional complementarities explaining the limits of change and evolution through processes of bricolage and translation (Campbell 2004) are common to both. So, too, are arguments about a mooted convergence towards a liberal model (see Hay and Wincott 2012: 164–93).

Different welfare regimes have distinct (in)egalitarian and redistributive properties, and thus shape the political economy of capitalism in diverse ways. Crucial dimensions of differentiation between regime types are conceptions and packages of social rights, social stratification and the relation between state, market and family (Esping-Andersen 1990: 29). Clusters of welfare state regimes provide 'a highly useful heuristic explanatory device' (Huber and Stephens 2001b: 108). The number of different clusters identifiable is disputed, but often-identified clustering of welfare capitalism types include the 'Nordic' (e.g. Denmark, Sweden), 'Continental/Bismarckian' (Germany, Austria), 'liberal' (UK, US), 'Southern' or 'Mediterranean' (Italy, Spain) and 'Antipodean wage-earner' (Australia, New Zealand) regimes (P. Pierson 2001; Ferrera et al. 2000, 2004; Huber and Stephens 2001a, 2001b; Hemerijck and Ferrera 2004).

Feminist political economy shines the light on iniquitous gendered effects of welfare regimes, an aspect often neglected in these comparative analyses. Jane Lewis' critique of the male breadwinner model premises of established welfare state typologies (1992; O'Connor 2015: 484–5; Orloff 2006, 2010) exposed the gendered division of labour and its implications. The institutional instantiation and reproduction of this gendered division of labour proceed through social and labour market policy, through employment law, through societal understandings of appropriate family life and in myriad other ways. 'Strong' male breadwinner states, such as post-war UK and Ireland, hindered female labour force participation.

Care work is typically under-valued and mostly unpaid, as reflected in levels of public provision of, for instance, childcare and care for other dependants, and also in wage rates for those (mostly women) carrying out care work. This contrasts with the Nordic experience, for example in Sweden, where women are/were compensated at market rates for care work and caring work is more valued.

There has been some evolution from the traditional 'male breadwinner' model since the post-war era. Lewis charts a shift towards a 'one and a half earner' family model or an 'adult worker model family' (in the US and Sweden; Lewis 2001: 163). The more gender-equitable 'dual earnership' model is becoming the norm according to the OECD (2010), thanks in part to sustained policy efforts at increasing the employment rates of women. The scale and speed of change towards less gender-unequal regimes and labour market conditions vary, and indeed broadly cluster according to welfare state types. Nordic societies have extensive institutional gender inequality infrastructures and gender equality is integral to public policy more broadly (O'Connor 2015: 489). Social democratic welfare states moved earliest and farthest, followed by the liberal, with Christian democratic states being the patriarchal laggards (O'Connor 2015: 485–6, table 25.1).

Others highlight interacting, intersecting class and gender inequalities within advanced capitalisms (Acker 1989), such that middle-class women and families benefit more than working-class women from state attempts to aid reconciling employment with family life through child care, parental leave and so on (Cantillon and Van Lancker 2013). Labour market reforms that enable female labour market participation, and facilitate combining this with caring work, arguably ignore ongoing structural gender inequality. Many attempts to improve the fit between family life and the labour market fail to deliver on the gender equality of adult women (Jenson 2009). Esping-Andersen (2009) sees female labour force participation as an 'incomplete revolution', since gender equality requires broader societal changes to generate a new 'gender equality equilibrium' (2009: 172). Thus at one level the feminization of the advanced economy workforce since the 1970s is a step towards a potentially more gender-equal society. Yet due to structural patriarchal power relations, women are still over-represented in part-time and lower-paid work (England 2005), the gender pay gap endures and gender equality in economic opportunities and outcomes remains an unattained goal (OECD 2013).

The biases in welfare state analysis relate not just to the neglect of gendered inequalities, but also to its inherent 'Eurocentrism'. Comparative welfare state analysis has primarily been developed to analyse the European (and to a lesser extent Antipodean and North American) welfare experience. Gough and Therborn point out: 'the European experience of post-agrarian societies dominated, at least relatively, by industrial employment was never repeated outside Europe'; economic development in other societies involves the 'informal sector' more, different patterns of urbanization and 'self-employment and tiny enterprises below the radar of the state and of social entitlements' (2010: 707). If capitalism and society develop in different ways, we might anticipate welfare provision differently too. Categories and typologies developed to explain European welfare states may have limited explanatory purchase elsewhere.

Here we recognize interlocked complementarities between the trajectories of welfare states and varieties of capitalism (Amable 2003; Gatti and Glyn 2006: 309–10; Iversen and Soskice 2006). Welfare states are important institutional elements of the 'complementary, coherent mutual "fitting" complexes' central to VoC, Manow argues, since 'social policy is a central domain for both direct and indirect state intervention into the employment relation'

(2001b: 154–6). Similar to VoC, identifying distinct welfare state 'families' invites CPE scholars to question whether there are specific welfare family trajectories in the changing global political economy. Some argue that 'Anglo-Saxon' liberal welfare capitalism displays greater compatibility with globalization, through its less generous, lower minimum standards and more deregulated labour market institutions. This more nimble, flexible welfare state and labour market regime, and broader model of capitalism, adapts more quickly and better, some contend, to fast-changing international competitive conditions.

On closer inspection, good economic and employment performance *can* be compatible with a variety of welfare state and labour market types, including those more regulated and securing higher minimum standards than, say, the UK economy (Hopkin and Wincott 2006). Sweden, the Netherlands and Denmark have all, at different times, been invoked as exemplars able to reconcile economic openness with generous social provision (Blanchard 2006). Thus generous, redistributive, egalitarian welfare regimes do not necessarily harm economic performance, since extensive social provision delivers public goods. Manow argues that 'the welfare state contributes substantially to the performance profile of national economies' and that 'generous welfare state programmes may enhance and not diminish international competitiveness' because of 'economically beneficial side-effects of social policy' (2001b: 146, 147).

Indeed, relatively generous Nordic welfare states often *outperform* liberal, more minimal provision: 'by some conventional analyses, all of Scandinavia should have long ago collapsed under the weight of its public spending'. Many Continental and Nordic welfare states consistently perform well in the Global Competitiveness Index, claiming three of the top four spots in 2005 (Scruggs 2006: 349). More generous welfare providers continued to hold their own in the top 10 in 2019, which included the Netherlands, Switzerland, Japan, Germany, Sweden and Denmark (World Economic Forum 2020). The different properties of different welfare state 'families' and their mooted 'goodness of fit' with the 21st-century global political economy lead us into an important underlying debate about economic openness and welfare. Interrogating the relationship between globalization and welfare state trajectories pits those asserting eroding welfare provision as a consequence of complex economic interdependence against those seeing *increased* social provision as a logical corollary of more open markets.

GLOBALIZATION AND WELFARE STATE RETRENCHMENT: A CONVERGENT 'RACE TO THE BOTTOM'?

Assessing the sustainability and viability of welfare regimes given changing international economic interdependence is a recurrent focus for CPE welfare state scholarship. One bold hypothesis posits that globalization is bearing down on all welfare states with equal force, inducing programme retrenchment and convergence on minimalist neo-liberal welfare norms. As Drezner puts it, 'once states decide to lower their barriers to exchange, a Pandora's box is unleashed which cannot be reversed' (2001: 75). At its strongest this thesis contends that globalization, understood as 'the cluster of technological, economic and political innovations that have drastically reduced barriers to economic, political and cultural exchange', induces 'an inexorable policy convergence' (ibid.: 53–5; see also Gray 1998; Schwartz 2001 for a discussion and critique). The mooted pressures for (downward) convergence towards the 'lowest common denominator' (Drezner 2001: 59) are the same as the 'race to the bottom' thesis we encountered briefly in Chapter 8.

The drivers inducing this convergence include the sheer scale of FDI flows which arguably empower capital (for example, transnational corporations) at the expense of other actors, including governments and unions. Increasingly mobile capital faces lower 'exit' costs and increased exit options, and capital will 'engage in regulatory arbitrage, moving to (or importing from) countries with the lowest regulatory standards. States, fearing a loss of their tax base, have no choice but to lower regulatory standards to avoid capital flight' (Drezner 2001: 58). This argument has a long pedigree. Adam Smith noted in the 1770s that 'the proprietor of stock is a citizen of the world ... He would be apt to abandon the country in which he was ... assessed to a burdensome tax, and would remove historical stock to some other country where he could either carry on his business or enjoy his fortune more at his ease' (Smith 1937: 800, quoted in Drezner 2001).

International capital mobility has increased exponentially since the early 1970s, let alone since Smith was writing. It brings 'tax jurisdictions into competition with one another'; capital is 'playing off the regulatory regimes of different economies one against another' (Hay and Wincott 2012: 69–70). This threat of capital exit constrains what kinds of tax and regulatory regimes governments can maintain, and tax competition undermines the fiscal basis of generous welfare provision. Eroding state tax-raising capacity is particularly problematic for costly welfare programmes, given 'the drain on profits that high non-wage labour costs and levels of corporate taxation are seen to represent' (ibid.: 69). Thus international pressures for (downward) convergence extend beyond taxation to include labour market regulation. Non-wage costs such as social security contributions are crucial for international competitiveness, since advanced economy firms compete with foreign firms spared these non-wage labour costs. Governments are thus limited in the labour market and fiscal institutions they may adopt.

This logic and reasoning lead some to anticipate ever more flexible labour markets and ever reducing welfare provision as the inevitable corollary of globalization. Strong versions include Przeworksi and Wallerstein's structural dependency of the state on capital thesis, rooted in Marxian assumptions (1988). There are also liberal variants (Cerny 1997a, 1997b; Gray 1998; Eichengreen 2008). Both types argue that globalization has changed state roles, inducing the pursuit of increasingly 'market-friendly' policies promoting labour market deregulation and lower direct taxation levels, which inevitably undermine welfare provision.

The 'race to the bottom' argument is bold and striking. It has potentially wide-ranging implications for contemporary capitalism's democratic legitimacy, since welfare provision enjoys enduring popular support (see e.g. P. Pierson 2001). Yet a very crude conception of the relation between globalization and welfare provision underpins this argument (for a critique, see Drezner 2001: 58–9). Hay and Wincott term the 'race to the bottom' argument the 'incommensurability thesis' (between welfare state and globalization; 2012: 71). This is derived from the assumptions of open economy macro-economics (ibid., Box 3.1), which emulate marginalist political economy (see pp. 74–8). Convergence on a minimal 'Anglo-Saxon' welfare model projects these assumptions, and a 'there is no alternative' argument, onto the global political economy. As Hay and Wincott note, these oversimplifying assumptions have a solid rationale when economists simplify the world economy to model it formally, but 'such a defence is simply not available to proponents of the incommensurability thesis', since their 'borrowings from neoclassical economics rarely if ever extend past the assumptions to the algebra' (2012: 72).

One problem in analysing the CPE of welfare is what social scientists call 'functionalism' (see pp. 117–20), wherein the welfare state is understood as a 'functional requisite for the reproduction of society and economy' (Esping-Andersen 1990: 13), called forth by mysterious systemic imperatives. Functionalist welfare state development accounts suffer from the Eurocentrism noted above. Thus when economic development reaches a particular stage, the demands of economic growth ultimately explains welfare expansion (Wilensky 1975, 1976; for a critique see C. Pierson 2006: 17–23). Functionalist retrenchment accounts argue that international competition in an ever more liberalized, globalizing economy bears down inexorably on welfare provision and labour market regulation.

These accounts lack a causal mechanism (Schwartz 2001: 19, 23, 25). Failure to define the mechanisms of change linking 'globalization' to welfare retrenchment leads to overstating the international origins of welfare state change (Manow 2001b: 164; C. Pierson 2001; Iversen 2005: 7, 184; Hay 2006). 'Race to the bottom' arguments also neglect how economic globalization's effects are mediated (and indeed contested) by states. This hinders convergence, since the domestic institutional contexts with which these international pressures interact vary greatly. Despite their shortcomings, 'race to the bottom' accounts have become highly influential. This has unsurprisingly provoked a robust counter-argument, the 'compensation' thesis.

THE COMPENSATION THESIS

We encountered the compensation thesis briefly in Chapter 8. This argues that exposure to economic insecurities and risks arising from globalization actually creates domestic political pressures for welfare state expansion, not retrenchment. Welfare states are thus becoming more, not less, significant players as societies seek responses to (and insulation from) the vulnerabilities and instabilities that increasing exposure to international economic competition can entail. This aligns with Karl Polanyi's prescient insights of the state setting the rules and framework for market activity, and of dialectical struggles between the forces of social protection and market liberalization within capitalism (2001 [1944]). The Polanyian 'double movement' logic (see p. 88, 148, 162) sees social protection as a necessary pre-condition to a viable market economy (Schwartz 2001: 44). Re-embedding market activity within its social context (from which it *cannot* be dis-embedded, except at the cost of dramatic social dislocation) is understood here as being essential to social reproduction.

Cameron analysed 'the expansion of the public economy' which accompanied the spread of freer markets after World War II, positing that such expansion 'was most pronounced in nations in which the economy is relatively "open", in the sense of being exposed to the vagaries of the international economy' (1978: 1251). Crucial here is the exposure of economies 'to pressures on markets and prices which are transmitted from other nations via international exchange' (ibid.: 1249). Such exposure exacerbates 'national anxieties and insecurities produced by economic interdependence' (ibid.: 1250; see also Lindbeck 1975: 56; Lehmbruch 1977; Frieden 1991). Advancing trade liberalization and heightened capital mobility and volatility after the 1960s (see pp. 207–8) increased societal exposure still further. Citizens' desires for protection 'bid up' electoral promises of public provision and expenditure through the so-called political business cycle (see pp. 133–6; Nordhaus 1975; Hibbs 1977; Cameron 1978: 1245). Thus governments promise increased social provision and insulation from globalization to secure re-election. Other office-seeking parties are loath to challenge these social programmes which, once established, become politically difficult to remove or erode (P. Pierson 2001). This provides the mechanism, underspecified by Polanyi (2001 [1944]), translating societal desires for social protection into policy outcomes. All this, of course, contradicts the 'race to the bottom' thesis.

Different compensation dynamics characterize large as opposed to small and particularly trade-dependent economies (Cameron 1978: 1249–50), generating a 'small states' subcategory of the compensation thesis. Katzenstein identified a causal relation between the small and most importantly *open* nature of European economies such as Sweden, Austria and the Netherlands and the large size of their governments (1985). Only following international liberalization beginning in the 1950s did the public sector assume 'such a prominent role in the small European states' (ibid.: 55), as they complemented 'their pursuit of liberalism in the international economy with a strategy of domestic compensation' (ibid.: 47). This took various forms, including investment, subsidies, incomes policy and most importantly transfer payments.

Rodrik's analysis shows the increased demands for social insurance arising from 'increased international economic interdependence' (1997: 49). Less skilled social groups 'perceive the expansion of unregulated markets as inimical to social stability and deeply held norms' (ibid.: 2); in Polanyian fashion (ibid.: 71) the result is rising government expenditures on social spending and income transfers as a proportion of GDP in the 40 years after World War II. Rodrik finds that more open economies have larger government spending, the latter 'performing an insulation function' (1998: 1011, 1021–3, 1997: 49–68; see also Swank 1998, 2001, 2002, 2003; Esping-Andersen 1990: 15; Huber and Stephens 2001a, 2001b).

Thus a consensus developed between Cameron (1978), Katzenstein (1985), Rodrik (1997, 1998), Garrett (1995, 1998) and others identifying a causal relationship, and 'not a spurious relationship' (Rodrik 1998: 1011), between welfare state expenditure growth and increased trade openness (see also C. Pierson 2006; Hay and Wincott 2012). For Manow, borrowing terminology from Ruggie's embedded liberalism (see pp. 10, 142–9, 255–6), 'social policy is conceived as a "functional equivalent" of protectionism, albeit one securing a higher welfare level for the entire society' (2001b: 162; see also Gough and Therborn 2010: 710).

The compensation thesis highlights the embeddedness of economic activity in social context logically implied by the symbiotic relationship between capitalism and welfare underlined in this chapter. Although concerned with complex international economic interdependence, the compensation thesis nevertheless focuses attention on domestic drivers of welfare state change, and on *endogenous* factors within the social and political context of market relations (Schwartz 2001). Paul Pierson identifies 'social and economic transformation occurring *within* affluent democracies' as primarily causing 'pressures on mature welfare states' (2001: 410, emphasis added). The degree of emphasis on such endogenous political factors contrasts starkly with a dominant focus on international economic factors of 'race to the bottom' convergence theorists.

EMPIRICAL ADJUDICATION: 'WELFARE EFFORT' AND WELFARE SPENDING

These, then, are the battle lines in the interpretive struggle over understanding the changing CPE of welfare capitalism. In this section and the next, I deploy the methods of CPE (see Chapter 13) to adjudicate empirically on the competing claims and widely differing interpretations of welfare trajectories discussed above. There are two main methodological approaches to such empirical examination. First, there are large 'n' quantitative cross-national diachronic analyses of overall levels of public expenditure, social transfers and tax takes in advanced economies. This allows us to identify broad patterns and regularities in evolving welfare provision. Second, in-depth qualitative analysis of a small number of countries or social programmes provides more fine-grained understandings of particular welfare trajectories. The combination of the two can generate a fuller picture – tackling that trade-off noted on p. 286 – between knowing 'less about more' and 'more about less'.

Beginning with the quantitative 'bigger picture', we analyse overall social spending levels and welfare provision in the advanced economies in recent decades. Obviously, as noted above, there are issues about *what* you measure and *how* you measure which will shape the story that gets told. Overall spending levels are not a perfect indicator of social welfare effort, or what Chris Pierson calls 'the character of any given welfare state' (C. Pierson 2006: 172). Nevertheless, charting aggregate spending provides a useful starting point. Furthermore, the relative ease of access to such data means corroboration from many scholars, making it easy to draw some relatively firm conclusions from a brief literature survey.

Cameron's analysis of the public economy's expansion in the decades following World War II finds that 'revenues of public authorities [in advanced capitalist economies] have increased dramatically – to a point where they are now equivalent to one-third to one-half of a nation's economic product' (1978: 1243). Substantial increases in government transfers to help the sick, the elderly, the unemployed and the poor in the post-war world account for this evolution. International economic integration is identified as an important catalyst: 'nations with open economies were far more likely to experience an increase in the scope of public funding than were nations with relatively closed economies' (ibid.: 1253). Partisanship is another key causal factor, with welfare states growing more under left-wing governments. Size also matters: 'larger nations with more closed economies experienced relatively modest increases in the scope of public economy compared to the smaller nations with open economies' (ibid.: 1254).

Garrett, though a proponent of the compensation thesis, nevertheless accepts the logic of capital mobility tightly constraining government economic and social policy-making. He employs cross-national quantitative analysis of government expenditure and deficit levels for 16 OECD countries between 1967 and 1990 to unearth how far welfare provision has been eroded. His findings support the compensation thesis and reveal considerable national variations in expenditure. Governments enjoy more room to manoeuvre than is generally appreciated (1995, 1998). Work deploying data up to the mid-2000s corroborates this picture (Obinger and Wagschal 2010).

Rodrik's analysis reveals a rise in public expenditure from 21 per cent in the 1930s to 47 per cent of GDP by the 1990s. Increases in social spending and especially income transfers drove this government expansion; this was 'particularly striking in countries such as the United States (from 9 to 34 percent), Sweden (from 10 to 69 percent), and the Netherlands (from 19 to 54 percent)' (1997: 49). Rodrik's analysis of 23 OECD countries during the 1990s also unearths an 'unmistakable' and 'robust positive association across countries between the degree of exposure to international trade and the importance of the government in the economy' (ibid.: 51–2). Greater openness does indeed mean bigger government spending: 'societies that expose themselves to greater amounts of external risk demand (and receive) a larger government role as shelter from the vicissitudes of global markets ... the welfare state is the flip side of the open economy!' (ibid.: 53). Extending the analysis beyond advanced economies, for 115 countries Rodrik finds a partial correlation (controlling for other determinants of government size) between openness and government size. However, in lower-income countries, government spending comes in the form of consumption, not social security and welfare. Rodrik finds 'a remarkably tight empirical association between openness to trade and government consumption' (ibid.: 52–3).

Swank's extensive systematic analysis explores the relationship between increasing financial openness and liberalization and levels of public spending, welfare spending and taxation across advanced economies since the 1970s. He finds no evidence that increased capital mobility is 'systematically associated ... with retrenchment in social welfare provision'. Indeed, contrary to convergence and 'race to the bottom' predictions, 'two dimensions of international capital mobility – borrowing on international financial markets and liberalization of capital controls – are actually positively and significantly related to total welfare spending' (2002: 86). Swank finds ongoing macro-economic room for manoeuvre and widely different levels of public expenditure and social provision. Thus 'internationalization has not resulted in large, systematic rollbacks of social welfare effort' (ibid.: 89). Swank's account is nuanced, noting that deficit levels (and how they are perceived in international bond markets) are a crucial contextual variable affecting the degree of government spending constraint. In short, when budget deficits become high, capital mobility engenders cuts in social welfare effort (ibid.: 94).

Thus, despite the dramatic shifts in political economic ideas, structures and international conditions charted in this book, the compensation thesis still applies. Iversen also finds 'no evidence of any broad-scale retrenchment of the welfare state' (2001: 45–8). These findings are corroborated by many studies: for example, Janoski's analysis of levels of spending on active labour market policies (1994) and Hicks' analysis of the social democratic corporatist model of economic performance (1994). Looking at advanced economy welfare states since the 1970s, Huber and Stephens find that 'not only have the cuts in entitlements and service in all but a few cases [notably the UK and New Zealand] been modest, the achievements of the welfare state in terms of income equalization and poverty reduction have largely been preserved, despite increased levels of unemployment' (2001b: 306).

Some contest the causal interrelation between openness and welfare state growth (Iversen 2001, 2005; Gatti and Glyn 2006: 303), but most comparative political economists agree that welfare states – in terms of levels of public (and publicly orchestrated private) social spending – have not been eroded. Kenworthy and Pontusson (2005: 24) identify reductions in generosity of benefits and transfers, but note that 'in most instances these were relatively minor' (see also Huber and Stephens 2001a, 2001b). For all the talk of welfare retrenchment, government spending funded by taxation still creeps up. Welfare state institutions have been remarkably robust, despite the neo-liberal rhetorical onslaught of recent decades. Threats of exit notwithstanding, corporations still pay very large sums in taxation (Swank 2002; Hines 2006).

The broad aggregate story indicates that, for both small and larger states, the amount of public money spent on welfare in advanced economies is not reducing. Hacker notes how US welfare provision, understood as a combination of public and publicly orchestrated private spending, has held up just as robustly as that of other advanced economies (2002). In short, claims that globalization erodes welfare provision by driving all societies towards a residual, minimalist, liberal model of social protection are without empirical foundation in cross-national quantitative analysis.

Thus there is little or no evidence of a race to the bottom, and welfare state convergence assumptions have rightly been questioned (Navarro et al. 2004). If anything, some detect a slight *upward* convergence of social provision (Gatti and Glyn 2006: 307). That said, evidence on social security expenditures and social transfer payments supports the notion of distinctive and enduring welfare regime 'families' (Obinger and Wagschal 2010: 348–52). Government spending and overall taxation levels indicate ongoing diversity, indeed divergence, with Anglo-Saxon and East Asian economies in the low tax, lower social spending bracket; continental 'Bismarckian' and southern European economies in the mid-range; and Scandinavian economies in the high tax, high social spending bracket (Hobson 2003; Perraton and Clift 2004: 205–15; Obinger and Wagschal 2010). While welfare state expansion has ceased, welfare institutions and programmes continue to deliver very substantial transfers of wealth and risk. Welfare states remain integral to advanced 'welfare capitalism', crucial sources of income and well-being for millions, and the principal mechanism for redistributing wealth and opportunities (C. Pierson 2001: 86–9).

Many governments retain relatively generous and partially redistributive welfare states in the global economy (Swank 2002: 271–2), yet it would be wrong to suppose that nothing has changed in the political economy of welfare state provision. The condition of 'permanent austerity' (P. Pierson 2001) is a reality. Even if the overall scale of welfare provision is not being eroded, the nature of welfare provision *is* changing through processes of recalibration and retrenchment. Rising income inequality and stagnating or declining living standards for many lower and middle income groups have been prevalent within 21st-century advanced capitalisms, especially since the GFC.

The different families of welfare deliver very significant differences in distributional consequences. These have remained stable over recent decades (Gatti and Glyn 2006: 308–9). The variety of different welfare regime properties and trajectories among the advanced economies is quite striking: 'differences between the most and least egalitarian OECD countries have been and remain huge ... unexciting sounding differences in Gini coefficients measuring income inequality mask really enormous differences in distributive patterns' (Glyn 2001: 6). Inequality is greatest in the Anglo-Saxon economies, lowest in the Nordic economies, with Bismarckian or continental European welfare states in the middle (Perraton and Clift 2004: 205–9, table 12.1). Yet inequalities are widening across all advanced political economies, spanning the various welfare state 'family' groups. The pace and degree of widening inequalities vary on welfare institutions and other factors – but rising inequality everywhere has adverse implications for the social and political settlements on which liberal market capitalism rests (see Chapter 12).

EMPIRICAL ADJUDICATION: SOCIAL RIGHTS AND WELFARE STATE 'RECALIBRATION'

Overall spending and taxation data can get a handle on the overall size of the welfare state, but it does not tell us enough about generosity of provision. We need to explore the qualitative welfare state changes with a bit more granularity. One approach follows T. H. Marshall, who identified social rights as at the core of a welfare regime (Marshall 1950; Esping-Andersen 1990: 21; Allan and Scruggs 2004; Scruggs 2006; Scruggs and Allen 2006). This apparently obvious observation generates a new take on the welfare retrenchment debates. A social rights perspective addresses generosity of provision and offers more fine-grained evidence of retrenchment (Allan and Scruggs 2004: 496–7).

Evolutions in aggregate spending levels can misleadingly conceal significant changes in the *logic* and *character* of welfare provision (Esping-Andersen 1990: 19–20; P. Pierson 2001: 421; Schwartz 2001: 19; C. Pierson 2006: 172). If the number of claimants increases significantly, then spending levels can increase, perhaps even substantially, while the *generosity* of benefits may be reduced – which surely meets a common-sense notion of retrenchment. This illustrates an important point: methodological choice is not a neutral dispassionate exercise; it may involve adopting an approach which fits the story you want to tell.

Paul Pierson, looking at overall welfare spending levels (which continued to rise in Britain from the 1970s to the 1990s), asserted that Thatcher's reputation for welfare state retrenchment was unjustified (1994). The use of different methodologies to quantify welfare state change has helped generate more nuanced understandings. Social rights approaches capture better the distributional goals and consequences of welfare provision (Stephens 2010). Work focusing on social rights tells a different story and helps to elucidate how welfare state retrenchment can change the logic, and generosity, of a welfare state (Allan and Scruggs 2004; Scruggs 2006; Scruggs and Allen 2006). Sure enough, in Britain under Thatcher,

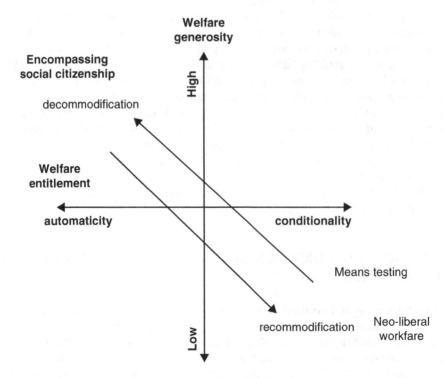

Figure 11.2 Logics of welfare restructuring

unemployment insurance and pensions reduced in generosity, and in that sense there was retrenchment (Esping-Andersen 1990; Scruggs 2006: 352).

Analysing a range of advanced welfare states and looking at social rights to unemployment insurance, sick pay and public pensions, analysed in terms of *replacement rates* and *coverage*, Scruggs assesses levels of benefits, duration of benefits and conditions necessary to qualify for and gain access to benefits. In this way he unearths 'social programme dynamics' with more nuance than crude spending measures can, enabling a more fine-grained assessment of 'welfare state resiliency' (Scruggs 2006: 349–50) and of the qualitative character of welfare provision (for example, in terms of generosity and universality).

The focus on evolving social rights, consistent with the broad aggregate data outlined above, leads Scruggs to reject unambiguously the 'race to the bottom' thesis, but he does unearth 'tangible signs of replacement rate retrenchment in all three [liberal, Nordic and continental] types of welfare states' (ibid.: 355). This retrenchment is greater in the most generous social democratic welfare states. However, 'it is worth noting that all of these (social democratic) countries had higher expected benefits in 2002 than in 1972' (ibid.: 362). The story is a complex one: 'while welfare state programmes are more generous than they were a generation ago, there has been a shift away from expanding entitlements and towards retrenchment' (ibid.). Summarizing a range of studies (C. Pierson 2006; Levy 2010; Hay and Wincott 2012), there have been cuts in levels of benefits and degrees of generosity in a number of cases (Figure 11.2).

A NEW WELFARE CAPITALIST SETTLEMENT?

The 21st-century costs of welfare in advanced economies are increasing, notably because of demographic changes (more elderly people, fewer working-age people) and technological advances in healthcare, which both raise the costs of treatment and mean increased longevity. Since the later 20th century, significant increases in unemployment in some political economies have meant increased dependency on the welfare state, combined with fewer people in work and paying the taxes to support that welfare state (Huber and Stephens 2001b: 305). These combined fiscal, social and demographic pressures are resulting in processes of 'recalibration' and 'recommodification' within welfare state restructuring in the contemporary period (see e.g. P. Pierson 2001 Levy 2010). The GFC and the European 'sovereign debt crisis' (actually a banking crisis) only made matters worse. The resultant deteriorations of advanced economy public finances increased austerity pressures still further. Reductions in social entitlements were seen as a primary means to both rebalance the books and reduce state liabilities (Hay and Wincott 2012; Blyth 2013). In Britain, the Coalition Government from 2010 to 2015 pursued harsh fiscal consolidation – focused overwhelmingly on spending cuts (Gamble 2012, 2014: 47; Lavery 2019: 116; Grimshaw 2013) – and drastically cut local government social services provision. The fiscal adjustment required of Greece, Spain, Ireland and Portugal during the Eurozone crisis also bore down on levels of welfare generosity and social provision (Vaughan-Whitehead 2013; Hopkin 2015; Petmesidou and Guillén 2017; Varoufakis 2016).

Successive governments have wrestled with these dilemmas, trying to deliver budgetary cuts while preserving popular social protection. Recent reforms in many countries have limited entitlements and increased means testing, rather than raising taxes, to cope with the funding shortfalls. The institutional organization of social protection is also changing, with similar patterns of change leading some to argue that fiscal pressures may have resulted in qualitative convergence between welfare states (Schwartz 1994). Reorganization within the state, particularly of welfare provision, has seen operational responsibility in some cases increasingly devolved to local levels, while control over spending becomes increasingly centralized and strict. NPM (see pp. 103–4) reforms increasingly introduced markets and quasi-markets, applying market efficiency structures and criteria to a widening range of welfare services provision. Illustrating the core political economy insight introduced in Chapter 2 about the interpenetration of state and market, welfare reforms have entailed increased 'marketization' of public services and social provision through 'contracting out' and increased private-sector involvement.

States can also require citizens to take out additional private health insurance or pension provision. Introducing direct competition for service provision with private-sector providers (for example, inviting private-sector actors to run state schools) and forms of quasi-competition between agencies have been part and parcel of the transformation of the welfare state. These reforms seek to diffuse welfare pressures by limiting the power of consumer and producer interest groups while strengthening the power of those state actors holding the purse strings. Rules-based fiscal policy regimes can also 'depoliticize' retrenchment and insulate policy-makers seeking to reduce spending (Schwartz 1994; Burnham 1999; Perraton and Clift 2004: 212). Such attempts to cut and contain costs and shift some of the financial burden of welfare provision off the public debt book began first in Anglo-Saxon economies such as the UK and New Zealand. Subsequently they have been undertaken in the Scandinavian social democratic heartlands, such as Sweden and Denmark (Glennerster 2010; Streeck 2017).

Arguably, a new political economic settlement is being reached within welfare capitalism, just as an 'embedded liberal' settlement was attained in the post-war period (Ruggie 1982). Yet the underpinnings of an emergent settlement involve less redistribution, higher levels of inequality, lower living standards, activation and recommodification. Rather than unconditional citizenship entitlements, more benefits are conditional upon recipients' behaviour or resources, for example means testing, requirements to be actively seeking work, or even 'workfare'-style obligations to undertake work in return for benefits. Through these and other mechanisms, contemporary welfare provision relies on returning citizens to the labour market to meet their needs. As such it is more unstable, not least because it lacks political support among large swathes of the population (see Chapter 12).

Esping-Andersen's classic study was organized around the notion of decommodification, yet this is ill-suited to capturing the marketization of welfare state provision that is proceeding apace across the advanced welfare states. The new political economy of welfare is more market conforming than the post-World War II 'golden age' of welfare. Its logic involves a greater reliance on recommodification, which means restricting 'the alternatives to participation in the labour market either by tightening eligibility or cutting benefits' (P. Pierson 2001: 422). The changing societal context and preferences have generated attempts to 'adapt social policy arrangements to the radically transformed interfaces between market, state and households' (ibid.: 427). For example, unemployment has not been the hammer blow to welfare states that many anticipated, in part because increased *male* unemployment has been offset by the increasing feminization of the labour market as patterns of family/work balance have changed in recent decades.

This emphasis on recommodification, returning citizens to the labour market or keeping them there for longer, is perhaps the key shift in the 21st-century welfare state settlement. Central to this is 'activation', seeking fresh employment after periods of sickness or inactivity (Kenworthy 2010; Hemerijck 2010). As Esping-Andersen himself notes, activation policies are not adequately captured by his central concept of decommodification (2000; Stephens 2010). Improving activation incentives operates through reforms to provision of employment services, or trying to increase demand for low-skill workers through targeted subsidies and 'making work pay' through work benefits. Similar activation-oriented or 'employment-centred' social policies were enacted throughout Europe and beyond in the 1990s and 2000s (Vandenbroucke 1999, 2002; Bonoli et al. 2000; Bonoli and Powell 2004), including in Denmark (Campbell and Pedersen 2007), France (Clasen and Clegg 2003), the Netherlands (Green-Pedersen et al. 2001) and Portugal (Costa Lobo and Magalhaes 2004: 91–2).

This emphasis on 'active' welfare spending, seen as an investment which contributes to human capital formation through education and training, has become widespread. Offering individual training and guidance and opportunities to improve skills are further common phenomena in welfare state change (see e.g. Hemerijck and Ferrera 2004). Jessop, informed by neo-Marxist Regulation School thinking, has talked of the 'Schumpeterian workfare state' superseding the 'Keynesian welfare state' (1993). Whether a new form of state has emerged is contested, but there is considerable evidence of a common direction of travel in welfare state restructuring. Activation measures often work out cheaper for governments than unemployment benefit.

Reforming pension systems to make them more fiscally sustainable can also involve activation, since one key goal is keeping citizens in the labour market longer by raising the retirement age and lengthening the contribution periods which secure eligibility to full pensions. Keeping people in work longer is seen as a good thing, not just for the public accounts and the national economy, but for the people themselves. Another recurrent theme is achieving cost savings in pension and health reforms by de-indexing entitlements (de-linking from inflation), reducing public-sector generosity and finding new ways to fund caring services (for childcare and the elderly). Cost-saving efforts, especially in pensions and healthcare, can lead to *de facto* rationing of provision (Hay and Wincott 2012).

The common trends towards activation should not, however, be seen as evidence of convergence. Partly, this is because of institutional path dependency within extant welfare families. In Sweden, the activation logic has always been integral to its welfare model. Active labour market policy, including retraining and assistance with job placement, was at the core of the Rehn–Meidner model developed in the 1950s (Kenworthy 2010; Rehn 1985). Thus a common turn towards activation is refracted through different institutional and ideational national settings and legacies. Nordic states long attuned to activation contrast with Bismarckian welfare states heavily predicated more upon passive welfare spending. In France, for example, early retirement schemes in the 1980s addressed unemployment by taking large numbers of potentially active citizens out of the labour market (Levy 2000, 2001). Turning the tanker of the French welfare state around and plotting a course towards activation has been difficult, though some success has been achieved (Milner 2001).

In general, Nordic welfare states spend similar amounts to continental (Bismarckian) welfare states, but the Nordics invest much more heavily in service provision and in human capital formation, skills, training and education, including higher education and activation policies (Iversen and Stephens 2008; Stephens 2010: tables 35.1, 35.2). This helps to explain the superior economic performance of Nordic welfare states and why retrenchment within European welfare states is distributed differently across welfare state clusters. Significantly for debates about welfare states in the 21st century, the liberal model is not alone in (fairly) successfully navigating the choppier waters of increasing economic interdependence. The (more generous and more egalitarian) Nordic model is faring well, too.

'Bismarckian' welfare states, by contrast, face greater pressures. Esping-Andersen describes their predicament as 'locked into a self-reinforcing negative spiral' (1996: 68; see also P. Pierson 2001: 445–56; Hay 2006: 9–13; Sapir 2006; Palier 2010; Palier and Thelen 2010). On a more optimistic note, Manow demonstrates how the 'social democratic corporatism' of post-World War II European welfare was, in hindsight, 'just one way to combine an open economy with a generous welfare state'. The Keynesian welfare state 'does not exhaust the source of potential linkages between domestic welfare and a liberal trade regime'; he posits a 'continental compromise between external openness and internal compensation' (2001a: 163) as one contemporary viable variant.

Even with a common direction of travel, social policy and labour market institutions retain their distinctiveness. Welfare state recalibration is an exercise in what Campbell calls 'bricolage' or 'translation', 'the combination of locally available principles and practices with new ones originating elsewhere' (2004: 65). As one looks closer, it becomes clear that commonalities of direction of travel mask widely divergent starting points (Hay 2004a, 2006) and differential degrees of commitment to activation. The result is differences in how much of the pre-existing (protected, less reformed) labour market remains and variation in the relative importance of 'new' activation-oriented contracts and programmes. Social minima, welfare programmes and labour market institutions continue to differ widely.

The Danish case is an exemplar of hybrid welfare state forms emerging within recalibration. Danish 'flexicurity' policies retain strong redistributive commitments alongside increasingly flexible work contracts and practices, with institutional decentralization of wage bargaining. There are three core elements. Firstly, there is limited private-sector employment protection (e.g. hiring and firing) and thus high job mobility. Secondly, there are generous universal unemployment, health insurance and other welfare benefits. These were increasingly tied to employment seeking, though levels were reduced and eligibility restricted in the 1990s. The levels of benefits remain comparatively high, even post-retrenchment (Scruggs 2006: table 1). Thirdly, there are extensive retraining and new skills acquisition opportunities, as well as assistance in locating new employment opportunities (Campbell and Pedersen 2007: 316–9). This model's combination of welfare generosity with an 'activating' state role has attracted admiring interest from other European countries with high unemployment.

Yet the new welfare 'settlement' may lack sufficient political and social support to endure (see Chapter 12), not least because 'replacement rates [are] declining ... [and] the conditions for receiving unemployment (and pension) benefits are becoming more stringent' (Allan and Scruggs 2004: 501). There may be further upheaval as governments and other social policy actors seek to wrestle with dilemmas over the welfare demands of their citizenry, the challenges of complex economic interdependence and the fiscal stresses they face. One thing is clear: while welfare states are restructuring, they are certainly not dismantling. There is less redistribution in the new welfare state settlement, though there is still plenty. Paul Pierson identifies three processes of change: 're-commodification, cost containment, recalibration' (P. Pierson 2001: 421). Different degrees of priority for each are accorded by 'families' of welfare regimes, with liberal ones focused on recommodification, continental ones on recalibration and cost containment, and Scandinavian ones on cost containment (ibid.: 427).

CONCLUSION

Cross-national comparative studies, both large N quantitative and small n qualitative, reinforce the picture of distinct welfare state 'families' of social policy provision in advanced governments with traceable trajectories. The differences between families of welfare regime and national social models have as yet not been eroded, and these welfare regimes remain *very* distinctive and clearly discernible in terms of taxation, spending and welfare outcomes (Glyn 2001; Swank 2002; Gatti and Glyn 2006); this despite globalizing pressures, 'permanent austerity' and common fiscal strains caused by demographic changes, and compounded by the GFC and Eurozone crises and their fiscal implications. Levels of societal inequality continue to vary, even if inequalities are widening across all early 21st-century advanced political economies (see Chapter 12).

Variety within the emergent new welfare capitalist settlement illustrates how the impact of globalizing forces on welfare state governance involves the complex interplay of endogenous and exogenous pressures. Reshaping the political economy of welfare state provision involves 'domestic' ideational and institutional variables playing a key mediating role. External influences on welfare states are refracted through national institutions: different aspects of welfare expenditure face different pressures and have distinct constituencies of support (Perraton and Clift 2004: 221).

The broader conception of welfare regime and 'welfare capitalism' facilitates appreciation of the multifaceted complexities of the processes of welfare restructuring and its politics. It also enables making the necessary connections between the political economy of welfare and comparative capitalisms. Appreciation of the embeddedness of state/market relations in a social context, of path dependency and institution complementarities, and of the interaction of the welfare state and the wider institutional matrix of capitalism all point to complex, configurative causation and contingent explanations. Even if globalization were the driver of welfare state change, and many deny that it is the prime suspect, the effects of economic globalization are mediated (and indeed contested) by states.

In terms of the gendered underpinnings of welfare state settlements, some progress has been made from the old 'male breadwinner' model towards the more gender-equitable 'dual earnership' model in many societies. However, the CPE of welfare is yet to escape the 'falsely universalizing (implicitly masculinist) analytic frames' of most welfare state analysis. Nor has much CPE analysis of welfare restructuring done enough to explore and challenge 'the gendered underpinnings of systems of social provision and the specific situations of women' (Orloff 2010: 253) within processes of recalibration and recommodification.

In this chapter I have argued that globalization is not driving a convergence in welfare state models, institutions and provision. While tax regimes have become flatter and less progressive, there remains scope to defend redistributive welfare programmes. The likely future trajectories of welfare states will involve cross-fertilization and hybridization of national social models. Amid recalibration and retrenchment, a new political settlement is emerging within advanced economies, whose welfare state regimes (of different family backgrounds) are all pushing recommodification and driving citizens into the labour market where possible. Furthermore, declining generosity and retreating redistribution struggle to offset the unequal outcomes inherent within capitalism. As we explore in the next chapter, the increases in inequality resulting from this new welfare 'settlement' threaten the very foundations of the liberal capitalist order, eroding the political and social support on which the system rests.

12 Inequality and the Political and Social Settlement Underpinning Advanced Capitalisms

INTRODUCTION

Widening inequalities within advanced economies are a notable feature of 21st-century capitalism. These inequalities have been especially pronounced among lower and middle income groups, and this has fuelled the disaffection which was readily mobilized around issues of 'globalization' and the 'losers' from it. The super rich, or 'the 1 per cent', were becoming much richer (Piketty 2014), extracting ever more exploitative monopoly rents from their economic activity. Meanwhile the rest of society, 'the 99 per cent', saw themselves as losing out (Milanovic 2016; Crouch 2019). The rising power of the largest corporations allows them to divert increasingly egregious amounts of income from ordinary workers and society at large to shareholders and top executives (Hager 2018; Hager and Baines 2020). As the 'Panama papers' and similar financial scandals have amply demonstrated, tax evasion, tax avoidance and illicitly squirreling away enormous wealth in shell companies in tax havens are rife. Fractured by these widening inequalities, the social and political underpinnings of liberal market capitalism, under strain for decades, began to pull apart in the early 21st century.

In this chapter we explore the drivers and dynamics of this inequality, and the increased strain it has placed on both the liberal institutional order, and the social and political settlement on which capitalism rests. Economic accounts of rising inequality tend to focus on globalization and technological change as the main drivers (for a review, see Hager 2018: 6–12). Yet this focus struggles to account for differential outcomes in political economies subject to similar pressures, suggesting certain blind spots in economistic assessments. The discipline of economics, in isolating economic processes, interactions and dynamics from their social, historical and political context through a series of simplifying assumptions (see Chapter 4), often neglects important social and political aspects of the reality of a capitalist market order. One of this book's key lessons is that the economy should not be studied in isolation from its political and social context.

CPE scholars readily appreciate that capitalism rests on a social and political settlement – entailing acceptance of the existing political economic order. A central insight of CPE analysis underscores how significant institutional infrastructure is needed to sustain any national 'model' of capitalism. Things like minimum wage regulations, labour market policies and institutions, company law and corporate governance norms, the degree of progressivity of tax regimes, and the nature and character of the welfare state are crucial intervening variables between global pressures and national distributional outcomes. The fact that economic orders rest on social and political foundations illustrates some of the core political economy insights, outlined in Chapter 2, on which this book repeatedly insists. Markets are not naturally occurring, but are better conceived as political constructs, and as resulting from political struggles over processes of market-making. Thus important roles are played by power and by politics in shaping and determining the institutional configuration and distributional outcomes of capitalism (Korpi 1983; Stephens 1979). These institutional and other factors profoundly affect the division of wealth across society in different political economies (see e.g. Glyn 2001; Hager 2018; Huber and Stephens 2014).

This chapter focuses on how any economic order of market relations, even one oriented towards freer markets and very limited state intervention, rests on a social and political settlement; that is, a broad acceptance within society and the political system of the underlying principles of political economy upon which that particular variant of capitalism is forged. This can encompass a range of aspects of how economy and society are ordered, including the levels of taxation (Scheve and Stasavage 2016) and social provision; how the fruits of growth are distributed within and across society; and how firms are constituted and regulated. During periods of relative stability, this political and social settlement becomes so taken for granted as to be almost invisible. A sense prevails within political debate that it could not be otherwise. The post-war 'embedded liberal compromise' (Ruggie 1982) is one good example that we explore further below. This compromise integrated elements of different traditions, notably international liberalism and economic nationalism, to forge a new capitalist order predicated upon domestic political economic interventionism.

In this chapter we use the comparative method – both synchronically (comparing different cases over the same time period) and diachronically (comparing a case or cases at different points in time) – in order to understand better the drivers and dynamics of contemporary capitalist inequality. Diachronic comparison across time throws into relief another core insight of political economy: that capitalism is a dynamic, not a static system, and that economic orders, and their social and political underpinnings, can and do change. A good example is provided by contrasting the common-sense understandings of how national political economies and the global economy should be ordered in the post-war era with the contemporary period. The assumptions about a supposedly settled liberal international order, and about the social and political foundations of national political economies, are periodically radically disturbed, even overturned.

After a brief summary of contemporary developments, we explore how evolutions in power relations within globalizing contemporary capitalism have affected the social and political settlement upon which it rests. Ever since Marx, political economists have appreciated that political power is linked to economic might – what some Marxists call the structural power of capital. This highlights how the owners of wealth can exploit the political system to their advantage and secure policies and regulations that increase their wealth at the expense of others. This structural power of capital (Przeworski and Wallerstein 1988), much focused on in various forms of Marxist analysis (see e.g. Arrighi 2010; Cox 1987; Bonefeld et al. 1992; Boyer and Saillard 2002), is ongoing and enduring within modern capitalism. Yet it interacts with contingent shifts in the political economic and institutional context.

The chapter excavates the back story of rising inequality through consideration of the embedded liberal compromise of the post-war era, and how that morphed under the New Right into 'dis-embedded neo-liberalism' from the 1970s onwards. The social fabric and political economic underpinnings of the old post-war 'embedded liberal' compromise, and its political settlement, had been eroding since the 1970s. Arguably the terms of that 'compromise' were renegotiated in the 1960s and 1970s with the ascendancy of the 'New Right'. Trade liberalization and increased capital mobility following the break-up of Bretton Woods advanced the globalizing push towards economic openness. The scope for domestic interventionism and insulation from the ravages of international market forces was scaled back. The 'dis-embedded' neo-liberalism of the 1980s and 1990s differed in crucial respects from embedded liberalism. Under dis-embedded neo-liberalism, economic growth in the advanced economies was no longer built upon full employment policies. New forms of precarious, low-skilled, short-term employment became a much more prominent feature of the labour market. The economic growth that episodically occurred was not delivering broad-based benefits for all of society (Bourguignon 2015; Milanovic 2016; Crouch 2019: 23–48).

This historical context prepares the ground for theorizing the rise of inequality, and understanding how and why it has risen still further in the wake of the GFC. The chapter explains how the general trend within late 20th-century/early 21st-century advanced capitalisms was rising inequality levels (Piketty 2014; Bourguignon 2015; Milanovic 2016). Yet identifying that wider trend misses national variation and differentiation over time. Analysing particular stories and trajectories, one sees a highly differentiated picture in terms of timings, patterns and drivers of rising inequality, shaped by political, societal and institutional factors (see e.g. Nolan 2018; Hager 2018).

TRUMP, BREXIT AND THE BACKLASH AGAINST LIBERAL MARKET INTEGRATION

Dis-embedded neo-liberalism provided a conducive context for delivering increasing economic benefits to the very affluent (Hacker and Pierson 2010; Hopkin and Lynch 2016; Hopkin and Shaw 2016; Hager 2018; Hager and Baines 2020). Embedded liberalism had promised what Lane Kenworthy termed 'jobs with inequality' (2008). By the early 21st century it was increasingly clear to larger swathes of the population that this was not being delivered. The sustained non-inflationary economic growth from the mid-1990s to the mid-2000s was celebrated as 'the Great Moderation' by self-congratulatory neo-liberals. New Classical economist Robert Lucas famously claimed that economics as a science had solved the problem of depression prevention (2003). Hubristic central bankers like Alan Greenspan, and politicians such as Gordon Brown, thought they had ended boom and bust and resolved capitalism's contradictions, and that their economic management would deliver enduring stability.

Obviously, the crash of 2008 punctured all that self-congratulatory nonsense. Yet perhaps the politically salient critique of the Great Moderation was less that it was built upon a hubristic myth that economic stability was now a permanent feature of capitalism. The more fundamental issue was exposed by asking the classic political economy question: *cui bono?* Or: 'who benefits?' The Great Moderation from the 1990s to 2007 had, in fact, *not* been great for large swathes of lower and middle income groups in society whose living standards, wages and future economic prospects were stagnating. Meanwhile enormous wealth was being created around them. For example, Jacobs and King highlight how the US Federal Reserve's prioritizing of price stability over employment (despite having a mandate to pursue both) increased US inequality (2016: 3). Milanovic's work underlines 'the diverging economic trajectories of people in the old rich world versus those in resurgent Asia ... the great winners have been the Asian poor and middle classes; the great losers the lower middle classes of the rich world' (2016: 20).

The rising inequality in 21st-century advanced capitalisms is a broad and common trend. Milanovic's famous 'elephant' graph shows gains or losses in real incomes across the global income distribution since the late 1980s. For most of the global population, significant real income gains were accrued. However, lower and middle income citizens of advanced economies are the only group whose real incomes have stagnated (2016: 3). In the same time period the top 1 per cent of global earners, nearly all living in these same advanced economies, have seen their wealth skyrocket upwards (2016: ch. 1, fig. 1.1; see also Forster and Nolan 2018: 12–14). Recent empirical work in CPE and economics has charted how the very top tenth, hundredth or thousandth of the income distribution is becoming vastly more wealthy (Atkinson 2015; Piketty 2015; Nolan 2018: 4–5; Milanovic 2016; Bourguignon 2015).

The widening of inequality within advanced capitalism needs situating in relation to the politics of austerity (Blyth 2013; Clift 2018). The periodization of 'austerity' can be helpfully understood on two timeframes. Firstly, it is conceived by some as one of 'permanent austerity' (Pierson 2001) under what we are calling in this chapter the dis-embedded neo-liberalism of the 1980s and 1990s, when welfare state retrenchment began in earnest in advanced economies (see Chapter 11). The Anglo-Saxon economies pushed hardest on both spending cuts and welfare retrenchment. The UK's majoritarian political system had earlier given Thatcher in the 1980s scope to sweep away the prior consensus and alter the welfare state settlement.

More pointedly, the post-crash politics of austerity saw a more truculent debt and deficit discourse which argued more aggressively that societies in advanced economies were 'living beyond their means'. This implored that scaled-back public spending, reduced social provision and a smaller state were an urgent necessity so that governments could cut the cloth to suit their purse (see Blyth 2013; Taylor-Gooby et al. 2017; Burton 2016; Gamble 2014; Schafer and Streeck 2013). In the UK after 2010, Conservative politicians David Cameron and George Osborne, although part of a coalition administration, came in with a strong commitment to change economic and social policy, pare down on public provision, reduce the size of the state and scale back welfare (Keegan 2014; Gamble 2012; Grimshaw 2013; Hopkin 2017; Hopkin and Shaw 2016). This post-GFC period of public-sector restructuring and squeezing public finances had important effects on the distributional consequences of advanced capitalism (Vaughan-Whitehead 2013).

The policy responses to the GFC only exacerbated the iniquitous tendencies of advanced capitalisms. In the wake of the crash, austerity policies cutting back welfare and public service provision became more firmly entrenched. This 'doubled down' on welfare state restructuring, which had been reducing the generosity of provision since the 1980s and 1990s (see Chapter 11). As a result, inequality levels soared even higher. It took time for the political repercussions of the GFC, and the inequality-exacerbating austerity policies that followed it, to be felt. It led in due course to a backlash against globalization and the liberal order (Crouch 2019; Gamble 2019).

One expression of disaffection at these political economic outcomes was resurgent populist politics in many countries. Seismic shifts in politics and political economy such as the rise of Donald Trump and the Brexit vote shook mainstream politics to its foundations. 'Patriotic' politicians (often themselves members of the global 1 per cent of super rich) mobilized and exploited the disaffection and dislocation of the 99 per cent, advancing a xenophobic agenda. They took against the 'globalists' and criticized selected aspects of international capitalism, notably freedom of movement and liberal immigration policies. These political economic shockwaves unleashed 'beggar-thy-neighbour' policies and jingoistic antagonism reminiscent of the inter-war years. Trump's strident 'America First' agenda saw increased protectionism and a protracted and acrimonious trade war with China. Meanwhile, Britain's diplomatic relations with European trading partners became frostier and decidedly more rancorous. Successive British Prime Ministers threatened a 'no-deal' crash out of the EU, which would entail greatly increased trade frictions and the UK abandoning numerous international agreements.

Ever since World War II, within advanced economies the norms and institutions of liberal markets had enjoyed acceptance nationally and internationally. The backlash against globalization called all that into doubt because many felt so 'left behind' within American and European societies. They were ready to question, and vote against, the familiar liberal promises that relatively open borders, expanding free trade and economic liberalization would deliver a tide of future and ongoing prosperity which would float all boats. Whole regions across Europe and North America begged to differ, bearing as they did the deep and unsightly scars of the de-industrialization that had re-shaped advanced economies from the 1970s onwards.

A changing international division of labour and alterations in global production networks saw heavy industries migrate away to far-flung parts of the world. The mines and factories had shut down long ago, but in many of these regions public policies had not intervened to facilitate economic adjustment and regeneration. The service industries that emerged to replace some of the manufacturing failed to develop or flourish in the regions hardest hit by de-industrialization. What new economic activity there was did not seem to require the skills of, or offer opportunities to, large swathes of the population. Regional inequalities grew and deprivation became entrenched. Those with low or moderate skill levels had to accept low wages and precarious working conditions (Crouch 2019: 32–3). Donald Trump in America, Marine Le Pen in France, Nigel Farage and Boris Johnson in the UK, and Matteo Salvini in Italy all found that their populist, nativistic and xenophobic messages resonated with these regions and groups. Promises to 'take back control' and to bring back jobs to the US rustbelt, or to de-industrializing parts of Europe, were seductive. Yet, as we shall explore later in this chapter, in failing to acknowledge the complexities of governing 21st-century economic interdependence, such posturing to restore 'control' was dubious, even duplicitous (Crouch 2019: 44–6). Nevertheless, the Brexit vote and the rise of Trump questioned, suddenly, the political settlement on which the economic order had been based (Gamble 2019). The political economic upheavals of the early 21st century revealed capitalism's social and political foundations to be vulnerable and unstable.

THE EMBEDDED LIBERAL COMPROMISE AND THE COMPARATIVE POLITICAL ECONOMY OF RISING INEQUALITY

Political economy scholars were somewhat blindsided by this backlash which arose in the liberal heartlands of the US and the UK – societies and political economies steeped in what Polanyi termed 'the liberal creed'. In order to understand how it came to this, it helps to explore how evolutions in power relations within globalizing contemporary capitalism have affected the social and political settlement on which it rests. This underlines the importance of another core CPE insight (Chapter 2), the crucial interaction of the domestic political economy with its international context. We use the comparative method to unearth this interaction by comparing *diachronically* over the second half of the 20th century. The relationship between capitalism and inequality had distinct characteristics and outcomes under the post-war regulated international liberalized market order which obtained between the 1940s and the 1970s. This changed during the 'dis-embedded liberalism' period from the late 1970s onwards due to legislative and regulatory changes that opened the door to higher and rising levels of economic inequality within advanced capitalisms. An international context of international capital mobility and light-touch regulation entailed increased 'exit' options for capital and more opportunities for tax avoidance or evasion. This increased the power of wealth holders (Cerny 1997a, 1997b; Crouch 2019: 33) and affected tax competition, reducing state capacity to tax capital (Streeck 2014; Hager and Baines 2020).

The assumptions of the post-war 'embedded liberal compromise' (see Chapter 7) suggested that advanced economies and societies accepted the expansion and deepening of market liberalization inherent in global capitalism. This was partly because the economic growth and employment this generated enabled governments to fund relatively extensive social provision and protection, limiting societal inequality. Thus, in theory, the whole of society could consider themselves 'winners' from the post-war capitalist order. Of course, such an interpretation ignores deep inequalities of gender (see pp. 5–6, 88–91, 132–3, 231–4, 299) and race that persisted and pervaded these societies. These were instantiated through the male breadwinner welfare state model, or through immigration policies and societal norms which sustained racially stratified labour markets. While it ignored these important injustices, the embedded liberal compromise did limit some kinds of inequalities. The 'social purpose', as Ruggie put it (1982), underpinning the political economic order embraced ideas of (some forms of) solidarity and collectivism, such that it was seen as the legitimate role of government and the state to seek to reduce certain social and economic inequalities. The post-war consensus on economic policy accepted a mixed economy, extensive trade union rights and redistribution through relatively high levels of progressive income tax – used to fund the welfare state. Broadly speaking, limiting inequality was seen as integral to economic efficiency on the assumption that 'fair is efficient'.

The fulcrum of the 'embedded liberal compromise' was a new institutionalized and regulated international legal settlement arrived at following World War II. Susan Strange referred to a 'more conscious effort at international management' of the global economy, whereby 'for the first time in history the governments of the leading economies had agreed on a set of rules, on a system of collective management' of the world economy (Strange 1994a, 1994b: 53, 55). Bretton Woods was an effort to avert the extremes of both nationalism and liberalism. As Ruggie put it, the new order sought to 'safeguard and even aid the quest for domestic stability without, at the same time, triggering the mutually destructive external consequences that had plagued the interwar period'. The 'compromise' Keynes and others crafted at Bretton Woods contrasted with both 'the economic nationalism of the thirties' and the 'liberalism of the gold standard and free trade' (1982: 393).

The thinker Ruggie evoked to capture the essence of the compromise was Karl Polanyi (see pp. 33–6, 86–8, 112, 142–5, 151, 162, 183, 230–1). His book *The Great Transformation* had done so much to deepen understanding of the interaction of the domestic and the international spheres in political economy analysis. Polanyi underlined the importance of compatibility and congruence between domestic policy regimes and the international sphere, and wrote starkly of the dangers to domestic political economies and societies of untrammelled international market forces. Economic relations and market activity must, he felt, be 'embedded' in the social order; otherwise 'human beings would perish from the effects of social exposure' (Polanyi 2001 [1944]: 76). Polanyi identified numerous shortcomings of the dominant economic ideas of 'the liberal creed' and presciently anticipated the hugely damaging environmental consequences of free market capitalism: 'Nature would be reduced to its elements, neighbourhoods and landscapes defiled, rivers polluted' (Polanyi 2001 [1944]: 76). *Laissez-faire* could 'not exist for any length of time without annihilating the human and natural substance of society' (Polanyi 2001 [1944]: 3). Thus the ultimate market failure of capitalism was that unfettered market operations would destroy the social order in which they are embedded.

At both the national and the international levels, society had, in short, to be protected from 'acute social dislocation' and 'the ravages of this satanic mill' (Polanyi 2001 [1944]: 76–7). For Polanyi, the 19th-century gold standard era, and efforts to revive it in the interwar years, illustrated the point. The return to the gold standard and freer movement of capital led to the Great Crash of 1929, and thereafter the Great Depression. The levels of inequality generated in the 1930s proved too great for society and the political systems in some advanced economies to bear the strain. The crash and its aftermath provoked policy responses of protectionist economic warfare between major economies, and political crises. This sowed the seeds of rising fascism, culminated in World War II and indicated the prescience of Polanyi's insights into embeddedness.

In Polanyian terms, there was – at the Bretton Woods conference towards the end of World War II – a conscious desire to 're-embed' (international) economic relations in the social and political context from which they became dangerously 'dis-embedded' in the first half of the 20th century. The new international order was, to a novel degree, 'multilateral in character', since this new economic policy regime was underpinned by the IMF, World Bank and other international economic institutions (Ruggie 1982: 393). It was a world away from what Polanyi called the 'pernicious nineteenth century dogma of the necessary uniformity of domestic regimes within the orbit of world economy' (Polanyi 2001 [1944]: 262). To avoid repeating the mistakes of freeing up markets too far and fast and failing to intervene to prevent a protracted slump, the post-war embedded liberal compromise was 'predicated upon domestic interventionism' (Ruggie 1982: 393). This carved out policy space for national governments to deliver a degree of social protection and economic stabilization, preventing inequality rising beyond socially bearable limits (Table 12.1).

THE RISE OF THE NEW RIGHT AND THE DECLINE OF EMBEDDED LIBERALISM

The particular balance between principles of political economy the 'embedded liberal compromise' struck was important for how capitalist growth was reconciled to reducing or limiting inequalities. On the one hand, there was a commitment to liberal international markets, especially in trade, but also facilitating international investment and capital flows. Furthermore, the founding agreements contained commitments to go further in liberalizing economic flows, reducing barriers to capital mobility and increasing trade flows as the regime developed. Yet – at the same time – the new political settlement created the domestic policy space and scope for national governments to pursue economic and welfare policies.

Table 12.1   Political economic orders and inequality

Epoch	International order	Dominant orthodoxy/ economic policy paradigm	Forms of state	Inequality in advanced economies
19th century – World War I	Gold standard Free trade Imperialism	Polanyi's 'liberal creed' *Laissez-faire*	Liberal state No safety net	High and rising
Post-war era – 1940s–1970s	Bretton Woods Pegged exchange rates Regulated (liberalizing) capital flows Trade liberalization	Embedded liberalism Keynesian demand management (full employment)	Keynesian welfare state	Moderate and reducing
1980s– 21st century	Globalization and deregulation High capital mobility Ever freer trade International division of labour	Dis-embedded neo-liberalism Monetarism and the New Right (low inflation, fiscal conservatism)	Competition state (Cerny)/ consolidation state (Streeck)	High and rising

These shielded citizens from some of the deprivations and hardships that befell vulnerable social groups during economic crises in earlier periods. Economic adjustment to changing international economic conditions had in the past often proceeded via deflation, recession or economic crisis.

Keynesian economics provided a rationale for redistribution of wealth to those poorer groups in society with a higher 'marginal propensity to spend' (i.e. they tend to spend what money they receive on meeting their immediate needs rather than saving it). This boosted aggregate demand in ways that had positive knock-on effects on confidence and economic activity that were good for the overall economic well-being of the nation (Glyn 1995). Reducing inequality seemed to be harnessed to the goal of securing prosperity. The apparently virtuous circle had 'worked' in a regime of mass production and mass consumption characterized by the French Regulation School of political economy (see pp 63–4, 177–8, 191–3) as the 'Fordist' regime of accumulation. The improving living standards of the working class were sustained by wage rises which were in turn enabled by increasing productivity. As wage claims accelerated, but productivity improvements failed to keep pace, this virtuous circle, and the wider regime of accumulation, began to unravel. The rapid growth rates of the 'Golden Age' of post-war capitalism came to an end in the 1960s amid rising industrial unrest. The alignment of pursuing greater equality and pursuing national prosperity came increasingly into question.

The embedded liberal compromise did not prove as stable as its originators might have hoped. The stresses and strains grew, notably after the move to convertibility of sterling with the dollar after 1958. As capital mobility increased, the bargain of accepting liberal globalization in return for rising living standards and insulation from international market forces began to break down. As growth faltered and stagnated, economic crises struck and economic policy problems increased, including flagging productivity, rising unemployment and rising inflation. This generated not only economic but also societal and political tensions. With the break-up of Bretton Woods in 1971, as the US Government 'closed the gold window' and effectively brought the managed international monetary system to an end (see pp. 10–11, 39, 206–8, 250–1), liberalized global market forces became less constrained by transnational law and regulation. The two oil crises of the 1970s dramatically increased the costs of production, and this only added to the economic difficulties faced by advanced economies.

The scale and speed of capital mobility had been rising sharply through the 1960s, resulting from the liberalization commitments within the initial Bretton Woods agreement. With the system's breakdown in the 1970s, the spectre of those social dislocations that Polanyi warned of was resurrected. In this febrile context, the neo-liberal 'New Right' rose to prominence, championing a different set of principles of political economy. Power within the political economy shifted from labour to capital. One indicator of this was that the proportion of added value accruing to capital increased substantially, at the expense of labour. Profit margins increased at the expense of wage earners within firms. The ideational reflection of the rising power of capital and the diminishing power of organized labour was a neo-liberal economic orthodoxy championed by Margaret Thatcher in the UK and Ronald Reagan in the US (King 1987; Gamble 1988). Domestic economic policy regimes such as increased progressive taxation or Keynesian 'demand management' to secure full employment were no longer the order of the day. The new priorities were keeping inflation down, freeing up markets and fiscal conservatism, notably curtailing state social spending. This was the economic policy agenda *par excellence* of wealthy holders of capital, and it became the cornerstone of sound economic management (Hall 1993; Blyth 2002a; Hay 2001; Clift 2020).

In the UK, the emergent Thatcherite settlement from 1979 onwards was a straw in the wind of how capitalism and state market relations were changing. It heralded an acceptance of the dominant role of free markets, and of modest state intervention and lower levels of taxation. Following the neo-liberal prescriptions of Hayek and others, unions were disempowered and systems of collective bargaining came under threat. As unions' rights were curtailed, their capacity to pursue the wage claims of their members was reduced (Walker 2014; Glyn 2001). Wage growth slowed or stagnated in many advanced economies and unemployment rose. Freeing firms from the shackles of social and other obligations and reducing regulation were prioritized. This policy programme, it was assumed, would provide a spur to entrepreneurialism that would revive the economy.

This all had major implications for the social and political settlement on which capitalism rested. Over time, Thatcherism altered what was considered acceptable in terms of the distribution of wealth and levels of inequality in society (Gamble 1988; Hall and Jacques 1983). The ideas informing New Right 'social purpose' were a far cry from the solidarity and collectivism of embedded liberalism. Individualism was the guiding principle of neo-liberalism. Thatcher, after all, famously declared that 'there is no such thing as society'. Her premierships delivered a growing divide between rich and poor, and her Governments' policy and discourse espoused a revival of Victorian notions of the undeserving poor – ideas that shaped her welfare reform agenda (Lavery 2019). This 'broke the post-war consensus on the structural causes of poverty and replaced it with individual explanations'. In the process it also 'blamed the poor for their poverty' and demonized 'dependency' (Walker 2014: 283).

The old Keynesian and embedded liberal notion that policies actively reducing inequality were good for the economy overall was overturned. As Thatcher put it in 1975, 'the relentless pursuit of equality' had caused 'damage to our economy' (quoted in Walker 2014: 283). Channelling the ideas of Hayek (see Chapter 4) and others, the neo-liberals argued that government intervention was harmful, instead favouring freeing up markets, and through that entrepreneurialism and economic dynamism. This would benefit national economic prosperity through its unleashing of individual economic potential.

Neo-liberalism entailed a different balance between state and market as compared to the post-war 'embedded liberal' order. Privatization of many industries saw a redrawing of the boundaries between public and private sectors. Governments in pursuit of welfare retrenchment even privatized public service provision, and introduced more market mechanisms such as 'contracting out' and increased competition for service delivery (see Chapter 11). This evolution in 'the role played by the state in shaping markets', as Mark Thatcher points out, altered 'the nature of the state' (2017: 179). The policies pursued changed the nature of the mutual constitution of state and market. These direct and indirect forms of market-making and market-shaping became conspicuous features of a new settlement. This political economic vision so pervaded society that, by the 1990s, parties of the mainstream Left – such as New Labour in the UK – had largely accepted the parameters of this neo-liberal policy agenda.

DYNAMICS OF INEQUALITY WITHIN 21ST-CENTURY CAPITALISM

The previous section used comparison across time to reveal how the political economic ideas underpinning capitalism can evolve over time. In this section the comparison is between countries. This returns us to one of the core insights of political economy developed in Chapter 2, how markets are embedded in specific social, political and historical contexts. The comparative method of CPE makes it possible to see more clearly how, in different national settings, the sedimented common-sense understandings about the appropriate approach to inequality differ and have diverse effects. This results in part from the different institutional constellations on which capitalism rests, which in turn reflect varied state traditions (see Chapter 7) and societal settlements around welfare provision (see Chapter 11). We can compare the array of national conceptions of social rights and entitlements, and of the appropriate role of the state in society, and see how these inform a variety of welfare regimes and economic policies. Such differing conceptions underpin, for example, 'Nordic' as compared to 'Anglo-Saxon' capitalism. The Scandinavian societies in the post-war era prioritized limiting social inequality, with higher personal and corporate taxation rates, very extensive public services and generous welfare provision. This contrasts with the prevailing view of minimum social standards, acceptable levels of taxation or the reach of the state into the lives of ordinary citizens underpinning 'Anglo-Saxon' capitalism in the UK or the US.

Societies developed differing conceptions of social rights and varied levels of generosity of benefits. They also had different social norms about how the fruits of growth should be distributed. Approaches varied as to what social and other responsibilities firms should be called upon to carry out in return for, for example, the privilege of limited liability afforded to joint stock companies. There were, in short, different views on what 'price' capital should be expected to pay for the benefits that it enjoyed from operating under the embedded liberal compromise. These benefits to capital were extensive and wide ranging, including

Table 12.2 Factors shaping inequality in the institutional framework of capitalism

Form of state	Social norms	Institutions	Policies	Firms	International economic relations
Neo-liberal state/ Keynesian welfare state	Extensive or minimal social rights	Individualized or collective bargaining; business lobbying, regulatory capture	Progressive or regressive income tax	Stakeholder or shareholder	Regulated (embedded liberal) or deregulated (dis-embedded neo-liberal)

massive state investment in infrastructure and education, the provision of stable conditions for investment and state-directed breakthroughs in research and development, to name but a few (Table 12.2).

Thus the widening inequality dynamics within contemporary capitalism outlined at the beginning of this chapter were refracted through the institutions of welfare capitalism (see Chapter 11) and mediated by state interventions (see Chapter 8) – which varied according to different national histories and trajectories. The development and evolution of these institutions, and the broader political economic norms underpinning them, were the subject of political struggles and contestation. Power and politics, as well as technological change and globalization, are key to explaining widening inequalities (Hager 2018). The changes in inequality levels therefore progress at different paces, affecting different parts of the income distribution in different countries (Hopkin and Lynch 2016: 336–7). For example, inequality is rising in all advanced economies, but is especially pronounced in the US and the UK – though the explanations as to why differ in important respects (Hacker and Pierson 2010; Hopkin and Shaw 2016). Furthermore, the timing of episodes of rising inequality also differs in different political economies – the rise occurring earlier for New Zealand and the UK, while it came later for Nordic countries.

These differences in how rising inequality plays out show the 'footprints' of the different social settlements and national negotiations of the appropriate institutional framework of capitalism. In recognition of national differentiation in the patterns of inequality, some argue that it is more helpful to see what is happening as a 'sequence of episodes' rather than a 'broad trend' (Atkinson 2015; Nolan 2018: 15, fig. 2.2; Forster and Nolan 2018). As Hager's exploration of the variety of explanations for variations in top incomes across advanced economies shows, these matters are multicausal and complex (2018). For Hager, public policies such as income tax rates matter, but so do a range of other social and political factors. These include corporate governance and power relations within the firm, the strength of unions within the political economy, the extent of financialization and the degree of prioritization of shareholder value norms (see 118, 196, 200–3, 207–11). Finally, political institutions (such as lobbying opportunities and veto points within the policy process) play a key role in shaping the distributional outcomes of capitalism. These political factors either facilitate or block tax and regulatory changes that suit the interests of very wealthy citizens and very large powerful companies (Hager 2018).

This level of complexity, and the array of intervening variables, suggests limits to the generalizability of findings from any one case study. There are grounds to suspect we should not generalize too widely from recent US experience (Hopkin and Lynch 2016; Hager 2018). Nevertheless, the evolution of the US political economy since the 1980s provides one salient example of a political economy of widening inequalities (see e.g. Eisner 2011: ch. 7; Solimano 2016: 98–110; Kenworthy 2018). Considering the US experience from a variety of perspectives broadens our understanding of the political drivers and evolving power relations shaping widening inequalities and US capitalist development.

Hacker and Pierson's account of *Winner Takes All Politics* tells a compelling story of rising inequalities resulting from the political power of the very wealthy. The US political system, and the role that money, campaign contributions and lobbying play within it, enabled wealthy corporations and individuals to shape tax and regulatory regimes and policies in their interests (2010; see also Lindsey and Teles 2017; Hager and Baines 2020). Financial deregulation fuelled the growing political power of financial interests, which triggered further deregulation and liberalization.

The SSA School (see pp. 174, 177, 191–3) offers a Marxist interpretation which takes some inspiration from the French Regulation School. SSA accounts identify widening inequalities as rooted in inherent class contradictions and antagonisms within US capitalism. Class-based power relations pit different fractions of capital against each other (notably with finance capital winning out over industrial capital), but more pervasively the US bourgeoisie exploits the US proletariat (Kotz et al. 1994; McDonough et al. 2010; Coates 2000: 41–2). Other scholars have, from a slightly different neo-Marxist perspective, highlighted the shift of value added from capital to labour in the US of the 'Golden Age' up to the 1970s, with the wealth of the top 1 per cent reducing (from 30 per cent of overall wealth in the 1950s, down to 22 per cent in the mid-1970s). This process then went into reverse. With the erosion of union power and the prioritizing of price stability (low inflation) over full employment in the neo-liberal era, class politics and the social relations of production shifted. By the late 1990s the top 1 per cent owned almost 40 per cent of national wealth (Duménil and Lévy 2002: 58).

Shifting economic orthodoxies and the rise of the New Right influenced the policies that transformed the distributive outcomes of US capitalism. Neo-liberal theories such as 'trickle-down economics' and 'supply-side economics' gained prominence under the Reagan administration. These favoured regressive low tax regimes allowing entrepreneurs to retain more of their wealth. Policy programmes took inspiration from ideas like the 'Laffer curve', which argued that if you reduced taxes on the rich as far as possible, it would unleash dynamism and entrepreneurialism which would substantially improve the economic health of the nation (Eisner 2011: 122–3, 128–31; Scheve and Stasavage 2016).

Hacker and Pierson's excellent analysis takes, perhaps, a rather narrow view of political power. Their view of 'organized combat' by extremely wealthy groups capturing the US political system through lobbying (Hacker and Pierson 2010) is largely rooted in what Lukes calls the first face of power. This is a behavioural approach focused on directly observable, demonstrably exercised power within the decision-making process: A makes B do something they otherwise would not have done (Lukes 1974; Hay 2002: 171–2). Other scholars analysing rising inequality do not confine their attention to 'narrow and specific acts of "organized combat"' (Hopkin and Lynch 2016: 339), but rather embrace a more encompassing view of political power. The 'second face' of power is agenda-setting power (Bachrach and Baratz 1962, 1963; Lukes 1974), which is broader and more complex. It includes the power of 'non-decision', or the capacity to set the agenda for the decision-making process in such a way that certain options are not even considered. This conception of power is focused on informal agenda-setting processes often outside formal political institutions (Hay 2002: 174–8). To this Lukes added a third face of power: preference-shaping power – such that people 'accept their role in the existing order of things, either because they can see or imagine no alternative to it, or because they see it as natural or unchangeable' (1974: 24; Hay 2002: 178–82).

Hopkin and Lynch (2016) foreground how 'economic elites can enjoy ever greater shares of income without actually having to act' (2016: 339–40). Their analysis deploys structural conceptions of power close to Lukes' second and third 'faces' (Lukes 1974). Comparable insights and views on power also underpin the neo-Marxist scholars discussed above. For constructivists, too, emergent common-sense understandings of appropriate state/market relations or appropriate economic policy which develop within society have a significant influence on political economic outcomes (see e.g. Rosamond 2002). This can close off policy options or trajectories of development in ways that recall Lukes' third face of power. These power dynamics were important in how the crash of 2008–9 was interpreted, and how this affected widening inequalities (Table 12.3).

Overall, the US case indicates the key role of ascendant neo-liberalism – at the levels of dominant economic ideas, of public policies and of state/market relations – in driving widening inequalities. The main policy outcomes of the New Right were much lower taxes for high earners (Scheve and Stasavage 2016), reduced union power and much lower levels of regulation of the financial sector (Hacker and Pierson 2010; Gourevitch 2013: 254). The growth of the financial services sector was a key source of increasing inequalities of wealth and power. That said, inequality had been rising in the US before the onset of financial deregulation. The origins can be sought in the period following the demise of the Bretton Woods system. David Coates identifies the 'erosion of the American dream' in the 1970s and 1980s as US growth faltered relative to key international competitors such as Japan. For individuals and their families, the wealth gains enjoyed by the post-war 'baby boomers' came to an end as Americans worked longer hours and society became more unequal (Coates 2000: 24–5; Gilbert 2018; Kenworthy 2018). Lower and median US incomes stagnated. The living standards of ordinary Americans did not improve even as the US economy grew more strongly in the 1990s (Coates 2000: 25). The trajectory of US capitalism as income inequality grew inexorably was summed up by Coates as 'a constellation of long hours, stagnating wages, low productivity and diminishing international competitiveness' (2000: 27).

These sections have explored how comparison across time and across cases can deepen understanding of the causes and consequences of widening inequalities within advanced capitalism. In the next section, the focus shifts to how the GFC and its aftermath affected inequality.

Table 12.3 Lukes' three faces of power and the politics of inequality

	Modes of power	Mechanisms and forms of power	Examples
1st face	Direct, behavioural, observable	Legislative lobbying for policy outcomes	'Organized combat'
2nd face	Indirect, structural, 'non-decision', agenda-setting	Structuring decision-making processes	Shaping the tax policy debate
3rd face	Structural, indirect, preference-shaping, acceptance of status quo	Socialization; dominant ideas close off policy options	Construction of economic crisis and response

THE GLOBAL FINANCIAL CRISIS, THE POLITICS OF AUSTERITY AND RISING INEQUALITY

The relationship between inequality and the GFC is interesting and complex. One theory identifies rising levels of inequality within advanced capitalism as an important cause of that crisis. Lysandrou focuses on the asset management industry and the proliferation of extraordinarily complex and opaque yet risk-filled financial services products such as collateralized debt obligations (CDOs). These became ever more significant parts of portfolios for advanced economy investors as immensely wealthy individuals looked for more ways to store and increase their wealth. This became a key driver of the GFC, which was, after all, triggered by non-performing 'sub-prime' loans bundled up in these CDOs. The overnight collapse in the value of these and many other complex, 'securitized' financial assets had very far-reaching and destabilizing consequences (Lysandrou 2011: 324; see also Gamble 2009; Crouch 2009; Skidelsky 2018; Tooze 2018; Helleiner and Pagliari 2009: 277–9).

When considering the implications for inequality of the GFC, one aspect that stands out is the prescience of a point made by constructivists and other ideationally attuned scholars (see Chapter 7) such as Andrew Gamble, Colin Hay, Mark Blyth, Vivien Schmidt, Andrew Baker and Wes Widmaier. How a political economic crisis like the GFC gets constructed and narrated is far from self-evident, but it is hugely consequential and politically significant. The GFC and Eurozone crises, and the recessions that followed in their wakes, mattered not only for what these events did to inequality levels, but also for how these crises were politicized, and how policy responses to them were discursively constructed.

The reason why the inequality issue came to such a head in the 2010s was not simply the occurrence of the GFC, but more specifically the macro-economic policy responses to it. Selecting crisis policy responses of public-sector cuts and other austerity policies increased social and political tensions. Firstly, the policies pursued arguably prolonged and aggravated the 'Great Recession' (Skidelsky 2018; Wren-Lewis 2011, 2019). Secondly, the huge burden of major economic adjustment to the crash and the Great Recession was not equitably shared. The poor, the vulnerable and the 'squeezed middle' (Parker 2013; OECD 2019) had to bear much of the strain. This ratcheted up already high levels of income inequality even further.

Consistent with the overarching arguments of this chapter, and indeed this book, austerity policies and the politics of 'fiscal squeeze' (Hood et al. 2014; Hood and Himaz 2017) played out differently in different societies. Some governments placed more emphasis on reducing government spending than on raising taxes, thus cutting more deeply into welfare state provision. We have already seen how, from the 1980s onwards in Anglo-Saxon economies, the increases in inequality proceeded faster and further than in many other societies (Nolan 2018). The US and the UK were also the bastions of financial capitalism, countries where the financial deregulation that drove the GFC was most advanced. In the UK, the financial sector was particularly large and important for the economy. It had always generated significant income for the state through taxation. This meant a double whammy whereby the bailouts of stricken financial institutions had to be especially large, and at the same time the collapse in financial sector activity had a particularly sizeable adverse effect on tax revenues and the public finances.

In 2010, the incoming Coalition Government in the UK branded the GFC 'New Labour's debt crisis', misleadingly implying that fiscal profligacy and excessive public spending before the crisis were the root cause (Gamble 2012, 2015; Hay 2013; Lavery 2019). The real reason why the public finances in advanced economies had deteriorated was that recession and credit crunch hit levels of economic activity, and therefore tax revenues, hard. As in any downturn, social spending goes up (on things like unemployment benefits) while government revenues go down. This is the normal working of the 'automatic stabilizers' limiting the cyclical fluctuations of the economy. Added to this, governments had bailed out troubled yet vast financial institutions. These had been trading in cavalier fashion in securitized fictitious financial commodities which neither they – nor anyone else, it seems – fully understood. Certainly, none of them could readily gauge, as the crisis hit in the autumn of 2008, their levels of exposure and liability arising from their portfolios. This activity massively increased systemic risks within the financial system, effectively making a broader collapse of capitalism more likely. As President Bush put it in a late-night crisis meeting seeking to avert the collapse of the US economy in September 2008, 'this sucker could go down'. The socialization of these banking risks was seen as necessary to avert such a systemic collapse, but the effect was to raise public debt levels sharply. This was especially true in the UK, but it applied more widely.

In the context of the heated post-crash politics of austerity, rather than laying the blame at the door of excessive risk-taking by 'too big to fail' banks, the crisis was interpreted as the 'fault' of a supposedly over-extended state. In what Blyth terms 'the greatest Bait and Switch in Modern History' (2013: 73–4), in its aftermath the GFC was construed, some might say re-invented, as a crisis of *public-sector* debt, not one of banking and financial system failings and private-sector debt. Yet most of these supposedly fiscally profligate states had enjoyed relatively healthy public finances in the pre-crash period. It 'followed' (if you followed the multiple steps in a rather convoluted and problematic train of reasoning) that states had to reduce deficits and debt as a matter of the highest priority. Doing so in the midst of a recession is contrary to a substantial body of economic reason, as many pointed out (Wren-Lewis 2011; Skidelsky 2009, 2014, 2018), but their objections were overlooked. The Coalition Government elected in the UK in 2010 seized the opportunity to attempt to scale back the size and scope of the state (Gamble 2012, 2015), resurrecting a rhetoric of balanced budgets and fiscal discipline which harked back to the Treasury view of the inter-war era (Morrison 2016). As Miroswski put it: '*Never let a serious crisis go to waste*' (2013). Ideas of the undeserving poor re-entered British political discourse (Lavery 2019; Stanley 2016a) and operated as a bulwark to the government's swingeing public-sector cuts. The importance of asset ownership in determining distributional outcomes (Piketty 2014) meant that those who were not, for example, homeowners struggled the most (Finlayson 2009; Watson 2010).

The cuts in public spending and services presented by the Coalition Government from 2010 onwards as a 'necessary' response to deteriorating public finances could, of course, have been interpreted differently (see Clift 2018: ch. 6). For one thing, restoring the public finances could have proceeded via increased taxes, or by attempting to nurture growth and live with the gradual and incremental paying down of debt. This approach, reputable bodies such as the IMF advised, would be appropriate for some countries (see e.g. Ostry and Ghosh 2015). Instead, the UK Government discursively constructed the economic problems facing Britain as a crisis of debt, rather than a crisis of growth (Hay 2013; Lavery 2019; Green and Lavery 2015; Stanley 2016b). The focus, therefore, was on cutting public expenditure and austerity policies. The extent to which it was based on spending cuts – and the scale of the cuts – rather than tax rises was a matter of political choice, not economic necessity. Many see austerity as having unnecessarily prolonged the recession (Wren-Lewis 2019).

Constructing the crisis in this way had powerful political effects in advanced economies already living with the legacies of decades of dis-embedded neo-liberalism. Higher levels of precarious employment, and increasingly iniquitous distributional outcomes, had already been fraying the social fabric for years, especially in Anglo-Saxon economies. Coming on top of this, the post-GFC austerity policies took a heavy toll. What economic growth there had been in the UK had become increasingly socially and geographically uneven since the 1970s. This 'precariousness in deindustrialised low growth areas' only increased as austerity policies continued (Hay and Bailey 2019: 7). The GFC and its after-effects were not, however, confined to the Anglo-Saxon economies. Similar patterns of de-industrialization and regionalized deprivation were found in other advanced economies.

In another powerful act of discursive construction, what was more accurately a banking crisis in the Eurozone beginning in 2010 was constructed as a sovereign debt crisis. This ignored the fact French and German banks' risky overseas investment strategies caused many of the problems, fragilities and instabilities experienced by the Southern periphery of the Eurozone. Nevertheless, the European 'sovereign debt' crisis was narrated echoing similar politics of austerity themes. Once again, fault was found with the state and with the public sector. The prevailing narrative pitted fiscally prudent Northern 'Saints' against supposedly profligate and feckless Southern 'sinners' (Matthijs and McNamara 2015; Hopkin 2015: 163–5). This ignored a range of other causal factors contributing to the Eurozone crisis, including the flawed structure of European Monetary Union (EMU; see e.g. De Grauwe 2017; Pisani-Ferry 2011; Jabko 2015; McNamara 2015), lacking, for example, fiscal transfer distribution mechanisms which common currency areas normally need.

One might argue that the real problem facing the Eurozone after 2010 was Germany's refusal to inject sufficient economic stimulus to restore Eurozone growth. Yet European authorities, the European Central Bank (ECB) and the European Commission presented the problem as insufficient competitiveness on the part of Europe's Southern political economies. This construction meant that the logical solution was 'structural reforms' to the supply side of these economies in the European periphery (Matthijs and Blyth 2015). Germany and the European authorities pushed a recipe of labour market deregulation akin to the package they had enacted a decade earlier (Jacoby 2015; Newman 2015). This would involve making their labour markets more flexible, their pension systems less generous and their product markets more competitive. Tackling anaemic or absent growth would proceed in this way to restore the competitiveness of these economies.

Many have highlighted the flaws of this recipe to tackle the European crisis and restore economic growth (Clift 2018; Matthijs and Blyth 2015). Pursuing 'structural reforms' as the way to get out of economic difficulties, if it worked at all, would take decades. The timescale of this 'solution' to Europe's economic plight largely served to compound the problems for many social groups struggling in an epoch of precarious de-industrialized growth. Some Keynesian political economists noted the 'demand denial' inherent in an account which only sees supply-side solutions (Wren-Lewis 2011). Germany and the ECB's standard responses to the Eurozone crisis ignore how inequality is especially bad for economic growth (see e.g. Berg and Ostry 2011; Clift and Robles 2020). The one-size-fits-all solution ignores all we know about CPE – and how policies will play out differently according to national experiences, institutional contexts and trajectories. Nevertheless, this was the strategy pursued to restore Europe's economic fortunes. On the European continent, as in the Anglo-Saxon economies, rising inequality and unemployment and stagnating or declining living standards befell large sections of society. Austerity was overlain on top of the legacies of earlier de-industrialization, aggravating patterns of regionalized deprivation. This undermined still further the social and political settlement upon which liberal market capital rests.

Both these constructions of crisis – the GFC as a 'crisis of debt' rather than a 'crisis of growth', and the Eurozone as a 'sovereign debt' rather than a banking crisis – indicate the structural power of capital. These discursive constructions, and the responses they led to, served the interests of the major financial institutions. In both the GFC and the Eurozone, the 'too big to fail' banks *had* to be saved by governments and central banks. The potential adverse consequences to the wider economy of allowing them to go under – the threat of another Great Depression or similar – were just too daunting to contemplate. The political and market power of these large banks meant they were able to ensure that responses to the crises bailed them out and bought up many of their tarnished assets (Clift 2012; Jabko and Massoc 2012; Woll 2014). This was unpopular, but governments faced with sizeable systemic risks and perhaps even the threat of financial systemic collapse saw no alternative. This all indicates the limits of state capacity and power to manage aspects of contemporary capitalism, and the difficulties of securing social and political support for the existing order.

THEORIZING RISING INEQUALITY AFTER EMBEDDED LIBERALISM

To recap the story, and refresh some of the core insights of political economy running through this book, the international context of domestic political economy crucially shapes the evolutionary trajectory of capitalism. Thus the demise of the embedded liberal compromise and the rise of dis-embedded neo-liberalism help explain the new politics of inequality. This distinctive international political economic context unleashed new pressures, and perhaps pathologies, within capitalism. Secondly, as CPE scholars consistently underline, capitalism must be analytically located within its social and political context. Capitalism is embedded in particular institutional and ideational conditions, and these sustain national differentiation such that, as Gamble puts it, 'capitalism need not be a single fate' (1999: 144). Thirdly, state/market interactions involve a mutual constitution of state and market. This evolves and shape-shifts over time. Understanding the nature and contours of this mutual constitution is crucial for a deeper grasp of contemporary capitalist dynamics. Inspired by these core insights, CPE scholars have developed fresh theoretical reflections to explain rising inequality in 21st-century advanced capitalisms (Figure 12.1).

One interpretation is the rather downbeat analysis of Wolfgang Streeck, who has taken a keen interest in the sources and consequences of the increasingly heavy debt burdens of many advanced economies (2014). He identifies a generic trend across advanced economies as governments and societies have struggled to manage the political economic pressures wrought by rising inequality levels and higher unemployment. Streeck's account of 'the crisis of democratic capitalism' in some ways updates earlier classic analyses of a *Fiscal Crisis of the State* developed by Marxian political economist James O'Connor in the 1970s (1973; Streeck 2014: 3). This analysis in some ways anticipated the crisis of Keynesian social democracy and the rise of the New Right. O'Connor explored the difficulties capitalist states were experiencing performing two crucial (yet contradictory) functions: 'accumulation' (ensuring capitalist firms make profits and the economy grows) and 'legitimization' (securing societal and financial market acceptance for the prevailing regime). Capitalist states struggle to secure the conditions for 'profitable capital accumulation' and 'social harmony' simultaneously, because capitalist growth increasingly aggravates inequalities of wealth and

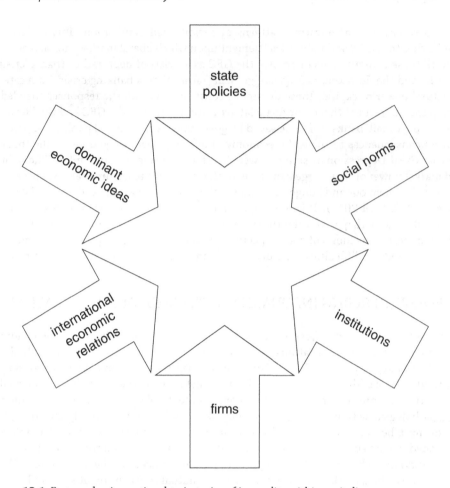

Figure 12.1 Factors shaping national trajectories of inequality within capitalism

power (O'Connor 1973: 6). Streeck's analysis offers a comparable interpretation of endemic increases in public borrowing, reducing taxation capacity and the rise of the 'debt state' (Streeck 2014, 2016, 2017; Hager and Baines 2020: 5–7). This new state form emerged in the 1980s and 1990s, in the period termed by Paul Pierson 'permanent austerity' (2001; see Chapter 11). This led to successive cuts in social welfare and other forms of public provision. Vulnerable social groups such as the young faced higher unemployment and widening inequalities. Often, what employment could be found was increasingly precarious.

Streeck highlights the steady ratcheting-up of public debt within the OECD economies since the 1970s, interpreting this as a new type of fiscal crisis of the state. Factors such as rising inflationary pressures (some caused by wage demands) and decreasing productivity led to rising unemployment in the 1980s. This put fresh burdens upon welfare states and various forms of state provision. Meanwhile, increasingly internationally mobile capital could exploit tax competition dynamics to secure lower corporate and income tax rates, reducing the state's capacity to raise revenue, especially from corporations and wealthy individuals (Hager and Baines 2020). Increased expenditures and reduced revenues put states in a double bind, spurring neo-liberal reforms and increasingly marketized social provision.

Other scholars have similarly linked the dismantling of the welfare state and the concomi-tant rise of private debt in advanced economies (Soederberg 2014). As a result of these policy dilemmas, public deficits and debt began to increase, a key facet of the advent of Streeck's 'debt state' (Streeck 2014: 47–96).

Advanced economy states took on increasing levels of public debt to prop up a struggling political economic regime. Yet this created dilemmas for governments, because at the same time, in a 'dis-embedded neo-liberalism' era of globalized financial markets, states had to maintain their credibility with bond market participants. Those buying up the government bonds, and hence funding these increasing public debt levels, welcome the opportunity to purchase relatively safe assets. Yet they require assurances 'that their sovereign debtors are in a position to comply with the terms of their loans, not just economically but politically' (Streeck 2017: 145). Thus bond markets are prone to favour fiscal discipline and sound money over other political economic priorities (Mosley 2003; Sinclair 2005). The 'debt state', Streeck argues, has given way to the rise of the 'consolidation state' as the prevalent regime in 21st-century advanced capitalism, wherein debt and inequality levels have risen in tan-dem (Streeck 2014: 97–164, 2017: 143–6; see also Solimano 2016). The 'consolidation state', Streeck argues, constitutes a new fiscal regime 'with public austerity as the fundamental principle governing the relationship between state and society' (Streeck 2017: 147), con-tributing to greater levels of economic inequality. Key to this fiscal regime is the securing of financial market confidence, something which came under threat for some advanced econo-mies under the increased debt burdens they have borne since the GFC.

This was an important driver behind evolving state/market relations that sought to bring down debts and deficits. One route to financial market credibility was by reducing public provision – hence the advent of the contracting-out of public services and the retrenchment of welfare state provision (see Chapter 11). Meanwhile, within the labour market there was an increasing prevalence of more precarious forms of employment, as well as higher levels of unemployment – some of it increasingly long term. As public provision was cut back, the adverse effects on aggregate demand threatened economic stagnation. The tension within capitalism between accumulation and legitimization identified earlier by O'Connor becomes increasingly acute. In ways which chime with accounts of financialization (see Chapter 10), and Colin Crouch's ideas of 'privatised Keynesianism' (2009), Streeck argues that integral to the 'consolidation state' is the increasing reliance on private household debt to fuel con-sumption and sustain economic growth. Streeck posits a new phase of late capitalist devel-opment, wherein households have had to take on increasing levels of private debt to sustain ailing capitalist growth.

Thus both state/market relations and the political and social settlement on which capital-ism rests look very different indeed under the 'consolidation state' as compared to the post-war embedded liberal compromise. In the 'consolidation state', individuals and families have to provide for their own social protection (for example through private pensions), to make up the shortfall of reduced public-sector provision. Fiscal consolidation and reducing public service provision become structural features of state reform across a range of economies (Streeck 2014: 117–25). Similar dynamics are identified in health (e.g. funding care for the elderly) and education (increasing private education, higher university fees) across some advanced economies. The capacity of the state to tackle inequality is much reduced in the recent period. More fundamentally, the very notion that the state *should* reduce inequality has been undermined. Streeck charts the shift from Keynesian to Hayekian principles. There has been an erosion of government intervention mechanisms (such as demand management economic policies or capital controls). Corporatist institutions reconciling capital and labour have also been undermined. These were institutions and policies that could limit the rise in inequalities and sustain some variant of the embedded liberal compromise within democratic capitalism. Instead, what has emerged is an approximation, under the consolidation state, of the 'Hayekian blueprint of a liberalized capitalist market economy immune from political pressure' (2014: 110–12).

As this chapter consistently underlines, there are deep tensions within this 21st-century capitalist regime – between what O'Connor termed 'accumulation' and 'legitimization'. Streeck puts this in stark terms of diminished democracy: 'whereas the politics of democratic capitalism was to protect society from the "vagaries of the market" (Polanyi), the politics of the consolidation state protects financial markets from what are the vagaries of democratic politics' (Streeck 2017: 148). The consolidation state leads to increasingly iniquitous outcomes compared to the embedded liberal compromise and the 'Golden Age' of post-war capitalism. There has been an erosion of the social rights of citizens (see Chapter 11). Even in Nordic countries, which were the former bastions of social democratic equality, the attrition of the old social and political settlement is quite far advanced. Sweden has historically been seen as a stronghold of egalitarian welfare policies and a place where protection from the vagaries of the market was extensive. Yet Streeck considered Sweden one of the most advanced on the path towards a 'consolidation state' (Streeck 2017: 151). In this reading, egalitarian social rights and public provision have been thoroughly hollowed out. The consequences of all this for 'legitimization' and political support for the market order are explored below.

WIDENING INEQUALITIES AND THE PARADOX OF NEO-LIBERAL DEMOCRACY

CPE, then, provides a series of telling insights into the sources of widening inequalities within contemporary advanced capitalisms. It helps us understand what drives rising inequalities, and why and how these threaten to fray the fabric of the social and political settlement upon which capitalism rests. The erosion of social rights and declining living standards under the current fiscal regime only increase the difficulties of resolving the tensions between 'legitimization' and 'accumulation' within capitalism (O'Connor 1973; Streeck 2014, 2017; Watson 2005a: 181–6). The consolidation state thesis has at its core not only structural causes of rising inequalities within advanced capitalisms, but also an account of the attenuation of democratic oversight over the management of the economy. The disaffections and frustrations of the poor, the vulnerable and the 'squeezed middle' within advanced capitalist societies seem well founded. CPE analysis of varieties of capitalism and of comparative welfare states, with distinctive conceptions of social rights and varied labour market dynamics, helps us make sense of why and how the rising sense of dislocation takes different forms in a variety of national settings.

The sense of disempowerment among those feeling 'left behind' amid advancing liberal globalization is even more readily understood if we consider how complex economic interdependence and internationalized market exchange are governed, regulated and managed in the modern world. Here it makes sense to return our gaze to the wider global political economy. Specifically, we are interested in the expansion of international institutions, rules, regulations and legal frameworks established to sustain liberal market integration globally.

These institutions built to manage trade, financial and other economic flows are enduring and pervasive features of contemporary capitalism and they have profoundly shaped domestic and international politics. Many of these regimes were first developed in the era of embedded liberalism, but the patchwork has been added to substantially since that system was challenged in the 1970s. National political economies are increasingly interwoven into global capitalism, and the sinews connecting the national and the global are embedded in a range of supranational legal frameworks and agreements. Any one nation's ability to reshape these transnational arrangements is limited at best. This explains why citizens, perhaps even whole societies, feel so disenfranchised by the way capitalism is evolving. International market integration and globalization have brought considerable gains – notably pulling vast numbers of people, especially in societies like China and India, out of abject poverty (see e.g. Bourguignon 2015; Crouch 2019: 25–8) – but this has arguably come at a price. Not only have lower and middle income groups in advanced economies seen their living standards stagnate (Milanovic 2016: 2016: ch. 1, fig. 1.1), but the scope for national democratic oversight and influence over international economic governance processes has been attenuated.

One under-appreciated consequence of the eras of embedded liberalism and then disembedded neo-liberalism is how the rules, laws and institutions needed to sustain and police integrated global markets have curtailed national autonomy and economic sovereignty. In a world characterized by overlapping frameworks of economic governance, national politicians face the 'paradox of neo-liberal democracy' (an idea developed by Colin Crouch), which reflects 'the gap between political debates and decisions, which remain obstinately national, and economic rule-making, which is fundamentally transnational' (Crouch 2019: 46). Thus policy-makers' 'political mandates are to pursue the political economic interests of their citizenry under conditions of complex economic, legal and regulatory interdependence where large parts of economic governance are no longer exclusively within their control' (Clift and Woll 2012a). This results from the overlaying of economic regimes and dense international jurisprudence regulating them in which national economies and governments are enmeshed. These institutions, although mostly multilateral in character, appear relatively impervious to democratic pressures from national citizenries (Figure 12.2).

The weaving together of multiple international regulatory frameworks exerts pressure on national economic policy to comply with supranational economic rules – such as those of the WTO, the North American Free Trade Agreement (NAFTA) or the European Single Market or Customs Union. Aspects like product and process standards, or safety, environmental and labour regulations for goods traded, have to be internationally agreed, recognized and maintained. There are limits that factors like rules-of-origin requirements associated with the European Single Market and WTO membership place on national economic policy-making, and what governments can do about them. These rules extend 'beyond the border' and into domestic politics, affecting competition policy, rules regarding state aid for industries, migration policy, labour law and other politically sensitive areas. For example, the integration of markets and the concurrent weaving together of regulatory frameworks put pressure on advocates of national economic intervention to eschew subsidies, positive discrimination in public procurement and other elements of old-style industrial policy (see Clift and Woll 2012a: 312–4). All this has implications for governments' capacity and autonomy to address the widening inequalities that, as we have seen in this chapter, are a prevalent feature of advanced capitalisms in the 21st century.

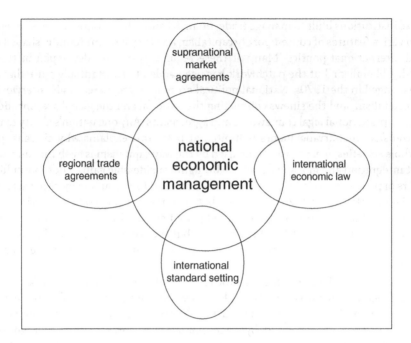

Figure 12.2 The paradox of neo-liberal democracy and the limits of taking back control

The profound if not self-evident contradictions between international market integration and spatially limited political mandates add substantially to the tensions faced by governments seeking to reconcile 'legitimization' and 'accumulation' as inequality levels rise in advanced economies. Policy-makers must seek to address these inequality issues in the context of binding international fiscal agreements and high levels of international capital mobility. All of this makes it harder to resolve the perennial dissonance between interdependent and globalizing economies and national political territoriality. Policy-makers face the increasing complexities of economic, legal and regulatory interdependence and these curtail the scope and capabilities of national economic management (Crouch 2019: 44–8). Such complexities help explain why it can take seven or more years to finalize a new international trade agreement.

The rules of the transnational market order and the disjuncture between international market integration and spatially limited national political mandates are endemic features of capitalism. This is the root of a cavernous gap between promises politicians articulate to their citizens about 'control' over economies and economic outcomes such as growth and jobs, and the much more complicated realities of 21st-century economic governance (Clift and Woll 2012a, 2012b). The GFC and banking crises in Europe brought about new forms of economic intervention, such as the construction of supranational banking resolution mechanisms and more stringent fiscal rules for the Eurozone. These brought the tensions between supranational governance and domestic economic autonomy into sharper focus.

To offer one salient example, the Greek economy after 2010 was in deep crisis, with very little prospect of the economic growth that would make debt repayment a realistic possibility. The tight and harsh conditionality of Troika bailouts, imposed by Germany, the ECB and others, required ever more austerity and public-sector cuts – exacerbating an already dire

Greek economic political and social crisis (Featherstone 2011; Lapavitsas et al. 2010; Lapavitsas 2012). In 2012, as further bailouts were being negotiated, governments and parties fighting a Greek general election were required to pre-commit ahead of polling to maintain the course of macro-economic policy agreed with Greece's international lenders. This despite unemployment at over 20 per cent, no prospect of growth, and inequality, hardship and poverty all at very high levels. In July 2015, the Greeks held a referendum on additional austerity policies that were a condition on a subsequent bailout. The people voted 'no' (61 per cent), but Alexis Tsipras' Syriza government ultimately said 'yes' to the stringent Troika conditions, seeing it as the only way to remain in the Eurozone (and avoid even deeper economic pain; Varoufakis 2017). The Greek population was expected to accept many further years of stagnating living standards and austerity policies. Hopkin characterizes the lot of those on the receiving end of European economic adjustment as 'years of sacrifice with no end in sight' and ongoing 'resilience in the face of a catastrophic and abrupt drop in living standards'. These Southern European countries were 'being invited to stagnate for an indefinite future, while implementing unpopular policies imposed upon them by largely unelected supranational institutions' (2015: 183, 184).

CAPITALISM, INEQUALITY AND THE POPULIST POLITICS OF 'TAKING BACK CONTROL'

It is not hard to see how populist politics rejecting the existing order could gain ground under such conditions. Across advanced economies in the post-GFC period, the cleavage of those social groups who felt 'left behind' by globalization was initially politicized by movements such as Occupy Wall Street in the US, the 'Indignados' in Spain, UK Uncut in Britain and the global Occupy movement as the struggle of 'the 99 per cent' against 'the 1 per cent'. These constituted significant 'breaches in the neoliberal political order' (Gamble 2019: 36). Many in those sections of society who felt they were without a stake or a say in the political economic order were mobilized, not least through their social media feeds, by the rise of 'Alt-Right' politicians and other populist movements. Forms of populist politics spanning the political spectrum from Left to Right emerged to challenge the established order – both political and economic. Each in their different way exploited the contradictions of the paradox of neo-liberal democracy and the social and political tensions of widening inequalities. The rise of Trump and the Brexit vote, both appealing to 'left behind' constituencies in varied ways (Crouch 2019: 1–3, 18–48), challenged mainstream political parties and traditional politics. These all form part of 'a wider populist rebellion against globalization and the western international economic and political order' (Gamble 2019: 36) with potentially far-reaching implications. More so than for many decades, contestation and dispute surrounded the relative merits of the liberal capitalist order. Populist and economic nationalist politicians such as Trump, in his nativist rhetorical assaults on 'globalism', exploited this powerful undercurrent of political debate.

The reconfiguration of economic governance and the interdependence of markets outlined above provide the context of the increased politicization of inequality and of the distributional consequences of 21st-century capitalism. The paradox of neo-liberal democracy helps explain the sense that citizens and indeed whole electorates felt unable to challenge and change the international order, even when its rules seem to run contrary to national, regional or some citizens' interests. The sentiment was especially pronounced among lower and middle income groups in advanced economies, those identified by Milanovic and others as the main losers from globalization. The stagnating living standards of lower and middle income groups fuelled 'anti-establishment sentiment' and a broad and deep discontent with capitalism, all of which fed the 'rise of right-wing populism' (Hay and Bailey 2019: 7).

Successive economic crises – from the GFC to the Eurozone crisis to Brexit and US/China trade wars – served only to exacerbate the incongruities revealed in the paradox of neo-liberal democracy, and to scale up these tensions. All these populist politicians and movements claimed to represent those left behind. The Trump Presidency and the Brexit saga unleashed protectionist impulses that generated fresh strains within international trade politics. Beppe Grillo's Five Star movement in Italy rose to power, auguring a much more Eurosceptic and hostile policy approach from one of the EU's largest core countries. In Greece, the populist left-wing party Syriza and the far right New Dawn overshadowed the established parties. Meanwhile, in Spain the populist left Podemos movement rose from nowhere to win 8 per cent support in the 2014 European elections. Spain's territorial debate, especially regarding Catalan independence, also became radicalized amid austerity policies (Hopkin 2015: 178–82).

Yet while these populist politicians fed off the paradox of neo-liberal democracy, they rarely if ever acknowledged the limits of their policy capacity. Instead, they stated unrealistically that they could 'take back control'. The likes of US President Donald Trump or UK Prime Ministers David Cameron, Theresa May and subsequently Boris Johnson consistently avoided acknowledging the inexorable constraints that economic interdependence places on policy and action. These constraints exist even for economic superpowers like the US – they are all the more manifest for more minor players on the global economic stage like the UK. Brexiteers, populist European leaders and Trump all fanned the flames of popular discontent with established politics and economic policy. Many of them also promoted exclusionary nationalistic 'patriotism' and denigrated 'globalism'. The failure by legions of politicians to explain or acknowledge the limits of their control over economic policy and governance increased the pressures on capitalism's social and political settlement.

Assuming away these facts of 21st-century economic life is detrimental to the quality of political economic debate. Le Pen, Trump, Johnson and others talk in demagogic terms, offering simplistic economic policy responses which fail to offer plausible or actionable 'solutions'. Crouch dismisses 'the illusion of economic sovereignty' (2019: 44–6) in a world where compromises have to be made in reaching international trade deals. He underlines 'the impossibility of separating individual national economic efforts from "the rest of the world"' (Crouch 2019: 44). This is because transnational production flows cross national borders multiple times before finished manufactures are ready for sale, such that the import content of exports for many economies is between 20 and 30 per cent. In such a world, erecting protectionist barriers to trade is likely to be an act of national economic self-harm.

The sharing and joint production of economic regulations – as in the European Single Market – is one means to reconcile national politics and global markets. Yet it is seen by some as an affront to cherished conceptions of sovereignty (Crouch 2019: 46). The problem is with outdated notions of sovereignty 'derived from military concepts of earlier centuries'. This ignores that 'in an increasingly integrated world, countries gain from pooling their sovereignty in order to secure transnational regulation of economic forces' (Crouch 2019: 46). Disingenuous promises to 'take back control' ignore these realities and sow the seeds of further disappointments among already disaffected voters and citizens, especially those whose income and living standards have been falling amid rising inequality.

This politics threatens the institutional edifices (such as the EU, WTO, NAFTA and so on) which instil and protect a broadly liberal approach to international economic relations – and have done since Bretton Woods (Gamble 2019). Harking back to a 19th-century-style trade politics, as in the 'Global Britain' blueprint aspired to by hyper-globalist neo-liberal Brexiteers (Daddow 2019; Baker et al. 1993; Seely and Rogers 2019), does not offer a realistic account of what political economic governance looks like within 21st-century capitalism. Trump displays a similar contradictory combination of xenophobic insularity and hyper-global free marketeering. His administration argues for the cutting of red tape and regulations, while also advancing jingoistic appeals to protect American jobs and keep immigrants out to 'make America great again'.

The revival of economic nationalist rhetoric in the mid-2010s was accompanied by nativistic appeals to build walls, strengthen border controls and tighten immigration regimes – and indeed to send 'them' home. Who constitutes 'them' and 'us' varies for different populist projects, since defining the limits of national inclusion is an important part of this chauvinist and xenophobic politics. Yet the complex economic interdependence inherent in 21st-century capitalism involves porous borders and extensive flows of people as well as goods and capital, all playing out within overlapping jurisdictions amid a density of international jurisprudence. The analytical tools of CPE can be applied to contemporary trade politics and debates about national and international economic governance. They reveal how the control promised in this populist discourse is illusory, based on a conception of sovereignty at odds with the way global capitalism works (Crouch 2019: 44–6; Siles-Brugge 2019; Rosamond 2019, 2020).

CONCLUSION

Political and social tensions are generated by the inherent tendencies of capitalism to exacerbate inequalities of wealth and power within and between societies. In understanding the political economy of rising inequality, it pays dividends to focus on the interactions of the international political economic order and domestic economic policy capacities which have long been a focus for CPE analysis. Under the gold standard in the 19th century and in the inter-war period, response to international economic pressure often took the form of harsh domestic deflationary adjustment – with damaging social consequences of recession and deprivation, as analysed by Polanyi and others. The post-World War II institutional context, and the novel economic ideas of the embedded liberal compromise (see Chapter 7), facilitated domestic economic interventionism to restrain instabilities and inequalities. Advanced economy societies accepted the deepening of market liberalization inherent in global capitalism, but had the capacity to mitigate its inegalitarian effects through the building of welfare states and the pursuit of full employment economic policies. Thus in one view, the whole of society could consider themselves 'winners' from the post-war order. Of course, such an interpretation ignores deep inequalities of gender (see pp. 5–6, 88–91, 132–3, 231–4, 299) and race that pervaded these societies. These were instantiated through things like the male breadwinner model and immigration policies selectively admitting a 'Gastarbeiter' underclass of workers that sustained racially stratified labour markets.

A closer CPE analysis reveals how differing national capitalisms (see Chapter 9) and welfare state settlements (see Chapter 11) are institutionalizations of societal negotiations and manifestations of the political and social settlements upon which any capitalist regime rests. This cross-national variance produces a variety of views about the desirable distribution of the fruits of growth within firms and across society (who is 'in' and who is 'out'?). All this generates ongoing political struggles over how best to regulate capitalism. Political contestation on these issues simmered beneath the surface for many years after World War II. This may be because welfare provision, progressive taxation and full employment economic policies kept the scale of inequality within what proved to be socially acceptable limits. With the end of the 'Golden Age' of capitalism, the social fabric and political economic underpinnings of the embedded liberal compromise began to feel the strain. Since the 1970s, as the distributive outcomes of advanced capitalisms became more unequal, they became more contested. One driver of widening inequalities was the steadily increasing economic openness sewn into the fabric of the post-war international political economic order. The tensions that ongoing liberalization generated were felt more keenly as the post-war economic boom faded.

Following the collapse of the Bretton Woods regime, embedded liberalism gave way to an international order of dis-embedded neo-liberalism. The aggressive liberalization and neo-liberal re-regulation pursued by the New Right from the 1980s onwards was an important spur to shifts in wealth and power within advanced political economies. They led to rising inequality, the erosion of workers' rights and an increasing share of value added accruing to capital rather than labour. Tax and regulatory changes enabled the wealthiest in society to retain ever more of their wealth. Meanwhile, real incomes for average workers stagnated and generosity of social provision was eroded amid 'permanent austerity'. De-industrialization and a changing international division of labour fuelled a rising sense of disempowerment and resentment among many vulnerable social groups.

The social fabric of the liberal capitalist settlement was already frayed by the erosion of social rights and of welfare state provision during decades of dis-embedded neo-liberalism. The scale of disaffection was exacerbated further by the post-GFC politics of austerity. In the face of rising advanced economy government debt levels and heightened fiscal pressures, welfare and social provision were whittled down. The social and political settlement upon which capitalism rested was buffeted by rising economic nationalism and populist anti-globalism as Trump, Johnson, Le Pen and others appealed to those 'left behind' by globalization. Yet the slogans of populist economic nationalism did not amount to a coherent economic policy programme capable of addressing these concerns or healing the social fractures.

All these simplistic 'solutions' ignored the realities of the politics of market-making, the density of international jurisprudence and the difficulties of securing a country's economic future within complex economic interdependence, overlapping jurisdictions and international regulatory regimes. As a result, they failed to offer answers to a series of complex and perhaps intractable problems. None faced up to the impossibility of 'taking back control' in many policy spheres, nor to the broader paradox of neo-liberal democracy. The rising level of inequality within capitalism, and the absence of effective policy programmes to mitigate or reverse it, indicate ongoing political and social instability for liberal market capitalism. Populist and economic nationalist disaffections and destabilizations threatened 'to unravel the western economic and political order which has been the framework of world politics for the last seventy years' (Gamble 2019). CPE as a field provides the analytical tools to make sense of these fascinating but deeply troubling complexities. In the next chapter, I consider debates about comparative methods and set out the logic of systematic comparative analysis and research design. This shows how comparative analysis can enhance our ability to apply CPE insights to explore particular aspects of capitalism through systematic scrutiny of themes, issues and cases.

13 The Comparative Method and Comparative Political Economy

INTRODUCTION: DISCIPLINARY POLITICS AND COMPARATIVE SOCIAL SCIENCE

The comparative element within CPE provides both the definitional boundaries of the sub-field and the core analytical resource which generates many of its most important insights. Comparative analysis can help us build knowledge in a number of ways. Firstly, it can provide contextual description of other political economies, thus expanding our understanding of the political economy. As the eminent comparative political scientist Seymour Martin Lipset put it, 'without examining social relations in different countries it is impossible to know to what extent a given factor actually has the effect attributed to it in a single country' (1963: 9–10). Secondly, comparative analysis can contribute to classification and the development of typologies, such as the varieties of capitalism explored in Chapter 9 or the welfare state 'families' in Chapter 11. These help us understand, explain and interpret broader political economic processes. In this way, comparing helps us develop new theories about political economy, or refine concepts which are the building blocks of these theories. The process of comparative analysis also helps us refine the concepts we use when analysing politics, by seeing how applicable they are in other contexts. This improves our clarity and explanation of politics and political economy. Thirdly, comparative analysis enables us to verify or falsify theories. We can check whether political economic generalizations, about welfare state erosion (Chapter 11) or of convergence among capitalisms (Chapter 6) or rising inequality within capitalism (Chapter 12), hold across cases. Thus comparison also tests theories and the hypotheses emanating from them (Landman 2000).

In Chapter 4 we considered the *Methodenstreit*, and how methodological differences between classical political economy and marginalism (and subsequently neo-classical economics) betrayed fundamentally different approaches to the study of political economy. In this chapter, we return to this theme of disciplinary politics and how it shapes choices of method within CPE. In what follows we explore what is 'at stake' in making these choices about methodology, and set out strengths and weaknesses of the various types and forms of comparative political analysis. After all, each type of research has the potential to tell us something revealing and interesting about political economy, and as a consumer of political economy scholarship, one is free to 'shop around'.

A focus on disciplinary politics will draw our attention to numerous assumptions which get made (only rarely explicitly) about how to understand the world around us, how best to go about using the comparative method, and what kind of knowledge the research process generates. These issues usually go under-explained, but it is my argument in this chapter that clear recognition of such issues – especially the choices researchers make over method and the trade-offs involved in those choices – helps comparativists appreciate the merits of the comparative method and get the most out of it. In order to understand how to go about engaging in systematic comparative social scientific inquiry, we need to familiarize ourselves with (selected highlights from) the literature on the comparative method within political science. In the process, we will grapple with some concepts within the philosophy of social sciences so as to understand the methodological underpinnings of different kinds of analysis.

On one side of the methodological debate we explored in Chapter 4 about how to analyse political economy, Ricardo and the Marginalists favoured simplifying assumptions, methodological individualism that assumes rational actors, and parsimonious theorizing. On the other side, Malthus, Marx and the German Historical School favoured historically contextualized interpretive analysis of socially embedded individuals. This debate has never been resolved, and nearly two centuries later some startlingly similar methodological disagreements endure between the 'two cultures' of social scientific research – qualitative and quantitative (Mahoney and Goertz 2006). Below we explore how the two cultures entail different approaches to comparative analysis. Each approach is trying to achieve something different, and we will illustrate these differences to give a flavour of what these complex and ideologically charged disciplinary debates about method hinge on. The fact that so many fine minds have for so long not decisively resolved the debate over method suggests that we should not look for who is right and who is wrong. We agree with Mark Blyth that 'to presume *a priori* that one approach is necessarily better than another is to engage in intellectual imperialism that curtails knowledge rather than adds to it' (2002b: 293). A more constructive approach – adopted in this book – recognizes the merit of various routes into political economy analysis, and appreciates that each generates valid and valuable insights.

Understanding a good deal about what is at stake in the selection of methods is an important precursor to a successful 'methodological pluralist' approach (see also Marsh and Stoker 2002: 311–18). We need to know what each kind of comparative analysis is trying to achieve and the 'health warnings' attached to each, if we are to interpret their findings and draw on their insights appropriately. Later in the chapter, we will consider in greater detail *why* and *how* we might conduct these comparisons and how to think systematically about the *method* and *logic* of comparative inquiry (Ragin 1987; Peters 1998: 28–57). This will prepare us both to engage in this kind of comparative reflection and to understand the implications of the various methodological and research design choices made along the way.

THE BUILDING BLOCKS OF THEORY: EPISTEMOLOGY AND ONTOLOGY

All research and analysis in CPE is rooted in some prior theoretical assumptions, whether it admits it or not. As Menger convincingly demonstrated in critiquing the early German Historical School, 'pure' empirical observation untainted by theory is not a realistic possibility for social scientific inquiry. This ubiquity of theory raises the question: what *is* a theory? A theory is a set of logically internally consistent statements that claim to explain an aspect of (in our case) political economic reality. Statements thus arranged contain concepts or terms important to the statements' making sense. For example, the concepts of capital and class are fundamental to Marx's theory of capitalism.

A theory also presupposes a number of other elements which are very important but rarely obvious. A bit like an iceberg, which is nine-tenths concealed below the water, a great number of the important intellectual moves and analytical choices that are bound up in selecting a theory and working within it go unseen and undiscussed. Any theory must be based on an account of the nature of the reality it tries to explain. In the philosophy of social science jargon, this is called an 'ontology'. An ontology is a theory of being or existence, a theory – if you like – of the way the world is, how it is put together and what makes it tick. As Peter Hall puts it, ontology refers to 'fundamental assumptions scholars make about the nature of the social and political world and especially about the nature of causal relationships within that world' (2003: 374). This is very important because 'the appropriateness of a particular set of methods for a given problem turns on assumptions about the nature of the causal relationships they are meant to discover' (ibid.). We return to the important issue of causality below. Since Adam Smith's philosopher friend David Hume wrote *Enquiries Concerning Human Understanding* in 1748, there has been a recognition that causal relationships cannot be 'read off' in a straightforward manner from the data. Correlation, in short, does not demonstrate causation, and therefore 'any scientific explanation involves the *assumption* of causal relationships' (Hodgson 2001: 9, emphasis added).

This understanding of causality, and of 'deep causal structures' (Hall 2003: 374), shapes what the core units of analysis are (individuals for classical liberal political economy, nations for economic nationalist political economy, capital and class for Marxist political economy). One's ontological position also determines how these units of analysis are conceived: are they rational, utility maximizing (as in Marginalist political economy and neo-classical economics) or socially and historically contingent and conditioned (as in Marxist or economic nationalist political economy)? An ontological position affects *where you look for answers* and, perhaps even more fundamentally, it conditions *what kinds of questions one asks* (see Blyth 2002b: 292–6).

As well as an understanding of the way the world is, a theory must also have an account of the status of the knowledge it generates. This must be based on a self-understanding of what the act of social scientific inquiry is for and what it can achieve. Is it seeking to make universal knowledge claims and generalizations of the kind built on *ceteris paribus* (all other things being equal) assumptions that we saw the Marginalists advancing in Chapter 4? Or is it interested in contingent, historically specific claims which are only deemed to operate under particular historical conditions, as is the case, in different ways, for both economic nationalist and Marxist political economy? In the philosophy of social science jargon this is called its 'epistemology', a theory of the kind and status of knowledge one can generate about society. Its status can be thought about as positioned somewhere on a continuum from Universal Truth (with a capital U and a capital T) at one end, and highly relativistic understandings at the other.

A theory also needs to have an account of *how* to go about acquiring this knowledge. In the social science jargon this is called a 'methodology'. This is the main focus of what follows, but it is important to keep in mind that the choice of method dovetails with positions on these issues of epistemology and ontology (Blyth 2002b: 293).

THE COMPARATIVE METHOD, POLITICAL ECONOMY AND DISCIPLINARY POLITICS

We have already encountered how fraught the debate over choice of social scientific method can be with the *Methodenstreit*, which tore the discipline of political economy apart in the 19th century. In this section we encounter similar kinds of debates within contemporary political science (sometimes considered the 'parent discipline' of CPE). Faced with the forbidding nature of the task of analysing global capitalism comparatively, choices must be made about focus, concepts and research methods. These choices of theories, methods and conceptual frameworks are not impartial, unbiased or 'purely' scientific. Questions of method are rooted in a set of pre-dispositions about the right way to go about political economy analysis. Are qualitative, interpretive, historical methods appropriate? Should one adopt quantitative and statistical methods?

From the 'sociology of knowledge' perspective we encountered in Chapter 4, focusing on what Wæver terms knowledge production regimes (1998), we can appreciate that such choices inevitably involve taking positions within disciplinary politics (see Clift et al. 2021). Protagonists discussing strengths and weaknesses of different methods of comparative political economic inquiry are often engaged in justifying and legitimizing their own assumptive foundations, ontological approaches, epistemological positions and methodological choices. In extreme cases, they may assert that only their position or approach is legitimate conduct in researching within the discipline, and only research carried out from these premises should be deemed admissible. The differing views of the merits of particular approaches to comparative analysis throw into relief how different disciplinary communities (say, CPE scholars in different continents, countries, universities or departments) tend to institutionalize in distinct ways the key aspects of academic inquiry. Arguably the most important issues are questions of admissibility and conduct: (a) what is considered to be acceptable or admissible work in a given field? (b) how should work be conducted and how and *where* should its results be presented (see Rosamond 2007; Clift and Rosamond 2009)? Each of these is intimately bound up with choice of method, logic of inquiry and research strategy in CPE. The next section sets out some of the key debates surrounding these issues within contemporary CPE.

The goal of comparison: the status of knowledge claims

Comparative social scientific analysis takes different forms, and it can be helpful to think about these differences in terms of the scholarly intent which motivates the research strategy. How do researchers conceive of the nature of social scientific research and what kind of knowledge claims do they want to make? Put differently, what is their epistemological position? For some political economists, the ultimate purpose of systematic academic inquiry is to discover general truths and make claims that are universal (or something close to it) about the political world. Their method of inquiry emulates the experimental research design of the natural sciences. They aspire to general theorizing, the discerning of law-like regularities, and something approaching a universal theory of political economy. One example of this is Niskanen's view of rent-seeking or bureaucratic budget maximization (see pp. 101–4). Another is Kenneth Waltz's account of the state in the international order (1979), and less rigorous versions in CPE include the capitalist convergence thesis (see pp. 123–6).

Other researchers assume that, given the complexities of the social world, it is difficult, and problematic, to be 'parsimonious' (i.e. include only a small number of factors or variables) in explanation and theorizing. They seek a more context-specific understanding, appreciative that there are good reasons to 'restrict the domain of their argument' (Mahoney and Goertz 2006: 238). Accordingly, these scholars recognize that their undertaking, while systematic and rigorous, is qualitatively distinct from inquiry within the natural sciences. Nevertheless, they seek to advance broader claims from their analysis. In place of bold claims of 'universality' or generalizability, they are more cautious about the status of their knowledge claims. As Meckstroth puts it:

> universality ... does not mean that the proposition must literally explain circumstances in all physical circumstances. Nor is evidence from all locations necessarily relevant for corroboration or falsification of such a proposition. This is due to the recognised status of 'initial conditions' in universal propositions which denote limiting circumstances under which a proposition is expected to operate. (1975: 135)

An example of this within CPE is the body of theorizing about and analysis of the welfare state and its development and evolution. This work focuses on and seeks to explain processes operating primarily within Western Europe since 1945. As we noted when highlighting the Eurocentric bias of comparative welfare state analysis (p. 234), and indeed VoC and comparative capitalisms analysis, these insights are not necessarily easily 'exportable' outside that context. For still others, the goal is to generate very contextualized and historically specific understandings of particular phenomena, highly idiographic accounts from which they do not seek to advance broader claims. An example of this is Chalmers Johnson's account of the Japanese 'developmental state' (see pp. 163–6), which he felt was a *sui generis* (one of a kind) explanation of a particular set of circumstances (1982).

We can hear echoes here of the *Methodenstreit* discussed in Chapter 4, which involved similar contending intellectual ambitions. The point, both then and now, is that all are legitimate positions on the vexed issues of conduct and admissibility. Each has a respectable and defensible epistemological position, but each will generate different kinds of work and insights. The implications for comparative analysis are important and developed further below. The ambit of one's study, or how many cases or data points one includes in one's research design, affects the kind of analysis one can conduct and the kind of knowledge one can generate. Thus an analysis of capitalist restructuring in every LME will operate at a higher level of generality, but be based on a lower level of in-depth knowledge, than an exploration of the transformation of the UK political economy. A prioritization of generalization suggests the study of a larger number of cases, which in turn suggests a statistical as opposed to interpretive historical approach (Table 13.1).

Table 13.1 Two cultures of CPE research: priorities in research conduct

Culture of research	Goal of comparison	Priorities in research design	Examples
Small N Interpretive	In-depth, contextual knowledge, limited portability of claims	Complexity – multiple interacting variables	German historical school, constructivism
Large N Positivist	Generalization, universal knowledge claims	Parsimony – *ceteris paribus* (all other things being equal)	Marginalism, neo-classical economics, public choice

The above are ideal types, and in reality stark oppositions between the approaches are often not obvious. Whereas many share some scepticism about generating law-like generalizations, most social scientists, Paul Pierson notes, want to 'develop claims about the social world that can potentially reach across time and space' (P. Pierson 2004: 7). This aspiration to what Pierson calls 'at least limited portability' of 'arguments that can "travel" in some form beyond a specific time and place' (ibid.: 6) is a useful way to think about the epistemological 'middle ground'. Most scholars are (I suspect rightly) infused with a degree of modesty about the status of knowledge claims. The key point is that methodological choices flow from a researcher's epistemological position.

Different assumptions about the nature of social scientific research and the knowledge claims issuing from it lend themselves to different kinds of research strategies and the use of different comparative methods.

What is at stake in research design? Positivism and interpretive social science

It should be clear by now that selecting a research strategy is not a neutral process. It entails important choices, with consequences for the kinds of debates a body of research contributes to, the kinds of places it is published, and who will read it and cite it. In the sociology of knowledge, these aspects of academia are recognized as sites of deeply political power struggles. Paul Pierson refers to the 'tribal, polarised character of much contemporary social science' (P. Pierson 2004: 10) – and he has a point. A lot is at stake: professional reputation, career prospects and visibility within an academic community. This helps to explain how such apparently technical questions can generate heated and charged methodological debate.

We noted above, and will explore further below, a schism between two cultures of research – qualitative and quantitative (Mahoney and Goertz 2006). A related schism is between positivism and interpretive social science. In the contemporary era, Payne and Gamble describe a methodological orthodoxy within much political economy work which they characterize as 'unquestioning positivism' entailing a 'commitment to a mode of production of knowledge dependent upon the belief that the separation of subject and object and fact and value are unproblematic' (1996: 6). Positivism assumes that social scientists stand outside the social world and observe it dispassionately and objectively (Ringer 2000: 19–26; Hay 2002: 80–8; Creswell 2008: 6–8). Researchers, and the research process, purportedly come with no bias or theoretical baggage attached. All salient phenomena in the social realm are deemed to be observable (and measurable); and all knowledge claims advanced about the real world are potentially falsifiable in the face of new empirical evidence. Positivism assumes the possibility of value-free or theory-free accumulation of evidence in testing hypotheses, emulating the natural sciences' methods as outlined above. These tenets constitute an influential set of shared understandings about appropriate social scientific method, especially dear to quantitative scholars.

Yet the idea of dispassionate social scientific investigation unbiased by prior theoretical assumptions is not a realistic characterization of the nature of social scientific research (Sanders 2002). What all political scientists engage in is not pure observation, but theoretically informed exploration. Thus there will inevitably be prior expectations (P. Pierson 2004: 7) informed by previous work. As Hodgson notes, in some realms of social science and philosophy, positivism began a retreat in the later 20th century in recognition that 'all descriptions of facts are theory-laden, and all descriptions are in fact dependent upon prior theories and conceptual frameworks' (Hodgson 2001: 75). Even if this positivist assumption may get relaxed somewhat, the others still hold for many.

An alternative, interpretive view holds that social scientific inquiry is just too different from the natural sciences to make a positivist strategy or approach viable. This sees it as spurious to proclaim to be dispassionate objective observers of the social world, not least because all researchers are part of that world. The assumed possibility of separation of subject and object is questioned; so too is the assumption that all that is relevant to political science analysis can be observed, measured or quantified. Again, different positions on these issues lead scholars to undertake different kinds of comparative analysis, adopting different research designs and different methods. On the whole, those comfortable with positivist assumptions are more likely to favour statistical approaches, as in Franzese's analysis of macro-economic policy-making (2002), or formal modelling which emulates neo-classical economics, as with rational choice political economy (see Chapter 5) or 'open economy politics' in IPE, using statistical analysis to examine domestic causes of foreign economic policy (Lake 2009; for a critique, see Oatley 2011). On the other hand, scholars sceptical of positivist precepts tend to engage in qualitative, interpretive, contextualized analysis, as, for example, in Wolfgang Streeck's analysis of German capitalist evolution (2009). Their research designs and research strategy may emulate historical methods. They are alive to the possibility of what Peter Hall calls 'deep causal structures' (2003: 374) playing an important part in explanation, without assuming that these can necessarily be observed or measured (Collier et al. 2004: 197–9; Table 13.2).

Some recent disciplinary history helps to explain certain dissimilarities in approaching these epistemological and methodological issues found within different national academic communities. In some academic cultures with loose academic disciplinary norms, such as the UK, there is a lack of an iron grip of any political science orthodoxy, positivist or otherwise. Such an intellectual context for the study of politics allows for dialogue between different disciplinary discourses. The behavioural revolution of the 1960s which shifted acceptable conduct in a quantitative, statistical and positivist methodological direction was a very powerful influence on US political science (Wæver 1998: 688). Yet what Wyn Grant calls 'the scientism of the behaviouralists' (Grant 2010: 35) never took hold within British political science. So in Britain, 'political science' was a disputed term, with many preferring 'studies' (with its less positivistic connotations).

Table 13.2   Two cultures of CPE research: research design and goals

Epistemology	Research goals	Observation of social world	Causation	Variables
Small N Interpretive	Explain outcomes; explore complexity	Theory-laden, separation of subject/object is not possible	Complex, configurative, necessary and sufficient cause, causes of effects	Not necessarily observable, measurable; deep causal structures
Large N Positivist	Emulate natural sciences, test hypotheses	Objective, pure science model	Statistical, correlational, effects of causes	All key variables observable, measurable

Qualitative and quantitative approaches to comparison

This distinction between interpretive political studies on the one hand and positivistic polit-ical science on the other is an important site of disciplinary politics, with significant implica-tions for stances on the appropriate conduct and admissibility of CPE research. This can be illustrated by the long-standing and 'tribal' debate in comparative methodology over the relative merits of qualitative and quantitative methods. Mahoney and Goertz describe the two approaches as 'alternative cultures. Each has its own beliefs, and norms. Each is some-times privately suspicious or sceptical of the other though usually more publicly polite' (2006: 227). Beck likens this cultural difference to the worship of alternative gods (2006; Schrodt 2006).

At the root of the 'cultural' difference, for Mahoney and Goertz, are 'different norms about research practices' which they trace back to 'the distinctiveness in basic goals' of research for each tradition (see also Ragin 2004: 124; Levi-Faur 2006: 371). For qualitative scholars, their 'core goal' is 'the explanation of outcomes in individual cases', and they 'adopt a "causes of effects" approach to explanation'. For quantitative, statistical scholars, by con-trast, the core research goal is 'to estimate the average effect of one or more causes across a population of cases', to which end they adopt 'the "effects-of-causes" approach [to causality] employed in experimental research', hence 'the explanation of specific outcomes in particu-lar cases is not a central concern' (Mahoney and Goertz 2006: 228–30). Thus some work on financialization seeks to explore general shifts in the role of finance in society across many advanced economies through analysis of broad quantitative data on stock market capitaliza-tion and so on (see Thatcher 2007; Engelen and Konings 2010; Karwowski and Stockhammer 2017), seeking to glean their average effects. Other work, conversely, looks in depth at establishing the causal linkages of change within – say – UK and US final salary pension regimes, seeking to establish the causal pattern of events and the implications of changes in particular cases (Langley 2004, 2008). The first is a variables-oriented approach; the second is a cases-oriented approach (Ragin and Zaret 1983; Ragin 2004).

These alternative points of departure and distinct research goals generate different kinds of comparison and suggest different ways to use the comparative method. How research is designed, how many cases are incorporated into the study and how they are analysed differ significantly within these distinct bodies of CPE analysis, each of which is trying to do dif-ferent things: 'if you really want to estimate average causal effects, you should not be in the business of trying to hunt down each causal factor that might affect outcomes in particular cases. But if you really want to explain outcomes in particular cases, it makes good sense to be in this business' (Mahoney and Goertz 2006: 244).

The core research goal of qualitative scholars tends to be to *understand* and *explain* par-ticularly interesting cases, political economic developments and processes in comparative context (see e.g. Collier and Collier 1991; Collier 1993), perhaps with a view to developing or refining theory. As Ragin puts it, the 'reciprocal clarification of empirical categories and theoretical concepts is one of the central concerns of qualitative research' (2004: 126). This is how different welfare state types, or varieties of capitalism, are identified, and how they are defined with incrementally greater precision. We can see here the contemporary legatees of the German Historical School we encountered in Chapters 3 and 4. Just like List, Schmoller and Weber, qualitative CPE work tends to be context-embedded and historically sensitive. It has a distinguished lineage within political science, building on the 'disciplined configura-tive approach' developed by Verba in the 1960s (1967). Yet there is an influential view, inspired by positivism, which argues that generalizable, universal propositions are 'better', and that quantitative methods using statistical analysis are more 'scientific' than qualitative analysis (Lijphart 1971, 1975).

Adam Przeworski and Henry Teune's *The Logic of Comparative Social Inquiry*, prioritizes generalizability of social science theories over accuracy (1970: 17). They also favour parsimony, which King et al. describe as 'a judgement, or even assumption, about the nature of the world: it is assumed to be simple' (1994: 20). Flowing from these proclivities is a preference for quantitative and statistical methods. Lijphart highlights 'special limitations' of the qualitative comparative method, deeming it insufficiently rigorous; and he advances forcefully the case against 'configurative' analysis (1971: 690). In this view, the qualitative approach to a small number of cases is seen as 'weaker', and wherever possible the statistical method is to be preferred (Lijphart 1975: 165). A similar position is taken in the influential qualitative methods text by King et al. (1994); for a critique, see Brady and Collier (2004). As Mahoney and Goertz note, the King et al. text 'assumes that quantitative researchers have the best tools for making scientific inferences, and hence qualitative researchers have to emulate these tools to the degree possible' (2006: 228; Table 13.3).

Agreement with this stance is very widespread, especially within US political science, where it has become somewhat hegemonic within some major journals' editorial policies. The prominence, not to say pre-eminence, of quantitative approaches (aligned with positivism) in US political science is explicable in part in terms of Ricardian comparative advantage. US PhD training is longer and rigorous than in many other countries, and it always contains extensive training in quantitative methodology – taught to a higher degree than in many other academic cultures (see e.g. Cohen 2007, 2008). As a result, US-trained social scientists tend to be more capable quantitative scholars. It is not that surprising that many within US academe value quantitative capabilities and technical sophistication highly. That said, US political science remains a vibrant, varied and somewhat pluralistic research community – as demonstrated by the thriving American Political Science Association (APSA) section on qualitative and multi-method research (see, for example, its journal *Qualitative and Multi-Method Research*).

An appreciation of disciplinary politics brings to the fore how this quantitative and positivist methodological position entails a set of assumptions about the '*rules of interpretation* and *criteria for admissible explanation*' (Holt and Turner 1970: 2). Lijphart's critique of qualitative, configurative analysis (1971, 1975: 172), King et al.'s interpretation of qualitative methodology (1994) and Przeworski and Teune's prioritizing of generalization and parsimony (1970) involve particular, and contestable, stances on conduct and admissibility. The

Table 13.3   Two cultures of CPE research: building blocks of research design

Epistemology	Focus of analysis	Mode of research	Research goals	Typical format
Small N Interpretive	Cases-oriented; complex, configurative causation	Qualitative, historical	Know more about less, 'thick' description	Case studies
Large N Positivist	Variables-oriented; correlation	Quantitative, statistical	Hypothesis testing, know less about more	Regression analysis

positivistic dismissal of qualitative, case-based comparative research assesses configurative and statistical analysis *by the same yardstick* and using *the same criteria*. Such a view ignores one central theme of this chapter – the differences between the two undertakings rooted in their distinct core research goals. The view of quantitative methods as more 'valid' and 'scientific' has been challenged recently (see Hall 2003; Brady and Collier 2004; Mahoney and Goertz 2006). Importantly, qualitative and quantitative research logically imply different understandings of causality. The point seems an obvious one, 'given that theories regularly posit alternative notions of cause, scholars should be open to working with different conceptions of causation' (Mahoney and Goertz 2006: 234). Yet the implications of this are under-appreciated.

Qualitative approaches, for example, tend to think in terms of necessary and sufficient causes (ibid.: 232–4; Ragin 1987, 2004; Weber 1949). This understanding of causality also underpins Mill's logic (1949 [1843]) that informs *all* comparative research design. Thus, at one level, all comparativists – be they qualitative or quantitative in orientation – accept and work with this version of causality. It is hardwired into the logic underpinning how comparative research gets designed, as we will discuss further below. The necessary and sufficient cause conception of causation underpins, for example, in-depth qualitative national case studies of particular models of capitalism and how they are evolving in the wake of international economic liberalization (see e.g. Clift 2004, 2012 on France; Deeg 1999 on Germany; Deeg 2012 on the USA; Matsuura et al. 2004 on Japan; Breslin 2007 on China; Ban 2013 on Brazil).

Yet, on another level, the quantitative approach to comparative analysis also thinks in terms of correlational causation: 'the statistical approach replaces the impossible-to-observe causal effect of T on a specific unit with the possible-to-estimate average causal effect of T over a population of units' (Mahoney and Goertz 2006: 233). The key point is that the statistical method entails distinctive probabilistic understandings of causation (Hall 2003). The necessary and sufficient cause conception of qualitative analysis 'cannot be unproblematically translated into the language of correlational causation' (Mahoney and Goertz 2006: 233) which underpins statistical analysis. This is one reason to consider the two as different kinds of undertakings.

An important dimension of qualitative comparative analysis is what Charles Ragin calls 'conjunctural causation' (1987, 2004: 133–5). This appreciation of causal complexity involves the configurative interaction of several, often interrelated, causal variables (Smelser 1976: 152–3). This is a necessary element of the 'explanation of outcomes' which is the qualitative scholar's core research goal because, in the real social and political world, given the multiplicity of different factors and variables exerting their influence and constantly interacting with each other, 'conjunctural causality' is likely to capture the reality of causal processes better than a simple A causes B model. Peter Hall focuses on this issue and its implications for methodological selection. He notes the *superiority* of the qualitative approach in being faithful to the way most comparativists think about causation, its ability to capture and deal with complexity in causation constituting an important strength (2003; Levi-Faur 2006: 371; Mahoney and Goertz 2006: 233).

On the other hand, this complex causation presents difficulties for quantitative statistical approaches. The interaction of variables means that 'the interaction effects are often so complex and the data so limited that regression analysis cannot test the relevant propositions' (Hall 2003: 386). Indeed, as Mahoney and Goertz point out in reviewing recent literature on interaction in statistical analysis, while 'one can include interaction in a statistical model', nevertheless 'the individual effect approach continues to be the norm in statistics as actually practised in the social sciences' (2006: 235). This leads Hall to argue that 'some of the most prominent theories in comparative politics now understand the world in terms that do not conform to the assumptions required by standard regression analysis' (Hall 2003: 384).

Hall also illustrates this lack of congruence of complex causality and statistical analysis with reference to path dependency (pp. 113–16), which is an important element in historical institutionalist explanations of political economy (see e.g. P. Pierson 1994, 2004; Hall 1986):

> a key development in the distant past (whether a fateful choice or a crucial event) often affects a case so deeply that it alters the impact of subsequent developments, thereby vitiating the assumption that such developments x, y, z can be expected to have the same impact across cases ... early developments can change the context of a case so radically that subsequent developments will have different effects in each of the cases ... it becomes unreasonable to suppose that an x occurring today has the same effect, y, across all settings. (Hall 2003: 385)

Notions of path dependency pose problems for statistical approaches looking to assess the average effect of a variable across numerous data points in different cases and across time (Mahoney and Goertz 2006). The question flowing from all this is: 'is there one logic of explanation in social scientific research, and is this logic statistical?' (Levi-Faur 2006: 372). The answer, for Hall (2003), Ragin (2004) and many others, is 'no'.

Indeed, Hall argues that views on optimal methods have evolved since the 'behaviouralist' revolution in the 1960s. The prioritizing of simple, parsimonious research designs limited to very few variables no longer holds sway (2003: 386–7). 'Parsimony', Hall claims, 'is no longer seen as a key feature of explanation in political science, and views about what constitutes an acceptable mode of explanation in political science have shifted towards the historical' (ibid.: 387). He elicits in support King et al.'s influential methodology text, which notes that parsimony 'is only occasionally appropriate ... we should never insist on parsimony as a general principle of designing theories' (1994: 20). The reason is a greater appreciation of conjunctural causation and innovations like the 'branching of a tree' conception of causality that underpins path dependence. Thus the logic that forms 'the basis of the qualitative view of cause and causal complexity are not more or less rigorous than the probability and statistics used by quantitative scholars' (Mahoney and Goertz 2006: 236; see also Ragin 2004: 138).

Large N and small N research designs

An issue closely linked to the above question of qualitative and/or quantitative method selection is the scale of a study. Put simply, how large is your 'N'? ('N' is jargon for the number of cases or data points incorporated in a research design.) This is a crucial question for comparative analysis because of the impact it has on the ambit and scope of the study (how much information do you need to gather, and how extensively can you familiarize yourself with what is going on in each case?). This choice will thus have an impact on the kind of comparative analysis one undertakes and the kind of knowledge it generates. Following a positivist logic, the rationale of the 'big N' approach is that, for results to be rigorous and reliable, you need a maximum possible number of cases to safely say your findings are 'generalizable'. Given their large scale, these studies tend towards statistical analysis, testing the average effect of one or a few measurable causes across many cases. Such studies may leave many factors untested or unmeasured. Big N comparativists trade off understanding in context, and of context, against generalizability. They know 'less about more'.

Meanwhile, small N studies favour a more interpretive, qualitative approach, prioritizing depth of knowledge. 'Small N' studies involve configurative understandings of causality (Ragin 1987) and can examine causal mechanisms within the cases with greater confidence arising from detailed understanding. The problems of reliability and validity of data, and reliance upon data which cannot be properly evaluated, which sometimes plague the statistical approach (Lijphart 1975: 171) are unlikely to occur. On the downside, it is not clear precisely how much the detailed grasp of these causal mechanisms in one or a few cases tells us about other, similar cases. The trade-off here sacrifices some of the generalizability in favour of depth of understanding – knowing more, and better, about less.

You can see that where one stands on what kinds of knowledge claims one wants to advance affects how one approaches these trade-offs. Some qualitative, case-oriented scholars prioritize depth of understanding as their main goal, while quantitative, variables-oriented scholars may prioritize generalizability and parsimony (Levi-Faur 2006: 371). Those warning against generalization from a few cases are clearly correct, but others engaging in a detailed study of a few cases may counter that their goal is not full-blown generalization, but perhaps Paul Pierson's 'limited portability' (2004: 6) of findings beyond their immediate context in time and place.

There are numerous ways in which the comparative method can contribute to the systematic and rigorous accumulation of knowledge in CPE, using both small and large N research designs. Comparative analysis of a small number of cases, perhaps even of only one case, can make a valuable contribution to building, honing and testing theory (Gerring 2007). There can be perfectly good theoretical or methodological reasons for limiting the number of cases under investigation. The 'critical' cases approach focuses on one case which previous research has shown to be particularly theoretically important (George and Bennett 2005; Mahoney and Goertz 2006: 242–4; Guy Peters 2013). Thus even a single study may show the limits of a theory: 'a case study is a study of a certain problem, proposition, or theory, and a case belongs to a larger category of cases' (Lijphart 1975: 160, 1971). For example, in the comparative analysis of social democracy and of welfare states, Sweden is often considered the paradigmatic case, and therefore single-country studies of the Swedish experience (see e.g. Pontusson 1992, 2011; Ryner 2002) are instructive for understanding the broader dynamics of social democracy and welfare state resilience as a phenomenon. Hence 'certain types of case studies' can be considered 'implicit parts of the comparative method' (Lijphart 1971: 691).

Comparison and case study can constitute mutually reinforcing and complementary undertakings. Collier's 'process-tracing' case study technique, for example, involves the systematic comparison (the logic of which is set out below) of carefully selected cases (Collier 1993; Bennett and Checkel 2014; George and Bennett 2005: ch 10). Here 'the goal is to assess whether the dynamics of change within each case plausibly reflect the same causal pattern suggested by the comparative appraisal of the case in relation to other cases' (1993: 115). Case studies can 'respond to theory', as Ragin puts it, 'by refuting and extending it or by illuminating important phenomena that are outside the scope of existing theory' (1992: 6, 2004: 128). Equally, there are 'hypothesis-generating' case studies which take 'a more or less vague notion of possible hypotheses, and attempt to formulate definite hypotheses to be tested subsequently among a larger number of cases' (Lijphart 1971: 692). There are also theory-infirming and theory-confirming case studies which 'are analyses of single cases within the framework of established generalisations' (ibid.).

Whether we opt for a large N or small N study, it is very important to calibrate carefully and appropriately the status of the knowledge claims we make on the back of our results (mindful of the various 'health warnings' attached to each method, given its shortcomings). For large N studies, the boldness of claims should be tempered by possible problems of reliability and validity of data, and reliance upon data which cannot be properly evaluated (Lijphart 1975: 171). For small N studies, it is important to recall that 'a single case can constitute neither the basis of a valid generalization nor the grounds for disproving an established generalization' (Lijphart 1971: 691). The findings of qualitative analysis of a small number of cases, even if at odds with the theory, cannot be considered a refutation of its premises. It should be a spur to possible refinement of the theory and its hypothesis, and possibly to quantitative work exploring whether the non-occurrence of the expected inter-relationship and causal connection is part of a broader pattern. If so, our suspicions about the validity of the theory will grow.

This is all part of the accretion of CPE knowledge by social scientists working in different traditions and deploying different methodologies. The stance taken in the big N 'versus' small N debate reflects the disciplinary political positions over conduct and admissibility discussed above and in Chapter 4. We have encountered both small N and large N approaches to comparative political economy in this book. This is partly to illustrate the merits of methodological pluralism. It is also because both approaches are very well represented within the CPE literature, and much can be learnt from reading the results of *both* types of analysis.

Where is your evidence?

Evidence, and the empirical adjudication of theories or propositions, is a crucial part of systematic political economy work. While most people can agree on this, disagreements are likely to creep in over what constitutes relevant and valid empirical evidence. Here again, different views on *rules of interpretation* and *criteria for admissible explanation* (Holt and Turner 1970) play a vital role, reflecting as they do different epistemological and ontological positions. These feed through into different stances on the crucial issues of admissibility and conduct – put crudely, what counts and how do you count it? Where one stands on these issues affects the kinds of comparisons undertaken.

Both qualitative and quantitative researchers in political economy are likely to draw on quantitative data, for example about economic performance in particular countries, to corroborate or confound the theories they are engaging with. Where the two cultures differ is in the range of other sources of evidence that they deem admissible, and how it should be analysed. Broadly speaking, quantitative scholars will tend to confine themselves to data that can be quantified in a way to render it malleable for statistical analysis. Qualitative scholars will deploy a range of techniques – historical analysis, archival research, interviews and so forth – building their analysis on a wider range of data to piece together a detailed understanding of the causal processes under scrutiny. Qualitative researchers, it has been noted, 'are in some ways analogous to criminal detectives: they solve puzzles and explain particular outcomes by drawing on detailed fact gathering, experience working with similar cases, and knowledge of general causal principles' (Mahoney and Goertz 2006: 241). They assign particular significance to certain observations which can constitute 'smoking guns' within their 'causal-process observation', corroborating or challenging a theoretical supposition (Brady and Collier 2004: 252–3). The quantitative approach, by contrast, weights all observations within their dataset equally (Mahoney and Goertz 2006: 241–2).

Both approaches to one's evidence base are valid, and each is appropriate to the different research goals the two 'cultures' are pursuing. Each strategy for evidence selection, however, has consequences. Within quantitative analysis, the crucial role of measurement and statistical analysis of data can affect the focus of inquiry. Yet what is readily measurable in this way does not necessarily equate to what is interesting or what is *really* important. Some questions go unasked because, quantitatively, it may be very difficult to gain analytical purchase on them. That is not to say they are not important questions (such as the role of dominant ideologies – see pp. 127–30). To come back to the assumptive basis of positivism, this work limits itself to the observable world, and indeed to those elements within it that are amenable to measurement to generate certain kinds of data. These approaches neglect, indeed cannot conceive of, what Hall calls 'deep underlying structures' (2003; Collier et al. 2004: 197–9).

On the other hand, qualitative research puts the onus upon the researcher to decide what constitutes relevant and appropriate evidence. Ragin talks of the 'constitution of cases' within qualitative research arising out of a dialogue between theory and evidence (2004: 128–33). Scholars must be careful to 'constitute cases' and sift evidence in a rigorous and systematic fashion, guarding against selection bias (choosing only evidence supporting their theoretical position). The variety of techniques and types of evidence drawn on by qualitative researchers makes it more difficult for other researchers to replicate their findings. This is a norm within natural sciences research to ensure the validity of findings, to which positivists in particular attach great importance (see also King et al. 1994: ch. 1). That is relatively straightforward within quantitative analysis, given the same datasets and the same statistical methods. Replication can be a much trickier proposition for interpretive social scientific analysis. The extent to which that is problematic depends on whether you see social science as so similar to the natural sciences that rules of interpretation should be the same or as similar as possible. In this book, we have approached issues of evidence base, admissibility and conduct in a methodologically pluralist manner.

Economics, rational choice and 'reflectivist' approaches

As comparative political economists there is one other issue of particular import, which concerns an aspect of 'borders' of the field (what lies outside the realms of the discipline) and 'external relations' with cognate disciplines. One set of 'external relations' stand out for political economy – those between political science and economics. To a significant degree, understandings of this relationship flow from the above stances on positivism, on 'scientific' methods and on the appeal of rigour, parsimony and the research designs of the natural sciences. Adam Przeworksi's approach to political economy, for example, sees the need to build on the foundations laid by marginalism and neo-classical economics (2003). This borrowing of method from economics, rooted in underlying *homo economicus* and *ceteris paribus* assumptions, is one familiar method in contemporary CPE analysis, most obviously exemplified by rational choice approaches (see Chapter 5).

'Rationalists' assume, as the Marginalists did, that all individuals are basically the same (utility maximizers). The attraction of this assumption is that a model built on such foundations can 'travel', as Paul Pierson puts it – perhaps everywhere (Pierson 2004). On the other hand, the alternatives to rationalist approaches are 'reflectivist' accounts. These tend to understand individuals in more socially embedded terms, and seek to comprehend the world views of the individuals they analyse with recourse to historical and cultural factors. We encountered this kind of analytical move when we looked at economic nationalists in Chapter 3. This reflectivist analytical stance can also be found within modern constructivist political economy (see pp. 134–8), seeing the political economic world in terms of multiple different rationalities shaped by particular historical, cultural and institutional conditions (Campbell 1998, 2004; Ruggie 1998; Schmidt 2008). These two radically different positions borrow in very different ways from the heritage of political economy. Unsurprisingly, each generates different kinds of knowledge claims and different kinds of knowledge.

COMPARATIVE POLITICAL ECONOMY AND METHODOLOGICAL PLURALISM

Of the various distinctions and methodological and epistemological choices outlined in the preceding sections, most can be grouped together within the two alternative 'cultures' of social scientific research – qualitative and quantitative (Mahoney and Goertz 2006; Ragin 2004). In the interests of the methodological pluralism advocated here, our priority is to recognize the relationship between qualitative and quantitative analysis. Both the case-oriented small N (qualitative) approach and the variable-oriented, large N (quantitative) approach 'are compatible with the goals of explanation and generalization, but they produce *different types of explanation* with *different degrees of abstraction*' (Ragin and Zaret 1983: 733). Both qualitative and quantitative methodology are very valuable parts of the CPE canon and arsenal, each generating tremendous insights into the CPE of capitalism. One should not damn either approach, but rather interrogate the underlying assumptions of both kinds of important and illuminating work (Blyth 2002b: 292). It is important to develop an understanding of the research process and appreciate the intellectual choices made within it in favour of particular analytical strategies and research techniques.

We reject the view that *either* positivistic (or quasi-positivistic), statistical, quantitative methods *or* qualitative, interpretive methods are inherently a more worthy pursuit. In all research designs there are difficult trade-offs, for example between parsimony and accuracy, or between generalizability and depth of understanding. An *a priori* assumption of superiority unwisely assumes away these trade-offs. It equally neglects that a different method, prioritizing different scholarly intentions, may generate complementary findings. For all the history of mutual suspicion between the 'two cultures', there have been some important developments in recent years. There has been an insistence from qualitative scholars (for the reasons outlined above) that their approach is no less scientific, merely that it is operating with a different conception of causation and adopting entirely appropriate and scientific methods to research from this standpoint (Hall 2003; Mahoney and Goertz 2006: 230–6; Levi-Faur 2006; Creswell 2008). As Mahoney and Goertz argue, both qualitative and quantitative approaches 'share the overarching goal of producing valid descriptive and causal inferences' (2006: 228–30; Table 13.4).

Table 13.4   Two cultures of CPE research and the trade-offs in research design

Quantitative Large N	Parsimony	Generalization	Breadth of understanding	Grasp of regularities/broad patterns
Qualitative Small N	Accuracy	Granularity	Depth of understanding	Grasp of context/specific detail

There are good reasons to draw on insights from both cultures. Much good qualitative political economy work is at its best when illuminating, in relation to particular cases, relationships, regularities and patterns detected within quantitative work. The idea of complementarities between the two cultures has led some to combine the two approaches more systematically than before. An important evolution here is the recent rise of 'mixed methods' approaches (see e.g. Hesse-Biber and Johnson 2015; Brady and Collier 2004), recognizing that 'both approaches are of value; in fact, they complement one another' (Mahoney and Goertz 2006: 231). The comparative politics canon offers a wealth of different research strategies and techniques. A methodologically pluralist approach and outlook can minimize the weaknesses and capitalize on the inherent strengths of various techniques (Lijphart 1971: 693). In this spirit, Collier's survey of comparative techniques and debates concludes 'the most fruitful approach is eclectic, one in which scholars are willing and able to draw upon these diverse techniques' (1993: 105). After all, one method rarely displays a perfect fit with substantive interest in CPE. For example, quantitative assessment of broad regularities and patterns of welfare state spending tell us a certain amount about the relationship between globalization and welfare. A fuller appreciation of this interrelationship is achieved when quantitative assessment is complemented with more in-depth, granular, qualitative analysis (see pp. 241–7). These kinds of calls for eclecticism in research design, coming from eminent comparativists such as Collier and Hall, bolster the case for the methodological pluralism advocated here.

HOW TO COMPARE: THE LOGIC OF COMPARATIVE ANALYSIS

We have seen the merits of a pluralistic, eclectic approach to methodology in CPE. Crucial to any analysis, however, is that research is carried out on a systematic basis informed by a clear logic. It is to this that we turn in this section. Comparisons are a useful way to build knowledge and understanding. We use the *logic of inference* (discussed below) to use facts we know to learn something about facts we do not know (King et al. 1994: 119; Mill 1949 [1843]).

In structuring comparative inquiry, the *systematic* element in comparison is very important. As political scientists, regardless of the stance we take on the status of our knowledge claims, we want to be as rigorous as possible in our comparative research design. This means knowing something about the logic of comparative inquiry and its terminology. First, we need to deconstruct the issue at hand into its component parts. We will use an example of a hypothetical piece of research to illustrate the choices and trade-offs faced by researchers in conducting their analysis. It will also help us to locate and understand social scientific terminology. Our focus will be on the increase in international capital mobility following the onset of what many term financial globalization (see e.g. Held et al. 1999) and its impact on politics and government policy. A broad area of interest such as this can be termed a 'problematic'. Cohen identifies the relevant problematic and maps out a research agenda for CPE analysis:

> The interesting question ... is not whether financial globalization imposes a constraint on sovereign states; it most clearly does. Rather, we should now be asking how the discipline works and under what conditions. What accounts for the remaining room for manoeuvre, and why do some countries still enjoy more policy autonomy than others? (1996: 283–4)

One interesting theme of research within this problematic is how globalizing financial markets have affected advanced state capacity in the field of macro-economic policy. It is often argued that the 1970s was a watershed, with heightening capital mobility reducing governmental macro-economic policy autonomy (Eichengreen 1996: ch. 5). In order to 'test' this thesis, it makes sense to identify specific theories in the CPE literature which posit relevant interrelationships and offer explanations. Such theories generate hypotheses, which are causal statements identifying expected outcomes and explanations of social phenomena. These can be broken down into their composite 'variables', which is how many social scientists describe the factors or elements within the explanation. These are the key 'moving parts' within the analysis. Two kinds of variables are most important and need to be clearly distinguished: firstly, the 'dependent variable' – or that which is being acted upon and explained; secondly, the 'independent variable' – that which, the hypothesis posits, causes or explains the observed outcome.

To take a prominent theory and hypothesis from the CPE literature on the role of states in the economy, the capital mobility hypothesis (CMH) posits a powerful constraining effect of financial capital mobility on states' economic policy (Andrews 1994: 194–201). The *dependent* variable, that being explained, is economic policy autonomy of a government or state. The *independent* variable – this is the thing which we think is causing the effect we are looking at – is international capital mobility. When thinking through a problem in CPE, it is helpful to formulate it in these terms to ensure one's approach to the research question is systematic and informed by a clear logic. Thinking in terms of dependent and independent variables, it becomes clearer how to go about establishing *causation* and offering corroboration for, or counter-evidence against, the theory you are exploring.

The CMH theory of economic policy autonomy in the context of capital mobility is part of a broader debate about the impact of globalization (Rodrik 1997, 1998; Garrett 1998; Gray 1998; Hirst and Thompson 1999). The CMH posits a set of causal interrelationships which Jerry Cohen terms the 'unholy trinity', identifying the intrinsic incompatibility of exchange rate stability, capital mobility and national policy autonomy (Cohen 1993: 147). In relation to exchange rates, one choice facing policy-makers is whether the rate should be fixed or floating. Under fixed exchange rates, capital mobility increases the efficacy of fiscal policy but eliminates monetary policy autonomy, while under floating rates, capital mobility renders fiscal policy ineffective, though monetary policy can be set independently (Andrews 1994; Oatley 1999: 1007–9).

According to the CMH, increasing financial liberalization and deregulation within the world economy since the 1970s have facilitated capital mobility, structurally empowering investors (and particularly large financial institutions) vis-à-vis governments (Frieden 1991). These empowered actors, Oatley argues, 'prefer low inflation and balanced budgets and rapidly shift their funds in response to macroeconomic policies that threaten to generate inflation or otherwise reduce the return on investment relative to other national markets' (1999: 1004). The 'stringent logic' of the 'unholy trinity' imposes, according to Cohen, 'an increasingly stark trade-off on policymakers' (1996: 286) which allegedly leads governments to eschew expansionary fiscal and monetary policies in favour of sound money, low inflation and balanced budgets. CMH theorizing argues that financial globalization leads governments to rein in their budgets. This has important implications, for example, for the relationship between globalization and the welfare state. Effectively, CMH predicts that globalization will lead (in a floating exchange rate context) to a scaling back of welfare state spending as part of a broader fiscal retrenchment and search for balanced budgets. We explored and critiqued such understandings of the relationship between the welfare state and economic globalization in detail in Chapter 11.

The CMH has its theoretical foundations in open economy macro-economics, based on a textbook version of a perfectly integrated open international economy. This is the international version of the liberal faith in the efficient operation of free markets (see pp. 44–7) transformed into a prior assumption. It is basically the same as the assumptions about general equilibrium, first advanced by Walras, which we encountered in Chapter 4. This is, obviously, a fairly heroic assumption – bold enough within one economy, but positively Herculean when transposed to the entire world economy.

Our hypothesis (CMH) states that the degree of economic policy autonomy is determined by the degree of international capital mobility, and that under current conditions of high mobility, *either* fiscal policy *or* monetary policy is tightly constrained (depending on the choice of fixed or floating exchange rates). CMH is a slightly more complex hypothesis because it involves an 'intervening variable' – the exchange rate regime – arguing that the precise impact on government economic policy autonomy varies according to whether exchange rates are fixed or floating.

CMH theorizing and hypothesizing have, in the interests of 'parsimony' (restricting the number of variables within comparative analysis), isolated a particular set of interrelationships. This research strategy has its attractions – in terms of the boldness of its predictions and explanations, the simplicity of its propositions and the clarity of its argument. However, as with any research strategy, there are 'costs' as well as 'benefits'. It risks neglecting other factors which might be having important effects on the outcomes we are interested in. How can we be sure that economic policy choices are not a result of purely domestic political factors, unrelated to the international economic environment? The honest answer is that we cannot be *sure*, but the extant literature on CPE and IPE gives us good grounds to reject an exclusively domestic explanation.

Indeed, in Chapters 8 and 11, we unearthed considerable grounds for doubt from the empirical record about the posited negative implications for state spending from increasing capital mobility which is at the heart of CMH theorizing. The story, it seems, is more complicated than the CMH framework recognizes. Thus, quite quickly, CPE analysis gets a bit messier than our nice neat CMH example, because the social world is so unlike the laboratory conditions which prevail in the natural sciences (from which social science methodologies are derived). The international economy, for example, is not likely to exhibit the properties of a perfectly integrated market as the CMH posits.

While there is an attraction (in terms of simplicity, parsimony and manageability of research design) in focusing on a very small number of variables which one anticipates will do the explaining, this, as with any other choice about method in social research, has costs as well as benefits. Much more often than not in conducting comparative social inquiry, there is a multiplicity of different possible independent 'variables' or factors – any or all of which may be having effects on our 'dependent variable'. It is in trying to work out *how* comparativists deal with these problems (too many variables, few if any of them subject to our control) that we have to consider the *method* and *logic* of comparative inquiry.

THE LOGIC OF COMPARATIVE RESEARCH DESIGN

The logic which informs comparative analysis can be traced back over 150 years to that great classical liberal political economist John Stuart Mill's *A System of Logic* (1949 [1843]), where he set out the logic of inference underpinning his methods of inductive inquiry (Box 13.1).

Box 13.1 Mill's logic of comparative research methods

1. **'Method of difference'**: *if there is an occurrence and a non-occurrence of a phenomenon* (the dependent variable) *and the conditions under which it occurs* (the independent variables) *are the same in all circumstances save one, then this one is the cause.* That is, factors that are common to the countries are irrelevant in determining the different patterns of behaviour being explained.
2. **'Method of agreement'**: *if several observations of the phenomenon* (the dependent variable) *have only one of several possible causes* (potential independent variables) *in common, then that one common factor is causal.* This method requires that the investigator identifies relevant instances of Y and then shows that all instances of Y have X and no other theoretically relevant cause or combination of causes in common.

Mill himself, it is important to note, was highly sceptical that such a logic of inquiry could be applied to the social sciences (for the 'too many variables' reasons outlined above). He felt that it was simply not plausible to apply his rigorous logical system to the design and conduct of social research. Nevertheless, it is his system which provides the bedrock of modern comparative research design. Mill's scepticism is another important health warning for us to bear in mind from here on. We cannot control for and manipulate every possible causal factor. These limitations should temper the boldness of claims and the firmness of conclusions drawn from our comparative analytical endeavours. That said, comparison can tell us a great deal, and that is why, Mill's misgivings notwithstanding, his logic still informs comparative social scientific research design.

Mill's logic has fostered two main types of research design: the most similar systems design (MSSD) and the most different systems design (MDSD) strategies (Przeworski and Teune 1970). The MDSD explores whether, if you have the supposed cause (the independent variable) present, the expected effect occurs, even if everything else about the cases is different. The MSSD is a more common approach and is the exact opposite. It attempts to emulate the controlled conditions of scientific experimental design, comparing cases where as many aspects as possible are similar *except* the supposed causal factor (the independent variable). This follows Lijphart's 'comparable cases strategy' (1971, 1975), where many variables are 'controlled' for by choosing (broadly) similar cases where a large number of factors are assumed to be (roughly) 'equal'. It allows greater confidence in focusing on particular 'variables' and attributing causal significance to them.

This indicates that case selection is very closely tied to research design and crucial to achieving systematic comparative analysis (see Ragin 2004: 125–8), especially for small N qualitative comparative analysis. Which cases will you look at and why? Building a research design from the ground up while paying close attention to these issues of logic is vital to successful *systematic* comparative analysis. Not all cases are equivalent, or of equivalent use in supporting or confounding a theory or hypothesis. The logic of comparative inquiry underpinning the MSSD informs case selection in much CPE analysis. Work on the advanced OECD states, for example, has selected cases that are similar in important respects, each country having an advanced economy, socio-economic structure and stable economic and political institutions, and being relatively well integrated into the world economy.

Applying all this to our CMH example, ideally we would conduct laboratory-type experiments: say, try out different economic policies to see whether CMH's predicted outcomes result. Yet this, of course, is not feasible. There are practical and ethical problems – we cannot render international capital immobile to see how economic policy-making might change, nor can we impose a change of exchange rate regime on a country to see if that frees up fiscal policy while constraining monetary policy. CPE researchers cannot run and then re-run economies under different conditions. This helps to explain why some CPE scholars (heeding Mill's cautionary scepticism) are wary of attempting a close emulation of the natural sciences. Instead, we have to resort to a comparison of what actually exists in the world: we can examine *variations* in *different factors* that *might* have important political consequences and see if variations in different possible causes (possible independent variables) have the posited effects and variations on our dependent variable.

The complexity of political economic phenomena demands caution in designing research. Alive to the 'too many variables' problem and the likelihood of complex configurative causation, comparative political economists are confronted with 'a multiplicity of conditions, a compounding of their influence on what is to be explained (the dependent variable) and an indeterminacy regarding the effect of any one condition or several conditions in combination' (Smelser 1976: 152–3). It is difficult to discern the effect of any one variable or of a series of them in combination. Chapter 4 introduced a 'solution' to this problem pursued by the Marginalists. They used the prior assumption of *ceteris paribus*, which holds everything else constant (apart from the very small number of key factors under scrutiny) in order to brush the complexity problem under the carpet. These kinds of simplifying assumptions are necessary for highly parsimonious explanations and formal model building. The same techniques are used in modern economics, as well as in rational choice political science (see pp. 97–100).

This 'solution' to the complexity problem clearly comes with certain health warnings attached. It has the downside of distancing the model and the analysis from the realities of the social and political world. For some, this is a price worth paying. Others are not so sure. This is all bound up with choices over epistemology, conduct and admissibility, though, as set out above, the various approaches display different strengths and weaknesses. This is not an issue that can be easily or satisfactorily resolved. It is important to recognize that any 'solution' to the complexity problem will involve trade-offs and compromises (see Table 13.4).

Nevertheless, the comparative political science literature does offer us some useful suggestions as to strategies which can help us focus our attention on what really matters in our comparative analysis.

Faced with the complexity problem of too many variables, what comparative political economists have to do is firstly to *reduce* the number of variables, drawing on previous CPE analysis to identify and eliminate obviously irrelevant variables. We can 'judiciously restrict' analysis to 'the really key variables, omitting those of only marginal importance' (Lijphart 1971: 690; Smelser 1976: 152–3; Ragin 2004: 125–8). Thus in our CMH example prior theoretical relevance has been attached to international capital mobility, and it is the role of this independent variable that the CMH explores. The restricting of variables involves theoretically informed interpretation, inevitably guided by prior theoretical assumptions. These will be different depending on which theory you select, so different variables could be omitted as irrelevant. Secondly, it is important to isolate one factor from another, thereby *making as precise as possible* what role each factor is playing and under what conditions. In the case of CMH this is done in relation to exchange rate regimes, with propositions derived from open economy macro-economics about economic policy constraints operating under fixed and floating exchange rates, respectively.

Once our key variables have been reduced as much as possible and isolated one from the other, we need logically and systematically to construct our research design to 'test' the CMH. One methodology would involve examining data on government economic policy for all advanced economies. This could subject to analytical scrutiny CMH assumptions about reduced economic policy autonomy given increased capital mobility. Statistical examination might establish whether the expected patterns of interrelationships between our key variables – capital mobility, exchange rate regime, fiscal policy, monetary policy – can be identified (Garrett and Lange 1991, 1995; Garrett 1998; Franzese 2002; Swank 2002; Mosley 2003).

An alternative strategy might be diachronic analysis (across time) of macro-economic policy-making (and constraints thereon) in a country over the last 50 years, which would cover the period before and after the rise in international capital mobility in the 1970s. The two 'cases' – Country A in the 1950s and 1960s, Country A in the 1990s and 2000s – would be 'similar', because they are in effect the same political economy, thus many factors could be assumed to be roughly equal. The crucial variable – the degree of international capital mobility – will be the key thing that has changed. Obviously, the change over time means that the two cases are not exactly the same in all other respects and other variables cannot be held constant. These are the compromises which have to be made in recognition that, in the social world, the neat and clean research designs of the natural sciences are not entirely plausible.

Another strategy would be to select cases of broadly similar political economies, at a similar size and stage of economic development, but which differ on the key intervening variable – that is, their exchange rate regime. One might choose, for example, the UK and France in the early 2000s, both among the world's leading advanced (post-)industrial economies. These cases should illustrate the different policy autonomy implications the CMH posits of choosing fixed or floating exchange rates. If we deploy a 'mixed methods' approach, these two strategies could be combined by looking at Britain and France across 50 years before and after the rise of international capital mobility (see Clift and Tomlinson 2004). This becomes a much more challenging research project, but claims that are advanced on the back of it carry more weight (Box 13.2).

Box 13.2 A 'checklist' of comparative analysis and research design

When constructing a comparative research design, follow Mill's logic and ask yourself:

- Which strategy am I using?
- What am I identifying as a cause?
- How have I ruled out all other potential factors?
- What is the logic of my 'research design'? Is it 'most similar systems' or 'most different systems'?
- What are my key variables? Are they independent, dependent or intervening variables?
- How am I managing or limiting the 'too many variables' problem?
- What is the hypothesis or theory I am drawing on?
- Why and how have I selected my cases?

We can use our CMH example to illustrate some of the different epistemological and methodological positions which are the stuff of the disciplinary politics discussed above, notably between proponents of large N versus those of small N studies. Of the different possible strategies to assess the CMH – qualitative analysis of a few cases or quantitative analysis of a large number of cases – which findings tell us more about CPE? (See Tables 13.1, 13.2 and 13.3.) The statistical study of all advanced economies can make fairly evident claims to inclusiveness and relevance. What of the analysis based on two cases? Given that the UK and France are both advanced, affluent political economies, one might argue that findings from work on them will be of relevance to similar kinds of economies.

One advantage of this kind of in-depth study is in capturing the historical specificity of contingent national state adaptation processes (see pp. 163–70) in the manner of the German Historical School discussed in Chapters 3 and 4. A small N study enables appreciation of these processes and the historically specific nature of economic policy-making in their complexity. The role of complex conjunctural causation, initial conditions and contextual factors in explanation will limit the extent to which findings can be seen as indicative of wider and broader trends. Such an account would probably fight shy of generalizing about 'the state' and capital mobility, preferring to clarify the degree and nature of policy autonomy in particular cases. Therefore these findings may not be easily 'portable' to other cases.

In the spirit of methodological pluralism, in investigating the CMH it makes sense to read work that approaches the question from a number of different angles. In Chapters 8–12, for example, I offered in-depth qualitative assessment of a variety of ways that a range of advanced political economies were changing in the wake of increasing financial market liberalization and internationalization. This was complemented with quantitative assessment of how far international capital mobility has increased since the 1970s. That way one can get a sense of the broad patterns of macro-economic policy-making in advanced economies and of some of their evolution since the onset of financial globalization, and a more detailed understanding of particular experiences, perhaps of 'critical' cases. This allows deeper understanding of the processes and causal mechanisms at work. Thereafter, one can assess whether the causes of change or stasis in macro-economic policy-making are indeed those posited by CMH theorists.

CONCLUSION

We have explored here how methodological choices involve trade-offs, such as that between generalizability and complexity. These reveal different researchers' stances on what price (in terms of selection of methods, logic of inquiry and the nature of our analysis) they are willing to pay to achieve generalizability of knowledge claims, weighed against the other research goals (such as depth of knowledge and complexity of understanding). For example, the focus of this book reflects choices about knowledge claims. Here we pitch camp on the epistemological middle ground. A CPE proposition may be limited, for example to affluent OECD economies. This may well be a valuable contribution to CPE analysis, in that we should not see such propositions as being less valid or less valuable than broader generalizations.

In this book, I have adopted a pluralist methodological stance, recognizing that qualitative and quantitative are potentially equally instructive, but that they are significantly different undertakings. I reject the notion that either qualitative or quantitative analysis is more scientific or more rigorous. The research goal of qualitative scholars is the explanation of outcomes in individual cases, while the research goal of quantitative scholars is estimating the average effect of one or more causes across a population of cases. The methodological choices made by each are appropriate to their different core aims. Any scholarship in CPE, including this book, has to make methodological choices, and these are never neutral. They rest on a set of assumptions about appropriate modes of social scientific inquiry and about what constitutes social scientific knowledge. It is important to recognize that different research strategies have different merits and that these strengths and weaknesses generate different kinds of insights. When approaching methodological choices and trade-offs, it is crucial to bear in mind the 'health warnings' attached to any research strategies and methods chosen. These are crucially important issues to consider when taking on a major research undertaking such as an extended essay, a research project, a dissertation or a PhD thesis. Full appreciation of what is at stake in these trade-offs is key when evaluating the results of research and the claims made by the scholars regarding the strength of their findings. That done, reading works from each perspective on a given topic or substantive theme is likely to generate a deepened understanding. CPE as a field develops through the accretion of knowledge from various perspectives and methodological standpoints.

14 Conclusion

In this book my central contention has been that a deepened understanding of contemporary capitalism is best founded on a thorough appreciation of the classical political economy progenitors of modern CPE. The chapters have explored key areas of substantive focus for CPE, such as the state, models of capitalism, finance, welfare and inequality. Along the way we have encountered and deployed many of the key insights of a rich lineage of influential thinkers, including Smith, Marx, List, Weber, Hayek, Keynes and Polanyi.

I have made the case for an approach to CPE of capitalism attuned to the social, institutional and ideational context in which capitalist market relations are embedded. This deepens an understanding of how political structures mediate and shape capitalism and its evolution at the global and national levels. CPE offers a rich variety of ways to analyse and understand better capitalisms' drivers, dynamics and implications for societies. It can shine the light on the instabilities and political struggles over capitalism, not just regarding its distributive outcomes, but also how capitalism destabilizes the social order. For example, the actions of large multinational corporations in pursuit of profit, and without regard for environmental consequences which currently lie outside the price mechanism, have been degrading the planet at an alarming rate for the last 100 years or more (Newell and Paterson 1998, 2010). Untrammelled capitalist market activity has devastating implications for climate change and the Earth's ecosystems.

The political economist Karl Polanyi presciently anticipated the hugely damaging environmental consequences of *laissez-faire* capitalism, which can 'not exist for any length of time without annihilating the human and natural substance of society' (Polanyi 2001 [1944]: 3). Thus the ultimate market failure of free market capitalism is that unfettered market operations destroy the social order in which they are embedded. The scale of the market failure involves nothing less than the annihilation of life on a planetary scale. Meanwhile international efforts to tackle the problem are hamstrung by corporations' profit motives and climate change–denying populist political leaders. This, surely, is the key political struggle over capitalism of the 21st century. CPE can offer the tools to understand the power relations within capitalism which hinder efforts to effectively address the climate crisis. In this conclusion, I briefly recap the position within disciplinary politics that such an approach to CPE entails, before revisiting CPE's core insights and some of the recurrent themes of contemporary CPE analysis of advanced capitalisms. I end by suggesting some future directions for the further development of CPE as a field of study.

DISCIPLINARY POLITICS AND CLASSICAL POLITICAL ECONOMY

What unites the classical political economy scholars is that they all share a *pre-disciplinary* view of political economy as a holistic field of study, integrating the political, the economic and the social into their understanding and analysis. Adam Smith, Karl Marx and Friedrich

List all characterize the market-making process, the nature of political intervention in market relations, its underlying dynamics, its consequences and implications in different ways, but they are agreed on the need for a thorough appreciation of the intimate intertwining of the political and the economic. They could not conceive of separating the study of the economic from the political, let alone establishing two rather disconnected academic disciplines – economics and political science – which institutionalized analytical divisions of labour between them.

There can be important, trenchant academic disagreements both between and indeed within disciplines about, among other things, what is considered to be acceptable or admissible work in a given field, how work should be conducted, and how and where its results should be presented. The capacity to define propriety on these issues is the stuff of a disciplinary politics which is sometimes submerged but always important. The approach to CPE adopted in this book attempts to overcome or transcend academic borders, drawing on economic sociology, history and heterodox economics, among others, as well as political science and IPE. This is hard to do, but at the very least it is important to recognize the merits of thinking outside the narrow confines of disciplinary boxes.

As regards thinking outside the box of mainstream political economy analysis, even scholarship inspired by classical political economy can have its shortcomings. We have identified limitations of much of the CPE canon, which struggles to take account of the gendered dimensions of the unequal power relations which stratify political economies. This has shaped, for example, how the political economy of the welfare state and labour markets gets analysed and understood. CPE work on welfare is one obvious sphere where patriarchal power relations and gendered assumptions (about who works, what counts as productive work, who provides social care) have significant effects.

The root causes of this can be found in underlying assumptions and conceptualizations in political economy which fail to take account of gendered inequalities. For feminist political economy scholars, 'gendering' political economy analysis entails 'a questioning of orthodox methods' as well as questioning 'gendered assumptions and biases' inherent in core concepts in political economy, such as what constitutes the 'productive economy', 'unproductive labour', 'work' or the public and private spheres (Spike Peterson 2005: 506–7; Steans 1999; Whitworth 2006; Elias and Roberts 2016, 2018a, 2018b; see pp. 5–6, 88–91, 132–3, 225–7, 231–4).

The post-war era is celebrated by some as a golden age when welfare states were constructed to redistribute wealth. Feminist political economy notes how they did so, but in ways that did not redistribute power between genders in a more equitable manner (see Chapter 11). The resultant institutional settlement of welfare capitalism assigned particular gendered social and economic roles – such as male 'breadwinner' and female 'housewife' and carer. Indeed, the post-war welfare states in many instances reinforced patriarchal social relations. These male breadwinner norms, and underlying unequal power relations, arguably account for women's often lower pay and marginalized position within the labour market. The 'falsely universalizing (implicitly masculinist) analytic frames' of most welfare state analysis explain the under-appreciation of the gendered underpinnings of welfare state settlements (Orloff 2010: 253). Women are substantially over-represented within underpaid, insecure, part-time, flexible employment. They remain under-represented in senior and management roles. These patriarchal assumptions can in turn be exploited by employers, who routinely pay women less and promote them less. As with so many other themes in the comparative analysis of capitalism, the story is a differentiated one. Socially conservative Bavaria took a different path from social democratic Sweden with regard to gender equality, for example.

As this indicates, power relations in societies in which political economies are embedded shape and stratify market relations in a range of different ways. The fundamental objective for CPE analysis, which is hard to achieve because it swims against the tide of the modern evolution of academic social sciences, is to recapture the 'pre-disciplinary' spirit of classical political economy inquiry. The genealogy of political economy charted in Chapter 4 unearthed why this presents such an intellectual challenge. The late 19th- and early 20th-century *Methodenstreit* dispute over the appropriate method and substantive focus of political economic analysis, and over how the individual should be conceptualized, had important implications for political economy and its study thereafter.

Jevons and the other Marginalists on the 'economics as a scientific enterprise' side of the divide held a tightly delimited view of what economics was and what it was not. Marginalism, both in the way it understood individuals and in its assumptions about the properties of markets, redirected the emphasis of political economy away from the categories of land, labour and capital as causes of a stratified, class-based social order riven with unequal power relations. Instead, it focused on a set of apolitical calculations, assuming the world to be populated by apolitical and classless, rational, utility-maximizing individuals. The differential distributional consequences of capitalism which had been so central to the analysis of Ricardo, and especially of Marx, were all simply assumed away; at which point the class struggle evaporates – in the model, at least.

From the broad-ranging concerns of classical political economy, social scientific inquiry into the economic narrowed to focus upon formal analysis of individual economic behaviours in the context of scarcity and the functioning of markets under certain assumed conditions, such as perfect information and perfectly clearing markets. The desire to hone the focus of political economy, identifying what its proponents saw as at its core and proposing a stripped-down, parsimonious, abstract model for analysing it, informed Marginalism's methodological techniques and substantive focus. Today we recognize these as the mainstays of the discipline of economics. The increasing technical specialization of economics meant it became difficult, if not impossible, to 're-embed' the study of the economic (at least as carried out by neo-classical economists) within the social and the political.

As I have argued in this book, despite this apparent 'victory' of Marginalism, *the economy is far too important a subject to leave exclusively to economists*, and CPE and political economy more broadly have a very important place and role to play in the study of the economic. One dramatic illustration of their import is provided by the climate crisis and the devastating global environmental consequences of free market capitalism. Ecological disaster lies outside the price mechanism and therefore market forces, and arguably much analysis in economics, are largely blind to it. The climate crisis constitutes a planetary form of what economists call market failure. The *laissez-faire* approach to economy and society has a cavernous blind spot where ecological sustainability is concerned and cannot be relied upon to resolve the issue or save the planet.

Mainstream economics cannot be relied upon to tackle the enormous environmental threat that growth-addicted global capitalism poses. It is not sufficiently attuned to power relations in the economy that impede efforts to generate effective mitigation. The powerful economic actors who benefit enormously from the existing ecologically unsustainable regime of accumulation will, under free market conditions, not be prevented from ecological destruction. Constructing an environmentally sustainable order, if it is to be achieved, will of necessity be a deeply political process at both domestic and international levels. Political economy, as always an ethical endeavour, can have much to say about how political economic orders should operate and be organized to more effectively address the global climate crisis.

These blind spots about power relations notwithstanding, the rise to dominance of neo-classical economics in the 20th century perhaps signals the 'victory' of the Marginalists over the historicists in the late 19th century. After the *Methodenstreit*, the classical political economy approach did not have anything like the prominence in the 20th century that it had enjoyed in the 19th. This disciplinary history helps us to contextualize the debates about method in modern political economy and CPE. It also helps to explain CPE's rather difficult and complex relationship with economics, which one might imagine to be a ready bedfellow. Some scholars kept the spirit of classical political economy alive in the 20th century, notably Weber, Keynes, Hayek, Veblen, Schumpeter and Polanyi. However, these were somewhat isolated voices, operating in a chasm between the two academic disciplines of politics and economics that were developing largely in isolation from one another.

Although occupying somewhat liminal space in the study of politics, political economy scholarship of burgeoning relevance to IPE and CPE scholars continued to be carried out through the 20th century. We encountered some of this work in the genealogy of CPE and political economy presented in Chapter 1. IPE as a field of study in many ways has a very long lineage (see Clift and Rosamond 2009; Watson 2005a), yet it was in the 1970s that IPE took on a more organized form as an academic sub-field, leading some to mistakenly see 1970 as 'year zero' (on this see Clift *et al.* 2021). In some ways IPE's growth as a field opened up more space for scholarship that was faithful to the classical political economy approach, reducing the marginality of political economy. Then, in the 1990s, an important intervention in disciplinary politics debates renewed efforts to reinvigorate the political economy field. Drawing on and further nurturing the by then vibrant sub-field of IPE, new journals, notably *New Political Economy* and *Review of International Political Economy*, were founded which sought to revitalize political economy, CPE and IPE as intellectual pursuits. These embraced intellectual heterodoxy and recognized the inseparability of economics from politics, and in these ways aimed to recapture some of the spirit of classical political economy (Gamble 1995; Gamble et al. 1996; Payne 2006; RIPE Editors 1994: 1–11). The project has enjoyed considerable success, and by the 2000s this kind of political economy work was routinely appearing with increasing frequency in the pages of a range of international, comparative and general political science journals. Both CPE and IPE were flourishing fields across the advanced economies and beyond. In this book, I have argued that the two should be seen as part of a similar broad intellectual project.

METHODOLOGICAL PLURALISM AND COMPARATIVE POLITICAL ECONOMY

At one level, the notion of 'victory' in the debate about social scientific method is, however, misleading. In the 21st century, strikingly similar issues to those at the heart of the 19th-century *Methodenstreit* continue to be discussed and debated, with no prospect of ultimate resolution. There is, in CPE as in all fields of political inquiry, a trade-off to be made between generalizability and complexity. The two cultures of social research – qualitative and quantitative – which inform the small N and large N approaches to comparative political analysis, respectively, are both reflected in the rich CPE literature. Different views continue to be found in CPE about the pros and cons in the perennial trade-off of knowing 'less about more' or 'more about less'.

The key point is that qualitative and quantitative scholarship represent different kinds of analysis, with distinct intellectual ambitions. Neither is 'better', but their differences must be recognized. For David Levi-Faur, 'if one adopts a more complex ontology' and a more complex understanding of causality, 'then accuracy and intimate knowledge of one's case might be elevated to the same importance as the search for generalization' (Levi-Faur 2006: 371). Thus for some more case-oriented than statistically minded scholars, 'intimate knowledge of one's case is not a secondary goal of social science analysis but at least equal in importance to other goals, such as generalization and parsimony' (ibid.). These are critically important questions for any CPE analysis facing the trade-offs inherent in social science methodologies and questions of research design. How they are resolved needs to be unpacked, evaluated and situated within the relevant disciplinary political context. Commitments to methodological positions should be 'worn on the sleeve', not left implicit or, worse, smuggled in and couched in loaded terms such as 'rigorous' and 'scientific'. It is in this spirit of methodological pluralism that the revitalization of CPE, and the dialogue with IPE, can proceed most fruitfully and be most generative of fresh insights.

COMPARATIVE POLITICAL ECONOMY: THE CORE INSIGHTS

I set out in Chapter 2 the four core insights which distil the essence of key intellectual moves, crucial to thinking like a political economist, which underpin CPE. Subsequent chapters have applied these in a range of theoretical and empirical contexts to provide a deeper understanding of the dynamics of contemporary capitalist restructuring. Here I will reiterate them briefly.

The first is the mutually constitutive understanding of states and markets. At the heart of CPE as a field of study is not 'state' or 'market' as conceptual abstractions, but the comparative analysis of particular sets of state/market relationships. This helps to 'bring the state back in' in a way which suffuses analysis with more of a sense of the politics in play within processes of capitalist restructuring. List, Polanyi, Marx, Keynes and others have all highlighted the inescapable, crucial and fundamental role of the state in shaping market activity and political economic outcomes. This is true within any capitalist economy, be it the archetypal post-war developmental state or a 21st-century 'neo-liberal' economy, because even 'free' markets require political and legal regulation, such as laws to protect property and contractual rights. Yet intervention is much broader and more variegated than that. This suggests posing questions not about more or less state intervention, but about the qualitative nature of state activity and state/economy relations. As a political economy scholar one is free to 'take sides' as to whether a particular set of market conditions do (or do not) deliver the beneficial outcomes for individuals and society that Smith and others posit they would. However, notwithstanding any possible disagreement on this issue, political economy scholarship recognizes that the political and the economic are intimately intertwined, that state and economy are mutually constitutive.

The second core insight is that markets are *not* natural, inevitable or self-sustaining. They are made. Capitalism as a social order is predicated on an active political process of creating market institutions. As such, markets should be conceived as politically constructed and politically maintained sets of institutions. There was nothing natural about changes in the form of companies since the mid-19th century, evolving from small concerns with individual capitalist owner-managers to large joint-stock enterprises. The rise of large-scale corporate economies required new laws, which were the subject of protracted political and ideological struggle. The resultant new political and corporate settlement eventually changed the face of capitalism. Similar dynamics are at play in the changes in finance, firms and national financial systems in the late 20th and early 21st centuries, as well as those which have followed the GFC. The enormous power of modern tech giants such Apple, Facebook and Google reflects a political struggle over how large corporations can organize – enabling, for example, corporate governance structures that limit accountability. Their colossal size, market valuation and market power, and their control of enormous amounts of data about us all, are key facets of their power. This is reinforced by their capacity to sustain oligopolistic dominance of their sectors. Their ability to operate in these ways reflects, again, political decisions by governments, regulators, states and international bodies. It is important to retain an expansive conception of the market-making interventions of states and other authorities, mindful that some market-shaping activity can sneak under the CPE radar. Much of it might not be the kind of thing that gets measured, or that can be measured, or about which data is collected.

The third core insight is that market relations need to be analysed in ways which recognize that political, economic and social processes and institutions are interlinked and should be studied as a complex and interrelated whole. Political economies are negotiated socio-economic orders. 'Embeddedness', a helpful concept dear to economic sociologists, has found its way increasingly into CPE, notably via the influential writings of Karl Polanyi (2001 [1944]). Drawing on Polanyi, much contemporary CPE analysis offers a socially embedded account of actors and institutions (Jackson and Deeg 2008: 683). Embeddedness entails recognition that capitalism's institutional infrastructural arrangements reflect the history, politics and culture of a country. Both at the institutional and the ideational levels, social embeddedness explains how 'common pressures may be refracted through different sets of institutions, leading to different sorts of problems and calling forth distinct solutions' (ibid.; see also Hay 2004a).

The fourth core insight is that capitalism is a dynamic social order. As Wolfgang Streeck puts it, 'all social-institutional orders are always in flux ... slow and gradual change is an ever-present condition of institutional structures' (Streeck 2010: 12). The embeddedness discussed above, after all, is a dynamic not a static phenomenon (Polanyi 2001 [1944]; Block and Evans 2005: 507). Path dependency, too, needs to be understood in ways that are non-deterministic and are built on nuanced understandings of institutions, the agents who animate them and their wider social context, appreciating that there is a good deal 'up for grabs' and amenable to contingent processes of change (Fligstein 1996; Campbell 2004: 71, 2011: 226; Lindberg and Campbell 1991). Key features of advanced political economies *have* changed and this throws down the gauntlet to social scientists to offer convincing *explanations* of change. Concepts like translation and bricolage, as introduced by John Campbell and discussed in Chapter 6, can help. They explain change as involving political choices by creative actors, wherein certain institutional recombinations win out over others (Campbell 2004: 65–71). This kind of thinking alerts us to the contingency of small-scale capitalist change. We also need to be alive to the theoretical possibility of 'great reversals' or dramatic changes, which have periodically occurred within capitalisms in the 20th and 21st centuries.

In light of the discussion in Chapters 11 and 12, a further core insight is the intimate connection between capitalism and increasing inequality. Political and social tensions are generated by the inherent tendencies of capitalism to exacerbate inequalities of wealth and indeed power within and between societies. Efforts to limit capitalism's iniquitous effects are the stuff of ongoing political struggles over how best to regulate capitalism. Inequality is affected by the interaction of the international political economic order and domestic economic policy capacities. Within post-war capitalism, advanced economy societies accepted the expansion and deepening of market liberalization inherent in global capitalism. In doing so, they took solace in government capacity to mitigate capitalism's inegalitarian effects through the building of welfare states and the pursuit of full employment economic policies. Then embedded liberalism gave way to an international order of dis-embedded neo-liberalism. Fast forward to the 21st century and the losers from globalization are legion, while the abilities of welfare states to insulate societies from social dislocation caused by international economic forces seem substantially reduced. The rich get very much richer, while real incomes for average workers stagnate and generosity of social provision is eroded amid 'permanent austerity'. CPE reveals how differing welfare state settlements are instantiations of societal negotiations, of the political and social settlements on which any capitalist regime rests. This cross-national variance produces a variety of views about the desirable distribution of the fruits of growth within firms and across society (who is 'in' and who is 'out'). Yet all face increased demographic and economic pressures in the 21st century.

RECURRENT SUBSTANTIVE THEMES FOR 21ST-CENTURY COMPARATIVE POLITICAL ECONOMY

Comparative political economy: the international and the domestic

This book has the distinctive characteristic of putting CPE in dialogue with IPE. Analysis has proceeded in the spirit of Katzenstein (1978, 1985), Gourevitch (1978, 1986) and Strange (1971, 1976), all of whom focused on the interplay of international and domestic forces, wherein little clear-cut distinction can be identified between the two. In this book we see domestic political economic actors, or entire advanced industrial states, as independent variables, as both 'architects' and 'subjects' of the world economy. The overall evolution of advanced capitalism in the late 20th and early 21st centuries has seen significant globalizing transformations: the rising overseas listing of firms and the development, expansion and internationalization of corporate bond markets and global shares trading, as well as the spread of financialization. These are changing firms, financial systems, societies and capitalisms, yet 'domestic' political economic actors are not simply passive recipients of such changes; rather, they mediate and contest it, as well as being the authors of such change.

Global capitalism has been transformed over recent decades and IPE scholarship, by identifying trends in trade, finance, production and development, provides much useful insight as to the underlying causes. CPE unearths how the impacts of these (similar) changes in the role of international markets within domestic capitalisms differ. The nationally specific institutional configurations and trajectories of capitalist evolution which have long been the mainstays of CPE analysis provide a set of initial conditions in the form of pre-existing norms and structures. These mediate the nature of a national political economy's articulation with the international context and *interact* with new influences. While there are common pressures, there are nonetheless separate paths of adjustment (Hay 2004a; see also Deeg and Jackson 2007: 155–6).

Institutions and comparative capitalisms

Market relations and institutions are always and everywhere intimately interwoven within capitalism. In fact, the institutional infrastructures and contexts are constitutive of market relations and the actual operation of markets. It does not make sense to talk about 'the market' in isolation from or abstracted from this institutional context. An important aspect of the CPE of capitalism is to understand these institutions and their role within and relationship to economic activity and to wider society. The empirical reality of the institutional embedding of market activity should be reflected in how we think about and analyse markets.

Comparativists armed with their typologies of capitalisms inevitably want to use them to discern overarching patterns, trajectories or directions of travel within capitalist restructuring. At the global level, the increasing prevalence and preponderance of market mechanisms are profoundly transforming state/market relations. The convergence thesis claims that this is happening in a way that asymmetrically targets different models of advanced capitalism because, this argument asserts, only the liberal model 'fits'. The LME model of shareholder capitalism, rooted in market mechanisms, can ride the wave of liberalization, while the co-ordination of CME or stakeholder capitalism, rooted in non-market mechanisms, flounders. A teleological evolution towards LME shareholder capitalism over time is posited as a consequence (Crouch and Streeck 1997: 13–15; see also Crouch 2005a, 2005b; Hay 2005).

The resurgence of economic nationalism, protectionism and economic interventionism in the second decade of the 21st century has given us Trump, Brexit and other dramatic upheavals. Whether fuelled by concerns about environmental unsustainability, austerity or inequality, or about inter-generational (in)justice, protests against aspects of liberal free market capitalism have become a more salient feature of the political landscape in advanced economies in recent years. These developments suggest that a teleological path towards an ever more liberal form of capitalism with ever freer and more lightly regulated markets may not be a helpful way to conceptualize the trajectory of contemporary capitalist restructuring (see Chapter 12).

Apart from its obvious difficulty explaining the anti-liberal backlash against globalization, we have encountered numerous other objections, both theoretical and empirical, to the convergence account of the trajectory of advanced capitalist change. Path dependency tells us that the institutions which are constitutive of markets instantiate distinct histories and trajectories of evolution within each economy. This makes convergence among the world's capitalisms an unlikely scenario. An alternative interpretation identifies emergent hybridization of advanced capitalisms. Different (evolving and dynamic) sets of institutional complementarities can in this account explain the *differential* effects of *similar* kinds of changes within capitalisms, potentially generating increased diversity. In analysing what he calls variously 'capitalist diversity' or 'the diversity of economic institutions', Crouch proposes a 'recombinant capitalism' approach to the models of capitalism problematic, which involves 'deconstructing into constituent elements and then being ready to recombine into new shapes the aggregated forms' (2005a: 440). Thus capitalisms should be analysed 'not to determine which (singular) of a number of theoretical types they should each be allocated, but to determine which (plural) of these forms are to be found within them, in roughly what proportions, and with what change over time' (ibid.).

Hybridization suggests a different role for ideal types within the research strategy, which avoids the 'square pegs in round holes' problem. It does not make sense to try to get cases to 'fit' squarely within one or other model. That constitutes a misuse of ideal types (see Hay 2019) and is putting the cart before the horse in comparing capitalisms. Instead, the models are best used to deepen analysis of the empirical realities of political economies. This more sophisticated use of VoC ideal types is harder to achieve and its findings are less likely to throw up clearly identifiable general trends. Nevertheless, this approach has the merit of doing justice to the empirical complexities of capitalist restructuring; hybridization also offers a more contingent, open-ended account of capitalist change.

21st-century welfare capitalism: recalibration or retrenchment?

Issues of inequalities of power and wealth are central to political economy analysis. This is but the latest iteration of a long-running concern to explain, explore and critique the distributional consequences of capitalism which began with the classical political economists. CPE underlines the importance of (historically specific) embedded institutional arrangements for welfare provision in shaping capitalism and the market economy from the 19th century onwards. In the advanced economies, this institutional infrastructure of social protection and labour market regulation intervenes to mitigate the adverse effects of market competition for the losers, and to shape the labour market's norms. In short, historically it was better to be poor and unemployed in Sweden than in the US, because of the configuration of capitalist institutions in each country, the properties and qualities they impart to market relations and their embedding in a societal context. Yet interestingly, capitalism's inequality is being politicized in similar ways across very different societies and welfare regimes. Xenophobic radical right-wing nationalists have had success in both the US and Sweden – and elsewhere – in mobilizing the poor, unemployed, disaffected and 'left behind' to embrace anti-immigration 'solutions' to joblessness and chauvinistic approaches to welfare reform.

Globalization, some argue, leads to a welfare 'race to the bottom', for reasons of tax competition and goodness of fit between a minimal welfare model and ever freer international product, labour and services markets. While change is afoot within advanced economy welfare provision, the 'race to the bottom' thesis does not capture the reality at all well. Thus closer empirical inspection shows that welfare state retrenchment pressures have been overstated (see Swank 2002; Hay 2006). The 'compensation thesis' we encountered in Chapter 11, following the logic of Polanyi's 'double movement' wherein the socially damaging consequences of freer markets provoke resistance within society, underlines how increased international economic exposure heightened the vulnerability of domestic actors to changing global economic conditions, generating calls for protection.

Yet this *is* an era of 'permanent austerity' (P. Pierson 2001) for advanced economy welfare provision, given demographic pressures, the increasing costs of care, high structural unemployment and debt-laden public finances. To manage this problem and address the inflationary pressures on state welfare spending, there is an emergent new welfare settlement which replaces an emphasis on 'decommodification' (Esping-Andersen 1990) with one on 'activation'. Returning men and women of all ages to the labour market, keeping them there for as long as possible and making the benefits system and labour market work in tandem (Haveman 1997) are central to the new political economy of welfare. In-work benefits and targeted tax breaks and subsidies seek to 'make work pay' and tackle poverty traps; meanwhile, many benefits are becoming less generous and some are increasingly contingent on job search efforts. Another dimension of the evolving political economy of welfare is increased reliance on market mechanisms in the delivery of public welfare services and the 'recommodification' of welfare. These evolutions are of wider significance for CPE because of the historically interconnected evolution of welfare regimes and models of capitalism. Without an appreciation of this symbiotic relationship, accounts of *both* the welfare regime *and* a given national capitalism are incomplete.

Growing inequalities and neo-liberal state transformations across advanced economies are altering the distribution of wealth and power within societies. Even in the former social democratic heartlands, public sectors are being privatized, marketized and transformed. Levels of public provision, and the generosity of welfare, are being scaled back. This has seen inequalities widen across all advanced economies and led to more disaffection and growing instability within the social and political settlement on which capitalism rests. Threats are posed to liberal welfare capitalism by resurgent political forces of economic nationalism, nativist anti-'globalism' and illiberal populism that have gained ground in various societies across the advanced capitalist world. The trajectories of national capitalisms are likely to alter as a result. The challenge to the institutional and regulatory edifice upon which liberal economic internationalism has been built over many decades is profound. This suggests different kinds of interactions between domestic and international forces than those that obtained during the complex economic interdependence which prevailed from the collapse of Bretton Woods in the 1970s up to the early 21st century and the GFC.

For all these changes and challenges, however, welfare states continue to play a hugely significant role, affecting the disposable incomes and life chances of great swathes of the OECD world. The overall volumes of advanced economy welfare spending continue to rise in reflection of this. As this demonstrates, capitalism and the welfare state institutions, programmes and regimes exist in an inextricably interactive relationship. The provision of non-economic public goods such as social stability and an educated workforce by the welfare state is but one aspect of its symbiotic relationship with capitalism.

COMPARATIVE POLITICAL ECONOMY: THE ROAD AHEAD

Comparative political economy and ongoing incorporation of the ideational dimension

A consistent emphasis in this book has been that Weberian notions of *Verstehen*, and how economic actors understand their environment, represent important insights for CPE scholarship (Weber 1978 [1922]; Swedberg 1998: 36). These ideational processes play out differently in different political economies, generating diverse national traditions of economic thought, state traditions (Dyson 1980) or shared understandings of markets, the state and capitalism. These social constructions of political economic ideas, distilled into paradigms, can shape material conditions. As Rosamond puts it, 'an idea can become sedimented and "banal" in the sense of becoming commonsensical and barely discussed'; and these 'emergent intersubjectivities' are important 'because of the ways they help to structure both perceptions and arguments amongst policy actors' (Rosamond 2002: 158; see also Hall 1989: 383–6; Campbell 1998: 378–82; Jackson and Deeg 2008: 683; Hay 2016).

Appreciation of the differentiated, ideationally distinctive kinds of state/society complexes of advanced political economies has been an important foundation of and focal point for the 'ideational turn' in CPE (see e.g. Schmidt 2002; Clift 2012). What Dyson has termed 'the underlying importance of ideas as real phenomena and of their internalization by domestic elites' has always been crucial to explanations in political economy, and is becoming increasingly recognized as such within CPE. It 'underlines the complex interweaving and mutual interdependence between the material and the ideational' (2000: 647). This is a fruitful avenue of inquiry which CPE can develop further. Weberian interpretive causality, wherein one can only explain social action through the understanding of the actor (Swedberg 1998: 23), can underpin a contemporary research agenda which 'goes beyond the comparison of state economic policies and formal institutions to examine differences in the social organization of private economic activity' (Hollingsworth et al. 1994: 4; Jackson and Deeg 2006). Ideationally attuned CPE has power to add to the understanding of contemporary capitalist restructuring in drawing attention to the contingency, context-specificity and contested nature of dominant economic ideas and understandings of how the economy works.

Combating Eurocentrism and OECD-centrism

One of the themes of this book is the potential for greater cross-fertilization between CPE and IPE, given significant commonalities of theorizing, approach and substantive analytical focus. IPE, especially when conceived as a continuation of the classical political economy tradition, can become a field that CPE draws on, feeds off and contributes to much more. Yet both IPE and CPE need to extend their gaze more systematically beyond the world's richer economies and the OECD states, at the very least to include the BRICS and other emerging markets. We have noted in a number of places how many of the theories, concepts and analytical frameworks developed within contemporary CPE have been primarily developed for the analysis of European (and to a lesser extent Antipodean and North American) experience. It therefore has 'Eurocentrism' health warnings attached, which some see as applying equally strongly to the classical political economy scholarship on which modern CPE builds (Hobson 2013a, 2013b; Helleiner and Wang 2018; Chey and Helleiner 2018).

The particular trajectory and character of economic development in Western Europe and North America are unlikely to be reproduced in the same way elsewhere. In the BRICS and beyond, the informal sector and self-employment often play larger roles, the displacement of the state and social entitlements within the economy are often considerably smaller, and patterns of urbanization differ markedly from the European experience (see Gough and Therborn 2010: 707). If capitalism and society develop in different ways, so the categories and typologies developed to explain European capitalist experience may have limited explanatory purchase elsewhere. To explore and address this issue, there needs to be a much fuller engagement between CPE and developmental political economy (see e.g. Lane and Ersson 1997; Hoogevelt 2001). The work of scholars such as Tony Payne (2005) and Nicola Phillips (2005) needs to be systematically engaged with in CPE, especially in a 21st century where China is now such a dominant power and other non-Western economies are on the rise.

While CPE has proved adept at analysing and explaining disparities of wealth and economic inequality *within* the advanced economies, its research agendas have often neglected the much larger and more significant gulfs between rich and poor between the global North and global South, or between rich and poor *within* the global South. Fuller engagement between CPE and developmental political economy would enhance its potential to address some of the most pressing political economic questions of the 21st century:

> would anyone freely choose a distributional pattern of scarce goods and services leading to hundreds of millions of people suffering serious harm and disadvantage independent of their will and consent (and 50,000 dying every day of malnutrition and poverty related causes)? (Held and McGrew 2003: 41)

Why is it that the amount spent on frivolous luxuries such as jewellery, cosmetics and things like pet food in Europe and North America each year dwarfs the amount of money which could be spent (but is not) on delivering clean water, basic sanitation, healthcare and education to all the world's poor (ibid.)? CPE tells us that institutions can and do make a huge difference to capitalism's distributional consequences. Surely more could be done to address these vast disparities, whose origins are to be found within the dynamics of global capitalism in general, and advanced 'post-industrial' capitalism specifically. It is in the narrow self-interest of the richer nations to do so, since one consequence of the levels of global inequality is continuing and accelerating environmental degradation.

Polanyi analysed the environmental threat that capitalism posed in terms of land (by which he meant nature) as a fictitious commodity. He wrote of the dangerous 'stark utopia' of a 'dis-embedded' market order and untrammelled international market forces for domestic political economies and societies (Polanyi 2001 [1944]: 3). He explored the shortcomings of the dominant economic ideas of 'the liberal creed' and the 'weaknesses and perils', indeed fundamental contradictions, in unregulated free markets. Economic relations and market activity must he felt, be 'embedded' in the social order, otherwise 'human beings would perish from the effects of social exposure' (Polanyi 2001 [1944]: 76). Society had, in short, to be 'protected against the ravages of this satanic mill' (Polanyi 2001 [1944]: 76–7). Without the 'protective covering of cultural institutions', the institutional, regulatory and social context within which the market is embedded, humanity would suffer from 'acute social dislocation through vice, perversion, crime, and starvation. Nature would be reduced to its elements, neighbourhoods and landscapes defiled, rivers polluted, military safety jeopardised, and the power to produce food and raw materials destroyed' (Polanyi 2001 [1944]: 76).

Political economy has always been an ethical endeavour, with much to say about how political economic orders should operate and be organized. There is scope for CPE to deliver much more on how these global inequalities could be mitigated and reduced through the mobilization of new social forces, changing approaches to governance and institutional innovation. CPE has scope to contribute in important ways to understandings of how the global climate crisis can be addressed.

CONCLUSION

CPE highlights the contingency and historical specificity of individual national state adaptation processes, and is accordingly wary of hasty generalization about a retreat of the state, capitalist convergence or a welfare 'race to the bottom'. The 'always embedded' notion of mutual constitution of state and market, and the expansive conception of market-making intervention which has informed the discussion in this book, indicates that there are many places to look for the new state activism and new kinds of state/market interaction – for example, within the authoring of global regulations and standards. In this way, CPE can 'break with the artificiality that characterizes the concept of the market in economic theory as well as in social science discourse in general' (Swedberg 2005: 233). At the core of CPE is an understanding of capitalist evolution since the 19th century, not as the natural working-out of inexorable economic logics, but as contingent and deeply political processes of market-making and re-regulation. It is this approach, built on the insights of classical political economy, that can help CPE deepen understandings of 21st-century capitalism.

A Guide to Further Reading

ADAM SMITH

Heilbroner, R. (1986) *The Essential Adam Smith* (Oxford: Oxford University Press).
Rothschild, E. (2001) *Economic Sentiments: Adam Smith, Condorcet and the Enlightenment* (Cambridge, MA: Harvard University Press).
Watson, M. (2005) *Foundations of International Political Economy* (Basingstoke: Palgrave Macmillan).

KARL MARX

Cox, R. (1987) *Power, Production and World Order* (New York: Columbia University Press).
Harvey, D. (1982) *The Limits of Capital* (Oxford: Blackwell).
Harvey, D. (2010) *A Companion to Marx's Capital* (London: Verso).
McLellan, D. (1980) *The Thought of Karl Marx* (Basingstoke: Macmillan).
Wolff, T. (2002) *Why Read Marx Today?* (Oxford: Oxford University Press).

KARL POLANYI

Dale, G. (2010) *Karl Polanyi: The Limits of the Market* (Cambridge: Polity).
Dale, G. (2016) *Reconstructing Karl Polanyi: Excavation and Critique* (London: Pluto Press).
Dale, G., Holmes, C. and Markantonatou, M. (eds) (2019) *Karl Polanyi's Political and Economic Thought* (Newcastle-upon-Tyne: Agenda Publishing).
Watson, M. (2005) *Foundations of International Political Economy* (Basingstoke: Palgrave Macmillan).

JOHN MAYNARD KEYNES

Backhouse, R. E. and Bateman, B. W. (eds) (2006) *The Cambridge Companion to Keynes* (Cambridge: Cambridge University Press).
Bleaney, M. (1985) *The Rise and Fall of Keynesian Economics: An Investigation of Its Contribution to Capitalist Development* (Basingstoke: Macmillan).
Clarke, P. (2009) *Keynes* (London: Bloomsbury).
Skidelsky, R. (2009) *Keynes: The Return of the Master: Why, Sixty Years After His Death, John Maynard Keynes Is the Most Important Economic Thinker in the World* (London: Allen Lane).

FRIEDRICH LIST AND ECONOMIC NATIONALISM

Chang, H.-J. (2002) *Kicking Away the Ladder: Development Strategy in Historical Perspective* (London: Anthem Press).

Crane, G. (1998) 'Economic Nationalism: Bringing the Nation Back In', *Millennium: Journal of International Studies*, 27(1): 55–76.

Harlen, C. (1999) 'A Reappraisal of Classical Economic Nationalism and Economic Liberalism', *International Studies Quarterly*, 43(4): 733–44.

Helleiner, E. (2002) 'Economic Nationalism as a Challenge to Economic Liberalism? Lessons from the 19th Century', *International Studies Quarterly*, 46(3): 307–29.

Helleiner, E. and Pickel, A. (eds) (2005) *Economic Nationalism in a Globalizing World* (Ithaca, NY: Cornell University Press).

Levi-Faur, D. (1997) 'Friedrich List and the Political Economy of the Nation-State', *Review of International Political Economy*, 4(1): 154–78.

FRIEDRICH VON HAYEK

Gamble, A. (1996) *Hayek: The Iron Cage of Liberty* (Cambridge: Polity Press).

Feser, E. (ed.) (2006) *The Cambridge Companion to Hayek* (Cambridge: Cambridge University Press).

IDEATIONAL ANALYSIS

Abdelal, R., Blyth, M. and Parsons, C. (eds) (2010) *Constructing the International Economy* (Ithaca, NY: Cornell University Press).

Blyth, M. (2002) *Great Transformations* (Cambridge: Cambridge University Press).

Campbell, J. (1998) 'Institutional Analysis and the Role of Ideas in Political Economy', *Theory and Society*, 27(3): 377–409.

Ruggie, J. (1998) *Constructing the World Polity* (Abingdon: Routledge).

Schmidt, V. (2008) 'Discursive Institutionalism: The Explanatory Power of Ideas and Discourse', *Annual Review of Political Science*, 11: 303–26.

Schmidt, V. A. (2010) 'Taking Ideas and Discourse Seriously: Explaining Change Through Discursive Institutionalism as the Fourth "New Institutionalism"', *European Political Science Review*, 2(1): 1–25.

Widmaier, W. W., Blyth, M. and Seabrooke, L. (2007) 'Exogenous Shocks or Endogenous Constructions? The Meanings of Wars and Crises', *International Studies Quarterly*, 51(4), 747–59.

INSTITUTIONALISM

Campbell, J. (1998) 'Institutional Analysis and the Role of Ideas in Political Economy', *Economy and Society*, 27(3): 377–409.

Campbell, J. (2004) *Institutional Change and Globalization* (Princeton, NJ: Princeton University Press).

Fioretos, O., Falleti, T. G. and Sheingate, A. (2016) 'Historical Institutionalism in Political Science', in *The Oxford Handbook of Historical Institutionalism* (Oxford: Oxford University Press).

Mahoney, J. and Thelen, K. (eds) (2010) *Explaining Institutional Change: Ambiguity, Agency and Power* (Cambridge: Cambridge University Press).

Pierson, P. (2004) *Politics in Time* (Princeton, NJ: Princeton University Press).

Streeck, W. and Thelen, K. (eds) (2005) *Beyond Continuity: Institutional Change in Advanced Industrial Economies* (Oxford: Oxford University Press).

THE STATE

Dyson, K. (1980) *The State Tradition in Western Europe* (Oxford: Martin Robertson).

Dyson, K. (2014) *States, Debt, and Power: 'Saints' and 'Sinners' in European History and Integration* (Oxford: Oxford University Press).

Jessop, B. (2002) *The Future of the Capitalist State* (Cambridge: Polity Press).

King, D. and Le Galès, P. (eds) *Reconfiguring European States in Crisis* (Oxford: Oxford University Press).

Levy, J. (ed.) *The State After Statism: New State Activities in the Age of Liberalization* (Cambridge, MA: Harvard University Press).

Schmidt, V. A. (2009) 'Putting the Political Back into Political Economy by Bringing the State Back in Yet Again', *World Politics*, 61(3): 516–46.

Weiss, L. (ed.) (2003) *States in the Global Economy* (Cambridge: Cambridge University Press).

Woo-Cumings, M. (ed.) (1999) *The Developmental State* (Ithaca, NY: Cornell University Press).

COMPARATIVE CAPITALISMS

Amable, B. (2003) *The Diversity of Modern Capitalism* (Oxford: Oxford University Press).

Crouch, C. (2005) *Capitalist Diversity and Change* (Oxford: Oxford University Press).

Crouch, C. and Streeck, W. (eds) (1997) *The Political Economy of Modern Capitalism: Mapping Convergence and Diversity* (London: Sage).

Hancké, B. (ed.) (2009) *Debating Varieties of Capitalism* (Oxford: Oxford University Press).

Hancké, B., Rhodes, M. and Thatcher, M. (eds) (2007) *Beyond Varieties of Capitalism: Conflict, Contradictions, and Complementarities in the European Economy* (Oxford: Oxford University Press).

Kotz, D., McDonough, T. and Reich, M. (1994) *Social Structures of Accumulation: The Political Economy of Growth and Crisis* (Cambridge: Cambridge University Press).

McDonough, T., Reich, M. and Kotz, D. (eds) (2010) *Contemporary Capitalism and Its Crisis: Social Structure of Accumulation Theory for the 21st Century* (Cambridge: Cambridge University Press).

Schmidt, V. (2002) *The Futures of European Capitalism* (Oxford: Oxford University Press).

BRETTON WOODS

Eichengreen, B. (1996) *Globalizing Capital* (Princeton, NJ: Princeton University Press).

Eichengreen, B. and Kenen, P. (1994) 'Managing the World Economy Under the Bretton Woods System: An Overview', in P. Kenen (ed.), *Managing the World Economy* (Washington, DC: Institute for International Economics), pp. 3–57.

Helleiner, E. (1994) *States and the Re-emergence of Global Finance* (Ithaca, NY: Cornell University Press).

FINANCE AND THE GLOBAL FINANCIAL CRISIS

Blyth, M. (2013) *Austerity: The History of a Dangerous Idea* (Oxford: Oxford University Press).

Clift, B. (2018) *The IMF and the Politics of Austerity in the Wake of the Global Financial Crisis* (Oxford: Oxford University Press).

Gabor, D. and Ban, C. (2016) 'Banking on Bonds: The New Links Between States and Markets', *JCMS: Journal of Common Market Studies*, 54(3): 617–35.

Gamble, A. (2009) *Spectre at the Feast* (Basingstoke: Palgrave Macmillan).

Gamble, A. (2014) *Crisis Without End?* (Basingstoke: Palgrave Macmillan).

Hardie, I. and Howarth, D. (eds) (2013) *Market-Based Banking and the International Financial Crisis* (Oxford: Oxford University Press).

Helleiner, E. (2014) *The Status Quo Crisis: Global Financial Governance After the 2008 Meltdown* (Oxford: Oxford University Press).

Maxfield, S., Winecoff, W. K. and Young, K. L. (2017) 'An Empirical Investigation of the Financialization Convergence Hypothesis', *Review of International Political Economy*, 24(6): 1004–29.

Pérez, S. (2019) *Banking on Privilege: The Politics of Spanish Financial Reform* (Ithaca, NY: Cornell University Press).

Tooze, A. (2018) *Crashed: How a Decade of Financial Crises Changed the World* (Harmondsworth: Penguin).

Van der Zwan, N. (2014) 'Making Sense of Financialization', *Socio-Economic Review*, 12(1): 99–129.

NEO-LIBERALISM

Crouch, C. (2011) *The Strange Non-death of Neoliberalism* (Cambridge: Polity Press).

Davies, W. (2016) *The Limits of Neoliberalism: Authority, Sovereignty and the Logic of Competition* (London: Sage).

Gamble, A. (1988) *The Free Economy and the Strong State* (Basingstoke: Macmillan).

Mirowski, P. (2013) *Never Let a Serious Crisis Go to Waste: How Neoliberalism Survived the Financial Meltdown* (London: Verso Books).

Peck, J. (2007) *Constructions of Neoliberal Reason* (Oxford: Oxford University Press).

Schmidt, V. and Thatcher, M. (eds) (2013) *Resilient Liberalism in Europe's Political Economy* (Cambridge: Cambridge University Press).

INEQUALITY

Bourguignon, F. (2015) *The Globalization of Inequality* (Princeton, NJ: Princeton University Press).

Hacker, J. and Pierson, P. (2010) 'Winner-Take-All Politics: Public Policy, Political Organization, and the Precipitous Rise of Top Incomes in the United States', *Politics and Society*, 38(2): 152–204.

Hager, S. B. (2018) 'Varieties of Top Incomes?', *Socio-Economic Review*. https://doi.org/10.1093/ser/mwy036.

Milanovic, B. (2016) *Global Inequality: A New Approach for the Age of Globalization* (Cambridge, MA: Harvard University Press).

Nolan, B. (ed.) (2018) *Inequality and Inclusive Growth in Rich Countries: Shared Challenges and Contrasting Fortunes* (Oxford: Oxford University Press).

Stiglitz, J. E. (2012) *The Price of Inequality: How Today's Divided Society Endangers Our Future* (New York: WW Norton).

WELFARE

Esping-Andersen, G. (1990) *The Three Worlds of Welfare Capitalism* (Cambridge: Polity Press).

Esping-Andersen, G. (ed.) (1996) *Welfare States in Transition: National Adaptations in Global Economies* (London: Sage).

Hay, C. and Wincott, D. (2012) *The Political Economy of European Welfare Capitalism* (Basingstoke: Palgrave Macmillan).

Offe, C. (1984) *Contradictions of the Welfare State* (London: Hutchinson).
Pierson, P. (ed.) *The New Politics of the Welfare State* (Oxford: Oxford University Press).

COMPARATIVE POLITICAL ECONOMY METHOD

Bennett, A. and Checkel, J. T. (eds) (2014) *Process Tracing: From Metaphor to Analytic Tool* (Cambridge: Cambridge University Press).
Brady, H. and Collier, D. (eds) *Rethinking Social Inquiry: Diverse Tools, Shared Standards* (Lanham, MD: Rowman & Littlefield).
George, A. and Bennett, A. (2005) *Case Studies and Theory Development in the Social Sciences* (Cambridge, MA: MIT Press).
Gerring, J. (2006) *Case Study Research: Principles and Practices* (Cambridge: Cambridge University Press).
Hall, P. (2003) 'Aligning Ontology and Methodology in Comparative Research', in J. Mahoney and D. Rueschemeyer (eds), *Comparative Historical Analysis in the Social Sciences* (Cambridge: Cambridge University Press), pp. 373–406.
Hay, C. (2002) *Political Analysis* (Basingstoke: Palgrave Macmillan).
Peters, B. G. (1998) *Comparative Politics: Theory and Methods* (New York: NYU Press).

FRANCE

Amable, B. (2017) *Structural Crisis and Institutional Change in Modern Capitalism* (Oxford: Oxford University Press).
Clift, B. (2004) 'The French Model of Capitalism: *Still* Exceptional?', in J. Perraton and B. Clift (eds), *Where Are National Capitalisms Now?* (Basingstoke: Palgrave Macmillan), pp. 91–110.
Clift, B. (2012) 'Comparative Capitalisms, Ideational Political Economy and French Post-*Dirigiste* Responses to the Global Financial Crisis', *New Political Economy*, 17(5): 565–90.
Loriaux, M. (1991) *France After Hegemony: International Change and Financial Reform* (Ithaca, NY: Cornell University Press).
Loriaux, M. (1999) 'The French Developmental State as Myth and Moral Ambition', in M. Woo-Cumings (ed.), *The Developmental State* (Ithaca, NY: Cornell University Press), pp. 235–75.
Schmidt, V. (1996) *From State to Market? The Transformation of French Business and Government* (Cambridge: Cambridge University Press).

UK

Berry, C. (2016) *Austerity Politics and UK Economic Policy* (Cham: Springer).
Coates, D. (2000) *Models of Capitalism* (Cambridge: Polity Press).
English, R. and Kenny, M. (1999) *Rethinking British Decline* (Basingstoke: Palgrave).
Gamble, A. (1990) *Britain in Decline* (Basingstoke: Macmillan).
Green, J. and Lavery, S. (2015) 'The Regressive Recovery: Distribution, Inequality and State Power in Britain's Post-Crisis Political Economy', *New Political Economy*, 20(6): 894–923.
Lavery, S. (2019) *British Capitalism After the Crisis* (Cham: Springer International).
Thompson, H. (2017) 'Inevitability and Contingency: The Political Economy of Brexit', *British Journal of Politics and International Relations*, 19(3): 434–49.
Tomlinson, J. (1990) *Public Policy and the Economy Since 1900* (Oxford: Clarendon Press).

US

Campbell, J., Hollingsworth, J. and Lindberg, L. (eds) (1991) *Governance of the American Economy* (New York: Cambridge University Press).

Coates, D. (2000) *Models of Capitalism* (Cambridge: Polity Press).

Davis, G. (2009) *Managed by the Markets: How Finance Re-shaped America* (Oxford: Oxford University Press).

Jacobs, L. R. and King, D. S. (2016) *Fed Power: How Finance Wins* (Oxford: Oxford University Press).

Krippner, G. (2011) *Capitalizing on Crisis* (Cambridge, MA: Harvard University Press).

Montgomerie, J. (2009) 'The Pursuit of (Past) Happiness? Middle-Class Indebtedness and American Financialisation', *New Political Economy*, 14(1): 1–24.

GERMANY

Deeg, R. (1999) *Finance Capitalism Unveiled: Banks and the German Political Economy* (Ann Arbor, MI: University of Michigan Press).

Haipeter, T. (2020) 'Financial Market Capitalism and Labour in Germany. Merits and Limits of a Sociological Concept', *German Politics*, 29(3): 382–403.

Lehrer, M. and Celo, S. (2016) 'German Family Capitalism in the 21st Century: Patient Capital Between Bifurcation and Symbiosis', *Socio-Economic Review*, 14(4): 729–50.

Röper, N. (2018) 'German Finance Capitalism: The Paradigm Shift Underlying Financial Diversification', *New Political Economy*, 23(3): 366–90.

Streeck, W. and Yamamura, K. (eds) (2003) *The Origins of Nonliberal Capitalism* (Ithaca, NY: Cornell University Press).

Yamamura, K. and Streeck, W. (eds) (2003) *The End of Diversity? Prospects for German and Japanese Capitalism* (Ithaca, NY: Cornell University Press).

JAPAN

Chiavacci, D. and Lechevalier, S. (2017) 'Japanese Political Economy Revisited: Diverse Corporate Change, Institutional Transformation, and Abenomics', *Japan Forum*, 29(3): 299–311.

Morris-Suzuki, T. and Takuro, S. (2016) *Japanese Capitalism Since 1945: Critical Perspectives*. Abingdon: Routledge.

Shibata, S. (2016) 'Resisting Japan's Neoliberal Model of Capitalism: Intensification and Change in Contemporary Patterns of Class Struggle', *British Journal of Industrial Relations*, 54(3): 496–521.

Streeck, W. and Yamamura, K. (eds) (2003) *The Origins of Nonliberal Capitalism* (Ithaca, NY: Cornell University Press).

Vogel, S. K. (2019) 'Japan's Ambivalent Pursuit of Shareholder Capitalism', *Politics & Society*, 47(1): 117–44.

Yamada, T. (2018) 'Analyses of Japanese Capitalism Based on the Régulation Approach: An Overview of 30 Years of Research', in *Contemporary Capitalism and Civil Society* (Singapore: Springer), pp. 127–49.

Yamamura, K. and Streeck, W. (eds) (2003) *The End of Diversity? Prospects for German and Japanese Capitalism* (Ithaca, NY: Cornell University Press).

KOREA

Pirie, I. (2007) *The Korean Developmental State: From Dirigisme to Neoliberalism* (Abingdon: Routledge).

Thurbon, E. (2016) *Developmental Mindset: The Revival of Financial Activism in South Korea* (Ithaca, NY: Cornell University Press).

CHINA

Breslin, S. (2007) *China and the Global Economy* (Basingstoke: Palgrave Macmillan).

Gruin, J. (2019) *Communists Constructing Capitalism: State, Market, and the Party in China's Financial Reform* (Manchester: Manchester University Press).

Zhao, S. (2017) 'Whither the China Model: Revisiting the Debate', *Journal of Contemporary China*, 26(103): 1–17.

Zhang, X. (2017) 'Chinese Capitalism and the Maritime Silk Road: A World-Systems Perspective', *Geopolitics*, 22(2): 310–31.

Bibliography

Abdelal, R. (2006) 'Writing the Rules of Global Finance: France, Europe, and Capital Liberalization', *Review of International Political Economy*, 13(1): 1–27.

Abdelal, R., Blyth, M. and Parsons, C. (2010) 'Constructing the International Economy', in R. Abdelal, M. Blyth and C. Parsons (eds), *Constructing the International Economy* (Ithaca, NY: Cornell University Press), pp. 1–20.

Acker, J. (1989) 'The Problem with Patriarchy', *Sociology*, 23(2): 235–40.

Adrian, T. and Shin, H. S. (2008) 'Financial Intermediaries, Financial Stability and Monetary Policy', Paper Prepared for the Federal Reserve Bank of Kansas City Symposium at Jackson Hole, 21–23 August.

Adrian, T. and Shin, H. S. (2010) 'The Changing Nature of Financial Intermediation and the Financial Crisis of 2007–09'. Federal Reserve Bank of New York Staff Reports No. 439.

Aglietta, M. (1979) *A Theory of Capitalist Regulation: The US Experience* (New York: Schocken Books).

Aglietta, M. (2000) 'Shareholder Value and Corporate Governance: Some Tricky Questions', *Economy and Society*, 29(1): 146–59.

Aglietta, M. and Breton, R. (2001) 'Financial Systems, Corporate Control and Capital Accumulation', *Economy and society*, 30(4): 433–66.

Aglietta, M. and Rebérioux, A. (2005) *Corporate Governance Adrift?* (Cheltenham: Elgar).

Ahmad, S. (1990) 'Adam Smith's Four Invisible Hands', *History of Political Economy*, 22(1): 137–44.

Albert, M. (1993) *Capitalism Against Capitalism* (Chichester: Wiley).

Alcouffe, C. (2000) 'Judges and CEOs: French Aspects of Corporate Governance', *European Journal of Law and Economics*, 9(2): 127–44.

Allan, J. and Scruggs, L. (2004) 'Political Partisanship and Welfare State Reform in Advanced Industrial Societies', *American Journal of Political Science*, 48(3): 493–512.

Alvarez, I. (2015) 'Financialization, Non-financial Corporations and Income Inequality: The Case of France', *Socio-Economic Review*, 13(3): 449–75.

Amable, B. (2003) *The Diversity of Modern Capitalism* (Oxford: Oxford University Press).

Amable, B. (2017) *Structural Crisis and Institutional Change in Modern Capitalism* (Oxford: Oxford University Press).

Amin, A. (1994) *Post-Fordism: A Reader* (Oxford: Blackwell).

Amsden, A. (2001) *The Rise of 'the Rest': Challenges to the West from Late- Industrializing Economies* (Oxford: Oxford University Press).

Anderson, P. (1974) *Lineages of the Absolutist State* (London: Verso).

Anderson, E. (2000) 'Beyond Homo Economicus: New Developments in Theories of Social Norms', *Philosophy and Public Affairs*, 29(2): 170–200.

Anderson, P. and Camiller, P. (eds) (1994) *Mapping the West European Left* (London: Verso).

Andersson, R. (2014) *Illegality, Inc.: Clandestine Migration and the Business of Bordering Europe* (Oakland, CA: University of California Press).

Andrews, D. (1994) 'Capital Mobility and State Autonomy: Towards a Structural Theory of International Monetary Relations', *International Studies Quarterly*, 38(2): 193–218.

Aoki, M. (2000) *Information, Corporate Governance and Institutional Diversity* (Oxford: Oxford University Press).

Arrighi, G. (1994) *The Long Twentieth Century: Money, Power, and the Origins of Our Times* (London: Verso).

Arrighi, G. (1996) *The Long Twentieth Century: Money, Power, and the Origins of Our Time* (London: Verso).

Arrighi, G. (2010) *The Long Twentieth Century: Money, Power, and the Origins of Our Times*, New Edition (London: Verso).

Arrow, K. (1951) *Social Choice and Individual Values* (New York: Wiley).

Arthur, W. (1989) 'Competing Technologies, Increasing Returns and Lock-In by Historical Events', *Economic Journal*, 99: 116–31.

Assa, J. (2012) 'Financialization and Its Consequences: The OECD Experience', *Finance Research*, 1(1): 35–9.

Assa, J. (2016) *The Financialization of GDP: Implications for Economic Theory and Policy* (New York: Routledge).

Atal, M. R. (2019) *When Companies Rule: Corporate Political Authority in India, Kenya and South Africa* (Doctoral thesis). https://www.repository.cam.ac.uk/handle/1810/289776.

Atkinson, A. B. (2015) *Inequality* (Cambridge, MA: Harvard University Press).

Bachrach, P. and Baratz, M. S. (1962) 'Two Faces of Power', *The American political science review*, 56(4): 947–52.

Bachrach, P. and Baratz, M. S. (1963) 'Decisions and Nondecisions: An Analytical Framework', *The American Political Science Review*, 57(3): 632–42.

Backhouse, R. (1994) *Economists and the Economy: The Evolution of Economic Ideas*, 2nd edn (London: Transaction Publishers).

Backhouse, R. (2002) *The Penguin History of Economics* (London: Penguin).

Backhouse, R. (2006) 'The Keynesian Revolution', in R. Backhouse and B. Bateman (eds), *The Cambridge Companion to Keynes* (Cambridge: Cambridge University Press), pp. 19–38.

Backhouse, R. E. and Bateman, B. W. (eds) (2006) *The Cambridge Companion to Keynes* (Cambridge: Cambridge University Press).

Baines, J. and Hager, S. B. (2019) 'Financial Crisis, Inequality, and Capitalist Diversity: A Critique of the Capital as Power Model of the Stock Market', *New Political Economy*: 1–18.

Bair, J. and Mahutga, M. (2012) 'Varieties of Offshoring? Spatial Fragmentation and the Organization of Production in 21st Century Capitalism', in G. Morgan and R. Whitley (eds), *Capitalism and Capitalisms in the 21st Century* (Oxford: Oxford University Press), pp. 270–97.

Bakker, I. (2007) 'Social Reproduction and the Constitution of a Gendered Political Economy', *New Political Economy*, 12(4): 541–56.

Baker, A. (2013a) 'The New Political Economy of the Macroprudential Ideational Shift', *New Political Economy*, 18(1): 112–39.

Baker, A. (2013b) 'The Gradual Transformation? The Incremental Dynamics of Macroprudential Regulation', *Regulation and Governance*, 7(2): 417–34.

Baker, A. (2014) 'Transnational Technocracy and the Macroprudential Paradox', in *Transnational Financial Regulation After the Crisis* (London: Routledge), pp. 45–65.

Baker, A. and Wigan, D. (2017) 'Constructing and Contesting City of London Power: NGOs and the Emergence of Noisier Financial Politics', *Economy and Society*, 46(2): 185–210.

Baker, D., Gamble, A. and Ludlam, S. (1993) 'Whips or Scorpions? The Maastricht Vote and the Conservative Party', *Parliamentary Affairs*, 46(2): 151–66.

Ban, C. (2013) 'Brazil's Liberal Neo-developmentalism: New Paradigm or Edited Orthodoxy?', *Review of International Political Economy*, 20(2): 298–331.

Ban, C. and Gabor, D. (2016) 'The Political Economy of Shadow Banking', *Review of International Political Economy*, 23(6): 901–14.

Bank of International Settlements (BIS) (2019) *Foreign Exchange Turnover in April 2019. Triennial Central Bank Survey*. https://www.bis.org/statistics/rpfx19_fx.htm.

Barber, W. (1967) *A History of Economic Thought* (London: Pelican).

Barca, F. and Becht, M. (eds) (2001) *The Control of Corporate Europe* (Oxford: Oxford University Press).

Bastagli, F., Coady, D. and Gupta, S. (2012) 'Income Inequality and Fiscal Policy', IMF Staff Discussion Note (Washington, DC: IMF).

Beck, N. (2006) 'Is Causal-Process Observation an Oxymoron?', *Political Analysis*, 14(3): 347–52.

Becker, G. (1983) 'A Theory of Competition Among Pressure Groups for Political Influence', *Quarterly Journal of Economics*, 98(3): 371–400.

Becker, G. (1985) 'Public Policies, Pressure Groups and Dead-Weight Costs', *Journal of Public Economics*, 28(2): 329–47.

Becker, U. (2013) 'Measuring Change of Capitalist Varieties: Reflections on Method, Illustrations from the BRICs', *New Political Economy*, 18(4): 503–32.

Becker, U. and Schwartz, H. (eds) (2005) *Employment 'Miracles'* (Amsterdam: Amsterdam University Press).

Becker, U. and Vasileva, A. (2017) 'Russia's Political Economy Re-conceptualized: A Changing Hybrid of Liberalism, Statism and Patrimonialism', *Journal of Eurasian Studies*, 8(1): 83–96.

Bedford, K. and Rai, S. M. (2010) 'Feminists Theorize International Political Economy', *Signs: Journal of Women in Culture and Society*, 36(1): 1–18.

Beeson, M. (2003) *The Rise and Fall (?) of the Developmental State: The Vicissitudes and Implications of East Asian Interventionism* (mimeo, University of Queensland).

Beeson, M. (2009) 'Developmental States in East Asia: A Comparison of the Japanese and Chinese Experiences', *Asian Perspective*, 33(2): 5–39.

Beneria, L. (2003) 'Economic Rationality and Globalization: A Feminist Perspective', in M. Ferber and J. Nelson (eds), *Feminist Economics Today: Beyond Economic Man* (Chicago, IL: University of Chicago Press).

Benhabib, S. (1994) *Situating the Self: Gender, Community and Postmodernism in Contemporary Ethics* (Cambridge: Polity Press).

Bennett, A. and Checkel, J. T. (eds) (2014) *Process Tracing: From Metaphor to Analytic Tool* (Cambridge: Cambridge University Press).

Berg, A. and Ostry, J. D. (2011) *Inequality and Unsustainable Growth: Two Sides of the Same Coin?* IMF Staff Discussion Note SDN/11/08 (Washington DC: International Monetary Fund).

Berger, S. (2013) *Making in America* (Cambridge, MA: MIT Press).

Berghoff, H. (2016) 'Varieties of Financialization? Evidence from German Industry in the 1990s', *Business History Review*, 90(1): 81–108.

Berle, A. and Means, G. C. (1932) *The Modern Corporation and Private Property* (New York: Macmillan).

Bhagwati, J. (1998) 'The Capital Myth: The Difference Between Trade in Widgets and Dollars', *Foreign Affairs*, 77(3): 7–12.

Blackburn, R. (2008) 'The Subprime Crisis', *New Left Review* 50: 63–106.

Blanchard, O. (2006) 'European Unemployment: The Evolution of Facts and Ideas', *Economic Policy*: 5–59.

Blaug, M. (1996) *Economic Theory in Retrospect* (Cambridge: Cambridge University Press).

Bleaney, M. (1985) *The Rise and Fall of Keynesian Economics: An Investigation of Its Contribution to Capitalist Development* (Basingstoke: Macmillan).

Block, F. (1994) 'The Roles of the State in the Economy', in N. Smelser and R. Swedberg (eds), *Handbook of Economic Sociology* (Princeton, NJ: Princeton University Press).

Block, F. (2003) 'Karl Polanyi and the Writing of the Great Transformation', *Theory and Society*, 32(3): 275–306.

Block, F. (2007) 'Understanding the Divergent Trajectories of the United States and Western Europe: A Neo-Polanyian Analysis', *Politics and Society*, 35(1): 3–33.

Block, F. (2008) 'Swimming Against the Current: The Rise of a Hidden Developmental State in the United States', *Politics and Society*, 36(2): 169–206.

Block, F. (2011) 'Crisis and Renewal: The Outlines of a Twenty-First Century New Deal', *Socio-Economic Review*, 9: 31–57.

Block, F. and Evans, P. (2005) 'The State and the Economy', in N. Smelser and R. Swedberg (eds), *Handbook of Economic Sociology* (Princeton, NJ: Princeton University Press), pp. 505–26.

Block, F. and Keller, M. (2009) 'Where Do Innovations Come From? Transformations in the US Economy, 1970–2006', *Socio-Economic Review*, 7: 459–83.

Block, F., Cloward, R., Ehrenreich, B. and Fox Piven, F. (1987) *The Mean Season: The Attack on the Welfare State* (New York: Pantheon).

Blyth, M. (2002a) *Great Transformations* (Cambridge: Cambridge University Press).

Blyth, M. (2002b) 'Institutions and Ideas', in D. Marsh and G. Stoker (eds), *Theory and Methods in Political Science*, 2nd edn (London: Red Globe Press), pp. 292–310.

Blyth, M. (2003) 'Same as It Never Was: Temporality and Typology in Varieties of Capitalism', *Comparative European Politics*, 1(2): 215–26.

Blyth, M. (ed.) (2009a) *Routledge Handbook of International Political Economy: IPE as a Global Conversation* (London: Routledge).

Blyth, M. (2009b) 'Torn Between Two Lovers? Caught in the Middle of British and American IPE', *New Political Economy*, 14: 329–36.

Blyth, M. (2013) *Austerity: The History of a Dangerous Idea* (Oxford: Oxford University Press).

Bohle, D. (2018) 'European Integration, Capitalist Diversity and Crises Trajectories on Europe's Eastern Periphery', *New Political Economy*, 23(2): 239–53.

Bonefeld, W. (1992) 'Social Constitution and Form of the Capitalist State', in W. Bonefeld, R. Gunn and K. Psychopedis (eds), *Open Marxism, Volume 1: Dialectics and History* (London: Pluto Press), pp. 93–132.

Bonefeld, W. (2012) 'Freedom and the Strong State: On German Ordoliberalism', *New Political Economy*, 17(5): 633–56.

Bonefeld, W., Gunn, R. and Psychopedis, K. (eds) (1992) *Open Marxism, Volume 1: Dialectics and History* (London: Pluto Press), pp. 93–132.

Bonizzi, B. (2014) 'Financialisation in Developing and Emerging Countries', *International Journal of Political Economy*, 42(4): 83–107.

Bonizzi, B. (2016) The Changing Impact of Finance Development. Financialisation, Economy, Society and Sustainable Development (FESSUD), Working Paper, No. 124, pp. 2–61. Available at: http://fessud.eu/wp-content/uploads/2015/03/The-Nature-Performance-and-Economic-Impact-of-Sovereign-Wealth-Funds-working-paper-135.pdf (Accessed: October 2017).

Bonoli, G. (2001) 'Political Institutions, Veto Points, and the Process of Welfare State Adaptation', in P. Pierson (ed.), *The New Politics of the Welfare State* (Oxford: Oxford University Press), pp. 238–64.

Bonoli, G. and Powell, M. (eds) (2004) *Social Democratic Party Policies in Europe* (London: Routledge).

Bonoli, G., George, V. and Taylor-Gooby, P. (2000) *European Welfare Futures: Towards a Theory of Retrenchment* (Cambridge: Polity Press).

Borsch, A. (2007) *Global Pressure, National System: How German Corporate Governance Is Changing* (Ithaca, NY: Cornell University Press).

Bourguignon, F. (2015) *The Globalization of Inequality* (Princeton, NJ: Princeton University Press).

Bowles, S. and Gintis, H. (1993) 'The Revenge of Homo Economicus: Contested Exchange and the Revival of Political Economy', *Journal of Economic Perspectives*, 7(1): 83–102.

Boyer, R. (1990) *The Regulation School: A Critical Introduction* (New York: Columbia University Press).

Boyer, R. (1998) 'Hybridization and Models of Production: Geography, History and Theory', in R. Boyer, E. Charron, U. Jurgens and S. Tolliday (eds), *Between Imitation and Innovation: The Transfer and Hybridization of Production Models in the International Automobile Industry* (Oxford: Oxford University Press).

Boyer, R. (2000) 'Is a Finance-Led Growth Regime a Viable Alternative to Fordism? A Preliminary Analysis', *Economy and society*, 29(1): 111–45.

Boyer, R. (2005a) 'Coherence, Diversity, and the Evolution of Capitalisms: The Institutional Complementarity Hypothesis', *Evolutionary and Institutional Economics Review*, 2(1): 43–80.

Boyer, R. (2005b) 'From Shareholder Value to CEO Power: The Paradox of the 1990s', *Competition & Change*, 9(1): 7–47.

Boyer, R. and Drache, D. (eds) (1996) *States Against Markets: The Limits of Globalization* (London: Routledge).

Boyer, R. and Juillard, M. (1995) 'Les Etats-Unis: adieu au fordisme!', in R. Boyer and Y. Saillard (eds), *Théorie de la régulation* (Paris: La Découverte).

Boyer, R. and Saillard, Y. (1995) *Théorie de la régulation. L'état des savoirs* (Paris: La Découverte).

Boyer, R. and Saillard, Y. (2002) *Regulation Theory: The State of the Art* (London: Routledge).

Brady, H. and Collier, D. (eds) (2004) *Rethinking Social Inquiry: Diverse Tools, Shared Standards* (Lanham, MD: Rowman & Littlefield).

Braithewaite, J. and Drahos, P. (2000) *Global Business Regulation* (Cambridge: Cambridge University Press).

Brassett, J. and Rethel, L. (2015) 'Sexy Money: The Hetero-normative Politics of Global Finance', *Review of International Studies*, 41(3): 429–49.

Brennan, G. and Buchanan, J. (1985) *The Reason of Rules* (Cambridge: Cambridge University Press).

Brenner, R. (1998) 'Uneven Development and the Long Downturn: The Advanced Capitalist Economies from Boom to Stagnation, 1950–1998', *New Left Review*, 229: 1–265.

Breslin, S. (1996) 'China: Developmental State or Dysfunctional Development?', *Third World Quarterly*, 17(1): 689–706.

Breslin, S. (2007) *China and the Global Economy* (Basingstoke: Palgrave Macmillan).

Breslin, S. (2008) 'How China Changed the Global Economy and the Global Economy Changed China: Thirty Years of Investment and Trade', Unpublished Working Paper, University of Warwick.

Breslin, S. (2011) 'The "China Model" and the Global Crisis: From Friedrich List to a Chinese Mode of Governance?', *International Affairs*, 87(6): 1323–43.

Breslin, S. (2012a) 'Government–Industry Relations in China: A Review of the Art of the State', in A. Walter and Xiaoke Zhang (eds), *East Asian Capitalism: Diversity, Change, and Continuity* (Oxford: Oxford University Press).

Breslin, S. (2012b) 'Paradigm(s) Shifting? Responding to China's Response to the Global Financial Crisis', in W. Grant and G. Wilson (eds), *The Consequences of the Global Financial Crisis: The Rhetoric of Reform and Regulation* (Oxford: Oxford University Press), pp. 226–46.

Breslin, S. (2014) 'Financial Transitions in the PRC: Banking on the State?', *Third World Quarterly*, 35(6): 996–1013.

Broome, A. (2014) *Issues and Actors in the Global Political Economy* (Basingstoke: Palgrave Macmillan).

Broome, A. and Seabrooke, L. (2012) 'Seeing Like an International Organisation', *New Political Economy*, 17: 1–16.

Brynjolfsson, E. and McAfee, A. (2011) *Race Against the Machine* (Lexington, MA: Digital Frontier Press).

Buchanan, J. (1975) *The Limits of Liberty: Between Anarchy and the Leviathan* (Chicago, IL: Chicago University Press).

Buckler, S. (2002) 'Normative Theory', in D. Marsh and G. Stoker (eds), *Theory and Methods in Political Science*, 2nd edn (London: Red Globe Press), pp. 172–96.

Bukharin, N. (1971 [1917]) *Imperialism and the World Economy* (London: Merlin).

Burnham, P. (1994) 'Open Marxism and Vulgar International Political Economy', *Review of International Political Economy*, 1(2): 221–31.

Burnham, P. (1999) 'The Politics of Economic Management in the 1990s', *New Political Economy*, 4(1): 37–53.

Burnham, P. (2001) 'Marx, International Political Economy and Globalisation', *Capital and Class*, 75: 7–16.

Burnham, P. (2003) *Remaking the Post-War World Economy* (Basingstoke: Palgrave Macmillan).

Burton, M. (2016) *The Politics of Austerity* (London: Palgrave Macmillan).

Byrne, J. and Davis, P. (2002) 'A Comparison of Balance Sheet Structures in Major EU Countries', *National Institute Economic Review*, 180(1): 83–95.

Cafruny, A. and Ryner, M. (eds) (2003) *A Ruined Fortress? Neo-Liberal Hegemony and Transformation in Europe* (New York: Rowman & Littlefield).

Cafruny, A. and Ryner, M. (2007a) *Europe at Bay: In the Shadow of US Hegemony* (Boulder, CO: Lynne Rienner).

Cafruny, A. and Ryner, M. (2007b) 'Monetary Union and the Transatlantic and Social Dimensions of Europe's Crisis', *New Political Economy*, 12(2): 141–65.

Cameron, D. (1978) 'The Expansion of the Public Economy: A Comparative Analysis', *American Political Science Review*, 72(4): 1243–61.

Campbell, J. (1998) 'Institutional Analysis and the Role of Ideas in Political Economy', *Theory and Society*, 27(3): 377–409.

Campbell, J. (2004) *Institutional Change and Globalization* (Princeton, NJ: Princeton University Press).

Campbell, J. (2010) 'Institutional Reproduction and Change', in G. Morgan, J. Campbell, C. Crouch, O. Pedersen and R. Whitley (eds), *The Oxford Handbook of Comparative Institutional Analysis* (Oxford: Oxford University Press), pp. 87–116.

Campbell, J. (2011) 'The US Financial Crisis: Lessons for Theories of Institutional Complementarity', *Socio-Economic Review*, 9: 211–34.

Campbell, J. and Lindberg, L. (1990) 'Property Rights and the Organization of Economic Activity by the State', *American Sociological Review*, 55(5): 634–47.

Campbell, J. and Pedersen, O. (2007) 'The Varieties of Capitalism and Hybrid Success: Denmark in the Global Economy', *Comparative Political Studies*, 40(3): 307–22.

Campbell, J., Hollingsworth, J. and Lindberg, L. (1991) *Governance of the American Economy* (Cambridge: Cambridge University Press).

Cantillon, B. and Van Lancker, W. (2013) 'Three Shortcomings of the Social Investment Perspective', *Social Policy and Society*, 12(4): 553–64.

Caporaso, J. and Levine, D. (1992) *Theories of Political Economy* (Cambridge: Cambridge University Press).

Carey, H (1848) *The Past, the Present and the Future* (Philadelphia, PA: Carey & Hart).

Carey, H. (1858-9) *Principles of Social Science, vol.1-3* (Philadelphia, PA: J.B. Lippincott).

Carstensen, M. (2011a) 'Paradigm Man vs. the Bricoleur: Bricolage as an Alternative Vision of Agency in Ideational Change', *European Political Science Review*, 3(1): 147-67.

Carstensen, M. (2011b) 'Ideas Are Not as Stable as Political Scientists Want Them to Be: A Theory of Incremental Ideational Change', *Political Studies*, 59: 596-615.

Castells, M. (2000) *The Rise of the Network Society* (Oxford: Blackwell).

Castles, F. (2004) *The Future of the Welfare State: Crisis Myths and Crisis Realities* (Oxford: Oxford University Press).

Cerny, P. (1989) 'The "Little Big Bang" in Paris: Financial Deregulation in a *Dirigiste* System', *European Journal of Political Research*, 17: 169-92.

Cerny, P. (1997a) 'Paradoxes of the Competition State', *Government and Opposition*, 32(2): 251-74.

Cerny, P. (1997b) 'International Finance and the Erosion of Capitalist Diversity', in C. Crouch and W. Streeck (eds), *The Political Economy of Modern Capitalism* (Oxford: Oxford University Press), pp. 173-81.

Chang, H.-J. (1996) *The Political Economy of Industrial Policy* (Basingstoke: Palgrave Macmillan).

Chang, H.-J. (1999) 'The Economic Theory of the Development State', in M. Woo-Cumings (ed.), *The Development State* (Ithaca, NY: Cornell University Press), pp. 182-99.

Chang, H.-J. (2002) *Kicking Away the Ladder: Development Strategy in Historical Perspective* (London: Anthem Press).

Chang, H. J. (2011, May) 'Industrial Policy: Can We Go Beyond an Unproductive Confrontation?', in *Annual World Bank Conference on Development Economics*, pp. 83-109.

Chang, H. J. and Andreoni, A. (2016) 'Industrial Policy in a Changing World: Basic Principles, Neglected Issues and New Challenges', Paper Presented at the *Cambridge Journal of Economics at 40 Years* Conference.

Chang, H. J., Andreoni, A. and Kuan, M. L. (2013) 'International Industrial Policy Experiences and the Lessons for the UK', in *The Future of Manufacturing, UK Government Office of Science* (London: BIS).

Charkham, J. (1995) *Keeping Good Company* (Oxford: Oxford University Press).

Chey, H. K. and Helleiner, E. (2018) 'Civilisational Values and Political Economy Beyond the West: The Significance of Korean Debates at the Time of Its Economic Opening', *Contemporary Politics*, 24(2): 191-209.

Chwieroth, J. (2014) 'Controlling Capital: The International Monetary Fund and Transformative Incremental Change from Within International Organisations', *New Political Economy*, 19(3): 445-69.

Cioffi, J. (2006) 'Building Finance Capitalism: The Regulatory Politics of Corporate Governance Reform in the United States and Germany', in J. D. Levy (ed.), *The State After Statism: New State Activities in the Age of Globalization and Liberalization* (Cambridge, MA: Harvard University Press), pp. 185-229.

Clarke, R. (1979) *The Japanese Company* (New Haven, CT: Yale University Press).

Clarke, S. (1983) *Marx, Marginalism and Modern Sociology* (London: Macmillan).

Clarke, P. (1988) *The Keynesian Revolution in the Making 1924-1936* (Oxford: Clarendon Press).

Clarke, S. (1992) 'The Global Accumulation of Capital and the Periodisation of the Capitalist State Form', in W. Bonefeld, R. Gunn and K. Psychopedis (eds), *Open Marxism, Volume 1: Dialectics and History* (London: Pluto Press), pp. 93-132.

Clarke, P. (1996) 'The Keynesian Consensus', in D. Marquand and A. Seldon (eds), *The Ideas That Shaped Post-War Britain* (London: Fontana Press).

Clarke, P. (2009) *Keynes* (London: Bloomsbury).

Clarke, T., Jarvis, W. and Gholamshahi, S. (2019) 'The Impact of Corporate Governance on Compounding Inequality: Maximising Shareholder Value and Inflating Executive Pay', *Critical Perspectives on Accounting*, 63: 102049.

Clasen, J. and Clegg, D. (2003) 'Unemployment Protection and Labour Market Reform in France and Great Britain in the 1990s: Solidarity versus Activation?', *Journal of Social Policy*, 32(3): 361-81.

Clift, B. (2004) 'The French Model of Capitalism: Still Exceptional?', in J. Perraton and B. Clift (eds), *Where Are National Capitalisms Now?* (Basingstoke: Palgrave Macmillan), pp. 91–110.

Clift, B. (2007) 'French Corporate Governance in the New Global Economy: Mechanisms of Change and Hybridisation Within Models of Capitalism', *Political Studies*, 55(4): 546–67.

Clift, B. (2009) 'Second Time as Farce? The EU Takeover Directive, the Clash of Capitalisms and the Hamstrung Harmonisation of European (and French) Corporate Governance', *Journal of Common Market Studies*, 47(1): 55–79.

Clift, B. (2012) 'Comparative Capitalisms, Ideational Political Economy and French Post-*Dirigiste* Responses to the Global Financial Crisis', *New Political Economy*, 17(5): 565–90.

Clift, B. (2013) 'Economic Patriotism, the Clash of Capitalisms, and State Aid in the European Union', *Journal of Industry, Competition and Trade*, 13(1): 101–17.

Clift, B. (2016) 'French Economic Policy: Theory Development and the Three 'I's', in R. Elgie, E. Grossman and A. G. Mazur (eds), *The Oxford Handbook of French Politics* (Oxford: Oxford University Press), pp. 509–34.

Clift, B. (2018) *The IMF and the Politics of Austerity in the Wake of the Global Financial Crisis* (Oxford: Oxford University Press).

Clift, B. (2019) 'Contingent Keynesianism: The IMF's Model Answer to the Post-crash Fiscal Policy Efficacy Question in Advanced Economies', *Review of International Political Economy*, 26(6): 1211–37.

Clift, B. (2020) 'The Hollowing Out of Monetarism: The Rise of Rules-Based Monetary Policy-Making in the UK and USA and Problems with the Paradigm Change Framework', *Comparative European Politics*: 18(3): 281–8.

Clift, B. and McDaniel, S. (2019) 'Capitalist Convergence? European (Dis?) Integration and the Post-crash Restructuring of French and European Capitalisms', *New Political Economy*: 1–19. https://doi.org/10.1080/135 63467.2019.1680963.

Clift, B. and Robles, M. (2020) 'The IMF, Tackling Inequality, and Post-neoliberal Re-globalisation: The Paradoxes of Political Legitimation Within Economistic Parameters',

Globalizations, 2020: 1–20. https://doi.org/10 .1080/14747731.2020.1774325.

Clift, B. and Rosamond, B. (2009) 'Lineages of a British International Political Economy', in Mark Blyth (ed.), *Routledge Handbook of International Political Economy: IPE as a Global Conversation* (London: Routledge), pp. 95–111.

Clift, B. and Tomlinson, J. (2002) 'Tawney and the Third Way', *Journal of Political Ideologies*, 7(3): 315–31.

Clift, B. and Tomlinson, J. (2004) 'Capital Mobility and Fiscal Policy: The Construction of Economic Policy Rectitude in Britain and France', *New Political Economy*, 9(4): 515–37.

Clift, B. and Tomlinson, J. (2008) 'Whatever Happened to the UK Balance of Payments "Problem"? The Contingent (Re)Construction of British Economic Performance Assessment', *British Journal of Politics and International Relations*, 10(4): 607–29.

Clift, B. and Tomlinson, J. (2012) 'When Rules Started to Rule: The IMF, Neo-Liberal Economic Ideas, and Economic Policy Change in Britain', *Review of International Political Economy*, 19(3): 477–500.

Clift, B. and Woll, C. (2012a) 'Economic Patriotism: Re-inventing Control Over Open Markets', *Journal of European Public Policy*, 19(3): 307–23.

Clift, B. and Woll, C. (2012b) 'The Revival of Economic Patriotism', in G. Morgan and R. Whitley (eds), *Capitalism and Capitalisms in the 21st Century* (Oxford: Oxford University Press), pp. 70–89.

Clift, B, Kristensen, P. M. and Rosamond, B. (2021) 'Remembering and Forgetting IPE: Disciplinary History as Boundary Work', *Review of International Political Economy*.

Coase, R. (1937) 'The Nature of the Firm', *Economica*, 4: 386–405.

Coates, D. (1994) *The Question of UK Decline* (Hemel Hempstead: Wheatsheaf).

Coates, D. (1999) 'Why Do Growth Rates Differ?', *New Political Economy*, 4(1): 77–96.

Coates, D. (2000) *Models of Capitalism* (Cambridge: Polity Press).

Coates, D. (ed.) (2005) *Varieties of Capitalism, Varieties of Approaches* (Basingstoke: Palgrave Macmillan).

Cohen, B. (1993) 'The Triad and the Unholy Trinity: Lessons for the Pacific Region', in R. Higgott, R. Leaver and J. Ravenhill (eds), *Pacific Economic*

Relations in the 1990s: Cooperation or Conflict? (Boulder, CO: Lynne Rienner).

Cohen, B. (1996) 'Phoenix Arisen: The Resurrection of Global Finance', *World Politics*, 48: 268–96.

Cohen, B. J. (2002) 'Bretton Woods System', in R. J. Barry Jones (ed.), *Routledge Encyclopedia of International Political Economy* (London, Routledge).

Cohen, B. J. (2007) 'The Transatlantic Divide: Why Are American and British IPE So Different?', *Review of International Political Economy*, 14(2): 197–219.

Cohen, B. J. (2008) *International Political Economy: An Intellectual History* (Princeton, NJ: Princeton University Press).

Cohen, B. J. (2019) *Advanced Introduction to International Political Economy*, 2nd edn (Cheltenham: Edward Elgar).

Collier, D. (1993) 'The Comparative Method', in A. Finifter (ed.), *Political Science: The State of Discipline II* (Washington, DC: American Political Science Association), pp. 105–19.

Collier, R. and Collier, D. (1991) *Shaping the Political Arena* (Princeton, NJ: Princeton University Press).

Collier, D., Brady, H. and Seawright, J. (2004) 'Critiques, Responses, and Trade-Offs: Drawing Together the Debate', in H. Brady and D. Collier (eds), *Rethinking Social Inquiry: Diverse Tools, Shared Standards* (Lanham, MD: Rowman & Littlefield), pp. 195–228.

Costa Lobo, M. and Magalhaes, P. (2004) 'The Portuguese Socialists and the Third Way', in G. Bonoli and M. Powell (eds), *Social Democratic Party Policies in Europe* (London: Routledge), pp. 83–101.

Cox, R. (1981) 'Social Forces, States and World Orders: Beyond International Relations Theory', *Millennium: Journal of International Studies*, 10(2): 126–55.

Cox, R. (1983) 'Gramsci, Hegemony and International Relations: An Essay in Method', *Millennium: Journal of International Studies*, 12(2): 162–75.

Cox, R. (1985) 'Social Forces, States and World Orders: Beyond International Relations Theory', in R. Keohane (ed.), *Neo-Realism and Its Critics* (New York: Columbia University Press), pp. 204–55.

Cox, R. (1987) *Power, Production and World Order* (New York: Columbia University Press).

Cox, R. (1995) 'Critical Political Economy', in B. Hettne (ed.), *International Political Economy: Understanding Global Disorder* (London: Zed Books), pp. 31–45.

Crane, G. (1998) 'Economic Nationalism: Bringing the Nation Back In', *Millennium: Journal of International Studies*, 27(1): 55–76.

Crane, G. and Amawi, A. (eds) (1997) *The Theoretical Evolution of International Political Economy*, 2nd edn (Oxford: Oxford University Press).

Creswell, J. W. (2008) *Research Design: Qualitative and Quantitative and Mixed Methods Approaches*, 3rd edn (London: Sage).

Creswell, J. W. (2015) 'Revisiting Mixed Methods and Advancing Scientific Practices', in S. N. Hesse-Biber and R. B. Johnson (eds), *The Oxford Handbook of Multimethod and Mixed Methods Research Inquiry* (Oxford: Oxford University Press).

Crotty, J. (2009) 'Structural Causes of the Global Financial Crisis: A Critical Assessment of the "New Financial Architecture"', *Cambridge Journal of Economics*, 33(4): 563–80.

Crouch, C. (1982) *The Politics of Industrial Relations*, 2nd edn (London: Fontana).

Crouch, C. (1993) *Industrial Relations and European State Traditions* (Oxford: Oxford University Press).

Crouch, C. (2004) 'The State and Innovations in Economic Governance', *Political Quarterly*, 75(1): 100–16.

Crouch, C. (2005a) 'Models of Capitalism', *New Political Economy*, 10(4): 439–56.

Crouch, C. (2005b) *Capitalist Diversity and Change* (Oxford: Oxford University Press).

Crouch, C. (2009) 'Privatised Keynesianism: An Unacknowledged Policy Regime', *British Journal of Politics and International Relations*, 11(3): 382–99.

Crouch, C. (2010) 'Complementarity', in G. Morgan, J. Campbell, C. Crouch, O. Pedersen and R. Whitley (eds), *The Oxford Handbook of Comparative Institutional Analysis* (Oxford: Oxford University Press), pp. 117–38.

Crouch, C. (2011) *The Strange Non-death of Neoliberalism* (Cambridge: Polity Press).

Crouch, C. (2016) *The Knowledge Corrupters* (Cambridge: Polity Press).

Crouch, C. (2017) 'The Limitations of the Limited State: Neoliberal Theory Meets the Real World', in D. King and P. Le Galès (eds),

Reconfiguring European States in Crisis (Oxford: Oxford University Press), pp. 232–50.

Crouch, C. (2019) *The Globalization Backlash* (Cambridge: Polity Press).

Crouch, C. and Le Galès, P. (2012) 'Cities as National Champions?', *Journal of European Public Policy*, 109(3): 405–19.

Crouch, C. and Streeck, W. (eds) (1997) *The Political Economy of Modern Capitalism: Mapping Convergence and Diversity* (London: Sage).

Culpepper, P. (2005) 'Institutional Change in Contemporary Capitalism: Coordinated Financial Systems Since 1990', *World Politics*, 57(2): 173–99.

Daddow, O. (2019) 'GlobalBritain™: The Discursive Construction of Britain's Post-Brexit World Role', *Global Affairs*, 5(1): 5–22.

Dahl, R. (1961) *Who Governs? Democracy and Power in an American City* (New Haven, CT: Yale University Press).

Dale, G. (2010) *Karl Polanyi: The Limits of the Market* (Cambridge: Polity Press).

Dale, G. (2016) *Reconstructing Karl Polanyi: Excavation and Critique* (London: Pluto Press).

Dale, G., Holmes, C. and Markantonatou, M. (eds) (2019) *Karl Polanyi's Political and Economic Thought* (Newcastle-upon-Tyne: Agenda Publishing).

Damro, C. (2004) 'Linking Competition Policy and Trade', in B. Hocking and S. McGuire (eds), *Trade Politics* (London: Routledge), pp. 194–207.

Davis, M. (1986) *Prisoners of the American Dream* (London: Verso).

Davis, G. (2009) *Managed by the Markets: How Finance Re-shaped America* (Oxford: Oxford University Press).

De Goede, M. (2001) *Virtue, Fortune, and Faith: A Genealogy of Finance* (Minneapolis, MN: University of Minnesota Press).

De Grauwe, P. (2017) *The Limits of the Market: The Pendulum Between Government and Market* (Oxford: Oxford University Press).

de Vries, M. G. (1987) *Balance of Payments Adjustment 1945 to 1986: The IMF Experience* (Washington, DC: IMF).

Deeg, R. (1999) *Finance Capitalism Unveiled: Banks and the German Political Economy* (Ann Arbor, MI: University of Michigan Press).

Deeg, R. (2001) 'Institutional Change and the Uses and Limits of Path Dependency: The Case of German Finance', Max Planck Institute Discussion Paper, 01/06.

Deeg, R. (2005) 'Path Dependency, Institutional Complementarity and Change in National Business Systems', in G. Morgan, R. Whitley and E. Moen (eds), *Changing Capitalisms* (Oxford: Oxford University Press), pp. 21–52.

Deeg, R. (2010) 'Institutional Change in Financial Systems', in G. Morgan et al. (eds), *The Oxford Handbook of Comparative Institutional Analysis* (Oxford: Oxford University Press), pp. 309–34.

Deeg, R. (2012) 'The Limits of Liberalization? American Capitalism at the Crossroads', *Journal of European Public Policy*, 19(8): 1249–68.

Deeg, R. and Jackson, G. (2007) 'Toward a More Dynamic Theory of Capitalist Variety', *Socio-Economic Review*, 5(1): 149–79.

Deeg, R. and O'Sullivan, M. (2009) 'The Political Economy of Global Finance Capital', *World Politics*, 61: 731–63.

Devetak, R. (2001) 'Critical Theory', in S. Burchill (ed.), *Theories of International Relations* (London: Red Globe Press).

Dicken, P. (2011) *Global Shift*, 6th edn (London: Sage).

DiMaggio, P. and Powell, W. (1983) 'The Iron Cage Revisited: Institutional Isomorphism and Collective Rationality in Organizational Fields', *American Sociological Review*, 48(2): 147–60.

Djelic, M.-L. (2010) 'Institutional Perspectives – Working Towards Coherence or Irreconcilable Diversity?', in G. Morgan, J. Campbell, C. Crouch, O. Pedersen and R. Whitley (eds), *Oxford Handbook of Comparative Institutional Analysis* (Oxford: Oxford University Press), pp. 15–40.

Djelic, M.-L. and Quack, S. (eds) (2010) *Transnational Communities* (Cambridge: Cambridge University Press).

Djelic, M.-L. and Sahlin-Andersson, K. (eds) (2006) *Transnational Governance: Institutional Dynamics of Regulation* (Cambridge: Cambridge University Press).

Dobb, M. (1967) *Studies in the Development of Capitalism* (London: Routledge & Kegan Paul).

Dobb, M. (1973) *Theories of Value and Distribution Since Adam Smith* (Cambridge: Cambridge University Press).

Dobbin, F. (1994) *Forging Industrial Policy: The United States, Britain and France in the Railway Age* (Cambridge, MA: Harvard University Press).

Dore, R. (1983) 'Goodwill and the Spirit of Market Capitalism', *British Journal of Sociology*, 33(4): 459–82.

Dore, R. (ed.) (2000) *Stock Market Capitalism: Welfare Capitalism Japan and Germany Versus the Anglo-Saxons* (Oxford: Oxford University Press).

Downs, A. (1957) *An Economic Theory of Democracy* (New York: Harper & Row).

Drezner, D. W. (2001) 'Globalization and Policy Convergence', *International Studies Review*, 3(1): 53–78.

Drezner, D. W. (2007) *All Politics Is Global: Explaining International Regulatory Regimes* (Princeton, NJ: Princeton University Press).

Driver, R. and Wren-Lewis, S. (1995) 'Jobs Without Inflation', *New Economy*, 2: 28–35.

Dudouet, F.-X. and Grémont, E. (2010) *Les grands patrons en France: du capitalisme d'état à la financiarisation* (Paris: Editions lignes de repères).

Duménil, G. and Lévy, D. (2002) 'The Profit Rate: Where and How Much Did It Fall? Did It Recover? (USA 1948–2000)', *Review of Radical Political Economics*, 34(4): 437–61.

Duménil, G. and Lévy, D. (2004) *Capital Resurgent: Roots of the Neoliberal* (Cambridge, MA: Harvard University Press).

Dunleavy, P. (1991) *Democracy, Bureaucracy and Public Choice* (Hemel Hempstead: Harvester).

Dunleavy, P. and O'Leary, B. (1987) *Theories of State* (Basingstoke: Macmillan).

Dyson, K. (1980) *The State Tradition in Western Europe* (Oxford: Martin Robertson).

Dyson, K. (1999) 'The Franco-German Relationship and Economic and Monetary Union: Using Europe to "Bind Leviathan"', *West European Politics*, 22(1): 25–44.

Dyson, K. (2000) 'EMU as Europeanization: Convergence, Diversity and Contingency', *Journal of Common Market Studies*, 38(4): 645–66.

Eatwell, J. and Milgate, M. (2011) *The Fall and Rise of Keynesian Economics* (Oxford: Oxford University Press).

Ebbinghaus, B. and Manow, P. (1998) 'Studying Welfare-State Regimes and Varieties of Capitalism: An Introduction', in *Conference on Varieties of Welfare Capitalism* (Cologne: Max Planck Institute for the Study of Societies), pp. 11–3.

Ebenau, M. (2012) 'Varieties of Capitalism or Dependency? A Critique of the VoC Approach for Latin America', *Competition & Change*, 16(3): 206–23.

Eichengreen, B. (1996) *Globalizing Capital* (Princeton, NJ: Princeton University Press).

Eichengreen, B. (2008) *The European Economy Since 1945: Coordinated Capitalism and Beyond* (Princeton, NJ: Princeton University Press).

Eichengreen, B. and Kenen, P. (1994) 'Managing the World Economy Under the Bretton Woods System: An Overview', in P. Kenen (ed.), *Managing the World Economy* (Washington, DC: Institute for International Economics), pp. 3–57.

Eisner, M. (2011) *The American Political Economy* (Abingdon: Routledge).

Ekelund, R. and Tomlinson, R. (1986) *Microeconomics* (Boston, MA: Little, Brown).

Elias, J. (2016) 'Whose Crisis? Whose Recovery? Lessons Learned (and Not) from the Asian Crisis', in A. A. Hozic and J. True (eds), *Scandalous Economics: Gender and the Politics of Financial Crises* (Oxford: Oxford University Press), pp. 109–25.

Elias, J. and Roberts, A. (2016) 'Feminist Global Political Economies of the Everyday: From Bananas to Bingo', *Globalizations*, 13(6): 787–800.

Elias, J. and Roberts, A. (eds) (2018a) *Feminist Global Political Economies of the Everyday* (London: Routledge).

Elias, J. and Roberts, A. (2018b) 'Introduction: Situating Gender Scholarship in IPE', in J. Elias and A. Roberts (eds), *Handbook on the International Political Economy of Gender* (Northampton: Edward Elgar).

Elster, J. (1985) *Making Sense of Marx* (Cambridge: Cambridge University Press).

Elster, J. (1989) *Nuts and Bolts for the Social Sciences* (Cambridge: Cambridge University Press).

Engelen, E. (2008) 'The Case for Financialisation', *Competition & Change*, 12(2): 111–9.

Engelen, E. and Konings, M. (2010) 'Financial Capitalism Resurgent: Comparative Institutionalism and the Challenges of Financialization', in G. Morgan, J. Campbell, C. Crouch, O. Pedersen and R. Whitley (eds), *The Oxford Handbook of Comparative Institutional Analysis* (Oxford: Oxford University Press), pp. 601–24.

Engelen, E., Erturk, I., Froud, J., Johal, S., Leaver, A., Moran, M., Nilsson, A. and Williams, K. (2011) *After the Great Complacence: Financial Crisis and the Politics of Reform* (Oxford: Oxford University Press).

England, P. (2005) 'Emerging Theories of Care Work', *Annual Review of Sociology*, 31: 381–99.

Enriques, L. and Volpin, P. (2007) 'Corporate Governance Reforms in Continental Europe', *Journal of Economic Perspectives*, 21(1): 117–40.

Epstein, G. (1996) 'International Capital Mobility and the Scope for National Economic Management', in D. Drache and R. Boyer (eds), *States Against Markets: The Limits of Globalization* (London: Routledge), pp. 211–26.

Epstein, G. A. (2005) 'Introduction: Financialisation and the World Economy', in G.A. Epstein (ed.), *Financialisation and the World Economy* (Cheltenham: Edward Elgar), pp. 3–16.

Epstein, G. and Gintis, H. (1995) 'International Capital Markets and National Economic Policy', *Review of International Political Economy*, 2(4): 693–718.

Erturk, I., Froud, J., Johal, S., Leaver, A. and Williams, K. (2007) 'The Democratization of Finance? Promises, Outcomes and Conditions', *Review of International Political Economy*, 14(4): 553–75.

Esping-Andersen, G. (1990) *The Three Worlds of Welfare Capitalism* (Cambridge: Polity Press).

Esping-Andersen, G. (ed.) (1996) *Welfare States in Transition: National Adaptations in Global Economies* (London: Sage).

Esping-Andersen, G. (1999) *Social Foundations of Postindustrial Economies* (Oxford: Oxford University Press).

Esping-Andersen, G. (2000) 'Multi-dimensional Decommodification: A Reply to Graham Room', *Policy and Politics*, 28(3): 353–9.

Esping-Andersen, G. (2009) *Incomplete Revolution: Adapting Welfare States to Women's New Roles* (Cambridge: Polity Press).

Estevez-Abe, M. (2008) *Welfare and Capitalism in Postwar Japan* (Cambridge: Cambridge University Press).

Estevez-Abe, M., Iversen, T. and Soskice, D. (2001) 'Social Protection and the Formation of Skills: A Reinterpretation of the Welfare State', in P. Hall and D. Soskice (eds), *Varieties of Capitalism: The Institutional Foundations of Comparative Advantage* (Oxford: Oxford University Press), pp. 145–83.

European Commission (2009) 'Report from the Commission: State Aid Scoreboard Report on State Aid Granted by the EU Member States Autumn 2009', Updates COM(2009)661 (Brussels: European Commission).

Evans, P. (1995) *Embedded Autonomy: States and Industrial Transformation* (Princeton, NJ: Princeton University Press).

Evans, P. (2004) 'Development as Institutional Change: The Pitfalls of Monocropping and the Potentials of Deliberation', *Studies in Comparative International Development*, 38(4): 30–52.

Evans, P. B., Rueschemeyer, D. and Skocpol, T. (1985) *Bringing the State Back In* (Cambridge: Cambridge University Press).

Farrall, S. and Hay, C. (2014) *The Legacy of Thatcherism: Assessing and Exploring Thatcherite Social and Economic Policies* (Oxford: Oxford University Press).

Farrell, H. and Newman, A. (2010) 'Making International Markets: Domestic Institutions in International Political Economy', *Review of International Political Economy*, 17(4): 609–38.

Farrell, H. and Quiggin, J. (2017) 'Consensus, Dissensus, and Economic Ideas: Economic Crisis and the Rise and Fall of Keynesianism', *International Studies Quarterly*, 61(2): 269–83. https://doi.org/10.1093/isq/sqx010.

Fasenfest, D. (2018) 'Is Marx Still Relevant?', *Critical Sociology*, 44(6): 851–5. https://doi.org/10.1177/0896920518784793.

Featherstone, K. (2011) 'The JCMS Annual Lecture: The Greek Sovereign Debt Crisis and EMU: A Failing State in a Skewed Regime', *JCMS: Journal of Common Market Studies*, 49(2): 193–217.

Featherstone, K. (2015) 'External Conditionality and the Debt Crisis: The "Troika" and Public Administration Reform in Greece', *Journal of European Public Policy*, 22(3): 295–314.

Feenstra, R. (1998) 'Integration of Trade and Disintegration of Production in the Global Economy', *Journal of Economic Perspectives*, 12(4): 31–50.

Fehn, R. and Meier, C. P. (2001) 'The Positive Economics of Labor Market Rigidities and Investor Protection', *Kyklos*, 54(4): 557–90.

Feldmann, M. (2019) 'Global Varieties of Capitalism', *World Politics*, 71(1): 162–96.

Feldstein, F. and Horioka, C. (1980) 'Domestic Savings and International Capital Flows', *The Economic Journal*, 90: 314–29.

Ferguson, T. and Rogers, J. (1987) *Right Turn: The Decline of the Democrats and the Future of American Politics* (New York: Hill & Wang).

Fernandez, R. and Wigger, A. (2016) 'Lehman Brothers in the Dutch Offshore Financial Centre: The Role of Shadow Banking in Increasing Leverage and Facilitating Debt', *Economy and Society*, 45(3–4): 407–30.

Ferrera, M. and Hemerijck, A. (2003) 'Recalibrating Europe's Welfare Regimes', in J. Zeitlin and D. M. Trubek (eds), *Governing Work and Welfare in a New Economy: European and American Experiments* (Oxford: Oxford University Press), pp. 88–128.

Ferrera, M., Hemerijck, A. and Rhodes, M. (2000) *The Future of Social Europe: Recasting Work and Welfare in the New Economy* (Oeiras: Celta Editora).

Ferrera, M., Hemerijck, A. and Rhodes, M. (2004) *The Future of European Welfare States: Recasting Welfare for a New Century* (Oxford: Oxford University Press).

Field, A. (1984) 'Microeconomics, Norms and Rationality', *Economic Development and Cultural Change*, 32: 683–711.

Fine, B. (2012) 'Neoliberalism in Retrospect? It's Financialisation, Stupid', in *Developmental Politics in Transition* (London: Palgrave Macmillan), pp. 51–69.

Fine, B. (2013) 'Financialization from a Marxist Perspective', *International Journal of Political Economy*, 42(4): 47–66.

Finlayson, A. (2009) 'Financialisation, Financial Literacy and Asset-Based Welfare', *British Journal of Politics and International Relations*, 11(3): 400–21.

Fioretos, O. (2009) 'The International Regulation of Corporate Identity', *Comparative Political Studies*, 42(9): 1167–92.

Fioretos, O. (2010) 'Capitalist Diversity and the International Regulation of Hedge Funds', *Review of International Political Economy*, 17(4): 696–723.

Fioretos, O. (2011a) *Creative Reconstructions: Multilateralism and European Varieties of Capitalism After 1950* (Ithaca, NY: Cornell University Press).

Fioretos, O. (2011b) 'Historical Institutionalism in International Relations', *International Organization*, 65(2): 367–99.

Fioretos, O., Falleti, T. G. and Sheingate, A. (2016) 'Historical Institutionalism in Political Science', in *The Oxford Handbook of Historical Institutionalism* (Oxford: Oxford University Press), pp. 3–30.

Flaherty, E. (2015) 'Top Incomes Under Finance-Driven Capitalism, 1990–2010: Power Resources and Regulatory Orders', *Socio-Economic Review*, 13: 417–47.

Fligstein, N. (1990) *The Transformation of Corporate Control* (Cambridge, MA: Harvard University Press).

Fligstein, N. (1996) 'Markets as Politics: A Political–Cultural Approach to Market Institutions', *American Sociological Review*, 61: 656–73.

Fligstein, N. (2001) *The Architecture of Markets: An Economic Sociology of Twenty-First Century Capitalist Societies* (Princeton, NJ: Princeton University Press).

Forster, M. and Nolan, B. (2018) 'Inequality and Living Standards: Key Trends and Drivers', in B. Nolan (ed.), *Inequality and Inclusive Growth in Rich Countries: Shared Challenges and Contrasting Fortunes* (Oxford: Oxford University Press), pp. 11–40.

Franzese, R. J. (2002) *Macroeconomic Policies of Developed Democracies* (Cambridge: Cambridge University Press).

French, S., Leyshon, A. and Wainwright, T. (2011) 'Financializing Space, Spacing Financialization', *Progress in Human Geography*, 35(6): 798–819.

Frieden, J. (1991) 'Invested Interests: The Politics of National Economic Policies in a World of Global Finance', *International Organization*, 45(4): 425–51.

Froud, J., Haslam, C., Johal, S. and Williams, K. (2000) 'Shareholder Value and Financialization: Consultancy Promises, Management Moves', *Economy and Society*, 29(1): 80–110.

Froud, J., Johal, S., Leaver, A. and Williams, K. (2006) *Financialisation and Strategy: Narratives and Numbers* (New York: Palgrave Macmillan).

Fukuyama, F. (1989) 'The End of History?', *The National Interest*, Summer, 1–8.

Fukuyama, F. (2006) 'After Neoconservatism', *New York Times*, 19 February.

Fuller, S. (2003) *Kuhn vs Popper: The Struggle for the Soul of Science* (London: Icon Books).

Gabor, D. (2018) 'Goodbye (Chinese) Shadow Banking, Hello Market-Based Finance', *Development and Change*, 49(2): 394–419.

Gabor, D. and Ban, C. (2016) 'Banking on Bonds: The New Links Between States and Markets', *JCMS: Journal of Common Market Studies*, 54(3): 617–35.

Galbraith, J. K. (1954) *The Great Crash* (London: Pelican).

Galbraith, J. K. (1956) *American Capitalism* (London: Pelican).

Gamble, A. (1984) 'Stabilisation Policy and Adversary Politics', in A. Gamble and S. Walkland (eds), *The British Party System and Economic Policy 1945–1983* (Oxford: Oxford University Press), pp. 40–91.

Gamble, A. (1986) 'The Political Economy of Freedom', in Ruth Levitas (ed.), *The Ideology of the New Right* (Cambridge: Polity Press).

Gamble, A. (1988) *The Free Economy and the Strong State* (Basingstoke: Macmillan).

Gamble, A. (1990) *Britain in Decline* (Basingstoke: Macmillan).

Gamble, A. (1995) 'The New Political Economy', *Political Studies*, 43(3): 516–30.

Gamble, A. (1996) *Hayek: The Iron Cage of Liberty* (Cambridge: Polity Press).

Gamble, A. (1999) 'Marxism After Communism: Beyond Realism and Historicism', *Review of International Studies*, 25(5): 127–44.

Gamble, A. (2004) 'British National Capitalism Since the War: Declinism, Thatcherism and New Labour', in J. Perraton and B. Clift (eds), *Where Are National Capitalisms Now?* (Basingstoke: Palgrave Macmillan), pp. 33–49.

Gamble, A. (2009) *Spectre at the Feast* (London: Red Globe Press).

Gamble, A. (2012) 'Economic Policy', in D. Seawright and T. Heppell (eds), *Cameron and the Conservatives* (Basingstoke: Palgrave Macmillan), pp. 59–73.

Gamble, A. (2014) *Crisis Without End?* (London: Red Globe Press).

Gamble, A. (2015) 'Austerity as Statecraft', *Parliamentary Affairs: A Journal of Representative Politics*, 68(1): 42–57.

Gamble, A. (2019) 'After Brexit: The Past and Future of the Anglo-Liberal Model', in C. Hay and D. Bailey (eds), *Diverging Capitalisms* (London: Springer), pp. 17–42.

Gamble, A. and Kelly, G. (2000) 'Three Politics of the Company', in J. Parkinson, G. Kelly and A. Gamble (eds), *The Political Economy of the Company* (Oxford: Hart).

Gamble, A. and Payne, T. (eds) (1996) *Regionalism and World Order* (Basingstoke: Macmillan).

Gamble, A., Payne, A., Dietrich, M., Hoogevelt, A. and Kenny, M. (1996) 'Editorial Policy Statement: New Political Economy', *New Political Economy*, 1(1): 5–11.

Gamble, A., Kelly, G. and Kelly, D. (eds) (1997) *Stakeholder Capitalism* (Basingstoke: Macmillan).

Gamble, A., Kelly, G. and Parkinson, J. (2000) 'Introduction: The Political Economy of the Company', in J. Parkinson, G. Kelly and A. Gamble (eds), *The Political Economy of the Company* (Oxford: Hart), pp. 1–20.

Garrett, G. (1995) 'Capital Mobility, Trade, and the Domestic Politics of Economic Policy', *International Organization*, 49(4): 657–87.

Garrett, G. (1998) *Partisan Politics in the Global Economy* (Cambridge: Cambridge University Press).

Garrett, G. and Lange, P. (1991) 'What's Left for the Left?', *International Organization*, 45(4): 537–64.

Garrett, G. and Lange, P. (1995) 'Internationalisation, Institutions and Political Change', *International Organization*, 49(4): 627–55.

Gatti, D. and Glyn, A. (2006) 'Welfare States in Hard Times', *Oxford Review of Economic Policy*, 22(3): 301–12.

George, A. and Bennett, A. (2005) *Case Studies and Theory Development in the Social Sciences* (Cambridge, MA: MIT Press).

Germain, R. (1997) *The International Organization of Credit* (Cambridge: Cambridge University Press).

Germain, R. (2010) *Global Politics and Financial Governance* (Macmillan International Higher Education).

Germain, R. (2019) 'International Political Economy', in G. Dale, C. Holmes and M. Markantonatou (eds), *Karl Polanyi's Political and Economic Thought* (Newcastle-upon-Tyne: Agenda Publishing), pp. 27–48.

Gerring, J. (2007) *Case Study Research: Principles and Practices* (Cambridge: Cambridge University Press).

Giddens, A. (1998) *The Third Way: The Renewal of Social Democracy* (Cambridge: Polity Press).

Gilbert, D. (2018) *The American Class Structure in an Age of Growing Inequality* (Thousand Oaks, CA: Sage).

Gill, S. (1998) 'European Governance and New Constitutionalism: Economic and Monetary Union and Alternatives to Disciplinary Neoliberalism in Europe', *New Political Economy*, 3(1): 5–26.

Gilpin, R. (1971) 'The Politics of Transnational Relations', *International Organization*, 25(3): 398–419.

Gilpin, R. (1975) *U.S. Power and the Multinational Corporation: The Political Economy of Foreign Direct Investment* (New York: Basic Books).

Gilpin, R. (1981) *War and Change in World Politics* (Cambridge: Cambridge University Press).

Glennerster, H. (2010) 'The Sustainability of Western Welfare States', in F. Castles, S. Liebfried, J. Lewis, H. Obinger and C. Pierson (eds), *The Oxford Handbook of the Welfare State* (Oxford: Oxford University Press), pp. 689–702.

Glyn, A. (1995) 'Social Democracy and Full Employment', *New Left Review*, 211: 33–55.

Glyn, A. (ed.) (2001) *Social Democracy in Neoliberal Times* (Oxford: Oxford University Press).

Glyn, A. (2006) *Capitalism Unleashed: Finance, Globalisation and Welfare* (Oxford: Oxford University Press).

Godechot, O. (2012) 'Is Finance Responsible for the Rise in Wage Inequality in France?', *Socio-Economic Review*, 10: 447–70.

Godechot, O. (2016) 'Financialization Is Marketization! A Study of the Respective Impacts of Various Dimensions of Financialization on the Increase in Global Inequality', *Sociological Science*, 3: 495–519.

Goodin, Robert (1996) 'Institutions and Their Design', in R. Goodin (ed.), *The Theory of Institutional Design* (Cambridge: Cambridge University Press), pp. 1–53.

Goodin, R. (2003) 'Choose Your Capitalism?', *Comparative European Politics*, 1(2): 203–14.

Gotoh, F. (2019) *Japanese Resistance to American Financial Hegemony: Global Versus Domestic Social Norms* (Abingdon: Routledge).

Gough, I. (1996) 'Social Welfare and Competitiveness', *New Political Economy*, 1(2): 209–32.

Gough, I. and Therborn, G. (2010) 'The Global Futures of Welfare States', in F. Castles, S. Liebfried, J. Lewis, H. Obinger and C. Pierson (eds), *The Oxford Handbook of the Welfare State* (Oxford: Oxford University Press), pp. 703–20.

Gourevitch, P. (1978) 'The Second Image Reversed: The International Sources of Domestic Politics', *International Organization*, 32: 881–911.

Gourevitch, P. (1986) *Politics in Hard Times: Comparative Responses to International Economic Crises*, Cornell Studies in Political Economy (Ithaca, NY: Cornell University Press).

Gourevitch, P. (1996) 'The Macro Politics of Micro-Institutional Differences in the Analysis of Comparative Capitalism', in S. Berger and R. Dore (eds), *Convergence or Diversity? National Models of Production and Distribution in a Global Economy* (New York: Cornell University Press).

Gourevitch, P. and Shinn, J. (2005) *Political Power and Corporate Control* (Princeton, NJ: Princeton University Press).

Gourevitch, P. A. (2013) 'Yet More Hard Times?' in M. Kahler and D. A. Lake (eds), *Politics in the New Hard Times: The Great Recession in Comparative Perspective* (Ithaca: Cornell University Press), pp. 253–74.

Goyer, M. (2001) 'Corporate Governance and the Innovation System in France: 1985–2000', *Industry and Innovation*, 8(2): 135–58.

Goyer, M. (2003) 'Corporate Governance, Employees, and the Focus on Core Competencies in France and Germany', in C. Milhaupt (ed.), *Global Markets, Domestic Institutions* (New York: Columbia University Press), pp. 183–213.

Goyer, M. (2006) 'Varieties of Institutional Investors and National Models of Capitalism: The Transformation of Corporate Governance in France and Germany', *Politics and Society*, 34(3): 399–430.

Goyer, M. (2011) *Contingent Capital* (Oxford: Oxford University Press).

Granovetter, M. (1985) 'Economic Action and Social Structure: The Problem of Embeddedness', *American Journal of Sociology*, 91: 481–510.

Granovetter, M. and Swedberg, R. (eds) (2001) *The Sociology of Economic Life* (Boulder, CO: Westview Press).

Grant, W. (2010) *The Development of a Discipline: The History of the Political Studies Association* (Oxford: Wiley-Blackwell).

Grant, W. and Wilson, G. (eds) (2012) *The Consequences of the Global Financial Crisis: The Rhetoric of Reform and Regulation* (Oxford: Oxford University Press).

Gray, J. (1998) *False Dawn* (London: Granta).

Green, J. and Lavery, S. (2015) 'The Regressive Recovery: Distribution, Inequality and State Power in Britain's Post-crisis Political Economy', *New Political Economy*, 20(6): 894–923.

Green, D. and Shapiro, I. (1994) *Pathologies of Rational Choice Theory: A Critique of Applications in Political Science* (New Haven, CT: Yale University Press).

Green-Pedersen, C., van Kersbergen, K. and Hemerijck, A. (2001) 'Neoliberalism, the "Third Way" or What? Recent Social Democratic Welfare Policies in Denmark and the Netherlands', *Journal of European Public Policy*, 8(2): 307–25.

Greer, I. (2016) 'Welfare Reform, Precarity and the Re-commodification of Labour', *Work, Employment and Society*, 30(1): 162–73.

Griffin, P. (2007a) 'Sexing the Economy in a Neo-liberal World Order: Neo-liberal Discourse and the (Re) Production of Heteronormative Heterosexuality', *British Journal of Politics and International Relations*, 9(2): 220–38.

Griffin, P. (2007b) 'Refashioning IPE: What and How Gender Analysis Teaches International (Global) Political Economy', *Review of International Political Economy*, 14(4): 719–36.

Griffin, P. (2010) 'Development Institutions and Neoliberal Globalisation', in L. J. Shepherd (ed.), *Gender Matters in Global Politics: A Feminist Introduction to International Relations* (Abingdon: Routledge), pp. 218–33.

Grimes, W. (2001) *Unmaking the Japanese Miracle: Japanese Macroeconomic Policy Making, 1985–2000* (Ithaca, NY: Cornell University Press).

Grimshaw, D. (2013) 'Austerity, Privatization and Levelling Down: Public Sector Reforms in the United Kingdom', in D. Vaughan-Whitehead (ed.), *Public Sector Shock in Europe: Between Structural Reforms and Quantitative Adjustment* (Cheltenham: Edward Elgar), pp. 576–626.

Gruin, J. (2013) 'Asset or Liability? The Role of the Financial System in the Political Economy of China's Rebalancing', *Journal of Current Chinese Affairs*, 42(4): 73–104.

Gruin, J. (2019) *Communists Constructing Capitalism: State, Market, and the Party in China's Financial Reform* (Manchester: Manchester University Press).

Guttmann, R. and Plihon, D. (2008, December) 'Consumer Debt at the Center of Finance-Led Capitalism', in *CEPN/SCEPA Conference "Globalization and Inequality: Are Growth Regimes in Open Economies Bound to be Biased*, pp. 17–8.

Guy Peters, B. (2013) *Strategies for Comparative Research in Political Science* (Basingstoke: Macmillan International Higher Education).

Hacker, J. (2002) *The Divided Welfare State* (Cambridge: Cambridge University Press).

Hacker, J. (2005) 'Policy Drift: The Hidden Politics of US Welfare State Retrenchment', in W. Streeck and K. Thelen (eds), *Beyond Continuity* (Oxford: Oxford University Press), pp. 40–82.

Hacker, J. and Pierson, P. (2010) 'Winner-Take-All Politics: Public Policy, Political Organization, and the Precipitous Rise of Top Incomes in the United States', *Politics and Society*, 38(2): 152–204.

Hager, S.B. (2018) 'Varieties of Top Incomes?', *Socio-Economic Review*. https://doi.org/10.1093/ser/mwy036.

Hager, S. B. and Baines, J. (2020) 'Jurisdictional Tax Rates: How the Structure of Corporate Taxation Fuels Concentration and Inequality', *Politics and Society*, forthcoming.

Haldane, A. (1995) *Rules, Discretion and the UK's New Monetary Framework* (London: Bank of England).

Hall, P. (1986) *Governing the Economy* (Cambridge: Polity Press).

Hall, P. (1989) 'Conclusion', in P. Hall (ed.), *The Political Power of Economic Ideas* (Princeton, NJ: Princeton University Press), pp. 361–92.

Hall, P. (1993) 'Policy Paradigms, Social Learning and the State', *Comparative Politics*, 25: 275–96.

Hall, P. (2003) 'Aligning Ontology and Methodology in Comparative Research', in J. Mahoney and D. Rueschemeyer (eds), *Comparative Historical Analysis in the Social Sciences* (Cambridge: Cambridge University Press), pp. 373–406.

Hall, P. (2007) 'The Evolution of Varieties of Capitalism in Europe', in B. Hancké, M. Rhodes and M. Thatcher (eds), *Beyond Varieties of Capitalism* (Oxford: Oxford University Press), pp. 39–88.

Hall, P. and Gingerich, D. (2009) 'Varieties of Capitalism and Institutional Complementarities in the Political Economy', *British Journal of Political Science*, 39(3): 449–82.

Hall, S. and Jacques, M. (eds) (1983) *The Politics of Thatcherism* (London: Lawrence and Wishart).

Hall, P. and Soskice, D. (2001) *Varieties of Capitalism: Institutional Foundations of Comparative Advantage* (Cambridge: Cambridge University Press).

Hall, P. and Soskice, D. (2003) 'Varieties of Capitalism and Institutional Change: A Response to Three Critics', *Comparative European Politics*, 1(2): 241–9.

Hall, P. and Thelen, K. (2005) 'The Politics of Change in Varieties of Capitalism', Paper Presented at the American Political Science Association Annual Meeting, Philadelphia, PA.

Hamilton ([1791] 1997) 'Report on Manufactures', in G. T. Crane and A. Amawi (eds), *The Theoretical Evolution of International Political Economy: A Reader* (Oxford: Oxford University Press).

Hancké, B. (2002) *Large Firms and Institutional Change* (Oxford: Oxford University Press).

Hancké, B. (ed.) (2009) *Debating Varieties of Capitalism* (Oxford: Oxford University Press).

Hancké, B., Rhodes, M. and Thatcher, M. (eds) (2007) *Beyond Varieties of Capitalism: Conflict, Contradictions, and Complementarities in the European Economy* (Oxford: Oxford University Press).

Hannah, L. (1983) *The Rise of the Corporate Economy*, 2nd edn (London: Methuen).

Haraway, D. J. (1991) *Simians, Cyborgs and Women* (London: Routledge).

Hardie, I. and Howarth, D. (eds) (2013) *Market-Based Banking and the International Financial Crisis* (Oxford: Oxford University Press).

Hardie, I., Howarth, D., Maxfield, S. and Verdun, A. (2013a) 'Banks and the False Dichotomy in the Comparative Political Economy of Finance', *World Politics*, 65(4): 691–728.

Hardie, I., Howarth, D. and Maxfield, S. (2013b) 'Introduction: Towards a Political Economy of Banking', in *Market-Based Banking and the International Financial Crisis* (Oxford: Oxford University Press), pp. 1–21.

Hardin, G. (1968) 'The Tragedy of the Commons', *Science*, 162: 1243–8.

Hargreaves Heap, S. (1992) *The New Keynesian Macroeconomics* (Aldershot: Edward Elgar).

Hargreaves Heap, S. (1994) 'Institutions and Macroeconomic Performance', *Journal of Economic Surveys*, 8(1): 36–56.

Harlen, C. (1999) 'A Reappraisal of Classical Economic Nationalism and Economic Liberalism', *International Studies Quarterly*, 43(4): 733–44.

Hartwell, R. (1971) '"Introduction" to Ricardo's', in *Principles of Political Economy and Taxation* (London: Pelican), pp. 7–46.

Harvey, D. (1982) *The Limits of Capital* (Oxford: Blackwell).

Harvey, D. (2010) *A Companion to Marx's Capital* (London: Verso).

Hassel, A. (1999) 'The Erosion of the German System of Industrial Relations', *British Journal of Industrial Relations*, 37(3): 483–505.

Haveman, R. (1997) 'Equity with Employment', *Renewal*, 5(3/4): 30–42.

Hay, C. (2001) 'The "Crisis" of Keynesianism and the Rise of Neoliberalism in Britain: An Ideational Institutionalist Approach', in J. Campbell and O. Pedersen (eds), *The Rise of Neoliberalism and Institutional Analysis* (Princeton, NJ: Princeton University Press), pp. 193–218.

Hay, C. (2002) *Political Analysis* (London: Red Globe Press).

Hay, C. (2004a) 'Common Trajectories, Variable Paces, Divergent Outcomes? Models of European Capitalism under Conditions of Complex Economic Interdependence', *Review of International Political Economy*, 11(2): 231–62.

Hay, C. (2004b) 'The Normalizing Role of Rationalist Assumptions in the Institutional Embedding of Neoliberalism', *Economy and Society*, 33(4): 500–27.

Hay, C. (2004c) 'Re-stating Politics, Re-politicising the State: Neoliberalism, Economic Imperatives, and the Rise of the Competition State', *Political Quarterly*, 75(1): 30–50.

Hay, C. (2005) 'Two Can Play at That Game ... or Can They? Varieties of Capitalism, Varieties of Institutionalism', in D. Coates (ed.),

Varieties of Capitalism, Varieties of Approaches (Basingstoke: Palgrave Macmillan), pp. 106–21.

Hay, C. (2006) 'What's Globalisation Got to Do with It? Economic Interdependence and the Future of European Welfare States', *Government and Opposition*, 41(1): 1–22.

Hay, C. (2009) 'Constructivist Institutionalism', in S Binder, R. Rhodes and B. Rockman (eds), *Oxford Handbook of Political Institutions* (Oxford: Oxford University Press), pp. 56–74.

Hay, C. (2011) 'Globalisation's Impact on States', in J. Ravenhill (ed.), *Global Political Economy* (Oxford: Oxford University Press), pp. 312–44.

Hay, C. (2013) *The Failure of Anglo-liberal Capitalism* (Basingstoke: Palgrave Macmillan).

Hay, C. (2016) 'Good in a Crisis: The Ontological Institutionalism of Social Constructivism', *New Political Economy*, 21(6): 520–35.

Hay, C. (2019) 'Does Capitalism (Still) Come in Varieties?', *Review of International Political Economy*: 1–18.

Hay, C. and Bailey, D. (2019) 'Introduction: Brexit and European Capitalism – A Parting of the Waves?', in *Diverging Capitalisms* (Cham: Palgrave Macmillan), pp. 1–16.

Hay, C. and Lister, M. (2006) 'Introduction: Theories of the State', in C. Hay, M. Lister and D. Marsh (eds), *The State: Theories and Issues* (London: Red Globe Press), pp. 1–20.

Hay, C. and Wincott, D. (1998) 'Structure, Agency and Historical Institutionalism', *Political Studies*, 46(5): 951–7.

Hay, C. and Wincott, D. (2012) *The Political Economy of European Welfare Capitalism* (London: Red Globe Press).

Hayek, F. (1945) *The Road to Serfdom* (London: Routledge & Kegan Paul).

Hayek, F. (1973) *Law, Legislation and Liberty: A New Statement of the Liberal Principles of Justice and Political Economy, Vol. 1: Rules and Order* (London: Routledge).

Hayward, J. (2007) *Fragmented France: Two Centuries of Disputed Identity* (Oxford: Oxford University Press).

Heilbroner, R. (1986) *The Essential Adam Smith* (Oxford: Oxford University Press).

Heilbroner, R. (1992) *The Worldly Philosophers* (New York: Touchstone/Simon & Schuster).

Heilbroner, R. (1996) *Teachings from the Worldly Philosophy* (New York: W. W. Norton).

Held, D. and McGrew, A. (2003) 'The Great Globalization Debate: An Introduction', in D. Held and A. McGrew (eds), *The Global Transformations Reader* (Cambridge: Polity Press), pp. 1–50.

Held, D., McGrew, A., Goldblatt, D. and Perraton, J. (1999) *Global Transformations* (Cambridge: Polity Press).

Helgadóttir, O. (2016) 'Banking Upside Down: The Implicit Politics of Shadow Banking Expertise', *Review of International Political Economy*, 23(6): 915–40.

Helleiner, E. (1994) *States and the Re-emergence of Global Finance* (Ithaca, NY: Cornell University Press).

Helleiner, E. (2002) 'Economic Nationalism as a Challenge to Economic Liberalism? Lessons from the 19th Century', *International Studies Quarterly*, 46(3): 307–29.

Helleiner, E. (2005) 'The Meaning and Contemporary Significance of Economic Nationalism', in E. Helleiner and A. Pickel (eds), *Economic Nationalism in a Globalizing World* (Ithaca, NY: Cornell University Press), pp. 220–34.

Helleiner, E. (2014) *The Status Quo Crisis: Global Financial Governance After the 2008 Meltdown* (Oxford: Oxford University Press).

Helleiner, E. (2019) 'Varieties of American Neomercantilism: From the Early American Republic to Trumpian Economic Nationalism', Paper Presented at the ISA Conference, Toronto.

Helleiner, E. (2020) 'The Diversity of Economic Nationalism', *New Political Economy*, forthcoming.

Helleiner, E. and Pagliari, S. (2009) 'Towards a New Bretton Woods? The First G20 Leaders Summit and the Regulation of Global Finance', *New Political Economy*, 14(2): 275–87.

Helleiner, E. and Pickel, A. (eds) (2005) *Economic Nationalism in a Globalizing World* (Ithaca, NY: Cornell University Press).

Helleiner, E. and Wang, H. (2018) 'Beyond the Tributary Tradition of Chinese IPE: The Indigenous Roots of Early Chinese Economic Nationalism', *Chinese Journal of International Politics*, 11(4): 451–83.

Hemerijck, A. (2006) *Recalibrating Europe's Semi-Sovereign Welfare States* (No. SP I 2006-103). WZB Berlin Social Science Center.

Hemerijck, A. (2010) *In Search of a New Welfare State* (Oxford: Oxford University Press).

Hemerijck, A. and Ferrera, M. (2004) 'Welfare Reform in the Shadow of EMU', in G. Ross and A. Martin (eds), *Euros and Europeans: Monetary Integration and the European Model of Society* (Oxford: Oxford University Press), pp. 248–77.

Henderson, W. (1983) *Friedrich List* (London: Cass).

Hernes, H. M. (1987) *Welfare State and Woman Power: Essays in State Feminism* (Oslo: Scandinavian University Press).

Hertig, G. (2018) 'Governance by Institutional Investors in a Stakeholder World', in W.-G. Ringe and J. N. Gordon (eds), *The Oxford Handbook of Corporate Law and Governance* (Oxford: Oxford University Press), pp. 1–23. https://doi.org/10.1093/oxfor dhb/9780198743682.013.35.

Hesse-Biber, S. N. and Johnson, R. B. (eds) (2015) *The Oxford Handbook of Multimethod and Mixed Methods Research Inquiry* (Oxford: Oxford University Press).

Hibbs, D. A. (1977) 'Political Parties and Macroeconomic Policy', *American Political Science Review*, 71(4): 1467–87.

Hicks, A. (1994) 'The Social Democratic Corporatist Model of Economic Performance in Short- and Medium-Run Perspective', in T. Janoski and A. Hicks (eds), *The Comparative Political Economy of the Welfare State* (Cambridge: Cambridge University Press), pp. 189–217.

Higgott, R. (1994) 'International Political Economy', in A. Groom and M. Light (eds), *Contemporary International Relations: A Guide to Theory* (London: Pinter), pp. 156–170.

Higgott, R. (1999) 'Economics, Politics and (International) Political Economy: The Need for a Balanced Diet in an Era of Globalisation', *New Political Economy*, 4(1): 23–36.

Hildebrand, B. (1848) *The National Economy of the Present and Future* (Frankfurt-am-Main).

Hilferding, R. (1981 [1910]) *Finance Capital. A Study of the Latest Phase of Capitalist Development*, ed. Tom Bottomore (London: Routledge & Kegan Paul).

Hindmoor, A. (2006) *Rational Choice* (London: Red Globe Press).

Hines, J. R. (2006) 'Will Social Welfare Expenditures Survive Tax Competition?', *Oxford Review of Economic Policy*, 22(3): 330–48.

Hirschman, A. (1970) *Exit, Voice and Loyalty: Responses to Decline in Firms, Organizations and States* (Cambridge, MA: Harvard University Press).

Hirschman, A. (1989) 'How the Keynesian Revolution Was Exported from the United States and Other Comments', in P. Hall (ed.), *The Political Power of Economic Ideas* (Princeton, NJ: Princeton University Press), pp. 347–60.

Hirschman, A. (1995) *A Propensity to Self-Subversion* (Cambridge, MA: Harvard University Press).

Hirst, P. and Thompson, G. (1999) *Globalisation in Question* (Cambridge: Polity Press).

Hiscox, M. J. (2002) *International Trade and Political Conflict: Commerce, Coalitions, and Mobility* (Princeton, NJ: Princeton University Press).

Hobson, J. A. (1988a [1938]) 'Confessions of an Economic Heretic', in M. Freeden (ed.), *J. A. Hobson: A Reader* (London: Unwin Hyman), pp. 29–33.

Hobson, J. A. (1988b [1938]) *Imperialism: A Study* (London: Unwin Hyman).

Hobson, J. A. (1988c [1901]) 'The Social Problem', in M. Freeden (ed.), *J. A. Hobson: A Reader* (London: Unwin Hyman), pp. 29–33.

Hobson, J. A. (1988d [1916]) 'The New Protectionism', in M. Freeden (ed.), *J. A. Hobson: A Reader* (London: Unwin Hyman), pp. 168–72.

Hobson, J. (2003) 'Disappearing Taxes or the "Race to the Middle"? Fiscal Policy in the OECD', in L. Weiss (ed.), *States in the Global Economy* (Cambridge: Cambridge University Press), pp. 37–56.

Hobson, J. M. (2012) *The Eurocentric Conception of World Politics: Western International Theory, 1760–2010* (Cambridge: Cambridge University Press).

Hobson, J. (2013a) 'Part 1 – Revealing the Eurocentric Foundations of IPE: A Critical Historiography of the Discipline from the Classical to the Modern Era', *Review of International Political Economy*, 20(5): 1024–54.

Hobson, J. (2013b) 'Part 2 – Reconstructing the Non-Eurocentric Foundations of IPE: From Eurocentric "Open Economy Politics" to Inter-Civilizational Political Economy', *Review of International Political Economy*, 20(5): 1055–81.

Hobson, J. M. and Seabrooke, L. (eds) (2007) *Everyday Politics of the World Economy.* (Cambridge: Cambridge University Press).

Hocking, B. and McGuire, S. (eds) (2004) *Trade Politics*, 2nd edn (London: Routledge).

Hodgson, G. (1988) *Economics and Institutions* (Cambridge: Polity Press).

Hodgson, G. (1999) *Economics and Utopia: Why the Learning Economy Is Not the End of History* (London: Routledge).

Hodgson, G. (2001) *How Economics Forgot History* (Abingdon: Routledge).

Hodgson, G. (2002) 'The Evolution of Institutions', *Constitutional Political Economy*, 13: 111–27.

Hodgson, G. M. (2016) 'Varieties of Capitalism: Some Philosophical and Historical Considerations', *Cambridge Journal of Economics*, 40(3): 941–60.

Hollander, S. (1992) *Classical Economics* (Toronto, ON: Toronto University Press).

Hollingsworth, J. (1991) 'The Logic of Coordinating American Manufacturing', in J. Campbell, J. Rogers Hollingworth and L. N. Lingberg (eds), *The Governance of the American Economy* (Cambridge: Cambridge University Press), pp. 35–73.

Hollingsworth, J. (1997) 'Continuities and Changes in Social Systems of Production: The Cases of Japan, Germany and the United States', in J. Hollingsworth and R. Boyer (eds), *Contemporary Capitalism: The Embeddedness of Institutions* (Cambridge: Cambridge University Press), pp. 265–310.

Hollingsworth, J. and Boyer, R. (eds) (1997) *Contemporary Capitalism: The Embeddedness of Institutions* (Cambridge: Cambridge University Press).

Hollingsworth, J., Schmitter, P. and Streeck, W. (eds) (1994) *Governing Capitalist Economies: Performance and Control* (Oxford: Oxford University Press).

Holloway, J. (2002) *Change the World Without Taking Power* (London: Pluto Press).

Holmes, C. (2009) 'Seeking Alpha or Creating Beta? Charting the Rise of Hedge Fund-Based Financial Ecosystems', *New Political Economy*, 14(4): 431–50.

Holmes, C. (2012) 'Problems and Opportunities in Polanyian Analysis Today', *Economy and Society*, 41(3): 468–84.

Holmes, C. (2019) 'Introduction', in G. Dale, C. Holmes, and M. Markantonatou (eds), *Karl Polanyi's Political and Economic Thought* (Newcastle-upon-Tyne: Agenda Publishing), pp. 1–7.

Holmes, C. and Yarrow, D. (2019) 'Economic Ideas', in G. Dale, C. Holmes and M. Markantonatou (eds), *Karl Polanyi's Political and Economic Thought* (Newcastle-upon-Tyne: Agenda Publishing), pp. 7–26.

Holt, R. and Turner, J. (eds) (1970) *The Methodology of Comparative Research* (New York: Free Press).

Hood, C., Heald, D. and Himaz, R. (2014) *When the Party's Over: The Politics of Fiscal Squeeze in Perspective* (Oxford University Press).

Hood, C. and Himaz, R. (2017) *A Century of Fiscal Squeeze Politics: 100 Years of Austerity, Politics, and Bureaucracy in Britain* (Oxford University Press).

Hoogevelt, A. (2001) *Globalization and the Post-Colonial World* (Basingstoke: Palgrave Macmillan).

Hopkin, J. (2015) 'The Troubled Southern Periphery', in M. Matthijs and M. Blyth (eds), *The Future of the Euro* (Oxford: Oxford University Press), pp. 161–84.

Hopkin, J. (2017) 'When Polanyi Met Farage: Market Fundamentalism, Economic Nationalism, and Britain's Exit from the European Union', *British Journal of Politics and International Relations*, 19(3): 465–78.

Hopkin, J. and Lynch, J. (2016) 'Winner-Take-All Politics in Europe? European Inequality in Comparative Perspective', *Politics and Society*, 44: 335–43.

Hopkin, J. and Shaw, K. A. (2016) 'Organized Combat or Structural Advantage? The Politics of Inequality and the Winner-Take-All Economy in the United Kingdom', *Politics and Society*, 44: 345–71.

Hopkin, J. and Wincott, D. (2006) 'New Labour, Economic Reform and the European Social Model', *British Journal of Politics and International Relations*, 8(1): 50–68.

Höpner, M. and Schäfer, A. (2010) 'A New Phase of European Integration: Organised Capitalisms in Post-Ricardian Europe', *West European Politics*, 33(2): 344–68.

Howell, C. (2006) 'The State and the Reconstruction of Industrial Relations After

Fordism: Britain and France Compared', in J. Levy (ed.), *The State After Statism: New State Activities in the Age of Globalization and Liberalization* (Cambridge, MA: Harvard University Press), pp. 139–84.

Hozic, A. A. and True, J. (eds) (2016) *Scandalous Economics: Gender and the Politics of Financial Crises* (Oxford: Oxford University Press).

Huber, E. and Stephens, J. (2001a) *Development and Crisis of the Welfare State* (Chicago, IL: University of Chicago Press).

Huber, E. and Stephens, J. (2001b) 'The Social Democratic Welfare State', in A. Glyn (ed.), *Social Democracy in Neoliberal Times* (Oxford: Oxford University Press), pp. 276–311.

Huber, E. and Stephens, J. D. (2014) 'Income Inequality and Redistribution in Post-industrial Democracies: Demographic, Economic and Political Determinants', *Socio-Economic Review*, 12: 245–67.

Huber, E., Charles R., Stephens, Brady, J. and Beckfield, J. (2004) 'Comparative Welfare States Data Set', Northwestern University, University of North Carolina, Duke University and Indiana University. Available at: www.nsd.uib.no/macrodataguide/set.html?id=8andsub=1.

Hundt, D. (2009) *Korea's Developmental Alliance* (London: Routledge).

Hunt, B. C. (1936) *The Development of the Business Corporation in England, 1800–1867* (Harvard, MA: Harvard University Press).

Hutton, W. (1994) *The State We're In* (London: Jonathan Cape).

Hveem, H. (2009) 'Pluralist IPE: A View from Outside the 'Schools', *New Political Economy*, 14(3): 367–76.

Ikenberry, G. J. (1992) 'A World Economy Restored: Expert Consensus and the Anglo-American Postwar Settlement', *International Organization*, 46(1): 289–321.

IMF (2013) 'United Kingdom 2013 Article IV Consultation Staff Report.' IMF Country Report No. 13/210 (Washington, DC: International Monetary Fund).

Iversen, T. (1999) *Contested Economic Institutions* (Cambridge: Cambridge University Press).

Iversen, T. (2001) 'The Dynamics of Welfare State Expansion: Trade Openness, Deindustrialization, and Partisan Politics', in P. Pierson (ed.), *The New Politics of the Welfare State* (Oxford: Oxford University Press), pp. 45–79.

Iversen, T. (2005) *Capitalism, Democracy, and Welfare* (Cambridge: Cambridge University Press).

Iversen, T. and Soskice, D. (2001) 'An Asset Theory of Social Policy Preferences', *American Political Science Review*, 95(4): 875–94.

Iversen, T. and Soskice, D. (2006) 'Electoral Institutions and the Politics of Coalitions: Why Some Democracies Redistribute More than Others', *American Political Science Review*, 100(2): 165.

Iversen, T. and Soskice, D. (2010) 'Economic Interests and Political Representation: Coordination and Distributive Conflict in Historical Perspective', in D. Coen, W. Grant and G. Wilson (eds), *The Oxford Handbook of Business and Government* (Oxford: Oxford University Press), pp. 208–47.

Iversen, T. and Stephens, J. D. (2008) 'Partisan Politics, the Welfare State, and Three Worlds of Human Capital Formation', *Comparative Political Studies*, 41(4–5): 600–37.

Jabko, N. (2006) *Playing the Market: A Political Strategy for Uniting Europe 1985–2005* (Ithaca, NY: Cornell University Press).

Jabko, N. (2015) 'The Elusive Economic Government and the Forgotten Fiscal Union', in M. Matthijs and M. Blyth (eds), *The Future of the Euro* (Oxford: Oxford University Press), pp. 70–89.

Jabko, N. and Massoc, E. (2012) 'French Capitalism Under Stress: How Nicolas Sarkozy Rescued the Banks', *Review of International Political Economy*, 19(4): 562–85.

Jackson, G (2001) 'The Origins of Nonliberal Corporate Governance in Germany and Japan', in W. Streeck and K. Yamamura (eds), *The Origins of Nonliberal Capitalism: Germany and Japan* (Ithaca, NY: Cornell University Press), pp. 121–70.

Jackson, G. (2008) 'Employment Adjustment and Distributional Conflict in Japanese Firms', in M. Aoki, G. Jackson and H. Miyajima (eds), *Corporate Governance in Japan* (Oxford: Oxford University Press), pp. 282–309.

Jackson, G. and Deeg, R. (2006) 'How Many Varieties of Capitalism? Comparing the

Comparative Institutional Analyses of Capitalist Diversity', MPIfG Discussion Paper, No. 06/2, Cologne, Max Planck Institute.

Jackson, G. and Deeg, R. (2008) 'From Comparing Capitalisms to the Politics of Institutional Change', *Review of International Political Economy*, 15(4): 680–709.

Jackson, G. and Miyajima, H. (2008) 'Introduction: The Diversity and Change of Corporate Governance in Japan', in M. Aoki, G. Jackson and H. Miyajima (eds), *Corporate Governance in Japan* (Oxford: Oxford University Press), pp. 1–50.

Jackson, G. and Vitols, S. (2001) 'Between Financial Commitment, Market Liquidity and Corporate Governance: Occupational Pensions in Britain, Germany, Japan and the USA', in B. Ebbinghaus and P. Manow (eds), *Comparing Welfare Capitalism: Social Policy and Political Economy in Europe, Japan and the USA* (London: Routledge).

Jackson, G., Aoki, M. and Miyajima, H. (eds) (2008) *Corporate Governance in Japan* (Oxford: Oxford University Press).

Jacobs, L. R. and King, D. S. (2016) *Fed Power: How Finance Wins* (New York: Oxford University Press).

Jacoby, S. (2005) *The Embedded Corporation* (Princeton, NJ: Princeton University Press).

Jacoby, W. (2015) 'Europe's New German Problem', in M. Matthijs and M. Blyth (eds), *The Future of the Euro* (Oxford: Oxford University Press), pp. 187–209.

James, H. (1996) *International Monetary Co-operation Since Bretton Woods* (Oxford: Oxford University Press).

Janoski, T. (1994) 'Direct State Intervention in the Labor Market', in T. Janoski and A. Hicks (eds), *The Comparative Political Economy of the Welfare State* (Cambridge: Cambridge University Press), pp. 54–92.

Janoski, T. and Hicks, A. (1994) *The Comparative Political Economy of the Welfare State* (Cambridge: Cambridge University Press).

Jenson, J. (2009) 'Lost in Translation: The Social Investment Perspective and Gender Equality', *Social Politics*, 16(4): 446–83.

Jessop, B. (1990) *State Theory: Putting the Capitalist State in Its Place* (Cambridge: Polity Press).

Jessop, B. (1993) 'Towards a Schumpeterian Workfare State? Preliminary Remarks on Post-Fordist Political Economy', *Studies in Political Economy*, 40: 7–39.

Jessop, B. (2002) *The Future of the Capitalist State* (Cambridge: Polity Press).

Jevons, W. (1871) *Theory of Political Economy* (London: Macmillan).

Jiang, Y. (2010) 'China's Pursuit of Free Trade Agreements: Is China Exceptional?', *Review of International Political Economy*, 17(2): 238–61.

Johnson, C. (1982) *MITI and the Japanese Miracle* (Stanford, CA: Stanford University Press).

Johnson, C. (1995) *Japan: Who Governs? The Rise of the Developmental State* (New York: W. W. Norton).

Johnson, J. (2001) 'Path Contingency in Postcommunist Transformations', *Comparative Politics*, 33(3): 253–74.

Johnston, A. and Regan, A. (2016) 'European Monetary Integration and the Incompatibility of National Varieties of Capitalism', *JCMS: Journal of Common Market Studies*, 54(2): 318–36.

Johnston, A. and Regan, A. (2018) 'Introduction: Is the European Union Capable of Integrating Diverse Models of Capitalism?', *New Political Economy*, 23(2): 145–259.

Johnston, A., Kornelakis, A. and d'Acri, C. R. (2011) 'Social Partners and the Welfare State: Recalibration, Privatization or Collectivization of Social Risks?', *European Journal of Industrial Relations*, 17(4): 349–64.

Jones, K. B. (1988) 'Towards the Revision of Politics', in K. B. Jones and A. G. Jónasdóttir (eds), *The Political Interests of Gender: Developing Theory and Research with a Feminist Face* (London: Sage), pp. 11–32.

Jung, J. (2015) 'Shareholder Value and Workforce Downsizing, 1981–2006', *Social Forces*, 93: 1335–68.

Kahn, R. (1931) 'The Relation of Home Investment to Unemployment', *Economic Journal*, 41: 173–98.

Kalecki, M. (1943) 'The Political Aspects of Full Employment', *Political Quarterly*, 14(4): 322–30.

Kamata, S. (1983) *Japan in the Passing Lane* (London: Pantheon).

Karwowski, E. and Stockhammer, E. (2017) 'Financialisation in Emerging Economies: A Systematic Overview and Comparison with Anglo-Saxon Economies', *Economic and Political Studies*, 5(1): 60–86.

Katzenstein, P. (ed.) (1978) *Between Power and Plenty: Foreign Economic Policies of Advanced*

Industrial States (Madison, WI: University of Wisconsin Press).

Katzenstein, P. (1985) *Small States in World Markets* (Ithaca, NY: Cornell University Press).

Keegan, W. (2014) *Mr Osborne's Economic Experiment: Austerity 1945–51 and 2010.* Searching Finance.

Kenworthy, L. (2006) 'Institutional Coherence and Macroeconomic Performance', *Socio-Economic Review*, 4: 69–91.

Kenworthy, L. (2008) *Jobs With Equality* (Oxford: Oxford University Press)

Kenworthy, L. (2010) 'Labour Market Activation', in F. Castles, S. Liebfried, J. Lewis, H. Obinger and C. Pierson (eds), *The Oxford Handbook of the Welfare State* (Oxford: Oxford University Press), pp. 435–47.

Kenworthy, L. (2016) 'Taxes', The Good Society Blog, July, accessed at https://lanekenworthy.net/taxes/.

Kenworthy, L. (2018) 'America's Great Decoupling', in B. Nolan (ed.), *Inequality and Inclusive Growth in Rich Countries* (Oxford: Oxford University Press), pp. 333–362.

Kenworthy, L. and Pontusson, J. (2005) 'Rising Inequality and the Politics of Redistribution in Affluent Countries', Paper, Maxwell School of Citizenship and Public Affairs, Syracuse University.

Keohane, Robert O. (2009) 'The Old IPE and the New', *Review of International Political Economy*, 16: 34–46.

Keynes, J. (1937) 'The General Theory of Employment', *Quarterly Journal of Economics*, 51(2): 209–23.

Keynes, J. M. (1964 [1936]) *The General Theory of Employment Interest and Money* (London: Macmillan).

Kindleberger, C. (1993) *A Financial History of Western Europe*, 2nd edn (Oxford: Oxford University Press).

King, D. (1987) *The New Right* (Basingstoke: Macmillan).

King, D. and Le Galès, P. (2017) 'A Reconfigured State? European Policy States in a Globalizing World', in D. King and P. Le Galès (eds), *Reconfiguring European States in Crisis* (Oxford: Oxford University Press), pp. 1–44.

King, D. and Le Galès, P. (2017a) 'Introduction: A Reconfigured State: European Policy States in a Globalizing World', in D. King and P. Le Galès (eds), *Reconfiguring European States in Crisis* (Oxford: Oxford University Press), pp. 1–44.

King, D. and Le Galès, P. (eds) (2017b) *Reconfiguring European States in Crisis* (Oxford: Oxford University Press).

King, D. and Wood, S. (1999) 'The Political Economy of Neoliberalism: Britain and the United States in the 1980s', in H. Kitschelt, P. Lange, G. Marks and J. Stephens (eds), *Continuity and Change in Contemporary Capitalism* (Cambridge: Cambridge University Press), pp. 371–97.

King, G., Keohane, R. and Verba, S. (1994) *Designing Social Inquiry* (Princeton, NJ: Princeton University Press).

Kıran, J. (2018) 'Expanding the Framework of the Varieties of Capitalism: Turkey as a Hierarchical Market Economy', *Journal of Eurasian Studies*, 9(1): 42–51.

Kirschner, J. (2009) 'Realist Political Economy: Traditional Themes and Contemporary Challenges', in M. Blyth (ed.), *Routledge Handbook of International Political Economy: IPE as a Global Conversation* (London: Routledge), pp. 39–47.

Kitschelt, H. (1994) *The Transformation of European Social Democracy* (Cambridge: Cambridge University Press).

Kitschelt, H., Lange, P., Marks, G. and Stephens, J. (eds) (1999) *Continuity and Change in Contemporary Capitalism* (Cambridge: Cambridge University Press).

Klaes, M. (2006) 'Keynes Between Modernism and Post-modernism', in R. Backhouse and B. Bateman (eds), *The Cambridge Companion to Keynes* (Cambridge: Cambridge University Press), pp. 257–70.

Klein, L. (1968) *The Keynesian Revolution* (London: Macmillan).

Klein, J. (1996) *Crossing Boundaries: Knowledge, Disciplinarities and Interdisciplinarities* (Charlottesville, VA: University of Virginia Press).

Knafo, S. (2013) *The Making of Modern Finance: Liberal Governance and the Gold Standard*, RIPE Series in Global Political Economy (Abingdon: Routledge).

Knafo, S. (2019) 'The Gold Standard', in G. Dale, C. Holmes and M. Markantonatou (eds), *Karl Polanyi's Political and Economic Thought* (Newcastle-upon-Tyne: Agenda Publishing), pp. 89–108.

Knight, J. and North, D. (1997) 'Explaining Economic Change: The Interplay Between Cognition and Institutions', *Legal Theory*, 3(3): 211–26.

Koelble, T. A. (1991) *The Left Unraveled: Social Democracy and the New Left Challenge in Britain and West Germany* (Durham, NC: Duke University Press).

Kohli, A. (2004) *State-Directed Development: Political Power and Industrialization in the Global Periphery* (Cambridge: Cambridge University Press).

Korpi, W. (1983) *The Democratic Class Struggle: Swedish Politics in Comparative Perspective* (London: Routledge & Kegan Paul).

Kotz, D., McDonough, T. and Reich, M. (1994) *Social Structures of Accumulation: The Political Economy of Growth and Crisis* (Cambridge: Cambridge University Press).

Kowalik, T. (2003) 'Introduction to the Routledge Classics Edition', in R. Luxemburg (ed), *The Accumulation of Capital* (London: Routledge), pp. ix–xiv.

Krasner, S. (1976) 'State Power and the Structure of International Trade', *World Politics*, 28(3): 317–47.

Krasner, S. (1978) *Defending the National Interest: Raw Materials Investments in U.S. Foreign Policy* (Princeton, NJ: Princeton University Press).

Krasner, S. (1984) 'Approaches to the State: Alternative Conceptions and Historical Dynamics', *Comparative Politics*, 16(2): 223–46.

Krippner, G. (2001) 'The Elusive Market: Embeddedness and the Paradigm of Economic Sociology', *Theory and Society*, 30: 775–810.

Krippner, G. (2011) *Capitalizing on Crisis* (Cambridge, MA: Harvard University Press).

Krippner, G. and Alvarez, A. S. (2007) 'Embeddedness and the Intellectual Projects of Economic Sociology', *Annual Review of Sociology*, 33: 219–40.

Krugman, P. (2012) *End This Depression Now!* (New York: W. W. Norton).

Kuhn, T. (1970) *The Structure of Scientific Revolutions* (Chicago, IL: Chicago University Press).

Kuisma, M. (2007) 'Nordic Models of Citizenship: Lessons from Social History for Theorising Policy Change in the "Age of Globalisation"', *New Political Economy*, 12(1): 87–95.

Kwon, R., Roberts, A. and Zingula, K. (2017) 'Whither the Middle Class? Financialization, Labor Institutions, and the Gap Between Top-and Middle-Income Earners in Advanced Industrial Societies', *Sociology of Development*, 3(4): 377–402.

Kydland, F. and Prescott, E. (1977) 'Rules Rather than Discretion: The Inconsistency of Optimal Plans', *Journal of Political Economy*, 67: 473–91.

Labbé, D. (1994) 'Trade Unionism in France Since the Second World War', *West European Politics*, 17(1): 146–67.

Lagarde, C. (2019) 'Forging a Stronger Social Contract – The IMF's Approach to Social Spending'. Speech at the International Labour Organisation. Geneva, 14 June. Available at: https://www.imf.org/en/News/Articles/2019/06/14/sp061419-md-social-spending.

Lagna, A. (2016) 'Derivatives and the Financialisation of the Italian State', *New Political Economy*, 21(2): 167–86.

Lai, H. (2010) 'Uneven Opening of China's Society, Economy, and Politics: Pro-growth Authoritarian Governance and Protests in China', *Journal of Contemporary China*, 19(67): 819–35.

Lake, D. (2006) 'International Political Economy: A Maturing Interdiscipline', in Donald A. Wittman and Barry A. Weingast (eds), *The Oxford Handbook of Political Economy* (Oxford: Oxford University Press), pp. 757–77.

Lake, D. (2009) 'Open Economy Politics: A Critical Review', *Review of International Organizations*, 4: 219–44.

Landman, T. (2000) *Issues and Methods in Comparative Politics: An Introduction* (London: Routledge).

Landreth, H. and Colander, D. (1994) *History of Economic Thought*, 3rd edn (Boston, MA: Houghton Mifflin).

Lane, J.-E. and Ersson, S. (1997) *Comparative Political Economy: A Developmental Approach* (London: Pinter).

Langley, P. (2004) 'In the Eye of the "Perfect Storm": The Final Salary Pensions Crisis and Financialisation of Anglo-American Capitalism', *New Political Economy*, 9(4): 539–58.

Langley, P. (2007) 'Everyday Investor Subjects and Global Financial Change: The Rise of Anglo-American Mass Investment', in L Seabrooke and J Hobson (eds), *Everyday Politics of the World Economy* (Cambridge: Cambridge University Press), pp. 103–19.

Langley, P. (2006) 'The Making of Investor Subjects in Anglo-American Pensions', *Environment and Planning D: Society and Space*, 24(6): 919–34.

Langley, P. (2008) *The Everyday Life of Global Finance: Saving and Borrowing in Anglo-America* (Oxford: Oxford University Press).

Langley, P. (2010) 'The Performance of Liquidity in the Subprime Mortgage Crisis', *New Political Economy*, 15: 71–89.

Lapavitsas, C. (2012) *Crisis in the Eurozone* (Verso Books).

Lapavitsas, C., Kaltenbrunner, A., Lindo, D., Michell, J., Painceira, J. P., Pires, E. and Teles, N. (2010) 'Eurozone Crisis: Beggar Thyself and Thy Neighbour', *Journal of Balkan and Near Eastern Studies*, 12(4): 321–73.

Lash, S. and Urry, J. (1987) *The End of Organised Capitalism* (Madison, WI: University of Wisconsin Press).

Lasswell, H. (1936) *Politics: Who Gets What, When, How?* (New York: McGraw-Hill).

Lavery, S. (2019) *British Capitalism After the Crisis* (Cham: Springer International).

Lazonick, W. (1993) *Business Organization and the Myth of the Market Economy* (Cambridge: Cambridge University Press).

Lazonick, W. and O'Sullivan, M. (2000) 'Maximizing Shareholder Value: A New Ideology for Corporate Governance', *Economy and Society*, 29(1): 13–35.

Lehmbruch, G. (1977) 'Liberal Corporatism and Party Government', *Comparative Political Studies*, 10(1): 91–126.

Lehmbruch, G. (2001) 'The Institutional Embedding of Market Economies: The German "Model" and Its Impact on Japan', in W. Streeck and K. Yamamura (eds), *The Origins of Nonliberal Capitalism: Germany and Japan* (Ithaca, NY: Cornell University Press), pp. 39–93.

Leijonhufvud, A. (1968) *On Keynesian Economics and the Economics of Keynes* (Oxford: Oxford University Press).

Lenin, V. I. (1950 [1917]) *Imperialism, the Highest Stage of Capitalism* (Moscow: Foreign Languages Publishing House).

Levi, M. (1997) 'A Model, a Method, and a Map: Rational Choice in Comparative and Historical Analysis', in Mark I. Lichbach and Alan S. Zuckerman (eds), *Comparative Politics: Rationality, Culture, and Structure* (Cambridge: Cambridge University Press), pp. 19–41.

Levi-Faur, D. (1997a) 'Economic Nationalism: From Friedrich List to Robert Reich', *Review of International Studies*, 23(3): 359–70.

Levi-Faur, D. (1997b) 'Friedrich List and the Political Economy of the Nation-State', *Review of International Political Economy*, 4(1): 154–78.

Levi-Faur, D. (2006) 'Varieties of Regulatory Capitalism: Getting the Most Out of the Comparative Method', *Governance*, 19(3): 367–82.

Levy, J. (2000) 'France: Directing Adjustment?', in F. Scharpf and V. Schmidt (eds), *Welfare and Work in the Open Economy: Volume Two* (Oxford: Oxford University Press), pp. 337–44.

Levy, J. (2001) 'Partisan Politics and Welfare Adjustment: The Case of France', *Journal of European Public Policy*, 8(2): 265–85.

Levy, J. (2006a) 'The State Also Rises', in J. Levy (ed.), *The State After Statism: New State Activities in the Age of Liberalization* (Cambridge, MA: Harvard University Press), pp. 1–30.

Levy, J. (2006b) 'The State After Statism: From Market Direction to Market Support', in J. Levy (ed.), *The State After Statism* (Cambridge, MA: Harvard University Press), pp. 367–94.

Levy, J. (2010) 'Welfare Retrenchment', in F. Castles, S. Liebfried, J. Lewis, H. Obinger and C. Pierson (eds), *Oxford Handbook of the Welfare State* (Oxford: Oxford University Press), pp. 552–68.

Levy, J., Muira, M. and Park, G. (2006) 'Exiting Etatisme? New Directions in State Policy in France and Japan', in J. Levy (ed.), *The State After Statism* (Cambridge: Harvard University Press), pp. 93–138.

Lewis, J. (1992) 'Gender and the Development of Welfare Regimes', *Journal of European Social Policy*, 2(3): 159–73.

Lewis, J. (2001) 'The Decline of the Male Breadwinner Model: Implications for Work and Care', *Social Politics: International Studies in Gender, State & Society*, 8(2): 152–169.

Leyshon, A. and Thrift, N. (2007) 'The Capitalization of Almost Everything: The Future of Finance and Capitalism', *Theory, Culture and Society*, 24(7–8): 97–115.

Lieberthal, K. G. and Lampton, D. M. (eds) (1992) *Bureaucracy, Politics, and Decision Making in Post-Mao China* (Berkeley, CA: University of California Press).

Lijphart, A. (1971) 'Comparative Politics and Comparative Method', *American Political Science Review*, 65: 682–93.

Lijphart, A. (1975) 'The Comparable Cases Strategy in Comparative Research', *Comparative Political Studies*, 8: 158–77.

Lin, J. and Chang, H. J. (2009) 'Should Industrial Policy in Developing Countries Conform to Comparative Advantage or Defy It? A Debate Between Justin Lin and Ha-Joon Chang', *Development policy review*, 27(5): 483–502.

Lin, K.-H. and Tomaskovic-Devey, D. (2013) 'Financialization and U.S. Income Inequality, 1970–2008', *American Journal of Sociology*, 118: 1284–329.

Lindbeck, A. (1974) *Is Stabilization Policy Possible? Time-Lags and Conflicts of Goals*. Institute for International Economic Studies, University of Stockholm.

Lindbeck, A. (1975) *The Changing Role of the National State*. Institute for International Economic Studies, University of Stockholm.

Lindberg, L. and Campbell, J. L. (1991) 'The State and the Organization of Economic Activity', in J. Campbell, J. Hollingsworth and L. Lindberg (eds), *Governance of the American Economy* (New York: Cambridge University Press), pp. 356–95.

Lindblom, C. (1977) *Politics and Markets: The World's Political Economic Systems* (New York: Basic Books).

Lindsey, B. and Teles, S. M. (2017) *The Captured Economy: How the Powerful Enrich Themselves, Slow Down Growth, and Increase Inequality* (Oxford: Oxford University Press).

Lipietz, A. (1992) *Towards a New Economic Order: Postfordism, Ecology, Democracy* (Oxford: Oxford University Press).

Lipset, S. M. (1963) *The First New Nation: The United States in Historical and Comparative Perspective* (New York: Basic Books).

Lipset, S. M. and Rokkan, S. (1967) *Party Systems and Voter Alignments* (New York: Free Press).

List, F. (1856 [1841]) *National System of Political Economy* (Philadelphia, PA: Lippincott).

Loriaux, M. (1991) *France After Hegemony: International Change and Financial Reform* (Ithaca, NY: Cornell University Press).

Loriaux, M. (1999) 'The French Developmental State as Myth and Moral Ambition', in M. Woo-Cumings (ed.), *The Developmental State* (Ithaca, NY: Cornell University Press), pp. 235–75.

Loriaux, M. (2003) 'France: A New "Capitalism of Voice"?', in L. Weiss (ed.), *States in the Global Economy* (Cambridge: Cambridge University Press), pp. 101–20.

Lucas, R. E. (1976) 'Econometric Policy Evaluation: A Critique', in *Carnegie-Rochester Conference Series on Public Policy, Vol. 1* (North-Holland), pp. 19–46.

Lucas, R. E. and Sargent, T. (1981) 'After Keynesian Macroeconomics', *Rational Expectations and Econometric Practice*, 1: 295–319.

Lucas Jr, R. E. (2003) 'Macroeconomic Priorities', *American economic review*, 93(1): 1–14.

Lütz, S. (1998) 'The Revival of the Nation-State? Stock Exchange Regulation in an Era of Globalized Financial Markets', *Journal of European Public Policy*, 5(1): 153–69.

Lütz, S. (2000) 'From Managed to Market Capitalism? German Finance in Transition', *German Politics*, 9(2): 149–71.

Lütz, S. (2004) 'Convergence Within National Diversity: The Regulatory State in Finance', *Journal of Public Policy*, 24(2): 169–97.

Luxemburg, R. (2003) *The Accumulation of Capital* (Abingdon: Routledge).

Lysandrou, P. (2011) 'Global Inequality as One of the Root Causes of the Financial Crisis: A Suggested Explanation', *Economy and Society*, 40(3), 323–44.

Lysandrou, P. and Nesvetailova, A. (2015) 'The Role of Shadow Banking Entities in the Financial Crisis: A Disaggregated View', *Review of International Political Economy*, 22(2): 257–79.

Macartney, H. (2011) *Variegated Neoliberalism: EU Varieties of Capitalism and the International Political Economy*, Routledge Series in Global Political Economy (Abingdon: Routledge).

Maclean, M. (1999) 'Corporate Governance in France and the UK: Long-Term Perspectives on Contemporary Institutional Arrangements', *Business History*, 41(1): 88–116.

Mahoney, J. and Goertz, G. (2006) 'A Tale of Two Cultures: Contrasting Quantitative and Qualitative Research', *Political Analysis*, 14(3): 227–49.

Mahoney, J. and Thelen, K. (eds) (2010) *Explaining Institutional Change: Ambiguity, Agency and Power* (Cambridge: Cambridge University Press).

Maliniak, D. and Tierney, M. (2009) 'The American School of IPE', *Review of International Political Economy*, 16: 6–33.

Mancias, P. (1987) *A History and Philosophy of the Social Sciences* (Oxford: Blackwell).

Manne, H. (1965) 'Mergers and the Market for Corporate Control', *Journal of Political Economy*, 73(2): 110–20.

Manow, P. (2001a) 'Business Coordination, Wage Bargaining and the Welfare State: Germany and Japan in Comparative Historical Perspective', in B. Ebbinghaus and P. Manow (eds), *Comparing Welfare Capitalism, Social Policy and Political Economy in Europe, Japan and the USA* (London: Routledge), pp. 27–51.

Manow, P. (2001b) 'Comparative Institutional Advantages of Welfare State Regimes and New Coalitions in Welfare State Reforms', in P. Pierson (ed.), *The New Politics of the Welfare State* (Oxford: Oxford University Press), pp. 146–64.

March, J. G. and Olsen, J. P. (1984) 'The New Institutionalism: Organizational Factors in Political Life', *American Political Science Review*, 78(3): 734–49.

Mares, I. (2001) 'Firms and the Welfare State: When, Why and How Does Social Policy Matter to Employers?', in P. Hall and D. Soskice (eds), *Varieties of Capitalism: Institutional Foundations of Comparative Advantage* (Oxford: Oxford University Press), pp. 184–212.

Mares, I. (2003) *The Politics of Social Risk: Business and Welfare State Development* (Cambridge: Cambridge University Press).

Marglin, S. and Schor, J. (eds) (1992) *The Golden Age of Capitalism: Reinterpreting the Postwar Experience* (Oxford: Clarendon Press).

Markus, S. (2008) 'Corporate Governance as Political Insurance: Firm-Level Institutional Creation in Emerging Markets and Beyond', *Socio-Economic Review*, 6: 69–98.

Marquand, D. (1988) *The Unprincipled Society* (London: Fontana).

Marsh, D. and Furlong, P. (2002) 'A Skin Not a Sweater: Ontology and Epistemology in Political Science', in D. Marsh and G. Stoker (eds), *Theory and Methods in Political Science*, 2nd edn (London: Red Globe Press), pp. 17–44.

Marsh, D. and Stoker, G. (2002) 'Conclusion', in D. Marsh and G. Stoker (eds), *Theory and Methods in Political Science*, 2nd edn (London: Red Globe Press), pp. 311–7.

Marshall, T. H. (1950) *Citizenship and Social Class: And Other Essays* (Cambridge: Cambridge University Press).

Marshall, T. H. (1963) 'The Welfare State: A Comparative Study', in T. H. Marshall (ed.), *Sociology at the Crossroads and Other Essays* (London: Heinemann).

Martin, R. (2002) *Financialization of Daily Life* (Temple University Press).

Martin, A. (2004) 'The EMU Macroeconomic Policy Regime and the European Social Model', in A. Martin and G. Ross (eds), *Euros and Europeans* (Cambridge: Cambridge University Press), pp. 20–50.

Martin, C.-J. (2005) 'Last Year's Model? Reflections on the American Model of Employment Growth', in U. Becker and H. Schwartz (eds), *Employment 'Miracles'* (Amsterdam: Amsterdam University Press), pp. 183–204.

Martin, C.-J. and Swank, D. (2008) 'The Political Origins of Co-ordinated Capitalism', *American Political Science Review*, 102(2): 181–98.

Marx, K. (1974) *Capital, Volume I* (London: Lawrence & Wishart).

Marx, K. (1977) *Karl Marx Selected Writings*, ed. David McLellan (Oxford: Oxford University Press).

Marx, K. and Engels, F. (1970) *The German Ideology* (London: Lawrence & Wishart).

Massó, M. (2016) 'The Effects of Government Debt Market Financialization: The Case of Spain', *Competition & Change*, 20(3): 166–86.

Matsuura, K., Pollitt, M., Takada, R. and Tanaka, S. (2004) 'Institutional Restructuring in the Japanese Economy', in J. Perraton and B. Clift (eds), *Where Are National Capitalisms Now?* (Basingstoke: Palgrave Macmillan), pp. 133–53.

Matthijs, M. and Blyth, M. (2015) 'Conclusion: The Future of the Euro', in M. Matthijs and M. Blyth (eds), *The Future of the Euro* (Oxford: Oxford University Press), pp. 249–69.

Matthijs, M. and McNamara, K. (2015) 'The Euro Crisis' Theory Effect: Northern Saints, Southern Sinners, and the Demise of the Eurobond', *Journal of European Integration*, 37(2): 229–45.

Maxfield, S., Winecoff, W. K. and Young, K. L. (2017) 'An Empirical Investigation of the Financialization Convergence Hypothesis', *Review of International Political Economy*, 24(6): 1004–29.

McDonough, T., Reich, M. and Kotz, D. (eds) (2010) *Contemporary Capitalism and Its Crisis: Social Structure of Accumulation Theory for the 21st Century* (Cambridge: Cambridge University Press).

McGrew, A. (2011) 'The Logics of Economic Globalisation', in J. Ravenhill (ed.), *Global Political Economy* (Oxford: Oxford University Press), pp. 275–311.

McLean, I. (1987) *Public Choice* (New York: Blackwell).

McLellan, D. (1980) *The Thought of Karl Marx* (Basingstoke: Macmillan).

McNally, C. A. (2019) 'Chaotic mélange: Neoliberalism and Neo-Statism in the Age of Sino-Capitalism', *Review of International Political Economy*, 27(2): 281–301.

McNamara, Kathleen. (2009) 'Of Intellectual Monocultures and the Study of IPE', *Review of International Political Economy*, 16: 72–84.

McNamara, K. R. (2015) 'The Forgotten Problem of Embeddedness', in M. Matthijs and M. Blyth (eds), *The Future of the Euro* (Oxford: Oxford University Press), pp. 21–43.

Meckstroth, T. (1975) 'A Study of the Logic of Comparative Enquiry', *Comparative Political Studies*, 8(2): 132–48.

Meek, R. (1956) *Studies in the Labour Theory of Value* (New York: Monthly Review Press).

Menz, G. (2017) *Comparative Political Economy* (Oxford: Oxford University Press).

Milanovic, B. (2016) *Global Inequality: A New Approach for the Age of Globalization* (Harvard, MA: Harvard University Press).

Mill, J. S. (1949 [1843]) *A System of Logic: Ratiocinative and Inductive* (London: Longman).

Mill, J. S. (1970 [1848]) *Principles of Political Economy* (London: Penguin).

Milner, S. (1995) 'France', in S. Berger and D. Broughton (eds), *The Force of Labour: The West European Labour Movement and the Working Class in the Twentieth Century* (Oxford: Berg), pp. 211–44.

Milner, S. (2001) 'Globalisation and Employment in France: Between Flexibility and Protection?', *Modern and Contemporary France*, 9(3): 327–38.

Mirowski, P. (1986) 'Institutions as a Solution Concept in a Game Theory Context', reprinted in G. Hodgson (ed.), *The Economics of Institutions* (Aldershot: Elgar), pp. 241–63.

Mirowski, P. (2013) *Never Let a Serious Crisis Go to Waste: How Neoliberalism Survived the Financial Meltdown* (London: Verso Books).

Miyajima, H. and Kuroki, F. (2008) 'The Unwinding of Cross-Shareholding in Japan: Causes, Effects and Implications', in M. Aoki, G. Jackson and H. Miyajima (eds), *Corporate Governance in Japan* (Oxford: Oxford University Press), pp. 79–124.

Miyajima, H., Ogawa, R. and Saito, T. (2018) 'Changes in Corporate Governance and Top Executive Turnover: The Evidence from Japan', *Journal of the Japanese and International Economies*, 47: 17–31.

Molina, O. and Rhodes, M. (2007) 'The Political Economy of Adjustment in Mixed Market Economies: A Study of Spain and Italy', in B. Hancke, M. Rhodes and M. Thatcher (eds), *Beyond Varieties of Capitalism* (Oxford: Oxford University Press), pp. 223–52.

Monks, R. and Minow, N. (2004) *Corporate Governance* (Oxford: Blackwell).

Montgomerie, J. (2006) 'The Financialization of the American Credit Card Industry', *Competition and Change*, 10(3): 301–19.

Montgomerie, J. (2007) 'The Logic of Neoliberalism and the Political Economy of Consumer Debt-Led Growth', in S. Lee and S. McBride (eds), *Neo-Liberalism, State Power and Global Governance* (Dordrecht: Springer), pp. 157–72.

Montgomerie, J. (2009) 'The Pursuit of (Past) Happiness? Middle-Class Indebtedness and American Financialisation', *New Political Economy*, 14(1): 1–24.

Moran, M. (2001) 'The Rise of the Regulatory State in Britain', *Parliamentary Affairs*, 54(1): 19–34.

Moran, M. (2003) *The British Regulatory State: High Modernism and Hyper-Innovation* (Oxford: Oxford University Press).

Morin, F. (2000) 'A Transformation in the French Model of Shareholding and Management', *Economy and Society*, 29(1): 36–53.

Morrison, J. A. (2016) 'Shocking Intellectual Austerity: The Role of Ideas in the Demise of the Gold Standard in Britain', *International Organization*, 70(1): 175–207.

Moschella, M. (2015) 'The Institutional Roots of Incremental Ideational Change: The IMF and Capital Controls After the Global Financial Crisis', *British Journal of Politics and International Relations*, 17(3): 442–60.

Mosconi, F. (2015) *The New European Industrial Policy: Global Competitiveness and the Manufacturing Renaissance* (London: Routledge).

Mosley, L. (2000) 'Room to Move: International Financial Markets and National Welfare States', *International Organisation*, 54(4): 737–73.

Mosley, L. (2003) *Global Capital and National Governments* (Cambridge: Cambridge University Press).

Mueller, D. (1979) *Public Choice* (Cambridge: Cambridge University Press).

Mueller, D. (2003) *Public Choice III* (Cambridge: Cambridge University Press).

Navarro, V., Schmitt, J. and Astudillo, J. (2004) 'Is Globalisation Undermining the Welfare State?', *Cambridge Journal of Economics*, 28(1): 133–52.

Nesvetailova, A. (2007) *Fragile Finance: Debt, Speculation and Crisis in the Age of Global Credit* (Basingstoke: Palgrave Macmillan).

Nesvetailova, A. (2010) *Financial Alchemy in Crisis: The Great Liquidity Illusion* (London: Pluto Press).

Nesvetailova, A. (2014) 'Innovations, Fragility and Complexity: Understanding the Power of Finance', *Government and Opposition*, 49: 542–68.

Nesvetailova, A. (2015) 'A Crisis of the Overcrowded Future: Shadow Banking and the Political Economy of Financial Innovation', *New Political Economy*, 20(3): 431–53.

Newell, P. and Paterson, M. (1998) 'A Climate for Business: Global Warming, the State and Capital', *Review of International Political Economy*, 5(4): 679–703.

Newell, P. and Paterson, M. (2010) *Climate Capitalism: Global Warming and the Transformation of the Global Economy* (Cambridge: Cambridge University Press).

Newman, A. (2015) 'The Reluctant Leader: Germany's Euro Experience and the Long Shadow of Reunification', in M. Matthijs and M. Blyth (eds), *The Future of the Euro* (Oxford: Oxford University Press), pp. 117–35.

Nicholls, A. (1994) *Freedom with Responsibility* (Oxford: Oxford University Press).

Niskanen, W. (1971) *Bureaucracy and Representative Government* (Chicago, IL: Aldane Atherton).

Niskanen, W. (1991) 'A Reflection on Bureaucracy and Representative Government', in A. Blais and S. Dion (eds), *The Budget-Maximising Bureaucrat* (Pittsburgh, PA: Pittsburgh University Press), pp. 13–32.

Nolan, B. (ed.) (2018) *Inequality and Inclusive Growth in Rich Countries: Shared Challenges and Contrasting Fortunes* (Oxford: Oxford University Press).

Nölke, A. (2010) 'A "BRIC" Variety of Capitalism and Social Inequality: The Case of Brazil', *Revista de Estudos e Pesquisas sobre as Américas*, 4(1): 1–14.

Nölke, A. and Perry, J. (2007a) 'The Power of Transnational Private Governance: Financialization and the IASB', *Business and Politics*, 9(3): 1–25.

Nölke, A. and Perry, J. (2007b) 'Coordination Service Firms and the Erosion of Rhenish Capitalism', in H. Overbeek, A. Nölke and B. van Apeldoorn (eds), *The Transnational Politics of Corporate Governance Regulation* (London/New York: Routledge), pp. 121–36.

Nölke, A. (2017) 'Financialisation as the Core Problem for a "Social Europe"', *Revista de economía mundial*, 46: 27–47.

Nölke, A., ten Brink, T., May, C. and Claar, S. (2019) *State-Permeated Capitalism in Large Emerging Economies* (London: Routledge).

Nordhaus, W. D. (1975) 'The Political Business Cycle', *Review of Economic Studies*, 42(2): 169–90.

North, D. (1981) *Structure and Change in Economic History* (New York: W. W. Norton).

North, D. (1990) *Institutions, Institutional Change and Economic Performance* (Cambridge: Cambridge University Press).

O'Brien, D. (1978) *The Classical Economists* (Oxford: Oxford University Press).

O'Brien, R. and Williams, M. (2013) *Global Political Economy*, 4th edn (London: Red Globe Press).

O'Brien, R. and Williams, M. (2016) *Global Political Economy*, 5th edn (London: Red Globe Press).

O'Connor (1973) *The Fiscal Crisis of the State* (New York: Transaction Publishers).

O'Connor, J. S. (2015) 'The State and Gender Equality', in S. Leibfried, E. Huber, M. Lange, J. D. Levy, F. Nullmeier and J. D. Stephens (eds), *The Oxford Handbook of Transformations of the State* (Oxford: Oxford University Press), pp. 482–98.

O'Connor, J. S., Orloff, A. S. and Shaver, S. (1999) *States, Markets, Families: Gender, Liberalism and Social Policy in Australia, Canada, Great*

Britain and the United States (Cambridge: Cambridge University Press).

O'Sullivan, M. (2003) 'The Political Economy of Comparative Corporate Governance', *Review of International Political Economy*, 10(1): 23–72.

O'Sullivan, M. (2007) 'Acting Out Institutional Change: Understanding the Recent Transformation of the French Financial System', *Socio-Economic Review*, 5(3): 389–436.

O'Sullivan, M. (2010) 'Finance Capital in Chandlerian Capitalism', *Industrial and Corporate Change*, 19(2): 549–89.

O'Sullivan, E., Andreoni, A., López-Gómez, C. and Gregory, M. (2013) 'What Is New in the New Industrial Policy? A Manufacturing Systems Perspective', *Oxford Review of Economic Policy*, 29(2): 432–62.

Oatley, T. (1999) 'How Constraining Is Capital Mobility? The Partisan Hypothesis in an Open Economy', *American Journal of Political Science*, 43(4): 1003–27.

Oatley, T. (2011) 'The Reductionist Gamble: Open Economy Politics in the Global Economy', *International Organization*, 65: 311–41.

Obinger, H. and Wagschal, U. (2010) 'Social Expenditure and Revenues', in F. Castles, S. Liebfried, J. Lewis, H. Obinger and C. Pierson (eds), *The Oxford Handbook of the Welfare State* (Oxford: Oxford University Press), pp. 333–52.

OECD (2006) *Competitive Cities in the Global Economy* (Paris: OECD).

OECD (2010) *Gender Brief*. OECD Social Policy Division. www.oecd.org/els/family/44720649.pdf.

OECD (2013) *The OECD Gender Initiative*. https://www.oecd.org/gender/.

OECD (2019) *Under Pressure: The Squeezed Middle Class* (Paris: OECD Publishing) https://doi.org/10.1787/689afed1-en.

Offe, C. (1984) *Contradictions of the Welfare State* (London: Hutchinson).

Offe, C. (2005) 'The European Model of "Social" Capitalism: Can It Survive European Integration?', in M. Miller (ed.), *World of Capitalisms: Institutions, Governance and Economic Change in the Era of Globalisation* (London: Routledge), pp. 146–78.

Offerlé, M. (2009) *Sociologie des organisations patronales* (Paris: La Découverte).

Ohmae, K. (1995) *The End of the Nation State* (London: HarperCollins).

Olson, M. (1965) *The Logic of Collective Action* (Cambridge, MA: Harvard University Press).

Olson, M. (1982) *The Rise and Decline of Nations: Economic Growth, Stagflation and Social Rigidities* (New Haven, CT: Yale University Press).

Onis, Z. (1991) 'The Logic of the Developmental State', *Comparative Politics*, 24(1): 109–26.

Orloff, A. S. (2006) 'From Maternalism to 'Employment for All'', in J. D. Levy (ed.), *The State after Statism: New State Activities in the Age of Liberalization* (Cambridge, MA: Harvard University Press), pp. 230–68.

Orloff, A. S. (2009) 'Gendering the Comparative Analysis of Welfare States: An Unfinished Agenda', *Sociological Theory*, 27(3): 317–43.

Orloff, A. S. (2010) 'Gender', in F. G. Castles, S. Leibfried, J. Lewis, H. Obinger and C. Pierson (eds), *The Oxford Handbook of the Welfare State* (Oxford: Oxford University Press), pp. 252–64.

Orloff, A. S. and Skocpol, T. (1984) 'Why Not Equal Protection? Explaining the Politics of Public Social Spending in Britain, 1900–1911, and the United States, 1880s–1920', *American Sociological Review*, 49(6): 726–50.

Ostrom, E. (1990) *Governing the Commons: The Evolution of Institutions for Collective Action* (Cambridge: Cambridge University Press).

Ostrom, E. (2007) 'Collective Action Theory', in C. Boix and S. Stokes (eds), *Oxford Handbook of Comparative Politics* (Oxford: Oxford University Press), pp. 186–210.

Ostry, J. D. and Ghosh, A. R. (2015) 'When Is Repaying Public Debt Not of the Essence'. *Blog post, IMF Direct*. Available at: https://blog-imfdirect.imf.org/2015/06/02/when-is-repayingpublic-debt-not-of-the-essence.

Oxelheim, L. (1996) *Financial Markets in Transition: Globalization, Investment, and Economic Growth* (London: Routledge).

Oxfam (2017) 'An Economy for the 99%', Oxfam Briefing Paper.

Palier, B. (ed.) (2010) *A Long Goodbye to Bismarck? The Politics of Welfare Reforms in Continental Europe* (Amsterdam: Amsterdam University Press).

Palier, B. and Thelen, K. (2010) 'Institutionalizing Dualism: Complementarities and Change in France and Germany', *Politics and Society*, 38(1): 119–48.

Palley, T. (2008) *Financialisation: What It Is and Why It Matters* (Washington, DC: Levy

Economics Institute and Economics for Democratic and Open Societies).

Pallister-Wilkins, P. (2016) 'Interrogating the Mediterranean "Migration Crisis"', *Mediterranean Politics*, 21(2): 311–15.

Parker, S. (ed.) (2013) *The Squeezed Middle: The Pressure on Ordinary Workers in America and Britain* (Bristol: Policy Press).

Pauly, L. (1997) *Who Elected the Bankers?* (Ithaca, NY: Cornell University Press).

Payne, A. (2005) *The Global Politics of Unequal Development* (London: Red Globe Press).

Payne, A. (2006) 'The Genealogy of New Political Economy', in A. Payne (ed.), *Key Debates in Political Economy* (Routledge: London), pp. 1–10.

Payne, A. and Gamble, A. (1996) 'Introduction: The Political Economy of Regionalism and World Order', in A. Gamble and A. Payne (eds), *Regionalism and World Order* (Basingstoke: Macmillan), pp. 1–20.

Peritz, R. (1996) *Competition Policy in America, 1888–1992: History, Rhetoric, Law* (Oxford: Oxford University Press).

Perraton, J. (2003) 'The Scope and Implications of Globalisation', in J. Michie (ed.), *The Handbook of Globalisation* (Cheltenham: Edward Elgar), pp. 37–60.

Perraton, J. (2009) 'Changes in Developed Countries' Economic Systems Since the 1980s', *Economy and Society*, 38: 177–201.

Perraton, J. and Clift, B. (eds) (2004) *Where Are National Capitalisms Now?* (Basingstoke: Palgrave Macmillan).

Perraton, J., Goldblatt, D., Held, D. and McGrew, A. (1997) 'The Globalisation of Economic Activity', *New Political Economy*, 2(2): 257–77.

Persky, J. (1995) 'Retrospectives: The Ethnology of Homo Economicus', *Journal of Economic Perspectives*, 9(2): 221–31.

Peters, B. G. (1998) *Comparative Politics: Theory and Methods* (Basingstoke: Macmillan).

Peters, B. G. (1999) *Institutional Theory in Political Science* (London: Continuum).

Peters, B. G., Piere, J. and King, D. (2005) 'The Politics of Path Dependency: Political Conflict in Historical Institutionalism', *Journal of Politics*, 67(4): 1275–300.

Peterson, V. S. (2005) 'How (the Meaning of) Gender Matters in Political Economy', *New Political Economy*, 10(4): 499–52.

Petmesidou, M. and Guillén, A. M. (eds) (2017) *Economic Crisis and Austerity in Southern Europe: Threat or Opportunity for a Sustainable Welfare State* (London: Routledge).

Phelan, L., Henderson-Sellers, A. and Taplin, R. (2013) 'The Political Economy of Addressing the Climate Crisis in the Earth System: Undermining Perverse Resilience', *New Political Economy*, 18(2): 198–226.

Phillips, A. W. (1950) 'Mechanical Models in Economic Dynamics', *Economica*, 17: 283–305.

Phillips, A. (1992) 'Must Feminists Give Up on Liberal Democracy?', *Political Studies*, 40: 68–82.

Phillips, N. (ed.) (2005) *Globalizing International Political Economy* (Basingstoke: Palgrave Macmillan).

Pickel, A. (2005) 'Introduction: False Oppositions: Reconceptualizing Economic Nationalism in a Globalizing World', in E. Helleiner and A. Pickel (eds), *Economic Nationalism in a Globalizing World* (Ithaca, NY: Cornell University Press), pp. 1–20.

Pierson, C. (2001) *Hard Choices: Social Democracy in the 21st Century* (Cambridge: Polity Press).

Pierson, C. (2006) *Beyond the Welfare State: The New Political Economy of Welfare*, 3rd edn (Cambridge: Polity Press).

Pierson, C. and Castles, F. (2000) 'Introduction', in C. Pierson and F. Castles (eds), *The Welfare State Reader* (Cambridge: Polity), pp. 1–10.

Pierson, P. (1994) *Dismantling the Welfare State?* (Cambridge: Cambridge University Press).

Pierson, P. (1996) 'The New Politics of the Welfare State', *World Politics*, 48(2): 143–79.

Pierson, P. (2000) 'Increasing Returns, Path Dependence, and the Study of Politics', *American Political Science Review*, 94(2): 251–67.

Pierson, P. (ed.) (2001) *The New Politics of the Welfare State* (Oxford: Oxford University Press).

Pierson, P. (2004) *Politics in Time* (Princeton, NJ: Princeton University Press).

Pike, A. and Pollard, J. (2010) 'Economic Geographies of Financialisation', *Economic Geography*, 86(1): 29–51.

Piketty, T. (2014) *Capital in the Twenty-First Century* (Cambridge, MA: Harvard University Press).

Piketty, T. (2015) 'Putting Distribution Back at the Center of Economics: Reflections on Capital in the Twenty-First Century', *Journal of Economic Perspectives*, 29(1): 67–88.

Piketty, T., Saez, E. and Zucman, G. (2018) 'Distributional National Accounts: Methods and Estimates for the United States', *Quarterly Journal of Economics*, 133: 553–609.

Piore, M. and Sabel, C. (1984) *The Second Industrial Divide: Possibilities for Prosperity* (New York: Basic Books).

Pirie, I. (2005) 'The New Korean State', *New Political Economy*, 10(1): 27–44.

Pirie, I. (2008) *The Korean Developmental State: From Dirigisme to Neo- Liberalism* (London: Routledge).

Pisani-Ferry, J. (2011) *The Euro Crisis and Its Aftermath* (Oxford: Oxford University Press).

Pisano, G. P. and Shih, W. C. (2013) *Producing Prosperity* (Boston, MA: Harvard Business Review Press).

Polanyi, K. (1957) 'The Economy as an Instituted Process', in K. Polanyi (ed.), *Trade and Market in the Early Empires* (New York: Free Press), pp. 243–69.

Polanyi, K. (2001 [1944]) *The Great Transformation: The Political and Economic Origins of Our Time* (Boston, MA: Beacon Press).

Pollitt, C. (2002) 'Clarifying Convergence: Striking Similarities and Durable Differences in Public Management Reform', *Public Management Review*, 4: 471–92.

Pontusson, J. (1992) *The Limits of Social Democracy: Investment Politics in Sweden* (Ithaca, NY: Cornell University Press).

Pontusson, J. (2011) 'Once Again a Model: Nordic Social Democracy in a Globalized World', in J. Cronin, G. Ross and J. Shoch (eds), *What's Left?* (London: Duke University Press), pp. 89–115.

Prasad, M. (2006) *The Politics of Free Markets* (Chicago, IL: Chicago University Press).

Przeworski, A. (1985) *Capitalism and Social Democracy* (Cambridge: Cambridge University Press).

Przeworski, A. (2003) *States and Markets: A Primer in Political Economy* (Cambridge: Cambridge University Press).

Przeworski, A. and Teune, H. (1970) *The Logic of Comparative Social Inquiry* (New York: John Wiley).

Przeworski, A. and Wallerstein, M. (1988) 'Structural Dependence of the State on Capital', *American Political Science Review*, 82(1): 11–29.

Quack, S. and Djelic, M.-L. (2005) 'Adaptation, Recombination and Reinforcement: The Story of Antitrust and Competition Law in Germany and Europe', in W. Streeck and K. Thelen (eds), *Beyond Continuity* (Oxford: Oxford University Press), pp. 255–81.

Quaglia, L. (2007) 'The Politics of Financial Service Regulation and Supervision Reform in the European Union', *European Journal of Political Research*, 46(2): 269–90.

Quaglia, L. (2010) 'Completing the Single Market in Financial Services: The Politics of Competing Advocacy Coalitions', *Journal of European Public Policy*, 17(7): 1007–23.

Quaglia, L. and Howarth, D. (2018) 'Brexit and the Battle for Financial Services', *Journal of European Public Policy*, 25(8): 1118–36.

Quiggin, J. (2012) *Zombie Economics: How Dead Ideas Still Walk Among Us* (Princeton, NJ: Princeton University Press).

Radice, H. (2004) 'Comparing National Capitalisms', in J. Perraton and B. Clift (eds), *Where Are National Capitalisms Now?* (Basingstoke: Palgrave Macmillan), pp. 183–94.

Ragin, C. (1987) *The Comparative Method* (Berkeley, CA: University of California Press).

Ragin, C. (1991) 'The Problem of Balancing Discourse on Cases and Variables in Comparative Social Science', *International Journal of Comparative Sociology*, 32(1): 1–8.

Ragin, C. (1992) 'Cases of "What Is a Case?"', in C. Ragin and H. Becker (eds), *What Is a Case? Exploring the Foundations of Social Inquiry* (Cambridge: Cambridge University Press), pp. 1–17.

Ragin, C. (2004) 'Turning the Tables: How Case-Oriented Research Challenges', in H. Brady and D. Collier (eds), *Rethinking Social Inquiry: Diverse Tools, Shared Standards* (Lanham, MD: Rowman & Littlefield), pp. 123–38.

Ragin, C. and Zaret, D. (1983) 'Theory and Method in Comparative Research: Two Strategies', *Social Forces*, 61: 731–54.

Rajan, R. and Zingales, I. (2003) 'Great Reversals: The Politics of Financial Development in the Twentieth Century', *Journal of Financial Economics*, 69(1): 5–50.

Ravenhill, J. (2008) 'In Search of the Missing Middle', *Review of International Political Economy*, 15: 18–29.

Ravenhill, J. (2011) *Global Political Economy*, 3rd edn (Oxford: Oxford University Press).

Ravenhill, J. (2017) *Global Political Economy*, 5th edn (Oxford: Oxford University Press).

Ravenhill, J. and Jiang, Y. (2009) 'China's Move to Preferential Trading: A New Direction in China's Diplomacy', *Journal of Contemporary China*, 18(58): 27–46.

Rehn, G. (1985) 'Swedish Active Labor Market Policy: Retrospect and Prospect', *Industrial Relations: A Journal of Economy and Society*, 24(1): 62–89.

Reich, R. (1984) *The New American Frontier* (London: Penguin).

Rethel, L. and Sinclair, T. (2012) *The Problem with Banks* (London: Zed Books).

Ricardo, D. (1971 [1817]) *Principles of Political Economy and Taxation* (London: Pelican).

Rieger, E. and Liebfried, S. (2003) *Limits to Globalization* (Cambridge: Polity Press).

Ringer, F. (2000) *Max Weber's Methodology: The Unification of the Cultural and Social Sciences* (Cambridge, MA: Harvard University Press).

RIPE (1994) 'Editorial: Forum for Heterodox International Political Economy', *Review of International Political Economy*, 1: 1–12.

Robinson, J. (2016) *The Accumulation of Capital* (Basingstoke: Springer).

Rodrik, D. (1997) *Has Globalization Gone Too Far?* (Washington, DC: Institute for International Economics).

Rodrik, D. (1998) 'Why Do More Open Economies Have Bigger Governments?', *Journal of Political Economy*, 106(5): 997–1032.

Rodrik, D. (2004) 'Industrial Policy for the Twenty-First Century', UNIDO Working Paper.

Roe, M. J. (1994) *Strong Managers, Weak Owners: The Political Roots of American Corporate Finance* (Princeton, NJ: Princeton University Press).

Roe, M. J. (2003) *Political Determinants of Corporate Governance: Political Context, Corporate Impact* (Oxford: Oxford University Press).

Roe, M. J. (2006) 'Legal Origins, Politics, and Modern Stock Markets', *Harvard Law Review*, 120: 460–527.

Rogers, C. (2009) 'From Social Contract to "Social Contrick": The Depoliticisation of Economic Policy Making Under Harold Wilson, 1974–75', *British Journal of Politics and International Relations*, 11(4): 634–51.

Rogowski, R. (1989) *Commerce and Coalitions: How Trade Affects Domestic Political Alignments* (Princeton, NJ: Princeton University Press).

Rosamond, B. (2002) 'Imagining the European Economy: "Competitiveness" and the Social Construction of "Europe" as an Economic Space', *New Political Economy*, 7(2): 157–78.

Rosamond, B. (2007) 'European Integration and the Social Science of EU Studies: The Disciplinary Politics of a Subfield', *International Affairs*, 83(2): 231–52.

Rosamond, B. (2019) 'Brexit and the Politics of UK Growth Models', *New Political Economy*, 24(3): 408–21.

Rosamond, B. (2020) 'European Integration and the Politics of Economic Ideas: Economics, Economists and Market Contestation in the Brexit Debate', *Journal of Common Market Studies*, 58(5): 1085–106.

Roscher, W. (1843) *Outline of Lectures on Political Economy According to the Historical Method* (Göttingen: Dieterich).

Rothschild, E. (2001) *Economic Sentiments: Adam Smith, Condorcet and the Enlightenment* (Cambridge, MA: Harvard University Press).

Rothstein, B. (1998) *Just Institutions Matter: The Moral and Political Logic of the Universal Welfare State* (Cambridge: Cambridge University Press).

Ruggie, J. (1982) 'International Regimes, Transactions and Change: Embedded Liberalism in the Post-War Economic Order', *International Organization*, 36(2): 379–415.

Ruggie, J. (1998) *Constructing the World Polity* (Abingdon: Routledge).

Ryner, M. (2002) *Capitalist Restructuring, Globalisation and the Third Way: Lessons from the Swedish Model* (London: Routledge).

Ryner, M. (2015) 'Europe's Ordoliberal Iron Cage: Critical Political Economy, the Euro Area Crisis and Its Management', *Journal of European Public Policy*, 22(2): 275–94.

Ryner, M. and Cafruny, A. (2016) *The European Union and Global Capitalism: Origins, Development and Crisis* (London: Macmillan International Higher Education).

Rosamond, B. (2019). Brexit and the politics of UK growth models. New political economy, 24(3), 408-421.

Sako, M. (2008) 'Organizational Diversity and Institutional Change: Evidence from Financial and Labour Markets in Japan', in M. Aoki, G. Jackson and H. Miyajima (eds), *Corporate Governance in Japan* (Oxford: Oxford University Press), pp. 399–426.

Salant, W. (1989) 'The Spread of Keynesian Doctrines and Practices in the United States', in P. Hall (ed.), *The Political Power of Economic Ideas* (Princeton, NJ: Princeton University Press), pp. 27–52.

Sanders, D. (2002) 'Behaviouralism', in D. Marsh and G. Stoker (eds), *Theory and Methods in Political Science*, 2nd edn (London: Red Globe Press), pp. 45–64.

Sapir, A. (2006) 'Globalisation and the Reform of European Social Models', *Journal of Common Market Studies*, 44(2): 369–90.

Sartori, G. (1970) 'Concept Misformation in Comparative Politics', *American Political Science Review*, 64(4): 1033–53.

Sassoon, D. (1996) *100 Years of Socialism* (London: I.B. Tauris).

Schafer, A. and Streeck, W. (eds) (2013) *Politics in the Age of Austerity* (Cambridge: Polity Press).

Scharpf, F. (1991) *Crisis and Choice in European Social Democracy* (Ithaca, NY: Cornell University Press).

Scharpf, F. (1997) *Games Real Actors Play: Actor-Centered Institutionalism in Policy Research* (Boulder, CO: Westview Press).

Scheve, K. and Stasavage, D. (2016) *Taxing the Rich: A History of Fiscal Fairness in the United States and Europe* (Princeton, NJ: Princeton University Press).

Schmidt, V. (1996) *From State to Market? The Transformation of French Business and Government* (Cambridge: Cambridge University Press).

Schmidt, V. (2002) *The Futures of European Capitalism* (Oxford: Oxford University Press).

Schmidt, V. (2003) 'French Capitalism Transformed, Yet Still a Third Variety of Capitalism', *Economy and Society*, 32(4): 526–54.

Schmidt, V. (2008) 'Discursive Institutionalism: The Explanatory Power of Ideas and Discourse', *Annual Review of Political Science*, 11: 303–26.

Schmidt, V. A. (2009) 'Putting the Political Back into Political Economy by Bringing the State Back in Yet Again', *World Politics*, 61(3): 516–46.

Schmidt, V. A. (2010) 'Taking Ideas and Discourse Seriously: Explaining Change Through Discursive Institutionalism as the Fourth "New Institutionalism"', *European Political Science Review*, 2(1): 1–25.

Schmidt, V. (2012) 'What Happened to the State-Influenced Market Economies (SMEs)? France, Italy and Spain Confront the Crisis as the Good, the Bad and the Ugly', in W. Grant and G. Wilson (eds), *The Consequences of the Global Financial Crisis: The Rhetoric of Reform and Regulation* (Oxford: Oxford University Press), pp. 156–86.

Schmidt, V. and Thatcher, M. (eds) (2013) *Resilient Liberalism in Europe's Political Economy* (Cambridge: Cambridge University Press).

Schmitter, P. (2010) 'Business and Neo-Corporatism', in D. Coen, W. Grant and G. Wilson (eds), *The Oxford Handbook of Business and Government* (Oxford: Oxford University Press), pp. 248–60.

Schmoller, G. (1902 [1884]) *The Mercantile System and Its Historical Significance* (New York: Macmillan).

Schneider, B. R. (2009) 'Hierarchical Market Economies and Varieties of Capitalism in Latin America', *Journal of Latin American Studies*, 41(3): 553–75.

Schneider, B. R. and Soskice, D. (2009) 'Inequality in Developed Countries and Latin America: Coordinated, Liberal and Hierarchical Systems', *Economy and Society*, 38(1): 17–52.

Scholte, J. A. (2005) *Globalisation: A Critical Introduction* (London: Red Globe Press).

Schrank, A. and Whitford, J. (2009) 'Industrial Policy in the United States: A Neo-Polanyian Interpretation', *Politics & Society*, 37(4): 521–53.

Schrodt, P. A. (2006) 'Beyond the Linear Frequentist Orthodoxy', *Political Analysis*, 14(3): 335–9.

Schwartz, H. M. (1994) 'Public Choice Theory and Public Choices: Bureaucrats and State Reorganization in Australia, Denmark, New Zealand, and Sweden in the 1980s', *Administration and Society*, 26(1): 48–77.

Schwartz, H. (2001) 'Round Up the Usual Suspects! Globalization, Domestic Politics, and Welfare State Change', in P. Pierson (ed.), *The New Politics of the Welfare State* (Oxford: Oxford University Press), pp. 17–44.

Schwartz, H. (2009) 'Subprime Nation: American Power', in *Global Capital, and the Housing Bubble* (Ithaca: Cornell University Press).

Schwartz, H. (2010) *States Versus Markets: The Emergence of a Global Economy*, 3rd edn (London: Red Globe Press).

Schwartz, H. and Seabrooke, L. (2008) 'Varieties of Residential Capitalism in the International Political Economy: Old Welfare States and the New Politics of Housing', *Comparative European Politics*, 6(3): 237–61.

Schwartz, H. M. and Seabrooke, L. (2009) 'Varieties of Residential Capitalism in the International Political Economy: Old Welfare States and the New Politics of Housing', in H. M. Schwartz and L. Seabrooke (eds), *The Politics of Housing Booms and Busts* (Basingstoke: Palgrave Macmillan), pp. 1–27.

Scott, J. (1998) *Seeing Like a State* (New Haven, CT: Yale University Press).

Scruggs, L. (2006) 'The Generosity of Social Insurance, 1971–2002', *Oxford Review of Economic Policy*, 22(3): 349–64.

Scruggs, L. and Allen, J. (2006) 'Welfare State Decommodification in Eighteen OECD Countries: A Replication and Revision', *Journal of European Social Policy*, 16(1): 55–72.

Scruggs, L. and Allen, J. (2008) 'Social Stratification and Welfare Regimes for the 21st Century: Revisiting the Three Worlds of Welfare Capitalism', *World Politics*, 60(4): 642–64.

Seabrooke, L. (2006) *The Social Sources of Financial Power: Domestic Legitimacy and International Financial Orders* (Ithaca, NY: Cornell University Press).

Seabrooke, L. (2007) 'Varieties of Economic Constructivism in Political Economy: Uncertain Times Call for Disparate Measures', *Review of International Political Economy*, 14(2): 371–85.

Seabrooke, L. and Wigan, D. (2017) 'The Governance of Global Wealth Chains', *Review of International Political Economy*, 24(1): 1–29.

Searle, J. (1995) *The Construction of Social Reality* (London: Penguin).

Seely, B. and Rogers, J. (2019) *Global Britain: A Twenty-First Century Vision* (London: Henry Jackson Society).

Self, P. (1993) *Government by the Market? The Politics of Public Choice* (Basingstoke: Macmillan).

Sen, A. (1977) 'Rational Fools: A Critique of the Behavioral Foundations of Economic Theory', *Philosophy and Public Affairs*, 6(4): 314–44.

Shapiro, J. (2001) *Mao's War Against Nature: Politics and the Environment in Revolutionary China* (Cambridge: Cambridge University Press).

Shapiro, J. (2016) *China's Environmental Challenges* (New York: John Wiley & Sons).

Sharman, J. C. (2006) *Havens in a Storm: The Struggle for Global Tax Regulation* (Ithaca, NY: Cornell University Press).

Shin, T. (2014) 'Explaining Pay Disparities Between Top Executives and Nonexecutive Employees', *Social Forces*, 92: 1339–72.

Shonfield, A. (1958) *British Economic Policy Since the War* (London: Penguin).

Shonfield, A. (1965) *Modern Capitalism: The Changing Balance of Public and Private Power* (Oxford: Oxford University Press).

Siles-Brügge, G. (2019) 'Bound by Gravity or Living in a "Post Geography Trading World"? Expert Knowledge and Affective Spatial Imaginaries in the Construction of the UK's Post-Brexit Trade Policy', *New Political Economy*, 24(3): 422–39.

Simon, H. (1982) *Models of Bounded Rationality* (Cambridge, MA: MIT Press).

Simon, H. (1985) 'Human Nature in Politics: The Dialogue of Psychology with Political Science', *American Political Science Review*, 79: 293–304.

Sinclair, T. (2001) 'International Capital Mobility: An Endogenous Approach', in T. Sinclair and K. Thomas (eds), *Structure and Agency in International Capital Mobility* (Basingstoke: Palgrave Macmillan), pp. 93–110.

Sinclair, T. (2005) *The New Masters of Capitalism: American Bond Rating Agencies and the Politics of Creditworthiness* (Ithaca, NY: Cornell University Press).

Sinclair, T. (2010) 'Round Up the Usual Suspects: Blame and the Subprime Crisis', *New Political Economy*, 15(1): 91–107.

Skidelsky, R. (1970) '1929–1931 Revisited', *Bulletin of the Society for the Study of Labour History*, 21: 6–8.

Skidelsky, R. (2009) *Keynes: The Return of the Master: Why, Sixty Years After His Death, John Maynard Keynes Is the Most Important Economic Thinker in the World* (London: Allen Lane).

Skidelsky, R. (2014) 'The Osborne Audit: What Have We Learned?' *New Statesman*, 17 March.

Skidelsky, R. (2018) *Money and Government: A Challenge to Mainstream Economics* (London: Penguin).

Skocpol, T. (1985) 'Bringing the State Back In: Strategies of Analysis in Current Research', in T. Skocpol, P. Evans and D. Rueschemeyer (eds), *Bringing the State Back In* (New York: Cambridge), pp. 3–36.

Skocpol, T. (1992) *Protecting Soldiers and Mothers: The Politics of Social Provision in the United States, 1870s–1920s* (Cambridge, MA: Harvard University Press).

Skocpol, T. (1995) 'Why I Am an Historical Institutionalist', *Polity*, 28(1): 103–6.

Skocpol, T. and Amenta, E. (1986) 'States and Social Policies', *Annual Review of Sociology*, 12(1): 131–57.

Skocpol, T. and Ikenberry, J. (1983) 'The Political Formation of the American Welfare State in Historical and Comparative Perspective', *Comparative Social Research*, 6(1): 5–87.

Skocpol, T. and Theda, S. (1979) *States and Social Revolutions: A Comparative Analysis of France, Russia and China* (Cambridge: Cambridge University Press).

Smelser, N. (1976) *The Comparative Method in Social Sciences* (Englewood Cliffs, NJ: Prentice-Hall).

Smelser, N. and Swedberg, R. (eds) (2005) *The Handbook of Economic Sociology* (Princeton, NJ: Princeton University Press).

Smith, A. (1993 [1776]) *An Inquiry into the Nature and Causes of the Wealth of Nations* (Oxford: Oxford University Press).

Smith, A. (2009 [1759]) *The Theory of Moral Sentiments* (London: Penguin).

Soederberg, S. (2009) *Corporate Power and Ownership in Contemporary Capitalism: The Politics of Resistance and Domination* (London: Routledge).

Soederberg, S. (2014) *Debtfare States and the Poverty Industry: Money, Discipline and the Surplus Population* (Abingdon: Routledge).

Solimano, A. (2016) *Global Capitalism in Disarray: Inequality, Debt, and Austerity* (New York: Oxford University Press).

Soskice, D. (1999) 'Divergent Production Regimes: Coordinated and Uncoordinated Market Economies in the 1980s and 1990s', in H. Kitschelt, P. Lange, G. Marks and J. Stephens (eds), *Continuity and Change*

in *Contemporary Capitalism* (Cambridge: Cambridge University Press), pp. 101–34.

Spencer, R. and Yohe W. (1970) 'The "Crowding Out" of Private Expenditures by Fiscal Policy Action', *Journal of Money, Credit and Banking*, Nov.: 461–72.

Squire, V. (2017) 'Governing Migration Through Death in Europe and the US: Identification, Burial and the Crisis of Modern Humanism', *European Journal of International Relations*, 23(3): 513–32.

Squire, V., Dimitriadi, A., Perkowski, N., Pisani, M., Stevens, D. and Vaughan-Williams, N. (2017) *Crossing the Mediterranean Sea by Boat: Mapping and Documenting Migratory Journeys and Experiences* (Coventry: University of Warwick).

Stanley, L. (2016a) 'Legitimacy Gaps, Taxpayer Conflict, and the Politics of Austerity in the UK', *British Journal of Politics and International Relations*, 18(2): 389–406.

Stanley, L. (2016b) 'Governing Austerity in the United Kingdom: Anticipatory Fiscal Consolidation as a Variety of Austerity Governance', *Economy and Society*, 45(3–4): 303–24.

Steans, J. (1999) 'The Private Is Global: Feminist Politics and Global Political Economy', *New Political Economy*, 4(1): 113–28.

Steele, G. R. (2001) *Keynes and Hayek: The Money Economy* (London: Routledge).

Stephens, J. (1979) *The Transition from Capitalism to Socialism* (London: Macmillan).

Stephens, J. (2010) 'The Social Rights of Citizenship', in F. Castles, S. Liebfried, J. Lewis, H. Obinger and C. Pierson (eds), *The Oxford Handbook of the Welfare State* (Oxford: Oxford University Press), pp. 511–25.

Stephens, J., Huber, E. and Ray, L. (1999) 'The Welfare State in Hard Times', in H. Kitschelt, P. Lange, G. Marks and J. Stephens (eds), *Continuity and Change in Contemporary Capitalism* (Cambridge: Cambridge University Press), pp. 164–93.

Sternberg, E. (1998) *Corporate Governance: Accountability in the Marketplace* (London: Institute of Economic Affairs).

Streeck, W. (2016) 'The Rise of the European Consolidation State', in H. Magara (ed), *Policy Change Under New Democratic Capitalism* (Abingdon: Routledge), pp. 39–58.

Stierl, M. (2018) 'A Fleet of Mediterranean Border Humanitarians', *Antipode*, 50(3): 704–24.

Stierl, M. (2020) 'Reimagining Europe Through the Governance of Migration', *International Political Sociology*, 14(3): 252–69.

Stigler, G. (1971) 'The Theory of Economic Regulation', *Bell Journal of Economics and Management Sciences*, 2: 137–46.

Stiglitz, J. E. (2012) *The Price of Inequality: How Today's Divided Society Endangers Our Future* (New York: WW Norton).

Stiglitz, J. E. (2015) *The Great Divide* (London: Penguin).

Stiglitz, J. E. (2018) 'Where Modern Macroeconomics Went Wrong', *Oxford Review of Economic Policy*, 34(1–2): 70–106.

Stiglitz, J. and Greenwald, B. (2014) *Creating a Learning Society* (New York: Columbia University Press).

Stiglitz, J., Lin, J. Y. and Patel, E. (eds) (2013) *The Industrial Policy Revolution II* (Basingstoke: Palgrave).

Stilwell, F. (2012) *Political Economy: The Contest of Economic Ideas*, 3rd edn (Oxford: Oxford University Press).

Stoffaes, C. (1989) 'Industrial Policy and the State: From Industry to Enterprise', in P. Godt (ed.), *Policy-Making in France* (London: Pinter).

Story, J. and Walter, I. (1997) *Political Economy of Financial Integration in Europe* (Manchester: Manchester University Press).

Strange, S. (1970) 'International Economics and International Relations: A Case of Mutual Neglect', *International Affairs*, 46(2): 304–15.

Strange, S. (1971) *Sterling and British Policy* (Oxford: Oxford University Press).

Strange, S. (1976) 'The Historical Perspective', in A. Shonfield (ed.), *International Economic Relations in the Western World 1959–1971*, Vol. 2 (Oxford: Oxford University Press), pp. 26–64.

Strange, S. (1994a) *States and Markets* (London: Pinter).

Strange, S. (1994b) 'From Bretton Woods to the Casino Economy', in S. Corbridge, R. Martin and N. Thrift (eds), *Money, Power and Space* (Oxford: Blackwell), pp. 29–48.

Strange, S. (1996) *The Retreat of the State* (Cambridge: Cambridge University Press).

Strange, S. (1997) 'The Future of Global Capitalism; or, Will Divergence Persist Forever?', in C. Crouch and W. Streeck (eds), *Political Economy of Modern Capitalism: Mapping Convergence and Diversity* (Thousand Oaks, CA: Sage), pp. 182–91.

Strange, G. (2011) 'China's Post-Listian Rise: Beyond Radical Globalisation Theory and the Political Economy of Neoliberal Hegemony', *New Political Economy*, 16(5): 539–59.

Streeck, W. (1997) 'German Capitalism: Does It Exist? Can It Survive?', *New Political Economy*, 2(2): 237–56.

Streeck, W. (2001) 'Introduction: Exploring into the Origins of Nonliberal Capitalism in Germany and Japan', in W. Streeck and K. Yamamura (eds), *The Origins of Nonliberal Capitalism* (Ithaca, NY: Cornell University Press), pp. 1–38.

Streeck, W. (2009) *Re-forming Capitalism: Institutional Change in the German Political Economy* (Oxford: Oxford University Press).

Streeck, W. (2010) 'Taking Capitalism Seriously: Towards an Institutionalist Approach to Contemporary Political Economy', Max Planck Institute MPIfG Discussion Paper 10/15, Cologne.

Streeck, W. (2011) 'The Crisis of Democratic Capitalism', *New Left Review*, 71: 5–29.

Streeck, W. (2014) *Buying Time: The Delayed Crisis of Democratic Capitalism* (London: Verso Books).

Streeck, W. (2016). The rise of the European consolidation state. In Magara, H. (Ed.). *Policy Change Under New Democratic Capitalism*. (Abingdon: Routledge), pp. 39–58.

Streeck, W. (2017) 'A New Regime: The Consolidation State', in D. King and P. Le Galès (eds), *Reconfiguring European States in Crisis* (Oxford: Oxford University Press), pp. 139–57.

Streeck, W. and Thelen, K. (eds) (2005) *Beyond Continuity: Institutional Change in Advanced Industrial Economies* (Oxford: Oxford University Press).

Steven, L. (1974) *Power: A Radical View* (London and New York: Macmillan).

Swank, D. (1998) 'Funding the Welfare State: Globalization and the Taxation of Business in Advanced Market Economies', *Political Studies*, 46(4): 671–92.

Swank, D. (2001) 'Political Institutions and Welfare State Restructuring', in P. Pierson (ed.), *The New Politics of the Welfare State* (Oxford: Oxford University Press), pp. 197–237.

Swank, D. (2002) *Global Capital, Political Institutions, and Policy Change in Developed Welfare States* (Cambridge: Cambridge University Press).

Swank, D. (2003) 'Withering Welfare? Globalisation, Political Economic Institution, and Contemporary Welfare States', in L. Weiss (ed.), *States and the Global Economy* (Cambridge: Cambridge University Press), pp. 58–82.

Swedberg, R. (1998) *Max Weber and the Idea of Economic Sociology* (Princeton, NJ: Princeton University Press).

Swedberg, R. (2005) 'Markets in Society', in N. Smelser and R. Swedberg (eds), *The Handbook of Economic Sociology* (Princeton, NJ: Princeton University Press), pp. 233–53.

Swenson, P. (2002) *Capitalists Against Markets: The Making of Labour Markets and Welfare States in the United States and Sweden* (Oxford: Oxford University Press).

Tabb, W. (1999) *Reconstructing Political Economy: The Great Divide in Economic Thought* (London: Routledge).

Tawney, R. H. (1961 [1921]) *The Acquisitive Society* (London: Collins).

Taylor-Gooby, P., Leruth, B. and Chung, H. (eds) (2017) *After Austerity: Welfare State Transformation in Europe After the Great Recession* (Oxford University Press).

Tetlow, G. and Stojanovic, A. (2018) 'Understanding the Economic Impact of Brexit', Institute for Government report.

Thatcher, M. (2007) *Internationalisation and Economic Institutions: Comparing the European Experience* (Oxford: Oxford University Press).

Thatcher, M. (2017) 'The Reshaping of Economic Markets and the State', in D. King and P. Le Gales (eds), *Reconfiguring European States in Crisis* (Oxford: Oxford University Press), pp. 179–200.

Thatcher, M., Hancké, B. and Rhodes, M. (eds) (2007) *Beyond Varieties of Capitalism: Conflict, Contradictions, and Complementarities in the European Economy* (Oxford: Oxford University Press).

Thelen, K. (2000) 'Why German Employers Cannot Bring Themselves to Dismantle the German Model', in T. Iverson, J. Pontusson and D. Soskice (eds), *Unions, Employers and Central Banks* (Cambridge: Cambridge University Press), pp. 138–72.

Thelen, K. (2001) 'Varieties of Labor Politics in the Developed Democracies', in P. Hall and D. Soskice (eds), *Varieties of Capitalism: Institutional Foundations of Comparative Advantage* (Cambridge: Cambridge University Press), pp. 71–103.

Thelen, K. (2004) *How Institutions Evolve: The Political Economy of Skills in Germany, Britain, the United States, and Japan* (Cambridge: Cambridge University Press).

Thelen, K. (2010) 'Beyond Comparative Statics: Historical Institutional Approaches to Stability and Change in the Political Economy of Labor', in G. Morgan, J. Campbell, C. Crouch, O. Pedersen and R. Whitley (eds), *The Oxford Handbook of Comparative Institutional Analysis* (Oxford: Oxford University Press), pp. 41–62.

Thelen, K. and Steinmo, S. (1992) 'Historical Institutionalism in Comparative Politics', in S. Steinmo, K. Thelen and F. Longstreth (eds), *Structuring Politics* (Cambridge: Cambridge University Press), pp. 1–32.

Therborn, G. (1986) *Why Are Some People More Unemployed Than Others?* (London: Verso).

Thiemann, M. (2014) 'In the Shadow of Basel: How Competitive Politics Bred the Crisis', *Review of International Political Economy*, 21(6): 1203–39.

Thiemann, M. (2018) *The Growth of Shadow Banking: A Comparative Institutional Analysis* (Cambridge University Press).

Thompson, G. (2004) 'The US Economy in the 1990s: The "New Economy" Assessed', in J. Perraton and B. Clift (eds), *Where Are National Capitalisms Now?* (Basingstoke: Palgrave Macmillan), pp. 12–32.

Thompson, G. (2012) 'What Is Happening to Corporations and What of Their Future?', in G. Morgan and R. Whitley (eds), *Capitalism and Capitalisms in the 21st Century* (Oxford: Oxford University Press), pp. 298–318.

Titmuss, R. (1963) *Essays on the 'Welfare State'* (London: George Allen & Unwin).

Titmuss, R. (1965) 'The Role of Redistribution in Social Policy', *Social Security*, 28(6): 14–20.

Tomlinson, J. (1990) *Public Policy and the Economy Since 1900* (Oxford: Clarendon Press).

Tooze, A. (2018) *Crashed: How a Decade of Financial Crises Changed the World* (London: Penguin).

Tooze, R. and May, C. (2002) 'Authority and Markets: Interpreting the Work of Susan Strange', in R. Tooze and C. May (eds), *Authority and Markets: Susan Strange's*

Writings on International Political Economy (Basingstoke: Palgrave Macmillan), pp. 1–16.

Tooze, R. and Murphy, C. (eds) (1991) *The New International Political Economy* (Boulder, CO: Lynne Rienner).

Tribe, K. (1988) 'Friedrich List and the Critique of "Cosmopolitical Economy"', *The Manchester School*, 56(1): 17–36.

Tribe, K. (2007) 'Historical Schools of Economics: German and English', in W. Samuels, J. Biddle and J. Davis (eds), *The History of Economic Thought* (Oxford: Blackwell), pp. 215–30.

True, J. (2016) 'The Global Financial Crisis's Silver Bullet: Women Leaders and "Leaning In"', in A. Hozic and J. True (eds), *Scandalous Economics: Gender and the Politics of Financial Crisis* (Oxford: Oxford University Press), pp. 41–56.

Tsakalotos, E. (2005) '*Homo Economicus* and the Reconstruction of Political Economy: Six Theses on the Role of Values in Economics', *Cambridge Journal of Economics*, 29(6): 893–908.

Tsebelis, G. (1990) *Nested Games: Rational Choice in Comparative Politics* (Berkeley, CA: University of California Press).

Tsuru, S. (1993) *Japanese Capitalism* (Cambridge: Cambridge University Press).

Tucker, T. (2019) *Industrial Policy and Planning: What It Is and How to Do It Better* (Roosevelt Institute).

Tullock, G. (1965) *The Politics of Bureaucracy* (Boston, MA: University Press of America).

Tullock, G. (1989) *The Economics of Special Privilege and Rent-Seeking* (Boston, MA: Kluwer Academic).

Tullock, G. (1990) 'The Costs of Special Privilege', in J. Alt and K. Shepsle (eds), *Perspectives on Positive Political Economy* (Cambridge: Cambridge University Press), pp. 195–211.

UNCTAD (2003) *World Investment Report* (New York: United Nations).

Underhill, G. (2000) 'State, Market, and Global Political Economy: Genealogy of an (Inter-?) Discipline', *International Affairs*, 76(4): 805–24.

van Apeldoorn, B. and Horn, L. (2007) 'The Marketisation of European Corporate Control: A Critical Political Economy Perspective', *New Political Economy*, 12(2): 211–35.

Van der Zwan, N. (2014) 'Making Sense of Financialization' *Socio-Economic Review*, 12(1): 99–129.

Van Gunten, T. and Navot, E. (2018) 'Varieties of Indebtedness: Financialization and Mortgage Market Institutions in Europe', *Social Science Research*, 70: 90–106.

van Kersbergen, K. and Manow, P. (eds) (2009) *Religion, Class Coalitions, and Welfare States* (Cambridge: Cambridge University Press).

Van Treeck, T. (2009) 'The Political Economy Debate on 'Financialisation' – A Macroeconomic Perspective', *Review of International Political Economy*, 16(5): 907–44.

Vandenbroucke, F. (1999) 'European Social Democracy: Convergence, Divisions, and Shared Questions', *Political Quarterly*, 69(5): 37–52.

Vandenbroucke, F. (2002) 'Foreword', in G. Esping-Andersen, with D. Gallie, A. Hemerijck and J. Myles (eds), *Why We Need a New Welfare State* (Oxford: Oxford University Press), pp. viii–xxiv.

Varoufakis, Y. (2016) *And the Weak Suffer What They Must?* (London: Vintage).

Varoufakis, Y. (2017) *Adults in the Room: My Battle with Europe's Deep Establishment* (London: Random House).

Vartiainen, J. (2004) 'Scandinavian Capitalism at the Turn of the Century', in J. Perraton and B. Clift (eds), *Where Are National Capitalisms Now?* (New York: Palgrave Macmillan), pp. 154–68.

Vasileva-Dienes, A. and Schmidt, V. A. (2019) 'Conceptualising Capitalism in the Twenty-First Century: The BRICs and the European Periphery', *Contemporary Politics*, 25(3): 255–75.

Vaughan-Whitehead, D. (ed.) (2013) *Public Sector Shock: The Impact of Policy Retrenchment in Europe* (Cheltenham: Edward Elgar).

Vaughan-Williams, N. (2015) *Europe's Border Crisis: Biopolitical Security and Beyond* (New York: Oxford University Press).

Veblen, T. (1904) *The Theory of the Business Enterprise* (New York: Charles Scribner's).

Veblen, T. (1919) 'Why Is Economics Not an Evolutionary Science?', in T. Veblen (ed.), *The Place of Science in Modern Civilisation and other Essays* (New York: B.W. Huebsch), pp. 56–81.

Verba, S. (1967) 'Some Dilemmas in Comparative Research', *World Politics*, 20(01): 111–27.

Verdier, D. (2002) *Moving Money: Banking and Finance in the Industrialized World* (Cambridge: Cambridge University Press).

Viner, J. (1984) 'Adam Smith and Laissez-faire', in J. C. Wood (ed.), *Adam Smith: Critical*

Assessments, Vol. 1 (London: Edward Elgar), pp. 143–67.

Vitols, S. (2003) 'From Banks to Markets: The Political Economy of Liberalisation of the German and Japanese Financial Systems', in K. Yamamura and W. Streeck (eds), *The End of Diversity? Prospects for German and Japanese Capitalism* (Ithaca, NY: Cornell University Press), pp. 240–60.

Vogel, D. (1995) *Trading Up: Consumer and Environmental Regulation in a Global Economy* (Cambridge, MA: Harvard University Press).

Vogel, S. (1996) *Freer Markets, More Rules?* (Ithaca, NY: Cornell University Press).

Vogel, S. (2003) 'The Re-organization of Organized Capitalism: How the German and Japanese Models Are Shaping Their Own Transformations', in K. Yamamura and W. Streeck (eds), *The End of Diversity? Prospects for German and Japanese Capitalism* (Ithaca, NY: Cornell University Press), pp. 306–33.

Vogel, S. (2005) 'Routine Adjustment and Bounded Innovation: The Changing Political Economy of Japan', in W. Streeck and K. Thelen (eds), *Beyond Continuity* (Oxford: Oxford University Press), pp. 145–68.

Vogel, S. (2006) *Japan Remodeled: How Government and Industry Are Reforming Japanese Capitalism* (Ithaca, NY: Cornell University Press).

Wade, R. H. (2003) 'What Strategies Are Viable for Developing Countries Today? The World Trade Organization and the Shrinking of "Development Space"', *Review of International Political Economy*, 10(4): 621–44.

Wade, R. H. (2012) 'Return of Industrial Policy?', *International Review of Applied Economics*, 26(2): 223–39.

Wæver, O. (1998) 'The Sociology of a Not So International Discipline: American and European Developments in International Relations', *International Organization*, 52(4): 687–727.

Walker, C. (2014) 'Don't Cut Down the Tall Poppies: Thatcherism and the Strategy of Inequality', in S. Farrall and C. Hay (eds), *The Legacy of Thatcherism* (Oxford: Oxford University Press), pp. 282–305.

Wallerstein, M. and Przeworski, A. (1995) 'Capital Taxation with Open Borders', *Review of International Political Economy*, 2(3): 425–45.

Walras, L. ([1954] 1873) *Elements of Pure Economics* (London: George Allen & Unwin).

Walter, A. (2006) 'From Developmental to Regulatory State? Japan's New Financial Regulatory System', *The Pacific Review*, 19(4): 405–28.

Waltz, K. (1979) *Theory of International Politics* (Reading, MA: Addison-Wesley).

Wan, M. (2011) 'The Domestic Political Economy of China's Preferential Trade Agreements', in V. K. Aggarwal and S. Lee (eds), *Trade Policy in the Asia-Pacific: The Role of Ideas, Interests, and Domestic Institutions* (New York: Springer), pp. 29–48.

Ward, H. (2002) 'Rational Choice', in D. Marsh and G. Stoker (eds), *Theory and Methods in Political Science*, 2nd edn (London: Red Globe Press), pp. 65–89.

Watson, M. (1999) 'Rethinking Capital Mobility: Re-regulating Financial Markets', *New Political Economy*, 4(1): 55–75.

Watson, M. (2002) 'The Institutional Paradoxes of Monetary Orthodoxy: Reflections on the Political Economy of Central Bank Independence', *Review of International Political Economy*, 9(1): 183–96.

Watson, M. (2003) 'Ricardian Political Economy and the "Varieties of Capitalism" Approach: Specialization, Trade and Comparative Institutional Advance', *Comparative European Politics*, 1(2): 227–40.

Watson, M. (2005a) *Foundations of International Political Economy* (London: Red Globe Press).

Watson, M. (2005b) 'What Makes a Market Economy? Schumpeter, Smith and Walras on the Coordination Problem', *New Political Economy*, 10(2): 143–61.

Watson, M. (2008) 'Constituting Monetary Conservatives via the "Savings Habit": New Labour and the British Housing Market Bubble', *Comparative European Politics*, 6(3): 285–304.

Watson, M. (2009) 'Headlong into the Polanyian Dilemma: The Impact of Middle-Class Moral Panic on the British Government's Response to the Sub-prime Crisis', *British Journal of Politics and International Relations*, 11(3): 422–37.

Watson, M. (2010) 'House Price Keynesianism and the Contradictions of the Modern Investor Subject', *Housing Studies*, 25(3): 413–26.

Watson, M. (2011) 'The Historical Roots of Theoretical Traditions in Global Political

Economy', in J. Ravenhill (ed.), *Global Political Economy* (Oxford: Oxford University Press), pp. 29–66.

Watson, M. (2012) 'Friedrich List's Adam Smith Historiography and the Contested Origins of Development Theory', *Third World Quarterly*, 33(3): 459–74.

Watson, M. (2016) 'The Historical Roots of Theoretical Traditions in Global Political Economy', in J. Ravenhill (ed.), *Global Political Economy* (Oxford: Oxford University Press), pp. 26–51.

Weber, M. (1949) 'Objective Possibility and Adequate Causation in Historical Explanation', in M. Weber (ed.), *The Methodology of the Social Sciences* (New York: Free Press), pp. 164–88.

Weber, M. (1978 [1922]) *Economy and Society, Volume 1* (Berkeley, CA: University of California Press).

Weber, M. (1994 [1895]) 'The Nation State and Economic Policy (Inaugural Lecture)', in P. Lassman and R. Speirs (eds), *Weber: Political Writings*, Cambridge Texts in the History of Political Thought (Cambridge: Cambridge University Press), pp. 1–28.

Weingast, B. (1996) 'Political Institutions: Rational Choice Perspectives', in R. Goodin and H.-D. Klingemann (eds), *A New Handbook of Political Science* (Oxford: Oxford University Press), pp. 167–90.

Weingast, B. (2002) 'Rational-Choice Institutionalism', in I. Katznelson and H. Milner (eds), *Political Science: The State of the Discipline* (New York: W. W. Norton), pp. 660–92.

Weir, M. (1989) 'Ideas and Politics: The Acceptance of Keynesianism in Britain and the United States', in P. Hall (ed.), *The Political Power of Economic Ideas* (Princeton, NJ: Princeton University Press), pp. 53–86.

Weiss, L. (1998) *The Myth of the Powerless State: Governing the Economy in a Global Era* (Cambridge: Polity Press).

Weiss, L. (ed.) (2003) *States in the Global Economy* (Cambridge: Cambridge University Press).

Weiss, L. (2004) 'Developmental States Before and After the Asian Crisis', in J. Perraton and B. Clift (eds), *Where Are National Capitalisms Now?* (Basingstoke: Palgrave Macmillan), pp. 154–68.

Weiss, L. (2014) *America Inc.?: Innovation and Enterprise in the National Security State* (Ithaca, NY: Cornell University Press).

Whitworth, S. (1988) 'Gender in the Inter-Paradigm Debate', *Millennium: Journal of International Studies*, 18(2): 265–72.

Whitworth, S. (2006) 'Theory and Exclusion: Gender, Masculinity, and International Political Economy', in *Political Economy and the Changing Global Order*, 3rd edn (Don Mills: Oxford University Press), pp. 88–99.

Widmaier, W. (2003a) 'The Keynesian Bases of a Constructivist Theory of the International Political Economy', *Millennium: Journal of International Studies*, 32(1): 87–107.

Widmaier, W. (2003b) 'Constructing Monetary Crises: New Keynesian Understandings and Monetary Cooperation in the 1990s', *Review of International Studies*, 29(1): 61–77.

Widmaier, W. (2004) 'The Social Construction of the "Impossible Trinity": The Inter-Subjective Bases of Monetary Cooperation', *International Studies Quarterly*, 48(2): 433–53.

Widmaier, W. (2009) 'Economics Are Too Important to Leave to Economists: The Everyday–and Emotional–Dimensions of International Political Economy', *Review of International Political Economy*, 16(5): 945–57.

Widmaier, W. (2016) *Economic Ideas in Political Time* (Cambridge: Cambridge University Press).

Widmaier, W. W., Blyth, M. and Seabrooke, L. (2007) 'Exogenous Shocks or Endogenous Constructions? The Meanings of Wars and Crises', *International Studies Quarterly*, 51(4): 747–59.

Wilensky, H. L. (1975) *The Welfare State and Equality: Structural and Ideological Roots of Public Expenditure* (Berkeley, CA: University of California Press).

Wilensky, H. L. (1976) *The 'New Corporatism,' Centralization, and the Welfare State* (London: Sage).

Wilks, S. (2009) 'The Impact of the Recession on Competition Policy: Amending the Economic Constitution?', *International Journal of the Economics of Business*, 16(3): 269–88.

Williams, F. (1995) 'Race/Ethnicity, Gender, and Class in Welfare States: A Framework for Comparative Analysis', *Social Politics: International Studies in Gender, State & Society*, 2(2): 127–59.

Williamson, O. (1975) *Markets and Hierarchies: Analysis and Anti-trust Implications: A Study of the Economics of Internal Organization* (New York: Free Press).

Williamson, O. (1985) *The Economic Institutions of Capitalism: Firms, Markets and Relational Contracting* (London: Macmillan).

Wilson, T. (1976) 'Sympathy and Self-Interest', in T. Wilson and A. Skinner (eds), *The Market and the State: Essays in Honour of Adam Smith* (Oxford: Clarendon Press), pp. 73–99.

Wilson, G. (2012) 'The United States: The Strange Survival of (Neo)Liberalism', in W. Grant and G. Wilson (eds), *The Consequences of the Global Financial Crisis: The Rhetoric of Reform and Regulation* (Oxford: Oxford University Press), pp. 51–66.

Winch, D. (2009) *Wealth and Life* (Cambridge: Cambridge University Press).

Wolff, T. (2002) *Why Read Marx Today?* (Oxford: Oxford University Press).

Woll, C. (2008) *Firm Interests: How Governments Shape Business Lobbying on Global Trade* (Ithaca, NY: Cornell University Press).

Woll, C. (2010) 'Firm Interests in Uncertain Times: Business Lobbying in Multilateral Service Liberalisation', in R. Abdelal, M. Blyth and C. Parsons (eds), *Constructing the International Economy* (Ithaca, NY: Cornell University Press), pp. 137–54.

Woll, C. (2014) *The Power of Inaction: Bank Bailouts in Comparison* (Ithaca, NY: Cornell University Press).

Woll, C. (2017) 'State Action in Financial Times', in D. King and P. Le Galès (eds), *Reconfiguring European States in Crisis* (Oxford: Oxford University Press), pp. 201–14.

Woo-Cumings, M. (1999) 'Introduction: Chalmers Johnson and the Politics of Nationalism and Development', in M. Woo-Cumings (ed.), *The Developmental State* (Ithaca, NY: Cornell University Press), pp. 1–31.

World Economic Forum (2020) *Global Competitiveness Report 2019* (Geneva: World Economic Forum).

Worswick, D. and Trevithick, J. (1983) *Keynes and the Modern World* (Cambridge: Cambridge University Press).

Wren-Lewis, S. (2011) 'Lessons from Failure: Fiscal Policy, Indulgence and Ideology', *National Institute Economic Review*, 217(1): 1–16.

Wren-Lewis, S. (2019) 'Macroeconomic Policy Beyond Brexit', *The Political Quarterly*, 90: 44–52.

Yamamura, K. (ed.) (1997) *The Economic Emergence of Modern Japan* (Cambridge: Cambridge University Press).

Young, B. (2014) 'German Ordoliberalism as Agenda Setter for the Euro Crisis: Myth Trumps Reality', *Journal of Contemporary European Studies*, 22(3): 276–87.

Youngs, G. (1999) *From International to Global Relations: A Conceptual Challenge* (Cambridge: Polity Press).

Zahariadis, N. (2008) *State Subsidies in the Global Economy* (Basingstoke: Palgrave Macmillan).

Zuboff, S. (2019) *The Age of Surveillance Capitalism: The Fight for a Human Future at the New Frontier of Power* (London: Profile Books).

Zysman, J. (1983) *Government, Markets, Growth: Financial Systems and the Politics of Industrial Change* (Ithaca, NY: Cornell University Press).

Index

9781352011302